T0321761

Security Solutions and Applied Cryptography in Smart Grid Communications

Mohamed Amine Ferrag
Guelma University, Algeria

Ahmed Ahmim
University of Larbi Tebessi, Algeria

A volume in the Advances in Information Security, Privacy, and Ethics (AISPE) Book Series

www.igi-global.com

Published in the United States of America by
    IGI Global
    Information Science Reference (an imprint of IGI Global)
    701 E. Chocolate Avenue
    Hershey PA, USA 17033
    Tel: 717-533-8845
    Fax: 717-533-8661
    E-mail: cust@igi-global.com
    Web site: http://www.igi-global.com

Library of Congress Cataloging-in-Publication Data

Names: Ferrag, Mohamed Amine, 1987- editor. | Ahmim, Ahmed, 1986- editor.
Title: Security solutions and applied cryptography in smart grid
  communications / Mohamed Amine Ferrag and Ahmed Ahmim, editors.
Description: Hershey PA : Information Science Reference, [2017] | Includes
  index.
Identifiers: LCCN 2016045997| ISBN 9781522518297 (hardcover) | ISBN
  9781522518303 (ebook)
Subjects: LCSH: Smart power grids--Security measures. | Data encryption
  (Computer science) | Computer networks--Security measures.
Classification: LCC TK3105 .S334 2017 | DDC 621.3190285/58--dc23 LC record available at https://lccn.loc.
gov/2016045997

This book is published in the IGI Global book series Advances in Information Security, Privacy, and Ethics (AISPE) (ISSN: 1948-9730; eISSN: 1948-9749).

British Cataloguing in Publication Data
A Cataloguing in Publication record for this book is available from the British Library.

All work contributed to this book is new, previously-unpublished material. The views expressed in this book are those of the authors, but not necessarily of the publisher.

For electronic access to this publication, please contact: eresources@igi-global.com.

Advances in Information Security, Privacy, and Ethics (AISPE) Book Series

Manish Gupta
State University of New York, USA

ISSN:1948-9730
EISSN:1948-9749

MISSION

As digital technologies become more pervasive in everyday life and the Internet is utilized in ever increasing ways by both private and public entities, concern over digital threats becomes more prevalent.

The **Advances in Information Security, Privacy, & Ethics (AISPE) Book Series** provides cutting-edge research on the protection and misuse of information and technology across various industries and settings. Comprised of scholarly research on topics such as identity management, cryptography, system security, authentication, and data protection, this book series is ideal for reference by IT professionals, academicians, and upper-level students.

COVERAGE

- Global Privacy Concerns
- Tracking Cookies
- Risk Management
- Internet Governance
- Network Security Services
- CIA Triad of Information Security
- Computer ethics
- Telecommunications Regulations
- Privacy Issues of Social Networking
- Data Storage of Minors

IGI Global is currently accepting manuscripts for publication within this series. To submit a proposal for a volume in this series, please contact our Acquisition Editors at Acquisitions@igi-global.com or visit: http://www.igi-global.com/publish/.

Titles in this Series

For a list of additional titles in this series, please visit: www.igi-global.com

Online Banking Security Measures and Data Protection
Shadi A. Aljawarneh (Jordan University of Science and Technology, Jordan)
Information Science Reference • copyright 2017 • 312pp • H/C (ISBN: 9781522508649) • US $215.00 (our price)

Developing Next-Generation Countermeasures for Homeland Security Threat Prevention
Maurice Dawson (University of Missouri-St. Louis, USA) Dakshina Ranjan Kisku (National Institute of Technology, India) Phalguni Gupta (National Institute of Technical Teachers' Training & Research, India) Jamuna Kanta Sing (Jadavpur University, India) and Weifeng Li (Tsinghua University, China)
Information Science Reference • copyright 2017 • 428pp • H/C (ISBN: 9781522507031) • US $210.00 (our price)

Security Solutions for Hyperconnectivity and the Internet of Things
Maurice Dawson (University of Missouri-St. Louis, USA) Mohamed Eltayeb (Colorado Technical University, USA) and Marwan Omar (Saint Leo University, USA)
Information Science Reference • copyright 2017 • 347pp • H/C (ISBN: 9781522507413) • US $215.00 (our price)

Managing Security Issues and the Hidden Dangers of Wearable Technologies
Andrew Marrington (Zayed University, UAE) Don Kerr (University of the Sunshine Coast, Australia) and John Gammack (Zayed University, UAE)
Information Science Reference • copyright 2017 • 345pp • H/C (ISBN: 9781522510161) • US $200.00 (our price)

Security Management in Mobile Cloud Computing
Kashif Munir (University of Hafr Al-Batin, Saudi Arabia)
Information Science Reference • copyright 2017 • 248pp • H/C (ISBN: 9781522506027) • US $150.00 (our price)

Cryptographic Solutions for Secure Online Banking and Commerce
Kannan Balasubramanian (Mepco Schlenk Engineering College, India) K. Mala (Mepco Schlenk Engineering College, India) and M. Rajakani (Mepco Schlenk Engineering College, India)
Information Science Reference • copyright 2016 • 375pp • H/C (ISBN: 9781522502739) • US $200.00 (our price)

Handbook of Research on Modern Cryptographic Solutions for Computer and Cyber Security
Brij Gupta (National Institute of Technology Kurukshetra, India) Dharma P. Agrawal (University of Cincinnati, USA) and Shingo Yamaguchi (Yamaguchi University, Japan)
Information Science Reference • copyright 2016 • 589pp • H/C (ISBN: 9781522501053) • US $305.00 (our price)

Innovative Solutions for Access Control Management
Ahmad Kamran Malik (COMSATS Institute of Information Technology, Pakistan) Adeel Anjum (COMSATS Institute of Information Technology, Pakistan) and Basit Raza (COMSATS Institute of Information Technology, Pakistan)
Information Science Reference • copyright 2016 • 330pp • H/C (ISBN: 9781522504481) • US $195.00 (our price)

www.igi-global.com
701 E. Chocolate Ave., Hershey, PA 17033
Order online at www.igi-global.com or call 717-533-8845 x100
To place a standing order for titles released in this series, contact: cust@igi-global.com
Mon-Fri 8:00 am - 5:00 pm (est) or fax 24 hours a day 717-533-8661

To Our Families

Table of Contents

Section 1
Vulnerabilities, Threats, and Attacks

Yona Lopes, Fluminense Federal University, Brazil
Natalia Castro Fernandes, Fluminense Federal University, Brazil
Tiago Bornia de Castro, Universidade Federal Fluminense, Brazil
Vitor dos Santos Farias, Universidade Federal Fluminense, Brazil
Julia Drummond Noce, Universidade Federal Fluminense, Brazil
João Pedro Marques, Universidade Federal Fluminense, Brazil
Débora Christina Muchaluat-Saade, Universidade Federal Fluminense, Brazil

Gurbakshish Singh Toor, Nanyang Technological University, Singapore
Maode Ma, Nanyang Technological University, Singapore

Swapnoneel Roy, University of North Florida, USA

Danda B. Rawat, Howard University, USA
Brycent A. Chatfield, Georgia Southern University, USA

Section 2
Authentication, Privacy, and Interoperability

Section 3
Intrusion Detection Systems and Cryptography Solutions

Section 4
Smart Energy and Network Management

Detailed Table of Contents

Yona Lopes, Fluminense Federal University, Brazil
Natalia Castro Fernandes, Fluminense Federal University, Brazil
Tiago Bornia de Castro, Universidade Federal Fluminense, Brazil
Vitor dos Santos Farias, Universidade Federal Fluminense, Brazil
Julia Drummond Noce, Universidade Federal Fluminense, Brazil
João Pedro Marques, Universidade Federal Fluminense, Brazil
Débora Christina Muchaluat-Saade, Universidade Federal Fluminense, Brazil

Advances in smart grids and in communication networks allow the development of an interconnected system where information arising from different sources helps building a more reliable electrical network. Nevertheless, this interconnected system also brings new security threats. In the past, communication networks for electrical systems were restrained to closed and secure areas, which guaranteed network physical security. Due to the integration with smart meters, clouds, and other information sources, physical security to network access is no longer available, which may compromise the electrical system. Besides smart grids bring a huge growth in data volume, which must be managed. In order to achieve a successful smart grid deployment, robust network communication to provide automation among devices is necessary. Therefore, outages caused by passive or active attacks become a real threat. This chapter describes the main architecture flaws that make the system vulnerable to attacks for creating energy disruptions, stealing energy, and breaking privacy.

Chapter 2

Gurbakshish Singh Toor, Nanyang Technological University, Singapore
Maode Ma, Nanyang Technological University, Singapore

The evolution of the traditional electricity infrastructure into smart grids promises more reliable and efficient power management, more energy aware consumers and inclusion of renewable sources for power generation. These fruitful promises are attracting initiatives by various nations all over the globe in various fields of academia. However, this evolution relies on the advances in the information technologies and communication technologies and thus is inevitably prone to various risks and threats. This work focuses on the security aspects of HAN and NAN subsystems of smart grids. The chapter presents some of the prominent attacks specific to these subsystems, which violate the specific security goals requisite for their reliable operation. The proposed solutions and countermeasures for these security issues presented in the recent literature have been reviewed to identify the promising solutions with respect to the specific security goals. The paper is concluded by presenting some of the challenges that still need to be addressed.

Chapter 3

Swapnoneel Roy, University of North Florida, USA

In this work, a denial of service (DoS) attack known as the clogging attack has been performed on three different modern protocols for smart grid (SG) communications. The first protocol provides authentication between smart meters (SM) and a security and authentication server (SAS). The second protocol facilitates secure and private communications between electric vehicles (EV) and the smart grid. The third protocol is a secure and efficient key distribution protocol for the smart grid. The protocols differ in either their applications (authentication, key distribution), or their ways of communications (usage of encryption, hashes, timestamps etc.). But they are similar in their purpose of design (for the smart grid) and their usage of computationally intensive mathematical operations (modular exponentiation, ECC) to implement security. Solutions to protect these protocols against this attack are then illustrated along with identifying the causes behind the occurrence of this vulnerability in SG communication protocols in general.

Chapter 4

Danda B. Rawat, Howard University, USA
Brycent A. Chatfield, Georgia Southern University, USA

The transformation of the traditional power grid into a cyber physical smart energy grid brings significant improvement in terms of reliability, performance, and manageability. Most importantly, existing communication infrastructures such as LTE represent the backbone of smart grid functionality. Consequently, connected smart grids inherit vulnerabilities associated with the networks including denial of service attack by means of synchronization signal jamming. This chapter presents cybersecurity in cyber-physical energy grid systems to mitigate synchronization signal jamming attacks in LTE based smart grid communications.

Section 2
Authentication, Privacy, and Interoperability

Chapter 5

Georgios Karopoulos, National and Kapodistrian University of Athens, Greece
Christoforos Ntantogian, University of Piraeus, Greece
Christos Xenakis, University of Piraeus, Greece

The introduction of information and communication technologies to the traditional energy grid offers advantages like efficiency, increased reliability, resilience, and better control of demand-response, while on the other hand poses customers' privacy at risk. By using information collected by a smart meter, an attacker can deduce whether a house is empty from its residents, which devices are being used, residents' habits and so on. In order to cope with such cases, many privacy-preserving aggregation solutions have been proposed that allow aggregation, while at the same time protect individual readings from attackers. In this book chapter, the authors provide a critical review of such methods, comparing them and discussing advantages and disadvantages.

Chapter 6

Sowmyarani C. N., R.V. College of Engineering, India
Dayananda P., JSS Academy of Technical Education, Bengaluru, India

Privacy attack on individual records has great concern in privacy preserving data publishing. When an intruder who is interested to know the private information of particular person of his interest, will acquire background knowledge about the person. This background knowledge may be gained though publicly available information such as Voter's id or through social networks. Combining this background information with published data; intruder may get the private information causing a privacy attack of that person. There are many privacy attack models. Most popular attack models are discussed in this chapter. The study of these attack models plays a significant role towards the invention of robust Privacy preserving models.

Chapter 7

Melesio Calderón Muñoz, Cupertino Electric, Inc., USA
Melody Moh, San Jose State University, USA

The electrical power grid forms the functional foundation of our modern societies, but in the near future our aging electrical infrastructure will not be able to keep pace with our demands. As a result, nations worldwide have started to convert their power grids into smart grids that will have improved communication and control systems. A smart grid will be better able to incorporate new forms of energy generation as well as be self-healing and more reliable. This paper investigates a threat to wireless communication networks from a fully realized quantum computer, and provides a means to avoid this problem in smart grid domains. We discuss and compare the security aspects, the complexities and the performance of authentication using public-key cryptography and using Merkel trees. As a result, we argue for the use of Merkle trees as opposed to public key encryption for authentication of devices in wireless mesh networks (WMN) used in smart grid applications.

Chapter 8

Cristina Alcaraz, University of Malaga, Spain
Javier Lopez, University of Malaga, Spain

Transparency in control transactions under a secure network architecture is a key topic that must be discussed when aspects related to interconnection between heterogeneous cyber-physical systems (CPSs) arise. The interconnection of these systems can be addressed through an enforcement policy system responsible for managing access control according to the contextual conditions. However, this architecture is not always adequate to ensure a rapid interoperability in extreme crisis situations, and can require an interconnection strategy that permits the timely authorized access from anywhere at any time. To do this, a set of interconnection strategies through the Internet must be studied to explore the ability of control entities to connect to the remote CPSs and expedite their operations, taking into account the context conditions. This research constitutes the contribution of this chapter, where a set of control requirements and interoperability properties are identified to discern the most suitable interconnection strategies.

Section 3
Intrusion Detection Systems and Cryptography Solutions

Chapter 9

SCADA (Supervisory Control and Data Acquisition) systems are a critical part of modern national critical infrastructure (CI) systems. Due to the rapid increase of sophisticated cyber threats with exponentially destructive effects, intrusion detection systems (IDS) must systematically evolve. Specific intrusion detection systems that reassure both high accuracy, low rate of false alarms and decreased overhead on the network traffic must be designed for SCADA systems. In this book chapter we present a novel IDS, namely K-OCSVM, that combines both the capability of detecting novel attacks with high accuracy, due to its core One-Class Support Vector Machine (OCSVM) classification mechanism and the ability to effectively distinguish real alarms from possible attacks under different circumstances, due to its internal recursive k-means clustering algorithm. The effectiveness of the proposed method is evaluated through extensive simulations that are conducted using realistic datasets extracted from small and medium sized HTB SCADA testbeds.

Chapter 10

The increase of the applications of numerous innovative technologies and associated devices has brought forward various new concepts like Cyber-Physical System (CPS), Internet of Things (IoT), Smart environment, Smart cities, and so on. While the boundary lines between these concepts and technologies are often kind of blur and perhaps, each one's development is helping the development of the other, M2M (Machine to Machine) communication would surely play a great role as a key enabler of all these emerging scenarios. When we see the same smart concept from different angles; for instance, from the participating device, or human being's angle, we get different definitions and concept-specific standards. In this chapter, our objective is to study M2M system and communication along with its security issues and intrusion detection systems. We have also proposed our framework in line with the standardization efforts for tackling security issues of M2M.

In recent years, it has been revealed that these critical infrastructures such as SCADA systems have been the target of cyber-terrorism. In general cyber-attacks are infrequent in nature and hence infrequent pattern identification in SCADA systems is an important research issue. Therefore, design and development of an efficient infrequent pattern detection technique is a research priority. In this chapter, the effectiveness of co-clustering which is advantageous over regular clustering for creating more fine-grained representation of the data and computationally efficient is explored for infrequent pattern identification in SCADA systems. A multi-stage co-clustering based infrequent pattern detection technique is proposed and applied on seven benchmark SCADA datasets which includes practical industrial datasets. The proposed method shows its superiority over existing clustering based techniques in terms of computational complexity which is essential for practical deployment in a SCADA framework.

Cyber Security of ICS/SCADA systems is a major aspect of current research focus. Cyber Ranges and Test-beds can serve as means of vulnerability and threat analysis of real SCADA systems with low costs. Significantly lacking from current research, is detailed documentation of the decision process and the potential difficulties that need to be considered when undertaking the creation of a Cyber Range (CR) in order to facilitate the capture of labelled datasets which is included in this paper. This paper makes several further contributions; a review of Cyber Ranges created by Academic Institutions that influenced the criteria in creating CYRAN, the De Montfort University CYber RANge. The article presents the design implementation, the process of creating effective rules of engagement, the management and running of a Cyber Range Event (CRE) with partners from Industry and Academia and the creation of labelled datasets.

Over the last decade, Internet of Things (IoTs) have brought radical changes to the means and forms of communication for monitoring and control of a large number of applications including Smart Grid (SG). Traditional energy networks have been modernized to SGs to boost the energy industry in the context of efficient and effective power management, performance, real-time control and information flow using two-way communication between utility provides and end-users. However, integrating two-way communication in SG comes at the cost of cyber security vulnerabilities and challenges. In the context of SG, node compromise is a severe security threat due to the fact that a compromised node can significantly impact the operations and security of the SG network. Therefore, in this chapter, Key Management Scheme for Communication Layer in the Smart Grid (KMS-CL-SG) has proposed. In order to achieve a secure end-to-end communication we assign a unique key to each node in the group.

Section 4
Smart Energy and Network Management

Chapter 14

Nazmus S. Nafi, RMIT University, Australia
Khandakar Ahmed, RMIT University, Australia
Mark A. Gregory, RMIT University, Australia

In a smart grid machine to machine communication environment, the separation of the control and data planes in the Software Defined Networking (SDN) paradigm increases flexibility, controllability and manageability of the network. A fully integrated SDN based WSN network can play a more prominent role by providing 'last mile' connectivity while serving various Smart Grid applications and offer improved security, guaranteed Quality of Service and flexible interworking capabilities. Hence, more efforts are required to explore the potential role of SDN in Smart Grid communications and thereby ensure its optimum utilization. In this chapter we provide a description of how SDN technology can be used in WSN with an emphasis on its end-to-end network architecture. We then present its novel application to Advanced Metering Infrastructure, Substation Automation, Distributed Energy Resources, Wide Area Measurement Systems, and Roaming of Electric Vehicles in Smart Grids.

Chapter 15

Imene Yahyaoui, Federal University of Espírito Santo, Brazil
Rachid Ghraizi, Indra, Spain
Fernando Tadeo, University of Valladolid, Spain
Marcelo Eduardo Vieira Segatto, Federal University of Espírito Santo, Brazil

This chapter is concerned with the energy management of a hybrid micro-grid composed of photovoltaic/ wind/ battery bank and diesel generator, which is used to supply domestic loads. Hence, a control strategy is proposed to manage the power flow between the power sources and the loads, which ensures the maximization of the renewable sources use, and therefore the minimization of the battery bank and diesel generator use. The control strategy allows the installation operating cost to be minimized and the safe operating for the battery bank to be guaranteed. The strategy is tested using measured data of some climatic parameters of the target area, showing its efficiency in fulfilling the fixed objectives.

This chapter presents a detailed study of renewable energy integrated charging infrastructure for electric vehicles (EVs) and discusses its various aspects such as siting requirements, standards of charging stations, integration of renewable energy sources for powering up charging stations and interfacing devices between charging facilities and smart grid. A smart charging station for EVs is explained along with its essential components and different charging methodologies are explained. It has been recognized that the amalgamation of electric vehicles in the transportation sector will trigger power issues due to the mobility of vehicles beyond the stretch of home area network. In this regard an information and communication technology (ICT) based architecture may support EVs management with an aim to enhance the electric vehicle charging and energy storage capabilities with the relevant considerations. An ICT based solution is capable of monitoring the state of charge (SOC) of EV batteries, health and accessible amount of energy along with the mobility of EVs.

The introduction of Electric Vehicle (EVs) has a great potential for the reductions of carbon emissions and air pollution. Whereas, EVs are more likely to run out of energy and need to be charged during their journeys. This is mainly due to the limited EV battery capacity and long trip distance in big cities. Practically, this concern could be substantially improved by recharging EVs' electricity at deployed public Charging Stations (CSs) during journeys. However, even if the flexibility of public CSs could be improved and adjusted following the rapid growth of EVs, major technical challenges and contributions in this chapter involve decision making intelligence for the selection of CSs as charging plans, and the provisioning communication infrastructure for secure information dissemination within network.

This research chapter is concerned with the control of a photovoltaic powered plant connected to a single-phase grid. The system is equipped with dc–dc converters, which allow the panels' maximum power point to be tracked, and the voltage at their terminals to be regulated. Power is injected into the grid using an adequate control of a single-phase inverter connected to a filter and loads. In this research chapter, the active and reactive powers are controlled using the Voltage Oriented Control strategy, taking into account the grid and the loads characteristics. The control strategy is tested by simulation, and the obtained results prove its performance even under solar radiation change.

Preface

Electrical energy storage is a key of modern and future life. The consumption of electrical energy (i.e. the use of air conditioning, audio and video devices or electric heating) is increasing every year due; firstly, to the increase of the population and secondly by the appearance of new form of consumption, such as electric cars. The dilemma with this increase consumption is, how to ensure the balance between supply and demand for electricity at all times? To address this problem, the idea of placing the new generation of smart grids to control this energy has appeared in recent literature in different flavors in order to provide electric power supply secure, sustainable and competitive to consumers. In addition, the revolution in smart grid involves a significant change in side of the consumer where consumers will also become producer with the ability of energy storage such as in the vehicle battery, or as a local generation sources such as photovoltaic panels.

The smart grid develops modern solutions for the next-generation network and digital communication in which many systems and subsystems are interconnected to provide services from end-to-end network between various actors and between intelligent devices that are deployed there. Within each network, a hierarchical structure is composed of different types of networks, such as the HANs (Home Area Networks), the BANs (Building Area Networks), the IANs (Industrial Area Networks), the NANs (Neighborhood Area Networks), the FANs (Field Area Networks), and the WANs (Wide Area Networks). In addition, large societies propose the use of cloud computing in smart grid applications connected with the electrical control center.

The main problem in the development of a smart grid is not located at the physical medium but mainly in delivery of reliability and security. The possibility of fitting with active or passive attacks in smart grid network is great to divulge privacy and disrupt energy (e.g. Wormhole Attack, False Data Injection Attack, Black Hole Attack, Grey Hole Attack, DoS Attack, Physical Layer Attack, Colluding Adversary Attack, Routing Table Overflow Attack etc.). Therefore, the security requirements, including authentication, accountability, integrity, non-repudiation, access control and confidentiality should be paid more attention in the future for high performance smart grids. This book will cover the current scope of various methodologies and mechanisms in the theory and practice of security, privacy, intrusion detection, and applied cryptography in smart grid communications in one place.

This book is organized as follows:

- Section 1 introduces the vulnerabilities, threats, and attacks in smart grid communications;
- Section 2 deals with authentication, privacy, and interoperability in smart grid communications;
- Section 3 presents intrusion detection systems and cryptography solutions for securing smart grid communications
- Section 4 discusses smart energy and network management in smart grid.

In more detail:

- Section 1 includes chapters titled "Vulnerabilities and Threats in Smart Grid Communication Networks," "Security Issues of Communication Networks in Smart Grid," "Denial of Service Attack on Protocols for Smart Grid Communications," and "Detecting Synchronization Signal Jamming Attacks for Cyber Security in Cyber-Physical Energy Grid Systems";
- Section 2 includes "Privacy-Preserving Aggregation in the Smart Grid," "Analytical Study on Privacy Attack Models in Privacy Preserving Data Publishing," "Authentication of Smart Grid: The Case for Using Merkle Trees," and "Secure Interoperability in Cyber-Physical Systems";
- Section 3 includes "Novel Intrusion Detection Mechanism with Low Overhead for SCADA Systems," "A Study on M2M (Machine to Machine) System and Communication: Its Security, Threats, and Intrusion Detection System," "Infrequent Pattern Identification in SCADA Systems Using Unsupervised Learning," "CYRAN: A Hybrid Cyber Range for Testing Security on ICS/SCADA Systems," and "A Key Management Scheme for Secure Communications Based on Smart Grid Requirements (KMS-CL-SG)";
- Section 4 includes "Modelling Software-Defined Wireless Sensor Network Architectures for Smart Grid Neighborhood Area Networks," "Smart Energy and Cost Optimization for Hybrid Micro-Grids: PV/Wind/Battery/Diesel Generator Control," "Feasibility Study of Renewable Energy Integrated Electric Vehicle Charging Infrastructure," "Enabling Publish/Subscribe Communication for On-the-Move Electric Vehicle Charging Management," and "Smart Control Strategy for Small-Scale Photovoltaic Systems Connected to Single-Phase Grids: Active and Reactive Powers Control."

This book aims to be an essential reference source, building on the available literature in the field of smart grid security in developing countries while providing for further research opportunities in this dynamic field. We hope it serves as a reference for technology developers and managers to adopt and implement smart grid platforms in developing nations across the globe.

Mohamed Amine Ferrag
Guelma University, Algeria

Ahmed Ahmim
University of Larbi Tebessi, Algeria

Acknowledgment

The book came into light due to the direct and indirect involvement of many researchers, academicians, advanced-level students, technology developers, and industry practitioners. Therefore, we acknowledge and thank the contributing authors, research institutions, and companies whose papers and study materials have been referred to in this book.

The success of this book would not have been possible without the cooperation of the three committees: the editorial board, the editorial assistant from IGI Global, and the contributing authors. Thus, we are very grateful for their support. In addition, we also thank those authors whose contributions could not be selected for the final book.

We are very thankful to the team of IGI Global for accepting our book proposal and giving us the opportunity to work on this book project. Particularly, we are thankful to Erin Wesser (Assistant Managing Editor, Acquisitions), Kayla Wolfe (Managing Editor, Acquisitions), Jan Travers (Director of Intellectual Property and Contracts), and Courtney Tychinski (Development Editor - Books).

Best Regards,

Mohamed Amine Ferrag
Guelma University, Algeria

Ahmed Ahmim
University of Larbi Tebessi, Algeria

Section 1
Vulnerabilities, Threats, and Attacks

Chapter 1
Vulnerabilities and Threats in Smart Grid Communication Networks

Yona Lopes
Fluminense Federal University, Brazil

Vitor dos Santos Farias
Universidade Federal Fluminense, Brazil

Natalia Castro Fernandes
Fluminense Federal University, Brazil

Julia Drummond Noce
Universidade Federal Fluminense, Brazil

Tiago Bornia de Castro
Universidade Federal Fluminense, Brazil

João Pedro Marques
Universidade Federal Fluminense, Brazil

Débora Christina Muchaluat-Saade
Universidade Federal Fluminense, Brazil

ABSTRACT

Advances in smart grids and in communication networks allow the development of an interconnected system where information arising from different sources helps building a more reliable electrical network. Nevertheless, this interconnected system also brings new security threats. In the past, communication networks for electrical systems were restrained to closed and secure areas, which guaranteed network physical security. Due to the integration with smart meters, clouds, and other information sources, physical security to network access is no longer available, which may compromise the electrical system. Besides smart grids bring a huge growth in data volume, which must be managed. In order to achieve a successful smart grid deployment, robust network communication to provide automation among devices is necessary. Therefore, outages caused by passive or active attacks become a real threat. This chapter describes the main architecture flaws that make the system vulnerable to attacks for creating energy disruptions, stealing energy, and breaking privacy.

DOI: 10.4018/978-1-5225-1829-7.ch001

INTRODUCTION

According to the NIST (National Institute of Standards and Technology) conceptual model (NIST, 2014), smart grids are composed of seven logical domains, which have distinct characteristics, actors, and intelligent devices that must be interconnected. End devices have become smarter and may communicate seamlessly with data and control centers.

In the past, communication networks for electrical systems were restrained to closed and secure areas, which guaranteed network physical security. Due to the integration with smart meters, clouds, and other information sources, physical security to network access is no longer available, which may compromise the electrical system control and management.

Smart grid deployment begins with a massive insertion of smart meters. Also, the number of Intelligent Electronic Devices (IED) increases in order to support Distribution Automation (DA). In general, the quantity of automation sensors, such as smart meters and IEDS, and the amount of data collected from these sensors increase significantly. Smart grids bring a huge growth in data volume, which must be managed.

In order to achieve a successful smart grid deployment, robust network communication to provide automation among devices is necessary. Such scenario involves several nodes, links, systems, protocols, and technologies. A composition of different types of networks forms a broad and complex architecture. It brings several advantages such as visibility, availability, and remote control that make possible several new operations from the utility. In addition, new energy applications, such as capacity planning and peak power shaving, will improve the system. Moreover, new applications will facilitate the deployment of new energy services such as energy audits, demand response programs, and electric vehicle charging (Budka, Deshpande, & Thottan, 2014).

However, the same interconnected system that makes the grid smarter also brings security threats and makes the grid vulnerable to attacks. Thereat smart grids cannot advance without dealing with security problems. Attacks against the electrical power grid can directly impact the population and would affect people, trade, companies, and anyone who cannot stand without electric power. Any possibility of event that impacts confidentiality, integrity, and availability of smart grid domains is considered a threat.

Attacks attempting to gain advantage of the information exchange system vulnerabilities are known as data-centric threats. Such threats can be elusive and might result in critical damage to industrial infrastructure. A worm might reprogram an industrial control facility to degrade the equipment and generate false operation logs, compromising maintenance. An attacker can take control of the system or steal confidential information without physical access to the plant (Wei & Wang, 2016). Attacks against nuclear facilities such as the Falliere et al. (2011) worm incident and the Assante (2016) attack are a demonstration of the dangerous potential of cyber threats.

For instance, SCADA (Supervisory Control and Data Acquisition), which is a very important system that monitors the electrical system operation, must be interconnected with all that network structure. SCADA system vulnerabilities are usually correlated to the use of the Human Machine Interface (HMI) and data historians (Wilhoit, 2013). Data historians are log databases that store trends and historical information about processes of an industrial control system.

Compromising the HMI can lead the attacker to access secure areas where he can modify set points or controls. An improper opening or closing circuit breaker can cause unnecessary consumer shutdowns. Besides, if a circuit was undergoing maintenance, an improper closing circuit breaker would threaten human life.

If an attacker can access the data historian, he can read the centralized database with all accounting information about the industrial control system environment. Hence, he will know information about security systems as well as a list of commands used in devices as Programmable Logic Controllers (PLCs) and IEDs.

Not only SCADA is vulnerable to attacks, but also smart meters and any IEDs. It is important to realize that every smart meter is close to customers, who are potential attackers. They could change consumption data, disclose privacy related information, and use smart meters as an entrance point to major attacks. Therefore, outages caused by passive or active attacks become a real threat. Motivations to attacks range from reducing costs in the energy bill to terrorism promotion.

This chapter discusses security issues related to smart grids, its main vulnerabilities, and threats. It describes the main architecture flaws that make the electrical system vulnerable to attacks for creating energy disruptions, stealing energy, and breaking privacy.

The remaining of the text is organized as follows. Firstly, we describe the main security concepts related to smart grids. Then, we present smart grid usual attacks, considering both substations and Advanced Metering Infrastructure (AMI). Next, we describe the main current solutions to create a secure environment for smart grid communications. In the last part of the chapter, conclusions and future research directions are presented.

BACKGROUND

Cyber Security in the Smart Grid

Understanding the impact of attacks on power grid communications depends on the comprehension of the concept of cyber incident. According to FIPS (Federal Information Processing Standards), this concept is defined as follows:

An occurrence that actually or potentially jeopardizes the confidentiality, integrity, or availability of an information system or the information the system processes, stores, or transmits or that constitutes a violation or imminent threat of violation of security policies, security procedures, or acceptable use policies. (FIPS PUB 200, 2006, p. 7)

Recently, the discussion about cyber security threats against electrical power grids has raised and has become a key issue for smart grids. The integration of information models and communication networks to power systems brings new security challenges related to authenticity, confidentiality, integrity, and availability. The interconnection of devices that are distributed in places without physical security is one of the main concerns.

For instance, the use of AMI places a special threat, because final users are able to directly introduce information in the system. The corruption of meters by individual users, virus, or hackers running DoS (Denial of Service) attacks could disrupt the power provision for an entire city.

Attacks against smart grids may be devastating, because they include the whole energy network, from substations and distribution networks to residences, industrial, and commercial installations. The outcomes of the attacks range from service outages to physical damages to buildings, in case an attacker is able to disturb the protection system, compromising the security in electrical installations. Solutions to those threats are still under discussion and may include well-known security techniques already applied in the Internet and new security protocols for smart grid communications.

To provide a better comprehension of those attacks and their countermeasures, we discuss the main security concepts related to this scenario: authentication, authorization, accountability, privacy, integrity, availability, and physical protection.

Authentication

Authentication is the ability to verify the identity of an entity. In smart grids, all entities in the system must have a verifiable identification. This means that all players, such as users, enterprises, IEDs, sensors, home devices, smart meters, electrical cars, etc. must be uniquely identified in the system in a secure way. In the Internet, this can be achieved by the use of a Public Key Infrastructure (PKI) or simpler identifying systems in the case of less sensitive devices. This could be applied in a simple way for smart grids. For instance, control systems, such as SCADA, which have an important function for substation automation and can control field devices, should be identified by the use of digital certification to avoid man-in-the-middle attacks. It implies buying a publicly verifiable certificate. This kind of investment, however, is not justifiable to devices inside a home network. In this case, in which devices are not expected to interact with sensitive systems, but only provide useful information and services for the user, devices could be authenticated by self-signed certificates or login/password schemes.

A good authentication system is the main base to provide all other security concepts. A simple use of a cyphered communication does not provide security, because malicious users can fake identities and corrupt the system. Hence, the ability to prove another entity's identity is a key factor for a successful environment.

Authorization

The authorization concept is closely related to the authentication concept. It represents the ability to verify system policies to grant or not access of an authenticated entity to a specific system. Authorization systems differ on the granularity of policies. A very simple policy would be to grant access to all authenticated users. For instance, in a home network, all devices that were registered by the user should be able to connect to the home management system. Nevertheless, this policy does not fit in a substation system access, where there are users with different priority levels, devices that should interact only with pre-specified set of devices, and so on. In these cases, policies related to attributes, roles, time, etc. apply.

Accountability

Another important issue to provide security in a communication system is the ability to register events. Hence, whenever an unusual event happens, the system administrator must be able to track down which previous events led to the situation. This is specially important to perform auditing and to discover attack causes, when they happen. This is the essence of accountability systems. An important characteristic is that system logs must be secured stored, in order to avoid that a user subverts the registered information to cover up a malicious action.

Privacy

Privacy is another important requirement for smart grids. In these networks, different kinds of sensitive information are being transmitted among different entities. This includes private information about users, such as the kind of devices they have at home, the times they are at home, the places where they have been with their cars, and information about electrical utilities. The last one has important economical aspects, as there is market competition among dealers that could be influenced by exposing internal system in substations. A common mistake is to associate privacy only to the use of cyphers. Indeed, cryptography is the main way to provide privacy, but only when authenticity of communication endpoints has already been proved.

Integrity

Integrity is the ability to guarantee that data will flow from senders to receivers without any changes in the content. Man-in-the middle attacks are used to spy the information, but also to change message content between its source and destination(s). Smart grid communication must guarantee integrity, because modifying sensor or actuator data on the fly could cause disruptions in the power grid. Moreover, communication between users and systems must be secured in order to avoid system misuse that could cause both financial losses to users and disruptions in the power grid.

Availability

The last security concept is availability, which is related to failures and DoS attacks. In a non-hostile environment, failures in the network, failures in the hardware and software, or an overcharge of users in a server could cause service unavailability. In hostile environments, hackers can use a small number or a high number of devices, usually remotely controlled, to interrupt a service. We call these attacks DoS and Distributed DoS (DDoS), respectively. These kinds of attacks usually cause service unavailability and consequently financial losses. One of the main concerns about DoS or DDoS is that they are usually hard to stop without harming legitimate users. The main reason is that the attacker traffic is similar to legitimate traffic and therefore firewall systems cannot block only the attacker traffic. Hackers are able to generate this kind of traffic coming from distributed sources because of botnets. Botnets are composed of a set of devices compromised by malicious code that can be remotely operated. Usually a user with a compromised device does not know that he/she is part of a botnet, because bots are usually transparent to the user and generate small amounts of traffic in very specific moments triggered by a remote malicious user.

This kind of attack is of main concern in smart grids, because the power system is composed of a huge number of devices that generate data to specific services, like SCADA. For instance, a hacker could compromise smart meters and use them to disrupt a service that collects smart meter measures and alarms.

Physical Protection

To disrupt those security concepts, a hacker needs to access devices and to perform an attack. In legacy power grids, control devices were physically protected. Hence, hackers would need to physically invade a power grid facility in order to access a device and disrupt the control network. With the advance of smart grids, the control network now reaches the end user through devices like smart meters. Hence, instead of trying to compromise a control device or service through the network, by searching for software vulnerabilities, the hacker can invade the network by tampering a smart meter that is in his/her house, for instance. When a hacker has physical access to a node, it becomes very easy to change codes and access data stored in the device, changing its behavior. Once a hacker controls a legitimate network node, he/she becomes an internal attacker. This means that the attacker controls a node that is trusted by the whole system. Hence, all injected messages will be considered as legitimate. After infecting a node, it becomes easier to compromise other legitimate nodes through the network, because security systems are configured to stop external threats and release communication between internal nodes. Hence, physical security of communicating devices is a main concern to power grids.

Information Technology Security x Industrial Control System Security

One of the main reasons for power-system security gaps is the difference between security in traditional Information Technology (IT) scenarios and in Industrial Control Systems (ICS).

Usually for security provision of the Internet world, confidentiality is one of the main issues, as user data cannot be disclosed. In ICS, even though confidentiality is important to protect industrial secrets, it is not the main concern. Integrity and availability are indeed the essential requirements for a correct execution of the control system even in the presence of internal or external attackers.

In traditional IT systems, a main rule is to keep the system updated. Patches to solve security issues must be applied as fast as possible to stop possible attacks using the exposed vulnerability. No engineer or system analyst would fear to update the system. This is a different reality in ICS. Indeed, devices usually have proprietary firmware, which may fail after an update. Usually, device manufacturers do not take responsibility on patch appliance and engineers do not feel comfortable to update the firmware running the risk to compromise very expensive devices. Hence, it is common to replace devices with more secure ones instead of updating device software (Lüders, 2011).

Another important difference is that, in traditional IT systems, devices are natively integrated with firewall, Access-Control Lists (ACL), and other security systems, which is not a reality in ICS. Also, computers connected to the Internet can count on secure communication protocols to share sensitive information, while devices in an ICS are based on naive communication protocols.

SMART GRID ATTACKS

This section describes smart grid scenarios in which attacks occur due to communication-network security weaknesses. Firstly attacks against substation and supervisory scenarios are discussed. The second part of this section presents AMI attacks.

Attacks Against Substations and Data and Control Center

Before discussing attacks, it is necessary to understand why a substation or a Data and Control Center (DCC) can represent a vulnerable scenario. It is related to the communication architecture and protocols used.

One of the main elements of a substation is the SCADA system. SCADA is used not only for substations, but also for different kinds of ICS. SCADA deployment has not varied much in the last 30 years in terms of information security, despite of several documented security issues (Wilhoit, 2013). In the context of smart grids, this evolution is of special concern since communication networks are evolving to interconnect the whole system, which implies more network threats.

SCADA remotely controls and monitors substation equipment from utility DCC, using Remote Terminal Units (RTUs) deployed at substations to accomplish it. More recently, IEDs are used to comprise the same functionality.

Data acquisition is related to the measurement and reporting of values such as currents and voltages, and status report of field devices such as circuit breakers and switches. Control is related to the command of substation devices as tripping of circuit breakers. It requires a communication network from SCADA (master station) to RTU (slave), as illustrated in Figure 1. Notice that IEDs can communicate directly with SCADA using a protocol, so RTUs could be removed. Solutions with a number of IEDs connected to RTUs are also used despite the fact that remote control could be performed directly on IED, as illustrated in Figure 1.

Communication between RTU and SCADA requires a protocol, which traditionally was based on the use of a serial communication line. One of the oldest protocols used is MODBUS, developed by Modicon (currently Schneider) for process control systems. However, Distributed Network Protocol 3 (DNP3) and IEC 60870-5, both from the 90s, are increasingly replacing MODBUS. Initially, DNP3 and IEC 61870-5 were created for a serial communication line, as MODBUS. However, soon after they have acquired versions for TCP/IP.

It is important to emphasize that communication with these protocols happens among RTUs/IEDs and SCADA. This communication is also possible among IEDs and RTU. DNP3, IEC 60870-5, and other SCADA protocols aims at performing remote control and supervision but do not perform electrical

Figure 1. Generic substation scheme

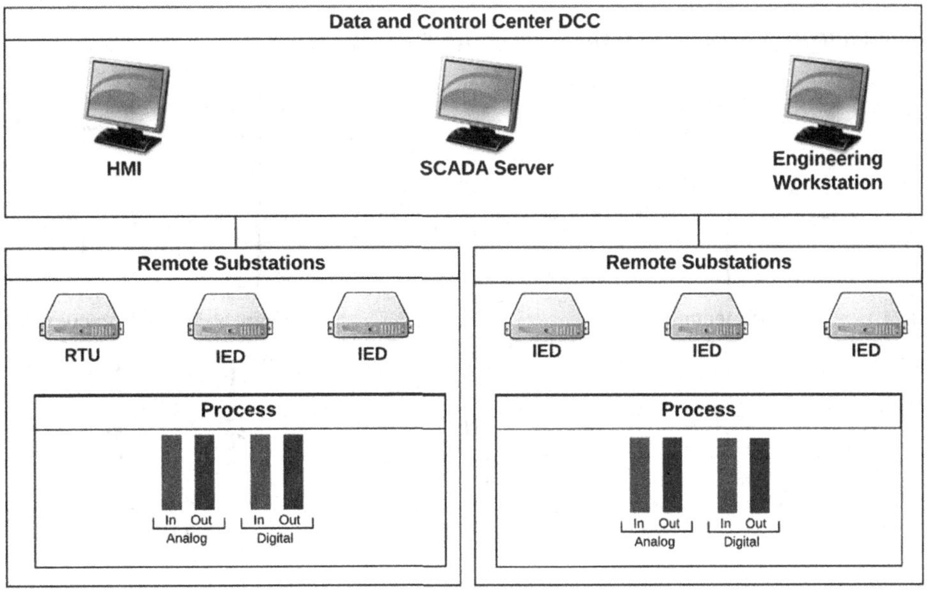

protection functions. Thus, a field device, such as a circuit breaker, receives commands through control cables from IEDs. For example, after detecting an abnormal condition (by cables), the IED could initiate an electrical protection command (a trip) to open a circuit breaker through control cables. SCADA protocols only report information or receive commands from the operator over the communication network. However, a trip command, which depends on protection schemes and control cables, is performed by a single IED. Moreover, with the substation modernization, those control cables can be replaced by a communication network, as it will be discussed in the following.

Indeed, in the last years, several substation automation protocols that are not often compatible with each other were proposed and implemented in substations. The deployment of a substation network with different protocols brought many substation automation problems. To couple with interoperability issues, the IEC 61850 standard was developed. This standard aims at reaching interoperability encompassing communication networks and systems in substations. Many utilities across the world have begun or are planning to deploy substation devices (IEDs) and substation communication networks based on IEC 61850 (Budka, Deshpande, & Thottan, 2014).

IEC 61850 defines object models that formally represent protection and control function, substation equipment, data communication, and others. Different vendors may implement it providing interoperability. It results in a strong difference between IEC 61850 and traditional communication schemes, such as the ones described for DNP3 or IEC 60870-5, as illustrated in Figures 2 and 3. In IEC 61850, field devices are connected by an Ethernet LAN, replacing traditional control cables. Therefore, conventional field devices, as Current Transformers (CTs), Voltage Transformers (VTs), and circuit breakers are replaced by modern devices that communicate with IEDs using a protocol.

The modeling of automation devices is object oriented and the communication model uses three types of protocols: GOOSE (Generic Object Oriented Substation Event), SV (Sampled Values), and MMS (Manufacturing Message Specification).

MMS is a SCADA protocol that is very similar to DNP3. This protocol uses a client-server model where IEDs are servers and SCADA is the client. MMS uses seven layers of OSI network architecture and its maximum delay ranges from 100 ms to 1000 ms.

Figure 2. Communication scheme of legacy substations

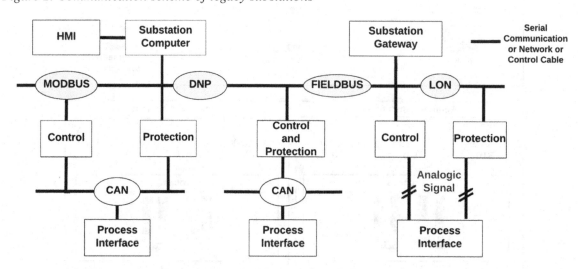

Figure 3. Substation scheme using IEC 61850

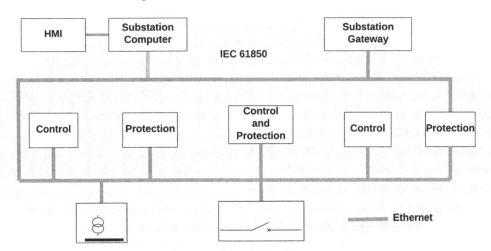

GOOSE and SV are delivered using a publish-subscribe model to multicast MAC addresses. SV can also use client-server model to unicast addresses. GOOSE and SV have severe time constraints up to 3 ms, and they are directly mapped to the link layer in order to provide fast response time. This is because GOOSE and SV are used for protection schemes. SV is used to send measures from instrument transformers or merging units and GOOSE is used for protection. Hence, GOOSE and SV allows communication between IEDs. For instance, TCs and TPs can send measurements using SV messages to IEDs. After detecting an abnormal condition, an IED can initiate a command to open a circuit breaker (trip command). However, if the circuit breaker fails, the IED can send a GOOSE message (breaker failure indication) to other IEDs as an effort to solve the problem as fast as possible.

Many smart grid energy applications have rigid time constraints in terms of communication availability and delay (IEC 61850-7-420, 2009). Therefore, specific characteristics of this new energy-delivery concept have driven several research projects aimed at designing an adequate communication infrastructure to meet the expected Quality of Service (QoS) and reliability for smart grids (Kounev, Lévesque, Tipper, & Gomes, 2016). For instance, IEC 61850 standard has addressed the problem of DER insertion (IEC 61850-7-420, 2009), recommending the same time threshold established for substation protection and control.

IEC 61850 recommends delays from 3 ms to 100 ms for protection messages according to the message type. Moreover, in 2010, the United States Department of Energy analyzed communication requirements for smart functions (e.g., Demand Response and DER) and defined millisecond values for smart grid protection and control and reliability levels for each service (U.S. Department of Energy, 2010). In addition, since 2005, rigid restrictions have been described by the IEEE 1646 standard (IEEE 1646, 2004). IEEE 1646 addresses delay requirements for some substation operations at as little as 4 ms and 5 ms, for 60 Hz and 50 Hz AC frequencies.

For applications requiring communication between substations, delay requirements are more relaxed. Thus remote activation of a protection scheme at a substation is needed within 8 ms to 10 ms after a fault at that substation has been remotely detected at an adjoining substation.

As a consequence of this new communication standard, the use of IEDs in substations resulted in many advantages such as high-speed communication and reduced costs. However, improvements of this digital system cause several security threats in substations. Attacks can change data being sent over the network, which can cause, for example, an improper opening or closing of circuit breakers, as discussed before. In the case of improper opening, the system will cease to supply loads without any fault, causing unnecessary consumer shutdown. In the case of an improper closure, system fault condition is reconnected, supporting a short-circuit. Moreover, if the circuit is undergoing maintenance, it threatens human life.

The next sections present the description of attacks that may cause massive damage in the substation, in both internal and external cyber structures. Attacks are subdivided in two types: type one represents attacks against SCADA; type two represents attacks that could be performed after attacks against SCADA, when the attacker is already local at the substation.

Type 1: Attacks Against Supervisor Systems

Attacks against supervisory systems happen in any kind of ICS. A recent study spread a number of honeypots over the world that emulated ICS operating with SCADA and the communication protocol MODBUS/DNP3 controlling a pump system. A honeypot is an installation that creates a fully mimicked version of a real installation. The idea is to create an environment attractive to hackers in order to study new forms of attacks (Wilhoit, 2013). That study registered 74 specific attacks to ICS installations in a period of three months. The number of attack attempts was even greater if we consider generic auto-mated attacks like SQL injections, reaching 33.466 attacks. Figure 4 shows the distribution of the origin of ICS specific attacks.

The observed attacks were related to vulnerabilities of SNMP (Simple Network Management Protocol), HMI server, absence of a proper authentication system, and VxWorks (File Transfer Protocol - FTP).

Figure 4. Origin of attacks against ICS honeypots
Source: Wilhoit, 2013

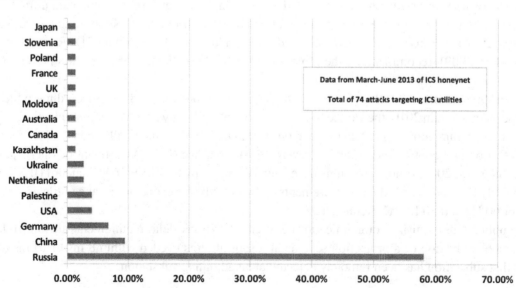

For better understanding attacks against SCADA, we will focus on the use of the DNP3 protocol. Other communication protocols such as MODBUS or MMS in IEC 61850 suffer from similar attacks, as none of these protocols was designed considering the existence of an untruthful communication environment. Hence, these protocols do not employ encryption, authentication, and authorization.

In general, attacks against systems using SCADA are divided in three categories: attacks that exploit communication protocol specifications; attacks that exploit vendor implementations, like configuration errors and code flaws; and attacks against the underlying infrastructure, which target information technology, network assets, and weak system security policies (East, Butts, Papa, & Shenoi, 2009).

From now on, we will focus on attacks against the DNP3 specification. DNP3 allows three communication models between the master unit, which represents the control center, and the outstation (slave) device, as shown in Figures 5-7. Communication between the master and outstations is modeled in three different modes: unicast, broadcast, and unsolicited responses. In the unicast mode, the master sends a request and waits for an answer of the target outstation. For instance, the master can request a circuit

Figure 5. DNP3 network configurations: One-to-one connection
(East, Butts, Papa, & Shenoi, 2009)

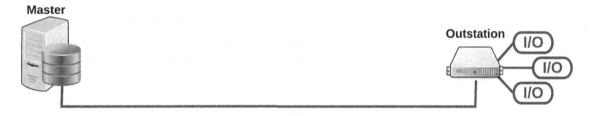

Figure 6. DNP3 network configurations: Multi-drop connection
(East, Butts, Papa, & Shenoi, 2009)

Figure 7. DNP3 network configurations: Hierarchical connection
(East, Butts, Papa, & Shenoi, 2009)

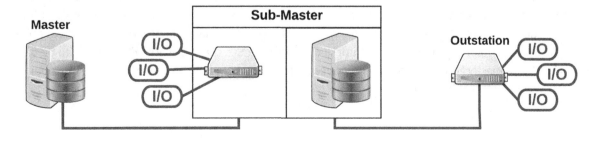

breaker status or perform a circuit breaker command and the outstation answers with the result of the operation, respectively. In broadcast transmission, a request is forwarded to all outstations and there is no answer to the master. In the unsolicited response, outstations send an unsolicited message to the master containing periodic updates, events, or alerts.

Attacks targeting/originating from the supervision system are based on message interception, fake message injection, and message modification. Attacks against DNP3 can be classified according to the network architecture layer where it occurs. In the following, we provide a few examples of attacks against DNP3 (East, Butts, Papa, & Shenoi, 2009):

- **Passive Network Reconnaissance:** The attacker with appropriate access captures and analyzes messages to discover information about network topology, devices in use, available functionalities, etc.
- **Baseline Response Replay and Man-in-the-Middle:** In these attacks, an attacker observes network traffic and injects messages to the master as outstations and to outstations as the master. In the case of the man-in-the-middle attack, a device is placed between the master and outstations capturing and modifying traffic and impersonating each other. The objectives of these attacks are to spy, stop the master and/or the outstations, modify the behavior of the master and/or outstations, and impersonate the master and/or outstations to cause failures in the service.
- **Link-Layer Field Modification:** This attack, which depends on the establishment of a man-in-the-middle attack, has many variations, according to the DNP3 message field that is modified. The DNP3 frame format is described in Figure 8. For instance, the attacker could modify the Length field to disrupt message processing; change the DFC Flag to send a fake signal of busy outstation to the master; or change the message to send Function Code 1, in order to promote an unnecessary restart of the outstation that causes temporary unavailability.
- **Pseudo-Transport Layer Field Modification:** This attack is another variation of the man-in-the-middle to disrupt the treatment of fragmented messages. In this case, the attacker could change transport message fields causing the destination to discard all incomplete fragments or yet to cause processing errors when joining fragmented information.
- **Outstation Write Attack:** In this application attack, the attacker uses Function Code 2 to write fake data in an outstation. This attack sends a DNP3 message with Function Code 2, which writes data objects to an outstation, causing errors in the device. Another variation sends Function Code 9 or 10 to freeze and clear data objects, creating inconsistent states in the system.
- **Configuration File Interception Attack:** This application attack aims at obtaining the configuration file of an outstation. To do so, the attacker sends a message indicating a corrupted configuration file impersonating the master. The victim outstation then resends the configuration file, which is intercepted by the attacker.
- **Denial of Service with a Single Packet:** In this attack, the attacker sends special crafted response packets that are able to crash the master. This attack explores both DNP3 and firmware exploits in order to disrupt the entire substation system, as it is able to stop the master. As a consequence, the control center can no longer monitor and control the SCADA network. The attack can be triggered by a master request or by any other event chosen by the attacker, as DNP3 allows unsolicited responses.

Figure 8. DNP3 frame format

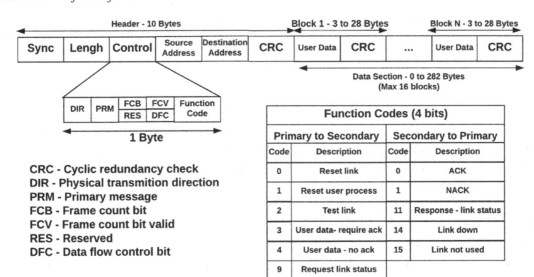

CRC - Cyclic redundancy check
DIR - Physical transmition direction
PRM - Primary message
FCB - Frame count bit
FCV - Frame count bit valid
RES - Reserved
DFC - Data flow control bit

Function Codes (4 bits)			
Primary to Secondary		**Secondary to Primary**	
Code	Description	Code	Description
0	Reset link	0	ACK
1	Reset user process	1	NACK
2	Test link	11	Response - link status
3	User data- require ack	14	Link down
4	User data - no ack	15	Link not used
9	Request link status		

It is important noticing that those attacks are documented and can be easily performed using open tools (Rodofile, Radke, & Foo, 2015). The main difficult is to gain access to the network running the SCADA system, which was supposed to be secure. Overcoming those threats, however, requires a redefinition of communication protocols considering that the network is no longer safe in a smart grid environment.

Type 2: Attacks Against Communications Between Local Devices

Attacks between local substation devices target the misuse of an IED to disrupt the electrical system. Those attacks' specific details depend directly on the communication protocol in use. To illustrate, we will describe the attacks using IEC 61850 standard definitions. Both remote unauthorized access and physical unauthorized access can lead to the attacks described in the following.

It is important noticing that there are different methods for an attacker to access an IED. The simplest way is when an insider attacker accesses the device and changes configuration parameters to damage the network. Another possible action of an internal attacker is to connect a malicious device to the network in order to inject traffic and impersonate devices in the network. Nevertheless, it is also possible to access an IED through external methods by exploring VPN software exploits, or by placing an attack against the device that connects the substation to the outside world. Another possibility is to access an IED through SCADA. Hence, once SCADA is compromised, it becomes very easy to access IEDs, because usually these devices are configured with a standard login and password.

One of the main concerns when analyzing the communication inside a substation is that QoS requirements of protection messages are not compliant with delays imposed by cryptographic methods. To provide authenticity and integrity, which are the most basic security requirements in control systems, we need to perform some cryptographic-based scheme. Since there is no authentication or integrity check in current communication protocols in addition to all other vulnerabilities of ICS described in the previous sections, a large number of attacks become possible.

This section focuses on attacks against IEC 61850, in order to illustrate the impacts of attacks against the communication between IEDs and also between any local devices. The GOOSE protocol was chosen as an example because it enables communication among IEDs. The main focus of the GOOSE protocol is to transmit data between two or more IEDs quickly and reliably. Even though, when using GOOSE, a substation is prone to different attacks, such as:

- **Denial-of-Service Attack:** This attack is used to prevent users from accessing network resources. The attacker sends a large number of messages to the machine under attack using one or more machines already compromised. In the substation scenario, this attack aims at stopping an IED. Also, the attacker most likely intends to slow the delivery of critical messages between substations and disable the remote control and other monitoring functions (Bayat, Arkian, & Aref, 2015). A powerful damage can occur in substations, once the communication is hijacked and the attacker prevents the reception of legitimate traffic. To perform this attack, the attacker must access the IED either using firmware exploits or by circumventing network security flaws. Once the attacker controls an IED, it generates a huge amount of GOOSE packets into the substation network. As GOOSE messages are sent in broadcast, all substation devices start receiving a large number of GOOSE messages. This attack is also called Flooding Attack (Li, et al., 2015). Two consequences arise: legitimate messages may not reach the destination in time because of message queues in network switches and in endpoints; IEDs may stop working because they are not designed to receive a large number of messages. This second consequence is easier to observe if the attacker uses malformed messages (Khaitan, McCalley, & Liu, 2015; Lopes, Muchaluat-Saade, Fernandes, & Fortes, 2015).
- **GOOSE Spoofing:** Since there is no authentication or integrity checks in GOOSE messages, attackers are able to send fake messages in the network. For injecting consistent traffic, an attacker can observe network traffic to discover data such as the current Status Number (stNum) of a GOOSE message flow. The stNum parameter works like a sequence number. Hence, the attacker can generate GOOSE messages with increasing stNum after inspecting an initial GOOSE frame. Fake GOOSE frames should be sent in multicast as rapidly as possible by the attacker. It is expected that once the attack traffic starts being processed by the subscriber, legitimate traffic with lower status numbers will be discarded (Kush, Ahmed, Branagan, & Foo, 2014). Therefore, the attacker stops the legitimate information flow as well as he can insert any kind of information that could disrupt the communication network or the power system.
- **Impersonate a Central Device:** In this attack, the compromised device is configured to impersonate a server of the supervisory system. It is easier to be deployed whether the attacker is able to connect a computer to the substation LAN. Indeed, industrial automation software that enables customers to implement a SCADA is easily available, which facilitates this attack.
- **Attacks against Ethernet:** GOOSE protocol specifies the use of Ethernet to connect substation devices in the LAN. Therefore, this network is prone to all layer-2 attacks against Ethernet, such as ARP attacks, MAC flooding attacks, spanning-tree attacks, multicast brute force attacks, VLAN trunking protocol attacks, private VLAN attacks, identity theft, VLAN hopping attacks, MAC spoofing and double-encapsulated 802.1Q/Nested VLAN attacks (Yoo & Shon, 2015).

Attacks in Advanced Metering Infrastructure

As the complexity and degree of automation in industrial plants and utility infrastructure have increased, the need for a reliable and flexible system that could enable the collection of measurements in sparse geographical locations or dangerous places in a plant drove the industry to develop an infrastructure of instrumentation devices with processing and telecommunication capabilities. These devices are known as smart meters.

Advanced Metering Infrastructure (AMI) is a command and control system that has millions of nodes and touches every consumer and almost every enterprise system. With the use of smart meters, which collect massive amounts of data, and with the implementation of AMI, the need for security in Power Distribution becomes evident. In this section, we discuss the kinds of attacks against AMI and also threats and vulnerabilities in the access network.

Advanced Metering Infrastructure Overview

The implementation of a bidirectional communication is the key element of smart grids. In the same fashion, the introduction of smart meters in the distribution network enables a better understanding of the demand and a better control of the energy usage and distributed generation. The advanced metering infrastructure is an essential part of a smart distribution system and refers to the network that connects the distribution operator to the customer. At the operator end, a system known as Meter Data and Management System (MDMS) interconnects electronic meters capable of collecting precise time-based information about the power consumption of customers.

Common approaches for meter networks are a direct connection with the MDMS inside the Data and Control Center (DCC) or via a meter concentrator, as shown in Figure 9. This local network of meters that communicates with a concentrator is known as a Neighborhood Area Network (NAN). An RF mesh or Power Line Communications over narrowband frequencies (PLC-NB) are popular technologies used for transmission. PLC limits the number of meters connected to devices in the secondary windings of the transformer where the concentrator is installed. Hence, PLC is usually less employed than a wireless alternative (Budka, Deshpande, & Thottan, 2014),

Some of the new functionalities introduced with the implementation of smart meters, such as dynamic price information and the high precision and real-time metering of the consumer power usage, insert a series of vulnerabilities that can expose consumer private data. This vulnerability is due to the precision of the information generated by these meters. The electrical signature of many house hold appliances and human activity can be tracked by an attacker. Private data can be used for burglary, kidnapping, and other criminal activities. Pricing information will encourage consumers to avoid power consumption in peak demand hours, and to control their power consumption in a more aware manner, but they can also be manipulated by an attacker to control the energy market. By relying in wireless technologies, a NAN is vulnerable to signal jamming, eavesdropping, replay attack, and data injection attacks. These are some examples of the importance of investing in a secure communication system for the AMI that will be better explained in the following sections (Finster & Baumgart, 2014).

In the following sections, this chapter describes attacks in internal cyber structures of the distribution network. Attacks against the Advanced Metering Infrastructure and home area networks such as

Figure 9. AMI structure in the smart grid context

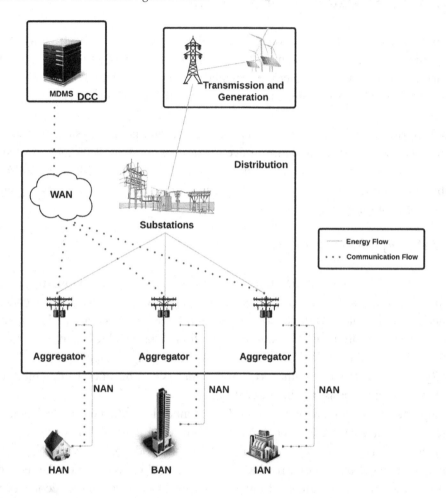

attacks against user privacy, attacks against distribution service, signaling jamming and other malicious usage of the communication network. According to the NIST report on cyber security for smart grids, as discussed before, three major objectives for a secure network are: availability, integrity, and confidentiality (Cyber Security Working Group, 2010). In the context of distribution automation and AMI, these concepts apply as following:

- **Availability:** Access to system functionalities must be ready when needed. If an attacker interrupts the communication between a smart home and the operation center, he compromises the system availability.
- **Integrity:** Information must be protected against falsification, modification or destruction. In the context of NANs, an example of loss of integrity is the modification of the power usage information by a malicious customer trying to deny his financial responsibility.
- **Confidentiality:** Information access must be restricted to authorized entities in order to protect privacy and proprietary information. This is a major concern for customers since an attacker can acquire a lot of personal information from such a precise power monitoring system.

Attacks Against Service Availability in Distribution Systems

This section presents examples of attacks targeting availability in distribution systems and their impacts. Denial-of-service attacks attempt to interrupt the normal operation of the service and can be performed at different communication layers. As NAN communication protocols are chosen, other vulnerabilities might emerge. Here we focus on channel jamming, a simple and generic physical layer attack. Jamming is a transmission of interfering signal that decreases the signal-to-noise ratio of a wireless communication channel.

Maintaining the balance between energy production and consumption is essential for the grid stability. With smart grids, the introduction of renewable energy sources increases. Hence, the prediction of produced energy becomes more difficult, due to renewable sources intermittent nature. Renewable power sources depend on environmental factors that make power generation prediction more complex and less accurate. Therefore, there is a paradigm change with the grid modernization: in traditional grid energy, production adapts to the demand, but in smart grids, demand adapts to the production and makes user consumption more efficient. Demand Side Management (DSM) programs arise as one of the solutions to adjust user consumption to supply. DSM is an action or decision made by utility to alter and model user pattern of consumption. DSM correct operation depends on a reliable communication between the grid and consumers. Two examples of jamming attacks against DSM programs are discussed in the following, with different motivations, that could result in power loss.

In a context of real-time demand response, we present the first example. In real-time programs, energy price is dynamic along the day. Market uses power demand, power generation cost, and constraints of transmission lines to calculate a price that reflects available grid resources. Then, users of this program receive messages from the market every time energy cost changes and adjust their consumption to the new price. Li and Han describe a possibility of market manipulation by jamming the real-time price signal between market and consumers, as show in Figure 10 (Li & Han, 2011). When there is low energy availability, the market sends a message with a higher price to users that reduce their consumption and expect for a lower price message to increase or normalize the consumption. The attacker blocks the price signal of a highly populated area, then the consumers system keeps working with the last price received and the attacker monitors the market price waiting for a significant change to stop jamming. Therefore, the jammer can control price changes and use it to profit, for example, if the attacker blocks the signal during a higher price, when price decreases, he stores energy, while the other users are working with a

Figure 10. Jamming price signal to manipulate power market

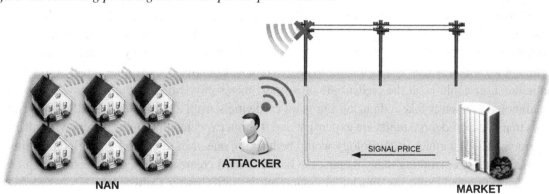

higher price. Then he stops jamming, when users will receive a lower price and increase their consumption, price will tend to increase again and in this moment, he sells the stored energy. Since the utility uses real-price to balance demand and supply, if a highly populated area does not receive a price increase and does not reduce its consumption, it can result in instability of the grid or even in a wide-area blackout.

The second example occurs at direct load control. Direct load control (DLC) is another alternative of a DSM program, in which a consumer receives incentives or discounts on electricity bill to allow the utility to have direct control of some appliances of his home. In emergency cases or when demand exceeds the available supply, a message command is sent to switch off some loads and protect the grid. Control commands to reduce energy consumption pass through the AMI network, and similar to the real-price programs, utility uses DLC to balance demand and supply, then an interception of a reduce command can affect the grid stability. Attacks against this communication could damage the grid, impact range from a discomfort of consumers to power loss in critical areas, compromising human lives. A malicious user can jam this communication and block messages to trick the program, so he/she receives discount on electricity bill for participating in the program without switching off any load. After an emergency case, the utility sends a switch on command to normalize user consumption. An adversary can jam during the switch on command preventing the normalization of the operation for a specific user. In the worst case, terrorist attacks may block the signal in a large area affecting the stability of the grid and causing blackout.

Attacks Against Data Integrity in Distribution Systems

Attacks that attempt to manipulate data instead of blocking services are typically more sophisticated than a jamming attack. Also, their consequences are usually more severe. An attacker can modify data to fraud power-consumption information in behalf of a customer. Another possibility involves issuing a service interruption command for a meter and leaving a residence without power. Also, the meter firmware is vulnerable to malware injection during update, or modified firmware might be uploaded compromising its billing capacity. Another possibility is to compromise a large number of devices to corrupt the global view of the sensing system. In this case, a large number of devices would be able to inject fake messages in the network, containing fake measurement data or fake alarms. A fake global view of the system could trigger wrong actions through the distribution supervision system, causing power failures.

The attack methodology is very similar to the ones against the Internet. For instance, an attacker could perform a man-in-the-middle, execute a replay attack or even create a botnet of smart meters. In the case of a man-in-the-middle attack, the malicious user will try to impersonate a trusted smart meter and the Data and Control Center (DCC). The attacker will connect to both communicating parties impersonating the end peers. This maneuver enables an attacker to eavesdrop on data, inject false packets, resend authentic data, and modify packet payload (Ur-Rehman, Zivic, & Ruland, 2015). Replay attacks are simpler to execute, since they are based in resending old messages, but they are also easier to avoid. Injecting new fake messages as a meter would be much more effective than a replay attack. For instance, a malicious user could steal the credentials of a smart meter physically corrupting the device. Then, the malicious user sends fake data using the valid credentials from a computer. Usually tamper-proof devices that avoid credential thefts are expensive and it is not expected that smart meters will fulfill this requirement. The last attack methodology would be hacking one or more meters through the communication network. By corrupting many meters, the hacker would create a botnet of meters. In both cases, it requires finding and exploring unpatched vulnerabilities of the meter firmware.

As explained before, using digital signatures for firmware authentication might not be enough to protect a smart meter (McDaniel & McLaughlin, 2009). From past experiences, we know that bugs and security breaches are inevitable, especially when dealing with a system where hacking can be so easily monetized. Hence, the communication network security must be based on different security techniques.

Attacks Against User Privacy in Distribution Systems

Having described possible DoS attacks and attacks against service integrity that could occur in distribution systems, we now move on to describe security issues against user privacy. In a traditional grid metering, utilities employees gather meter measurements monthly. With the advances promoted by AMI, meter data becomes more detailed and reported in shorter time intervals (Siddiqui, Zeadally, Alcaraz, & Galvao, 2012). Although detailed and granular data are important to enable several smart grid services, they create major privacy vulnerabilities.

The main kinds of attacks against user privacy are eavesdropping and traffic analysis. Both take advantage of NAN wireless communication to obtain intimate details of user's life. Eavesdropping is an unauthorized listening of a private conversation, in this case secretly intercepting a wireless communication channel. In traffic analysis, traffic pattern is monitored with the intention to infer user daily habits.

Periodic data exchange between smart appliances and the Energy Management System (EMS) allows users to monitor consumption in real-time and remotely control home devices. However an adversary could eavesdrop this communication, acquire device consumption and use a load-profiling algorithm to identify which device is switched on. Each device has a load signature, a unique electric behavior, that might be used in a process of recognition of electrical devices (Rahimi, Chan, & Goubran, 2011), and in a deeper analysis, the attacker might obtain even multimedia content like the television channel a user is watching (Greveler, Justus, & Loehr, 2012). The privacy issue is serious not only because of the exposure of the user's intimate life, but also for the fact that this information can compromise the user's own safety. Through traffic analysis, a consumption profile can be traced and a user's routine details can be inferred, what time he/she wakes up, what time he/she goes to sleep, if he/she is traveling, which people are at home at a specific hour, as shown in Figure 11. This information may be used for theft, robbery, and even kidnapping.

Detection of these types of attacks becomes difficult due to their passive nature. The adversary just wants to steal information without alteration of data and without modifying the system operation. Thus, prevention is more important than detection.

SOLUTIONS AND RECOMMENDATIONS

After describing the main attacks against the smart grid communication network, we now describe the main solutions to create an integrated communication architecture, which provides reliability, privacy, and non-repudiation.

Substations and AMI Cryptography

As previously discussed, the smart grid communication network is vulnerable to several types of attacks. Unencrypted data communication is one of the reasons that increase vulnerability. In order to understand

Figure 11. Example of energy consumption measurements that could be used to spy private data of user routine
Source: Molina-Markham, Shenoy, Fu, Cecchet, & Irwin, 2010

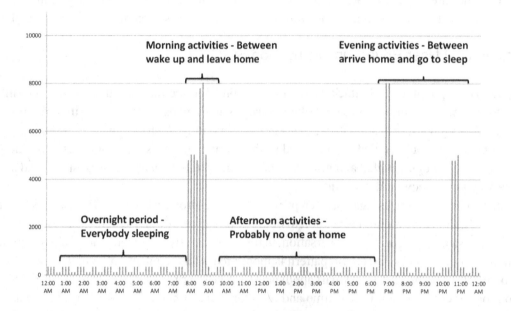

better this scenario and where cryptography can be used, it is necessary to understand which kind of protocols are in use. In this section, we classify them in three types. The first type is called SCADA protocols, which is responsible for the communication between supervisory systems and devices as smart meters and IEDs. SCADA protocols usually have milder time constrains than others. It is because its goal is to display devices for users and allow interaction between them. Supervisory goals comprise data acquisition and controls. Data acquisition is used to show information for users. Controls, which are made by commands from the supervisory to devices, are started by user decisions. Therefore, user interface is part of the supervisory system and delays depend on user activity. Thus, network delays from 200 ms to 1000 ms are very well accepted.

The second type of protocol is called protection protocols. Opposed to the previous type, this kind of protocol has strong time constraints ranging from 3 ms to 100 ms according to scenario requirements. In this case, in order to prevent faults or to limit service loss due to an electrical failure, network protection messages are sent after an electrical event. Faults may affect a big part of the electrical system very quickly, so all protection messages require rigid time constraints. It is important to highlight that protective devices (e.g., IEDs) can detect fault conditions and send protection messages to another device (e.g., a smart breaker or an IED that can operate a breaker) only in modern and more recent systems. In traditional systems, a protection device detects fault conditions and directly operates a circuit breaker by control cables, without communication.

The third type is aimed at measuring and sampling values. The idea comprises sampling instantaneous values of power system quantities, mainly primary currents and voltages, and transmitting them over the network. These values are published in the network and protection or control devices (or any device that can make use of them) are able to subscribe to it. Sampled values are used for protection and control devices for identifying a fault due to an electrical failure. Therefore, time constrains are so rigid as protection protocols, or more, as it is necessary for failure identification.

The protocol time constraints are one of the main keys for cryptography use in this scenario. In general, cryptography or encryption is the transformation of information from a comprehensive state to apparent nonsense. Thus, cryptography transmits data in a particular form to whom it is intended for, in a way that just them can process it. Thus, the sender of an encrypted message shares the decoding technique needed to recover the original information only with the intended receiver. Cryptographic tools include symmetric key cryptography and asymmetric key cryptography. Symmetric cryptography requires less computational resources and causes less delay in the communication. Examples of symmetric algorithms are AES (Advanced Encryption Standard) and DES (Data Encryption Standard) (Mishra, Dinh, Thai, Seo, & Shin, 2016). A secure key management is essential for information encryption.

However, cryptography adds delay to network communication. As encoding and decoding are performed across packets, the total time from an event to an operation, for example, can considerably increase. Recognizing this fact, most encryption solutions are not suitable for use in protocols with rigid time constraints as sampled value protocol and protection protocols. It is necessary that encryption methods not only satisfy real time performance requirements of those protocols, but also ensure message security. As there are few works about this issue published in the literature (Fangfang, Huazhong, Dongqing, & Yong, 2013), it is a good research opportunity: a method to provide safety combined with quality of service. Extensive testing should be made to ensure that solutions with encryption do not exceed smart grid delay requirements. In (Fangfang, Huazhong, Dongqing, & Yong, 2013), authors show by simulation with software OPNET that, with a hybrid encryption method, it is possible. However deeper tests need to be done.

On the other hand, cryptography could be added to SCADA protocols without problems, since this kind of protocols do not have many delay constraints. Several researchers have proposed cryptograph methods and key-management schemes for SCADA. This is because SCADA protocols were not designed with a security mindset. As showed by (Amoah, Camtepe, & Foo, 2016), many researchers have proposed solutions to this end but much work remains to be done. Literature solutions are very specific, with many peculiarities. Some solutions are presented below together with solutions for a safe communication.

Standardized Solution for Security in Substations

Due to historical reasons, cyber security issues are not part of industrial protocols. DNP3, 60870-5, and IEC 61850 were published when security was not an industrial major worry. To overcome this issue, IEC 62351 standard was developed by the IEC Technical Committee (TC) 57 in order to provide security requirements in energy automation networks. In fact, IEC 62351 already uses current methods as far as possible. For instance, it uses Transport Layer Security protocol (TLS) in order to preserve the integrity of the messages based on a strong identity management scheme. Also, it proposes the use of Role-Based Access Control (RBAC). This means that not only it intends to securely identify every system entity, but also to define policies for access control based on role of the entity in the system. The standard objectives also comprise integrity, confidentiality, prevention of spoofing, intrusion detection, authentication through digital certificates, and so on. This standard is divided in 10 parts, as illustrated in Figure 12.

A well-known solution already applied is an Intrusion Detection System (IDS). The purpose of IDS is to detect abnormal behavior in the network by scanning packets and generating alerts to operators. An IDS is typically classified as network-based or host-based. A network-based IDS monitors local network

Figure 12. IEC 62351 structure

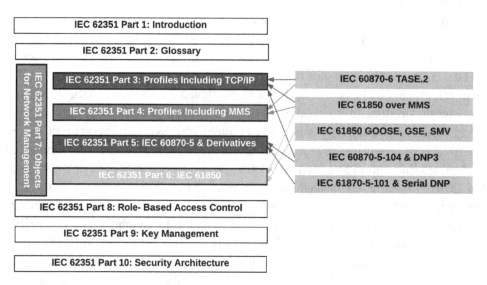

traffic and has access to all transmitted packets, while a host-based IDS scans packets in one or more servers individually (Sun, Liu, & Xie, 2016). A recent work of Mishra et al. (2016) has demonstrated an optimal method for packet scan as an affordable defense against attacks, offering security without compromising strict QoS requirements.

Solutions for Providing Security in AMI

Security solutions for AMI are under discussion and there are a high number of proposals about how to provide security in the network. In this section, we show solutions and protection schemes for attacks against internal cyber structures of a distribution network and the challenges of improving safety in this scenario.

The jamming attack was presented as a threat to availability of the grid. A few works propose solutions for this kind of wireless attack, most of them are frequency-hop based techniques. For instance, there is a proposal that suggests the use of multiple alternate frequency channels (Aravinthan, Namboodiri, Sunku, & Jewell, 2011). If meters detect interference in the current channel, all meters move through a predefined and common random sequence of channels. When a meter completes the authentication process, it receives the frequency hopping sequence through an encrypted channel. Another proposal consists of a random spread-spectrum scheme called Frequency Quorum Rendezvous (FQR) (Lee, Oh, & Gerla, 2011). FQR exploits a quorum system that allows each node to build a hopping sequence independently during the key establishment phase. The intersection property of the quorum system guarantees that a pair of nodes meets within a bounded amount of time, during which they share a common key used for future spread spectrum communications. This mechanism not only avoids jamming, but also eavesdropping.

Preventing false data injection and fraud can be achieved with strong end-to-end encryption in communication channels of the AMI and HAN (Home Area Network) network. Since delay constraints for this application are not critical, many end-to-end encryption options used in the Internet are readily available. A list of works related to false-data attack prevention can be found at Sharma and Saini (2015).

Authentication is also of major importance since false or fraudulent meters might be inserted into the network giving attacker the ability to execute commands and degrade service. Nicanfar et al. (2014) present a smart grid mutual authentication (SGMA) that provides an efficient authentication between smart meter and authentication server using passwords, and a smart grid key management (SGKM) protocol using public key infrastructure (PKI).

New improvements were also proposed to protect user privacy. In this case, a mechanism partially obscures the user load profile using a rechargeable battery, and protects user privacy (Varodayan & Khisti, 2011). The consumption reported by the smart meter to the utility company is a combination of appliances and battery consumption. At any time, a battery may perform a combination of the following actions (or none of them) subject to its capacity: relay power directly from the utility to the appliances; store energy from the utility company for future use; deliver previously stored energy to the appliances. This way, charging and discharging a battery can manipulate the output load, obscuring the real consumer information. Other solutions for privacy are based on key management schemes to protect the content being transmitted inside the home and between the meter and the control systems (Kazienko, Silva Filho, Moraes, & Albuquerque, 2015).

FUTURE RESEARCH DIRECTIONS

In this chapter, we addressed smart grid vulnerabilities from customer and smart meters to substations and control centers. We described attacks and threats and its consequences. Besides, we highlighted possible solutions and researches, which might help us to achieve a secure smart grid. However, the deployment of a secure smart grid communication network is still a huge challenge. Some research directions include:

- Proposals as IEC 62351 promise results, but they require extensive tests and experimentations. They must be tested with industrial protocols to attest that the quality of service required by energy applications cannot be affected. In addition, that standard proposal is being updated with new methods or evolution of already known methods, which confirms the need of constant evaluation.
- Standardization is also a main concern. The smart grid architecture is complex and composed of different kinds of domains and networks. The success of smart grid commercial deployment depends on standard mechanisms that enable different vendors to interoperate and interface in a standard manner. A universal standard could be used in order to provide interoperability, flexibility, cost reduction, and so on. The use of the same information model will improve communication and mainly security researches. There are indications of IEC 61850 use, however there are still many issues to be assessed.
- The establishment of a universal smart grid framework for secure communication is very important. This framework must take into consideration a "defense-in-depth" protection (Lüders, 2011). Hence, every communication layer must be addressed, as well as hardware and software. Traditional IT security techniques must also be addressed in smart grid context, including issues like:
  - An easy and inexpensive process to apply security patches in IEDs and smart meters;
  - The use of identity management frameworks to provide secure authentication and authorization;
  - The use of configuration management systems to IEDs and smart meters;

- ◦ The use of new firewalls and intrusion detection techniques in substations and AMI networks.
  - ◦ The use of big data techniques to discover important information among data collected from smart meters to help to discover botnets, energy theft, and even terrorism actions.
- The proposal of more secure authentication and integrity methods for multicast communication without incurring in high process power requirements or high communication delays. This is of special importance for providing a communication between IEDs that is more resilient against internal and external attackers.
- The proposal of a complete solution, which comprises interoperability between different cryptographic systems, is also needed. Different communication technologies and protocols are used in smart grid infrastructure that results in unique cryptography requirements for each one. A secure and interoperable approach is essential.
- The balance between information availability and privacy preservation is not trivial and is a very interesting research direction. While a great set of information results in smarter decisions and better optimizations, it also represents a threat to user privacy. Smart metering information makes it possible to infer consumer behavior, which will possibly offend consumers.

CONCLUSION

The advance of smart grid communication sets new security challenges. As the scenario in substations and in distribution systems change, old concepts fell to the ground. Now it is clear that attackers are a reality for field networks in substations, even if firewalls, virtual private networks (VPN), intrusion detection systems (IDS), and a few encryption techniques are in use.

There is no ultimate solution for security in smart grid communication networks as well as this complete solution does not exist for the Internet either. Security must always evolve because hackers are always looking for new exploits. Legacy processes to manage ICS networks are no longer acceptable. Practices such as not using firewalls, not using anti-virus, not applying patches, using default configurations and default accounts, not using digital certification, etc. are no longer acceptable. In addition, vendors must assume responsibility for developing secure and robust devices. Much effort has been placed in the last years for developing devices that were safe against explosions or failures in the electrical system and that were robust to different scenarios of power faults. Nevertheless, those devices are not tested under abuse cases and cannot be considered secure.

Many of those observations rise from the fact that there are many IT network security experts, but just a few that understand both network security and industrial control systems. Hence, there is a strong need to train more professionals able to work in this multidisciplinary area.

REFERENCES

Amoah, R., Camtepe, S., & Foo, E. (2016). *Securing DNP3 Broadcast Communications in SCADA Systems. IEEE Transactions on Industrial Informatics.*

Aravinthan, V., Namboodiri, V., Sunku, S., & Jewell, W. (2011). Wireless AMI Application and Security for Controlled Home Area Networks. *IEEE Power and Energy Society General Meeting.*

Assante, M. J. (2016). *Confirmation of a Coordinated Attack on the Ukrainian Power Grid.* Retrieved from SANS Industrial Control Systems Security Blog: https://ics.sans.org/blog

Bayat, M., Arkian, H. R., & Aref, M. R. (2015). A revocable attribute based data sharing scheme resilient to DoS attacks in smart grid. *Wireless Networks, 21*(3), 871–881. doi:10.1007/s11276-014-0824-9

Bhaiji, Y. (2008). *Network Security Technologies and Solutions.* CCIE Professional Development Series.

Budka, K. C., Deshpande, J. G., & Thottan, M. (2014). *Communication Networks for Smart Grids.* Springer-Verlag London. doi:10.1007/978-1-4471-6302-2

Cheung, J. C., Chim, T., Yiu, S., Hui, L. C., & Li, V. O. (2011). Credential-based Privacy-preserving Power Request Scheme for Smart Grid Network.*IEEE Global Telecommunications Conference (GLOBECOM).* doi:10.1109/GLOCOM.2011.6134566

Cyber Security Working Group. (2010). The Smart Grid Interoperability Panel - Guidelines for smart grid cyber security. *NISTIR, 7628,* 1–597.

Detken, K.-O., Genzel, C.-H., & Jahnk, M. (2014). Integrity protection in a smart grid environment for wireless access of smart meters. *Wireless Systems within the Conferences on Intelligent Data Acquisition and Advanced Computing Systems: Technology and Applications (IDAACS-SWS), 2nd International Symposium on,* (pp. 79-86).

East, S., Butts, J., Papa, M., & Shenoi, S. (2009). A Taxonomy of Attacks on the DNP3 Protocol. In C. Palmer, & S. Shenoi (Eds.), Critical Infrastructure Protection III (pp. 67-81). Springer Berlin Heidelberg. doi:10.1007/978-3-642-04798-5_5

Falliere, N., Murchu, L., & Chien, E. (2011). *W32.Stuxnet Dossier.* Symantec.

Fan, Z., Kulkarni, P., Gormus, S., Efthymiou, C., Kalogridis, G., Sooriyabandara, M., & Chin, W. H. et al. (2012). Smart Grid Communications: Overview of Research Challenges, Solutions, and Standardization Activities. *IEEE Communications Surveys and Tutorials,* 21–38.

Fangfang, W., Huazhong, W., Dongqing, C., & Yong, P. (2013). *Substation Communication Security Research Based on Hybrid Encryption of DES and RSA* (pp. 437–441). Intelligent Information Hiding and Multimedia Signal Processing. doi:10.1109/IIH-MSP.2013.115

Finster, S., & Baumgart, I. (2014). Privacy-Aware Smart Metering: A Survey. *IEEE Communications Surveys and Tutorials, 16*(3), 1732–1745. doi:10.1109/SURV.2014.052914.00090

FIPS PUB 200. (2006). *Minimum Security Requirements for Federal Information and Information Systems.* Federal Information Processing Standards Publication.

Greveler, U., Justus, B., & Loehr, D. (2012). *Multimedia Content Identification Through Smart Meter Power Usage Profiles.* CPDP.

Hoyos, J., Dehus, M., & Brown, T. X. (2012). *Exploiting the GOOSE protocol: A practical attack on cyber-infrastructure.* IEEE Globecom Workshops.

IEC 61850-7-420. (2009). *Basic communication structure - Distributed Energy Resources logical nodes.* International Electrotechnical Commission.

IEC 61850: Communication networks and systems for power utility automation. (n.d.). International Electrotechnical Commission Std.

IEEE 1646. (2004). IEEE Standard Communication Delivery Time Performance Requirements for Electric Power Substation Automation.

Katzir, L., & Schwartzman, I. (2011). Secure firmware updates for smart grid Devices. *Innovative Smart Grid Technologies (ISGT Europe),2nd IEEE PES International Conference and Exhibition on*, (pp. 1-5).

Kazienko, J. F., Silva Filho, P. R., Moraes, I. M., & Albuquerque, C. V. (2015). On the Performance of a Secure Storage Mechanism for Key Distribution Architectures in Wireless Sensor Networks. *International Journal of Distributed Sensor Networks, 2015*, 1–14. doi:10.1155/2015/392495

Khaitan, S. K., McCalley, J. D., & Liu, C. C. (2015). *Cyber Physical Systems Approach to Smart Electric Power Grid*. Springer-Verlag Berlin Heidelberg. doi:10.1007/978-3-662-45928-7

Kim, J. C., & Kim, T. H. (2014). Implementation of Secure IEC 61850 Communication. *CIRED Workshop*.

Kounev, V., Lévesque, M., Tipper, D., & Gomes, T. (2016). Reliable Communication Networks for Smart Grid Transmission Systems. *Journal of Network and Systems Management, 24*(3), 629–652. doi:10.1007/s10922-016-9375-y

Kush, N., Ahmed, E., Branagan, M., & Foo, E. (2014). Poisoned GOOSE: Exploiting the GOOSE Protocol. *Proceedings of the Twelfth Australasian Information Security Conference*, (pp. 17-22).

Lee, E.-K., Oh, S. Y., & Gerla, M. (2011). Frequency Quorum Rendezvous for Fast and Resilient Key Establishment under Jamming Attack. *Mobile Computing and Communications Review, 14*(4), 1–3. doi:10.1145/1942268.1942270

Li, H., & Han, Z. (2011). Manipulating the Electricity Power Market via Jamming the Price Signaling in Smart Grid. *IEEE International Workshop on Smart Grid Communications and Networks*. doi:10.1109/GLOCOMW.2011.6162363

Li, Q., Ross, C., Yang, J., Di, J., Balda, J. C., & Alan, H. (2015). The effects of flooding attacks on time-critical communications in the smart grid. *Innovative Smart Grid Technologies Conference (ISGT)*. IEEE Power & Energy Society. doi:10.1109/ISGT.2015.7131802

Lopes, Y., Fernandes, N. C., Bastos, C. A., & Muchaluat-Saade, D. C. (2015). SMARTFlow: a solution for autonomic management and control of communication networks for smart grids. *Proceedings of the 30th Annual ACM Symposium on Applied Computing*, (pp. 2212-2217). doi:10.1145/2695664.2695733

Lopes, Y., Muchaluat-Saade, D. C., Fernandes, N. C., & Fortes, M. Z. (2015). Geese: A traffic generator for performance and security evaluation of IEC 61850 networks. *IEEE 24th International Symposium on Industrial Electronics (ISIE)*, (pp. 687-692).

Lüders, S. (2011). Why Control System CyberSecurity Sucks. *GovCERT.NL Symposium*.

McDaniel, P., & McLaughlin, S. (2009). Security and Privacy Challenges in the Smart Grid. *IEEE Security and Privacy, 7*(3), 75–77. doi:10.1109/MSP.2009.76

McGhee, J., & Goraj, M. (2010). Smart High Voltage Substation Based on IEC 61850 Process Bus and IEEE 1588 Time Synchronization. *Smart Grid Communications (SmartGridComm), First IEEE International Conference on*, (pp. 489-494).

Mishra, S., Dinh, T. N., Thai, M. T., Seo, J., & Shin, I. (2016). Optimal packet scan against malicious attacks in smart grids. *Theoretical Computer Science, 609*, 606–619. doi:10.1016/j.tcs.2015.07.054

Molina-Markham, A., Shenoy, P., Fu, K., Cecchet, E., & Irwin, D. (2010). Private Memoirs of a Smart Meter.*Proceedings of the 2nd ACM Workshop on Embedded Sensing Systems for Energy-Efficiency in Building*, (pp. 61-66). doi:10.1145/1878431.1878446

Nicanfar, H., Jokar, P., Beznosov, K., & Leung, V. C. (2014). *Efficient Authentication and Key Management Mechanisms for Smart Grid Communications. IEEE Systems Journal*.

NIST. (2014). *NIST Framework and Roadmap for Smart Grid Interoperability Standards, Release 3.0.* NIST.

Pappu, V., Carvalho, M., & Pardalos, P. M. (2013). *Optimization and Security Challenges in Smart Power Grids*. Springer-Verlag Berlin Heidelberg. doi:10.1007/978-3-642-38134-8

Pothamsetty, V., & Malik, S. (2009). *Smart grid leveraging intelligent communications to transform the power infrastructure*. CISCO.

Rahimi, S., Chan, A. D., & Goubran, R. A. (2011). Usage Monitoring of Electrical Devices in a Smart Home.*33rd Annual International Conference of the IEEE EMBS*. doi:10.1109/IEMBS.2011.6091313

Rodofile, N. R., Radke, K., & Foo, E. (2015). Real-Time and Interactive Attacks on DNP3 Critical Infrastructure Using Scapy.*Proceedings of the 13th Australasian Information Security Conference (AISC)*, pp. 67-70.

Selga, J. M., Zaballos, A., & Navarro, J. (2013). Solutions to the Computer Networking Challenges of the Distribution Smart Grid. *IEEE Communications Letters, 17*(3), 588–591. doi:10.1109/LCOMM.2013.020413.122896

Sharma, K., & Saini, L. M. (2015). Performance analysis of smart metering for smart grid: An overview. *Renewable & Sustainable Energy Reviews, 49*, 720–735. doi:10.1016/j.rser.2015.04.170

Siddiqui, F., Zeadally, S., Alcaraz, C., & Galvao, S. (2012). Smart grid privacy: Issues and solutions.*21st International Conference on Computer Communications and Networks (ICCCN)*.

Sun, C.-C., Liu, C.-C., & Xie, J. (2016). *Cyber-Physical System Security of a Power Grid: State-of-the-Art*. Electronics.

Ur-Rehman, O., Zivic, N., & Ruland, C. (2015). Security issues in smart metering systems. *Smart Energy Grid Engineering (SEGE), IEEE International Conference on*, (pp. 1-7).

U.S. Department of Energy. (2010). *Communication requirements of smart grid*. Author.

Varodayan, D., & Khisti, A. (2011). Smart meter privacy using a rechargeable battery: Minimizing the rate of information leakage.*IEEE International Conference on Acoustics, Speech and Signal Processing (ICASSP)*. doi:10.1109/ICASSP.2011.5946886

Wei, M., & Wang, W. (2016). Data-centric threats and their impacts to real-time communications in smart grid. *Computer Networks*, *104*, 174–188. doi:10.1016/j.comnet.2016.05.003

Wilhoit, K. (2013). *The SCADA That Didn't Cry Wolf.* BlackHat Security Conference.

Yan, Y., Hu, R. Q., Das, S. K., Sharif, H., & Qian, Y. (2013). An efficient security protocol for advanced metering infrastructure in smart grid. *IEEE Network*, *27*(4), 64–71. doi:10.1109/MNET.2013.6574667

Yan, Y., Qian, Y., Sharif, H., & Tipper, D. (2012). A Survey on Smart Grid Communication Infrastructures: Motivations, Requirements and Challenges. *IEEE Communications Surveys and Tutorials*, 5–20.

Yang, H.-S., Kim, S.-S., & Jang, H.-S. (2012). Optimized Security Algorithm for IEC 61850 Based Power Utility System. *Journal of Electrical Engineering & Technology*, *7*(3), 443–450. doi:10.5370/JEET.2012.7.3.443

Yoo, H., & Shon, T. (2015). Novel Approach for Detecting Network Anomalies for Substation Automation based on IEC 61850. *Multimedia Tools and Applications*, *74*(1), 303–318. doi:10.1007/s11042-014-1870-0

KEY TERMS AND DEFINITIONS

Botnets: A number of Internet-connected programs that communicate with other similar programs usually aiming at performing a malicious task. For instance, botnets have been used to participate in distributed DoS attacks.

Data Historians: Log databases that store trends and historical information about processes of an industrial control system.

Device: An element designed to serve a purpose or perform a function for instance, a smart meter, a circuit breaker, a relay, etc.

Exploits: A program or a sequence of commands that aims at causing accidental or unexpected computer behavior through system vulnerability. Usually used to gain control of a computer system.

Intelligent Electronic Device: Any device incorporating one or more processors, with the capability to receive or send data/control from, or to, an external source.

Master: An entity that requests a service from a slave, receives unsolicited data from a slave, or sends commands to a slave.

Remote Terminal Unit: A slave/outstation in a supervisory system that acts as an interface between the communication network and the substation equipment reporting information.

Slave: An entity that provides data to a device or allows access to its resources.

Chapter 2
Security Issues of Communication Networks in Smart Grid

Gurbakshish Singh Toor
Nanyang Technological University, Singapore

Maode Ma
Nanyang Technological University, Singapore

ABSTRACT

The evolution of the traditional electricity infrastructure into smart grids promises more reliable and efficient power management, more energy aware consumers and inclusion of renewable sources for power generation. These fruitful promises are attracting initiatives by various nations all over the globe in various fields of academia. However, this evolution relies on the advances in the information technologies and communication technologies and thus is inevitably prone to various risks and threats. This work focuses on the security aspects of HAN and NAN subsystems of smart grids. The chapter presents some of the prominent attacks specific to these subsystems, which violate the specific security goals requisite for their reliable operation. The proposed solutions and countermeasures for these security issues presented in the recent literature have been reviewed to identify the promising solutions with respect to the specific security goals. The paper is concluded by presenting some of the challenges that still need to be addressed.

INTRODUCTION

The ever growing demand of energy all over the globe has compelled a shift from the traditional power distribution system to a more sustainable and efficient system incorporating the advances of information technology and communication and networking technologies. This new energy infrastructure is envisioned not only to provide more optimal energy consumption and better real-time power requirement assessment but also to incorporate renewable energy generation sources at both consumer and provider

DOI: 10.4018/978-1-5225-1829-7.ch002

sides for environment friendly power generation. The future grids will allow a two-way flow of energy and information (Zhang et al. 2011) between the consumers and the utility to conquer these future goals.

This evolution brings forward the deployment of smart appliances and smart meters at the consumer end (Zaballos, Vallejo & Selga 2011), capable of not only monitoring the power utilization but also optimizing it via real time evaluation of the energy flow in the power infrastructure, thus enabling the consumers to contribute to the smart future. These smart meters not only report the power consumption to the grid but also allow the grid to send control signals to the user end appliances in order to manage the power consumption based on dynamic pricing, peak consumption hours, system load requirements etc., making the users more energy aware (Ipakchi & Albuyeh 2009).

Smart grid deployment provides benefits to both the consumer and the utility ends in multitude of scenarios. Smart grid communication infrastructure allows the monitoring of real-time information regarding the power generation, transmission and user consumption. This data collaborated with the market price set by the service provider or by the users generating power at their end (renewable energy sources), will allow to rate the energy dynamically rather than having a fixed rate at all times. For instance, if the user wants energy resource during peak hours, they have to pay higher amounts. Thus by referring to these dynamic prices the users can optimize their utilization to reduce their bills and enables the service providers to help maintain efficient grid operations and automated management (Kim et al. 2014).

Smart grid infrastructure supports the exploitation of renewable energy at both the consumer and provider ends. This approach will reduce the burden on the environment to meet the current energy needs. Also the users producing the energy can sell it to other users or to the utility based on the market price or by negotiating their own price (Wu et al. 2012).

Smart grid also provides improvement in load shedding, the power supply is intentionally switched off under critical situations to avoid damage to the grid system. If the demand suddenly increases in a particular section or the supply of power significantly shortfalls to meet the demand, the demand has to be reduced instantly to stabilize the grid. Usually high priority feeders feeding to hospitals, water supply stations etc. are the last ones to have the impact and the first ones to recover in such a scenario, whereas the residential and commercial sectors have the lower priority. However, if due to time limitation selection cannot be made, the high priority sections could be impacted first as well (Hassan, Abdallah & Radman 2012).

Although smart grid deployment provides multiple benefits, the implementation of such infrastructure demands the deployment of an efficient communication system between the various entities of the system. The architecture of such a network tends to be highly distributed, heterogeneous and complex, incorporating different communication standards and resources. Every entity should be able to communicate with any other entity in a time sensitive scenario in such a complex network to achieve the desired outcomes. Such degree of complexity provides various venues for the adversaries to compromise the security of the system. The corresponding consequences resulting from these vulnerabilities can range from minimal harm, to entire system shutdown. Such impacts may lead to economic collapse, terrorist invasion and even loss of lives. If the users or the governments cannot trust the reliability of the system, the benefits will be easily over shadowed by the possible threats, defying the deployment of this novel future technology.

The motive of this chapter is to investigate the security aspects of Home Area Network (HAN) Neighborhood area network (NAN) subsystem of smart grids in detail. These domains have been emphasized because although the power generation and transmission system pose highly critical security demand and primary focus but a system is as strong as its weakest link. The unintended exploitation of the customer domain can jeopardize the entire system and cause a severe impact that we may not be accustomed to face.

ARCHITECTURE

The model architecture provided by National Institute of Standards and Technology (NIST) describes the smart grid framework in terms of seven domains: Bulk generation, transmission, distribution, operations, service providers, markets and customer domains (National Institute of Standards and Technology 2010). However, the layered model architecture has been usually considered in the recent literature which is merely the conversion of the conceptual model provided by NIST, into three layers HAN, NAN and Wide Area Network (WAN) as shown in Figure 1. The lowest layer can also include Business Area Network (BAN) or Industrial Area Networks (IAN) as well.

HAN should enable a constant interaction between the smart appliances and the Advanced Metering Infrastructure (AMI) and also interaction with the smart grid. Major HAN entities are smart appliances, smart meters and HAN gateway. Some other entities could be distributed energy resources for renewable energy generation, Plug in Electric Vehicles (PHEV) or Plug in Electric Hybrid Vehicles (PEHV). The smart home appliances of prime consideration are the heavy load appliances such as Air Conditioners, washers and dryers, pool pumps etc., whose operation can be optimized as their delayed availability can be accepted (Namboodiri et al. 2014). The smart appliances interact with the smart meters for reporting the energy consumption and also to receive the control commands for operation optimization. The smart meter interacts with a data aggregation entity i.e. a HAN gateway which further interacts with NAN data aggregation unit.

NANs are the communication facility of the distribution domain of smart grids. The NAN allows the distribution domain to monitor the energy delivered to the customer domain and optimize the dis-

Figure 1. General architecture of smart grid

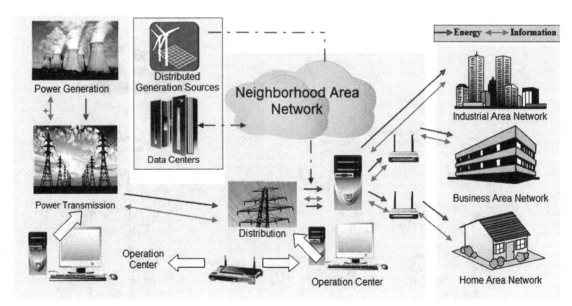

tribution according to the demand and availability options. NAN gateway collects the data from various HANs and forwards it to access points, where the data is aggregated and is further relay it to the upper layer. Similarly, the control signals from the control centers are relayed back to HAN via NAN. Thus it bridges the gap between HAN and WAN (Meng, Ma & Chen 2014). Figure 2 shows the mesh network topology of NAN.

The final layer consists of a Wide area networks accommodating various NANs. All the aggregated data from various NAN is acquired and processed in this layer by the supervisory control and data acquisition system (SCADA). The operation of billing based on consumer consumption, load management according to the demand response paradigm and other functionalities such as outage management, acquisition and management of customer information can all be included in the final layer.

As the traditional communication networks are not suitable according to the requirements of the future grids, advanced communication systems are being analyzed in various research works to select the ones capable to satiate the needs of current power grids. The most optimal communication standard considered for HAN is ZigBee, also known as low-rate wireless personal area networks (LR-WPANs) (Bou-Harb et al. 2013; Farooq & Jung 2014). It is based on IEEE 802.15.4 standard and employs small power digital radios. The communication standards considered for NANs are IEEE 802.15.4g and IEEE 802.11s standards. 802.15.4g is the newly developed standard derived from IEEE 802.15.4 making amendments in the PHY and MAC layer to specify the requirements of Wireless Smart Metering Networks (SUNs). This standard operates on license exempt bands and thus vulnerable. Another standard IEEE 802.11s, derived from IEEE 802.11 to extend its MAC protocol for Wireless Mesh Networks. Hence it is oriented towards addressing the network operation issues of NANs (Meng et al. 2014). A WAN connects several NANs and the coverage area is the high up to thousands of square miles. Thus the bandwidth requirements are up to 10-100Mbps and hence for WAN, optical fibers, WiMAX or cellular networks are most optimum options (Farooq & Jung 2014).

Figure 2. Mesh network topology of smart grid NAN

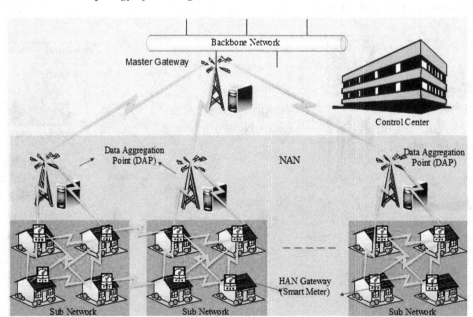

SECURITY OF SMART GRID NETWORKS

Although smart grid technology provides us with numerous benefits, it is highly vulnerable to various cyber or physical attacks. As the communication medium used amongst the various entities is not standardized for smart grids, they become an attractive target for the adversaries. Also the highly distributed network with large number of entities makes the problem more complex. To ensure the security of the system we must first analyze what are the requirements or goals that are to be met to make it a reliable system. This can help us to identify the possible threats that can breach these requirements and thus the possible countermeasures for these threats can be proposed.

Security Goals

The authors consider the following generally security goals (Namboodiri et al. 2014), requiring the prime importance. Prime goal of security is to mitigate risk, factoring in both the likelihood of the risk and the impact it will have on the system.

1. **Integrity:** Integrity is to ensure that the data communicated between the entities does not undergo unintentional alterations. Similarly, to ensure that the control commands sent to customer gateway, have not been manipulated in any manner. For example, control command sent by an impersonator to switch on all the appliances to millions of users during the peak hour can lead to a blackout.
2. **Authentication:** It is used by the communicating node to validate that the other node claiming to be the intended node is in fact the intended node and similar validation for the massages sent by them. For e.g. in NAN the customer should be ensured of the NAN gateway's authenticity to which it is communicating with and gateway should be ensured that it is communicating with the assigned user equipment.
3. **Privacy:** To ensure that the sensitive data is received by the intended party only and should not be disclosed to anyone else. For instance, the power usage information of a customer should be concealed from adversaries or neighboring HANs and NANs so that only utility receives it. The customer may even want that that the individual equipment usage data should not be disclosed to the utility, hence only aggregate of such data is to be sent.
4. **Availability:** The data or resources should be available to any authorized entity at all times. Since smart grids aim at optimizing the power consumption based on real time usage data for more sustainable usage and unavailability of system resources will hinder the transmission of such data. Thus this requirement becomes more crucial as opposed to the traditional energy infrastructures.
5. **Authorization:** Only the intended entities have the access to data or system resources to avoid the unintentional exploitation. For instance, the usage data of customers stored in the system should be accessible to different users such as customers, researchers or service providers according to their access priorities, like the fine grained data to be accessed by users and the utilities get only aggregated data.
6. **Non-Repudiation:** Non-repudiation is critical to verify the claim of truthfulness of any entity so that no authorized entity can deny the claim of sending specific information. This is a critical requirement especially in case of financial information transactions. For example, the users might try to manipulate the usage data to reduce the bill amount or even the service provider can do so to achieve higher revenues.

Since smart grid communication technology is still developing and possesses unique vulnerabilities, the design of smart grid communication networks must also fulfill the following requirements:

- **Forward Security:** The designed security protocols must retain the security efficacy in all the consecutive runs and the information passed on in the previous runs should not affect the security of the consecutive protocol runs. Hence it should be ensured that the security aspects are refreshed or renewed periodically to maintain the security requirements over a long haul.
- The architecture of smart grid infrastructure is divided into different domains and each domain has different security requirements according to the functionality of these domains. Hence, the security protocols must be designed to accommodate the requirements of each of the domains accordingly and also provide a seamless transition among different domains.
- The computation and storage costs incurred by the proposed security protocols must not be dependent on the number of users present in the network. As the number of users and the smart devices in smart homes are predicted to increase significantly in the near future, the security protocols must adhere to the computational resources of these devices and make the computational cost to achieve the desired security standards independent of the number of users.

Security Attacks

An action either intentional or unintentional that jeopardizes the achievement of above stated goals is a security threat. These security threats are dependent various factors and can impact the system to various degrees. Some of the major and commonly considered attacks to the HAN and NAN are stated below (Lee, Gerla and Oh 2012; McBride and McGee 2012). The attacks have been categorized into insider attacks and external attacks:

1. **Insider Attacks:** In case of insider attacks, the intruder either has access to the network or collaborates with other authorized users to attack the network.
   a. **Customer Impersonation:** In this attack the adversary impersonates as a legitimate client to the NAN. The impersonator can request the control system for the detailed consumption information of the client it is impersonating to gain the personal information, exploiting the privacy of the customer for the reasons mentioned earlier. The impersonator can also cause requests of switching off or switching on all the devices or repeated alternate switching.
   b. **Replay Attacks:** It is another type of false data sent to the entities. In this case, an older message or signal is repeatedly used to cause system disruption. The adversary can intercept a data consumption message and replay it to the smart meter causing to report false readings. In another scenario a signal could be replayed to the consumer equipment. For example, the replay signal sent to a dryer may cause it to dry the clothes over and over again. Such overburdening of a specific device may even damage the device or may even lead to injury to the consumer whose is unaware of the altered signal.
   c. **Repudiation:** Repudiation can also be a threat to the HAN under various scenarios. If the control center finds certain problem in the aggregated data consumption due to a significantly varying data consumption report of a consumer, then the consumer should be able to prove the authenticity of its data. For example, during import export of the distributed power of

a consumer, the consumer should follow the control signals under the collaboration with a utility. If any discrepancy is incurred the user should not be able to deny for the actions that had been conducted during this distributed energy management. A HAN or a smart meter can deny to have received the control signals from NAN entities such as demand response signals, claiming it to be the reason for avoiding the commands. In another case the compromised NAN entities can also be put up to these scenarios claiming not to have sent fraudulent signals to the respective HANs.

d. **Man in the Middle Attack:** The attacker can impersonate to be a NAN aggregator to all the HANs under it. This will lead the attacker to control the entre information flow of that specific NAN. This attack can not only cause false data reporting to the utility but can also enable the attacker to alter the control signals to large number of smart meters leading to sudden significant increase in demand or drop of demand in the system. This will lead to undesired load shedding, even to high priority feeders such as hospitals or airports, leading to loss of life and decrease in economy.

2. **External Attacks:** In case of external attacks, the intruder acts as an outside node and tries to abrupt the network security without access to the network.

a. **Eavesdropping:** Eavesdropping refers to the unauthorized monitoring of information communication between two entities with the aim of intercepting some useful information from it. The adversary gains hold of the content being communicated but does not alter it. Thus it becomes very difficult to detect such attacks. One of the scenarios for eavesdropping could be an unauthorized user trying to interpret the energy consumption patterns of an individual. This data if subjected to profiling algorithms can reveal information about an individual's lifestyle, such as when he is at home or not, what devices are being used at what times, even the travelling patterns can be revealed by monitoring his PEV data. Such adversaries maybe manufacturing industries of some specific equipment trying to improve marketing plans based on consumer usage or a burglar trying to intercept the living patterns of the individuals (Lisovich, Mulligan and Wicker 2010).

b. **False Data Injection:** In case of false injection of data, the adversary attempts to alter the data or introduce fraudulent data in some specific pattern rather than sending random bogus signals. The attacker gains access to the communication network. Then it can confuse the system involving large number of subscribers by sending fraudulent signals (Lu et al. 2010). This can cause disruption of service for a long duration impacting the availability as well as integrity of the system. In case of NAN the data being transferred to the NAN aggregation unit could be altered resulting in false aggregated reporting. This will mislead the utility in estimating the demand of a specific NAN region and significant alteration may even lead to load shedding or inaccurate demand response schemes (Grochocki 2012).

c. **Jamming:** Jamming is one of the physical layer attacks where a jammer fills the communication medium with noise, rendering the entities from communicating. Such attacks can also lead to distortion or destruction of sensitive and valuable data (Lu et al. 2010). This may lead to non-recovery of the intended message. The adversary may send noise signals to the medium at random intervals so that it can impact the availability and still being difficult to be detected.

d.   **Access Restriction:** This is similar to jamming attack but here the number of targeted entities is larger. The jammer tries to occupy the communication medium first every time so that other nodes will sense the medium busy and suspend their transmissions, thus blocking the legitimate nodes from communication initiation or may cause packet collision. An attacker impersonating to be a jammer may block all the other smart meters in the region to communicate with the NAN aggregator.

Motivation for Security Solutions in Smart Grid

Although the deployment of smart grids is a profitable affair, the security of such complex system has to be fully guaranteed before deployment as it is the involvement of power supply and consumption. The attacks on the power sector of any region can lead to major disasters. Hence the authors discuss some of the biggest security attacks on the power systems that provide a perspective of the reasons to that the security of smart grid architecture is so important.

One of the most well-known attacks is Stuxnet, a 500 Kbyte computer worm which was discovered in mid-2010. This advanced piece of malware targeted to reprogram industrial control systems without being detected. It infected the software of about 14 industrial units in Iran. One of these units was a Uranium-enrichment plant. The self-replicating property enabled it to impact large number of systems, although it was targeted towards the Siemens SCADA system to impact specific industrial processes. It first attacked machines operating Microsoft Windows, then the Siemens step7 software and finally the programmable logic controllers (PLC). The author of the malware had enough control to damage the centrifuges without the knowledge of the operators at the plant. It had the capability to spread onto systems not even connected to the internet. Although the attack was detected in 2010, its early variants stemming at least a year ago have been confirmed (Kushner 2013; Karnouskos 2011).

Another well documented attack is Shamoon also known as Disttrack that was encountered in Saudi Arabia. This attack was detected in 2012 by Seculert. This destructive cyber-attack had an impact on nearly 30,000 systems targeting one of the largest oil producers in Saudi Arabia. After gaining access to the domain controller, the malware was injected onto various systems. The major aim was to disrupt the functioning of various computer systems causing downtime at the targeted company (Dehlawi & Abokhodair 2013).

These malwares not only demonstrate that the security of critical infrastructures can be breached but also the impact that these attacks can lead to. This emphasizes the criticality of updating and improving the security aspects of power infrastructures. As smart grid infrastructure will rely heavily on advanced wireless technologies, these security threat become that more prevalent.

EXISTING SOLUTIONS

In this section, the authors review some of the proposed solutions in the recent literature to counteract the security issues in HAN and NAN domains. The reviews have to categorized based on their compliance with the security goals mentioned earlier. However, some of the work in the literature has a general approach towards these security measures, rather than having specific orientation to a domain. Some of these solutions have also been reviewed in this section.

Solutions for Privacy

In the deployment of smart grids, the major concern about privacy requirements turns out in terms of user acceptance. Customers' lack of trust towards the safety of their private information revealing their habits or daily consumption patterns bring this concern to light. Threat to the customer's privacy does not affect the system in a critical manner but the user acceptance towards the deployment of this new technology makes it a primary concern.

Min Lu et al. (2013) present 'Practical Privacy Preserving Aggregation (PPPA) scheme', where the differential privacy technique and cryptographic techniques have been jointly used. The goal of differential privacy is to provide the information as a whole, without disclosing individual details. This notion has been tailored for the smart grid design. The user nodes have been arranged into a quad tree structure with users representing the leaf nodes. The next level in the tree corresponds to a set of four users and so on. The root node's sum estimate gives the electricity consumption of the user area. If one of the users fails to respond, the control center calculates the estimate of all yellow blocks, as shown in Figure 3 and forwards it to the relays. The relays add a path signature to the aggregated data and forward it. Receiving all the reports, the control center estimates residential area's overall electricity usage.

Sook-Chin Yip et al. (2014) employ an incremental hash function to conceal the consumer data yet allowing the utility company to check the integrity of user data. The approach has been divided into three steps procedure:

1. **Consumer's Electricity Consumption Report Generation:** The real time power consumption of consumer is converted to corresponding cost using a quadratic cost function which is then hashed with an incremental hash function before being sent to operation center i.e. the data aggregator.
2. **Privacy Preserving Report Aggregation:** The collected hash energy cost per consumer is then summed by the operation center and then forwarded to the utility provider.
3. **Report Integrity Validation:** The utility provider verifies the integrity of the received report by comparing the total hashed energy cost received from operation center to the hashed total energy cost of the power that has been generated.

Figure 3. A special case of the proposed PPPA scheme

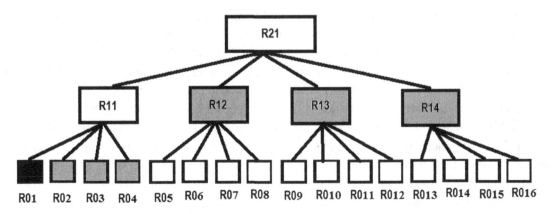

Weiwei Jia et al. (2014) introduce a new type of attack, Human–factor-aware Differential Aggregation (HDA) attack, in which human factor has been taken into consideration. They have suggested that even with privacy preserving protocols applied, an attacker can infer sensitive information about an individual by monitoring the aggregation data before and after the user leaves his residence. In their system model, they have assumed n users and an aggregator. Every consumer sends the consumption information after a particular time slot. Every meter divides its reading into different shares and computes the time-series information of each time slot. Using this information and the private key, each share has been encrypted by the meter. To aggregate a specific time slot's readings, the time-series information has been computed by the aggregator as well and using its own private key, the data has been further encrypted and aggregated. To secure against HDA attack, they used differential privacy with the variation that the noise is added by each meter, as the aggregator is considered untrustworthy.

Summary

Most of the proposed schemes have employed homomorphic encryption or data masking as well as differential data aggregation. However, the proposed schemes have certain vulnerabilities. The scheme by Min Lu et al. (2013), makes an assumption that only external adversaries are present and no internal attacks can be achieved. The incremental hashing employed by Sook-Chin Yip et al. (2014) has large computational expense and other innovative schemes such (Jia et al. 2014) will induce other vulnerabilities due to human errors.

Solutions for Integrity

Lei Yang and Fengjun Li (2013) claim that the individual smart meter data has been encrypted using homomorphic encryption and then aggregated to conceal individual readings. However, the malleable property of such encryption makes it difficult to detect malicious nodes which maybe injecting false data or some malfunctioning node causing unintentional data disruption leading to false data interpretation. To tackle this issue, they have proposed a distributed outlier localization scheme based on dynamic grouping and data re-encryption. In their scheme, the data aggregation tree has been partitioned into logical groups, with the root of each group storing historical data of the member meters. If the collector detects an anomaly, these root nodes are employed to find the malicious node in their sub tree. But the validation of individual meter reading by decrypting the historical data will require key updating after every outlier localization. To avoid this overhead, re-encryption has been used. They employ 'extended kernel density estimation based mechanism' for detection. But this scheme has been used in WSN and could not be directly deployed for NAN as it requires plaintext data and the data should be accessible to detector nodes. Thus a 'revised aggregation scheme' has been devised so that the verifiers can access the metering data as time-series data for detection but do not violate the privacy goals.

Kebina Manandhar et al. (2014) introduce the use of Kalman filters to detect various system attacks including false data injection. As the attacks in the power system are reflected in the form of voltage current or phase change, they derive the state space representation using the power grid voltage signal having amplitude and phase as variables. Euclidian distance metric based detector has been employed for detection of complicated false data injection attacker. Kalman filter uses the measurement vector collected from sensors and the state equation to compute the next state of the system. The X^2 detector compares a predefined threshold with the test statistics generated from the Kalman filter. If the detected difference between the projected estimates and actual value is large, the system indicates a possible attack.

Another work (Reed & Gonzalez 2012) provide intrusion detection enabling detection of zero-day and other elusive cyber-attacks without being confined to a specific platform. Their technique of 'power finger printing', as the name suggests, has been based on fine grained measurements of a processor's power consumption. These measurements have been compared alongside the references of trusted software using signal processing and pattern recognition techniques. If the traces do not match the corresponding stored signature to a bearable tolerance, an intrusion is indicated.

Mohammad Esmalifalak et al. (2014) propose two techniques for stealth attack detection based on machine-learning approach. The first method employs statistical based anomaly detection algorithm. The historical data collected from SCADA has been preprocessed and mapped to a low-dimension space. Then a Gaussian density function has been applied to the preprocessed data and the newly generated data has been compared with historical data for anomaly detection. The second approach employs distributed Support Vector Machine (SVM) to detect the stealthy false data injection. Firstly, the historical data has been prepared for each of the groups that work together to train the SVM. Then the local and local optimization parameters have been initialized and updated. The basic approach is that if the historical data contains class labels, identifying normal and tempered data, then a classifier can be trained to detect the attacks.

Summary

The work presented in the literature for integrity preservation is very limited. Most of the proposed solutions do not take into consideration the resource limitation of network devices of HAN and NAN domains. The process of re-encryption (Yang & Li 2013) and employment of kalman filters (Manandhar et al. (2014) make a significant increase in the computational costs. Also the schemes (Reed & Gonzalez 2012; Esmalifalak et al. 2014) tend to require hardware changes in the entire network which may not be feasible for the smart grid architecture.

Solutions for Availability

The availability of the network is jeopardized when the access to a resource is restricted. Major attacks causing this restriction include jamming, denial of service, replay attacks, flood attacks etc. Recent literature shows various proposed schemes for intrusion detection and combating jamming.

Beigi-Mohammadi Nasim et al. (2014) propose a low cost in band solution for intrusion detection specifically tailored for NAN. Wireless Mesh Networks (WMN) technology has been considered in their work, oriented to tackle different types of wormhole attacks, compromising the availability of NAN. The proposed approach is a combination of signature based and anomaly based detection systems. Collectors in each NAN have been assigned as monitoring. After turning on, a smart meter starts discovering the neighbor nodes to connect to the NAN. After authentication the best path for sending data to the collector is searched. This best will give minimum number of hop counts in the packet's field. Euclidean distance estimation estimates the smallest hop count. If the number of hop counts indicated in the sent packet's field has been smaller than the estimated minimum hop count, a wormhole attack is detected.

Yichi Zhang et al. (2011) propose another distributed intrusion detection scheme. In this approach several analyzing modules employing artificial immune system (AIS) have been deployed at level of smart grid network, specific to the requirements of that level. These modules communicate with each other for a better detection. The Authentication Module at HAN has three parts: Intrusion data acquisition, AIS models for normal and abnormal classification and result recording and awareness evaluation. Similarly the AM of NAN consist of HAN IDS results, its own AIS model and interface among HAN IDS. The classification of intrusion detection greatly enhances the detection ability as shown by their simulation results.

HongboLiu et al. (2013) provide a communication subsystem that has intelligent local controller. This approach allows sufficient meter readings to be communicated for system requirement estimation under jamming attack, hence gives the system self-healing capabilities. The basic approach is to exploit all the available resources on hand. Their proposed framework allows a smart meter to communicate not only with its local controller but any other controller in its nearby vicinity from which it can hear on any current available channel. This controller switching approach combined with spread spectrum techniques promises to provide better resilience under jamming. Their work also provides an optimal controller placement evaluation for effective switching.

Summary

Denial-of-service attacks are equally as crucial to the availability of communication network. Many intrusion detection schemes have been proposed in the recent literature to tackle this issue and to upgrade the available countermeasures. The intrusion detection systems can be divided into three major categories based on their operation: signature based- can detect only known attack patterns stored in the database. Anomaly based – can detect new attacks but high rate of false positives. Specification based- combination of better haves of other two having capability to detect new attacks with low false positive rate.

Solutions for Authorization

Next we review the work for achieving the authorization goal, the purpose of which is to allow only intended parties to access the network. However, the work for this goal is still limited.

Sushmita Ruj and Amiya Nayak (2013) consider HAN, BAN and NAN gateways for data privacy and access control. The data collected by various HANS is forwarded to the BAN gateways and the NAN gateway further aggregate the readings from the gateway BANs and send it to the nearest substations. The aggregated data at each step has been encrypted using Paillier encryption. To obtain the access control, the authors have tailored an attribute-based encryption, so that it can be efficiently implemented according to the smart grid requirements. The data collected by substations has been monitored by Remote Terminal Units (RTUs). Several Key Distribution Centers (KDCs) have been deployed to distribute cryptographic keys and attributes to the users and the RTUs. The RTUs encrypt the collected data under a set of these attributes before sending it to the repository to be stored. Different types of users such as researchers, maintenance units, consumers etc. have varied access structures. They obtain the secret key from the KDC corresponding to the attributes they are allowed to access.

Qinghai Gao (2012) claims that the cyber security related to authorization weakens due to the challenge of password management. Using biometric techniques such as fingerprinting a more secure and reliable access to the network can be obtained. However, the issue related to such biometric data is that it is not exactly reproducible for every measurement and hence such data cannot be protected using cryptographic techniques. They provide two methods for protecting the fingerprint data. First method is for protecting minutiae-sparse fingerprint, containing less than 60 minutiae points, where chaff minutiae points are added to the original template to get a chaffed template. This template is stored for enrollment but during authentication, original template is constructed but never stored. Hence a hacker could not identify the chaffed minutiae from real minutiae. For minutiae-rich fingerprint, containing more than 60 minutiae points, a sub template is created by random selection of minutiae points from the original template. This template is stored for enrollment and the original template is constructed during authentication but never stored.

Summary

The work oriented to tackle the issue of efficient authorization is still very limited in the current literature. Although the work (Ruj & Nayak 2013) has been tailored for smart grid architecture, the issue of key management and excessive cryptographic operation still lies. The work by Qinghai Gao (2012) would not only demand extra equipment such a fingerprint devices which will not only increase the installation cost but also the cost for recording and processing fingerprint data.

Solutions for Non-Repudiation

Jaeduck choi et al. (2011) provide message authentication and non-repudiation taking into account the power consumption issue for cryptographic operations. Their work has made use of two secret keys a1 and a2 in a hash chain relationship a1 = h(a2). The SM releases a2 to AMI and stores a1. Then these keys have been used by SM to generate two MAC values for transmitting authenticated data to AMI. The key a1 serves for non-repudiation goal. Similarly, AMI generates two keys b1 and b2 and b1 serves for non-repudiation. In case for non-repudiation verification the SM or AMI request for the secret key a1 or b2 respectively and ensure that the key shared with them has been generated from these keys.

Another work (Xiao, Xiao & Du 2013) present a mutual inspection strategy to resolve the issue of non-repudiation in smart grid neighborhood network. The approach proposes the installation of two smart meters with one electric wire for connection between the subscriber and the service provider. The bill readings exchanged between them have been used to calculate the difference between these readings. However, due to power loss during transmission or some dynamic factors caused by the environment, some inevitable difference would be there in the readings. So a threshold value is computed and if the dispute does not lie within the range of this threshold value, the accountability is lost and the service is terminated.

Other work (Irfan, Taj & Mahmud 2015) uses Software Defined network (SDN) and Lng Term Evolution (LTE) based architecture for smart grid security. Some user specific attributes such as the meter number, are sent along with the sum of the past 24-hour metering data to the utility. A designated program at the utility generates the sum of the last 24-readings and compares it to the received data. Using user specific details and the record of the metering data from the two communication channels i.e. SDN and LTE, ensures the repudiation of the network.

Summary

The goal of non-repudiation has also not been researched in depth for the smart grid network requirements. The work (choi et al. 2011) presents a novel and simple scheme however use of only two keys without any key refreshment makes the scheme very vulnerable over a long haul. The approach (Xiao, Xiao & Du 2013) raises the question of increased cost for installation of double the number of smart meter to support this scheme. But the author claims that the cost incurred due to energy theft every year is considerably larger than the initial investment cost and could be covered in smaller duration of time if the scheme is successfully implemented. The work (Irfan, Taj and Mahmud 2015) tends to incorporate the upcoming technologies such as SDN to make it more compatible to the future communication systems.

Solutions for Authenticity

Fangming Zhao et al. (2012) introduce a key exchange and revocation scheme while utilizing broadcast encryption cryptographic protocol and using a media key block. Two sub protocols have been employed. In first protocol the unrevoked devices share a media key which is encrypted from a broadcast encryption using their device keys. This protocol is mandatory. The first protocol has been executed in two phases: key sharing and confirmation. In first phase, a device A encrypts a randomly generated number using elliptical curve cryptography and sends it to device B and vice-versa. Then both of them calculate a common key by applying an Advanced Encryption Standard (AES) based hash function to the media key, the received encrypted message and the generated random number. The confirmation phase is optional for advanced security. Second sub protocol is for identity confirmation. Using the randomly generated number and its encryption as in first protocol, device A calculates a parameter along with its leaf number and open ID and device B does the same. With their public keys they verify the corresponding signatures and confirms if the open ID is surely of the intended device.

Sangji Lee et al. (2014) provide a coupled ID based authentication and Public Key infrastructure (PKI) mechanism for mutual device authentication. As ID based authentication does not provide mutual authentication and PKI increases data exchange overhead. The proposed scheme has combined the benefits of both the techniques. A certificate authority has been employed to provide authorization to meter data management system for certificate issuance to smart meters. SA and SM perform mutual authentication using the issued certificates. The MDMS sends authentication request to CA. After verification CA sends a CA_List to MDMS and authorizes it. SM sends authentication request to MDMS. After verification new certificates are generated and authentication reply with the new certificate is sent to SM. Similar procedure has been followed by SA. Now SA and SM authenticate using their own certificate encrypted by partner's public key which they decrypt using their own private key and thus perform mutual authentication.

Rongxing Lu et al. (2013) propose an efficient aggregate authentication protocol (EATH). In their protocol, all the smart grid sensor nodes aggregate their collected data and send it to the control center once they receive a request from it for state estimation. First the public and private keys of the control center and the sensor nodes are calculated and two secure cryptographic hash functions are selected. To determine the carrying capacity of a transmission line, the control center sends a request to all the nodes attaching a signature using its private key and a timestamp. Each sensor node collects their sensed data and computes its hash value. Then attributing a signature to it using their private keys, the data is sent to the aggregation node which is randomly chosen each time. The aggregation node verifies the data received from each node and then aggregates all the signatures to one aggregated signature. This collected data along with the aggregated signature is sent to the control center which again verifies it. A detailed security analysis demonstrates that the proposed protocol is secure for both source authentication and data integrity.

The use of SDN based authentication schemes is also gaining recent interest. Xiaoyu Duan and Xianbin Wang (2015) proposed an authentication handover scheme for 5G hetnets using the SDN architecture. They employ an authentication module at root controller and use user dependent secure context information for authentication handover. However, the system model followed by (Duan and Wang 2015) has the authentication management uses only one centralized controller, thereby making it a critical target point for the network security, which if compromised will jeopardize the security of the entire network. Also the security of the context information being transferred has not been proved.

Another work (Irfan, Taj & Mahmud 2015) proposed an SDN based architecture for the smart grid security. Their proposed scheme employs multiple SDN switches connected in mesh topology. Using a LTE module, they send the sum of the past 24-hour readings. All the data has been encrypted using AES-128 encryption following the NIST recommendation. The network has been divided into three sectors using a specialized SDN controller. The database of each sector is locked that can be unlocked only using biometric challenge/response handshake protocols to ensure the authentication.

Hamid Gharvi and Bin Hu (2013) present a dynamically updating key distribution scheme for wireless mesh networks (WMN), which are considered for deployment in NAN. They suggest that the newly adopted standard IEEE 802.11s for WMN has Simultaneous Authentication of Equals (SAE) protocol for security but since is based on single shared password it is vulnerable. Another protocol EMSA (Efficient Mesh Security Association) which uses 4-way handshaking protocol is a good replacement for SAE. But in this protocol the unprotected message1 and message3 can be forged to cause denial of service attack. They propose a hash based encryption scheme for the protection of these messages. They assume a multi-gate mesh network, having master gateway as the Mesh Authenticator (MA). First each gateway establishes a link with the MA, followed by authentication. After authentication, each supplement gateway initiates 4-way handshake, to obtain PTK (Pair wise Transit Key) for unicast communication and GTK (Group Transit Key) for multicast communication. Before the supplicate gateway takes the role of authenticator itself, the key PTK-KD also need to be established. Then the authenticated supplement can authenticate its children mesh points (MPs). Since message1 from authenticator to the supplement is not encrypted, a forged message will cause generation of new PTK which is not consistent with the one in authenticator and hence will halt the process. Similarly, forged message3 will lead to mismatch of RSNE (Robust Security Network Element). To avoid this issue, one way hashing scheme has been proposed. MA uses this hash function to encrypt PMK information and insert ii in the message1. After receiving, the supplicant uses its own PMK to compute the hashed value and then compares it with the one included in the message to verify it without the PMK information the intruder cannot forge this message. Similar process is followed for message3, where the hashed value is checked and compared before verifying AA RSNE. Through key refreshment scheme the PTK, GTK and PMK are also periodically updated.

Summary

Most of the work proposed for authentication uses complex cryptographic operations without taking into consideration the resource limitation of the HAN and NAN devices. Also only a couple of solutions have tailored their scheme to the smart grid architecture requirements. The work by Fangming Zhao et al. 2012 and Rongxing Lu et al. 2013 use multiple cryptographic encryption and decryption operations. The scheme (Lee et al. 2014) relies on a secure third party and also has the issue of key management. The work (Duan &Wang 2015) has a novel approach but does not provide the proof of the security of the context information being transferred. The work by Hamid Gharvi and Bin Hu (2013) improves the reliability of the system but key refreshment but leads to vulnerabilities such as DoS attacks in the consecutive key refreshment cycles.

OPEN ISSUES

Although researchers all over the world have contributed a lot of promising solutions for smart grid security and continue to do so, but still significant amount of work is required to make the deployment of smart grid technology a complete success so that the benefits of this fruitful innovation can be achieved to the fullest. Based on the work that has thus far been present in the literature and the security issues and requirements specific to smart grid architecture, we list some the areas that still need in depth research.

- **NAN Security:** Most of the work presented thus far has been highly oriented towards HAN domain and smart metering systems and the high end research focuses on the security of the final processing utility end. However the NAN has not been researched as much and the corresponding security solutions specifically tailored to the requirements of this domain are limited. Also the communication standards that are being used as the basis of most of the available solutions are the ones used to similar communication requirements that mimic the architectural behavior of smart grid infrastructure. But as these standards have not been specifically designed for NAN domain, the security flaws of these standards will migrate to the smart grid networks as well. Thus, unified and specially tailored communication standards for NAN domain are required.
- **WAN Security:** As we move from the HAN domain to the higher domains the security requirements become more and more stringent. Hence the security solutions in the WAN domain require much complex and reliable outcomes. Although the computation power of devices in these domains are high and can accommodate already established complex cryptographic schemes, but the consideration of the smart grid architecture and the transition from NAN to WAN domain in terms of security aspects are also to be considered. Very limited work has been presented in the literature to tackle the security requirements of the WAN domain and most of the security reliability is assumed on the protocols that a specific utility will adopt. Hence unified security solutions are to be developed for the WAN domain also.
- The integration of renewable energy is also one of the major benefits of smart grid deployment. This will allow the consumer party to become the generator of the energy simultaneously. However the legitimacy of those users and the authorization for certain users to generate and sell energy to other users and the security of this energy transaction are still areas where suitable research is pending. Also the power quality being fed to the smart grid will be influenced which should also be considered during the network automation of the smart grid.

In addition to the above mentioned potential research areas, there are several open-research issues related to smart grid security. Hence the future research could focus on the following aspects as well:

- **Uniformity:** Most of the solutions tend to focus on certain specific aspects of security requirements such as privacy and authenticity. However, the implementation of a combination of multiple complex mechanisms makes the process much more cumbersome. Also the network devices have certain resource restrains on the computational and storage capabilities and hence it may not be viable to implement multiple solutions for complete security of the system. Also the different schemes must be able to function smoothly simultaneously. Hence, rather uniform security architecture should be devised that fulfills all the corresponding security requirements.

- **Computational Complexity:** The network devices, especially in the lower domains are resource limited and hence cannot sustain highly complex and computationally burdensome security mechanisms. Also for the smart grid infrastructure to be effective, the time constraints on data communication are also very stringent which cannot be met using complex mechanisms. Many proposed solutions provide effective solutions but tend to use complex cryptographic tools. Hence schemes enabling a good balance between computational cost and system security still need to be devised.
- **Flexible:** As the smart grids consists of highly distributed networks with large number of network devices, any changes to the security protocols will require changes down to the network device hardware which is very ineffective. However, as the communication technologies will advance, changes will be inevitable. So architecture that can accommodate such changes without requiring changes to network hardware every time can be devised.

CONCLUSION

In this chapter, we have first introduced the architecture of smart grid communication infrastructure considering the three-domain layered architecture model and the corresponding communication standards most suitable to the requirements of each domain. Then, we have addressed the security requirements and security goals for the communication networks in smart grid followed by the introduction of the challenges and the security threats faced by the system that violate the corresponding security goals. Furthermore, we have reviewed the existing state-of-the-art solutions for HAN and NAN domains of the communication infrastructure and categorized these solutions based on the security goals. Finally, we have summarized the classification of security issues and corresponding requirements of communication networks in smart grid and then correspondingly envisioned the future research directions specific to HAN and NAN domains. We believe that under the protection of the security solutions in the future, the smart grid deployment will bring about significant fruitful changes to both of user power consumption and power supplies and improve the user experience considerably.

REFERENCES

Beigi-Mohammadi, N., Mišić, J., Khazaei, H., & Mišić, V. B. (2014). An intrusion detection system for smart grid neighborhood area network. In *Proceedings of IEEE International Conference on Communications (ICC)*. Sydney: IEEE. doi:10.1109/ICC.2014.6883967

Bou-Harb, E., Fachkha, C., Pourzandi, M., Debbabi, M., & Assi, C. (2013). Communication security for smart grid distribution networks. *IEEE Communications Magazine*, *51*(1), 42–49. doi:10.1109/MCOM.2013.6400437

Choi, J., Shin, I., Seo, J., & Lee, C. (2011). An Efficient Message Authentication for Non-repudiation of the Smart Metering Service. In *Proceedings of First ACIS/JNU International Conference on Computers, Networks, Systems and Industrial Engineering (CNSI)*. Korea, Jeju Island: IEEE. doi:10.1109/CNSI.2011.28

Dehlawi, Z., & Abokhodair, N. (2013). Saudi Arabia's response to cyber conflict: A case study of the Shamoon malware incident. In *Proceedings of IEEE International Conference on Intelligence and Security Informatics (ISI)*. Seattle, WA: IEEE. doi:10.1109/ISI.2013.6578789

Duan, X., & Wang, X. (2015). Authentication handover and privacy protection in 5G hetnets using software-defined networking. *IEEE Communications Magazine, 53*(4), 28–35. doi:10.1109/MCOM.2015.7081072

Esmalifalak, M., Liu, L., Nguyen, N., Zheng, R., & Han, Z. (2014). Detecting Stealthy False Data Injection Using Machine Learning in Smart Grid. *IEEE Systems Journal,* (99), 1-9.

Farooq, H., & Jung, L. T. (2014). Choices available for implementing smart grid communication network. In *Proceedings ofInternational Conference on Computer and Information Sciences (ICCOINS)*. IEEE.

Gao, Q. (2012). Biometric authentication in Smart Grid. In *Proceedings of International Energy and Sustainability Conference (IESC)*. New York, NY: IEEE.

Gharavi, H., & Hu, B. (2013). 4-way handshaking protection for wireless mesh network security in smart grid. In *Proceedings of IEEE Global Communications Conference (GLOBECOM)*. Atlanta, GA: IEEE. doi:10.1109/GLOCOM.2013.6831169

Grochocki, D. (2012). AMI threats, intrusion detection requirements and deployment recommendations. *InProceedings of IEEE Third International Conference on Smart Grid Communications (SmartGridComm)*. Taiwan: IEEE. doi:10.1109/SmartGridComm.2012.6486016

Hassan, R., Abdallah, M., & Radman, G. (2012). Load shedding in smart grid: A reliable efficient Ad-Hoc broadcast algorithm for smart house. In *Proceedings of IEEE Southeastcon*. IEEE. doi:10.1109/SECon.2012.6196919

Ipakchi, A., & Albuyeh, F. (2009). Grid of the future. *IEEE Power and Energy Magazine, 7*(2), 52–62. doi:10.1109/MPE.2008.931384

Irfan, A., Taj, N., & Mahmud, S. A. (2015). A Novel Secure SDN/LTE Based Architecture for Smart Grid Security. In *Proceedings of IEEE International Conference on Computer and Information Technology; Ubiquitous Computing and Communications; Dependable, Autonomic and Secure Computing; Pervasive Intelligence and Computing (CIT/IUCC/DASC/PICOM)*. Liverpool, UK: IEEE. doi:10.1109/CIT/IUCC/DASC/PICOM.2015.112

Jia, W., Zhu, H., Cao, Z., Dong, X., & Xiao, C. (2014). Human-Factor-Aware Privacy-Preserving Aggregation in Smart Grid. *IEEE Systems Journal, 8*(2), 598–607. doi:10.1109/JSYST.2013.2260937

Karnouskos, S. (2011). Stuxnet worm impact on industrial cyber-physical system security. In *Proceedings of 37th Annual Conference on IEEE Industrial Electronics Society (IECON 2011)*. Melbourne, Vic: IEEE. doi:10.1109/IECON.2011.6120048

Kim, B. G., Zhang, Y., van der Schaar, M., & Lee, J. W. (2014). Dynamic pricing for smart grid with reinforcement learning. In *Proceedings of IEEE Conference on Computer Communications Workshops (INFOCOM WKSHPS)*. Toronto, ON: IEEE. doi:10.1109/INFCOMW.2014.6849306

Kushner, D. (2013). The real story of stuxnet. *IEEE Spectrum*, *50*(3), 48–53. doi:10.1109/MSPEC.2013.6471059

Lee, E. K., Gerla, M., & Oh, S. Y. (2012). Physical layer security in wireless smart grid. *IEEE Communications Magazine*, *50*(8), 46–52. doi:10.1109/MCOM.2012.6257526

Lee, S., Bong, J., Shin, S., & Shin, Y. (2014). A security mechanism of Smart Grid AMI network through smart device mutual authentication. In *Proceedings of the International Conference on Information Networking (ICOIN2014)*. IEEE.

Lisovich, M. A., Mulligan, D. K., & Wicker, S. B. (2010). Inferring Personal Information from Demand-Response Systems. *IEEE Security and Privacy*, *8*(1), 11–20. doi:10.1109/MSP.2010.40

Liu, H., Chen, Y., Chuah, M. C., & Yang, J. (2013). Towards self-healing smart grid via intelligent local controller switching under jamming. In *Proceedings of IEEE Conference on Communications and Network Security (CNS)*. Washington, DC: IEEE.

Lu, M., Shi, Z., Lu, R., Sun, R., & Shen, X. S. (2013). PPPA: A practical privacy-preserving aggregation scheme for smart grid communications. In *Proceedings of IEEE/CIC International Conference on Communications in China (ICCC)*. IEEE. doi:10.1109/ICCChina.2013.6671200

Lu, R., Lin, X., Shi, Z., & Shen, X. (2013). EATH: An efficient aggregate authentication protocol for smart grid communications. In *Proceedings of IEEE Wireless Communications and Networking Conference (WCNC)*. IEEE. doi:10.1109/WCNC.2013.6554840

Lu, Z., Lu, X., Wang, W., & Wang, C. (2010). Review and evaluation of security threats on the communication networks in the smart grid. In *Proceedings of MILITARY COMMUNICATIONS CONFERENCE (MILCOM 2010)*. San Jose, CA: IEEE. doi:10.1109/MILCOM.2010.5679551

Manandhar, K., & Cao, X., Fei Hu & Liu, Y. (2014). Combating False Data Injection Attacks in Smart Grid using Kalman Filter. In *Proceedings of International Conference on Computing, Networking and Communications (ICNC)*. Honolulu, HI: IEEE. doi:10.1109/ICCNC.2014.6785297

McBride, A. J., & McGee, A. R. (2012). Assessing smart Grid security. *Bell Labs Technical Journal*, *17*(3), 87–103. doi:10.1002/bltj.21560

Meng, W., Ma, R., & Chen, H. H. (2014). Smart grid neighborhood area networks: A survey. *IEEE Network*, *28*(1), 24–32. doi:10.1109/MNET.2014.6724103

Namboodiri, V., Aravinthan, V., Mohapatra, S. N., Karimi, B., & Jewell, W. (2014). Toward a Secure Wireless-Based Home Area Network for Metering in Smart Grids. *IEEE Systems Journal*, *8*(2), 509–520. doi:10.1109/JSYST.2013.2260700

National Institute of Standards and Technology. (2010). *NIST Framework and Roadmap for Smart Grid Interoperability Standards (NIST Special Publication 1108)*. U.S. Department of Commerce.

Reed, J. H., & Gonzalez, C. R. A. (2012). Enhancing Smart Grid cyber security using power fingerprinting: Integrity assessment and intrusion detection. In *Proceedings of Future of Instrumentation International Workshop (FIIW)*. Gatlinburg, TN: IEEE. doi:10.1109/FIIW.2012.6378346

Ruj, S., & Nayak, A. (2013). A Decentralized Security Framework for Data Aggregation and Access Control in Smart Grids. *IEEE Transactions on Smart Grid, 4*(1), 196–205. doi:10.1109/TSG.2012.2224389

Wu, Y., Lau, V. K. N., Tsang, D. H. K., Qian, L., & Meng, L. (2012). Optimal exploitation of renewable energy for residential smart grid with supply-demand model. In *proceedings of 7th International ICST Conference on Communications and Networking in China (CHINACOM)*. IEEE.

Xiao, Z., Xiao, Y., & Du, D. H. (2013). Non-repudiation in neighborhood area networks for smart grid. *IEEE Communications Magazine, 51*(1), 18–26. doi:10.1109/MCOM.2013.6400434

Yang, L., & Li, F. (2013). Detecting false data injection in smart grid in-network aggregation. In *Proceedings of IEEE International Conference on Smart Grid Communications (SmartGridComm)*. Vancouver, Canada: IEEE. doi:10.1109/SmartGridComm.2013.6687992

Yip, S. C., Wong, K., Phan, R. C. W., Tan, S. W., Ku, I., & Hew, W. P. (2014). A Privacy-Preserving and Cheat-Resilient electricity consumption reporting Scheme for smart grids. In *Proceedings of International Conference on Computer, Information and Telecommunication Systems (CITS)*. IEEE doi:10.1109/CITS.2014.6878971

Yu, R., Zhang, Y., Gjessing, S., Yuen, C., Xie, S., & Guizani, M. (2011). Cognitive radio based hierarchical communications infrastructure for smart grid. *IEEE Network, 25*(5), 6–14. doi:10.1109/MNET.2011.6033030

Zaballos, A., Vallejo, A., & Selga, J. M. (2011). Heterogeneous communication architecture for the smart grid. *IEEE Network, 25*(5), 30–37. doi:10.1109/MNET.2011.6033033

Zhang, Y., Wang, L., Sun, W., Green, R. C., & Alam, M. (2011). Artificial immune system based intrusion detection in a distributed hierarchical network architecture of smart grid. In *Proceedings of IEEE Power and Energy Society General Meeting*. Detroit, MI: IEEE. doi:10.1109/PES.2011.6039697

Zhao, F., Hanatani, Y., Komano, Y., Smyth, B., Ito, S., & Kambayashi, T. (2012). Secure authenticated key exchange with revocation for smart grid. In *Proceedings of IEEE PES conference on Innovative Smart Grid Technologies (ISGT)*. Washington, DC: IEEE.

KEY TERMS AND DEFINITIONS

Asymmetric Encryption: A process of encryption where the specific information is encrypted using one key can only be decrypted by the corresponding pair key.

Cryptography: A field of study used to hide the meaning of specific content with the intent to protect its confidentiality and secrecy.

Digital Signatures: The proof for sender's identity and the contents of the electronically sent information by attaching a digital code to the information.

Hash Functions: A function that outputs fixed size data when applied to arbitrary sized message and in computationally difficult to invert.

Homomorphic Encryption: The encryption process where the results of computations performed on the encrypted text can be retrieved from the decrypted plain text.

Symmetric Encryption: A process of encryption where one secret key is used to both encrypt and decrypt the specific information.

Zero-Knowledge Proofs: When one user is able to prove that a certain information is true to another party without revealing any details of the information to the other party.

Chapter 3
Denial of Service Attack on Protocols for Smart Grid Communications

Swapnoneel Roy
University of North Florida, USA

ABSTRACT

In this work, a denial of service (DoS) attack known as the clogging attack has been performed on three different modern protocols for smart grid (SG) communications. The first protocol provides authentication between smart meters (SM) and a security and authentication server (SAS). The second protocol facilitates secure and private communications between electric vehicles (EV) and the smart grid. The third protocol is a secure and efficient key distribution protocol for the smart grid. The protocols differ in either their applications (authentication, key distribution), or their ways of communications (usage of encryption, hashes, timestamps etc.). But they are similar in their purpose of design (for the smart grid) and their usage of computationally intensive mathematical operations (modular exponentiation, ECC) to implement security. Solutions to protect these protocols against this attack are then illustrated along with identifying the causes behind the occurrence of this vulnerability in SG communication protocols in general.

INTRODUCTION

The collective nature of a smart grid (SG) with many subsystems and networks, working together as a system of systems makes its components vulnerable to various kinds of attacks most of which can be performed remotely. Therefore, security has become a first class parameter in the development of SG, and many authentication and key management protocols have been designed and are continually being designed. Security protocols for the smart grid can be broadly classified into two major classes according to their functions:

DOI: 10.4018/978-1-5225-1829-7.ch003

1.   Authentication, and
2.   Key Management.

User authentication can enable a perimeter device (e.g., a firewall, proxy server, VPN server, or remote access server) to decide whether or not to approve a specific access request to gain entry to a computer network. It is necessary to be able to identify and authenticate any user with a high level of certainty, so that the user may be held accountable should his/her actions threaten the security and productivity of the network. The more confidence a network administrator has regarding the user's identity, the more confidence the administrator will have in allowing that user specific privileges, and the more faith the administrator will have in the internal records regarding that user.

Multi-factor authentication is an approach to cyber-security in which the user is required to provide more than one form of verification in order to prove his/her identity and gain access to the system. It takes advantage of a combination of several authentication factors. Commonly used factors include verification by:

1.   Something a user knows (such as a password),
2.   Something the user has (such as a smart card or a security token), and
3.   Something the user is (such as the use of biometrics) (Stallings & Brown, 2008).

Due to their increased complexity, multi-factor authentication systems are harder to breach than those using any single factor.

Multiple factor authentication is needed to provide high-level security. But with the introduction of more factors, there are possibilities to introduce more vulnerability in the protocols that an attacker can exploit to launch an attack on them. Vulnerabilities are detected by static analysis before they are exploited. The root causes of CPU, stack, and other resource-exhaustion vulnerabilities (DoS) are often design flaws rather than programming errors. Several multi-factor authentication protocols in the literature involving smart cards, RFIDs, wireless networks, or digital signatures, rely on the usage of complex mathematical operations (e.g. ECC) for their security. Hence some level of protection should be added to them to guarantee total security against various kinds of attacks.

Key management is the management of cryptographic keys in a cryptosystem. This includes dealing with the generation, exchange, storage, use, and replacement of keys. It includes cryptographic protocol design, key servers, user procedures, and other relevant protocols. Key management concerns keys at the user level, either between users or systems. This is in contrast to key scheduling; key scheduling typically refers to the internal handling of key material within the operation of a cipher. Successful key management is critical to the security of a cryptosystem. In practice it is arguably the most difficult aspect of cryptography because it involves system policy, user training, organizational and departmental interactions, and coordination between all of these elements.

The nodes are all non-interactive in distributed key management protocols that are conventional. Every node is assumed to be able to independently learn about the keys shared with other nodes, without the assistance or intervention of any trusted third parties. The memory cost of each node in a non-interactive network has been proved to be N-1, where N is the total number of nodes in the network. This number does not depend on the kind of algorithms used to determine the pairwise keys. The pairwise key model, the Blom model and the Blundo model are optimum as non-interactive schemes in terms of their memory cost. However, as N grows, the memory requirement of non-interactive schemes grows exponentially.

This high memory requirement restricts their applications in many large-scale networks, such as ad hoc networks or sensor networks, which may involve hundreds to thousands of individual nodes.

To fix the problem of large memory requirements, and increase scalability of networks, interactions between nodes are implemented. Models like the Key Distributing Center (KDC) or the Key Trustee Center (KTC) have been developed to keep only a shared key with a trusted server that takes care of the key exchanging and agreement between nodes. However, KDC and KTC models have worse security issues than the non-interactive scheme, since they are single-point failure models. New key management protocols are developed that achieves a trade-off between the two extremes (fully-interactive (KDC/KTC), and the non-interactive) approaches. This way a balance between the memory cost, and security is made.

The way research works in the field in security especially while designing cryptographic protocols (for authentication and key management) is the security vulnerability analysis of one or more protocols leads to the design of new protocols. However, in most of these works, the authors present attacks on a previous protocol and propose a new protocol with assertions of the superior aspects of their protocol, while ignoring benefits that their new protocol does not attempt (or fails) to provide, and thus overlooking dimensions on which it performs poorly. Despite the lack of evaluation criteria, another common feature of these studies is that, there is no proper security justification (or even an explicit security model) presented, which explains why these protocols previously claimed to be secure turn out to be vulnerable.

One such vulnerability found in protocols is the denial of service (DoS). In a DoS attack, the adversary attempts to bring down a service thus preventing legitimate users access it. There are several ways to perform a DoS. DoS attacks when performed on a larger scale are called distributed denial of service (DDoS).

In this chapter, three recent communication protocols for the SG are analyzed for vulnerability to the *clogging attack*, which is a form of DoS. The first one by Nicanfar *et al.* (2014) is a protocol that provides authentication between smart meters (SM) and a security and authentication server (SAS). This protocol does not use timestamps. The second protocol we consider for analysis is by Tseng (2012). This protocol facilitates secure and private communications between electric vehicles (EV) and the smart grid, and uses timestamps. The third protocol by Xia *et al.* (2012) is a secure and efficient key distribution protocol for the smart grid.

Objectives of this Chapter

In order to demonstrate the vulnerabilities of the three modern protocols for smart grid communication considered a generalized cryptanalysis algorithm is applied to perform clogging attacks on these SG protocols that use computationally intensive operations like modular exponentiation and elliptic curve cryptography to guarantee security in the communication process. The attack results in the server side of the SG being forced to perform useless computationally intensive operations. This results in wastage of time and resources on the part of the server, and thus denial of service for legitimate users.

The first one by Nicanfar *et al.* (2014) is a protocol that provides authentication between smart meters (SM) and a security and authentication server (SAS). This protocol does not use timestamps. This protocol is shown to be vulnerable to the clogging attack. The vulnerability lies in the use of computationally intensive modular exponentiation by the server in the authentication process. In this analysis it is observed that using a timestamp would prevent clogging attack vulnerability in this protocol.

The second protocol we consider for analysis is by Tseng (2012). This protocol facilitates secure and private communications between electric vehicles (EV) and the smart grid, and uses timestamps. The vulnerability to clogging attack arises from the fact that no verification for the validity of the timestamps is performed in this protocol. A validity checking on timestamp added to the protocol makes it secure against the clogging attack.

The third protocol by Xia *et al.* (2012) is a secure and efficient key distribution protocol for the smart grid. It involves a trusted third party called the Trust Anchor (TA) that facilitates communication (in form of efficient key distribution) between the smart meters and service providers. The TA involves computationally intensive modular exponentiation that makes it vulnerable to clogging attack. Again, it is observed that the usage of timestamps with verification can make this protocol secure against clogging attack.

The three protocols differ in either their applications (authentication, key distribution), or their ways of communications (usage of encryption, hashes, timestamps etc.). But they are similar in their purpose of design (for the smart grid) and their usage of computationally intensive mathematical operations (modular exponentiation, ECC) to implement security.

It is observed that the usage of modular exponentiation or elliptic curve cryptography in protocols guarantees a higher level of security against much vulnerability, but it might also create vulnerability if it is used without an additional level of protection. The communication protocols analyzed in this chapter rely on either modular exponentiation or elliptic curve cryptography for their security. Hence some level of protection should be added to them to guarantee increased security against the clogging attack.

We conclude that additional techniques like usage of timestamps, usage of nonce, and encryption can be applied on these protocols to make them secure against the clogging attack.

Organization of this Chapter

The rest of this book chapter is organized as follows. The next section (Background) gives a brief overview of the research done in this area prior to this work and discusses the techniques employed in this work. The subsequent section (DoS attack on SG communication protocols) first describes the generic algorithm developed to launch the clogging attack on the various protocols analyzed in this chapter. Next the section describes each SG communication protocol in detail, performs clogging attack on them, and provides solutions for preventing the attack. Finally, the next sections summarize the work, discuss its significance, and propose possible future research directions.

BACKGROUND

This section summarizes the research done in the field of multi-factor authentication and key exchanging protocols in general, and also specifically for the smart grid (SG). The various kinds of attacks that are generally performed against these protocols are discussed, followed by two approaches to dealing with these attacks. Finally the approach taken in this chapter is briefly described.

A Research Snapshot of Security Protocols

The design and security analysis of authentication and key exchanging protocols has been an active area of research in recent years. Generally the security vulnerability analysis of one or more protocols leads to the design of new protocols. However, inmost of these studies, the authors present attacks on previous schemes and propose new protocols with assertions of the superior aspects of their schemes, while ignoring benefits that their schemes don't attempt (or fail) to provide, thus overlooking dimensions on which they perform poorly.

In addition to the lack of evaluation criteria, another common feature of these studies is that there is no proper security justification (or even an explicit security model) presented, which explains why these protocols previously claimed to be secure turn out to be vulnerable. Such an approach has generated a lot of literature, yet as far as we know, little attention has been paid to systematic design and analysis. The research history of this area can be summarized in Figure 1.

In particular, the design of security protocols for the smart grid (SG) has picked momentum as a topic of research recently. Several protocols designed can be broadly classified as Authentication and Key Management according to their functions. Authentication protocols for the SG that mostly use more than one factor (are multi-factor) have been recently designed by (Lee *et al.* 2014; Nicanfar *et al.*, 2014; Saxena & Choi, 2015; Tseng, 2012). Some recent key management protocols for the SG have been designed by (Badra & Zeadally, 2013;, Benmalek & Challal, 2015; Demertzis *et al.*, 2015; Xia & Wang, 2012).

Most of these protocols have been designed on top of other protocols in the process making the previous protocols secure against various kinds of attacks (vulnerabilities). Figure 2 provides a chronological snapshot of security protocols. In this figure, protocols appearing below have evolved from making ones on top more secure, by finding out vulnerabilities in them. As an example, the evolution and subsequent enhancement of one of the protocol analyzed and enhanced in this chapter (Xia *et al.*, 2012) has been shown in Figure 2.

Various Kinds of Attacks on Protocols

Some common attacks that are generally considered during security analysis are man-in-the-middle, dictionary, password guessing, brute force, replay, denial of service, etc.

1. **Brute-Force Attack:** In this kind of attack, the adversary simply tries out all possible combinations of alphabets to obtain the correct password. Alternatively, the adversary could be a bit more intelligent to try to guess the password by obtaining some information about the user. Usually, users choose passwords, which are easy for them to remember. Hence passwords contain things like the year of birth, or a part of the user name or user ID. The adversary could gather such information to simplify his efforts to break the password (Apostol, 2012).
2. **Impersonation Attack:** In this kind of attack, the adversary pretends to be a legitimate user and gains access to the services meant for the legitimate user. The adversary might spoof the IP address of the legitimate user, or could intercept the messages sent by the user and use them to gain access to the server (Wei-Chi & Chang, 2005).
3. **Replay Attack:** In this kind of attack, the adversary intercepts a message with the identity and the password of the legitimate user. The adversary then waits till the legitimate user logs out of

Figure 1. The design of security protocols

$$\text{New Protocol} \rightarrow \text{Broken} \rightarrow \text{Improved Protocol} \rightarrow \text{Broken Again}$$

$$\rightarrow \text{Further Improved Protocol} \rightarrow \cdots$$

Figure 2. A snapshot of the evolution of security protocols

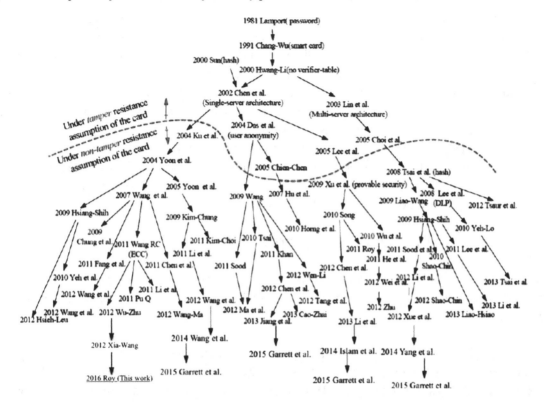

the service. Then he replays the message with the identity and the password to the server and gains access. Replay attacks are possible even when the user identity and password are encrypted (Syverson, 1994).

4. **Stolen Smart Card Attack:** In a password authentication scheme employing smart cards, the smart card contains the identity and password of the legitimate user. The stealing of the smart card by an adversary is equivalent to the stealing of a credit card. The adversary could enjoy service until all the servers to which the legitimate user has access are notified about the stolen smart card (Chen *et al.*, 2014).

5. **Stolen Server Database Attack:** In this kind of attack, the adversary steals the database maintained by the server that contains the user identities and passwords of the legitimate clients. Databases are not secured properly in most of the organizations. Database configurations are weak and insecure and easy to exploit. Database attacks go unnoticed as it takes less than 10 seconds to hack in and out of a database that is a major threat to organizations. Attackers use simple methods to break into databases, such as exploiting weak authentication, using default passwords and capitalizing on known vulnerabilities. The front-end client-server authentication store their passwords in their back-end databases and this connection are usually not secure. If the password is compromised, then the schema becomes vulnerable to attack which makes the protocol insecure. The adversary now has enormous power to do anything at his will (Wei-Chi *et al.*, 2004).

6. **Man-in-the-Middle Attack:** A man-in-the-middle attack is a similar strategy and can be used against many cryptographic protocols. One example of man-in-the-middle attacks is active eavesdropping,

in which the attacker makes independent connections with the victims and relays messages between them to make them believe they are talking directly to each other over a private connection, when in fact the entire conversation is controlled by the attacker. The attacker must be able to intercept all relevant messages passing between the two victims and inject new ones. Man-in-the-middle attacks are abbreviated in many ways, such as MITM, MitM, MiM or MIM.

7. **Insider Attack:** A legitimate user of one server could try to hack the credentials of another user. The victim might have access to some other service, which the adversary does not. The adversary thus gains access to that service (Wood, 2000).

8. **Denial of Service Attack:** The adversary tries to prevent legitimate users from obtaining the designated service. The adversary to achieve this goal adopts various techniques. This attack prevents the availability of a service rather than compromising any information (confidentiality), or modifying unauthorized information (integrity) (Houle *et al.*, 2001).

Approaches to Analyze and Security Protocols

Security has become an integral part of software design. Nowadays security is considered during the design and implementation of software rather than as add-on. There are two approaches to analyzing software for security:

1. **Static Analysis:** In this approach, the algorithm and the code after implementation are analyzed to find security vulnerabilities (Chess and McGraw, 2004; Garrett *et al.*, 2015; Harish and Roy, 2014; Roy *et al.*, 2011; Talluri and Roy, 2014). The advantage of static analysis is that it can find potential security violations without executing the application or, in the case of an algorithm analysis, even before the implementation is done.

2. **Dynamic Analysis:** In this approach, the software is executed and tested for potential vulnerabilities (Rahimi *et al.*, 1993; Russo & Sabelfeld, 2010; Sobajic & Pao, 1989; Yasinsac, 2001). One well-known technique is penetration testing in which the tester tries to be a hacker to break into a system (Petukhov & Kozlov, 2008).

Methodology Adopted in this Chapter

In this chapter, static vulnerability analysis is employed on three communication protocols for the SG. Specifically, static vulnerability analysis is performed to conclude if these protocols are vulnerable to clogging attack, a form of denial of service.

Static Analysis Technique

In this section, static analysis technique is illustrated in details, and how static analysis can be applied to detect security vulnerabilities is explained. Gary A. Kildall in (Kildall, 1973) introduced Data flow analysis. The general idea is to compute for each elementary program statement a set of information, which may reach it. The information could be variable names, arithmetic expressions, or values of variables. This depends on the objective of the specific analysis. A static program analysis, evaluates software, without executing it. This stands in contrast to a dynamic analysis that executes the code and observes its runtime behavior. Common techniques used in static analysis include model checking and data flow analysis. Model checking decides if a model of a system satisfies a given property. A data flow analysis computes information that reaches the program points of a program. As mentioned earlier, this work performs Static Vulnerability Analysis of various security protocols for the SG.

Static Analysis approach involves primarily three steps:

1. A Threat Model will be first formulated where the assumptions will be mentioned, and the common threats investigated for in the protocols would be identified.
2. The actual threat (vulnerability) analysis would be then performed on the protocols to find whether they are indeed vulnerable to the threats, and
3. Solutions to make the protocols secure against the threats will be then identified, and the application of the same on the protocols will be proved to make them secure against the identified threats.

The first step in the analysis of the protocols would be to design a threat model. Threat modeling is an approach for analyzing the security of an application. It looks at a system from a potential attacker's perspective. In the threat model, the assumptions under which the protocols would be analyzed statically to identify threats (vulnerabilities) in them are specified. The threat model would also consist of the various threats the protocols would be analyzed for.

Conventional multi-factor authentication and key exchanging protocols assume the attacker to have complete control over the communication channel between the parties in communication. In other words, the communication channel is considered insecure, and that the attacker can perform activities like eavesdropping, intercepting, inserting, deleting, and modifying any information (transmitted messages) over the communication channel.

The next step would be to choose authentication protocols to perform static cryptanalysis. As mentioned before, this work will only focus on protocols designed for the SG. Some of the other factors that will be considered to select protocols are:

1. How recent they are?
2. Different factors they use (e.g. Smart Cards, RFIDs, Memory drives, etc.).
3. What other means do they use to implement additional security (e.g. timestamps, nonce, encryption, hashes)?

The threat vulnerability analysis will be performed on these protocols to find whether they are indeed vulnerable to the threats. The last step would be to suggest solutions to prevent the identified attack in order to make the protocols more secure.

DoS ATTACK ON SG COMMUNICATION PROTOCOLS

The way most SG communication protocols (either authentication or key exchanging) work is that the client (usually a smart meter, or an electric vehicle, etc.) sends its credentials to the server (an authentication server, or a key distributing server, etc.) which then applies some mathematical operations (functions) to verify those credentials. These protocols usually work in different phases. The DoS attack illustrated in this chapter is applicable to various phases of the protocols cryptanalyzed.

The Denial of Service Attack

The main idea of the attack is the interception of the messages from the client to server containing the login credentials by the attacker. These messages are unencrypted in some protocols, while encrypted in others. They might (or might not) contain timestamps. The attacker then replays this intercepted messages several times to force the server perform computationally intensive mathematical operations (like modular exponentiation, elliptic curve cryptography, etc.) forcing the server to waste computational time and resources. Legitimate users are denied of any services that way. Algorithm 1 depicts the DoS attack, which is also known as the clogging attack (Garrett *et al.*, 2015).

Conditions for the Attack

The clogging attack can be successfully performed on a protocol that uses computational resource intensive operations to perform authentication. Two such operations used by the protocol that are crypt-analyzed in this work are modular exponentiation and elliptic curve cryptography (ECC) operations. In the following section their computational resource intensiveness is illustrated.

Modular Exponentiation

Modular exponentiation ($y \equiv g^x \pmod{n}$) is an operation widely used in authentication protocols to guarantee security. In practice, the modulus n is a very large prime, and the exponent x, which is often a chosen random secret value, should be very large as well. Harish and Roy (2014) computed the energy consumed in computing the modular exponentiation y for fixed values of the parameters g, x, and n. They then compared it with common operations like addition, exclusive-OR, and multiplication. Figure 3 shows their result.

As seen in Figure 3, modular exponentiation consumer over a hundred times more (computational) energy over the other common operations. This proves the computational intensiveness of modular exponentiation. Therefore any protocol that uses modular exponentiation is vulnerable to the DoS attack in which, the attacker can exploit the computational resource intensiveness of modular exponentiation to launch the attack.

Algorithm 1. The general algorithm for clogging attack

```
Intercept login message from client to server
if Timestamp is present then
   Modify timestamp to match requirements
else
   Keep message as is
end if
while The server is not completely clogged! do
   Replay the message to the server
end while
```

Figure 3. Comparison of normalized energy consumption of different operations (on log scale)
Source: Harish and Roy, 2014

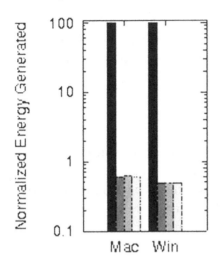

Elliptic Curve Cryptography

The ECC based operations are an alternative to modular exponentiation to perform authentication. The most commonly used ECC operations in authentication protocols are:

1. Bilinear pairing.
2. Scalar multiplication in group *G*.
3. Map-to-point conversion.

Let *Tp*, *Ts*, and *Tmap* respectively be the time taken to perform a single bilinear pairing, scalar multiplication, and map-to-point conversation. The following have been proved in (Xu & Wu, 2015):

1. $Tp > Ts > Tmap$
2. $Tp \approx 3 \times Ts$
3. $Tp \approx 4 \times Tmap$

Further let *Tmodex* be the time taken by one modulo exponentiation operation. It has been shown in (Farash and Ahmadian-Attari, 2014) that $Tp \approx 2 \times Tmodex$ to guarantee same level of security.

Elliptic Curve Cryptography (ECC) is a very widely used technique in multi factor authentication. ECC had been developed and used to reduce computational costs, but to provide the same level of security as other similar operations (e.g. modular exponentiation) provides. ECC thus finds its applications in various authentication protocols involving smart cards, RFIDs, wireless networks, digital signatures, and other factors. However, as the authors observe in (Farash and Ahmadian-Attari, 2014), the cost of one bilinear pairing that is an important operation of ECC is about two times higher than that of one modular exponentiation operation at the same security level. Therefore, the computationally intensive nature of ECC leaves a security loophole in the protocols by its usage. An attacker can force the server or the client to perform ECC operations repeatedly to clog them. This again results in one or all of them to waste resources by performing unnecessary computations.

It can be therefore concluded that all the ECC based operations bilinear pairing; scalar multiplication, and map- to-point conversation are quite computationally intensive. Therefore, a protocol that uses ECC operation has a potential vulnerability to DoS in which the attacker exploits the computational intensive nature of ECC operations.

Protocols Cryptanalyzed

Table 1 lists the protocols that have been shown to be vulnerable to the DoS attack by performing cryptanalysis on them. All the protocols considered are modern protocols designed for the smart grid. They differ in the usage of the type of mathematical operations, and the functionalities they provide.

In the next sections, each of the protocols is illustrated, cryptanalyzed (attacked), and then a solution with its security analysis is provided to make the protocol secure against the DoS attack.

Nicanfar *et al.* (2014)

The protocol by Nicanfar *et al.* (2014) is a secure and efficient smart grid mutual authentication (SGMA) protocol. This protocol provides authentication between smart meters (SM) and a security and authentication server (SAS). In their paper, they propose a secure and efficient SG mutual authentication (SGMA) scheme and an SG key management (SGKM) protocol. SGMA claims to provide efficient mutual authentication between SMs and the security and authentication server (SAS) in the SG using passwords.

For a detailed description of the protocol the reader is referred to (Nicanfar *et al.*, 2014). Figure 4 briefly describes the protocol.

Attack on the Protocol

It is assumed that the attacker A has unlimited access to message sent back and forth the (insecure) channel. A performs the following steps:

1. Intercept the message $\{SN_{sm}, ID_{sm}, G_{sm}\}$ from SM to SAS.
2. Replay $\{SN_{sm}, ID_{sm}, G_{sm}\}$ to SAS.
3. SAS is forced to calculate G_{sas} each time it receives that message.

Table 1. Protocols cryptanalyzed to perform DoS attack

Protocol	Tool(s) used for Authorization	Purpose of Protocol
Nicanfar *et al.* (2014)	Modular Exponentiation	Authentication for Smart Grid Communications.
Tseng (2012)	ECC (Bilinear pairing)	Authentication for Vehicle to Grid Network Communications.
Xia *et al.* (2012)	Modular Exponentiation	Key Exchanging for Smart Grids.

Figure 4. The SGMA protocol
Source: Nicanfar et al., 2014

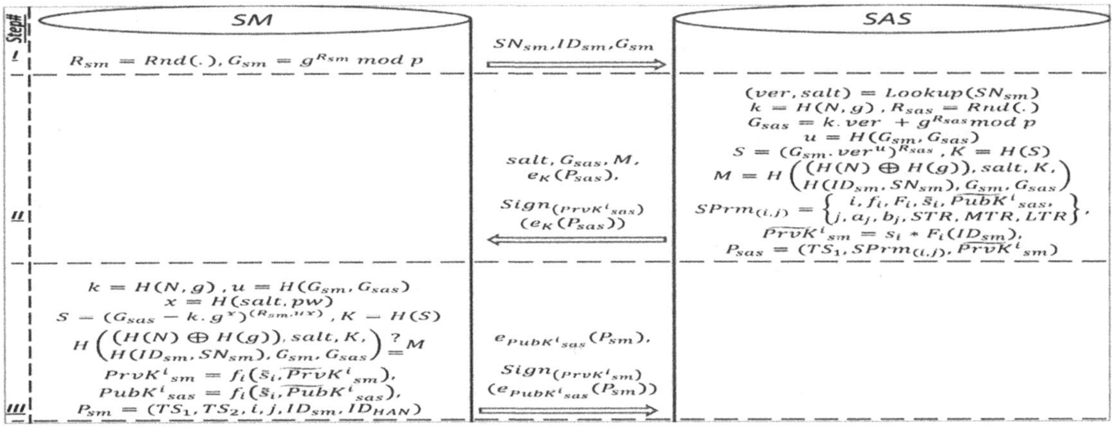

Since calculation of G_{sas} involves modular exponentiation computation, SAS will be clogged after some time only computing useless modular exponentiations, hence legitimate SMs would be denied of service.

It should be noted that even DoS-resilient mechanisms (e.g. timeout or locking an SM's account for a period of time after a predefined number of login failures) are introduced on the SAS's side (as mentioned in (Nicanfar *et al.*, 2014)), it may be not a real obstacle for attacker A as it can initialize new sessions with different intercepted identities in an interleaving manner. Hence, A can potentially perform the above attack procedure continuously, which will make the victimized SAS keep computing useless expensive modular exponentiation operations rather than any real work. Thus A clogs SAS with useless work and therefore A denies any legitimate SM service. If distributed DoS attacks are launched based on this strategy, the consequences will be more serious.

Proposed Countermeasures from the Attack

1. **Usage of Time Stamps:** One countermeasure from this attack for the SGMA protocol will be the addition of timestamp with the message $\{SN_{sm}, ID_{sm}, G_{sm}\}$. Let T_{sm} be the current system time of the SM while it sends the message to SAS. A hash of T_{sm} ($h(T_{sm})$) has to be added with the message. Therefore the SM sends the message $\{SN_{sm}, ID_{sm}, G_{sm}, T_{sm}, h(T_{sm})\}$. Upon receipt, SAS first recalculates $h(T_{sm})$ and compares it with the received hash value to ensure the timestamp has not been modified. SAS next checks whether $T_{sas} - T_{sm} \leq \Delta T$, where T_{sas} is the current system time of the SAS. This rules out the chances of DoS resulting from replays.

2. **Usage of Encryption:** Though this is not a good solution in terms of overhead, it will still prevent the DoS attack, if the message $\{SN_{sm}, ID_{sm}, G_{sm}\}$ is encrypted using either symmetric key, or public key encryption. This will however add overhead of key exchanging, and the encryption/decryption processes.

Tseng (2012)

Tseng's (2012) protocol is a protocol to facilitate secure and private communications between electric vehicles (EV) and the smart grid. In their paper, they claim to propose a secure and privacy-preserving communication protocol in certificateless public key settings for V2G networks, which utilizes the restrictive partially blind signature to protect the identities of the EV owners and is also designed to simplify the certificate management as in traditional public key infrastructure and to overcome the key escrow problem as in ID-PKC. Moreover, their proposed protocol has been claimed to achieve the property of completeness, identity and location privacy, confidentiality and integrity of the communications, and known-key security, and is claimed to be secure against the replay attacks and existential adaptively chosen message attacks.

The relevant portion of this protocol for the cryptanalysis purpose is the communication part between any electric vehicle (EV) and a central aggregator (CAG), which belongs to the vehicle to grid (V2G) network (the pass generation phase of the protocol). For a detailed description of the protocol the reader is referred to (Tseng, 2012). Figure 5 briefly describes the relevant portion of the protocol for our attack purpose.

Attack on the Protocol

It is again assumed that the attacker A has unlimited access to message sent back and forth along the (insecure) channel. A performs the following steps:

1. Intercept the message $\{ID_i, M, t_1, Sig_i(H_1(ID_i \| M \| t_1))\}$ from EV_i to CAG.

Figure 5. The pass generation phase of Tseng's protocol
Source: Tseng, 2012

EV_i		CAG
1. Send $\{ID_i, M, t_1, Sig_i(H_1(ID_i\|M\|t_1))\}$ to the CAG	$\rightarrow$	**2.** Receive $\{ID_i, M, t_1, Sig_i(H_1(ID_i\|M\|t_1))\}$ Check the validity of the signature Compute $U = rP$, $a = e(P,Q)$, $b = e(M,Q)$ Compute $z = e(M, SK_j)$ Compute $k_1 = e(D_j, Q_i)$
3. Receive $\{U, a, b, z, t_2, HMAC_{k_1}(U\|a\|b\|t_2)\}$ Compute $k_1 = e(D_i, Q_j)$ Check the message integrity Compute $M' = \alpha M + \beta P$, $A = e(M', Q_j)$, $z' = z^\alpha y^\beta$ Compute $a' = a^u g^v$, $b' = a^{u\beta} g^{u\alpha} A^v$ Compute $U' = \lambda Q_j + U + \mu P$ Compute $c = H_2(M', U', A, z', a', b') + \lambda H_1(\Delta)$ Compute $c' = cu$ Send $\{c, t_3, HMAC_{k_1}(c\|t_3)\}$ to the CAG	$\leftarrow$ $\rightarrow$	Send $\{U, a, b, z, t_2, HMAC_{k_1}(U\|a\|b\|t_2)\}$ to EV_i **4.** Receive $\{c, t_3, HMAC_{k_1}(c\|t_3)\}$ Check the message integrity Compute $S_1 = Q + cSK_j$ and $S_2 = cD_j + rH_1(\Delta)P_{pub}$
5. Receive $\{S_1, S_2, t_4, HMAC_{k_1}(S_1\|S_2\|t_4)\}$ Check the message integrity Check whether the following equations hold $e(P, S_1) = ay^c$ and $e(M, S_1) = bz^c$ If so, compute $S_1' = uS_1 + vQ_j$ and $S_2' = S_2 + \mu H_1(\Delta)P_{pub}$ The restrictive partially blind signature on (Δ, M') is $\{U', z', c', S_1', S_2'\}$ $Pass_i$ is $\{(\Delta, M'), (U', z', c', S_1', S_2')\}$	$\leftarrow$	Send $\{S_1, S_2, t_4, HMAC_{k_1}(S_1\|S_2\|t_4)\}$ to EV_i

2. Replay $\{ID_i, M, t_1, Sig_i(H_1(ID_i \| M \| t_1))\}$ to CAG.
3. CAG is forced to calculate U, a, b, z, k_1 each time it receives that message.

Since calculation of the above parameters involve bilinear pairing (ECC) computation, the CAG will be clogged after some time only computing useless bilinear pairings, hence legitimate EVs would be denied of service.

Again, A can potentially perform the above attack procedure continuously by replaying messages it intercepted from every single EV. This will make the victimized CAG keep computing the useless expensive ECC operations rather than any real work. Thus A clogs the CAG with useless work and therefore A denies any legitimate EV service. Again, if distributed DoS attacks are launched based on this strategy, the consequences will be more serious.

Proposed Countermeasures from the Attack

1. **Usage of Time Stamps Checking:** It is quite surprising to note that this protocol includes time-stamps and their hashes in the messages from the EVs, but verifications of the timestamps are not done by the CAG, which makes this protocol vulnerable to this DoS attack. One countermeasure from this attack for the protocol will be the verification of timestamp t_1 by the CAG upon receipt of the message $\{ID_i, M, t_1, Sig_i(H_1(ID_i \| M \| t_1))\}$ from EV_i. CAG first recalculates $H_1(ID_i \| M \| t_1)$ and compares it with the received hash value to ensure the timestamp t_1 has not been modified. CAG next checks whether $t_2 - t_1 \leq \Delta T$, where t_2 is the current system time of the CAG. This rules out the chances of DoS resulting from replays.
2. **Usage of Encryption:** Though this is not a good solution in terms of overhead, it will still prevent the DoS attack, if the message $\{ID_i, M, t_1, Sig_i(H_1(ID_i \| M \| t_1))\}$ is encrypted using either symmetric key, or public key encryption. This will however add overhead of key exchanging, and the encryption/decryption processes.

Xia *et al.* (2012)

The protocol by Xia *et al.* (2012) is a secure and efficient key distribution protocol for the smart grid. They motivate the design of their scheme by mentioning that most of the proposed key management methods for the SG that uses either using public key or symmetric key have a lot of drawbacks. As mentioned earlier the Public Key Infrastructure (PKI) scheme, which is essentially a non-interactive scheme, has the memory usage issue that they term the manageably sized certificate revocation list (CRL) problem. The third-party setting schemes (e.g., Kerberos) may have a disconnection problem if the third-party server is out of power - the single point failure problem that was mentioned earlier. To avoid these concerns, they consider a third-party setting for key distribution for the SG letting the server work as a lightweight directory access protocol (LDAP) server without losing security, in an attempt to balance between the two extreme schemes.

Since the cost of a LDAP server is not too high, it is affordable that the server could be duplicated a few times in case one server loses the communication. Their proposed system is claimed to be able to provide secure communication between the smart meter and the service provider.

Figure 6. The key distribution protocol by Xia et al
Source: Xia et al., 2012

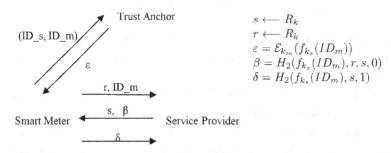

The relevant portion of their protocol for the cryptanalysis purpose is the message exchange between the smart meter (SM) and the trust anchor (TA). The TA is a trusted third party that manages the key distribution between the SMs and the service providers. For a detailed description of the protocol the reader is referred to (Xia *et al.*, 2012). Figure 6 briefly describes the protocol.

Attack on the Protocol

It is again assumed that the attacker A has unlimited access to message sent back and forth the (insecure) channel. A performs the following steps:

1. Intercept the message $\{ID_m, ID_s\}$ from SM to TA.
2. Replay $\{ID_m, ID_s\}$ to TA.
3. TA is forced to compute $k_s = H_1(ID_s^x \bmod p)$ each time it receives that message.

Since calculation of k_s involves modular exponentiation computation, the TA will be clogged after some time only computing useless modular exponentiations, hence legitimate SMs would be denied of service.

A can easily launch this attack on TA in a distributive manner (since the identities of the smart meters and the service providers are assumed to be public anyway).

Proposed Countermeasures from the Attack

1. **Usage of Time Stamps:** One countermeasure will be the addition of timestamp with the message $\{ID_m, ID_s\}$. Let T_m be the current system time of the SM while it sends the message to TA. A hash of T_m ($H(T_m)$) has to be added with the message. Therefore the SM sends the message $\{ID_m, ID_s, H(T_m)\}$. Upon receipt, the TA first recalculates $H(T_m)$ and compares it with the received hash value to ensure the timestamp has not been modified. TA next checks whether $T_{ta} - T_m \leq \Delta T$, where T_{ta} is the current system time of the TA This rules out the chances of DoS resulting from replays.
2. **Usage of Encryption:** Again, it will prevent the DoS attack, if the message $\{ID_m, ID_s\}$ is encrypted using either symmetric key, or public key encryption. This will however add overhead of key exchanging, and the encryption/decryption processes.

SOLUTIONS AND RECOMMENDATIONS

Table 2 summarizes the results obtained in this work. All the protocols have been found vulnerable against the clogging attack, a form of DoS. How the usage of timestamps can make them secure against this attack has been further illustrated.

The usage of encryption has been noted to be another solution against the DoS attack. However, it must be emphasized that as everything has costs involved, the level of security needed will determine the nature of the countermeasure.

FUTURE RESEARCH DIRECTIONS

Research in security is continuous. Authentication protocols for various applications are designed, vulnerabilities are discovered in them, and new protocols secure against the vulnerabilities are designed as a result. The vulnerability of modern authentication and key exchanging protocols for smart grids illustrated in this work will lead to future protocols designs secure against this attack.

Of particular interests would be to design better solutions against the vulnerability than the ones designed in this work. For example, with the usage of timestamps, there is the problem of clock synchronization between various entities in the smart grid. With the usage of encryption comes a lot of overhead that increases costs.

Another solution might be to use nonce in place of timestamp in the protocols. But it remains to be seen how effective will that be. Also a dynamic analysis of the solutions (implementations) and their comparison is an interesting future research direction to pursue.

CONCLUSION

In this research, three advanced protocols for smart grids have been shown to be vulnerable to the clogging attack, which is a form of denial of service. The goal of this work has been to uncover the subtleties and challenges in designing this type of protocols. While mathematical operations like modular exponentiation and elliptical curve cryptography guarantee a certain level of security, this work shows that their usage might lead to an easily-exploitable vulnerability just in case they are used without an additional level of protection. Several other such protocols in the literature rely on the usage of such mathematical operations for their security. Therefore some level of protection should be added to them to guarantee total security against clogging attack.

Table 2. Summary of the results and solutions

Protocol	Vulnerability	Countermeasure
Nicanfar *et al.* (2014)	Denial of Service (Clogging attack)	• Usage of Timestamps • Usage of Encryption
Tseng (2012)	Denial of Service (Clogging attack)	• Implementing timestamps verification (checks) • Usage of Encryption
Xia *et al.* (2012)	Denial of Service (Clogging attack)	• Usage of Timestamps • Usage of Encryption

REFERENCES

Apostol, K. (2012). *Brute-force attack*. Salu Publishing.

Badra, M., & Zeadally, S. (2013, April). Key management solutions in the smart grid environment. In *Wireless and Mobile Networking Conference (WMNC), 2013 6th Joint IFIP* (pp. 1-7). IEEE. doi:10.1109/WMNC.2013.6549050

Benmalek, M., & Challal, Y. (2015, August). eSKAMI: Efficient and Scalable multi-group Key management for Advanced Metering Infrastructure in Smart Grid. In Trustcom/BigDataSE/ISPA, 2015 IEEE (Vol. 1, pp. 782-789). IEEE.

Chen, B.-L., Kuo, W.-C., & Wuu, L.-C. (2014). Robust smart-card-based remote user password authentication scheme. *International Journal of Communication Systems*, 27(2), 377–389. doi:10.1002/dac.2368

Chess, B., & McGraw, G. (2004). Static analysis for security. *IEEE Security and Privacy*, 2(6), 76–79. doi:10.1109/MSP.2004.111

Demertzis, F. F., Karopoulos, G., Xenakis, C., & Colarieti, A. (2015). Self-organised Key Management for the Smart Grid. In Ad-hoc, Mobile, and Wireless Networks (pp. 303-316). Springer International Publishing. doi:10.1007/978-3-319-19662-6_21

Farash, M. S., & Ahmadian-Attari, M. (2014). A Pairing-free ID-based Key Agreement Protocol with Different PKGs. *International Journal of Network Security*, 16(2), 143–148.

Garrett, K., Talluri, S. R., & Roy, S. (2015). On vulnerability analysis of several password authentication protocols. *Innovations in Systems and Software Engineering*, 11(3), 167–176. doi:10.1007/s11334-015-0250-x

Harish, P. D., & Roy, S. (2014, May). Energy oriented vulnerability analysis on authentication protocols for cps. In *Distributed Computing in Sensor Systems (DCOSS), 2014 IEEE International Conference on* (pp. 367-371). IEEE. doi:10.1109/DCOSS.2014.52

Houle, K. J., Weaver, G. M., Long, N., & Thomas, R. (2001). *Trends in denial of service attack technology*. Retrieved from: https://resources.sei.cmu.edu/asset_files/WhitePaper/2001_019_001_52491.pdf

Kildall, G. A. (1973, October). A unified approach to global program optimization. In *Proceedings of the 1st annual ACM SIGACT-SIGPLAN symposium on Principles of programming languages* (pp. 194-206). ACM. doi:10.1145/512927.512945

Lee, W. B., Chen, T. H., Sun, W. R., & Ho, K. I. J. (2014, May). An S/Key-like one-time password authentication scheme using smart cards for smart meter. In *Advanced Information Networking and Applications Workshops (WAINA), 2014 28th International Conference on* (pp. 281-286). IEEE.

Nicanfar, H., Jokar, P., Beznosov, K., & Leung, V. (2014). Efficient authentication and key management mechanisms for smart grid communications. *Systems Journal, IEEE*, 8(2), 629–640. doi:10.1109/JSYST.2013.2260942

Petukhov, A., & Kozlov, D. (2008). *Detecting security vulnerabilities in web applications using dynamic analysis with penetration testing. Computing Systems Lab*. Department of Computer Science,Moscow State University.

Rahimi, F. A., Lauby, M. O., Wrubel, J. N., & Lee, K. L. (1993). Evaluation of the transient energy function method for on-line dynamic security analysis. *Power Systems. IEEE Transactions on, 8*(2), 497–507.

Roy, S., Das, A. K., & Li, Y. (2011). Cryptanalysis and security enhancement of an advanced authentication scheme using smart cards, and a key agreement scheme for two-party communication. In *Performance Computing and Communications Conference (IPCCC), 2011 IEEE 30th International*. IEEE. doi:10.1109/PCCC.2011.6108113

Russo, A., & Sabelfeld, A. (2010). Dynamic vs. static flow-sensitive security analysis. In *Computer Security Foundations Symposium (CSF), 2010 23rd IEEE*, (pp. 186–199). IEEE.

Saxena, N., & Choi, B. J. (2015). State of the Art Authentication, Access Control, and Secure Integration in Smart Grid. *Energies, 8*(10), 11883–11915. doi:10.3390/en81011883

Sobajic, D. J., & Pao, Y.-H. (1989). Artificial neural-net based dynamic security assessment for electric power systems. *Power Engineering Review, IEEE, 9*(2), 55–55. doi:10.1109/MPER.1989.4310480

Syverson, P. (1994). A taxonomy of replay attacks [cryptographic protocols]. In *Computer Security Foundations Workshop VII, 1994. CSFW7. Proceedings*, (pp. 187–191). IEEE.

Talluri, S. R., & Roy, S. (2014). Cryptanalysis and security enhancement of two advanced authentication protocols. In Advanced Computing, Networking and Informatics (vol. 2, pp. 307–316). Springer. doi:10.1007/978-3-319-07350-7_34

Tseng, H. R. (2012, April). A secure and privacy-preserving communication protocol for V2G networks. In *Wireless Communications and Networking Conference (WCNC)* (pp. 2706-2711). IEEE. doi:10.1109/WCNC.2012.6214259

Wei-Chi, K., & Chang, S.-T. (2005). Impersonation attack on a dynamic id-based remote user authentication scheme using smart cards. *IEICE Transactions on Communications, 88*(5), 2165–2167.

Wei-Chi, K., Hao-Chuan, T., & Tsaur, M.-J. (2004). Stolen-verifier attack on an efficient smart card-based one-time password authentication scheme. *IEICE Transactions on Communications, 87*(8), 2374–2376.

Wood, B. (2000). An insider threat model for adversary simulation. SRI International. *Research on Mitigating the Insider Threat to Information Systems, 2*, 1–3.

Xia, J., & Wang, Y. (2012). Secure key distribution for the smart grid. Smart Grid. *IEEE Transactions on, 3*(3), 1437–1443.

Xu, L., & Wu, F. (2015). An improved and provable remote user authentication scheme based on elliptic curve cryptosystem with user anonymity. *Security and Communication Networks, 8*(2), 245–260. doi:10.1002/sec.977

Yasinsac, A. (2001). Dynamic analysis of security protocols. In *Proceedings of the 2000 workshop on New security paradigms*, (pp. 77–87). ACM.

Chapter 4
Detecting Synchronization Signal Jamming Attacks for Cybersecurity in Cyber–Physical Energy Grid Systems

Danda B. Rawat
Howard University, USA

Brycent A. Chatfield
Georgia Southern University, USA

ABSTRACT

The transformation of the traditional power grid into a cyber physical smart energy grid brings significant improvement in terms of reliability, performance, and manageability. Most importantly, existing communication infrastructures such as LTE represent the backbone of smart grid functionality. Consequently, connected smart grids inherit vulnerabilities associated with the networks including denial of service attack by means of synchronization signal jamming. This chapter presents cybersecurity in cyber-physical energy grid systems to mitigate synchronization signal jamming attacks in LTE based smart grid communications.

INTRODUCTION

Traditional power grids undoubtedly play a critical role in the functioning of society. thus, common luxuries such as computers, cellular phones, tablets, television, music, and most importantly, power within homes are enjoyed daily. Energy demands by consumers, industries, and civilians alike, remain a daily challenge in terms of efficiency. There is no real-time interaction between consumers and utility providers in traditional energy grids. The transformation of traditional energy networks to cyber physical smart energy grids can assist in revolutionizing the energy industry in terms of reliability, performance, and manageability in almost real-time (Rawat, 2015, (Rawat, Rodrigues, & Stojmenovic, 2015)). In

DOI: 10.4018/978-1-5225-1829-7.ch004

cyber physical smart energy grid, there are seven domains associated with the design. These domains include: bulk generation, transmission, distribution, customer, markets, service provider, and operations as in Figure 1. The first four domains are to feature two-way power and information flow whereas the latter three consist of information collection and power management.

The vastness of the smart grid, as aforementioned, is a major parameter that must be orchestrated in a highly distributed and hierarchal manner to achieve efficient and reliable communication. Communications in cyber physical smart grid is divided into three tiers: Home Area Networks, Neighborhood Area Networks, and Wide Area Networks as shown in Figure 2.

A Home Area Network (HAN) consists of all appliances residing in a consumer's premise. Smart appliances within the premise transmit real-time power usage to a smart utility meter serving as the HAN gateway node. Real-time power usage along with pricing provided by utility companies grants consumers real-time insight of their power bill along with knowledge of which devices are consuming the most power.

Neighborhood Area Network (NAN) compiles all data transmitted from HANs. NAN provides the opportunity for utility companies to control end user devices, send real time commands, and control the distribution grid devices [2, 10, 11]. Another function of NAN is delivering information provided by HANs to Wide Area Networks (WAN).

WAN collects information from NANs to that is ultimately delivered to utility companies through variety of technologies such LTE cellular, WiMAX, etc. The WAN also cover power generation to transmission.

Drastic differences in latency requirement for the smart grid, in comparison to the internet, are indicative of how critical the delays are within the smart energy grid. Performance wise, internet focuses on

Figure 1. Seven domains of smart cyber-physical grid
Source: NIST Smart Grid Model, 2010

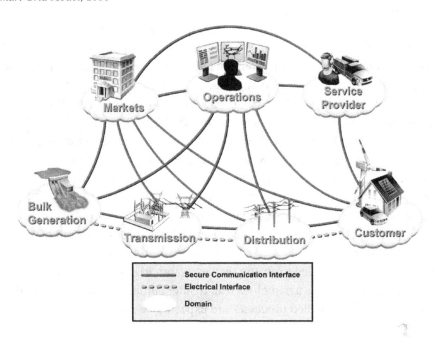

Figure 2. HAN, NAN, and WAN for cyber physical smart energy grid
Source: Bajracharya, et. al., 2016

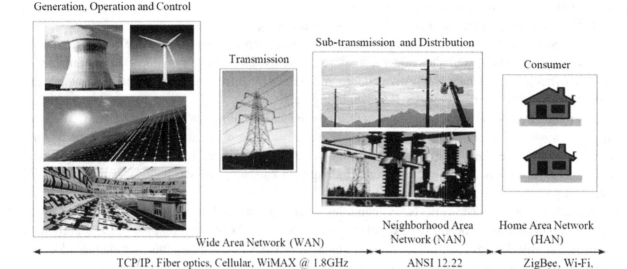

high throughput and fairness amongst users. Power communication focuses to ensure reliable, secure, real-time message delivery instead of focusing on throughput.

In general, communication across internet tends to exhibit a random burst like behavior adopting the World Wide Web (www) protocol as a major standard. In power networks, traffic flow is very periodic which is necessary for consistent monitoring in SCADA systems. In short, smart grid traffic differs entirely from internet traffic though they share the same vulnerabilities.

There are two common power system communication protocols: Distributed Network Protocol 3.0 and International Electro-technical Commission 61850. Distributed Network Protocol 3.0 (DNP) was originally developed by General Electric in 1993 for SCADA applications. Initially, DNP 3.0 communication protocols were based on serial communication in the physical layer. Today, four layers are supported: physical, data link, transport, and application. DNP3 is widely used in electrical, water, oil, gas and other industries. International Electro-technical Commission 61850 (IEC 61850) protocol is the current standard for Ethernet based communications. IEC 61850 provides TCP/IP protocols just as the updated DNP3 with the addition of UDP/IP and applications necessary for time-critical messages. Through IEC 61850, timing requirements for time critical messages are defined.

Aspiration for security in the smart grid infrastructure is commonly based on the CIA triad. The three components CIA is comprised of is: Confidentiality, Integrity, and Availability. Confidentiality is necessary for ensuring that correct information falls into the right hands. Confidentiality is intrinsically linked to privacy aspects where consumer and power market information should be taken into consideration (Holfeld et. al., 2015).

Integrity in the smart grid is needed to ensure that an unauthorized user does not modify data. Information getting into the hands enables a malicious user to alter automated processes. With the enormous magnitude of the smart grid, automated processes are expected be routine.

Availability signifies information being available to authorized personnel at any given time. In the smart grid, availability is a crucial factor. Power systems are expected to be available 100% of the time thus data availability also involves preventing denial-of-service attacks leading to blackouts (Du & Qian, 2012).

The smart grid features a relatively open communication network as it covers over large geographical areas. Therefore, ensuring invulnerability of every device within the network becomes a very challenging task. When wireless network is used this challenge becomes even more complex as wireless signal can be overheard and jammed by the attackers/jammers.

There are various forms of jamming attacks. Jamming attacks target radio signals by continuously or randomly emitting random signals into the channel with an aim of jamming the channel or deteriorate the signal quality at the receiver. MAC layer jamming prevents a node from determining channel availability.

Channel jamming could be executed to block Synchronization Signal which is known as Synchronization Signal Jamming (SSJ) (Hwang et. al., 2009). Note that whenever a node wants to connect to another, a series of synchronization steps are required before transmission begins. A Primary Synchronization (PS) signal is transmitted from one node to the other for initial establishment of communications. Following the PS signal is a Secondary Synchronization (SS) signal which consecutively makes way for reception of a Master Information Block (MIB).

Due to the critical nature of the smart grid, with respect to time-critical messages, launching any kind of jamming attack proves catastrophic. Cost wise, a utility company could potentially find themselves victims to the tariff of dispatching technicians to resolve issues. Also, a network rendered to this type attack may leave many homes subject to blackout and more.

LONG TERM EVOLUTION (LTE) AND JAMMING WAVEFORM MODEL FOR SMART ENERGY GRID

This section presents the overview of Long Term Evolution (LTE) systems, synchronization in LTE OFDM system and jamming waveform model for Synchronization Signal Jamming (SSJ).

Figure 3. CIA triad for cyber physical smart energy grid

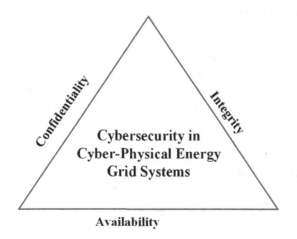

Overview

The LTE is one of the most advanced wireless networks deployed today and is diligently paving its way as the primary cellular standard. Additionally, LTE's ease of access, ubiquity, high data rates, flexibility, and mobility signify major application in the realm of smart grids.

The smart grid concept presents itself as a viable solution to the currently limited power grid in a revolutionary manner. Enhancements are expected to be noticed in every domain in addition to SCADA operations. Incorporating a two-way communication infrastructure grants utility companies an upper hand in combating the issues of efficiency and manageability.

The advancement of the smart grid concept has brought attention to LTE networks as a communication infrastructure of choice. LTE's robust nature and ease of implementation in devices with limited computational abilities is ideal for control of smart meters and other network components within the home, neighborhood, and wide area networks that are essential for operation. The usage of LTE in smart grid communications is extensively covered in the literature (Xu, et. al., 2012; Granelli, et. al., 2014; Du & Qian, 2012; Gözde, et. al., 2015; Holfeld et. al., 2015).

Smart metering utilized within the smart grid is related to the measurement of the power consumption of a building or apartment, and provides information about the Quality Electronic Report as well as feedback for the users of the power grid (Granelli, et. al., 2014). Furthermore, a utility company would be able to access instantaneous power readings of a given meter without having to dispatch technicians. Another improvement to note would be faster response time to issues that may arise.

Due to computational limits of smart meters, incorporation of LTE protocols is ideal to obtain two-way communication. In this study, an intrusion detection system (IDS) is proposed to detect jamming of the primary synchronization signal transmitted from base station to user equipment (UE).

The underlying technology of LTE is Orthogonal Frequency Division Multiplexing (OFDM). In OFDM, the entire channel is divided into many narrow bandwidth sub-channels, which maintain high data rate transmission and at the same time increase the symbol duration to combat inter-symbol interference (ISI) (Hwang et. al., 2009). To achieve OFDMA, the subcarriers are dynamically divided amongst mobile devices to enable access. In general, the input data stream is divided amongst the subcarriers. The subcarriers are spaced 15 KHz apart to achieve orthogonality as shown in Figure 4.

Figure 4. Orthogonality of subcarriers in OFDM systems

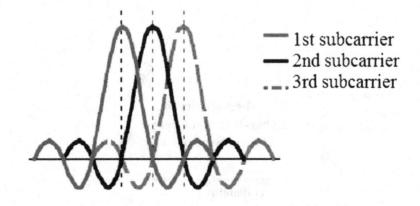

Each subcarrier in OFDM based LTE comprises of 7 symbols in which a scheme such as QPSK, 16 QAM or 64 QAM modulates the bits. After mapping and modulating the data onto the subcarriers, the Inverse Fast Fourier Transform (IFFT) is performed on data associated with each subcarrier. IFFT transforms the data into a time domain signal as

$$x(t) = \sum_{k=0}^{N-1} x_k e^{\frac{j2\pi kt}{NT_s}} \tag{1}$$

The IFFT signal, x(t), is a function of the summation of the data symbols x_k, number of subcarriers N, and the symbol time T_s. To mitigate ISI, a cyclic prefix is appended in each subcarrier stream. Cyclic prefix is obtained by placing a copy of the end of a symbol at the beginning of the symbol thus increasing symbol length. The increase in symbol length counteracts multipath fading effects. Finally the parallel streams of data are converted to serial for transmission. In LTE, a Resource Block constitutes 12 subcarriers with 7 symbols each. Moreover, a resource block constitutes a 0.5 millisecond slot within the standard 10 ms time frame. Two resource blocks are associated with the 1 millisecond sub-frames. The number of resource blocks for communications is determined by bandwidth. Bandwidths utilized in LTE are 1.25 MHz with 6 resource blocks, 2.5 MHz with 12 resource blocks, 5 MHz with 25 resource blocks, 10 MHz with 50 resource blocks, 15 MHz with 75 resource blocks, and 20 MHz with 100 resources blocks (Scheme, 2009).

Synchronization in LTE OFDM System

In LTE, primary synchronization signal (PSS), secondary synchronization signal (SSS) and master information block (MIB) synchronization signal are designed to be detected by all types of UE. They are transmitted twice per 10 ms radio frame. Importantly, synchronization signals in LTE always occupy the central 62 subcarriers of the channel making the cell search procedure the same regardless of bandwidth (Rumney, 2013). The primary synchronization signal (PSS) enables a UE to access a cell ID as the initial step of communication establishment. Note that the PSS and the SSS are transmitted periodically on the last and second to last OFDM symbols of slot 0 of the first and the sixth sub-frames within a radio frame in frequency division duplex mode. PSS is constructed from a Zadoff-Chu sequence, which are complex valued sequences that have constant amplitude as

$$x_q(k) = e^{-j\left(\frac{\pi q k(k+1)}{N}\right)} \tag{2}$$

where N is the length of the sequence and q is the Zadoff-Chu sequence root index. The secondary synchronization signal (SSS) provides timing information, FDD or TDD configuration, and cyclic prefix length. Lastly, the master information block (MIB) contains the downlink bandwidth of the cell, configuration, and system frame number.

Jamming Waveform Model for Synchronization Signal Jamming (SSJ)

In SSJ, the typical waveform deployed for jamming is noise. Though signals are subject to noise in an AWGN channel, the addition of a second source of noise proves to be effective in altering primary synchronization (PS) delivery. A received signal $x(t)$ can be represented by the OFDM signal generated at the transmitter as (Pejanovic-Djurisic 2012)

$$x(t) = \sum_{k=0}^{N-1} x_k e^{j2\pi kFt} \tag{3}$$

where x_k is the symbol transmitted on the kth subcarrier, F is the kth subcarrier frequency given by:

$$F = k\left(\frac{B}{N}\right) \tag{4}$$

where B is the given bandwidth and N is the total number of subcarriers. Thus the jamming waveform is modeled as

$$n(t) = He^{j2\pi kF't} \tag{5}$$

with H denoting the jamming tone and F' constituting a given subcarrier frequency for a PS symbol during the fifth sub-frame.

DETECTION OF SYNCHRONIZATION SIGNAL JAMMING

Implementing an Intrusion Detection System (IDS) to detect whether a communication channel is jammed plays a major role in mitigating such attacks. With an IDS, the synchronization process is to be monitored to ensure completion. Additionally, periodic PS signals could be transmitted for a desired number of packets to detect jamming during transmission. For the scope of this study, the primary focus is detection for the initial PS signal for each message needing to be transmitted.

The framework for the IPS includes sensing a PS signal for establishment of a communication channel and comparing the received signal power to an expected power level. To do so, the IDS detects a PS signal when a channel is presumed idle. In this case, the PS signal is transmitted with an expected power which can be determined by using a statistical method or historic data as

$$\left|P_{received} - P_{expected}\right| < \alpha \tag{6}$$

Once the signal is received, the difference in signal strengths is compared to a predetermined threshold, α. The predetermined value is set by user to a quantity that best fits the respective application. If the threshold is exceeded, then the system is assumed to be compromised thus sending an alert to the utility company for corrective action.

Furthermore, the instantaneous data stream 'a' can be compared against the expected data value 'b' in smart grid communication to detect an attack. One approach that could detect attacks is cosine similarity matching, that is,

$$similarity = \cos(\theta) = \frac{a.b}{|a||b|} \tag{7}$$

where $0 \leq \cos(\theta) \leq 1$. Note that when observed value 'a' is equal to expected value 'b', similarity score should be 0. If not, the similarity value would not be 0. This could help detect cyber-attacks that insert false data (Rawat et. al., 2015) or wrong value because of signal jamming.

NUMERICAL RESULTS

Performance evaluation is carried out using numerical results obtained from simulations. First we plotted the power difference for PSS signal vs. the time as shown in Figure 5. To see LTE synchronization signal jamming, the detection systems received PS signal strengths over a period of 200 milliseconds thus translating to 40 observed PS signals. Comparing power of the received signal with the expected to an applied threshold of $\alpha = 2.5$, a total of 13 PSS was presumed "jammed" as represented by Figure

Figure 5. Detected jammed PSS (primary synchronization signal) after applied threshold of 2.5

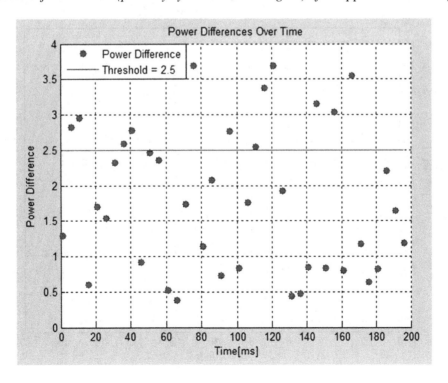

5. After calculating the difference in signal strengths and plotting them in relation to time, the results for every PS signal are obtained. Figure 5 infers, once the 2.5 threshold is applied at times t = 5ms, t = 35ms, t=100ms, t = 120ms, and t = 180ms, to name a few, the selected channel for transmission was deemed "jammed". For the mentioned times, utility companies are notified and corrective action, such as establishing an alternative or preferable link by switching to another frequency in place of the jammed frequency, are viable options.

Next, Figure 6 demonstrates the expected OFDM signal in relation to the signal altered by jamming effect. Ideally, the difference between expected signal and observed signal was expected to be zero. Alternatively both signals should overlap with each other when there is jamming attack.

Similarly Figure 7 illustrates the correlation between jamming signal and targeted PS signal. Ideally these two signal should have overlapped if there was no jamming attack. Difference indicates that there is jamming attack in the system. When an attack is detected, the detector reports to the administer at monitoring center or takes the corrective action to avoid attack as quickly as possible.

CONCLUSION

In the tiered WANs, NANs, and HANs infrastructure in cyber-physical smart energy grid system, wireless technologies are candidate solutions to establish communication between utility company and consumer. Connected systems bring networking opportunity to different entities along with several vulnerabilities. Since wireless mediums are very susceptible to several cyber-attacks including channel jamming. This

Figure 6. Expected OFDM Signal vs. Jammed OFDM Signal

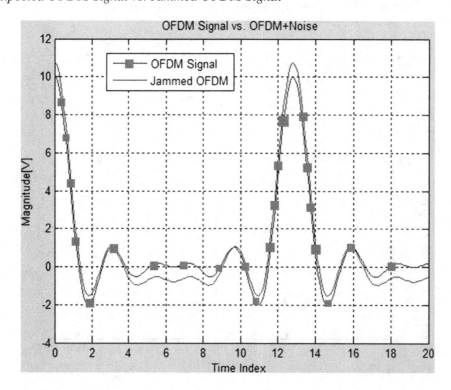

Figure 7. Jamming waveform compared to PSS

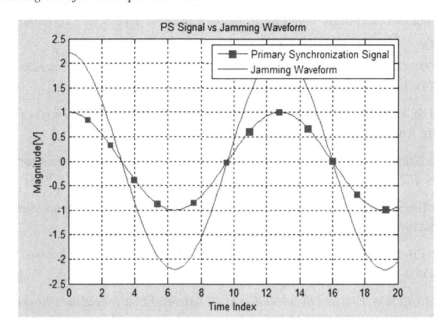

chapter has presented an intrusion detection system to detect/mitigate jamming attacks in LTE based smart grid communication system. Once a channel is declared jammed, system can send an alert signal and corrective actions could be taken by the administrators or systems dynamically. Performance is evaluated using numerical results obtained from experiments.

REFERENCES

Bajracharya, C., & Rawat, D. B. (2016). Dynamic spectrum access enabled home area networks for smart grid communications. *Int. J. Smart Grid and Green Communications*, *1*(2), 130–142. doi:10.1504/IJSGGC.2016.078946

Du, J., & Qian, M. (2012, August). Research and application on LTE technology in smart grids. In *Communications and Networking in China (CHINACOM), 2012 7th International ICST Conference on* (pp. 76-80).

Gözde, H., Taplamacıoğlu, M. C., Arı, M., & Shalaf, H. (2015, April). 4G/LTE technology for smart grid communication infrastructure. In Smart Grid Congress and Fair (ICSG), 2015 3rd International Istanbul (pp. 1-4).

Granelli, F., Domeniconi, D., Da Fonseca, N. L., & Tsetsgee, B. (2014, July). On the Usage of WiFi and LTE for the Smart Grid. In *2014 7th International Conference on Ubi-Media Computing and Workshops*. doi:10.1109/U-MEDIA.2014.49

Holfeld, B., Jaeckel, S., Thiele, L., Wirth, T., & Scheppelmann, K. (2015, May). Smart grid communications: LTE outdoor field trials at 450 MHz. In *2015 IEEE 81st Vehicular Technology Conference (VTC Spring)* (pp. 1-5).

Hwang, T. (2009). OFDM and its wireless applications: A survey. *IEEE Transactions on Vehicular Technology*, *58*(4), 1673–1694. doi:10.1109/TVT.2008.2004555

Pejanovic-Djurisic, M., Kocan, E., & Prasad, R. (2012). *OFDM Based Relay Systems for Future Wireless Communications*. River Publishers.

Rawat, D. B., & Bajracharya, C. (2015). Detection of false data injection attacks in smart grid communication systems. *IEEE Signal Processing Letters*, *22*(10), 1652–1656. doi:10.1109/LSP.2015.2421935

Rawat, D. B., & Bajracharya, C. (2015, April). Cyber security for smart grid systems: Status, challenges and perspectives. In SoutheastCon 2015 (pp. 1-6).

Rawat, D. B., Rodrigues, J. J., & Stojmenovic, I. (Eds.). (2015). *Cyber-physical systems: from theory to practice*. CRC Press. doi:10.1201/b19290

Rumney, M. (Ed.). (2013). *LTE and the evolution to 4G wireless: Design and measurement challenges*. John Wiley & Sons. doi:10.1002/9781118799475

Scheme, B. T. (2009). LTE: The evolution of mobile broadband. *IEEE Communications Magazine*, 45.

Xu, Y., & Fischione, C. (2012, May). Real-time scheduling in LTE for smart grids. In *Communications Control and Signal Processing (ISCCSP), 2012 5th International Symposium on* (pp. 1-6). doi:10.1109/ISCCSP.2012.6217872

Section 2
Authentication, Privacy, and Interoperability

Chapter 5
Privacy–Preserving Aggregation in the Smart Grid

Georgios Karopoulos
National and Kapodistrian University of Athens, Greece

Christoforos Ntantogian
University of Piraeus, Greece

Christos Xenakis
University of Piraeus, Greece

ABSTRACT

The introduction of information and communication technologies to the traditional energy grid offers advantages like efficiency, increased reliability, resilience, and better control of demand-response, while on the other hand poses customers' privacy at risk. By using information collected by a smart meter, an attacker can deduce whether a house is empty from its residents, which devices are being used, residents' habits and so on. In order to cope with such cases, many privacy-preserving aggregation solutions have been proposed that allow aggregation, while at the same time protect individual readings from attackers. In this book chapter, the authors provide a critical review of such methods, comparing them and discussing advantages and disadvantages.

INTRODUCTION

Traditional energy grid infrastructure is being upgraded into a smart grid. The smart grid is the result of the modernization of the existing energy grid in such a way that customers, as well as utilities, have the ability to monitor, control, and predict energy usage. To this end, the EU has plans to replace at least 80% of its electricity meters with smart ones by the year 2020 (European Commission, 2009). Moreover, according to a US report (The Edison foundation, 2014), the smart meter installations in the USA have reached 50 million of devices as of July 2014.

The advantages of the smart grid in a large scale are national energy independence, emissions control, and global warming combat. In the grid operator/utility level it enables more granular defini-

DOI: 10.4018/978-1-5225-1829-7.ch005

tion of pricing policy, better capacity and usage planning, increased resilience and protection against cyber- physical attacks, while it provides more flexibility to energy markets. Regarding customers, the smart grid will enable them manage actively their energy usage, control energy bills, and be involved as renewable energy producers.

Despite the numerous benefits from its adoption, the smart grid comes with several security and privacy concerns. In the smart grid, customers need to frequently share information on energy usage with the utility, something that exposes them to privacy invasions. In the proposed book chapter, the authors will study energy metering data aggregation in the Advanced Metering Infrastructure (AMI) and its privacy implications. An indicative example of the latter is an attacker that observes energy usage reports of a smart meter, in order to infer when nobody is in the house.

In the past few years, several privacy-preserving billing and metering data aggregation schemes have been proposed. The idea behind these schemes is to use cryptographic tools, like homomorphic or traditional symmetric/asymmetric encryption, so that smart meters transmit measurements to utility providers in a secure manner. In order not to overwhelm utility servers with excessive traffic, aggregators are used, which are nodes that aggregate consumption data for a geographic area before sending the result to the utility operator. Privacy- preserving aggregation approaches need to protect customers from third parties, that wish to gain access to their consumption data, but also aggregators, since they cannot always be considered trusted. Moreover, such schemes need to meet several other requirements to be considered appropriate for the smart grid, like security and scalability.

The rest of this book chapter is organised as follows. In the next section, the authors present a reference architecture for privacy-preserving aggregation, the security model and requirements. Next, existing work in privacy-aggregation in the smart grid is categorised and presented in detail. Also, a discussion regarding findings from the analysis and comparison of the aforementioned proposed schemes is provided, followed by conclusions of this study.

BACKGROUND

In this section, the authors present a generic smart grid architecture that will assist in the analysis of the privacy-preserving aggregation schemes. Next, the authors will present the considered security model for consumption aggregation, and the requirements that derive from it.

Architecture

Regarding metering data transmission, there are mainly two types found in the literature that operate in parallel (WELMEC, 2010; Efthymiou & Kalogridis, 2010):

- **High Frequency:** Where readings are collected every 15 minutes (this is common practice for electricity meters), and
- **Low Frequency:** Where readings are collected for longer periods for billing purposes (every week or month).

Here, the authors focus on high frequency data only, where each measurement does not need to be associated to the respective smart meter in order for the utility to perform the required actions (e.g. respond to electricity demand, load forecasting, and outage management). On the other hand, low frequency data need to be correlated with each smart meter, because they are used for billing individual customers.

The target of privacy-preserving aggregation schemes is to protect the privacy of consumers, while they report their high frequency electricity consumption data to the utility. For this reason, the authors only consider a limited reference architecture for the purposes of usage data aggregation, shown in Figure 1. This architecture comprises the Utility, several aggregators that aggregate consumption data from smart meters (i.e., Aggregator 1, Aggregator 2,..., Aggregator w), and finally smart meters that reside in a large area or neighbourhood (i.e., SM 1, SM 2,..., SM n).

- **Utility:** The utility server needs to collect high-frequency (i.e. every 15 minutes) aggregated values, in order to perform some action like respond to electricity demand, load forecasting, and outage management; in this case, the individual readings are not necessary, and do not offer any benefit to the server. It also collects low-frequency (every week or month) metering data for billing purposes.
- **Aggregators:** The aggregators sum the individual readings received by smart meters, and transmit the result to the utility server. It is possible for a smart meter to play the role of an aggregator.
- **Smart Meters:** The smart meters reside in houses, or other buildings, and are responsible for collecting electricity consumption readings. These readings are transmitted either for aggregation or billing. The number of smart meters in each building varies, depending on the size of the building; usually, detached houses have one smart meter, while apartment buildings have one smart meter per apartment. In some cases, the architecture might not include aggregators, and smart meters can play their role, by aggregating consumption data they receive from other smart meters.

Security Model

In the model the authors present in the following, they consider the cases that are meaningful for privacy-preserving aggregation only. First, they analyse internal entities of the smart grid, followed by external attackers.

Figure 1. Smart grid aggregation reference architecture

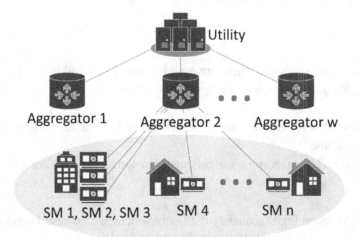

- **Utility:** The utility is considered a fully trusted entity, that has low incentive in attacking end customers' privacy.
- **Aggregators:** The aggregators follow the honest-but-curious model, which is what most related works on privacy-preserving aggregation depend on. According to this model, aggregators are considered honest, in the sense that they follow the privacy-preserving aggregation protocol properly. On the other hand, they are considered curious, meaning that they can misbehave by storing or forwarding to adversaries all messages received by other parties and intermediate computational results, in order to obtain or infer knowledge of others' private data. The result is that aggregators are assumed not to drop or modify messages routed through them, allowing the system to run smoothly, while at the same time try to get access to customers' electricity usage data. Therefore, the aggregators are only trusted to deliver aggregated consumption readings correctly; it is not taken for granted that they will not store or forward the received messages to other parties, inside or outside the smart grid.
- **Smart Meters:** The smart meters also follow the honest-but-curious model. Similar to aggregators, smart meters are assumed to send valid energy consumption data to the aggregators and the utility, while they do not drop or modify messages routed through them, if they are used for relaying usage data of other smart meters. At the same time, they may attempt to retrieve or infer other smart meters' electricity usage data.

External Adversaries

There is also the possibility of external adversaries, that might want to execute the following attacks:

- Determine a customer's consumption
- Determine that a customer's consumption is zero or close to zero, which means that no one is in the house
- Discover customer habits and activities, like watching television, which have detectable power consumption signatures
- Inject false data
- Mount Denial of Service (DoS) attacks.

Requirements

Based on the aforementioned security model, as well as the operational goals of the smart grid, the authors specify the following requirements for a privacy-preserving aggregation solution:

- **Data Confidentiality:** This requirement ensures that a metering is only known to the utility and the consumer. This protection should be offered against honest-but-curious nodes and adversaries that:
    - Eavesdrop communication links, and
    - Have access to reports send by smart meters and aggregators.
    Confidentiality should be preserved even in the presence of colluding adversaries.

- **Message Authentication:** The aggregators should be capable of verifying that individual metering reports to be aggregated come from authorized smart meters. The utility should be able to verify that aggregation reports come from authorized aggregators.
- **Data Integrity:** The entities of the smart grid should have the means to verify that the received data have not been altered en route. The utility should be able to verify that meterings have not been altered by malicious aggregators or third parties.
- **Non-Repudiation:** A privacy-preserving aggregation scheme should preserve the non repudiation of exchanged messages. There should be a way to prove that a smart metering report was send by a specific smart meter; the same applies to an aggregator report.
- **Efficiency:** Privacy-preserving aggregation schemes introduce additional computational overhead to protect consumer privacy. Thus, a good privacy- preserving aggregation scheme should keep that overhead as small as possible.
- **Accuracy:** An aggregation scheme should preserve consumers' privacy without affecting the accuracy of the gathered data, and without allowing other smart meters know the exact metering of an individual meter.
- **Adaptability:** A smart grid is expected to have nodes joining and leaving the network. An aggregation scheme should be flexible enough and adapt to such events, with minimum reconfiguration cost.
- **Scalability:** A privacy-preserving aggregation scheme should be able to support large numbers of entities, in the order of millions of devices.
- **No Single Point of Failure:** The smart grid has high availability requirements; thus, it should not be easy for an attacker to mount a Denial-of-Service attack. Entities of the smart grid that are not redundant or duplicated are considered single points of failure and should be avoided.

PRIVACY-PRESERVING AGGREGATION

Existing work on privacy-preserving aggregation in the smart grid can be classified in four main categories, based on the data protection method employed:

- Homomorphic encryption,
- Traditional encryption,
- Data masking, and
- Steganography

It should also be noted here that there is a recent survey on privacy-preserving smart metering (Finster & Baumgart, 2015) that uses a different classification approach. That survey focuses on architectural differences, examining mainly whether a Trusted Third Party (TTP) is used or not. Since the vast majority of smart grid entities, which are the smart meters, have computation, storage and memory limitations, the authors believe that efficiency is one of the most important properties. Thus, the authors chose to categorize existing work based on the data protection method, which is the design choice that mostly affects efficiency.

In this section related work is analysed in detail, following the classification defined above. A comparison of the existing privacy-preserving aggregation protocols for the smart grid is shown in Table 1. Most of the criteria of Table 1 are self-explained. By computation overhead the processing cost to achieve privacy-preserving aggregation is defined, and is studied separately for the three main node classes found in the smart grid: smart meters, aggregators, and utility servers. Where smart meters act as aggregators as well, the computation overhead is indicated in the smart meter column only. The computation overhead can take three values: high, medium, and low. A node shows high computation overhead if it performs homomorphic encryption/decryption/multiplications (J. Liu, Lu, & Koh, 2010), it performs too many asymmetric encryption/decryption operations, or when a node has a huge number of other nodes directly connected to it involving similar cryptographic operations. If a node performs several non homomorphic encryption/decryption operations, additions following an homomorphic protocol, or when a node has a huge number of other nodes directly connected to it involving similar cryptographic operations, then the authors argue that it shows medium computation overhead. Finally, if the node mainly performs arithmetic operations with just a couple of cryptographic operations, it is considered as having low overhead.

Table 1. Characteristics of related work on privacy-preserving aggregation

Scheme	Data encryption	Aggregation node	Computation overhead		
			Smart meter	Aggregator	Utility
(Li, Luo, & Liu, 2010)	homomorphic	smart meter	high	-	high
(Garcia & Jacobs, 2011)	homomorphic	aggregator	high	medium	high
(Lu, Liang, Li, Lin, & Shen, 2012)	homomorphic	aggregator	high	medium	high
(Cho, Li, & Choi, 2014)	homomorphic	utility	high	low	high
(Vetter, Ugus, Westhoff, & Sorge, 2012)	homomorphic	outside the smart grid	high	low	high
(Marmol, Sorge, Ugus, & P'erez, 2012)	homomorphic	utility	high	-	high
(Efthymiou & Kalogridis, 2010)	asymmetric	aggregator	medium	medium	medium
(Seferian, Kanj, Chehab, & Kayssi, 2014)	symmetric	utility	medium	-	high
(X. Liu, Zhang, Wang, & Wang, 2014)	asymmetric/ symmetric	utility	medium	-	high
(Bohli et al., 2010) #1	asymmetric	TTP	medium	medium	medium
(Bohli et al., 2010) #2	masking	utility	low	-	medium
(Finster & Baumgart, 2013)	masking	smart meter	medium	-	low
(Finster, 2013)	masking	smart meter	low	-	medium
(Kursawe, Danezis, & Kohlweiss, 2011)	masking	aggregator	medium	medium	medium
(Zhang, Lu, Liang, Qiao, & Shen, 2013)	masking	aggregator	medium	medium	medium
(Feng, Wang, Zhang, & Ruan, 2008)	masking	aggregator	low	low	low
(Abuadbba & Khalil, 2015)	steganography	-	medium	-	medium

Apart from characteristics affected by design choices, in Table 2 the authors present a comparison of existing works based on the requirements defined previously; the comparison is based on the following signs: +, ○, –, (+), (○), (–). The plus sign shows that the method fulfils the requirement. A small circle shows that a requirement is partially met. The minus sign shows that the requirement is not met. When the three signs above are put into parentheses, it means that the respective work does not include all the details needed, and the authors had to make assumptions to come to a conclusion.

Homomorphic Encryption-Based Schemes

Several existing schemes depend on homomorphic encryption, mainly due to its ability to allow aggregators sum encrypted readings, without actually knowing the plain text value. As a next step, the utility sums the encrypted results from aggregators and decrypts the final result; this decryption discloses the total consumption without revealing any information about the consumption of each individual house. These schemes can be further divided into those using asymmetric, and those using symmetric encryption.

Table 2. Requirements fulfilment of related work

Scheme	Data conf.	Msg auth.	Data integr.	Non-rep.	Effic.	Acc.	Adapt.	Scal.	No sin. point of fail.
(Li, Luo, & Liu, 2010)	+	+	+	+	-	+	-	-	+
(Garcia & Jacobs, 2011)	-	+	+	+	-	+	-	+	+
(Lu, Liang, Li, Lin, & Shen, 2012)	+	+	+	+	-	+	+	+	+
(Cho, Li, & Choi, 2014)	+	+	+	+	-	+	+	-	+
(Vetter, Ugus, Westhoff, & Sorge, 2012)	(+)	(+)	(+)	-	-	+	+	-	-
(Marmol, Sorge, Ugus, & Pérez, 2012)	+	+	+	-	-	+	-	-	+
(Efthymiou & Kalogridis, 2010)	-	+	+	+	○	+	+	+	-
(Seferian, Kanj, Chehab, & Kayssi, 2014)	+	+	+	-	○	+	○	-	-
(X. Liu, Zhang, Wang, & Wang, 2014)	+	+	+	+	○	+	+	-	+
(Bohli et al., 2010) #1	○	○	○	(-)	○	+	+	+	+
(Bohli et al., 2010) #2	○	(-)	(-)	(-)	(+)	-	-	+	+
(Finster & Baumgart, 2013)	○	(-)	(-)	(-)	+	+	-	+	+
(Finster, 2013)	+	+	+	+	+	+	+	○	+
(Kursawe, Danezis, & Kohlweiss, 2011)	+	+	+	-	○	+	-	+	+
(Zhang, Lu, Liang, Qiao, & Shen, 2013)	+	+	+	+	○	+	+	+	+
(Feng, Wang, Zhang, & Ruan, 2008)	-	(-)	(-)	-	+	+	+	+	+
(Abuadbba & Khalil, 2015)	-	+	+	-	○	+	+	-	+

In (Li et al., 2010), the aggregation is actually performed by smart meters that reside on the way to a collector node, in an in-network incremental aggregation approach without dedicated aggregators. In each neighbourhood, an aggregation tree is constructed where the collector node is the root. A careful network design for the tree is essential for the method to perform well; according to the authors:

1. The height of the tree should be small for communication efficiency, and
2. An internal tree node should not have too many children for computation and communication efficiency.

The design choice of not having dedicated aggregators poses a high overhead to low resource smart meters, for executing several homomorphic operations; high overhead is also applied to the utility, due to homomorphic decryptions. Moreover, the two design requirements mentioned above affect adaptability and scalability; as the number of nodes increases, special care should be given to fulfil them.

The approach proposed in (Garcia & Jacobs, 2011), comprises homomorphic encryption and additive secret sharing. The aggregator sends the public key certificates of all users in the neighbourhood to all of them. Each meter divides its readings into shares, encrypts each one with a different public key except one, and sends them all to the aggregator. The aggregator aggregates $N - 1$ shares that are encrypted using the public key of a smart meter, and forwards this encrypted value to the smart meter, repeating the same procedure for all meters. Each smart meter decrypts the received message, adds the value that held back in the previous step to this, and sends the new outcome back to the aggregator which aggregates all received values resulting in the total consumption. This method poses: high computation overhead to smart meters due to several homomorphic encryptions and decryptions performed, medium overhead to aggregators since they only perform homomorphic additions, and high computation to the utility due to homomorphic decryptions. If the assumption that, at least, two of the smart meters belonging to the same group/neighbourhood are honest is not met, then there is a data confidentiality issue. Finally, this method presents adaptability issues during node join and leave, since new smart meter groups must be formed and exchange digital certificates.

EPPA (Lu et al., 2012) follows a more straightforward approach, where asymmetric homomorphic encryption is used; smart meters encrypt their consumption data, the aggregation is performed by the aggregators directly on these encrypted data, and the result is forwarded to the utility. The main difference from other similar methods is that EPPA can be performed on multidimensional data, which include energy consumption, consumption time and purpose, processing them all together in the same round. Thus, it achieves better overall performance compared to traditional one-dimensional methods, which have to process every dimension separately. Regarding computation cost, smart meters present high overhead due to homomorphic encryptions, aggregators medium overhead since they only perform homomorphic additions, and the utility servers high overhead because of homomorphic decryptions.

In PALDA (Cho et al., 2014), smart meters use homomorphic encryption for encrypting readings, and send these to the aggregator, which forwards these single encrypted values to the utility. Having all the readings in its possession, the utility server can respond to two different types of requests:

1. The total power usage of a single user for a given period, and
2. The total power usage of a group of users.

The main characteristic of this scheme is that the aggregators do not really aggregate readings, but only forward them to the utility, which performs all the needed processing. This results to smart meters showing high overhead due to homomorphic encryptions, aggregators with low overhead, and the utility showing high overhead due to homomorphic decryptions. This solution is not expected to scale well, since all processing, consisting of cryptographic and non- cryptographic operations, is performed on the utility servers; moreover, a large number of smart meters will create bottlenecks to utility responses, if requests are expected to be served in real time.

In Vetter et al. (2012), a scheme based on symmetric homomorphic encryption is proposed, which allows aggregation to take place outside the smart grid, in an external entity; the authors argue that this processing operation can be outsourced to a cloud provider. First, each smart meter sends its encrypted consumption to the aggregator, which stores it in a database. This database can be queried by interested parties (like the utility), using selective SQL queries. The result is aggregated energy consumptions from different smart meters, encrypted using different keys. The decryption of the aggregated value is performed using an aggregated key, which is the result of the aggregation of the individual keys used for the consumptions' encryption. Actually, a TTP should exist in order to manage the encryption keys, and their aggregations to form decryption keys. Regarding computation cost, smart meters will show high overhead due to homomorphic encryption, aggregators low overhead since they only forward encrypted values to the database, and the utility high overhead because it performs homomorphic decryptions to reveal the aggregated values it receives from the external entity. Also, there is medium overhead to the external entity that performs homomorphic additions of the encrypted measurements, and medium overhead on the TTP that performs key aggregation, since, in this case, homomorphism applies to the key space as well. Outsourcing the aggregation procedure to a third party involves risks in data confidentiality, message authentication and data integrity, since these depend on the policies and procedures implemented by the third party, or cloud provider. Moreover, due to the use of symmetric encryption, non-repudiation cannot be preserved. This solution will not scale well for large numbers of smart meters, due to the large amounts of data that would need to be decrypted in real time, during the execution of the SQL queries. Finally, the TTP can be considered a single point of failure.

Another scheme, which is based on symmetric homomorphic encryption, is (Marmol et al., 2012); here bi-homomorphic encryption is used, which is additively homomorphic on both the plaintext and key space. Initially, smart meters are organised into groups, where one smart meter per group is periodically designated as the key aggregator. Each smart meter encrypts its reading with a key, and sends the encrypted reading to the utility through a secure channel. The key is sent to the key aggregator through a secure channel as well. Smart meters do not have access to the individual readings, while the utility does not have access to the individual keys. The key aggregator sends the aggregated key to the utility through a secure channel, so that the latter can decrypt the aggregated consumptions. This way, the utility does not have access to the plaintext readings of each smart meter, but only their aggregation. This scheme presents high complexity, while the organization of the groups and the election of the key aggregation node is not discussed and poses an attack vector. Smart meters are expected to have high computation overhead, due to homomorphic encryptions and the burden put on key aggregators; the utility will also have high computation overhead, due to homomorphic decryptions and lack of aggregators, which causes all smart meters to connect directly to it. Non-repudiation is not preserved, since symmetric encryption is used. This scheme presents also adapt- ability issues, because of the reconfiguration needed when nodes join or leave the network, as well as scalability issues, since, for large numbers of smart meters, the utility will need to perform a large number of aggregation operations.

Conventional Cryptography

In this category, schemes utilise symmetric or asymmetric cryptography and the individual consumption readings should be decrypted before they are summed. This makes privacy protection difficult, leading to complex architectures and additional computation and communication overhead.

One of the most well-known and cited works in this category is (Efthymiou & Kalogridis, 2010); in this scheme, two meter IDs are created: an anonymous, and an attributable one. The manufacturer of the smart meter knows both IDs, while the utility knows only the attributable one; correspondingly, each smart meter has two profiles, using two different certificates: an anonymous and an attributable one. During the bootstrapping phase, each smart meter communicates with the TTP to send both the anonymous and attributable profiles/certificates, and then the TTP sends the anonymous profile/certificate to the aggregator. The key management is performed by a Certification Authority (CA) and a TTP is used to keep the correspondence between the two IDs, and authenticate the anonymous readings received by the smart meters. The high-frequency, privacy critical measurements (the vast majority of metering data) are send to the designated aggregator using anonymous identifiers, while low-frequency, billing related measurements are re- ported with known smart meter identifiers. In the former case, the aggregator decrypts measurements, performs the aggregation and forwards the result to the utility. The efficiency of this solution is medium due to the use of asymmetric cryptography for consumption reading transmission: smart meters encrypt consumption readings, aggregators decrypt them and encrypt the aggregation result, and the utility decrypts the received aggregated results. The main is- sue with this scheme is that both the TTP and the smart meter manufacturer should be fully trusted; if they behave maliciously, then confidentiality is at risk. Moreover, the privacy offered is not adequate according to (Jawurek, Johns, & Rieck, 2011), since it is possible to correlate pseudonymous consumption traces with real consumer identities, either by identifying anomalies in consumption during unusual events (e.g., a house repair), or by linking consumption patterns. Finally, the TTP is a single point of failure, and should be adequately protected.

A different approach is the one proposed in (Seferian et al., 2014), where smart meters send their readings directly to the utility, encrypting them with symmetric keys. The generation of these symmetric keys is based on Physical Unclonable Functions (PUFs). The exchange of symmetric keys among the smart meters is performed by the utility, which acts as a Private Key Generator (PKG) in an ID-based cryptosystem. Smart meters can also act as relays of their direct neighbours to forward their messages, relying on the aforementioned ID-based key distribution. Regarding computation cost, smart meters present medium overhead, since they perform several cryptographic operations, and they also act as relays for other smart meters; the utility has high overhead, mainly due to the fact that all smart meters are directly connected to it and, moreover, it acts as a PKG. Also, non-repudiation cannot be guaranteed, since readings are encrypted using pairwise symmetric keys. The adaptability of this scheme is medium, due to the procedures needed to generate private keys on node join, as well as revoke the respective credentials on node leave. Another drawback of this scheme is low scalability, since all smart meters are directly connected to the utility servers. This scheme depends on the utility to perform key management as a PKG; this, however, could potentially convert the utility into a single point of failure.

In (X. Liu et al., 2014), a system for multidimensional data aggregation is presented, using asymmetric, as well as symmetric encryption. Here, the authors do not assume that there exists a TTP; however, the utility performs all needed key management operations, and can be considered as such. The system is based on bilinear pairing cryptography and blind signatures, and both additive and non-additive aggregation functions can be performed. High overhead is put on the utility, which needs to manage all smart meters that are directly connected to it, while smart meters present medium overhead due to the symmetric and asymmetric cryptographic operations required. Another serious drawback of this scheme is low scalability, since all smart meters are directly connected to the utility servers.

In Bohli et al. (2010), a solution that is based on conventional asymmetric encryption is proposed, where smart meters send encrypted readings to a TTP; the latter forwards to the utility only the aggregation of these readings. Regarding billing, the TTP sums up the readings of each smart meter and sends the result together with the identity of the meter to the utility. The computation overhead of this scheme is medium for all involved entities, due to the many cryptographic operations involved. The TTP should be fully trusted, since it has access to all customers' data and identities; this, however, does not follow the usual honest- but-curious model, and can create issues in data confidentiality, authentication, and integrity. Moreover, in the paper it is stated that readings are sent using "some form of encrypted communication" without any further details; this means that non-repudiation might not be preserved, depending on the protocol used.

Data Masking

In the next category, which comprises solutions that are based on data masking, the real consumption is obfuscated without the use of cryptography, to provide more lightweight schemes.

In the last mentioned paper (Bohli et al., 2010), a second scheme is proposed that is based on data masking. In this scheme, no TTP is used, and each smart meter masks readings with random values before sending them; this random noise follows a known distribution, such that the final aggregation will be close to the real one. Therefore, using this method the smart meters do not actually send accurate consumption data to the utility. The computation overhead of the smart meters is expected to be low, since it is a masking method; this, however, is not clear, since there is no information about the security of the channel used to transmit masked values to the utility. Regarding the utility, it is expected to have medium overhead, since all smart meters will be directly connected to it. The main issue here, according to the authors, is that large groups of smart meters are needed, in order to achieve an acceptable level of privacy. This can have two consequences: inadequate confidentiality protection when small groups are used, and adaptability issues during node join and leave for group formation. Also, in this scheme, only a random value is added to the reading, and there no information about how this value is transferred to the utility, something that cannot ensure message authentication, data integrity and non-repudiation.

Another similar scheme is Elderberry (Finster & Baumgart, 2013). In this scheme, smart meters are organised randomly into P2P groups, forming an aggregation tree with small groups of smart meters as leaf nodes. Each smart meter breaks a consumption reading into random numbers that sum up to the actual reading, following the Slice-Mix-Aggregate algorithm (He, Liu, Nguyen, Nahrstedt, & Abdelzaher, 2007), and sends these numbers, except one, to its group members. Then, each meter adds the number it kept with the ones received by its neighbours; every meter in the group does the same, so that the final sum is the total consumption of the group. Finally, the root of the aggregation tree sends this value to the utility. This scheme imposes low computation overhead to most smart meters, and medium overhead to those smart meters that serve as aggregation tree roots, playing the role of aggregators; the utility presents low overhead, due to the low number of cryptographic operations needed. There are some issues which are not discussed in the paper, like link encryption, billing and key management. Regarding data confidentiality, it is possible for colluding neighbours (even when link encryption is employed) to recover a metering. What is more, the authors argue that only by eavesdropping on all outgoing and all incoming communication links of a smart meter, the anonymisation of this meter can be broken; this, however, can be possible in rural areas where smart meters will have only a few neighbours. While the use of TLS and client certificates are described in the paper, these are limited to the overlay bootstrapping, and are not compulsory for consumption messages trans- mission; since there seems to be no other measure taken to preserve message authentication, data integrity, and non-repudiation, these properties cannot be guaranteed. Also, the proposed scheme has potentially high complexity to construct the aggregation tree, leading to adaptability issues when nodes join or leave the smart grid.

Smart Meter Speed Dating (SMSD) (Finster, 2013) is another lightweight scheme that also uses the Slice-Mix-Aggregate algorithm. In this case, the algorithm is simplified for two nodes, and the resulting pairs of smart meters mask their readings cooperatively, using a Diffie-Hellman key exchange operation and key certificates stored in them during manufacture. Then, the masked readings are sent to the utility, and the sum of the two masked readings equals the sum of the actual readings of the two meters, without being possible for the utility to infer the original readings. Regarding computation cost, smart meters are expected to have low overhead, since they do not execute many cryptographic operations, while utility servers will present medium overhead, since half of the smart grid's meters will connect directly to the utility, due to the lack of aggregators. Masked readings are signed, thus, message authentication, data integrity and non-repudiation are preserved. An issue is scalability: supposing that a smart grid can comprise up to millions of devices, all smart meters should operate using two lists of this size; moreover, half of the smart grid's meters will need to directly connect to the utility.

In (Kursawe et al., 2011) four protocols for privacy-preserving aggregation are presented, where each party masks their measurements in such a way that, when these values are summed, masking values cancel each other out or add up to a known value, so that the aggregator can obtain the total consumption. The proposed protocols present better efficiency compared to an homomorphic solution (in the paper they are compared to (Garcia & Jacobs, 2011)), but they show increased complexity, affecting resilience during node join and leave. While the existence of signature keys is referenced, there are no details of a non-repudiation mechanism for the messages exchanged among smart grid nodes. The only protocol which is efficient, namely the low-overhead protocol, should be initialised with the public keys of all other smart meters in a group; this affects resilience when meters join or leave the group.

While PARK (Zhang et al., 2013) is described as using symmetric keys, it is essentially a masking scheme, since the "secret key" produced is simply added to the consumption. Smart meters also have in their possession digital certificates, and the result of the aforementioned addition is signed by the public key of the smart meter. The secret key is produced using two independent hash chains; one value from the first chain is concatenated to one value from the second chain, and the secret key is the hash of this concatenation. The seeds used for the hash chains are selected by the utility, and transmitted securely to the smart meters. An aggregator can sum the received values, and subtract from them the added secret keys; the secret keys are sent to the aggregator by the utility, which has knowledge of the respective hash chains. This method requires from each smart meter to keep a potentially large volume of data in its memory (depending on how long the hash chains are), because the two hash chains are of opposite direction; this is a significant drawback taking into account smart meters' hardware limitations. The computation cost will be medium for smart meters, since they need to perform 3 hash operations to create a single secret key, let alone the operations required for digitally sign the message. For aggregators, the overhead will also be medium, due to the many asymmetric decryptions needed to verify digital signatures of the messages received by smart meters. Finally, the utility overhead will be medium, due to the operations needed in order to produce the secret keys for all smart meters. The efficiency of this method is also affected by the additional communication between the aggregator and the utility: the utility sends the secret keys to the aggregator, which computes and sends back to the utility the real aggregated consumption, while it would be sufficient for the aggregator to send the masked aggregated consumption to the utility.

A similar method is (Feng et al., 2008), even though it is intended for wireless sensor net- works. In this scheme, the sink (which plays a similar role as the utility) shares a secret value with each sensor node; this value can be different for each application. Sensor nodes form clusters with one node acting as cluster head; when a sensor node has a reading to send, it sends the sum of the reading and the secret value to the cluster head, which aggregates all received values and sends the result to the sink. The sink receives all the perturbed values and subtracts the secret values of all sensor nodes. This way, intermediate or third parties do not know the exact readings of sensor nodes. While this is a lightweight method, it cannot be applied to the smart grid as is, and the reason is that the secret value is static and never updated or changed. Knowing beforehand that in most houses the consumption curve follows a similar pattern (e.g. lower consumption during working hours and higher during after work hours), it is possible for an attacker to infer the secret value or a good approximation of it, in order to figure out when nobody is in the house. Thus, data confidentiality is not preserved with this method. The computation overhead is low for both sensor nodes and the sink without, however, taking into consideration further protection mechanisms which are not described. Moreover, non-repudiation is not guaranteed since no measures to this direction are taken.

Steganography

Finally, the last category has only one work which is based on steganography (Abuadbba & Khalil, 2015). This work, however, cannot fulfil the main requirement expected from such schemes, which is consumption data confidentiality; instead, it focuses on personal data protection only. This method, protects personal customer data by hiding them in smart meter readings, and not the readings themselves, as in the rest of related works; therefore, the authors argue that this method does not preserve consumption data confidentiality. First, a symmetric key that is known to the smart meter and the utility should be generated; this key is used for confidential data encryption (like IDs, geolocation, date of birth, address, and total consumption), and random sequence generation. Private data are hidden into sub-bands coefficients, that result after applying Discrete Wavelet Transform (DWT) to the smart meter's readings. The confidentiality of the private data is protected by using the aforementioned symmetric key:

1. To encrypt these data, and
2. Select the positions of the hiding matrix where these data will be hidden.

Drawbacks of this method include medium efficiency, due to the numerous cryptographic and non-cryptographic operations needed to be performed by the smart meters and the utility, while all smart meters connect directly to the latter. Finally, the use of symmetric keys cannot preserve non-repudiation, while it is also responsible for low scalability.

DISCUSSION

In this section, the authors summarise their findings from reviewing privacy-preserving aggregation solutions for the smart grid. Referring to Table 1, a first observation has to do with the diverse design choices of the node performing the aggregation. While the obvious choice would be a dedicated aggregator node, existing proposals use the following smart grid entities as aggregation nodes as well: smart meters, the utility, TTPs, and the cloud (implied by aggregation outside the smart grid). The main issue from using a smart meter as an aggregator is the additional overhead, taking also into account their computational and storage constraints. Additional overhead is an issue when using the utility as well, but for a different reason: the large volume of smart meters in a smart grid (in the order of millions of nodes) that need to directly communicate with the utility can create bottlenecks or other connection issues. Using a TTP as an aggregator can have the same issues as the utility case; moreover, the TTP can also become a single point of failure and provide an easy way for an attacker to mount a DoS attack. The outsourcing of aggregation to the cloud can create trust and legal issues, especially in cases where the cloud servers and the utility network reside in different countries or even continents.

Regarding computation overhead, schemes belonging to the homomorphic category present efficiency issues due to the high computation overhead imposed by homomorphic encryption (Naehrig, Lauter, & Vaikuntanathan, 2011). In (J. Liu et al., 2010), it is experimentally shown that computation on encrypted data using homomorphic encryption is several orders of magnitude slower compared to computation on plain data. The most efficient category tends to be masking methods which avoid the use of cryptography as much as possible in order to provide more lightweight solutions, at least for the resource-constrained smart meters. This is the reason why standardisation bodies recommend masking for meeting the efficiency and privacy requirements of a privacy-preserving mechanism for the smart grid (CEN-CENELEC-ETSI, 2014). A major concern affecting the efficiency of masking methods is the protection of the transmitted data, since most methods do not explicitly define the mechanisms to provide this protection and just mention that data are exchanged through a "secure channel". For example, if the secure channel of a method A is created using asymmetric cryptography while for a method B symmetric cryptography is used, then it is expected that B will be more efficient than A but B will not provide non-repudiation. Apart from overall efficiency, solutions that choose not to utilise a dedicated aggregator are expected to pose additional overhead to the rest of the smart grid entities.

Table 2 presents which of the requirements set previously are met by each existing work. Regarding data confidentiality, things are mixed with almost half solutions meeting this requirement, while the rest of them partially meet or not meet it at all. For message authentication and data integrity, most solutions (around 75%) meet these requirements; a small number of solutions meet partially or not meet them at all under assumptions the authors have made. Non-repudiation is preserved only from approximately half of the proposals; the rest of them do not meet this requirement either directly or under assumptions. Efficiency is mainly affected by the consumption data protection method; thus, homomorphic solutions are less efficient, conventional cryptography-based ones have medium efficiency and most masking methods are considered efficient. Only one method does not meet the accuracy requirement by sending imprecise consumption data. A bit more than half of the proposals meet the adaptability requirement; those that do not are mainly schemes that organise smart grid nodes into complex or inflexible architectures in order to operate correctly. Half of the proposals present adequate scalability; most of the remaining methods do not follow a distributed aggregation model, resulting in non-scalable schemes. Finally, the majority of the proposals do not include a single point of failure.

Summarising, on the main drawbacks of each category of solutions, common issues in homomorphic solutions are efficiency, scalability and, to a lesser extent, lack of adaptability. Solutions belonging to the conventional cryptography category present medium efficiency, due to the overhead of cryptography. In some cases, such schemes are not scalable and make use of TTPs, which render them susceptible to attacks that target single points of failure. In masking methods, the most common issue is the lack of protection against non-repudiation, since schemes belonging to this category usually do not provide such countermeasures. Other issues include lack of adaptability and inadequate confidentiality under certain conditions. Drawbacks of the steganography method include lack of consumption data confidentiality and medium efficiency, due to the numerous cryptographic and non-cryptographic operations needed to be performed by the smart meters and the utility, while all smart meters connect directly to the latter. Finally, the use of symmetric keys cannot preserve non-repudiation, while it is also responsible for low scalability.

FUTURE DIRECTIONS

In spite that considerable research has been conducted in the area of privacy-preserving aggregation for the smart grid, there are still some open issues that deserve to be explored more thoroughly. First, the majority of existing solutions protect the exact measurements of each individual smart meter; however, the target of aggregation is not billing, where inaccurate measurements are translated to inaccurate bills, but a clear picture of the consumption of an area comprising multiple smart meters. Thus, aggregation protocols that are not strict on individual readings accuracy might lead to more efficient and less complex solutions.

Another future research direction could be the decoupling of consumption readings from the smart meter/consumer identity. Again, since the main concern of aggregation is the sum of consumption in an area, there is no need to link a single reading to the exact device or person; instead, a proof that the smart meter belongs to the aggregated area is sufficient. Research in this area can lead to schemes with advanced privacy preserving characteristics and less complexity for aggregation and credential management.

Third, most solutions require the AMI to be organised into special structures like trees, smart meter groups and pairs. Taking into consideration the size of a smart grid together with the large number of smart meters, the requirement of organising new and existing AMI nodes into a single structure would increase the complexity of the infrastructure substantially. Therefore, future solutions should be flexible enough in order to support diverse architectures and levels of smart meter organisation.

CONCLUSION

In this book chapter, the authors have reviewed related work on privacy-preserving aggregation for the smart grid, providing a detailed analysis and comparison of related schemes. First, a minimal smart grid architecture was provided to present the main entities that take part in aggregation. Then, the security model of privacy-preserving aggregation for each individual entity was analysed and the requirements that an ideal privacy-preserving aggregation solution for the smart grid should meet were studied. For better organisation of their study, the authors divided related work into four categories according to the employed data protection method. The main part of this work was the individual analysis and comparison of pro- posed schemes together with comments about their advantages and disadvantages, followed by a discussion about our findings. This review showed that, while extensive work in the field of privacy-preserving aggregation for the smart grid has been performed, no scheme covers adequately all requirements and each one of them presents one or more inefficiencies.

ACKNOWLEDGMENT

This research has been funded by the European Commission as part of the SMART-NRG project (FP7-PEOPLE-2013-IAPP Grant number 612294).

REFERENCES

Abuadbba, A., & Khalil, I. (2015). Wavelet based steganographic technique to protect household confidential information and seal the transmitted smart grid readings. *Information Systems*, *53*, 224–236. Retrieved from http://www.sciencedirect.com/science/article/pii/S0306437914001355 doi:10.1016/j.is.2014.09.004

Bohli, J.-M., Sorge, C., & Ugus, O. (2010). A privacy model for smart metering. In Communications workshops (ICC), 2010 IEEE international conference on (pp. 1–5). doi:10.1109/ICCW.2010.5503916

CEN-CENELEC-ETSI. (2014, December). *Smart grid information security*. Author.

Cho, S., Li, H., & Choi, B. J. (2014). Palda: Efficient privacy-preserving authentication for lossless data aggregation in smart grids. In Smart grid communications (smartgridcomm), 2014 IEEE international conference on (pp. 914–919).

Efthymiou, C., & Kalogridis, G. (2010). Smart grid privacy via anonymization of smart metering data. In *Smart grid communications (smartgridcomm), 2010 first IEEE international conference on* (pp. 238–243). doi:10.1109/SMARTGRID.2010.5622050

European Commission. (2009). *Smart grids and meters*. Retrieved from http://ec.europa.eu/energy/en/topics/markets-and-consumers/smart-grids-and-meters

Feng, T., Wang, C., Zhang, W., & Ruan, L. (2008). Confidentiality protection for distributed sensor data aggregation. In *Infocom 2008. the 27th conference on computer communications*. IEEE. doi:10.1109/INFOCOM.2008.20

Finster, S. (2013). Smart meter speed dating, short-term relationships for im- proved privacy in smart metering. In Smart grid communications (smart- gridcomm), 2013 IEEE international conference on (pp. 426–431).

Finster, S., & Baumgart, I. (2013). Elderberry: A peer-to-peer, privacy-aware smart metering protocol. In Infocom, 2013 proceedings IEEE (pp. 3411– 3416).

Finster, S., & Baumgart, I. (2015). Privacy-aware smart metering: A survey. *IEEE Communications Surveys and Tutorials*, *17*(2), 1088–1101. doi:10.1109/COMST.2015.2425958

Garcia, F. D., & Jacobs, B. (2011). Privacy-friendly energy-metering via homomorphic encryption. In *Security and trust management* (pp. 226–238). Springer. doi:10.1007/978-3-642-22444-7_15

He, W., Liu, X., Nguyen, H., Nahrstedt, K., & Abdelzaher, T. (2007). PDA: Privacy-preserving data aggregation in wireless sensor networks. In *Infocom 2007. 26th IEEE international conference on computer communications* (pp. 2045–2053).

Jawurek, M., Johns, M., & Rieck, K. (2011). Smart metering de- pseudonymization. In *Proceedings of the 27th annual computer security applications conference* (pp. 227–236).

Kursawe, K., Danezis, G., & Kohlweiss, M. (2011). Privacy-friendly aggregation for the smart-grid. In Privacy enhancing technologies (pp. 175–191). doi:10.1007/978-3-642-22263-4_10

Li, F., Luo, B., & Liu, P. (2010). Secure information aggregation for smart grids using homomorphic encryption. In *Smart grid communications (smartgridcomm), 2010 first IEEE international conference on* (pp. 327–332). doi:10.1109/SMARTGRID.2010.5622064

Liu, J., Lu, Y.-H., & Koh, C.-K. (2010). *Performance analysis of arithmetic operations in homomorphic encryption. Purdue University e-Pubs*. ECE Technical Reports.

Liu, X., Zhang, Y., Wang, B., & Wang, H. (2014). An anonymous data aggregation scheme for smart grid systems. *Security and Communication Networks*, *7*(3), 602–610. doi:10.1002/sec.761

Lu, R., Liang, X., Li, X., Lin, X., & Shen, X. (2012). EPPA: An efficient and privacy-preserving aggregation scheme for secure smart grid communications. Parallel and Distributed Systems. *IEEE Transactions on*, *23*(9), 1621–1631.

Marmol, F. G., Sorge, C., Ugus, O., & Perez, G. M. (2012). Do not snoop my habits: preserving privacy in the smart grid. *Communications Magazine, IEEE, 50*(5), 166–172.

Naehrig, M., Lauter, K., & Vaikuntanathan, V. (2011). Can homomorphic encryption be practical? In *Proceedings of the 3rd acm workshop on cloud computing security workshop* (pp. 113–124). doi:10.1145/2046660.2046682

Seferian, V., Kanj, R., Chehab, A., & Kayssi, A. (2014). PUF and ID-based key distribution security framework for advanced metering infrastructures. In Smart grid communications (smartgridcomm), 2014 IEEE international conference on (pp. 933–938).

The Edison Foundation. (2014, September). *Utility-scale smart meter deployments: Building block of the evolving power grid* (Tech. Rep.). The Edison Foundation.

Vetter, B., Ugus, O., Westhoff, D., & Sorge, C. (2012). Homomorphic primitives for a privacy-friendly smart metering architecture. In Secrypt (pp. 102– 112).

WELMEC. (2010, May). *Guideline on time depending consumption measurements for billing purposes* (interval metering). Author.

Zhang, K., Lu, R., Liang, X., Qiao, J., & Shen, X. (2013, Aug). PARK: A privacy-preserving aggregation scheme with adaptive key management for smart grid. In Communications in China (ICCC), 2013 IEEE/CIC international conference on (p. 236-241). doi:10.1109/ICCChina.2013.6671121

Chapter 6

Analytical Study on Privacy Attack Models in Privacy Preserving Data Publishing

Sowmyarani C. N.
R.V. College of Engineering, India

Dayananda P.
JSS Academy of Technical Education, Bengaluru, India

ABSTRACT

Privacy attack on individual records has great concern in privacy preserving data publishing. When an intruder who is interested to know the private information of particular person of his interest, will acquire background knowledge about the person. This background knowledge may be gained though publicly available information such as Voter's id or through social networks. Combining this background information with published data; intruder may get the private information causing a privacy attack of that person. There are many privacy attack models. Most popular attack models are discussed in this chapter. The study of these attack models plays a significant role towards the invention of robust Privacy preserving models.

INTRODUCTION

Data publishing includes 3 entities such as,

1. **Publisher:** The one who publishes the collected data on web
2. **Data Owner:** The one who owns the data or the data is about that individual
3. **Data Recipient:** The one who can access the published data

Publisher will collect the data from data owners. Data owners will have trust over the publisher and give their data. Publisher will publish it by removing the data which may directly leads to breach of privacy of data owners. The data recipients will receive the data from publisher and use the data for analysis purpose to process the data to come out with analogy or decision making.

DOI: 10.4018/978-1-5225-1829-7.ch006

Publisher before publishing the data should remove the attributes which directly identifies the individual. For example, consider hospital data related to patient entity. Name and complete address will directly identify the individual. So, such attributes will be removed from the data base and rest of attributes will be published. But, this is not sufficient to provide privacy. The person who is interested to know the private information of other individual, can threat privacy of that person. This can be achieved by having background knowledge (Martin, D.J. 2007) about that person and linking the same with the published data. Consider the following data in table form:

Intruder, who is interested in private information of other individual, will have background knowledge (RASTOGI V, 2007) about the person like, where he lives. The area zip code will be 146254. He knows that, that person's age is in 30's. If this background information is linked to the Table 1, intruder can easily conclude that, that person is having hepatitis disease causing a privacy breach. Many privacy preserving methods (Hua-jin Wang 2007, Qinghai Liu 2014) came into existence to avoid privacy breach. Some popular traditional methods are: Perturbation (DUNCAN G 1998, Xiao-Bai Li 2006) and Inference control (Haibing Lu; 2008, Yingjiu Li 2006, R. Brand 2002).

The data in detail which is subject-specific will contain sensitive data which will identify the individuals uniquely. This may lead to violation of individual privacy. There are many laws being enforced to protect privacy. This is the motivation for researchers to work on many privacy preserving models and come up with new techniques which will preserve privacy.

Figure 1. Privacy preserving data publishing

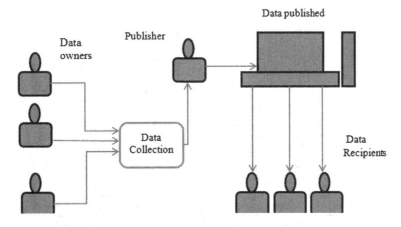

Table 1. Tabular data

Age	Zipcode	Disease
25	146234	Jaundice
35	146245	Gastritis
35	146254	Hepatitis
45	146267	Asthma

Need for Data Privacy in Enterprises

Many enterprises will produce data as part of their daily work such as HealthCare centers, Government Agencies, Manufacturing Industries, Outsourcing, Retail Business, Insurance Companies, Finance and Banking etc. In each and every enterprise which collects person-specific data will contain sensitive information related to persons. So, privacy preservation in needed in all wide varieties of enterprises. At the same time, enterprises need to publish their data for analysis purpose where the outcomes of this data analysis will lead to a great decision making which helps the enterprise growth. But the same data published to utilize should not lead to threat of privacy. Balancing this utility and privacy of these enterprise data is crucial.

For example, as shown in Table 2. In health care centers, history of disease for particular person may be considered as sensitive information. In the same way, in other enterprises, sensitive information of individual will be recorded.

These data need privacy preservation. The Table 2 shows the different enterprises and types of data collected in those enterprises.

Government Regulations in Different Parts of the World

There are many privacy legislations enforced to protect privacy of individuals. These legislations will play an important role in protecting privacy.

The different countries and their privacy legislations are listed in the Table 3.

Table 2. Different types of data collected from various enterprises

Sln	Enterprise	Type of data being collected
1.	HealthCare centers	Medical details of individuals, History of diseases, research data related to health
2.	Government Agencies	Census records, medical surveys, economic surveys
3.	Manufacturing Industries	Process details, Blueprints, Production data
4.	Outsourcing	Customer data, Business Process Outsourcing, Knowledge Process Outsourcing
5.	Retail Business	Inventory records, individual credit card detail, audits.
6.	Insurance Companies	Claims records, Accident History, Policy details
7.	Finance	Portfolio information, credit history, Transaction records, Investment details
8.	Banking	Bank Statements, Account details, Loan details, Transaction details.

Table 3. Government regulations

Country	Privacy Legislation
Australia	Privacy Amendment Act of 2000
European Union	Personal Data Protection Directive 1998
Hong Kong	Personal Data (Privacy) Ordinance of 1995
United Kingdom	Data Protection Act of 1998
United States	Security Breach Information Act (S.B. 1386) of 2002 Gramm-Leach-Bliley Act of 1999 Health Insurance Portability and accountability Act of 1996

Personal Information About Individual

The publically available information on the web may help the intruder or attacker to gain background knowledge about an individual. This background information can be combined with the published data which may lead to privacy disclosure. There are many means to gain background knowledge about individual such as,

- E-Mails
- Information available by searching using search engines (Google etc)
- Profiles in social networking available publically
- Personal information at e-commerce sites/organizations
- Documents on computer/network

PERTURBATION

Perturbation is a technique which is mainly used to preserve statistical data. The main idea behind this technique is to replace the original data with synthetic data.

Synthetic data will not have meaning in real world. The statistical information collected from perturbed data will be similar to statistical information collected from original data. Even with the background knowledge, the intruder cannot get the private information of individual. Because, the perturbed data is not directly correspond to the real world data.

The methods to achieve perturbation include:

- Additive noise
- Synthetic data generation.
- Data swapping

Additive Noise

Additive noise is used to provide protection in control over statistical disclosure. It is a replacement of original data which have sensitive information such as salary of a person or disease of a patient etc. Sensitive value 'v' will be replaced with sensitive value "v+r1", where r1 is random generated value with some distribution. Privacy can be measured by how modified value is close to original value. By adding the random noise, statistical information such as means, correlations etc will be preserved.

Synthetic Data Generation

To achieve this method, statistical models should be built from original data. After that, some sample points are chosen from the statistical model, which will act as synthetic data for publication instead of original data.

Perturbation approach has its own limitations such as, perturbed data is not meaningful in real world. Data received by recipients will be meaningless in real world. The statistical information is only preserved which is explicitly selected by the publisher.

Data Swapping

Data swapping (REISS, S. P., 1984;MOORE, R. A., JR., 1996) protects attribute with numerical value and categorical value. Swapping is exchanging values of the sensitive attributes, among the individual records. While swapping, the lower order frequency is maintained for aggregated values such as counts which help for statistical analysis in such a way that, statistical information should be real as per the original data.

Another alternative approach to swapping is rank swapping. Rank swapping is achieved by ranking values of sensitive attribute 'S' in ascending order and then exchange value 'x' with 'y' which also belongs to same sensitive attribute 'S' by ranking values of sensitive attributes. The value says 'u' is randomly selected within a range which is restricted to %p of v. This method will preserve the statistical information than ordinary data swapping

INFERENCE CONTROL

This technique is basically used for statistical disclosure control. It protects sensitive data in such a way that, data published can be mined without breaching the private information of individual. Inference control is applied in many areas including official statistics, Healthcare and E-Commerce. The challenge in inference control is balancing data quality level and privacy level. Sufficient protection for data should be provided by maintaining the data quality. Researchers or analysts will be utilizing the published data. Data utilization is the major use or main purpose of data publishing.

If privacy is preserved by affecting the data quality, such data cannot be utilized for analysis purposes. As the main objective to publish data is data utility, this will not be met. So, there is an always tradeoff between the privacy for data and data quality. There are 3 important sub disciplines under data protection:

- Tabular data protection
- Dynamic databases
- Micro data protection

Tabular Data Protection

This is one of the tradition ways of structuring the data in table form. The goal was to publish static aggregated information, in such a way that, private information of individual whose information can be inferred from the published table should be preserved.

Dynamic Databases

The user who is using the database should not be able to get private information of individuals by querying the database by aggregate queries. The aggregate information retrieved by the user should not infer to individual information. This may be subjected to tracker attack (Rathindra Sarathy, Krish Muralidhar, 2010). Some aggregate queries which reveal the private information will be refused. The query is required to be answered without refusing it, then, the perturbed result will be displayed. Finally if the aggregate information is required, and it will not lead to privacy threat, the results will be produced.

Micro Data Protection

The main objective is to preserve static data of individual, which is called micro data. Recently, the date is been collected and published in the form of micro data. The major drawback of inference control was probabilistic attack. To overcome this drawback, various data anonymization techniques came into existence.

There are popular approaches to preserve data privacy by allowing the published data get utilized at the same time. One of the major techniques is Anonymization.

DATA ANONYMIZATION

Data anonymization is evolving as a research area under privacy preservation. Important operation included under data anonymization process is generalization and suppression.

Generalization

Data generalization is replacing the actual values of attribute with the generalized value. For example, if the attribute called disease is containing values such as "gastritis", "stomach ulcer" and "peptic ulcer". Since these diseases belong to stomach, these values can be replaced with generalized values such as "stomach disease". There are different techniques existing for Generalization. Popular techniques among generalization are discussed as follows:

Full-Domain Generalization

Full domain generalization method, the values of attribute are generalized to value present in the same level. In Figure 2, tree structure for generalization is shown for attribute Animal. In level 0, attribute is there. In level 1, the generalized vales are there. In level 2 actual values of animal attribute is there. In this method of generalization, values of attribute such as Tiger and Goat are generalized to value mammal which is at level1. Since it is full domain generalization, snake and lizard values are generalized to value Reptile which is also at same level 1.

Sub-Tree Generalization

In sub-tree generalization method, as name indicates, in sub tree, all non-leaf nodes are generalized otherwise none are generalized. As shown in Figure 2, if Tiger is generalized to mammal, it requires that, Goat should also generalize to mammal. But, Snake and Lizard need not be generalized to Reptiles. It requires that, if generalization is done, it is done at sub tree level. One sub-tree in the complete tree may be generalized. Other sub-tree may not be generalized.

Figure 2. Generalization hierarchy of tree structure

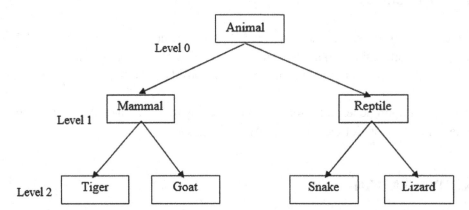

Sibling Generalization

Sibling generalization method is similar to sub-tree generalization. But, it requires that, some siblings of generalized value as node are left ungeneralized. As shown in Figure 2. Tiger will be generalized to mammal. But, Goat need not be generalized.

Cell Generalization

There are two ways of achieving cell-generalization method such as Global recoding and Local recoding. If all the occurrences of particular value are generalized to some value, it is called as global recoding. If some occurrences of attribute values are generalized and some other occurrences are not generalized, it is called as local recoding.

ANONYMIZATION MODELS

K-Anonymity

- **K-Anonymity Property:** For a given table T(A1, A2, …, An), and its Quasi-identifier Q-id, table T satisfies the k-anonymity property if and only if, each sequence of values in T[Q-id] appears with at least k occurrences in T[Q-id] where T[Q-id] denotes the projection of attributes in Q-id, maintaining with duplicate tuples.
- **Quasi-Identifiers (QIDs):** These are the attributes, which together helps the intruder to know more details about the individual and leads to identification of individual record inturn determining sensitive attribute value. For example, in Table 4, values of Zipcode and Age together helps determining sensitive attribute value in each record.
- **Equivalence Class:** If QIDs are unique, its easy for intruder to determine sensitive attribute value of particular record. IF, QIDs consists of same values within a group of records, then, individual information cannot be identified particularly within same group of records called Equivalence class. For example, Table 5 contains three equivalence classes containing three records each.

Table 4 shows original data. Before this data is published, k-anonymization is applied on this data. To apply k-anonymity, first we should choose quasi-identifiers and decide on which attribute should be considered as sensitive attribute. Table 4 has three attributes namely, Zipcode, Age and Disease.

The original data may supposed to have address field instead of zipcode. Since the address directly hampers privacy, only zipcode is retained for analysis purpose based on areas of different regions. So, since disclosing age and zipcode may not directly threat privacy, these two attributes are chosen to be part of data published. As disease is the sensitive information of individual, age and zipcode are chosen as Q-ids.

The following example which includes table 4 and 5 will explain the form of original data and the anonymized data obtained after applying k-anonymity technique. Table 5 includes data for value of k=3.

P-Sensitive, K-Anonymity

- **P-Sensitive K-Anonymous Property:** For a given table T, it satisfies p-sensitive k-anonymity (Xiaoxun Sun, 2009) property if and only if it satisfies k-anonymity property, and then, for each equivalence class (EC) in T, total number of distinct values for each sensitive attribute will occur at least p number times within same equivalence class (EC).

This model extends the features of popular k-anonymity model with sensitivity concept where the sensitivity level of attribute values considered as important aspect.

Table 6 shows one such 2-sensitive 4-anonymous data, where in each equivalence class there is at least 2 times the occurrence of sensitive attribute. Hence the intruder cannot be able to determine the exact health condition of a person with available background knowledge.

If any equivalence class has all the disease attributes as fever, if intruder gets to know that, that information belongs to particular person. Then, that may not be so sensitive information.

So, the importance should be given more to very sensitive information. Depending on this scenario, sensitivity levels are categorized.

Table 4. Original patterns table

ID	Zipcode	Age	Disease
1	18677	35	Heart Attack
2	18602	33	Heart Attack
3	18678	36	Heart Attack
4	18905	56	Stomach ulcer
5	18909	67	Heart Attack
6	18906	54	Lung Cancer
7	18605	42	Heart Attack
8	18673	48	Lung Cancer
9	18607	43	Lung Cancer

Table 5. 3-Anonymous version of Table4

ID	Zip Code	Age	Disease
1	186**	3*	Heart Attack
2	186**	3*	Heart Attack
3	186**	3*	Heart Attack
4	189**	>=50	Stomach ulcer
5	189**	>=50	Heart Attack
6	189**	>=50	Lung Cancer
7	186**	4*	Heart Attack
8	186**	4*	Lung Cancer
9	186**	4*	Lung Cancer

Table 6. 2-sensitive 4-anonymous data

ID	Country	Age	Zipcode	Disease
1	America	<=30	153**	Hep-B
2	America	<=30	153**	Hep-B
3	America	<=30	153**	Lung cancer
4	America	<=30	153**	Lung cancer
5	Asia	>=40	138**	HIV
6	Asia	>=40	138**	Tuberculosis
7	Asia	>=40	138**	Sinusitis
8	Asia	>=40	138**	Heart Attack
9	America	3*	153**	Cough
10	America	3*	153**	Cough
11	America	3*	153**	Cough
12	America	3*	153**	Gastric Ulcer

l-Diversity

l-diversity (Machanavajjhala, 2006; Samarati, 2001) states that, for a table T to satisfy l-diversity, every equivalence classes should contain l well represented values for sensitive attribute.

Definition: A table T is said to satisfy l-diversity and only if each equivalence class should have at least l well-represented values for sensitive attribute.

Table 7 shows the original pattern of the data that has been collected and Table 8 gives the 2-diverse pattern after applying the l-diversity technique.

T-Closeness

Definition: t-closeness. An equivalence class satisfies t-closeness (Ninghui Li, 2010) principle if and only if the distance between distribution of values of sensitive attribute within the equivalence class and distribution of values of the attribute in the whole table is no more than particular threshold t. A table satisfies t-closeness then, it has to have all equivalence classes satisfy t-closeness.

Table 7. Original pattern

ID	Age	Zip Code	Disease
1	22	18024	Stomach Ulcer
2	24	18064	Headache
3	46	17249	Fever
4	49	17274	Fever

Table 8. 2-diversity micro data

ID	Age	Zip Code	Disease
1	2*	180**	Stomach Ulcer
2	2*	180**	Headache
3	4*	172**	Fever
4	4*	172**	Fever

t-closeness technique does not maintain the correlation among the quasi-identifiers. Since the values of sensitive attribute will be distributed, this distribution will affect the co-relation among the quasi-identifiers. This leads to the degradation of data quality. The limitation of closeness approach is degradation of data quality.

PRIVACY ATTACK MODELS

Privacy attack means, an intruder who is interested to know the private information of particular person of his interest, will have background knowledge about the person. This background knowledge may be gained though publically available information like voter's id or through social networks. Combining this background information (T. Li and N. Li.2008) with published data; intruder may get the private information causing a privacy attack of that person. There are many privacy attack models. Few of those models are discussed in this chapter in the next section

BACKGROUND KNOWLEDGE ATTACK

An adversary can gain the background knowledge on targeted person. This knowledge may be gained by publically available data such as census, voter information etc.

Background knowledge can be helpful to infer the information about the person by linking it with published data. Say, adversary knows the person X's information through publically available database such as his name, age and zip code as shown in the Table 9 and he is aware that, X is admitted to hospital with some liver problem. When he observes published data shown in Table 9 (a), he can easily identify that, X record belong to first equivalence class. Since the Table 9 (a) is 3 –anonymous, adversary should identify X's record among first 3 records. As he knows that, X is admitted with liver related problem, he can conclude that, he is diagnosed with Hepatitis-B. In this scenario, background knowledge about the adversary lead to threat of privacy leading to background knowledge attack (T. Li, N. Li, & J. Zhang 2009).

The records in the first equivalence class are having only 2 different values for sensitive attribute diagnosis such as Hepatitis-B and Bronchitis. Since adversary has knowledge that, X is admitted with liver related problem and another sensitive value apart from Hepatitis-B is bronchitis which is respiratory problem, he easily concluded the diagnosis for X is Hepatitis-B.

Table 9a. Publically available data

ID	Name	Age	ZIP code
1	X	25	14523
2	Y	30	14548
3	Z	35	14598

Table 9b. Published data

ID	Age	Zip code	Diagnosis
1	20-25	1452*	Hepatitis-B
2	20-25	1452*	Hepatitis-B
3	20-25	1452*	Bronchitis
4	30-35	1462*	Bronchitis
5	30-35	1462*	HIV
6	30-35	1462*	Swine Flu

If adversary is having poor background knowledge where he cannot determine that, to which equivalence class, the target person's record belongs to, and then this type of attack can never occur.

ATTRIBUTE DISCLOSURE ATTACK

Attribute disclosure attack occurs; when a record of individual is identified in published data and sensitive attribute value is disclosed. This type of attack is called as attribute disclosure attack. Attribute disclosure (Fienberg, S. E., Makov, E. U., & Steel, R. J. 1998) occurs in the following scenario. For example, assume that, Person X is a patient in some hospital. X is having Disease "HIV" as sensitive attribute value. His record store following data age=35, zipcode=152890 and disease=HIV.

When the intruder gets the background information of person about age and zipcode, if the equivalence class is having the disease attribute value for all records in the same equivalence class as HIV, he can conclude that, person X is having disease HIV. Attribute disclosure occurs. Even with the less amount of background information, attribute disclosure may occur. But if the disclosure occurs mainly due to background knowledge gained by the adversary, then it is called as background knowledge attack as the background knowledge plays a major role in identifying the individual record.

MEMBERSHIP DISCLOSURE ATTACK

Membership disclosure attack (Yedukondalu, Mohiddin, & Kirankumar, July-2013) is an adversary concluding that, the record of targeted individual is present in the database. For Example, Say, Table T contains n number of records. By linking background information of person X with published table, intruder may conclude that, person X record belongs to table T is called as membership disclosure attack.

HOMOGENEITY ATTACK

Homogeneity attack (L. Sweeney, "k-anonymity 2002) occurs; when all the records in the particular equivalence class (which is identified as it contains target person's record) have same value for sensitive attribute.

Consider Table 10 with 4-anonymous data which contains number of records which has sensitive attribute value disease. In an adversary has background knowledge on some target person as, his age is in 20's and he lives in area with zip code starting from 178. Now if he observes the Table 10, he can easily identify first equivalence class as, it contains target person's record. Since all the records in this equivalence class contain the same values for disease attribute, adversary can conclude that, target person is having gastritis. All the values for disease attribute were homogeneous which lead to disclosure of private information. This attack is called as homogeneity attack.

If all the records in the same equivalence class contain different values for sensitive attribute, this type of attack can never occur.

Table 10. Table with Homogeneity attack

Age	Zip_Code	Disease
20-30	178***	Gastritis
20-30	178***	Gastritis
20-30	178***	Gastritis
20-30	178***	Gastritis
40-50	176***	Pneumonia
40-50	176***	Pneumonia
40-50	176***	Heart attack
40-50	176***	Heart attack

Table 11. Table with Similarity attack

Age	Zip_Code	Disease
25-30	178***	Pneumonia
25-30	178***	Heart attack
25-30	178***	Frver
25-30	178***	Gastric ulcer
45-50	176***	Gastritis
45-50	176***	Stomach cancer
45-50	176***	Stomach ulcer
45-50	176***	Gastric ulcer

SIMILARITY ATTACK

Similarity attack (Domingo-Ferrer & Torra, 2008) occurs; when the sensitive attribute value for all the records in particular equivalence has similar value. For example, adversary get to know that, person X's record belongs to particular equivalence class, if all the records in that equivalence class are having similar value for sensitive attribute disease, intruder can conclude the type of disease causing privacy disclosure.

If adversary observes the published data shown in Table 11, with the background knowledge that, target person say X's record belongs to second equivalence class, he can easily conclude that, X is having some stomach related disease. Since the values for sensitive attribute in that equivalence class are similar where all the diseases belongs to stomach, adversary got the private information of X leading to privacy disclosure.

Even though the sensitive attribute values are different within same equivalence class, but there is a similarity among them, which became an advantage for adversary to conclude the type of disease that, target person may suffered from. This type of attack is called as similarity attack.

If all the records in the particular equivalence class contain dissimilar values for sensitive attribute, this type of attack can never occur.

SKEWNESS ATTACK

Skewness attack occurs, when the distribution of data values for sensitive attribute is skewed. For example, Consider senses data for 1000 records, where the self-employed attribute will have value as "yes" or "no". Say 10% of persons have "no" as value for self-employed attribute. Then, in any equivalence class with 5 records may contain "yes" as value for 4 records and "no" for 1 record.

In this equivalence class, distribution of this sensitive attribute value is skewed in such a way that, it leads an intruder to conclude value as "yes" so that, 80% of records says "yes" compared to 20% of records as "no" in equivalence class and 10% of overall records says "no". This attack is called as skewness attack.

For example, consider the records shown in Table 12. There are totally 10 records and table is 5-anonymous. Many people were tested for HIV. The test results are shown in Table 12. If any adversary observes these records, out of 10 records, 8 records are having test result as NO and 2 records are having as YES.

Table 12. Data under Skewness attack

Age	Zip_Code	HIV +ve
20-35	128***	NO
20-35	128***	NO
20-35	128***	NO
20-35	128***	NO
20-35	128***	YES
35-50	136***	NO
35-50	136***	NO
35-50	136***	NO
35-50	136***	NO
35-50	136***	YES

Table 13. Table with Probabilistic inference attack

Age	Zip_Code	Disease
25-35	628***	Bronchitis
25-35	628***	Bronchitis
25-35	628***	Bronchitis
25-35	628***	Heart attack
25-35	628***	Heart attack
35-40	156***	Asthma
35-40	156***	Asthma
35-40	156***	Pneumonia
35-40	156***	Pneumonia
35-40	156***	Pneumonia

If he get to know that, target person's record belongs to any one among these two equivalence classes, he can conclude that, result of the targeted person may be negative with 90% confidence.

The 90% of records say result is negative and if he observes distribution of value with respect to overall table, it is 80%. Since the distribution of result values are skewed, it is easy for adversary to conclude the sensitive attribute value by disclosing the privacy.

If the sensitive attribute values within the same equivalence class are well distributed without skewed, this type of attack can never occur.

PROBABILISTIC INFERENCE ATTACK

Probabilistic inference attack (Bagai, R.; Bin Tang; Euna Kim, 2013) occurs when adversary can determine the probability of sensitive attribute value belonging to target person's record.

If equivalence class contains 4 records and sensitive attribute value any two records in that have same value, then probability of being that value as target person's attribute value will be 2/4 i.e., 0.5. Adversary can conclude, there is 50% chance of his assumption being right.

If the probability of any sensitive value occurrence within the equivalence class is more then usually, such value may be predicted as the value belonging to target person record identified within that particular equivalence class.

Consider the Table 13 which contains 5-anonymous data. If adversary determines that, target person's record belongs to any of 2 equivalence classes, then he can derive the probability of his assumption being right. If adversary assumes that, Target person is having disease Bronchitis, the probability of being Bronchitis is 3/5 ie, 0.6 compared to probability of Heart attack being right, which is 2/5 ie, 0.2.

If all the records in the equivalence class contain different value, then all will have equal probability. With these equal probabilities, adversary cannot conclude any information belongs to target person. In this scenario, this type of attack never occurs.

TEMPORAL ATTACK

Data which is published periodically or with time gap can lead to temporal attack. When the data about some subject is published for first time and the data about the same subject is published after some period of time may lead to attack of privacy.

The difference between these published data with time gap may lead to additional information gained by the adversary. With is learned information adversary gains knowledge. With this knowledge, adversary can infer the sensitive information of an individual.

To overcome temporal attack, before publishing the data, the old data published should be considered and all the attributes from that table should be considered as quasi-identifiers for the subsequent releases.

UNSORTED MATCHING ATTACK

If the order of records appear in the original table is same as the order of records appear in the published table, adversary can learn additional information. This information will be helpful for adversary to infer the sensitive information.

Hence, to overcome this attack, the order in the published data should be different compared to original data.

COMPLEMENTARY RELEASE ATTACK

When the different anonymized versions of same original data is released, those versions can be linked together which may leads to privacy breach. This type of privacy attack is called as complementary release attack. Each release may be complement to one another.

Consider the Table 14 which contains original records. An adversary is interested to know the details of some person X with background knowledge such as he is male, his age as 52 years and his zip code as 345678.

With this knowledge, when he observes Table 15 he can determine that, X record may be any of first three records, as first three records contains sex value as male. When he observes the published table i.e. Table 16 he can easily conclude that X is having AIDS as the first 2 records which belongs to first equivalence class are containing only one male record.

When adversary got the 2 different versions of published tables of the same original data, he can link those published records and learn much information and link them to get the identification of individual person.

When table is published, the previous version of same data published should be considered and then the second version should be published in such a way that, sensitive information should not be disclosed. In this way, complementary release attack can be avoided.

Table 14. Original data for Complementary Release attack

Age	Sex	Zipcode	Disease
52	M	345678	AIDS
61	M	345627	AIDS
62	M	345627	Flu
58	F	345691	Flu
56	F	345691	Fever
51	F	345678	Flu

Table 15. Published table 1

Age	Sex	Zipcode	Disease
50-65	M	3456**	Flu
50-65	M	3456**	AIDS
50-65	M	3456**	AIDS
50-65	F	3456**	Flu
50-65	F	3456**	Fever
50-65	F	3456**	Flu

Table 16. Published table 2

Age	Sex	Zipcode	Disease
50-55	F	34567*	Flu
50-55	M	34567*	AIDS
55-60	F	34569*	Flu
55-60	F	34569*	Fever
60-65	M	34562*	Flu
60-65	M	34562*	AIDS

COMPARATIVE ANALYSIS

Existing privacy preserving techniques are compared with the new techniques implemented with respect their drawbacks and privacy attacks. The popular privacy attacks are considered for the comparative study where these attacks are important part of privacy preservation.

The privacy attacks included in this comparative study are as follows:

- Background Knowledge Attack (BKA)
- Attribute Disclosure Attack (ADA)
- Membership Disclosure Attack (MDA)
- Homogeneity Attack (HA)
- Similarity Attack (SMA)
- Skewness Attack (SKA)
- Probabilistic Inference Attack (PIA)
- Temporal Attack (TA)
- Unsorted Matching Attack (UMA)
- Complementary Release attack (CRA)
- Correlation among Quasi identifiers (CQ)
- Data utility (DU)

Following privacy preserving techniques are analyzed with respect to their vulnerability to privacy attacks and drawbacks in Table 17.

- k-anonymity
- p-Sensitive, k-anonymity
- l-diversity
- t-closenes

This comparative study shows that, new privacy preserving techniques are robust and provide improved privacy.

The Table 17 shows comparison of privacy models with respect to their attacks. ($\sqrt{}$) indicates that, technique is not under/overcomes respective privacy attack. (X) Indicates that, it is vulnerable/under respective attack.

K-Anonymity

K-anonymity is vulnerable to Background Knowledge Attack (BKA), Attribute Disclosure Attack (ADA), Membership Disclosure Attack (MDA), and Homogeneity Attack (HA) as shown in Table 17. This technique will not consider the amount of background information known by the intruder. Assumption about the intruder's background knowledge is made prior to anonymize the data. But, exact knowledge is unpredictable and under all sorts of background knowledge, k-anonymity may not provide sufficient protection.

P-Sensitive K-Anonymity

This technique is an extension of k-anonymity. It is vulnerable to Membership Disclosure attack. Even though the attribute values are manipulated according to their sensitivity, intruder can identify that, targeted person's record is belonging to anonymized table. While distributing the sensitive values of attributes among the equivalence class, a measure need to be taken to overcome the table from attack.

Table 17. Comparison of privacy models with respect to attack models

Privacy preserving models	Attack Models								
	BKA	ADA	MDA	HA	SMA	SKA	PIA	TA	UMA
k-anonymity	X	X	X	X	$\sqrt{}$	$\sqrt{}$	$\sqrt{}$	X	X
p-Sensitive, k-anonymity	$\sqrt{}$	$\sqrt{}$	X	$\sqrt{}$	$\sqrt{}$	$\sqrt{}$	$\sqrt{}$	$\sqrt{}$	$\sqrt{}$
l-diversity	$\sqrt{}$	$\sqrt{}$	$\sqrt{}$	$\sqrt{}$	X	X	$\sqrt{}$	$\sqrt{}$	$\sqrt{}$
t-closeness	$\sqrt{}$	$\sqrt{}$	$\sqrt{}$	$\sqrt{}$	$\sqrt{}$	X	$\sqrt{}$	$\sqrt{}$	$\sqrt{}$

L-Diversity

L-diversity is under similarity and skewness attacks. Even though the sensitive attribute values within the equivalence class are diverse, those values may be semantically/relatively same as one other. This tends to similarity attack. If the 80% of values within the equivalence class are similar and 20% are dissimilar, it may leads to skewness attack as the values will be skewed over equivalence class.

The distribution of sensitive attribute values should be taken care about the similarity of those values in relative aspects and then table should be anonymized.

The proportion of similar and dissimilar values should also be balanced to overcome the inference attacks such as skewness attacks.

T-Closeness

This technique overcomes the limitations of k-anonymity and l-diversity. But, as shown in Table 17 it is vulnerable to skewness attack. The values of sensitive attributes are distributed to satisfy the threshold level t. But the distribution of values within the equivalence class may be skewed.

The drawbacks of t-closeness as shown in Table 17 are, it does not maintain the correlation among quasi-identifiers and data utility is reduced. Since the records are distributed to satisfy the threshold, the correlation among the quasi-identifiers is not maintained.

The generalization of quasi-identifier values are achieved based on the threshold, not based on the correlation. This will lead to the degradation of data quality.

CONCLUSION

The privacy attacks are very common challenges in the field of Privacy preserving Data Publishing (PPDP). The privacy preserving techniques should be implemented with the main aim of being robust against these types of attacks. But the data on which the anonymization technique is applied is also considered as part of being robust against the attacks. The raw data or the real time data may have characteristics where, the categorical attribute values may not be always distinct. These structure of data becomes a hurdle for preserving private or sensitive data. Any technique which is invented to preserve privacy should be tested against the known attacks in the field before being implemented as a successful technique. This chapter narrates the known attacks existing in the field of PPDP which may lead to understand the possible privacy threats.

REFERENCES

Bagai, R., Tang, & Kim. (2013). Effectiveness of Probabilistic Attacks on Anonymity of Users Communicating via Multiple Messages. *Systems Journal, IEEE, 7*(2), 199-210.

Domingo-Ferrer, J., & Torra, V. (2008). *A Critique of k-Anonymity and Some of Its Enhancements*. Academic Press.

Duncan, G., & Fienberg, S. (1998). Obtaining information while preserving privacy: A Markov perturbation method for tabular data. In Statistical Data Protection, (pp. 351–362).

Fienberg, S. E., Makov, E. U., & Steel, R. J. (1998). Disclosure Limitation using Perturbation and Related Methods for Categorical Data. *Journal of Official Statistics*, *14*, 485–502.

Fung, B. C. M., Wang, K., Chen, R., & Yu, P. S. (2010, June). Privacy-preserving data publishing: A survey of recent developments. *ACM Computing Surveys*, *42*(4), 14. doi:10.1145/1749603.1749605

Hua-jin, W., Hu, & Liu. (2010). Distributed Mining of Association Rules Based on Privacy-Preserved Method. *Information Science and Engineering (ISISE),2010International Symposium on*.

Kargupta, H., Datta, S., Wang, Q., & Ravikumar, K. (2003). *Random Data Perturbation Techniques and Privacy Preserving Data Mining*. Paper from the IEEE International Conference on Data Mining, Orlando, FL.

Li & Sarkar. (2006). A Tree-Based Data Perturbation Approach for Privacy-Preserving Data Mining. *Knowledge and Data Engineering, IEEE Transactions on, 18*(9), 1278-1283.

Li, N., Li, T., & Venkatasubramanian, S. (2010). Closeness: A New Privacy Measure for Data Publishing. *IEEE Transactions on Knowledge and Data Engineering*, *22*(7), 943–956. doi:10.1109/TKDE.2009.139

Li, T., & Li, N. (2008). Injector: Mining background knowledge for data anonymization. In ICDE.

Li, T., Li, N., & Zhang, J. (2009). Modeling and integrating background knowledge in data anonymization. In ICDE. doi:10.1109/ICDE.2009.86

Liu, Q., Shen, H., & Sang, Y. (2014). A Privacy-Preserving Data Publishing Method for Multiple Numerical Sensitive Attributes via Clustering and Multi-sensitive Bucketization. *Parallel Architectures, Algorithms and Programming (PAAP),2014Sixth International Symposium on*.

Machanavajjhala, A., Gehrke, J., Kifer, D., & Venkitasubramaniam, M. (2006). L-diversity: Privacy beyond k-anonymity. In *Proc. 22nd Intnl. Conf. Data Engg. (ICDE)*. doi:10.1109/ICDE.2006.1

Martin, D. J., Kifer, D., Machanavajjhala, A., Gehrke, J., & Halpern, J. Y. (2007). Worst-Case Background Knowledge for Privacy-Preserving Data Publishing. *ICDE 2007. IEEE 23rd International Conference on*.

Moore, R. A., Jr. (1996). Controlled data-swapping techniques for masking public use microdata sets. Statistical Research Division Report Series RR 96-04. U.S. Bureau of the Census.

Rastogi, V., Suciu, D., & Hong, S. (2007). The boundary between privacy and utility in data publishing. In *Proceedings of the 33rd International Conference on Very Large Data Bases* (VLDB) (pp. 531–542).

Reiss, S. P. (1984). Practical data-swapping: The first steps. *ACM Trans. Datab. Syst., 9*(1), 20–37.

Reiter, J. P. (2002). Satisfying Disclosure Restrictions with Synthetic Data Sets. *Journal of Official Statistics*, *18*, 531–543.

Samarati, P. (2001). Protecting respondents identities in microdata release. *IEEE Transactions on Knowledge and Data Engineering*, *13*(6), 1010–1027. doi:10.1109/69.971193

Sarathy, R., & Muralidhar, K. (2010). Some additional insights on applying differential privacy for numeric data. *Proceeding PSD'10 Proceedings of the 2010 international conference on Privacy in statistical databases* (pp. 210-219). doi:10.1007/978-3-642-15838-4_19

Sowmyarani, C. N. (2012). Article: Survey on Recent Developments in Privacy Preserving Models. *International Journal of Computers and Applications*, *38*(9), 18–22. doi:10.5120/4636-6884

Sun, X., Wang, H., & Li, J. (2009). Achieving P-Sensitive K-Anonymity via Anatomy. *ICEBE '09. IEEE International Conference on e-Business Engineering*.

Sweeney, L. (2002). k-ANONYMITY: A Model for Protecting Privacy. *International Journal of Uncertainty, Fuzziness and Knowledge-based Systems*, *10*(5), 557–570. doi:10.1142/S0218488502001648

Vora, P. L. (2007). An Information-Theoretic Approach to Inference Attacks on Random Data Perturbation and a Related Privacy Measure. *Information Theory, IEEE Transactions on, 53*(8), 2971-2977.

Yuan, Y., Yang, J., Zhang, J., Lan, S., & Zhang, J. (2011). Evolution of privacy-preserving data publishing. In *Anti-Counterfeiting, Security and Identification (ASID),2011IEEE International Conference on*.

Chapter 7
Authentication of Smart Grid:
The Case for Using Merkle Trees

Melesio Calderón Muñoz
Cupertino Electric, Inc., USA

Melody Moh
San Jose State University, USA

ABSTRACT

The electrical power grid forms the functional foundation of our modern societies, but in the near future our aging electrical infrastructure will not be able to keep pace with our demands. As a result, nations worldwide have started to convert their power grids into smart grids that will have improved communication and control systems. A smart grid will be better able to incorporate new forms of energy generation as well as be self-healing and more reliable. This paper investigates a threat to wireless communication networks from a fully realized quantum computer, and provides a means to avoid this problem in smart grid domains. We discuss and compare the security aspects, the complexities and the performance of authentication using public-key cryptography and using Merkel trees. As a result, we argue for the use of Merkle trees as opposed to public key encryption for authentication of devices in wireless mesh networks (WMN) used in smart grid applications.

ORGANIZATION BACKGROUND

Cupertino Electric Inc. is a private company founded in 1954 and headquartered in San José, CA. It provides electrical engineering and construction services.

San José State University (SJSU) was founded in 1857 as a normal school and has matured into a metropolitan university in the Silicon Valley. It is one of 23 campuses in the California State University system, offering more than 145 areas of study with an additional 108 concentrations.

DOI: 10.4018/978-1-5225-1829-7.ch007

INTRODUCTION

The electrical power grid has served humanity well up to now, but as we seek new ways to generate energy and improve efficiency, we find that the existing grid will not be able to meet our needs. It is expected that by 2050 worldwide consumption of electricity will triple (Kowalenko, 2010). Furthermore, power grids are still susceptible to large-scale outages that can affect millions of people (U.S.-Canada Power System Outage Task Force, 2004). These are the motivations for the creation of an "advanced decentralized, digital, infrastructure with two-way capabilities for communicating information, controlling equipment and distributing energy" (National Institute of Standards and Technology (NIST, 2010). This infrastructure will be better able to incorporate new forms of energy generation, as well as be self-healing and more robust. Each device in a smart grid will likely have its own IP address and will use protocols like TCP/IP for communication. Thus they will be vulnerable to similar security threats that face present day communication networks (Yan, Qian, Sharif, Tipper, 2012); however, the stakes will be much higher. That is to say, in the information technology industry the highest priority is the confidentiality, integrity and availability of information. In the electrical power industry the highest priority is human safety. For the smart grid cyber security measures must not get in the way of safe and reliable power system operations (NIST, 2010).

Problem Statement

"The smart grid is a long-term and expensive resource that must be built future proof" (NIST, 2014). That is to say it must be designed and implemented to be able to meet future scalability and functionality requirements. At the same time it also needs to be able to survive future malicious attacks. With this in mind, and with our knowledge of the threat posed to some types of public key encryption from the quantum computer, it must be concluded that if the quantum computer is realize and public key encryption is extensively used in the smart grid we will have a very serious situation on our hands.

While many may still think that the era of quantum computing is in the far horizon, according to the Wall Street Journal, China launched the world's first quantum communication satellite in August 16 2016 (Wall Street Journal, August 2016). While this has "set to launch Beijing far ahead of its global rivals in the drive to acquire a highly coveted asset in the age of cyber espionage: hack-proof communications," it has also shown that cyber attacks that are based on quantum computing may be more eminent that what many initially thought. Finding alternatives to public key encryption that is vulnerable to quantum-computing based attacks for smart grid at this stage is therefore timely, and is in line with NIST goals of making the smart grid "future proof."

This chapter looks at the threat to public key encryption systems from the quantum computer in the context of smart grid security. The authors argue for the use of Merkle (Hash) trees as opposed to public key on the smart grid, specifically when used to authenticate devices in WMN. Results of this chapter have been presented as a poster (Muñoz, Moh, & Moh, October 2014) and a conference paper (Muñoz, Moh, Moh, December 2014). This is a continuation of our research effort in smart grid (Kapoor & Moh, 2015) and in mobile network and cloud security (Wong, Moh, & Moh, 2012; Yang, & Moh, 2012; Gaur, Moh, & Balakrishnan, 2013).

For this chapter a Merkle tree authentication scheme is implemented, and incorporated into the ns-3 Network Simulator. It is then compared to the performances of a publicly available version of RSA, a public key encryption system. The goal is to show that Merkle trees are a reasonable alternative to public key cryptography system for smart grid networks.

Current State of Affairs

The evolution of the power grid is already under way. We see the development and discussions today around the Internet of Things (IoT) and smart buildings are already starting to show up on the landscape. Smart buildings are defined as buildings that use technology and processes to effectively control their environments. This is accomplished through the use of IT-aided sensors and controls that allow for better building management and maintenance. These sensors and controls are developed using open systems and protocols and it is understood that "all cybersecurity defense are potentially breakable." Therefore, it is necessary to develop back-up plans that identify the minimum level of functionality, particularly when it comes to the safety of human life. Hardwired equipment with hands-on controls should also be a part of this functionality. Industry is taking note of these issues. "Investigating the issue of cyber threats in smart buildings is timely and pertinent" (Khaund, 2015).

A recent work (Fernandes, Jung, & Prakash, 2016) gives a good evaluation of the Samsung-owned SmartThings. This is currently the largest smart home platform. It supports motion sensors, fire alarms and door locks. SmartThings is comprised of three main components namely, hubs, the cloud backend and a smart phone app. This work focuses on design flaw vulnerabilities, not bugs and oversights. The findings showed a number of problems related to controls, privilege and access to devices. As a result of these flaws the authors were able to steal lock pin-codes, disable vacation mode, and cause fake fire alarms. SmartApps was not *allowed* to carry out these operations, nor was physical access to the home required. This study has demonstrated how insecure smart homes can be.

The study described above looked at over-the-shelf smart home appliances. On top of the flaws demonstrated, one cannot ignore the cyber threats brought by quantum computing technologies. An evident is the recent launch of quantum satellite by China, which has shown that the era of quantum computing (and therefore its enabling of cybersecurity attacks) is no longer in a far-distant future (Wall Street Journal, August 2016).

BACKGROUND

The Threat of Quantum Information Processing

Today's computer architecture is based on the transistor and the binary number system. Invented in 1948 at Bell Labs, within 10 years the solid-state transistor completely replaced its predecessor the vacuum tube (Tanenbaum, 1990). The transistor opened the door to the modern computer age by allowing computers to do more with smaller and smaller components. In recent years the trend has been to increase computing power by increasing the number of cores on a processor, i.e., increasing computing power by adding more transistors. Multicore processors do indeed seem to be the future for computers in the near term, and the potential for greater computational power seems close at hand as a result of the progress of miniaturization, "but this trend cannot continue indefinitely" (Stajic, 2013). Yet for the security of public key there is a greater threat; namely, a fully realized quantum computer that can break the factorization and discrete log problems with a brute force attack.

The quantum computer is not bound to the limits of transistors or the binary system architecture. Quantum Information Processing (QIP) uses atoms held in a magnetic field instead of transistors. These units are called qubits. The underlying principle behind the quantum computer involves Einstein's wave-particle duality. QIP exploits the laws of quantum mechanics and as a consequence a single qubit can take infinitely many quantum states. This "allows for a much more powerful information platform than is possible with conventional components" (Stajic, 2013). It is more than just that a quantum computer would be faster, it is that in the realm of quantum physics a computer can solve the factorization or discrete log problem in polynomial time rather than exponential time (Shor, 1997).

The modern computer's design closely resembles the classic conceptual model called the Turing machine. Developed by the British computer scientist Alan Turing in the 1930s, the Turing machine can effectively compute any function that is computable (Kozen, 1997). It can only have a finite amount of states and it can only read and write one symbol at a time on a one-dimensional tape (Rosen, 1995). This is how modern computers work, executing instruction after instruction, linearly on a CPU; even multicore processors work like this. The classic Turing machine can be thought of as having a single fixed state at any given time; the quantum machine on the other hand "has an internal wave function, which is a superposition of a combination of the possible basis states." Transforms of the wave function can then alter the entire set of states in a single operation (Schneier, 1996).

The quantum computer is currently in its infancy, and it will be a great challenge to get hundreds and thousands of atoms to act in unison and function correctly (Kaku, 2008). Large-scale quantum computer hardware requires that each qubit be extremely well isolated from the environment, yet precisely controlled using external fields. These problems are far from trivial (Monroe, Kim, 2013) and currently beyond our technological capabilities to overcome. That being said, "no fundamental physical principles are known that prohibit the building of large-scale and reliable quantum computers" (Rieffel, Polak, 2011).

Public key encryption systems are secure today, but in 1994 Peter Shor of Bell Labs showed that factorization and discrete logarithm based public key systems could be broken with a brute force attack by a quantum computer (Kaku, 2008). Shor's algorithm attacks the problem of finding the period of a function. It uses quantum parallelism to produce a superposition of all the values of this function in a single step. It then uses a quantum Fourier transform and, measuring the yields, gives the period. This is then used to factor (Rieffel, Polak, 2011).

Electrical Power Grid

Electrical equipment is installed with the intention that it will be in service for many years, even decades. To do otherwise would not be efficient or acceptable. Computer and communication technologies advance at a much more rapid pace. As a result, technology on the grid tends to lag. Many functions in the grid today continue to use communications technologies similar to those that were used in the 1980s and 90s, such as dial-up connections used for personal computers (IEEE-USA Board of Directors, 2010). Considering the expense, potential for disruption, and difficult to reach locations of some of this equipment, it seems clear why it is not updated with the latest trends in the computer world; the electrical power grid does not abide by Moore's Law.

In the U.S., *The Energy Independence and Security Act of 2007* established that the NIST has "primary responsibility to coordinate development of a framework that includes protocols and model standards for information management to achieve interoperability of smart grid devices and systems" (NIST, 2010). NIST is a part of the U.S. Department of Commerce, and issues standards and guidelines in the hope that they are adopted by industry. This promotes interoperability that will in turn promote economic development (Schneier, 1996).

In recent years NIST has generated many important documents related to the smart grid, particularly the *NIST Framework and Roadmap for Smart Grid Interoperability Standards* and the *NIST Guidelines for Smart Grid Cyber Security*. Updated revisions for documents are ongoing.

Wireless Mesh Networks

WMN have become popular network topologies in recent years due to their cost effectiveness and robustness. WMN are already being used in the Advanced Metering Infrastructure (AMI) component of the smart grid. Some smart meters currently being used in the AMI are using the ZigBee protocol to form WMN.

The ZigBee standard defines a set of communications protocols for low-data-rate short-range wireless networking (ZigBee Alliance, 2008). ZigBee beholds to the IEEE 802.15.4 standard, which defines the two bottom layers of the protocol, but then goes beyond that to implement two additional layers. ZigBee is well suited for controls applications because it is a low power, low data communications protocol, which can support a mesh topology. ZigBee is simple and inexpensive when compared to WiFi and Bluetooth (http://www.youtube.com/watch?v=BkVcElfOVyw).

In a WMN nodes are peers that forward messages for the network. Each node is connected to several other nodes, thus improving reliability since multiple routes exist from source to sink. WMN do have drawbacks, particularly they are vulnerable to attacks to their dynamically changing topology, their lack of conventional security infrastructure and wireless nature (Siddiqui & Huong, 2007).

When a node joins the network establishing trust among the devices is done through the process of authentication. Authentication allows a node to ensure the identity of the peer it wants to communicate with. Public key encryption, as well as Merkle trees, offers means by which nodes in networks can authenticate. However, the Merkle tree based scheme's security rests on the use of cryptographically secure hash functions, which we understand to be resistant to a quantum computer attack (Stallings, 1999).

Authentication Using Public Key Encryption

Public key encryption uses a public-private key pair; one used to encrypt, the other to decrypt. This has many advantages. The strength of public key encryption rests on difficult to solve math problems. For this chapter the authors are concerned with those based on the factorization problem and the discrete logarithms problem. The experiment will deal specifically with the factorization problem.

Public key can be used to authenticate two devices in the following manner. For clarity call one device *Alice* and the other *Bob*. *Alice* sends a message to *Bob* claiming to be *Alice*. *Bob* needs more proof than this, so *Bob* encrypts a message *R* using *Alice*'s public key. Since the public key is public, anybody can encrypt a message, but only the holder of the private key can decrypt the message. Alice receives the message *R*, decrypts it then sends it back to Bob. Since she is the only holder of her private key, she has authenticated herself (Stamp, 2011).

It is not known for certain at this point if factoring is "difficult" (Stamp, 2011). That is to say, the best factoring algorithm asymptotically is the *number field sieve*, which is an exponential-time algorithm (Shor, 1997). Solving the factorization problem in a timely manner today is beyond the reach of the most powerful computers and most efficient algorithms (Cormen, Leiserson & Rivest, 2009).

The concern with information security is not just is it safe today, but will it be safe in the future? At one time the German Enigma machine was the state of the art in data encryption; today, breaking it is a challenging graduate level homework problem.

The probability that modern cryptographic algorithms will become completely insecure is low. However, technological and theoretical breakthroughs are always possibilities (NIST, 2014). In 2018 the European Commission is set to start a 10-year, €1 billion effort called the Quantum Technology Flagship to support and coordinate the research and development of the quantum computer. Elsewhere governments, academia, and industry are also investing and seeking to develop this revolutionary technology (Hellemans, 2016)

RSA

This chapter focuses on factorization problem based public key encryption systems, but several well-known and widely used discrete log problem systems are worth mentioning, namely Diffie-Hellman, El Gamal, and elliptic curve cryptography (ECC) (Rieffel & Polak, 2011). NIST approves of their use in smart grid and some are already finding use (https://www.certicom.com/index.php/device-authentication-service/smart-energy-device-certificate-service). All of these systems are vulnerable to a quantum attack.

RSA is a public key encryption system that is based on the factoring problem. The system works with the use of public-private key pairs. To create a key pair two large prime numbers p and q are multiplied together to generate N.

That is,

$$N = pq$$

Then a value e is chosen at random that is the relative prime (i.e., their greatest common divisor is 1) of the product $(p-1)(q-1)$.

Then we compute the private key, such that

$$ed \equiv 1 \bmod (p-1)(q-1)$$

That is,

$$d = e^{-1} \bmod ((p-1)(q-1))$$

Note that d and n are also relative prime. At this point p and q can be discarded.
The RSA key pairs then are:

Public Key: (N, e)
Private Key: d

Now let M represent our plaintext message and let C be our cipher text. To encrypt we calculate the following:

$$C = M^e \bmod N$$

To Decipher we calculate:

$M = C^d \bmod N$

Here is a simple example (Schneier, 1996):

$p = 47, q = 71$

Then

$N = p\,q = 3337$
$(p - 1)(q - 1) = 46 * 70 = 3220$

Choose a random number e (must be relative prime to 3220) say 79. Then

$d = 79^{-1} \bmod 3220 = 1019$

e and N are published and d is kept secret.
Then to encrypt a message say:

$M = 688232$

Break into blocks:

$M^1 = 688$
$M^2 = 232$

Then:

$688^{79} \bmod 3337 = 1570 = C^1$
$232^{79} \bmod 3337 = 2756 = C^2$

Then your cipher text is *1570 2756*.
To decipher:

$1570^{1019} \bmod 3337 = 688 = M^1$
$2756^{1019} \bmod 3337 = 232 = M^2$

RELATED STUDIES

This section presents first related works on the justification of using WMN for smart grid, followed by a security framework of smart grid, and finally some relevant studies on using Merkel trees for smart grid authentication.

Modeling Smart Grid Using WMN

Smart grid technologies have gradually been developed through the combined efforts of electronic control, metering, and monitoring. Early experiments used the term broadband over power lines (BPL) to represent networks that connect millions of homes via smart meters, yet researchers used the WMN technology, notably for more reliable connections to home devices as well as supporting metering of other utilities (gas, water, etc.) (Burger & Iniewski, 2012). This was partly prompted by the successful initial deployments of smart grids using WMNs, such as the 2003 implementation in Austin, Texas (Sectoral e-Business Watch, 2009).

An important work of justifying the use of WMN model for smart grid network is by Xu and Wang (Xu & Wang, 2013). Recognizing the importance of providing time-critical communications in the power system, they modeled the smart grid network as a WMN, and provided the delay analysis in typical deployment scenarios. They specified the delay bounds, which would be useful for guiding smart grid network design to meet its communication demands.

One early theoretical study of using WMN as the communication environment of smart grid is by Zhang et al (Zhang, 2011). Recognizing that such environment needs to be robust, reliable, and efficient, the authors proposed a smart grid communication network, deploying WMN technologies including 802.15.4 Zigbee (Zigbee Alliance, 2008), 802.11s WLAN WMN standard (IEEE 802.11s, 2011) in different levels of smart grid networks, and verified its reliability through robust, efficient primal-dual routing.

Another theoretical study using WMN to model smart grid network is by Kim et al (Kim, Kim, Lim, Ko, Lee, 2012). The authors suggested using IEEE 802.11s standard (IEEE 802.11s, 2011) as the backbone for smart grid infrastructure, and analyzed the default routing protocol for the 802.11s standard, Hybrid Wireless Mesh Protocol (HWMP). They then proposed an enhancement, HWMP-RE (HWMP-Reliability Enhancement) for improving the routing reliability.

Smart Grid Security Framework

An important work on smart grid, or smart distribution grid (SDG), security was by Wang and Yi (Wang, Yi, 2011). They investigated two issues. First, they proposed a security framework for SDG based on a WMN topology and analyzed the potential security attacks and possible counter-attack measures. Next, they developed a new intrusion detection and response scheme (smart tracking firewall). They evaluated its performance and found that the smart tracking firewall can detect and respond to security attacks in real-time, and thus is a good fit for use in SDG.

The authors note that NIST guidelines document the usefulness and importance of WMN for smart grid. By their nature WMN are robust and economic so they are well suited for SDG applications. For an SDG to function properly they must meet the following requirements:

1. Collect power usage information
2. Monitor the status of electrical equipment
3. Send control messages from the control centers to electrical devices
4. Send pricing information to customers

WMN are vulnerable to signal jamming, eavesdropping and attacks from inside the network. It is argued that WMN need to cooperate with wired networks to deliver critical messages via secure and reliable paths within the shortest time. It is currently unknown if existing security of WMN can meet SDG requirements. Further research on this point is required.

Smart Grid Authentication using Merkel Trees

A recent work (Hu & Gharavi, 2014) evaluates authentication schemes for multi-gate mesh network in smart grid applications. This work provides additional support for the use of Merkle trees in smart grid. The most recently adopted IEEE 802.11s standard supports simultaneous authentication of equals (SAE) for its security protocol. This protocol uses one password shared by all devices. The standard also offers efficient mesh security association (EMSA) as an alternative approach. Both protocols use 4-way handshaking during which a network is vulnerable to denial of service (DoS) attacks.

The first step of the four-way handshake is to use a pre-shared key (PSK) or an authentication server to establish the authentication of the server. From this a secret key is generated that is called the pairwise master key (PMK). The client and server then exchange encrypted messages and decrypt them to authenticate themselves. 4-way hand shaking is a means for the client and server to independently prove to each other that they know the PSK/PMK, without disclosing it. The PMK usually lasts the entire session, but the traffic between needs to be encrypted as well. The handshake establishes a new key called the Pairwise Transient Key (PTK). It is prior to the establishment of the PTK that a denial of service could be launched. The goal of the attack would be to prevent the establishment of the PTK key. It is assumed that the attacker can eavesdrop and is able to forge messages. The Merkle tree is used during the exchange of the first message and without the PTK information the attacker is unable to derive the Merkle tree root. By using new Merkle trees during subsequent four-way hand shakings, this scheme is also able to prevent replay attacks.

The authors used ProVerif to analyze the vulnerabilities of the network and the resilience added by use of Merkle trees to defend against DoS attacks. This work does not look at quantum computer attacks on WMN.

Additional research has been done (Li, Lu, Zhou, Yang, & Shen, 2013) that uses Merkle trees for authentication to defend against message injection, message modification, message analysis and replay attacks. The work stresses the importance of authentication to the proper function of the smart grid. This work continues the discussion related to performance and security of Merkle trees in a smart grid application.

PROPOSED SOLUTION

This section describes the proposed solution. First, the Merkle tree and its construction are explained. As Merkle tree authentication scheme rests on a secure hash function, the second subsection expounded on secure hash functions and their desired properties. An important strength of hash functions is its resistance on birthday attack, which is illustrated in the last subsection.

Merkle Trees

A Merkle tree is a complete binary tree constructed from a set of secret leaf tokens where each internal node of the tree is a concatenation, then a hash of its left and right child. The leaves consist of a set of

m randomly generated secret tokens. Since it is a complete binary tree, $m = 2^h$ where h is the height of the tree and m is the number of leaves. The root is public, and is the result of recursive applications of the one-way hash function on the tree, starting at the leaves (Santhanam et al., 2008).

Merkle trees offer low cost authentication for mesh clients. Compared to public key, they are lightweight, quick to generate and are resistant to quantum attacks (http://en.wikipedia.org/wiki/Merkle_tree). The strength of the Merkle tree authentication scheme rests on having a secure hash function and practical cryptographic hash functions do exist. The purpose of a hash function is to produce a "fingerprint" of a message, that is, a hash function $s()$ is applied to a file M and produces $s(M)$, which identifies M, but is much smaller (Stamp, 2011).

Figure 1 shows a Merkle tree with 8 leaves ($m = 8$). This tree therefore has 8 one-time authentication tokens to offer. In a mesh application the client generates the tree, and the root of the tree is made public. The client can prove its identity to any mesh router, by comparing the published root against the root that is generated when the hash function and authentication path are provided. Note that it is computationally infeasible to determine the secret token from the published root of the tree (Santhanam et al., 2008).

Here is an example of a client authenticating itself with leaf Y_5 (referring to Figure 1):

Let F be a mapping function that we define by:

$$F(i,i) = s(Y_i)$$

$$F(i, j) = s(F(i,k), F((k+1), j))$$

$$\text{where } k = \frac{i + j}{2}$$

1. $F(1,8)$ is the root and is public, made known by the router
2. The client sends F(1, 4) and F(5, 8) and the router computes: s(F(1, 4), F(5, 8)) = F(1, 8)
3. The client sends F(5, 6) and F(7, 8) and the router computes: s(F(5, 6), F(7, 8)) = F(5, 8)
4. The client sends F(5, 5) and F(6, 6) and the router computes: s(F(5, 5), F(6, 6)) = F(5, 6)

Figure 1. A Merkel tree with authentication path

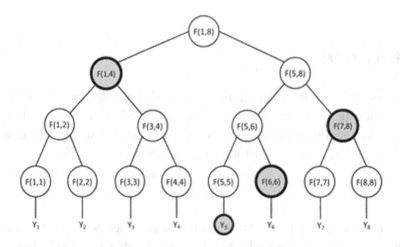

5.   The client sends Y_5 and the router computes: $s(Y_5) = F(5, 5)$
6.   The router has now authenticated the client through authenticating Y_5

Note that using this method, only $log_2 n$ transmissions are required to authenticate. However, only half of the transmissions are actually required because the router is generating half of the values itself.

To recap, the client transmits to the mesh router the secret token Y_i and the path to the root. The root is public so there is no need to transmit that. The client is authenticated by the fact that the mesh router is able to regenerate the value of the root based on the hash function $s()$ and the path provided by the client (Merkle, 1979).

Secure Hash Functions

Public key algorithms use expensive modular arithmetic, exponential operations and are therefore not good fits for mesh clients (Santhanam et al., 2008). An alternative to the use of resource-hungry, quantum computer-vulnerable public key authentication is a system based on Merkle trees. It is well known that hash based algorithms like MD5 and SHA-2 are computationally less expensive than symmetric key algorithms, which in turn are computationally less expensive that public key algorithms.

Popular cryptographic hash functions like SHA-1 or MD5 work much like block ciphers. That is they take plain text and split them into fixed sized blocks then iterated by way of a function for some number of rounds (Stamp, 2011). They are considered secure if no collisions have been found; SHA-1 was broken in 2005 (https://www.schneier.com/blog/archives/2005/02/sha1_broken.html). Hash functions must be fast and have the effect that small changes to the input result in large changes in the output. This is known as the *avalanche effect* (Stamp, 2011).

A cryptographic hash function must provide:

1.   **Compression:** The input file can be of any size, but the output must always be the same size.
2.   **Efficiency:** It must be relatively easy for the computer to compute the output.
3.   **One-Way:** Given only y of $y = s(x)$, it must be computationally infeasible to compute x.
4.   **Weak Collision Resistance:** It is not feasible to modify a message without changing its hash value. That is, given x and $s(x)$ to find any y, with $y \neq x$ and $s(x) = s(y)$ is infeasible.
5.   **Strong Collision Resistance:** We cannot find any two inputs that produce the same hash output. That is, it is infeasible to find any x and y, such that $y \neq x$ and $s(x) = s(y)$.

The last item here refers to how resistant the hash function is to the *birthday attack*.

The Birthday Attack

The birthday paradox is a classic topic in probability, the result being that with only 23 people in a room you have a 50% chance of having two people with the same birthday. The paradoxical part of this problem is that at first glance it would appear 23 is too small a number.

The number of comparisons required with n people in a room is:

$$\frac{n(n-1)}{2} \approx n^2$$

There are 365 days in a non-leap year and we get the following:

$$n^2 = 365$$
$$n = \sqrt{365} \approx 19$$

Appling this to hash functions, if we have $s(x)$ that has an output with n bits, then there are 2^n different possible hash values—all values being equally likely. Since

$$\sqrt{2^n} = 2^{n/2}$$

Then by the birthday problem we can expect to have a collision after $2^{n/2}$ different inputs. As a consequence to prevent this sort of attack, n must be substantially so large that a brute force attack is not reasonable (Stamp, 2011).

The goal of the birthday attack on a hash function is not to find a message x such that $s(x) = s(y)$, rather it is to find two random messages x and y such that $s(x) = s(y)$ (Schneier, 1996). "The strength of a hash function against brute-force attack depends solely on the length of the hash code produced by the algorithm" (Stalling, 1999). This is a key point; to defend against a quantum attack the hash code only needs to be increased in length.

ANALYSIS AND PERFORMANCE EVALUATION

This section first presents the complexity analysis, which includes the analyses of time, memory, and message complexities of Merkel trees and RSA. It then describes the experiment setup, including WMN representing a smart grid network, the Merkle tree for authentication nodes, and the RSA implementation. Finally it illustrates the experimental results consisting of build time and authentication time.

Complexity Analysis of Merkle Trees

Complexities of Build-Time and Authentication-Time

Since a Merkle tree is a complete binary tree the number of nodes at height h is 2^h. The height of the tree with n leaves is $log_2 n$. The number of internal nodes in such a tree of height h is:

$$1 + 2 + 2^2 + \ldots + 2^{h-1} = \sum_{i=0}^{h-1} 2^i = \frac{2^h - 1}{2 - 1}$$

Therefore, there are $(2^h - 1)$ internal nodes (Cormen et al., 2009). To build a Merkle tree in each node we have an asymptotic upper bound of $O(2^h)$ with additional cost for the hash function.

For our experiment the *hash( )* function available with the *tr1/functional* library of *C++* was used. *C++* uses *MurmurHashNeutral2* as its hash function, which uses a "Merkle-Damgard-esque" construction for its hash (https://sites.google.com/site/murmurhash/). This has a padding scheme on the front end to make sure all input into the compression function is of the same length. The input is broken into blocks that are then compressed. The compression involves taking the result so far and combining it with the next block. Many cryptographic hash functions work this way (http://en.wikipedia.org/wiki/Merkle-Damgard_construction). We can say that asymptotically the time complexity of the hash function is $O(\beta)$, where β is the key size.

The total build time is therefore $O(2^h) + O(\beta)$. The time to authenticate is bounded by the height of the tree, as illustrated in the previous section and Figure 1, and the hash function, i.e., $O(\beta\ h)$.

Memory Complexity

The amount of memory a Merkle tree requires is proportional to the size of the tree and the key size. Its memory complexity is therefore:

$$\beta * (2^h + 1) = O(\beta\ 2^h).$$

Message Complexity

As shown in previous sections, the Merkle tree sends an authenticating path back to the request. Each entry is $O(\beta)$ and there are h entries in this path, so we have $O(\beta\ h)$ message complexity.

Complexity Analysis of RSA

Computational Time Complexity

Public-private key generation relies on modular exponentiation. This is when an operation is raising one number to a power modulo another number. This is resource heavy, i.e., time, power and processor resources. Assume the *public key: (N, e)* and *private key: d*, satisfy:

$$\lg e = O(1),\ \lg d \le \beta \text{ and } \lg N \le \beta$$

Applying a public key requires $O(1)$ modular multiplications and uses $O(\beta^2)$ bit operations. Therefore the build time complexity is $O(1) + O(\beta^2) = O(\beta^2)$.

For authentication time, to apply a secret key requires $O(\beta)$ modular multiplications, for a total of $O(\beta^3)$ bit operations (Cormen et al., 2009).

Memory Complexity

In terms of memory consumption RSA does hold an advantage since it does not require a tree, and with one set of keys it can authenticate with an unlimited number of devices. Each node only needs to hold their own private key. Since public keys are public, the nodes do not need to retain that information. Therefore the amount of memory used is $O(\beta)$.

Message Complexity

RSA works in three exchanges. The message complexity is therefore also $O(\beta)$.

Comparison of Complexities

Table 1 summarizes the time, memory and message complexities of Merkle tree and of RSA.

Performance Experimental Setup

The experiments were set up using ns-3, a discrete event network simulator widely used in industry and academia for the purposes of testing and evaluating networks. Both Merkle tree and RSA authentication schemes were added into ns-3. This experiment was run on a MacBook Air running OS X 10.8.5, with a 1.8 GHz Intel Core i5 and 4 GB 1600MHz DDR3 of memory.

Wireless Mesh Network

In industry today we are starting to see utilization of WMN particularly in wireless lighting control systems. Currently these networks are limited to discrete sections of buildings, not entire buildings, and are often limited in size. For this reason we defined this experiment to have a network of 64 nodes.

Merkle Trees

The Merkle tree algorithm was coded as described in the previous sections. The Merkle trees were added into the existing ns-3 node structure, which represent devices in the WMN; this would be the build time. Later when the nodes are being linked into a network, we add a functionality of authentication of nodes; this would be the authentication time.

The initial assumption was that a Merkle tree with 16 leaves (depth of 4) would be sufficient. Assuming a network of 64 devices, and if every node can authenticate with 16 other nodes around it, that should be sufficient to create a robust system. Deep trees are no more secure than shallow ones.

Table 1. Complexity analysis

		MERKLE TREE	RSA
COMPLEXITIES	BUILD TIME	$O(2^h) + O(\beta)$	$O(\beta^2)$
	AUTH TIME	$O(\beta\,h)$	$O(\beta^3)$
	MEMORY	$O(\beta\,2^h)$	$O(\beta)$
	MESSAGE	$O(\beta\,h)$	$O(\beta)$

RSA

The RSA software used was obtained from *rsa Project* (https://code.google.com/p/rsa/). In the RSA scheme a private key is stored at the node. The public key is made public so there is no need for it to be stored in the node. This functionality was added in the same locations as the Merkle tree in ns-3.

RSA is able to use a public-private key pair to authenticate itself with any number of other nodes; this is an advantage over Merkle trees. That is, the Merkle tree scheme needs to know ahead of time how many nodes (devices) it will need to be able to authenticate with.

RSA key generation calculations depend on the length of the keys. For the sake of this test we choose 32 bits. We also have the length of our Merkle root at 32 bits. Albeit this would not be secure in a real system, it gives us good modeling data in a reasonable amount of time. We do test larger keys to see what impact the length has on calculation times.

Performance Results

The authors wanted to evaluate how the size of a Merkle tree effected build and authentication times. A large Merkle tree offers more authentication tokens, but takes longer to build and traverse. RSA on the other hand can authenticate with an unlimited number of devices, yet it requires intensive calculations to generate and use. To evaluate the Merkle tree time measurements were taken during the construction of the node, that is, when the Merkle tree is also built. Then when the node is linked into the network, this is the authentication time.

Build Time

Figure 2 shows that RSA is very slow to build compared to Merkle, taking on the order of 350,000 milliseconds to build. When compared to a Merkle tree of shallow depth, we see the Merkle scheme has a clear advantage. The Merkle scheme does slow down as the tree grows larger. Around a depth of 16

Figure 2. Build time comparison

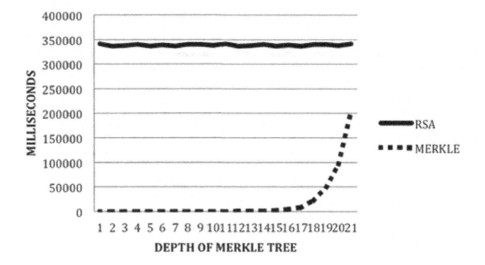

we start to see noticeable slowing in the Merkle scheme. At a depth of 16 each node has 65,536 leaves to authenticate with.

It was not possible to see at what depth the Merkle tree equaled RSA's time because at depth 25, the computer that was running the tests started to report memory problems, then seized up. At that depth we were building a Merkle tree with 33,554,432 leaves.

Authentication Time

For the Merkle trees we can see from Figure 2 that the larger the tree the more traversing of the tree we need to do to provide our authentication path. Still Merkle continues to do better than RSA for authentication. In these plots RSA is using a 32-bit key. With the 256-bit key, RSA did much worse than the Merkle tree taking about 3 minutes to authenticate one single node. This number would then be proportional to the size of the network and number of links. What we can see from all of this is that Merkle trees are a viable alternative to the use of public key for authentication.

FUTURE RESEARCH DIRECTIONS

For this chapter the authors proposed and evaluated Merkel tree-based authentication, to offer an alternative where public-key encryption would be vulnerable to quantum attack (Kaku, 2008). The immediate next step would be to build a network with an RSA key of up to 2048 bits, which today is considered a secure length, and compare with Merkel tree approach.

A study on public key encryption systems that are not vulnerable to a quantum computer attack, such as the NTRU Cryptosystem (http://tbuktu.github.io/ntru/), would also be useful. Yet, it seems reasonable that both RSA and NTRU-based systems would be slower than a Merkle tree scheme.

Another future direction would be to look at the alternatives that improve over the use of Diffie-Hellman key exchange. Diffie-Hellman is based on the discrete log problem and allows users to establish

Figure 3. Authentication time comparison

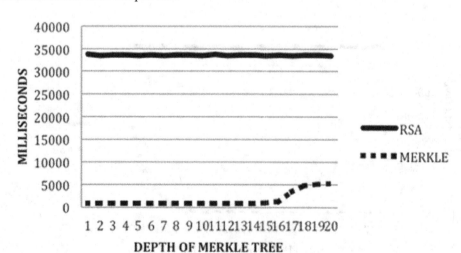

a shared symmetric key (Stamp, 2011). It is part of the NIST-approved cryptographic techniques, known as NSA Suite B, and is approved for use on the smart grid (NIST, 2014). Finding the pros and cons of Diffie-Hellman and providing superior alternatives would be valuable for future realization of secure smart grid systems.

CONCLUSION

"Cybersecurity is one of the key technical areas where the state of the art falls short of meeting the envisioned functional, reliability, and scalability requirements of the smart grid" (NIST, 2014). It is understood that public key encryption may not be desirable for use in the smart grid. Issues related to key servers and certificate authorities are high on the concerns.

Although people see the threat of a quantum computing attack to be low, it is understood to be a long-term possibility (NIST, 2014). An evident is the recent launch of quantum satellite by China, which has shown that the era of quantum computing (and therefore its enabling of cybersecurity attacks) is no longer in a far-distant future (Wall Street Journal, August 2016).

The main objective of this chapter is to discourage the use of discrete log and factorization-based public key encryption that is vulnerable to quantum-computing attacks in smart grid communication domains. The build-time and authentication-time complexities, memory and message complexities of RSA, a public key authentication method, and our proposed Merkel-tree-based authentication methods are analyzed and compared based on build and authentication times. The proposed Merkel tree-based method took less time to build and to authenticate than RSA. These studies show that Merkle tree-based authentication is lightweight, secure, resistant to quantum computer attacks and should be considered for use in smart grid applications.

An important factor in the quality of our lives in the future will depend on energy; how we get it, how we use it, how we distribute it. Smart grid is an important step toward a future with a quality of life better than the one we have today. Smart grid will take a generation to complete yet everything that is to come must be built on a solid foundation of information security.

REFERENCES

Berger, L. T., & Iniewski, K. (Eds.). (April2012). *Smart Grid - Applications, Communications and Security*. John Wiley and Sons.

Cormen, T., Leiserson, C., Rivest, R., & Stein, C. (2009). *Introduction to Algorithms* (3rd ed.). Cambridge, MA: The MIT Press.

Fernandes, E., Jung, J., & Prakash, A. (2016). *Security Analysis of Emerging Smart Home Applications*. Retrieved from https://cdn2.vox-cdn.com/uploads/chorus_asset/file/6410049/Paper27_SP16_Camera-Ready_SmartThings_Revised_1_.0.pdf

Gaur, S., Moh, M., & Balakrishnan, M. (December2013). Hiding behind the Clouds: Efficient, Privacy-Preserving Queries via Cloud Proxies. In *Proc. of International Workshop on Cloud Computing Systems, Networks, and Applications*. doi:10.1109/GLOCOMW.2013.6825035

Hellemans. (2016). Europe Bets €1 Billion on Quantum Tech. *IEEE Spectrum*.

Hu & Gharavi. (2014). Smart Grid Mesh Network Security Using Dynamic Key Distribution With Merkle Tree 4-Way Handshaking. *IEEE Transactions on Smart Grid, 5*. doi: 10.1109/TSG.2013.2277963

IEEE 802.11s. (2011). *Part11: Wireless LAN medium access control (MAC) (PHY) specifications amendment 10: Mesh networking*. IEEE Press.

IEEE-USA Board of Directors. (2010). *Building a Stronger and Smarter Electrical Energy Infrastructure*. Author.

Kaku, M. (2008). *Physics of the Impossible*. New York: Anchor Books.

Kapoor, A., & Moh, M. (2015). Implementation and evaluation of the DFF protocol for Advanced Metering Infrastructure (AMI) networks. *Proceedings of 11th IEEE International Conference on Design of Reliable Communication Networks*.

Khaund, K. (2015). *Cybersecurity in Smart Buildings*. Frost & Sullivan Collaborative Industry Perspective. Retrieved from http://23873b0b5ea986687186-fddd749ce937721293aa13aa786d4227.r31.cf1.rackcdn.com/Documentation/Cybersecurity%20in%20Smart%20Buildings_White%20Paper.pdf

Kim, Kim, Lim, Ko, & Lee. (2012). Improving the Reliability of IEEE 802.11s Based Wireless Mesh Networks for Smart Grid Systems. *Journal of Communications and Networks, 14*(6).

Kowalenko (2010). The Smart Grid: A Primer. *The Institute, IEEE*.

Kozen, D. (1997). *Automata and Computability*. Ithaca, NY: Springer. doi:10.1007/978-1-4612-1844-9

Li, H., Lu, R., Zhou, L., Yang, B., & Shen, X. (2013). An Efficient Merkle-Tree-Based Authentication Scheme for Smart Grid. *IEEE Systems Journal, 8*(2), 655–663. doi:10.1109/JSYST.2013.2271537

Merkle, R. (1979). *Secrecy Authentication and Public Key Systems*. Information Systems Laboratory, Stanford Electronics Laboratories. Retrieved from http://www.merkle.com/papers/Thesis1979.pdf

Monroe, C., & Kim, J. (2013, March). Scaling the Ion Trap Quantum Processor. *Science, 339*(6124), 1164–1169. doi:10.1126/science.1231298 PMID:23471398

Muñoz, M., Moh, M., & Moh, T.-S. (2014). Improving Smart Grid Security using Merkle Trees. *IEEE Conference on Communications and Network Security* (CNS). doi:10.1109/CNS.2014.6997535

Muñoz, M., Moh, M., & Moh, T.-S. (2014). Improving Smart Grid Authentication using Merkle Trees. *Proc. IEEE International Conference on Parallel and Distributed Systems*. doi:10.1109/PADSW.2014.7097884

NIST 7628. (2010). *Guidelines for Smart Grid Cyber Security*. Retrieved from http://www.nist.gov/smartgrid/upload/nistir-7628_total.pdf

NIST 7628 Revision 1. (2014). *Guidelines for Smart Grid Cyber Security*. Retrieved from http://nvlpubs.nist.gov/nistpubs/ir/2014/NIST.IR.7628r1.pdf

Rieffel, E., & Polak, W. (2011). *Quantum Computing, A Gentle Introduction*. Cambridge, MA: The MIT Press.

Rosen, K. (1995). *Discrete Mathematics And Its Applications* (3rd ed.). New York: McGraw-Hill, Inc.

Santhanam, L., Xie, B., & Agrawal, D. (2008). Secure and Efficient Authentication in Wireless Mesh Networks.*33rd IEEE Conference on Local Computer Networks*. doi:10.1109/LCN.2008.4664310

Schneier, B. (1996). *Applied Cryptography* (2nd ed.). New York: Wiley & Sons Inc.

Sectoral e-Business Watch. (2009). *Case study: Smart grid journey at Austin Energy, Texas, USA*. Author.

Shor, P. (1997, October). Polynomial-Time Algorithms for Prime Factorization and Discrete Logarithms on a Quantum Computer. *SIAM Journal on Computing, 26*(5), 1484–1509. doi:10.1137/S0097539795293172

Siddiqui, M. S., & Huong, C. S. (2007). Security Issues in Wireless Mesh Networks.*International Conference on Multimedia and Ubiquitous Engineering (MUE)*.

Stajic, J. (2013, March). The Future of Quantum Information Processing. *Science, 339*(6124), 1163. doi:10.1126/science.339.6124.1163 PMID:23471397

Stallings, W. (1999). *Cryptography and Network Security* (2nd ed.). Upper Saddle River, NJ: Prentice Hall.

Stamp, M. (2011). *Information Security Principles and Practices* (2nd ed.). Hoboken, NJ: Wiley & Sons Inc. doi:10.1002/9781118027974

Tanenbaum, A. (1990). *Structured Computer Organization* (3rd ed.). Englewood Cliffs, NJ: Prentice Hall.

The Wall Street Journal. (2016). *China's Latest Leap Forward Isn't Just Great—It's Quantum. Beijing launches the world's first quantum-communications satellite into orbit*. Retrieved 8/17/2016 from: http://www.wsj.com/articles/chinas-latest-leap-forward-isnt-just-greatits-quantum-1471269555

U.S.-Canada Power System Outage Task Force. (2004). *Final Report on the August 14, 2003 Blackout in the United States and Canada: Causes and Recommendations*. Retrieved from: http://energy.gov/sites/prod/files/oeprod/DocumentsandMedia/BlackoutFinal-Web.pdf

Wang, X., & Yi, P. (2011, December). Security Framework for Wireless Communications in Smart Distribution Grid. *IEEE Transactions on Smart Grid, 2*(4), 809–818. doi:10.1109/TSG.2011.2167354

Wong, R., Moh, T.-S., & Moh, M. (2012). Efficient Semi-Supervised Learning BitTorrent Traffic Detection: An Extended Summary. In *Proc. of 13th Int. Conf on Distributed Computing and Networking – ICDCN 2012 (LNCS)*, (vol. 7129). Springer. doi:10.1007/978-3-642-25959-3_40

Xu & Wang. (2013). Wireless Mesh Network in Smart Grid: Modeling and Analysis for Time Critical Communications. *IEEE Transactions on Wireless Communications, 12*(7), 3360 – 3371.

Yan, Y., Qian, Y., Sharif, H., & Tipper, D. (2012, January). A Survey on Cyber Security for Smart Grid Communications. *Communication Surveys and Tutorials, IEEE, 14*(4), 998–1010. doi:10.1109/SURV.2012.010912.00035

Yang, L., & Moh, M. (2011). Dual Trust Secure Protocol for Cluster-Based Wireless Sensor Networks. In *Proc. IEEE 45th Asilomar Conference on Signals, Systems and Computers*. doi:10.1109/ACSSC.2011.6190298

Zhang, Y., Sun, W., Wang, L., Wang, H., Green, R. II, & Alam, M. (2011). A multi-level communication architecture of smart grid based on congestion aware wireless mesh network. *43rd North American Power Symposium (NAPS)*.

ZigBee Alliance. (2008). *ZigBee Specifications 053474r17*. Retrieved from http://www.zigbee.org/

KEY TERMS AND DEFINITIONS

Factor: To decompose an integer into a product of primes.

National Institute of Standards and Technology (NIST): A measurement standards laboratory and part of the U.S. Department of Commerce.

One-Way Hash Function: A function that takes a variable length input and converts it to a fixed length output.

Public Key Encryption: Type of encryption where encrypting and decrypting are done with different keys.

Quantum Computing: Theoretical computing system that makes use of quantum mechanics to perform operations.

Ralph Merkle: Computer scientist and pioneer in the field of cryptography.

Tree: A connected acyclic graph.

Wireless Mesh Network (WMN): A wireless network topology where all nodes are peers that relay data for the network.

Chapter 8
Secure Interoperability in Cyber–Physical Systems

Cristina Alcaraz
University of Malaga, Spain

Javier Lopez
University of Malaga, Spain

ABSTRACT

Transparency in control transactions under a secure network architecture is a key topic that must be discussed when aspects related to interconnection between heterogeneous cyber-physical systems (CPSs) arise. The interconnection of these systems can be addressed through an enforcement policy system responsible for managing access control according to the contextual conditions. However, this architecture is not always adequate to ensure a rapid interoperability in extreme crisis situations, and can require an interconnection strategy that permits the timely authorized access from anywhere at any time. To do this, a set of interconnection strategies through the Internet must be studied to explore the ability of control entities to connect to the remote CPSs and expedite their operations, taking into account the context conditions. This research constitutes the contribution of this chapter, where a set of control requirements and interoperability properties are identified to discern the most suitable interconnection strategies.

INTRODUCTION

In the last few years, we have witnessed how the advent of new technologies, such as the Internet and wireless communication infrastructures, has radicalized the current control systems, the infrastructures of which are becoming smarter with a strong dependence on heterogeneous cyber-physical systems (CPSs). CPSs are collaborative systems comprising autonomous and intelligent control devices (e.g., smart meters, gateways, servers working as front-ends, remote terminal units (RTUs), sensors, smart industrial engineering devices, mobile robots, smart-phones, and many other cyber-physical control elements) capable of managing data flows and operations, and monitoring physical entities integrated as part of critical infrastructures (CIs). A Smart Grid system is a clear example of the composition of these

DOI: 10.4018/978-1-5225-1829-7.ch008

systems based on complex communication infrastructures (Yan et al., 2012). Their technologies, from diverse vendors or manufactures, manage a set of fundamental services according to the real demand, facilitating effective energy production, the management and notification of electricity pricing, as well as the provision of customizable services to end-users.

However, the composition of diverse types of networks requires addressing aspects related to the interoperability, so as to ensure control from anywhere and at any time. Cyber-physical devices located at different locations should be managed irrespective of the types of devices and protocols, and they must allow control entities to assist in a situation when needed. To address this heterogeneity, it is necessary to include a set of fundamental requirements linked to the underlying interconnection system, among them: authentication, authorization and policy management because:

1. Any unauthorized access to restricted devices may become a threat, and
2. Authorized access under different policies may hamper the monitoring tasks.

Intermediary policy enforcement systems with support for dynamic access could be an easy way of ensuring interoperable communication between different CPSs. If, in addition, the context has to consider dynamic access, the resulting system is a decision-making system with the capability to adapt the access to the type of context. These fundamental conditions are primarily related to the connectivity phase in which control entities may require the absolute connection with the desired destination node; and this connection is strongly linked to the privileges assigned to the control entities (human operators, processes), the intentions of these entities in the field and the contextual conditions.

However, the construction of specific interoperability architectures may lead to certain questions related to:

1. Whether these architectures may directly connect with the end cyber-physical devices instead of going through the main interfaces (gateways or front-ends) that generally comprise the current control systems; or
2. To directly connect with the control devices (e.g., RTUs, sensors, actuators).

To do this, it is necessary to analyze the existing interconnection strategies of CPSs to the Internet to determine which approach is the most suitable for maintaining the interoperability in restricted control contexts, assessing the connection level and timely access in extreme situations. The result of all this research constitutes the main contribution of this chapter, which is organized as follows. First we contribute with a generic interconnection architecture based on decision points, so as to provide the architectonic basis required for subsequent research. In the third section we identify the control requirements that all CPSs and their devices have to comply with, and present the different interconnection strategies to substations (where the CPSs are deployed). Lastly, we evaluate and discuss the properties of the CPSs in the fourth section according to the present constraints of the control systems, and provide the conclusions and future work.

Secure Interoperability: Diversity, Interaction, and Collaboration

As mentioned, in the majority of CIs and their physical systems all activity must be supervised, either locally or remotely, by complex and decentralized monitoring systems comprising large and small communication infrastructures. All these infrastructures base their communications on wired and wireless infrastructures, and are responsible for transferring evidence from one point of the CI to another. The back-haul and the Internet constitute, in this case, the main communication infrastructures that connect the different network distributions, while wireless technologies favor the monitoring and control transactions at local. The result is a road-map of interconnections comprising two heavily interconnected systems based on both cyber and physical elements.

Cyber-Physical Devices: Technologies and Communication Systems

The new smart CPSs adapted to the new Industry bring about fresh research challenges: *to provide connectivity without compromising the operating performance, security and safety-critical of the underlying systems* (Alcaraz & Lopez, 2012). For example, data streams have to be transmitted between different types of networks and computed on different types of devices with very different computational capacities (Alcaraz et al., 2015). Specifically, cyber-physical devices can be categorized according to their software (SW) and hardware (HW) capacities:

- **Weak:** It corresponds to those devices that are extremely constrained computationally but have sufficient capacity to run simple (arithmetic and logical) operations or predefined instructions.
- **Heavy-Duty:** Includes those devices that are relatively expensive from a computational point of view whose components are able to execute simple or complex operations or processes. Within this category, the industrial WSNs (IWSNs) are considered as an alternative, fundamental to the control. Their communications, mostly dependent on gateways, can support diverse communication standards, such as ZigBee PRO/Smart Energy (Zigbee, 2010), WirelessHART (HART, 2010) and ISA100.11a (ISA, 2010), and all of them rely on the IEEE 802.15.4 technology (IEEE, 2006). These CPS-specific protocols share certain functions and topologies, such as secure connectivity through symmetric and asymmetric cryptography, capacity to gain local access in substations and compatibility with 6LowPAN (Montenegro et al., 2007), energy saving, coexistence with other systems, data reliability and mesh communication (Alcaraz & Lopez, 2010).
- **Powerful-Duty:** Contains all those devices with significant and sufficient capacity to address any complex operation with a significant computational cost.

Table 1 summarizes the computational differences of existing CPSs and the diversity in their communications; where connection to the real world is generally reached through specific interfaces. These interfaces can range from gateways to traditional servers working as front-ends (e.g., data concentrators or RTUs). In this context, any adversarial influence may impact on the availability of resources given that the main interfaces are generally considered as single failure points. Any congestion could isolate the network, and interrupt control activities such as the typical 'store-and-forward' between RTUs. This also means that the availability of the different control points is critical to ensure controllability from anywhere at any time, meaning that security is a key requirement for interconnection. One easy way to ensure this requirement in a complex interoperability architecture would be through the following components (Alcaraz et al., 2016a):

- Authentication and access control across the different distributions, considering the existing network topologies and the different roles of the control entities, which may also be mobile.

Table 1. Typical cyber-physical devices and protocols

Weak	Heavy-duty	Power-duty
~ 4MHz, 1KB RAM and 4KB-16KB ROM (home-appliances, sensors)	~ 13MHz-180MHz, 256KB-512KB RAM and 4MB-32MB ROM (RTUs, smart meters, concentrators), or ~ 4MHz- 32MHz, 8KB-128KB RAM, 128KB-192KB ROM (industrial wireless sensor networks (WSNs))	Working at GHz with more than 2 processors per system and with at least a cache per processor, 16-32 GB RAM (servers, proxies or gateways)
6LowPAN	Zigbee PRO/Smart Energy Wireless HART ISA100.11a 6LowPAN Modbus-TCP/IP, DNP3, IEC-104 TCP/IP	TCP/IP Modbus-TCP/IP, DNP3, IEC-104 Zigbee PRO/ Smart Energy Wireless HART ISA100.11a

- Authorization is a security concept that allows interconnected systems to check and prove the identity of an entity, either a process or a human operator, and its rights to manage critical data associated with measurements, alarms, events or instructions.
- Interoperability is, contrarily, a property related to compatibility, where interfaces can interact and work with each other, not only in the present but also in the future without any type of access or implementation restrictions, in addition to permitting useful information to be exchanged between interfaces.

The composition of these three requirements comprises the functional stages of any policy enforcement point (PEP) together with its distributed policy decision points (PDPs). A PEP corresponds to a network device in which policy decisions are established according to the kind of access and its permissions. However this policy enforcement also depends on the decision taken by the PDPs in charge of evaluating and issuing authorization decisions.

Policy Enforcement Point: Architecture and Connectivity

The architecture that we consider here is decentralized, where the interconnection of CPSs is basically focused on a few proxies (see Figure 1). These proxies, linked to the functionality of the PDPs, are responsible for connecting different types of networks, offering peer- to-peer communication and relaying via the Internet. However, the connectivity to the different individual elements that comprise the CPSs is not always established through a direct connection from PDPs. Rather these connections are carried out through intermediary nodes serving as front-ends or gateways (as was stated in the previous section), which are in charge of controlling all the incoming and outgoing connections from their networks towards their closest PDPs. However, these connections must be restricted under specific authentication and authorization procedures, following access control schemes like those recommended by the IEC-6235-8 (IEC-62351, 2007).

The IEC-62351-8 is part of the IEC-62351 series (IEC-62351, 2007) that establishes end-to-end security in control systems and the protection of the communication channels. Concretely, the IEC-62351-8 recognizes the RBAC model as a potentially efficient mechanism for wide use in control systems and distributed services. Only authorized users and automated agents can gain access to restrictive

Figure 1. General architecture for distributed cyber-physical control systems

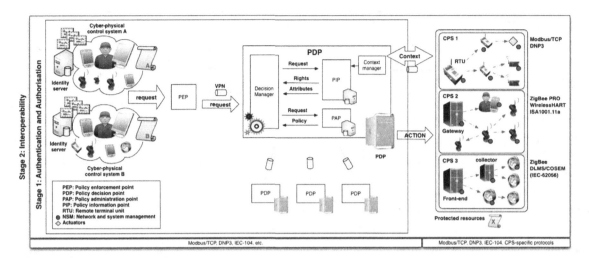

data objects, which may be located at distant geographical points and close to the observation scenario. Moreover, through RBAC it is possible to reallocate system controls and their security as defined by the organization policy, where the purpose is:

1. To introduce authorization aspects under the condition of subjects-roles-rights where a limited number of roles can represent many entities, and roles can be assigned to entities by non-expert personnel (Coyne & Weil, 2013);
2. Boost role-based access control in the power system management; and
3. Enable heterogeneity and audited interoperability between the different elements of a CPS (sensors, meters, etc.).

However, RBAC can be problematic when the application context is dynamic, where the access is limited to contextual states such as the saturation or isolation degree in substations, or the availability of nodes or objects. In this case, ABAC could solve these weaknesses by simplifying the model and applying labelled objects and dynamic attributes instead of permissions, and complement the tasks of RBAC by considering roles as attributes. Notwithstanding, ABAC has certain limitations in accountability terms where it is not possible to audit which entities have access and what permissions have been granted to an entity (Coyne & Weil, 2013). So the implementation of both approaches together could be a good approach to promote their potential features. To combine them, it is necessary to define specific rules to control the different access modes, which, in turn, have to be instanced according to the characteristics of the context. In this case, the decision managers of both approaches must be integrated inside the policy information points (PIPs), where the PIP modules have to determine the type of permission for a specific entity and the associated attributes, which are primordially related to the characteristics of the context.

This is also represented in Figure 1, where each entity belonging to an infrastructure or CPS has to authenticate itself to its own identity server corresponding to its own infrastructure. At this point, IEC-62351-8 recommends depending on a third entity (e.g., the security administrator) responsible for assigning roles to subjects and managing access tokens; generating and maintaining the basic security

Table 2. Roles and permissions established by the IEC-62351-8 standard

Roles	View	Read	Dataset	Reporting	Fileread	Filewrite	Filemgnt	Control	Config	Settinggroup	Security
Viewer	✓			✓							
Operator	✓	✓		✓				✓			
Engineer	✓	✓	✓	✓		✓	✓		✓		
Installer	✓	✓		✓		✓			✓		
SECADM	✓	✓	✓			✓	✓	✓	✓	✓	✓
SECAUD	✓	✓		✓	✓						
RBACMNT	✓	✓					✓		✓	✓	
Viewer	Capacity to view data objects.										
Operator	Capacity to view data objects and values, and perform control.										
Engineer	Capacity to view data objects and values, access datasets and files, and configure servers.										
Installer	Capacity to view data objects and values, write files and configure servers.										
SECADM	Capacity to manage users-roles-rights, and change security setting.										
SECAUD	Capacity to audit the system by viewing audit logs.										
RBACMNT	Hereditary role from the SECADM with only the ability to manage roles and rights.										

credentials (e.g., the typical tuple, username and password) in conjunction with X.509 certificates. If this first stage for the interconnection is overcome, the identity server provides an authentication token holding the information related to the requester and the protected object/device in the destination.

Once the authentication token has been obtained, the requester needs to have the tools necessary for access in the field. For that, a PEP service associated with the infrastructure has to be connected with the closest PDP with connectivity to the remote substation. When the PEP service establishes such a connection, the decision manager of the PDP has to first validate the authentication token (e.g., verify the entity and check the correctness of the token such as its type, size, content and format) and obtain information from the PIP module to proceed with the authorized connection. This authorization contains the final access decision managed by the decision manager in charge of computing: (i) the heterogeneity of the system, (ii) the information provided by the PIP module, and (iii) the security policies (e.g., IEC-62351-(4-6)) and the actions (see Table 2) given by the policy administration point (PAP). The information provided by the PIP module is related to the type of permission associated with the role of the requester and the attributes related to the natural state of the context requested. Observing Figure 1 it is possible to see that a great deal of this information can come from the context manager, also restrained inside the PIP modules. These managers are responsible for periodically examining the state of the application context, as well as the degree of criticality and/or accessibility of the resources, such as nodes and links. Although this information is crucial to determine the level of access to an entity, it also requires that the gateways periodically validate their contexts where the states may be subject to NSM (network and system management) objects, also defined as part of the IEC-62351-7 standard.

NSM objects are dynamic processes running through the different cyber-physical systems to monitor the health of the critical systems and their subsystems. The information from these objects should be managed for each CPS so as to detect possible anomalies that should be notified to the closest context managers. Depending on the context, the interconnection system can, in addition, activate one of the special functional features of RBAC, known as dynamic separation of duties (DSD). DSD allows multiple mutually exclusive roles (e.g., either Engineer or Operator) working independently but not at the same time or simultaneously. In this way, in crisis contexts only authorized personnel with capacity for the 'control' (see Table 2) is able to gain access, thereby avoiding bottlenecks and delays in the operational tasks. However, there may be the extreme case in which the rate of congestion may become quite notable, and the main interfaces (gateways, front-ends) may not be able to connect to the primary PDPs. In this case, one possible solution would be to let the cyber-physical devices with TCP/IP or 6LowPAN compatibility to promptly connect with the context managers integrated as part of the PDPs. To determine this possibility and its validity for holistic protection of the entire system, the remainder of this chapter focuses on analyzing the different connection measures and the current constraints of the context.

REQUIREMENTS AND INTEGRATION STRATEGIES FOR INTEROPERABILITY

There are currently several ways to connect cyber-physical elements to the Internet and, therefore, several interconnection strategies that enable the connection to different control entities (Christin et al., 2009). However, the process of determining which strategy is more effective for an architecture deployed within a CI can also require assessing the effectiveness of the existing approaches according to specific requirements of the application context and the interoperability requirements.

Control and Automation Requirements

Five control requirements are defined in (Alcaraz & Lopez, 2012) and considered in this study: two of them related to operating performance, i.e., real-time performance and sustainability, and three associated with security, i.e., dependability, survivability and safety-critical. The nature of these requirements, however, also obliges us to consider a subset of attributes associated with the control and the characteristics of the CPSs, since they can all have a direct influence on the properties of interoperability and automation. For example, any new upgrade of the system not only involves important changes to the network architecture, but also significant overheads in the end-devices, where any intermediary connection process (e.g., agreement algorithm, access control, authorization, and policy management) and the TCP/IP-based routing may result in important delays in the control. Given this, this section introduces the basic requirements that both control systems and CPSs must consider:

- Real-time performance subject to certain operational deadlines and delays, and linked to the effectiveness of the maintainability, upgrading of the system and the interoperability of its components. At this point, we consider the overhead as a main attribute where
  - It is essential to comply with a suitable trade-off between the number of devices and their overall cost within the system, and
  - The devices should not have an excess of workloads and unnecessary resources.
- Within this requirement, we identify three properties:
  - *Computational overhead* to comprise those technological capacities (e.g., memory, CPU cf. Table 1) that are needed within an end-device to implement specific control algorithms, applications and protocols, such as NSM, ZigBee, DNP3 or ISA100.11a. Note that in the PDPs, the computational cost invested in the negotiation algorithms and policy management also has a direct effect on the time needed for the access.

○ *Communication overhead* includes all those characteristics associated with a wireless communication channel, such as bandwidth, delays and complexities related to the header size of the protocols. For example, most of the devices shown in Table 1 follow the IEEE 802.15.4 standard with a transfer rate of 250 Kbit/s, and others can manage various protocols (e.g., Modbus-TCP/IP) complicating the header space, thus reducing the bytes available for the transmission of data. Moreover, the abuse of the channel and the authorized access through specific roles may also increase the rate of communication overhead between the PDPs and the main interfaces, thereby producing significant congestions in the substations.

○ Efficient *responsiveness* by optimizing resources and protocols. Concretely, this property is related to the functional features of the existing CPS-specific protocols (e.g., WirelessHART), which deal with the specific characteristics of the application context and its networks to promote their best services (Alcaraz & Lopez, 2010), such as: redundancy, link robustness through frequency hopping and blacklisting methods, control of packet collisions through a specific TDMA (time division multiple access) with a fixed time-slot, routing discovery, low-duty cycle, maintenance tasks through hand-held devices, prioritization and alert management, as well as diagnostic mechanisms with support in NSM objects. This optimization in PDPs is related to the optimization of PIP and PAP modules, and the decision managers.

- Sustainability defined as "*that development that is able to meet the needs of the present without compromising the ability of future generations to meet their own needs*" in (UNGA, 2007); i.e., the system has to continue to function like the day it was deployed irrespective of any extension of components or systems, updates, upgrades or modifications. Its main properties are:

○ *Maintenance* corresponds to the ability of the system to update resources, prevent the occurrence of faults and errors caused by vulnerabilities, or upgrade services through patches. To do so, the system must locally and/or remotely validate the functionality of resources and periodically test functions. The properties associated with maintainability are:

  ▪ *Addressing* through unique identifiers to locate and reach up processes and cyber-physical devices. Therefore, this property is linked to how the different nodes are accessed and who is responsible for storing and managing these identities.

  ▪ *Access* to (locally or remotely) address validation tasks of resources. This also means that this property is concerned with the current complexity of accessing the cyber-physical devices through IP connections or specific protocols.

  ▪ *Maintainability*, to the contrary, focuses on all those upgrading, updating, modification and optimization processes of HW/SW components. So this property aims to consider the number of changes or improvements made to a CPS.

○ *Scalability* and *extensibility* with regard to the capacities of the system to add new HW and SW components, respectively. Substations composed of complex CPSs tend to last for a long time, and this entails adapting new devices, applications, services and objects.

  ▪ As part of the scalability, *mobility* is an elemental property to be considered here. It is related to the system's capacity to permit the dynamic access in wireless networks. Any new joining or leaving from the network should not impact on the overall performance of the network. This property is in turn linked to rapid *addressing* in the field and the *access* at local or remote.

- Dependability defined as "*the ability of the system to properly offer its services on time, avoiding frequent and severe internal faults*" in (Al-Kuwaiti, 2009), includes reliability, maintainability, safety and security as main attributes. The first attribute is detailed below, and the rest, except maintainability, are described later.

- ◦ *Reliability* is a concept that refers to the capacity of the system to offer its services within desired quality thresholds, irrespective of the criticality of the context. Concretely, this property holds two fundamental properties:
  - ▪ *Availability* of data, resources and links, but focused on terms of fault-tolerance through redundancy strategies, and on terms of security through defense and self-healing mechanisms. If a resource does not offer the correct service at a given moment, then the resource will be unavailable and therefore unreliable. Moreover, if this situation is not controlled properly, it may take on a corrosive nature, since control components are closely interconnected, exponentially increasing the costs of maintainability.
  - ▪ *Robustness* through preventive and corrective measures, where the repair of states and parameters must be achieved in an acceptable time average and at an acceptable quality. This property is closely related to resilience and self-healing because it allows the system to continue its services, despite security breaches caused within the system.
- • Survivability comprises *"the capability of a system to fulfil its mission and thus to face malicious, deliberate or accidental faults in a timely manner"* in (Knight & Strunk 2004). Note that this feature is what distinguishes it from dependability. Survivability is part of the dependability, but in this case, dependability is intended to provide services in the presence of internal faults, which may be later exploited by malicious actions. Under this concept, a survivable system also assumes as attributes, resilience, availability - both described above -, safety and security, but here we primarily focus on security. In this sense, if the security is not fully addressed, any threat may potentially impact on the control and its performance, harming not only the safety of the CI itself, but also social and economic welfare. As this may also affect the integrity of the system itself, only authorized entities with restrictive permissions (IEC-62351-8, see Table 1) should have access to execute, modify or read sensitive data, and any action in the field should be subject to accountability. Therefore, its properties are as follows:
  - ◦ *Secure channel* includes all those security mechanisms and services (e.g., cryptography, key management systems, virtual private networks (VPNs) or firewalls) that favor the confidentiality and integrity of communication channels. And this compromise involves not only the security of communication channels of the CPSs but also the channels between PDPs and CPSs.
  - ◦ *Authentication* and *authorization*. Both properties deal with the types of mechanisms (e.g., decentralized in PDPs), credentials (e.g., certificates, keys) and tools (e.g., RBAC, ABAC) that can be used to validate identities and verify whether a given entity is able to perform a determined operation in a cyber-physical device, in a process or in an object (e.g., IEC 61850).
  - ◦ *Detection* and *response* refer to the main traceability structures and inspection of packets, as well as all those mechanisms that permit the automatic response to incidents with support for alert management (Alcaraz & Lopez, 2016b). At this point, NSM objects may have a significant influence on the detection processes.
  - ◦ *Accountability* to log any activity in the system, and includes the use of specific accountability protocols and external systems to offer support for massive critical data streams. These

systems can range from simple systems (local servers, external hard devices) to complex infrastructures such as cloud-computing or fog-computing.

- ◦ *Trust* and *privacy* due to the need to collaborate between cyber-physical devices. Both properties are related to the nature of the mechanisms, where trust management systems help measure the degree of collaboration; whereas privacy schemes prevent or reduce the exposure of sensitive data (e.g., energy usage) or the location of nodes.
- Safety-critical contemplates *"those systems that can potentially lead to serious consequences due to the existence of unplanned events, which could result in human deaths or injuries, or even significant physical damage"* (Bowen & Stavridou, 1993). This requirement embraces all those basic protection requirements described above, in order to manage the preparedness and mitigation of a critical system against advanced threats.

Once the control requirements have been addressed according to the properties of the CPSs, four interoperability requirements can be identified:

1. Ease and speed of access;
2. Transparency in and during the connection;
3. Availability of resources (links and nodes) and data; and
4. Reliability of the communication.

The access is related to the capacity of the system to gain virtual access to specific devices and operate through them in the field. Any overhead in the computation and/or communication in the destination nodes may affect the access, so there is an intrinsic dependence between the properties of cyber-physical networks and the interoperability properties. Precisely, Table 3 shows this characteristic, in which it is possible to see how the network properties, corresponding to the performance, sustainability and dependability of control systems, have a certain repercussion on the access.

As for communication, it concerns the capacity of the system to offer communication resources and robustness in case of an emergency, where there exists the probability of activating the DSD mechanisms to permit the access to restricted entities (e.g., Operators or SECADM), devices or objects. If the communications are feasible, it is also necessary to consider the capacity of the end-nodes to properly

Table 3. Dependence on control requirements and interconnection properties

Interoperab.	Performance			Sustainability					Depend		Survivability						
	Comp. overhead	Com. overhead	Responsiveness	Scalab. & extensib.	Mobility	Addressing	Access	Maintainability	Availability	Robustness	Secure channel	Authentication	Authorization	Detection & response	Accountability	Trust	Privacy
Rapid access	✓	✓	✓	✓	✓	✓	✓	✓	✓	✓	✓	✓	✓	✓	✓	✓	✓
Transparency				✓	✓	✓	✓	✓				✓	✓				
Availability	✓	✓	✓	✓	✓	✓	✓	✓	✓	✓		✓	✓				
Reliability	✓	✓	✓	✓	✓	✓	✓	✓	✓	✓	✓	✓	✓	✓	✓	✓	✓

manage and process actions on time. A great deal of this communication can be related to the context, where context managers (linked to or integrated inside PIPs) can request general conditions about the nature of the network and their devices, and in this way establish the access or activate the DSD in extreme cases (e.g., congestion or isolation of areas, inoperative devices, manipulation of variables, etc.). So the management of NSM objects throughout the network is crucial to maintain a correct functionality in PDPs y CPSs, and therefore, the access in the field.

Interconnection Strategies between PDPs and CPSs

To address the interoperability, it is necessary to analyze the existing interconnection strategies that help Internet entities connect to the different elements of a CPS. Currently, there are five connectivity models, classified as *stack-based* and *topology-based* (see Figure 2) (Christin et al., 2009). In the stack-based class, the remote interconnection depends on the topological characteristics, the protocols and the capacities of the nodes; whereas the topology-based connectivity depends on the location of those nodes that provide access to the Internet.

Concretely, the stack-based class holds three approaches: *front-end* (SbC-1), *gateway* (SbC-2) and *TCP/IP* (SbC-3). The front-end solution, still in force in substations, permits control entities (e.g., SCADA centres) to reach CPSs without communicating directly with each other. In this scenario, the CPSs are completely independent from the Internet and can implement their own stack of protocols (e.g., ZigBee, ISA100.11a, or WirelessHART). This allows the front-ends to act as intermediary nodes with the capacity to interpret communication protocols and serve as data concentrators. The gateway

Figure 2. Interconnection strategies

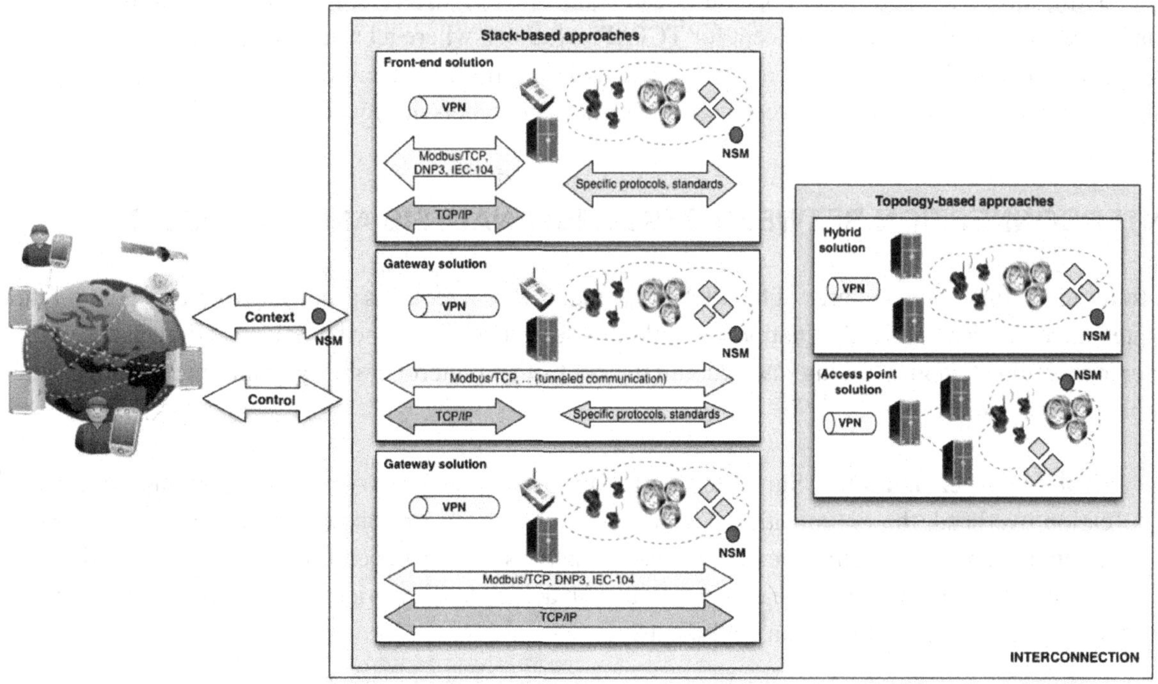

solution, to the contrary, translates the lower layer protocols (e.g., TCP/IP and CPS-specific protocols, or legacy protocols and CPS-specific protocols) and routes the information from one point to another, separating the control network from the Internet. In this sense, PDPs and cyber-physical devices or processes can exchange information without establishing a direct connection, where any operational transaction needs to traverse the gateway to convert the input request in a packet that can be understood by the destination node.

As for the third approach, the TCP/IP solution, it assumes that cyber-physical devices are able to implement the TCP/IP stack or have a certain compatibility with 6LoWPAN, promoting the paradigm of the *Internet of Things* (IoT) (Ovidiu, 2009). In this way, the application context remains fully integrated in the Internet via IPv6 or 6LowPAN, where PDPs, Internet entities (e.g., human operators, the central system or processes) and cyber-physical elements (e.g., smart sensors) can establish a direct connection with each other. However, this characteristic unfortunately does not always work. The approach still relies on the computational capacities of CPSs to support the TCP/IP stack and its payloads, in which devices classified as weak or heavy-duty may have certain difficulties to adapt the stack.

Regarding the topology-based classification, it comprises two kinds of approaches: *hybrid solutions* (TbC-1) and *access point* (TbC-2) solutions. The hybrid solution assumes the existence of a few nodes within the network with the ability to directly access the Internet. Generally, these nodes are associated with front-ends, where the devices have to traverse them to connect with the control entities, and vice-versa. The specific features of this type of approach are related to its capacity to offer redundancy (more than one front-end or gateway) and autonomy by allowing each substation to implement its own intelligence. On the other hand, when hierarchical CPSs can be built, it is advisable to consider the access point solution, where the top of the tree is composed of Internet-enabled nodes (backbones) and the connection to the Internet is done through them. The backbones permit the adaptation or addition of complex resources, in addition to implementing faster and more complex networks (e.g., WiFi, Bluetooth), through which human operators can connect using hand-held interfaces. Note that hybrid configurations are also possible, except for TCP/IP solutions, where a backbone-type distribution with the Internet-enabled nodes can act as front-ends, isolating the CPS from the Internet, or as gateways, allowing direct data exchange between control entities and cyber-physical devices.

INTERCONNECTION BETWEEN SYSTEMS: ANALYSIS AND DISCUSSION

Assuming the functional features of the PDPs to manage access requests according to privileges and the contextual conditions of the destination network, this section analyzes the benefits and drawbacks of the interconnection strategies, taking into account the control and interoperability requirements introduced in previous sections.

- **Real-Time Performance:** Supported by the properties related to computational and communication overhead, the optimization degree of the underlying protocols and the algorithms implemented. However, the effectiveness of these properties heavily depends on the architecture defined for the interoperability and the computational capacities of the devices. For example, although the authentication in the PDPs can be done using:

○   A PULL model (first gains access to the cyber-physical control object so that it can authenticate the identity of the requester using the authentication servers) or

○   A PUSH model (first fetches the access token from the identity servers before accessing the objects), the on-demand PULL model requires additional communication for the authentication, resulting in quite a costly procedure (Hong et al., 2009).

And if, in addition, PDPs connect with areas based on heavy-duty devices (e.g., RTUs), these may have certain capacities to support solutions that demand enough intelligence to:

- Execute control applications, security services (cryptography primitives, link-layer security, end-to-end security, authentication and authorization (both in local), accountability, detection mechanisms, etc.) and diagnostic mechanisms; and
- Implement the TCP/IP stack and/or legacy protocols (e.g., Modbus-TCP, DNP3).

These computational features vary significantly in weak devices, where large and complex operations may not be processed properly. Moreover, these HW/SW differences also affect the connectivity model, and concretely *stack-based* ones (SbC-1/-2/-3) or *topology-based* ones (TbC-1/-2).

Communication overhead also heavily depends on the design of the network. The interoperability architectures should be built following the cache philosophy in which front-ends or gateways (SbC-1/-2) not only serve as mere interconnection interfaces but also as data storage interfaces for the rapid provision of data or actions in the field. Nonetheless, the processing of packets in such interfaces (i.e., in SbC-1/-2/-3) may add an extra penalty to the overall performance of the CPSs. Concretely, this penalty in TCP/IP solutions (SbC-3) is limited to the size of the 6LowPAN headers − of the current industrial protocols are compatible to 6LowPAN (e.g., ISA100.11a) −, and SbC-1/-2 solutions depend on the optimization of the local headers of the CPS-specific protocols and on header compressors (optional). On the other hand, the functional features of the communication infrastructures also help the correct functioning of the automation and monitoring tasks. For example, high-speed communication technologies (e.g., the use of back-hauls for large distances, and the use of 802.15.4-based networks working at 250 Kbit/s and 802.11b-based networks at 11 Mbit/s for local control) allow rapid data management.

Optimization of services is also essential to reduce overheads. Many of the current communication protocols (e.g., WSN-specific protocols) are designed to optimize resources, the use of which can improve the behavior of all the interconnection solutions (SbC-1/-2, TbC-1/-2), except for those based on SbC-3 where the routing is associated with IP addresses. In addition, WSN-specific protocols generally define their own MAC layer services. For example, WirelessHART and ISA100.11a implement a specific TDMA with a fixed time slot to improve the quality of service of the data-link layer, a hopping/black-listing method to avoid disturbances in the channel, and a redundant mesh routing (Alcaraz & Lopez, 2010). Likewise, the optimization of interoperability services incorporated inside PDPs is also key to reducing the access time in the field. For example, the implementation of rule-based expert systems to manage authorization aspects according to the security policies could be a good approach. Intelligent engines could manage different security policies associated with different CPSs and manage the access according to their security policies.

- Sustainability led by the properties related to scalability, extensibility and maintenance. It is clear that any rise in terms of resources and services, certainly adds functional complexities to the access. Fortunately, this increase does not necessarily hamper the inclusion of new interconnection services to the Internet. Namely, for the inclusion of new members or the leaving of existing nodes, SbC-1/-2 only require updating the routing table and the mechanisms of the CPS-specific protocols in the main interfaces of the network (front-ends, servers or gateways); whereas SbC-3 requires updating the routing table of each Internet-enabled device. TCb-1/-2 is similar to SbC-3, but if the communication infrastructure is totally distributed, the changes made within the table have to be addressed in all the end-devices or depend on centralized interfaces. Regarding extensibility, this property largely depends on the capacity of the nodes to add or adapt new SW services.

The properties associated with maintenance are addressing, (local or remote) access and maintainability. For the management of addressing, both SbC-1 and SbC-2 require translating the identities (e.g., ID in DNP3 Address to ID in WirelessHART EUI-64 Address) from substations; whereas in SbC-3 the translation is managed from the central system to open a direct connection with the devices in the field. The complexity increases in decentralized networks, i.e., in the TbC-1/-2 approaches, as it is necessary to replicate the translation tables in the Internet-enabled nodes or to create a centralized service that provides a translation interface.

Regarding the access, if human operators, with the roles of Engineer, Installer or SECADM (or RBACMNT) have to have access in the field to manage maintenance tasks (e.g., with permissions of configuration − cf. Table 2) via PDPs or locally, they can use the device to execute data retrieval services. In distant controls, these entities particularly have to request the access through intermediary interfaces (gateways/front-ends) and establish TCP/IP direct connection with the network devices. If the communication is, to the contrary, done locally, operators can take advantage of the local services of the CPS-specific protocols. They can, for example, use the services offered by the internal protocols through external connections offered by other networks, such as mobile ad hoc networks, to gain access to the front-end or the gateway (SbC-1/-2). In contrast, in SbC-3, the access has to be carried out through specific addresses, the IP of which has to be known beforehand; and in TbC-2 there exists the need to know the location of the interface that manages the services/data of the node that human operators want to connect to.

As for SW upgrading, this can be executed from the central system to all the interconnection architecture, including PDPs and the CPSs. And in this case, the effectiveness of the updates depends on the interconnection strategies. For example, SbC-1 and TbC-2 are the simplest solutions, as the updating is only carried out in one device (the front-end or backbone node, respectively), but this process unfortunately disables the access. This drawback does not appear in SbC-2/-3 and TbC-1 since the updating is gradually addressed in each network device.

- Dependability is a fundamental property for context managers, which receive network status directly from gateways and front-ends (SbC-1/-2), or directly from Internet-enabled cyber-physical devices. To ensure this, dependability has to be supported by the properties related to availability and robustness, but the notion of availability is a weak property in SbC-1 and SbC-2. Both front-ends and the gateways are single failure points where attackers may consciously launch denial of services (DoS) attacks, leaving the network uncontrolled from the remote point of view. But even so, the smart nature of many of the nodes belonging to the SbC-2 solution may allow the underlying system to temporarily work in a standalone fashion, as happens with IWSNs. So, an easy way to overcome the problem in SCb-1-based networks would be through the replication of the main interfaces, as provided by the TbC-1 solution. Other replication-based strategies for resilience are, for example:

- ○ Checkpoint-based rollback with dependency on storage points (e.g., concentrators of SbC-1/-2 or external infrastructures such as cloud-computing), or
- ○ Log-based rollback (also known as message logging protocols) composed of checkpoints and a record of non-deterministic events (Bansal et al., 2012; Treaster, 2005).

However, the checkpoints are, in general terms, expensive and experts like Ruchika in (Ruchika, 2013) and Veronese et al. in (Bessani et al., 2009) recommend applying heterogeneous replication-based checkpoints to enhance performance and guarantee tamper-resistance to faults.

This also means that the implementation of robust solutions can also bring about significant complexities in determined solutions, especially in SbC-2/-3 y TbC-1/-2. Namely, SbC-1 may be able to implement self-healing mechanisms (e.g., store-and-forward) that ensure transparency in the connection and restoration in the case of incidences. However the self-healing mechanisms in solution SbC-2 may generally be less transparent since data messages are transferred as are, to the destination node. Likewise, TCP/IP solutions (i.e., SbC-3 and TbC-2) depend on the HW/SW resources, and for this reason they tend to be quite susceptible to threats to availability (e.g., DoS attacks). Similarly, PDPs are also single failure points where primary PDPs may be disabled or remain inoperative, thereby affecting the access. In this case, the corresponding PEP services should connect to other PDPs following a specific delegation scheme.

- Survivability led by a set of security properties such as authentication, authorization, detection, response, accountability, trust and privacy. Here, the adversarial scope is relevant because depending on the network configuration, the attacker may target a particular node. In SbC-1, TbC-1/-2, the most attractive nodes are precisely those that are located in the main interfaces that divide the CPS from the rest of the network, where attackers can modify measurement values, produce false injection, manipulate data (measurements, commands or alarms), impersonate identities, and so on. Although this problem is apparently controlled by SbC-3 and partially so by SbC-2, because the services are provided directly by the nodes, they are more likely to draw attention and be used to lead advanced attacks (Cárdenas et al., 2011).

Many advanced attacks target the integrity or availability of resources, sensitive data and identity. So one way of protecting the communication channels would be through the TCP/IP security services (relevant in SbC-3) and taking into account the security standards for industrial communication networks such as the IES-62351-(3-6). Series 3-6 of the standard specify the use of TLS/SSL together with key exchange algorithms (Diffie–Hellman, RSA), digital signature (Digital Signature Standard, RSA), encryption algorithms (RCA-128, 3DES or AES-128/256 bits) and secure hash algorithm. As a complement, VPNs in specific sections of the network, i.e., between PDPs and the main interfaces (SbC1/-2, see Figures 1 and 2) can also help in the network designs.

In substations, the SbC-1 and SbC-2 solutions can protect the communication channels by applying the primitive security measures offered by the CPS-specific protocols; e.g., Zigbee PRO/Smart Energy and ISA100.11a, which support key management through symmetric/asymmetric cryptography and certification. Similarly, intrusion detection mechanisms with support for automated response could also be considered as possible additional measures for the protection of the different system assets. However, this protection in distributed environments (SbC-2/-3) may become quite costly since each device needs to inspect each input data and the actions carried out in the surroundings. If these actions are based on simple techniques (e.g., based on statistical data) or are managed by powerful (de)centralized systems (e.g., front-ends and gateways in SbC-1/-2, respectively), the computational cost may be less.

Authentication and authorization in CPSs are two other security measures, in which it is important to determine the location of the authentication services. Although, the approach proposed in this chapter is based on an architecture in which the access request from external entities is validated by PDPs, the IEC-62351-8 standard recommends verifying the access in each end-point. This means that the authentication in SbC-1 should center on the front-ends and the rest of the solutions should fall on the end-points. To reduce costs in the latter case, the authentication could, for example, depend on additional (de)centralized services (e.g., lightweight directory access protocol, remote authentication dial-in user service or Kerberos) to avoid replication in distributed environments. On the other hand, the management of authentication and authorization databases can become expensive, as their maintenance depends on the size of the network and on the security policies specified for each area. Furthermore, this problem may even be higher in the authorization databases where roles and permissions (e.g., IEC-62351-8 reserves 32.767 roles for private use) may change more frequently than the identities.

With respect to accountability, it is advisable to specify centralized approaches in which the evidence can be stored in a single entity. However, this condition only works in SbC-1/2 solutions, but with the exception that the gateway can only extract statistical data from the packets. As for SbC-3, where the interactions are stored in all sensor nodes, the amount of information that can be stored is limited by the storage capacity of the network nodes. To solve these limitations, it is possible to download the information to external infrastructures (e.g., in a fog/cloud system (Alcaraz et al., 2011)) or powerful dedicated devices (e.g., TbC-1/-2), thereby favoring auditing and forensic tasks.

Trust and privacy are two other security measures needed to increase trust in the collaborations between nodes (e.g., PDPs-to-front-end, gateway-to-end-devices, etc.), and protect the data beyond the confidentiality and the location of these nodes. In this respect, the cyber-physical devices developed in SbC-2/-3 solutions could require reserving (i) the communication space to manage the interconnection to the Internet and (ii) the computational space to ensure secure end-to-end communication. In addition, SbC-3 also requires each connection to verify the trust values before making a decision; a condition that is not required in SbC-1. Concentrators, i.e., the front-ends, have a more holistic vision of the network as a whole, so they can, a priori determine the most suitable nodes for the execution of actions.

Privacy in CPS contexts can be achieved in two ways: through data privacy and location-based privacy. Data privacy involves protecting the communication channels (either via the Internet or wireless networks) and any activity associated with users' lifestyle routines. This principally affects the hierarchical interconnection solutions (SbC-1/-2, TbC-2). At this point, privacy becomes an important issue when:

- The activity pattern may be deduced by analyzing the signals received from home-appliances, known as load signatures or power fingerprints (Zeadally et al., 2012); and
- Lightweight mechanisms have to be supported to process and coordinate specific strategies as proposed in (Kalogridis, 2010).

In contrast, location privacy consists in preventing external entities from inferring the location of devices by, for example, analyzing the network traffic (Pai, 2008). However, current techniques still require complex synchronization methods, and HW and SW resources that may be excessive for some devices classified as weak and heavy-duty. This also means that the integration of privacy techniques might be too costly for some interconnection strategies because the computation of the approaches is normally implemented in the end-nodes (such as SbC-2/-3).

FURTHER DISCUSSION AND FUTURE WORK

Once the interoperability and control requirements together with the interconnection strategies have been presented, it is now necessary to discuss which interconnection strategy or strategies are the most suitable for critical scenarios. We first discuss the strategy SbC-3, as nowadays, many CPSs are part of the IoT (e.g., smart industrial sensors), and leave the rest of the solutions to be discussed later; i.e.:

- **TCP/IP Solution:** SbC-3 could certainly provide rapid access and availability of resources when sensitive parts of the system are seriously compromised (e.g., isolated areas of a CPS). In this case, Internet-enabled devices could take decisions by themselves to alert human operators to a situation in time, without traversing the front-ends or gateways; and operators could act accordingly while these devices still conduct monitoring tasks. Unfortunately, depending on the capacities of these elements and their susceptibility to specific attacks on the availability (e.g., DoS), the alert in these critical situations may not reach the control entity in time, affecting, in this case, the access. On the other hand, the availability of the resources largely depends on (i) the capacity of the nodes to support different types of services and complex applications, and on (ii) the functional features of the interconnection approaches. For example, SbC-3 is able to provide gradual updates for the entire network and to ensure resilience in the advent of severe faults, significantly favoring partial access to end-devices. However, this interconnection approach is not able to provide redundancy-based/roll-back-based restoration mechanisms as they demand replication of resources or keeping evidence to ensure the roll-back process. In contrast, SbC-1 or SbC-2 with TbC-1 are able to provide the service by relying on possible additional powerful devices for redundancy or roll-back. Regarding communication within SbC-3, it does not benefit from the optimized services that some CPS-specific protocols offer, such as WirelessHART or ISA100.11a. They, for example, provide a selective range of network topologies (e.g., mesh, many-to-one, star) with the capacity to offer routing mechanisms that allow the path redundancy and the specification of the special services of the link layer like those for the coexistence, collision and congestion. In addition, the network architecture is fully distributed, which makes it difficult to adapt store and forward mechanisms and capacities for support interfaces working as cache. This deficiency further complicates the monitoring tasks of the context managers in charge of continuously requesting the network status, which, together with the overhead implicit in the channels (due to complex IP headers), can, sooner or later, impact on the access.
- **Front-End Solution:** Solves some of the problems of SbC-3, but even so it still has certain drawbacks that affect the access. For example, control entities have to traverse the concentrator, which has to proceed with the translation of identities and the conversion of packets (e.g., Modbus/TCP to ISA100.11a), thereby increasing the time periods for the access and/or assistance in the

field. Additionally, the front-end is a concentrator that permits implementing diverse security mechanisms (authentication, authorization, detection, response and accountability) and complex resilience mechanisms, which probably require computational capacities and the adaptation of other approaches, like TbC-1, for redundancy. This redundancy helps protect the entire CPS from adversarial influences, and at least, in the main input points.

Unlike SbC-3, SbC-1 can take advantage of the optimized services of the CPS-specific protocols, such as redundant paths to reach a determined node in the network. This feature benefits, in parallel, the work of the NSM objects, which have to go through the system to determine the saturation levels, quality of service and activity of each resource included within a CPS. If there is isolation or congestion in certain parts of the system, these NSM objects can reach the concentrator using the mesh properties and the redundant services that many of the internal protocols offer. This way of concentrating the data at a single point favors the context management, and therefore the access management in the field.

- **Gateway Solution:** Adds certain functional features of the SbC-1 solution and the SbC-3 solution. Namely, SbC-2 is able to:
  - Configure communication environments based on CPS-specific protocols with support for store and forward mechanisms; and
  - Provide a direct connection to the nodes.

    However, these functionalities increase the complexity in the end-nodes, and therefore the execution of a critical action in the field. In addition, control entities have to traverse the gateway to analyze the incoming connections, detect threats (in the application layer) and log actions and events, further complicating the access. As for the management of the context, SbC-2 has similar capacities to SbC-1.

- **Hybrid and Access Point Solutions:** Two approaches that benefit the control architectures for maintenance and redundancy purposes. For example, TbC-1 solutions favor the access even when the primary interfaces (the front-ends or gateways) are subverted. In this case, redundant mechanisms are activated together with the DSD mechanisms to leave the access free to only authorized personnel with the specific roles and privileges (e.g., Operators or SECADM with specific control actions). However, the replication of resources (e.g., routing tables) is a handicap that may hamper the access and the management of the context. A way to lessen these complications would be through the implementation of suitable communication infrastructures composed of technologies potentially capable of processing and maintaining large databases with the capacity to ensure a high rate of replications.

Table 4 and Table 5 summarize all of these features and conclude this chapter. Specifically, we conclude that the full integration of the Internet-enabled devices to the Internet may produce high computational and communication costs where each device must process and maintain a routing table. This characteristic, certainly undesirable for the operational performance, is, to the contrary, beneficial in certain critical situations where the access to network interfaces is not always possible. Given this, we also believe that the hybrid configuration based on SbC-1/2 and TbC-1 in '*normal situations*' may still be effective to gain a desired interoperability, where the reliability of the communication can be subject

Table 4. Association of interconnection strategies and control requirements in CPSs

	Performance			Sustainability						Depend.		Survivability						
	Comp. overhead	Com. overhead	Responsiveness	Scalability	Mobility	Extensibility	Addressing	Access	Maintainability	Availability	Robustness/ resilience	Secure channel	Authentication	Authorization	Detection & response	Accountability	Trust	Privacy
SbC-1	★	O	★,O	+	+	★	◇	◇,O	−	−	◇	◇	◇	◇	◇	+	◇	◇
SbC-2	★	O	★,O	+	+	★	+	O	−	−	◇	◇	◇	◇	◇	+	◇	◇
SbC-3	★	−	★	+	+	★	−	+	+	+	+	●	●	●	◇	★,●	◇	◇
TbC-1	★	●	★,O	◇,●	+	★	−	+	+	+	+	◇	●	●	◇	+	◇	◇
TbC-2	★	●	★,O	◇,●	+	★	−	−	−	−	●	◇	●	●	◇	●	◇	◇

+	property provisioned ('−' is the opposite). Note that '+' is integrated as part of the rest of the symbols described below.
★	depends on the type of devices: weak, heavy-duty or powerful-duty.
●	depends on architecture (e.g., centralized or distributed) and technologies (e.g., TCP/IP).
O	depends on the optimization of the CPS-specific protocols.
◇	depends on the overhead implied in the services integrated (security, translation).

Table 5. Characteristics of the integration and their strategies in interoperability

	Interoperability			
	Rapid access	Transparency	Availability	Reliability
SbC-1	◇,O	+	−	★,◇,O
SbC-2	O	+	−	★,◇,O
SbC-3	+	+	+	★,◇
TbC-1	−	+	+	+
TbC-2	−	+	★	●

to the redundancy given by TbC-1. Only in emergency situations, can the solution SbC-3 be of special relevance where PDPs can transparently access the cyber-physical devices to manage '*critical situations*'.

To incorporate these combinations (i.e., SbC-1 or SbC-2 and TbC-1; and SbC-3) in complex systems, the interoperability architecture defined in Figure 1 must, therefore, be configured so that: *all the PDPs are able to access the front-ends or gateways in normal situations, and in turn, be able to directly access Internet-enabled devices in extreme situations.* But while these solutions can be effective for today's industry, it is still necessary to find a way to create self-sufficient systems where end-devices should form part of the IoT despite their current HW/SW constraints. So as future work, it would useful to study how to bring all the functionality of the Internet to specific cyber-physical devices and vice versa, and not in exceptional cases only.

ACKNOWLEDGMENT

The first author receives funding from the *Ramón y Cajal* research programme financed by the Ministerio de Economía y Competitividad. In addition, the work presented her has also been partially supported by PERSIST (TIN2013-41739-R) financed by the same ministry.

REFERENCES

Al-Kuwaiti, M., Kyriakopoulos, N., & Hussein, S. (2009). A comparative analysis of network dependability, fault-tolerance, reliability, security, and survivability. *IEEE Communications Surveys and Tutorials*, *11*(2), 106–124. doi:10.1109/SURV.2009.090208

Alcaraz, C., Agudo, I., Nuñez, D., & Lopez, J. (2011). Managing incidents in smart grids á la cloud. In The IEEE CloudCom 2011 (pp. 527–531). IEEE Computer Society.

Alcaraz, C., Cazorla, L., & Fernandez, G. (2015). Context-awareness using anomaly-based detectors for Smart grid domains. In *The 9th International Conference on Risks and Security of Internet and Systems* (vol. 8924, pp. 17–34). Springer.

Alcaraz, C., & Lopez, J. (2010). A security analysis for wireless sensor mesh networks in highly critical systems. *IEEE Transactions on Systems, Man and Cybernetics. Part C, Applications and Reviews*, *40*(4), 419–428. doi:10.1109/TSMCC.2010.2045373

Alcaraz, C., & Lopez, J. (2012). Analysis of requirements for critical control systems. *International Journal of Critical Infrastructure Protection*, *5*(3-4), 137–145. doi:10.1016/j.ijcip.2012.08.003

Alcaraz, C., Lopez, J., & Choo, K-K. (2016). Dynamic restoration in interconnected RBAC-based cyber-physical control systems. In *14th International Conference on Security and Cryptography (SECRYPT 2016) (vol. 4*, pp. 19-27). SCITEPRESS.

Alcaraz, C., Lopez, J., & Wolthunsen, S. (2016). Policy enforcement system for secure interoperable control in distributed Smart Grid systems. *Network and Computer Applications, Elsevier*, *59*, 301–314. doi:10.1016/j.jnca.2015.05.023

Bansal, S., Sharma, S., & Trivedi, I. (2012). A detailed review of fault tolerance techniques in distributed systems. *International Journal on Internet and Distributed Computing Systems*, *1*(1), 33–39.

Bessani, A., Veronese, G., Correia, M., & Lung, L. (2009). Highly-resilient services for critical infrastructures. In *Proceedings of the Embedded Systems and Communications Security Workshop*.

Bowen, J., & Stavridou, V. (1993). Safety-critical systems. Formal Methods and Standards. *Software Engineering Journal*, *8*(4), 189209. doi:10.1049/sej.1993.0025

Cárdenas, A., Amin, S., Lin, Z., Huang, Y., Huang, C., & Sastry, S. (2011). Attacks against process control systems: Risk assessment, detection, and response. In *The 6th ACM Symposium on Information, Computer and Communications Security* (pp. 355–366). ACM.

Christin, D., Reinhardt, A., Mogre, P., & Steinmetz, R. (2009). Wireless sensor networks and the internet of things: Selected challenges. In *8th GI/ITG KuVS Fachgespr¨ach Drahtlose Sensornetze*.

Coyne, E., & Weil, T. (2013). ABAC and RBAC: Scalable, flexible, and auditable access management. *IT Professional*, *15*(3), 14–16. doi:10.1109/MITP.2013.37

HART Communication Foundation IEC 62591. (2010). *Industrial communication networks Wireless communication network and communication profiles WirelessHART*. Retrieved on May, 2016, from http://www.hartcomm.org/

Hong, J., Suh, E., & Kim, S. (2009). Context-aware systems. *Expert Systems with Applications*, *36*(4), 8509–8522. doi:10.1016/j.eswa.2008.10.071

IEC-62351. (2007). *IEC-62351 (1-8): Information security for power system control operations, international electrotechnical commission*. Retrieved in May 2016, from http://www.iec.ch/smartgrid/standards/

ISA100. 11a - IEC 62734. (2009). *Wireless systems for industrial automation: Process control and related applications*. Retrieved on May 2016, from http://www.isa.org/

Kalogridis, G., Efthymiou, C., Denic, S., Lewis, T., & Cepeda, R. (2010). Privacy for smart meters: Towards undetectable appliance load signatures. In IEEE SmartGridComm (pp. 232–237). IEEE.

Knight, J., & Strunk, E. (2004). Achieving critical system survivability through software architectures. In *Architecting Dependable Systems II* (Vol. 3069, pp. 51–78). Springer. doi:10.1007/978-3-540-25939-8_3

Kuzlu, M., & Pipattanasomporn, M. (2013). Assessment of communication technologies and network requirements for different smart grid applications. In Innovative Smart Grid Technologies (pp. 1–6).

Montenegro, G., Kushalnagar, N., Hui, J., & Culler, D. (2007). *RFC 4944: Transmission of IPv6 packets over IEEE 802.15.4 networks*. RFC.

Ovidiu, V., Harrison, M., Vogt, H., Kalaboukas, K., Tomasella, M., Wouters, K., Gusmeroli, S., & Haller, S. (2009). Internet of things strategic research roadmap. *European Commission - Information Society and Media DG*.

Pai, S., Meingast, M., Roosta, T., Bermudez, S., Wicker, S. B., Mulligan, D. K., & Sastry, S. (2009). Transactional confidentiality in sensor networks. *IEEE Security and Privacy*, *6*(4), 28–35. doi:10.1109/MSP.2008.107

Ruchika, M. (2013). *Schemes for surviving advanced persistent threats* (Dissertation). Faculty of the Graduate School of the University at Buffalo, State University of New York.

IEEE Standard 802.15.4-2006. (2006). *Wireless medium access control and physical layer specifications for low-rate wireless personal area networks*. IEEE.

Treaster, M. (2005). *A survey of fault-tolerance and fault-recovery techniques in parallel systems*. CoRR, abs/cs/0501002.

United Nations General Assembly. (1987). Towards Sustainable Development, Commission on Environment and Development: Our Common Future. Document, A/42/427. Author.

Yan, Y., Qian, Y., Sharif, H., & Tipper, D. (2012). A survey on smart grid communication infrastructures: Motivations, requirements and challenges. *IEEE Communications Surveys & Tutorials*, (99), 1–16.

Zeadally, S., Pathan, A., Alcaraz, C., & Badra, M. (2012). Towards privacy protection in smart grid. *Wireless Personal Communications*, *73*(1), 23–50. doi:10.1007/s11277-012-0939-1

ZigBee Alliance. (2010). *Zigbee specifications*. Retrieved in May 2016, from http://www.zigbee.org/

Section 3
Intrusion Detection Systems and Cryptography Solutions

Chapter 9
Novel Intrusion Detection Mechanism with Low Overhead for SCADA Systems

Leandros Maglaras
De Montfort University, UK

Jianmin Jiang
Shenzhen University, China

Helge Janicke
De Montfort University, UK

Andrew Crampton
University of Huddersfield, UK

ABSTRACT

SCADA (Supervisory Control and Data Acquisition) systems are a critical part of modern national critical infrastructure (CI) systems. Due to the rapid increase of sophisticated cyber threats with exponentially destructive effects, intrusion detection systems (IDS) must systematically evolve. Specific intrusion detection systems that reassure both high accuracy, low rate of false alarms and decreased overhead on the network traffic must be designed for SCADA systems. In this book chapter we present a novel IDS, namely K-OCSVM, that combines both the capability of detecting novel attacks with high accuracy, due to its core One-Class Support Vector Machine (OCSVM) classification mechanism and the ability to effectively distinguish real alarms from possible attacks under different circumstances, due to its internal recursive k-means clustering algorithm. The effectiveness of the proposed method is evaluated through extensive simulations that are conducted using realistic datasets extracted from small and medium sized HTB SCADA testbeds.

INTRODUCTION

In order to modernize the national critical infrastructure, cyber-physical systems are becoming a vital part of them. Cyber-attacks tend to target important assets of the system, taking advantage of vulnerabilities on the architecture design or weaknesses of the defense systems. Lately several research efforts have revealed the importance of human factor on the cyber security assurance of a system (Evans, 2016; Ayres, 2016). Most of the weaknesses in CIs arise from the fact that system architects tend to adopt off-the-shelf technologies from the IT world, without a significant change, thus relying on the "airgap"

DOI: 10.4018/978-1-5225-1829-7.ch009

security principle that falsely assumes that an apparently isolated and obscure systems are implicitly secure. The integration of new technologies, especially Internet-like communications networks, may introduce some new threats to the security of a smart grid. In such a network there are three crucial aspects of security that may be threatened due to the CIA-triad, these being: confidentiality, integrity, and availability (Woo, 2015)

- Confidentiality is the property that information is not made available or disclosed to unauthorized individuals, entities or processes. An attack on this occurs when an unauthorized person, entity or process enters the system and accesses the information.
- Integrity refers to safeguarding the accuracy and completeness of assets, which ensures that the information in the system will not be modified by attacks.
- Availability pertains to the property of being accessible and usable upon demand by an authorized entity. The resources need to be kept accessible at all times to authorized entities or processes.

The integration of new technologies such as smart meters and sensors can bring new vulnerabilities to a smart grid that combined with the traditional cyber threats like malware, spyware and computer viruses make the situation complex and hard to deal with. (Sadeghi, 2015). In the three main control systems of a CI, the SCADA is the central nerve system that constantly collects the latest status from remote units, such as RTUs and PLCs. The communication between the different sub networks and the control system of a power grid can be blocked or cut off due to component failures or communication delays. If one of the crucial communication channels fails to connect in the operational environment, the control of important facilities may be impossible leading to possible power outages. In this situation, the effect of some widely known attacks can have devastating consequences on SCADA systems.

Intrusion detection systems can be classified into centralized intrusion detection systems (CIDS) and distributed intrusion detection systems (DIDS) depending on how the different components are distributed (Kenkre, 2014). In a CIDS the analysis of the data is performed in some fixed locations independently on the number of hosts that are monitored, while in a DIDS several IDS can be located in different places inside the smart grid. DIDS has specific advantages over CIDS. For instance, it is highly scalable easily extensible and scalable (Vasilomanolakis, 2014). It is evident that the development of distributed IDS specifically designed for SCADA systems, being able to ensure an adequate balance between high accuracy, low false alarm rate and reduced network traffic overhead, is needed. The above discussion clearly indicates that specific intrusion detection systems that reassure both high accuracy, low rate of false alarms and decreased overhead on the network traffic need to be designed for SCADA systems. Based on this need, new IDSs are constantly introduced belonging to two main categories; signature based and misuse detection. There has been considerable amount of work regarding SCADA intrusion and anomaly detection. Some IDS solutions involve combining network traces and physical process control data (Gao, 2010), other focus on detection of anomalies on network traffic (Yang, 2014) while there exist approaches that use machine-learning techniques (Maglaras, 2014), among others.

BACKGROUND

Intrusion detection can be categorized based on principal system characteristics as anomaly detection, signature detection and hybrid/compound detection. Countless research has been con- ducted in an attempt to answer the question of how to study the effectiveness of intrusion detection systems and how to handle attacks against intrusion detection systems themselves (Khan, 2007; Mukkamala, 2002; Maglaras, 2016; Cook, 2016). Although many quality contributions exist in this area, there is still plenty of space to improve areas in IDS development. Based on expert opinions there is a general consensus regarding the current state of network IDS. Many organizations are opting into purchasing signature based intrusion detection systems, due to the fact that they require less supervision, offer more automation and consume less time in setting features; therefore there is a belief that chances of human error are reduced. Furthermore, its widely stated that the majority of these organisations will employ IDSs that are not suited to their system needs as they simply pick the biggest brands, which may offer simplicity but on the same time they are left without an understanding of how to use these systems. Many experts state that issues still remain in identifying new forms of intrusion and in order to stay ahead, the cyber security industry must continue to develop IDS and organisations train key staff on how to use these devices rather than relying solely on automation

Misuse Detection Systems, commonly referred to as signature based detection systems since they work by using patterns of recognized attacks or known critical points in a system, can be used in order to find and match known intrusions. One big family of such intrusion detection algorithms is rule based algorithms (Roesch, 1999). Misuse detection offers greater accuracy and can efficiently detect variations of recognized attacks. Furthermore, such IDS also offer more meaningful intrusion diagnostics when an alarm is triggered by detailing diagnostic information about the cause of an alarm. In real applications though, during abnormal situations, the behavior of the system cannot be predicted and does not follow any known pattern or rule. This characteristic makes rule based algorithms incapable of detecting novel intrusions.

An anomaly detection based system uses the normal profile of a system or user to determine its decision making process, (Ahmed, 2016; Maglaras L. A., 2014; Shang, 2015). Development begins at the point at which the detector forms a judgment on behavior that constitutes to normal for the observed object in question and then a percentage of this activity may be flagged as suspicious and a preserved action is then taken. Generally, anomaly detection can be regarded as binary classification problem and thus many classification algorithms which are utilized for detecting anomalies, such as neural networks, support vector machines, K-nearest neighbor (KNN) and Hidden Markov model can be used. However, strictly speaking, they are not intrusion detection algorithms, as they require knowing what kind of anomaly is expecting, which deviates the fundamental object of intrusion detection. In addition these algorithms may be sensitive to noise in the training samples.

Segmentation and clustering algorithms (Portnoy, 2001) seem to be better choices because they do not need to know the signatures of the series. The shortages of such algorithms are that they always need parameters to specify a proper number of segmentation or clusters and the detection procedure has to shift from one state to another state. Negative selection algorithms (Kim, 2001) on the other hand, are designed for one-class classification; however, these algorithms can potentially fail with the increasing diversity of normal set and they are not meant to the problem with a small number of self-samples, or general classification problem where probability distribution plays a crucial role. Furthermore, negative selection only works for a standard sequence, which is not suitable for on line detection. Other algorithms, such as time series analysis (Viinikka, 2006) are also used as anomaly detection systems, but again, they may not be suitable for most of the real application cases.

To minimize the above mention drawbacks an intelligent approach based on OCSVM [One- Class Support Vector Machine] principles is proposed for intrusion detection. OCSVM is a natural extension of the support vector algorithm to the case of unlabeled data, especially for detection of outlier. The OCSVM algorithm maps input data into a high dimensional feature space (via a kernel) and iteratively finds the maximal margin hyperplane which best separates the training data from the origin.

OCSVM principles have shown great potential in the area of anomaly detection (Wang, 2004; Ma, 2003; Li, 2003). IDS can provide active detection and automated responses during intrusions (Dasgupta, 2001). The CockpitCI Framework detailed in (Cruz, 2014) uses a number of separate OCSVMs which are individually modelled for different parts of the ICS. The output of these is aggregated by a Main Correlator before being reported to the Security Management Platform Commercial IDS products such as NetRanger, RealSecure, and Omniguard Intruder alert work on attack signatures. These signatures needed to be updated by the vendors on a regular basis in order to protect from new types of attacks. Most of the current intrusion detection commercial software are based on approaches with statistics embedded feature processing, time series analysis and pattern recognition techniques. Several extensions of OCSVM method have been introduced lately (Glazer, 2013), (Song, 2008). OCSVM similar to other one-class classifiers e.g. GDE (Eskin, 2002), PGA (Knorr, 1997), suffer from false positive and over fitting situations. Intrusion detection systems (IDS) fail to deal with all kinds of attacks, while on the other hand, false alarms that are arisen from high sensitive IDS arise high economic risks.

For the OCSVM with an RBF kernel, two parameters σ and ν need to be carefully selected in order to obtain the optimal classification result. A common strategy is to separate the data set into two parts, of which one is considered unknown. The prediction accuracy obtained from the unknown set more precisely reflects the performance on classifying an independent data set. An improved version of this procedure is known as cross-validation. Cross-validation is a model validation technique for assessing how the results of a statistical analysis will generalize to an independent data set. It is mainly used in settings where the goal is prediction, and one wants to estimate how accurately a predictive model will perform in practice.

In ν-fold cross-validation (Burman, 1989; Friedman, 2001), the training set is divided into ν subsets of equal size. Sequentially one subset is tested using the classifier trained on the remaining ν-1 subsets. Thus, each instance of the whole training set is predicted once so the cross-validation accuracy is the percentage of data which are correctly classified. The cross-validation procedure can prevent the over fitting problem.

Using an ensemble of decision mechanisms with different parameters is another method to have an optimal result. An ensemble of classifiers (Menahem, 2013) is a set of classifiers whose individual decisions are combined in some way. more trusted final decision. Ensemble systems of classifiers are widely used for intrusion detection in networks. Classifier ensemble design aims to include mutually complementary individual classifiers which are characterized by high diversity either in terms of classifier structure (Tsoumakas, 2004), internal parameters (Kim M. J., 2010) or classifier inputs (Krawczyk, 2014).

Unnthorsson (2003) proposed another method to select parameters for the OCSVM. In their method, ν was first set to a user-specified allowable fraction of misclassification of the target class (e.g. 1% or 5%), then the appropriate σ value was selected as the value for the classification accuracy curve of training samples first reaches $1 - \nu$. The obtained ν and σ combination can then be used in the OCSVM classification.

OCSVM similar to other one-class classifiers suffer from false positive and over fitting. The former is a situation that occurs when the classifier fires an alarm in the absence of real anomaly in the system and happens when parameter σ has too large vale. The latter is the situation when a model begins to memorize training data rather than learning to generalize from trend and it shows up when parameter σ is given relatively small value (Li X. L., 2008).

In this book chapter we present a novel method that is based on the combination of OCSVM method with a recursive k-means clustering (Maglaras L. A., 2014, 2015, 2014) separating the real from false alarms in real time and with no pre-selection of parameters σ and ν. The proposed method is a natural extension of the support vector algorithm to the case of unlabeled data, especially for detection of outliers. The novel $K-OCSVM$ mechanism is trained offline by network traces, after the attributes are extracted from the network dataset. Output of the detection module is communicated to the system by IDMEF files that contain information about the source, time and severity of the intrusion. After the execution of the $K-OCSVM$ method only severe alerts are communicated to the system by IDMEF files that contain information about the source, destination, protocol and time of the intrusion. The main feature of $K-OCSVM$ module is that it can perform anomaly detection in a time-efficient way, with good accuracy and low overhead.

OCSVM METHOD

The one-class classification problem is a special case of the conventional two-class classification problem, where only data from one specific class are available and well represented. This class is called the target class. Another class, which is called the outlier class, can be sampled very sparsely, or even not at all. This smaller class contains data that appear when the operation of the system varies from the normal, due to a possible attack. In general cases, the outlier class might be very difficult or expensive to measure. Therefore, in the one class classifier training process, mainly samples from the target class are used and there is no information about its counterpart. The boundary between the two classes has to be estimated from data in the only available target class. Thus, the task is to define a boundary around the target class, such that it encircles as many target examples as possible and minimizes the chance of accepting outliers.

Scholkopf (2007) developed an OCSVM algorithm to deal with the one-class classification problem. The OCSVM may be viewed as a regular two-class SVM, where all the training data lie in the first class, and the origin is taken as the only member of the second class. The OCSVM algorithm first maps input data into a high dimensional feature space via a kernel function and then iteratively finds the maximal margin hyperplane, which best separates the training data from the origin. Using the kernel function to project input vectors into a feature space, nonlinear decision boundaries are allowed. Generally, four types of kernel are often used: linear, polynomial, sigmoid and Gaussian radial basis function (RBF) kernels.

Although the OCSVM requires samples of the target class only as training samples, some studies showed that when negative examples (i.e. samples of outlier classes) are available, they can be used during the training to improve the performance of the OCSVM. In this paper only normal data were used for the training of the method, though a similar to the one proposed by Tax (Tax, 2001), which includes a small amount of samples of the outlier class, will be also applied and evaluated in the near future.

OCSVM FOR SCADA SYSTEM

Cyber-attacks against SCADA systems (Barbosa, 2010) are considered extremely dangerous for Critical Infrastructure (CI) operation and must be addressed in a specific way (Zhu, 2011). Presently one of the most adopted attacks to a SCADA system is based on fake commands sent from the SCADA to the RTUs. OCSVM (Jiang, 2013; Zhang, 2008) possesses several advantages for processing SCADA environment data and automate SCADA performance monitoring, which can be highlighted as:

- In the case of SCADA performance monitoring, which patterns in data are normal or abnormal may not be obvious to operators. Since OCSVM does not require any signatures of data to build the detection model it is well suited for intrusion detection in SCADA environment.
- Since the detection mechanism does not require any prior information of the expected attack types, OCSVM is capable of detection both known and unknown (novel) attacks.
- In practice training data, taken from SCADA environment, could include noise samples. Most of the classification based intrusion detection methods are very sensitive to noise. However, OCSVM detection approach is robust to noise samples in the training process.
- Algorithm configuration can be controlled by the user to regulate the percentage of anomalies expected.
- Due to the low computation time, OCSVM detectors can operate fast enough for online performance monitoring of SCADA systems.
- Typically monitoring data of SCADA systems consists of several attributes and OCSVM is capable of handling multiple attributed data.

K–OCSVM

The proposed $K-OCSVM$ combines the well-known OCSVM classifier with the RBF kernel with a recursive K-means clustering module. Figure 1 illustrates the procedure of intrusion detection of our proposed K–$OCSVM$ *model*.

The OCSVM classifier runs with default parameters and the outcome consists of all possible outliers. These outliers are clustered using the k-means clustering method with 2 clusters, where the initial means of the clusters are the maximum and the minimum negative values returned by the OCSVM module. From the two clusters that are created from the K-means clustering, the one that is closer to the maximum negative value (severe alerts) is used as input in the next call of the K-means clustering. This procedure is repeated until all outcomes are put in the same cluster or the divided set is big enough compared to the initial one, according to the threshold parameter k_{thres}.

K-means clustering method divides the outcomes according to their values and those outcomes with most negative values are kept. That way, after the completion of this recursive procedure only the most severe alerts are communicated from the K–OCSVM. The division of the data need no previous knowledge about the values of the outcomes which may vary from -0.1 to -160 depending of the assigned values to parameters σ and ν. The method can find the most important/possible outliers for any given values to parameters σ and ν.

One important parameter that affects the performance of K–OCSVM is the value of threshold kthres. For given value 2, the final cluster of severe alerts that the method communicates to other parts of the IDS system is limited to 2 to 4 alarms. For bigger value (3 or more) the number of alerts also rises till

Figure 1. K−OCSVM module

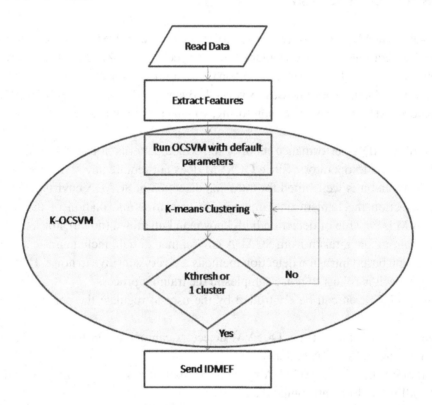

the method degrades to the initial OCSVM. The optimal value for the given parameter kthres is a matter for future investigation. In order to cooperate with the other modules the OCSVM module needed to be integrated in the *PID* system and communicate with the other modules. Once an intrusion is detected several actions can be taken by the *IDS* (intrusion detection system. These actions include recording of intrusions in log files, sending of alert messages, limit the bandwidth of the intruder or even block all connections from the intruder. In order to better cooperate with the other components/modules that are being used in parallel as detection agents, the OCSVM model sends IDMEF files.

PERFORMANCE EVALUATION

Training of OCSVM Model

The initial training of both the OCSVM and the *K−OCSVM* modules is conducted using several trace files

- A trace file that is sniffed out of a typical wireless network that consists of 10.000 lines each representing a packet send in the network.
- Datasets of a testbed under normal operation
- Datasets of a medium sized SCADA system under normal operation

To train the OCSVM, we adopt the *RBF* for the kernel equation. This kernel nonlinearly maps samples into a higher dimensional space so it can handle the case when the relation between class labels and attributes is nonlinear.

The training model that is extracted after the training of the OCSVM is used for on line detection of malicious data. Since the model is based on features that are related to network traffic, and since the traffic of the system varies from area to area and from time period to time period, possible generation of multiple models could improve the performance of the module.

The network traffic in electric grids varies according to the activity which is not constant during the day. Also in some areas the activity follows different patterns according to the local demand. These characteristics maybe be critical for the proper training of the module and the accurate detection of intruders.

Testing of OCSVM Model

We evaluate the performance of the method using data from the wireless network of the University campus, from a testbed that mimics a small-scale SCADA system and from a Hybrid testbed of a medium sized SCADA system. The parameters used for the evaluation of the performance of $K-OCSVM$ are listed in Table 1.

Wireless Network

In order to test our model we use another network trace file sniffed from the wireless network. The testing trace file consists of it 30.000 lines. We compare the performance of our proposed model against OCSVM classifiers having the same values for parameters σ and ν. We name each OCSVM classifier according to the parameters σ and ν: OCSV M0.07,0.01 stands for OCSVM classifier with parameters $\sigma = 0.07$ and $\nu = 0.01$.

In Table 2 we show the number of observed anomalies detected from OCSVM and $K-OCSVM$ respectively. From this table it is shown how parameters σ, ν affect the performance of OCSVM. Even for a value of ν equal to *0.005*, OCSVM produces over *400* possible attacks, making the method inappropriate for a SCADA system where each false alarm is costly.

In Figure 2 and Figure 3 we present the outcome that OCSVM produces for the training network trace under different values of parameters σ and ν. From these figures it is obvious that the outcome is strongly affected by the values of these parameters, making $K-OCSVM$ necessary tool for proper intrusion detection.

Table 1. Evaluation parameters

Parameter	Range of Values	Default value
σ	0.1 - 0.0001	0.007
ν	0.002 - 0.05	0.01
k_{thresh}	2 - 3	2

Table 2. Number of detected attacks for the wireless dataset (Kthres =2)

Parameter σ	Parameter ν	K−OCSVM	OCSVM
0.007	0.002	3	408
0.007	0.01	3	299
0.007	0.005	2	408
0.0001	0.01	3	274
0.1	0.01	2	295

Figure 2. OCSVM classification outcome (parameters: σ =0.007, ν=0.001)

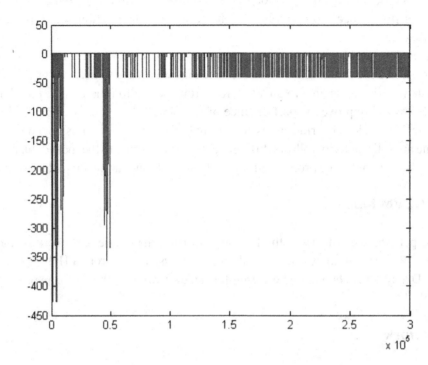

Figure 3. OCSVM classification outcome (parameters: σ =0.01, ν=0.05)

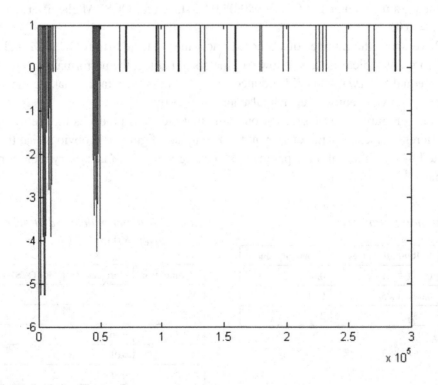

Testbed Scenario

The second trial is conducted off line with the use of two datasets extracted from the testbed. The testbed architecture mimics a small-scale SCADA system, comprising the operations and field networks and including a Human-Machine Interface Station (for process monitoring), a managed switch (with port monitoring capabilities, for net- work traffic capture), and two Programmable Logic Controller Units, for process control. The NIDS and OCSVM modules are co-located on the same host, being able to intercept all the traffic flowing on the network scopes. During the testing period several attack scenarios are simulated in the testbed. These scenarios include network scan, network flood and MITM attack.

Three kinds of attacks are being evaluated:

- **Network Scan Attack:** In typical network scan attack, the attacker uses TCP/FIN scan to deter- mine if ports are closed to the target machine. Closed ports answer with RST packets while open ports discard the FIN message. FIN packets blend with background noise on a link and are hard to be detected.
- **ARP Cache Spoofing - MITM Attack ARP Cache Spoofing:** A technique where an attacker sends fake ARP messages. The aim is to associate the attacker's MAC address with the IP address of another host, causing any traffic meant for that IP to be sent to attacker instead. The attacker could choose to inspect the packets, modify data before forwarding (man-in-the-middle attack) or launch a denial of service attack by causing some of the packets to be dropped.
- **DoS Attack:** Network flood is the instance where the attacker floods the connection with the PLC by sending SYN packets. In a TCP SYN flooding attack, an attacker sends many SYN messages, with fictitious (spoofed) IP addresses, to a single node (victim). Although the node replies with SYN/ACK messages, these messages are never acknowledged by the client. As a result, many half open connections exist on the victim, consuming its resources. This continues until the victim has consumed all its resources, hence can no longer accept new TCP connection requests.

In Table 3 we show the number of alert messages (IDMEF) sent from OCSVM and K−OCSVM respectively. From this table it is shown how parameters σ, ν affect the performance of OCSVM for the testbed scenario. While for the same network trace file OCSVM produces from 10529 to *10704* alert messages according to the values of the parameters, $K-OCSVM$ produces the same *120* alert messages. All the reported attacks are concerning the *DoS* attack that creates the biggest fluctuation in the network traffic.

Table 3. Number of produced IDMEF messages for the testbed scenario (Kthers = 2)

Parameter σ	Parameter ν	K−OCSVM	OCSVM
0.007	0.002	120	10529
0.007	0.01	120	10703
0.007	0.005	120	10584
0.0001	0.01	120	10602
0.1	0.01	120	10704

1. **Testbed Scenario with Split Testing Periods:** Since the attacks are performed during different time periods we divide the testing dataset in several smaller ones, each containing a different attack. Testing data consists of normal data and attack data and the composition of the data sets are as follows:

   a. Testing set-A': *1 - 5000*: Normal data
   b. Testing set-B': *5000 - 10000*: Normal data + **Arp spoofing** attack + **Network scan**
   c. Testing set-C': *10000 - 25000*: Normal data + **Flooding Dos attack** + **Network scan**
   d. Testing set-D': *25000 - 41000*: Normal data + **MITM attack**

From Table 4 we observe that not only the most important intrusions are detected and reported but also the total overhead on the system is limited. For all time periods the messages communicated reflect actual attacks in the network, except from the testing set-A'. In this time period *HMI* station demonstrated a significant variation in the rate that it injected packets in the system between testing and training of the module. This is due to the limited training of the OCSVM and can be avoided if training dataset consists of data that represent the traffic in the network during under workloads. The increased number of alarms created from $K-OCSVM$ for the dataset B' is due to the fact in this time period the attacker uses an excessive number of SYN packets in order to flood the communication channel.

2. **Hybrid Testbed Scenario:** The third trial is conducted off line with the use of large datasets extracted from a Hybrid Testbed (*HT B*) scenario. The Hybrid testbed architecture mimics a medium-scale SCADA system, comprising the operations and field networks and including Human-Machine Interface Stations (for process monitoring), six managed switches (with port monitoring capabilities, for network traffic capture), and several Programmable Logic Controller Units, for process control. The initial dataset consists of over *3* million rows, each representing a packet sent in the system, capturing network of several days. The dataset is split in *65* smaller ones of *50.000* rows. The datasets contain only data from a normal operation of the *HTB*.

Both OCSVM and $K-OCSVM$ are trained and tested with these datasets, using cross validation. The mean number of alert messages sent by the two modules is shown in Table V.

Using real datasets of a medium sized HTB SCADA system the performance of the proposed $K-OCSVM$ method is very stable compared to a simple OCSVM under the same configuration. This behavior is very promising since $K-OCSVM$ method has a very low false alarm rate (*lower than 0.02%*) while on the same time the overhead induced by the method is negligible (C.F. Subsection V-C. We must state

Table 4. Aggregated alarms produced by the K-ocsvm mechanism, compared to the initial alarms

Dataset	Initial alarms	Aggregated alarms
A	129	2
B	658	3
C	9273	120
D	203	3
All	10507	120

Table 5. Number of produced IDMEF messages for the Hybrid Testbed scenario (Kthers = 2)

Parameter σ	Parameter ν	K–OCSVM	OCSVM
0.007	0.002	1 - 2	40
0.007	0.01	1 - 2	207
0.007	0.005	1 - 2	105
0.0001	0.01	1 - 2	85
0.1	0.01	1 - 2	271

here that for the *HT B* we had available only non-malicious datasets for the evaluatioin of the proposed method. In the future when datasets containing malicious attacks are available an extensive evaluation of the *K−OCSVM* method is going to be conducted in terms of accuracy and false alarm rate.

Computational Cost and Time Overhead

Complexity of an intrusion detection system can be attributed to hardware, software and operation factors. For simplicity, it is usually estimated as the computing time required for performing classification of the dataset and outputting the final alarms. In order to evaluate the complexity of the proposed method we calculate the execution time and compare it to a simple OCSVM module. The evaluation is conducted on a PC with Intel core *2* duo *1.7* Mhz CPU, *2*GB main memory, *80*GB hard disk *7200* rpm hard disk and Microsoft windows *7 64*bit. In Figure 4 we represent the time performance of the method compared to a simple OCSVM module for the testbed scenario.

According to Figure 4 execution time of the proposed *K−OCSVM* is slightly bigger compared to a simple OCSVM method. The performance gap is around *5%* to *10%* for all the datasetsused in the simulation. Based on these observations we conclude that the system, performs a classiffication in a comparable time to that of a simple OCSVM classifier, and it thus can be adopted in soft real-time applications. We have to mention that the performance evaluation which is conducted in this subsection, does not include the time that each detection mechanism needs in order to create and disseminate IDMEF messages. It is evident that the OCSVM classifer, compared to the proposed *K−OCSVM*, needs significant additional time in order to send all the detected alarms.

Figure 4. Computational cost for the testbed scenario

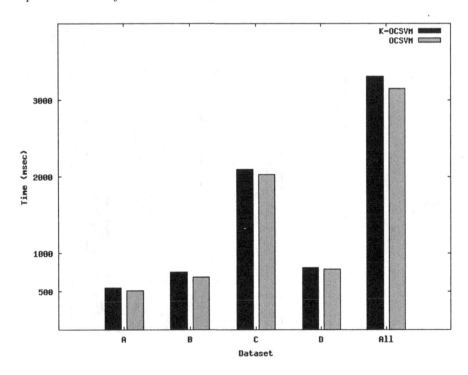

FUTURE RESEARCH DIRECTIONS

The proposed $K-OCSVM$ can significantly reduce the produced alarms from the OCSVM module that is the heart of the detection mechanism. The profound advantages of low overhead and low false alarm rate come with the cost of lower accuracy and higher computational overhead. In this section we discuss some enhancements of the proposed method that can improve its performance.

Parameter k_{thres}

As stated is Section IV $K-OCSVM$ method is a recursive clustering of the alarms produced by the OC-SVM module. This recursive procedure is used in order to distinguish severe from possible alarms and finally disseminate only those that represent an actual misbehavior of the system. This way the OCSVM module is enhanced in both the decreased overhead that induces to the system from the disseminated alarm files and in the decreased false alarm rate that it has. The recursive method stops when either all initial alarms are put in the same cluster or when the divided set is big enough compared to the initial one, according to the threshold parameter $k_{thre.}$

In the simulations presented in Subsection V the parameter is set to 2. When raising the value of this parameter the produced final alarms of the proposed $K-OCSVM$ method raises (See Figure 5). This raise also leads to a raise in the false alarm rate. On the other hand the accuracy of the method raises since less profound attacks are detected. By raising the value of the parameter above one limit the method degrades to the initial OCSVM. The optimum value for parameter $K-OCSVM$ varies according to the architecture

Figure 5. Parameter kthres affects the performance of the K−OCSVM mechanism (Testbed scenario with default parameters σ and ν)

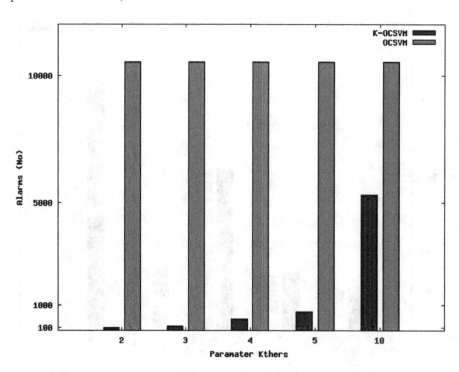

of the network. For big disperse networks large value of the parameter would lead to the creation of too many alarms from the module, while on the same time in a medium sized network very small value of the parameter would lead to a dangerous decrease of the detection capabilities of the module.

Except from the static configuration of the network, traffic conditions can also affect the performance of the method. In real SCADA systems the network traffic varies between daytime and night, weekdays and weekends. In order to cope with both static and dynamic features of the network an enhanced K−OCSVM method that dynamically adapts the parameter kthres, similar to (Campbell, 1999), (Cao, 2002) could be effective.

Multi Stage K−OCSVM

The proposed method uses only the values of the initial alarms in order to filter out those that don't represent an actual attack. That way attacks that cause significant variation in certain features of the OCSVM module are detected, while on the same time other more insidious attacks are passing undetected. A multi stage $K-OCSVM$ where both the number of attacks that share common characteristics, like origin, destination, port number e.t.c., and the actual values of the attacks can be developed in order to better detect different kinds of attacks.

Figure 6 represents a possible architecture of a two stage $K-OCSVM$ module. The number of the stages can be increased and the alarms produced by each stage can be further aggregated. The fusion of the outputs of the different stages can be done using any of the existing ensemble methods.i.e. majority voting, performance weighting, distribution summation, order statistics e.t.c.

The proposed $K-OCSVM$ may not be sufficient to build effective IDS on its own but is highly valuable when coupled with other methods, especially as an integrated part of a larger framework. It is likely that while anomaly detection provides opportunity to detect unknown attacks it will be necessary to combine them with signature and ruled based IDS components to achieve the greatest accuracy. Yang et al (Yang, 2014) have shown that multiple techniques can be used to create a highly effective IDS and Maglaras (Maglaras L. A., 2014) argue that model based systems alone are insufficient. Wang (Wang, 2004) crucially note that a greater understanding of the range of SCADA applications and protocols is required to achieve truly effective model based IDS components.

CONCLUSION

We have presents an intrusion detection module for SCADA systems that is based in OCSVM classifier and a recursive k-means clustering method. The module is trained off-line by network traces, after the attributes are extracted from the network dataset. The intrusion detection module is part of an distributed IDS system.

The method is tested on three different datasets. For the first testing scenario, traces of a wireless network are used. This test shows that the method is stable and its performance is not influenced by the selection of parameters ν and σ. For the second scenario, testing of the proposed module is conducted with datasets that are sniffed of a testbed that mimics a small-scale SCADA system under different attack scenarios. After the completion of the test, not only the most important intrusions are detected and reported by $K-OCSVM$ but also the total overhead on the system is limited. Finally extensive testing of the $K-OCSVM$ module with real datasets extracted from a medium sized HTB SCADA system shows

Figure 6. Architecture of a Multi stage K−OCSVM

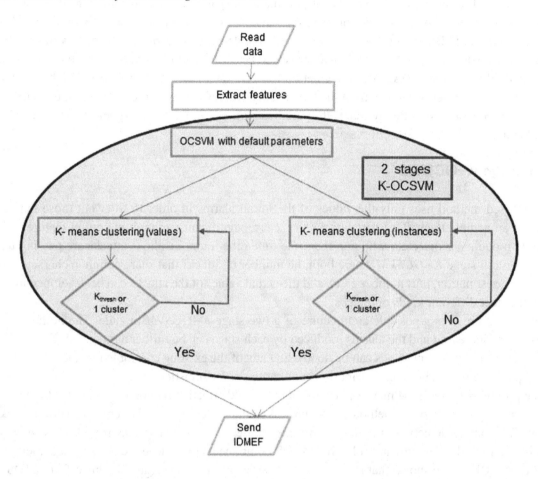

that the performance of the proposed *K−OCSVM* method remains very stable under different configurations. After the execution of the *K−OCSVM* method, for all the simulated scenarios, only severe alerts are communicated to the system by IDMEF files that contain information about the source, destination, protocol and time of the intrusion.

The main feature of *K−OCSVM* module is that it can perform anomaly detection in a time- efficient way, with good accuracy and low overhead. Low overhead is an important evaluation metric of a distributed detection module that is scattered in a real-time system, since frequent communication of IDMEF files from detection agents degrade the performance of the SCADA network. Recursive k-means clustering, reassures that small fluctuations on network traffic, which most of the times cause OCSVM to trigger false alarms, are ignored by the proposed detection module. The added computational time of the method compared to a simple OCSVM varies between 5% and 10% which results in a neglective time overhead. This overhead does not include the time that each detection mechanism needs in order to create and disseminate IDMEF messages. By adding the time needed in order to create and send each IDMEF file to the IDS management system the proposed *K−OCSVM* method prevails on the overall performance in terms of time efficiency. Finally we investigate how parameter k_{thres} affects the performance of the method and proposed a multi-stage *K−OCSVM* method for better accuracy.

REFERENCES

Ahmed, M., Mahmood, A. N., & Hu, J. (2016). A survey of network anomaly detection techniques. *Journal of Network and Computer Applications, 60*, 19–31. doi:10.1016/j.jnca.2015.11.016

Ayres, N., & Maglaras, L. A. (2016). Cyberterrorism targeting the general public through social media. Security Comm. *Networks*. doi:10.1002/sec.1568

Barbosa, R. R. R., & Pras, A. (2010, June). Intrusion detection in SCADA networks. In *IFIP International Conference on Autonomous Infrastructure, Management and Security* (pp. 163-166). Springer Berlin Heidelberg.

Burman, P. (1989). A comparative study of ordinary cross-validation, v-fold cross-validation and the repeated learning-testing methods. *Biometrika, 76*(3), 503–514. doi:10.1093/biomet/76.3.503

Campbell, C., Cristianini, N., & Shawe-Taylor, J. (1999). Dynamically adapting kernels in support vector machines. *Advances in Neural Information Processing Systems, 11*, 204–210.

Cao, L., & Gu, Q. (2002). Dynamic support vector machines for non-stationary time series forecasting. *Intelligent Data Analysis, 6*(1), 67–83.

Cook, A., Nicholson, A., Janicke, H., Maglaras, L., & Smith, R (2016). Attribution of Cyber Attacks on Industrial Control System. *EAI Transactions on Industrial Networks and Intelligent Systems*, 1-15.

Cruz Cruz, T., Proença, J., Simões, P., Aubigny, M., Ouedraogo, M., Graziano, A., & Yasakhetu, L. (2014, July). Improving cyber-security awareness on industrial control systems: The CockpitCI approach. In *13th European Conference on Cyber Warfare and Security ECCWS-2014*(p. 59).

Dasgupta, D., & Gonzalez, F. A. (2001, May). An intelligent decision support system for intrusion detection and response. In *International Workshop on Mathematical Methods, Models, and Architectures for Network Security* (pp. 1-14). Springer Berlin Heidelberg. doi:10.1007/3-540-45116-1_1

Eskin, E., Arnold, A., Prerau, M., Portnoy, L., & Stolfo, S. (2002). A geometric framework for unsupervised anomaly detection. In Applications of data mining in computer security (pp. 77-101). Springer US. doi:10.1007/978-1-4615-0953-0_4

Evans, M., Maglaras, L. A., He, Y., & Janicke, H. (2016). Human Behaviour as an aspect of Cyber Security Assurance. *arXiv preprint arXiv:1601.03921*

Friedman, J., Hastie, T., & Tibshirani, R. (2001). The elements of statistical learning (Vol. 1). Springer.

Gao, W., Morris, T., Reaves, B., & Richey, D. (2010, October). On SCADA control system command and response injection and intrusion detection. *IneCrime Researchers Summit, 2010*, 1–9.

Glazer, A., Lindenbaum, M., & Markovitch, S. (2013). q-ocsvm: A q-quantile estimator for high-dimensional distributions. In Advances in Neural Information Processing Systems (pp. 503-511).

Jiang, J., & Yasakethu, L. (2013, October). Anomaly detection via one class svm for protection of scada systems. In *Cyber-Enabled Distributed Computing and Knowledge Discovery (CyberC), 2013 International Conference on* (pp. 82-88). IEEE. doi:10.1109/CyberC.2013.22

Kenkre, P. S., Pai, A., & Colaco, L. (2015). Real time intrusion detection and prevention system. In *Proceedings of the 3rd International Conference on Frontiers of Intelligent Computing: Theory and Applications (FICTA) 2014* (pp. 405-411). Springer International Publishing. doi:10.1007/978-3-319-11933-5_44

Khan, L., Awad, M., & Thuraisingham, B. (2007). A new intrusion detection system using support vector machines and hierarchical clustering. *The VLDB Journal—The International Journal on Very Large Data Bases, 16*(4), 507-521.

Kim, J., & Bentley, P. J. (2001, July). An evaluation of negative selection in an artificial immune system for network intrusion detection. In *Proceedings of GECCO* (pp. 1330-1337).

Kim, M. J., & Kang, D. K. (2010). Ensemble with neural networks for bankruptcy prediction. *Expert Systems with Applications, 37*(4), 3373–3379. doi:10.1016/j.eswa.2009.10.012

Knorr, E. M., & Ng, R. T. (1997, August). *A Unified Notion of Outliers: Properties and Computation* (pp. 219–222). KDD.

Krawczyk, B., & Woźniak, M. (2014). Diversity measures for one-class classifier ensembles. *Neurocomputing, 126*, 36–44. doi:10.1016/j.neucom.2013.01.053

Li, K. L., Huang, H. K., Tian, S. F., & Xu, W. (2003, November). Improving one-class SVM for anomaly detection. In *Machine Learning and Cybernetics, 2003 International Conference on* (Vol. 5, pp. 3077-3081). IEEE.

Li, X., Wang, L., & Sung, E. (2008). AdaBoost with SVM-based component classifiers. *Engineering Applications of Artificial Intelligence, 21*(5), 785–795. doi:10.1016/j.engappai.2007.07.001

Ma, J., & Perkins, S. (2003, July). Time-series novelty detection using one-class support vector machines. In *Neural Networks, 2003. Proceedings of the International Joint Conference on* (Vol. 3, pp. 1741-1745). IEEE. doi:10.1109/IJCNN.2003.1223670

Maglaras, L. A., & Jiang, J. (2014). A real time OCSVM Intrusion Detection module with low overhead for SCADA systems. *International Journal of Advanced Research in Artificial Intelligence, 3*(10).

Maglaras, L. A., & Jiang, J. (2014, August). Intrusion detection in scada systems using machine learning techniques. In *Science and Information Conference (SAI)* (pp. 626-631). IEEE doi:10.1109/SAI.2014.6918252

Maglaras, L. A., & Jiang, J. (2014, August). Ocsvm model combined with k-means recursive clustering for intrusion detection in scada systems. In *Heterogeneous Networking for Quality, Reliability, Security and Robustness (QShine), 2014 10th International Conference on* (pp. 133-134). IEEE. doi:10.1109/QSHINE.2014.6928673

Maglaras, L. A. & Jiang, J. (2015). A novel intrusion detection method based on OCSVM and K-means recursive clustering. *EAI Transactions on Security and Safety*, 1-10.

Maglaras, L. A., Jiang, J., & Cruz, T. (2014). Integrated OCSVM mechanism for intrusion detection in SCADA systems. *Electronics Letters, 50*(25), 1935–1936. doi:10.1049/el.2014.2897

Maglaras, L. A., Jiang, J., & Cruz, T. J. (2016). Combining ensemble methods and social network metrics for improving accuracy of OCSVM on intrusion detection in SCADA systems. *Journal of Information Security and Applications*.

Menahem, E., Rokach, L., & Elovici, Y. (2013, October). Combining one-class classifiers via meta learning. In *Proceedings of the 22nd ACM international conference on Conference on information & knowledge management* (pp. 2435-2440). ACM doi:10.1145/2505515.2505619

Mukkamala, S., Janoski, G., & Sung, A. (2002). Intrusion detection using neural networks and support vector machines. In *Neural Networks, 2002. IJCNN'02.Proceedings of the 2002 International Joint Conference on* (Vol. 2, pp. 1702-1707). IEEE. doi:10.1109/IJCNN.2002.1007774

Portnoy, L., Eskin, E., & Stolfo, S. (2001). Intrusion detection with unlabeled data using clustering. In *Proceedings of ACM CSS Workshop on Data Mining Applied to Security* (DMSA-2001).

Roesch, M. (1999). Snort: Lightweight Intrusion Detection for Networks. *LISA*, 229-238.

Sadeghi, A. R., Wachsmann, C., & Waidner, M. (2015, June). Security and privacy challenges in industrial internet of things. In *Proceedings of the 52nd Annual Design Automation Conference* (p. 54). ACM. doi:10.1145/2744769.2747942

Schölkopf, B., Platt, J. C., Shawe-Taylor, J., Smola, A. J., & Williamson, R. C. (2001). Estimating the support of a high-dimensional distribution. *Neural Computation*, 13(7), 1443–1471. doi:10.1162/089976601750264965 PMID:11440593

Shang, W., Li, L., Wan, M., & Zeng, P. (2015, December). Industrial communication intrusion detection algorithm based on improved one-class SVM. In *2015 World Congress on Industrial Control Systems Security (WCICSS)* (pp. 21-25). IEEE. doi:10.1109/WCICSS.2015.7420317

Song, X., Fan, G., & Rao, M. (2008). Svm-based data editing for enhanced one-class classification of remotely sensed imagery. *IEEE Geoscience and Remote Sensing Letters*, 5(2), 189–193. doi:10.1109/LGRS.2008.916832

Tax, D. M. (2001). One-class classification. TU Delft, Delft University of Technology.

Tsoumakas, G., Katakis, I., & Vlahavas, I. (2004, September). Effective voting of heterogeneous classifiers. In *European Conference on Machine Learning* (pp. 465-476). Springer Berlin Heidelberg.

Unnthorsson, R., Runarsson, T. P., & Jonsson, M. T. (2003, August). Model selection in one-class SVMs using rbf kernels. In *Proc. 16th Int. Congress and Exhibition on Condition Monitoring and Diagnostic Engineering Management*. doi:10.1109/iThings/CPSCom.2011.34

Vasilomanolakis, E., Karuppayah, S., Mühlhäuser, M., & Fischer, M. (2015). Taxonomy and survey of collaborative intrusion detection. *ACM Computing Surveys*, 47(4), 55. doi:10.1145/2716260

Viinikka, J., Debar, H., Mé, L., & Séguier, R. (2006, March). Time series modeling for IDS alert management. In *Proceedings of the 2006 ACM Symposium on Information, computer and communications security* (pp. 102-113). ACM. doi:10.1145/1128817.1128835

Wang, Y., Wong, J., & Miner, A. (2004, June). Anomaly intrusion detection using one class SVM. In *Information Assurance Workshop, 2004. Proceedings from the Fifth Annual IEEE SMC* (pp. 358-364). IEEE. doi:10.1109/IAW.2004.1437839

Woo, P. S., Kim, B. H., & Hur, D. (2015). Towards Cyber Security Risks Assessment in Electric Utility SCADA Systems. *Journal of Electrical Engineering and Technology, 10*(3), 888–894. doi:10.5370/JEET.2015.10.3.888

Yang, Y., McLaughlin, K., Sezer, S., Littler, T., Im, E. G., Pranggono, B., & Wang, H. F. (2014). Multi-attribute SCADA-specific intrusion detection system for power networks. *IEEE Transactions on Power Delivery, 29*(3), 1092–1102. doi:10.1109/TPWRD.2014.2300099

Zhang, R., Zhang, S., Lan, Y., & Jiang, J. (2008). Network anomaly detection using one class support vector machine. In *Proceedings of the International MultiConference of Engineers and Computer Scientists* (Vol. 1).

Zhu, B., Joseph, A., & Sastry, S. (2011, October). A taxonomy of cyber attacks on SCADA systems. In *Internet of things (iThings/CPSCom), 2011 international conference on and 4th international conference on cyber, physical and social computing* (pp. 380-388). IEEE. doi:10.1109/iThings/CPSCom.2011.34

KEY TERMS AND DEFINITIONS

Critical Infrastructure: A term used to describe assets that are essential for the functioning of a society and economy.

IDS (Intrusion Detection System): A device or software application that monitors a network or systems for malicious activity or policy violations.

Kernel Methods: A class of algorithms for pattern analysis, whose best known member is the support vector machine (SVM).

SCADA (Supervisory Control and Data Acquisition): An industrial automation control system at the core of many modern industries.

SVM (Support Vector Machines): Supervised learning models with associated learning algorithms that analyze data used for classification and regression analysis.

SNORT: A free and open source network intrusion prevention system (NIPS) and network intrusion detection system.

Testbed: A platform for conducting rigorous, transparent, and replicable testing of scientific theories, computational tools, and new technologies.

Chapter 10

A Study on M2M (Machine to Machine) System and Communication:
Its Security, Threats, and Intrusion Detection System

Rami Haidar Ahmad
Technische Universität Berlin (TU Berlin), Lebanon

Al-Sakib Khan Pathan
Southeast University, Bangladesh

ABSTRACT

The increase of the applications of numerous innovative technologies and associated devices has brought forward various new concepts like Cyber-Physical System (CPS), Internet of Things (IoT), Smart environment, Smart cities, and so on. While the boundary lines between these concepts and technologies are often kind of blur and perhaps, each one's development is helping the development of the other, M2M (Machine to Machine) communication would surely play a great role as a key enabler of all these emerging scenarios. When we see the same smart concept from different angles; for instance, from the participating device, or human being's angle, we get different definitions and concept-specific standards. In this chapter, our objective is to study M2M system and communication along with its security issues and intrusion detection systems. We have also proposed our framework in line with the standardization efforts for tackling security issues of M2M.

INTRODUCTION

According to a prediction by Ericsson, by the year 2020, 50 billion devices will be connected to the Internet ("More than,", 2011). We have already started seeing the effects of Internet-based communications in a massive scale. A key aspect of this kind of communication is the underlying technology

DOI: 10.4018/978-1-5225-1829-7.ch010

of Machine to Machine (M2M) communication. M2M basically refers to technologies that allow both wireless and wired systems to communicate with other devices of the same type. In practice, Machine to machine (M2M) is a broad label which is applied to describe any technology that enables networked devices to exchange information and perform actions without the manual assistance of human beings. M2M is considered an integral part of the Internet of Things (IoT) and its nervous system (Duquet, 2015), which brings several benefits to industry and business. It is expected that in the coming years, both of our personal life and business life would be heavily influenced by M2M communication technologies. Usually, M2M systems allow a large number of diverse devices to communicate with each other over converged networks without human intervention. Recent studies (Duquet, 2015; Świątek, Tarasiuk, & Natkaniec, 2015; Hakiri & Berthou, 2015; Pathan, Khanam, Saleem, & Abduallah, 2013) mention a significant increase in the number of connected devices in various application domains such as eHealth, city automation, and smart metering, which will make a significant impact in the way we live today.

To get a better picture of M2M, we need to know that for quite a long time, it has been a real challenge to connect smart devices, sensors, meters to a network or to the Internet and to enable all these devices to share an application (bidirectional: sending and receiving information) without any manual effort of humans. After years of research works, with the advancements of various technologies, this objective has been somewhat achieved today. The enhancements of the capabilities of the end devices have truly started changing our daily life and more innovating business opportunities are expected from these in near future ("The Global," 2009; W. Ren, Yu, Ma, & Y. Ren, 2013). This scenario is what we call as M2M, i.e., Machine to Machine communication. Figure 1 shows a conceptual diagram.

A representative example of practical usage of M2M is in smart grid networks. The smart grid is an electronically controlled electrical grid that connects power generation, transmission, distribution, and consumers using Information and Communication Technologies (Zeadally, Pathan, Alcaraz, & Badra, 2013). Smart grid needs the support for bi-directional information flow between the consumer of electricity and the utility provider. To implement such an intelligent electricity network, smart metering system in M2M can facilitate flexible demand management in which case, a smart meter (SM)

Figure 1. Basic M2M concept

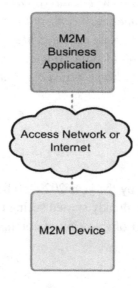

would be a two-way communicating device that would measure energy (e.g., electricity, gas, water, heat) consumption and communicate that information via some communications channels back to the local utility (Tan, Sooriyabandara, & Fan, 2011). In addition to that, there are models of M2M based sensor communications or mobile networks (Dohler, Boswarthick, & Alonso-Zárate, 2012) which could add more functionalities to the smart grid environment.

The European Telecommunications Standards Institute (ETSI) is now working as one of the leading standardization organizations producing globally-applicable standards for M2M sector (the readers are encouraged to see various M2M standards available at (W. Ren et al., 2013; "Machine-to-Machine communications," 2015; Chang, Soong, Tseng, & Xiang, 2011). The fundamental idea is to develop the existing vertical M2M applications, which use a multitude of technical solutions and diverse standards, into a fully interoperable M2M service platform that would permit horizontal business models (as shown in Figure 2 (diagram generated based on (Koss, 2014)). To clarify a bit, a vertical application basically refers to any software or other application that can support a specific business-process and targets a relatively smaller number of users with specific skill sets and job responsibilities within an organization. The horizontal M2M architecture would allow applications to share common data, infrastructure and network elements.

Figure 2. From vertical applications to horizontal business model

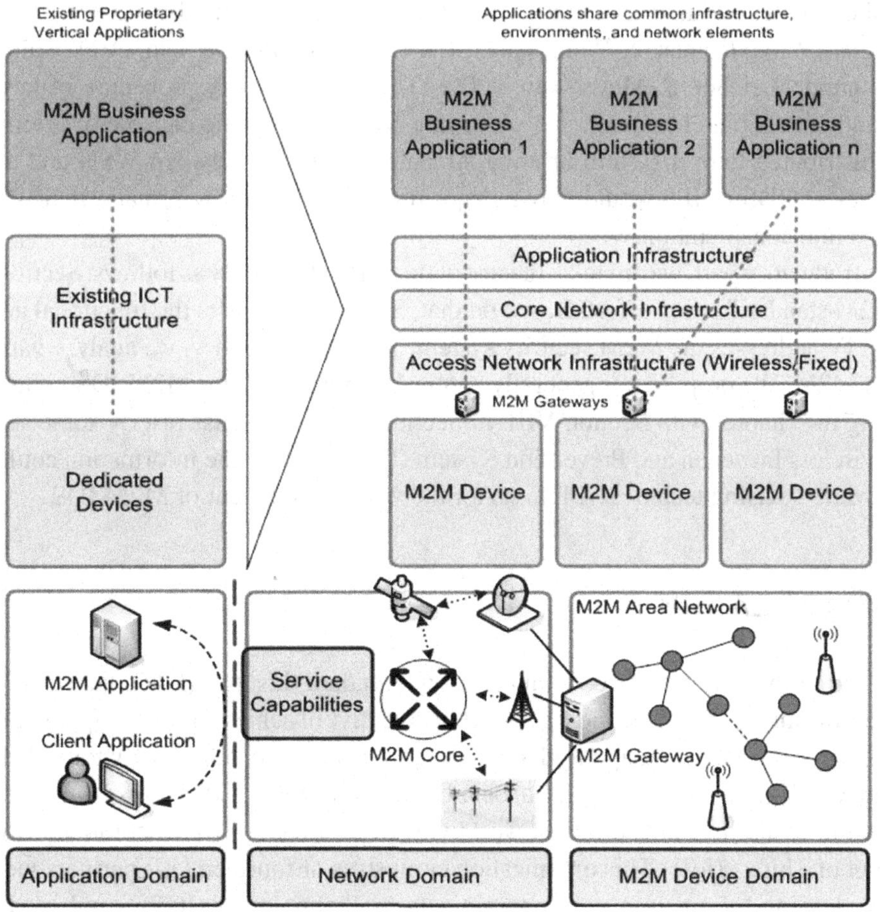

Security in Machine to Machine communication is addressed especially in the later ETSI specifications releases ("Machine-to-Machine communications (M2M)," 2011). Bootstrapping (e.g., Generic Bootstrapping Architecture (GBA), Extensible Authentication Protocol (EAP) based) key provisioning and hierarchy derivation, service connection and registration are well defined in the specifications alongside the Security Service Capability, xSEC ('x' can be the device gateway or the network).

While research in the field of M2M Intrusion Detection System (IDS) or Intrusion Prevention System (IPS) is still in its infancy stage and a big gap still exists, M2M systems have inherited many new challenges and security threats either from Wireless Sensor Networks (WSNs) or from other emerging computer networking technologies. Therefore, M2M IDS (MIDS) system has to combine the two features; first, of the IDS for computer networks and second, of the IDS for the WSNs or similar low-resource networks. This makes the intrusion detection/prevention issue even more complicated in this case. For instance, Wireless Sensor Networks (WSN) have a major vulnerability like the Denial of Service (DoS) (Wood & Stankovic, 2002), which would affect the functions of this network by causing the stop of transmission of valuable sensed information which would in turn cause the collapse of the whole decision making system that is based on the sensors (i.e., tiny physical device). Again, M2M can be affected by many others threats (as in a computer network) such as virus, unauthorized access of services, and so on (Lee, 2013; Qiu & Ma, 2015).

As M2M systems often have many small devices with low computational power and battery power, and they are implemented in a wide geographical area, such systems face relatively more security threats than the usual computer communication networks (Pathan et al., 2013; Aboelaze & Aloul, 2005; Abduvaliyev, Pathan, Zhou, Roman, & Wong, 2013; Lu, Li, Liang, Shen, & Lin, 2011; Shih et al., 2013; Cha, Shah, Schmidt, Leicher, & Meyerstein, 2009). The usual security procedure of key generation, distribution, authentication, encryption and so on, are not anyway alone capable of affording security for a widely distributed hybrid system or environment (like that is between WSN and computerized systems). Therefore, IDS or IPS would play a major role here, and any pragmatic IDS/IPS has to take all these details into consideration.

With this introductory part, we organize the rest of the part of this study as follows: Section II discusses the ETSI's M2M standardization effort. Based on that, Section III depicts the functional architecture of M2M, Section IV addresses the M2M security system. Then, in Section V, we analyze various security threats against M2M. We propose our generally applicable framework for M2M IDS in Section VI. Before concluding the chapter with Section VIII, in Section VII, we discuss briefly some supplementary issues about wireless Intrusion and Prevention System (IDPS) so that the information could be used for future works while devising technical solutions for the wireless segment of M2M IDS.

M2M STANDARDIZATION

As mentioned before, the European Telecommunications Standards Institute (ETSI) has been generating the common standardization of M2M technology with the objective of achieving global applicability. Another related organization, oneM2M, is supposed to be also a new standardization body for M2M technology. oneM2M ([oneM2M], 2015; Swetina, Lu, Jacobs, Ennesser, & Song, 2014) was launched in 2012 as a global initiative to ensure the most efficient worldwide deployment of M2M communications systems and the Internet of Things (IoT). This organization comprises of fourteen (14) partners including ETSI and seven other leading Information and Communications Technologies (ICT) Standards Development

Organizations (SDOs) representatives of different industry sectors. Existing vertical M2M applications use a multitude of technical solutions and diverse standards; hence, these formally established bodies are working towards developing fully interoperable M2M service platform to support various horizontal business models. The high level architecture of M2M is shown in Figure 3.

Based on such M2M architecture, the M2M system can be divided into different components which will be presented in the following subsections.

Device and Gateway Domain

- **M2M Device:** This is the end-user device, which can be either mobile or a static one. It can be a device with M2M application and M2M service capabilities (ETSI standardized device) or any other device such as Zigbee device, android or others (Non-ETSI standardized device).
- **M2M Gateway:** It is a device that acts as a proxy between the M2M devices and the network domain. It would run M2M application and use M2M service capabilities.
- **M2M Area Network:** It is any network that facilitates the connectivity between the M2M device and the M2M Gateway.

Figure 3. M2M architecture
Adopted from ("Machine-to-Machine communications (M2M)," 2011)

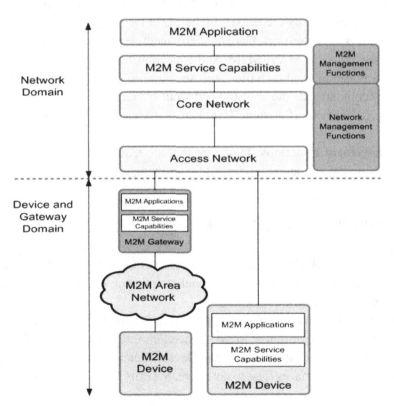

Network Domain

- **Access Network:** Allows M2M Device and Gateway domain to communicate with the Network domain, Access network may be but not limited to xDSL (Digital Subscriber Line - the '*x*' in xDSL is a variable that can change depending upon the speed and application of the xDSL technology like for instance, ADSL, VDSL, etc.), HFC (Hybrid Fiber-Coaxial), satellite, GERAN (GSM/EDGE Radio Access Network), UTRAN (Universal Terrestrial Radio Access Network), W-LAN (Wireless Local Area Network) and WiMAX (Worldwide Interoperability for Microwave Access).
- **Core Network:** It can provide the IP (Internet Protocol) connectivity, the service and network control functions, Interconnection (with other networks), Roaming and other services. Access network and the core network can be assumed together as a mobile operator providing the M2M services.
- **M2M Service Capabilities:** Provide M2M functions that are to be shared by different applications by exposing them through a set of open interfaces. M2M service capabilities use Core Network functionalities.
- **M2M Applications:** These applications run using M2M service capabilities so they are accessible through open interfaces.
- **M2M Management Functions:** These are the functions required for managing M2M Service Capabilities in the Network Domain. MSBF (M2M Service Bootstrap Function) is the first function and is realized within an appropriate server. It is responsible of facilitating the bootstrapping of M2M service layer security credentials in the M2M Device (or M2M Gateway) and the M2M Service Capabilities in the Network Domain. Permanent security credentials that are bootstrapped using MSBF are stored in MAS (M2M Authentication Server), a safe location, which can be an AAA (Authentication, Authorization, and Accounting) server. MSBF can be included within MAS, or it may communicate the bootstrapped security credentials to MAS, through an appropriate interface (e.g., Diameter (Calhoun, Zorn, Pan, & Akhtar, 2001) for the case where MAS is an AAA server).
- **Network Management Functions:** Functions that are required to manage the Access and Core Networks: Provisioning, Supervision, Fault Management, etc.

FUNCTIONAL ARCHITECTURE OF M2M

After knowing the overview of M2M system architecture as mentioned in the previous section, it is necessary to get some knowledge about the functional architecture of M2M, including the service capabilities and the reference points.

The main strength of M2M system is in the Service Capabilities Layer (SCL) which provides M2M functions that are to be exposed to different M2M applications through a set of interfaces. In this section, we will mention all these service capabilities in the Device, Gateway and Network sides. Also, we will learn about various types of interfaces (just to note here, Security Service Capability will be mentioned in the security system part later).

M2M Service Capabilities List

Service Capabilities ("Machine-to-Machine communications (M2M)," 2011) are in the three main parts of an M2M system, i.e., in the device, gateway and network (see Figure 4). Therefore, '*x*' here (as noted below) can be gateway, device, or network.

- Application Enablement (xAE)
- Generic Communication (xGC)
- Reachability, Addressing and Repository (xRAR)
- Communication Selection (xCS)
- Remote Entity Management (xREM)
- SECurity (xSEC)
- History and Data Retention (xHDR)
- Transaction Management (xTM)
- Compensation Broker (xCB)
- Telco Operator Exposure (xTOE)
- Interworking Proxy (xIP)

It should be noted here that, not all M2M Service Capabilities are needed to be instantiated in different parts of the system, but rather the interfaces are considered obligatory.

Figure 4. M2M functional architecture

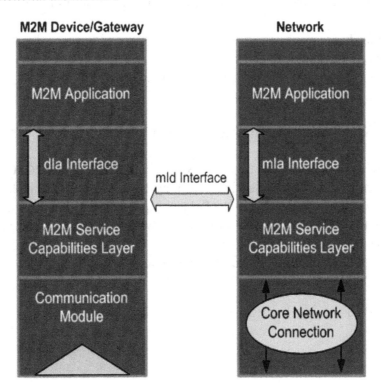

M2M Reference Points

- **mIa:** The *mIa* reference point ("Machine-to-Machine communications (M2M)," 2015) offers generic and extendable mechanism for Network Applications (NA) interactions with the NSCL (Network Service Capability Layer). The *mIa* reference point, between NA and NSCL, supports the following functions:
  - Registration of NA to the NSCL.
  - Requesting to Read/Write, subject to proper authorization, information in the NSCL, GSCL (Gateway Service Capabilities Layer), or DSCL (Device Service Capabilities Layer).
  - Requesting device management actions (e.g., software upgrade, configuration management).
  - Subscription and notification to specific events.
- **dIa:** The *dIa* reference point ("Machine-to-Machine communications (M2M)," 2015) offers generic and extendable mechanism for Device Application (DA)/Gateway Application (GA) interactions with the DSCL/GSCL. The *dIa* reference point supports the following functions:
  - Registration of DA/GA to GSCL.
  - Registration of DA to DSCL.
  - Requesting to Read/Write, subject to proper authorization, information in the NSCL (Network Service Capabilities Layer), GSCL, or DSCL.
  - Subscription and notification to specific events.
  - Requesting the creation, deletion and listing of group(s).
- **mId:** The *mId* reference point offers generic and extendable mechanism for SCL interactions. *mId* reference point usually exists between SCLs and supports the following:
  - Registration of a DSCL/GSCL to NSCL.
  - Requesting to Read/Write, subject to proper authorization, information in the NSCL, GSCL, or DSCL.
  - Requesting device management actions (e.g., software upgrade, configuration management).
  - Subscription and notification to specific events.
  - Requesting the creation, deletion and listing of group(s).
  - Providing security related features.

These reference points are mapped in the system overall as follows:

- **The Gateway:** It provides M2M Gateway Service Capability Layer (GSCL), communicates through the *mId* to the Network Service Capability Layer (NSCL) and it should communicate with the Gateway Application (GA) or the Device Application (DA) through the *dIa* interface.
- **The Device (with M2M service capabilities):** Communicates with an NSCL using the *mId* reference point and to DA using the *dIa* reference point.
- **The Device (not implementing an M2M service capability):** Communicates with the Gateway (GSCL) through the *dIa* interface.

ETSI-SPECIFIED M2M SECURITY SYSTEM

Given the status quo, Machine to Machine (M2M) is still a growing field, hence various studies and research works (Suo, Wan, Zou, & Liu, 2012; Roman, Zhou, & Lopez, 2013; Chen & Chang, 2012) insisted on the security issues of M2M, noting that we do not like to repeat the same mistake of the Internet - that the *Internet-boom* occurred first and afterwards, everyone began searching for solutions to the security threats (such as viruses and hackers). So, our take from this is that it is better to take security issues into practical consideration when first building a system.

While M2M is still being standardized, in parallel, some research works (Chang et al, 2011; Hongsong, Zhongchuan, & Dongyan, 2011; Barnhart & Bokath, 2011; Lai, Li, Zhang, & Cao, 2012; Bojic et al, 2014) are studying the security aspects of M2M. These studies are mainly concerned about how it is formed (Maras, 2015; Jover, 2015; Granjal, Monteiro, & Silva, 2013), its functional architecture, different mechanisms and topologies. Also, some other studies focus on the implementation of M2M in different domains and the tailoring of the security mechanism to fit in the new sectors where the M2M technology is expected to be implemented (Jover, 2015; Bartoli, 2013; Demblewski, 2015; Cimler, Matyska, Balik, Horalek, & Sobeslav, 2015; Arnoys, 2015; Satyadevan, Kalarickal, & Jinesh, 2014; John-Green & Watson, 2014; Sicari, Rizzardi, Coen-Porisini, Grieco, & Monteil, 2015; Jaber, Kouzayha, Dawy, & Kayssi, 2014). ETSI, by its turn, worked on the specification for standardization of M2M security system in most of its aspects, as a mechanism or as technical details. In this section, we will focus mainly on the different security mechanisms presented by ETSI without going into deep technical details of every mechanism since that is out of the scope of this chapter.

First, we will present the key hierarchy and realization, then the bootstrapping and service provisioning, security procedures for service connection between M2M Device/Gateway and the network, mId security, and finally, the security service capability in the device/gateway and in the network which governs all these procedures.

Second, we will present the supposed overall security mechanism; in other words, all the above mentioned functions and procedures - how they are supposed to work together so that the connection between the M2M device and the network is secured.

Key Hierarchy and Realization

In M2M, we have three types of keys: *Kmr*, *Kmc*, and *Kma* (see Figure 5). *Kmr* is the M2M root key, *Kmc* is the M2M connection key, and *Kma* is the M2M application key. *Kmc* is derived from *Kmr*, while *Kma* is derived from Kmc ("Machine-to-Machine communications (M2M)," 2011; "Machine-to-Machine communications (M2M)," 2015).

- **M2M Root Key (*Kmr*):** This key is used for mutual authentication and key agreement between the Device/Gateway M2M node and the M2M Service Provider. *Kmr* is also used for deriving an M2M Connection Key (*Kmc*). At the Network side, *Kmr* is stored in a Secured Environment within MAS (M2M Authentication Server). The Secured Environment should protect the information within (e.g., *Kmr* and the *Kmc* derivation process) from access or manipulation by unauthorized entities; also, in the device gateway side, *Kmr* must be stored within a Secured Environment Domain controlled by the M2M Service Provider ("Machine-to-Machine communications (M2M)," 2011; "Machine-to-Machine communications (M2M)," 2015).

Figure 5. Different types of keys of M2M system
Based on ("Machine-to-Machine communications (M2M)," 2011)

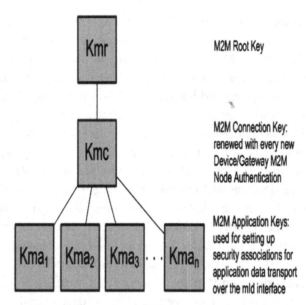

- **M2M Connection Key (Kmc):** This key is derived from Kmr, after successful mutual authentication of the Device/Gateway M2M node. Upon derivation, Kmc is delivered from MAS (wherein, it is derived within the same Secured Environment as Kmr) to NSEC (Network Security Capability Service), where it is stored in a local Secured Environment. Kmc expires upon termination of the corresponding M2M Service connection. Lifetime of Kmc is less than or equal to the lifetime of Kmr. A different Kmc is generated for every new M2M Service connection procedure of the Device/Gateway (D/G) M2M node with the same or a different Network M2M node ("Machine-to-Machine communications (M2M)," 2011; "Machine-to-Machine communications (M2M)," 2015).
- **M2M Application Key (Kma):** This optional key is used as symmetric shared secret for setting up secure application data sessions between NGC (Network Generic Communication) and DGC (Device Generic Communication) and/or between NGC and GGC, for authorized applications. Kma keys are derived from Kmc, after successful mutual authentication between D/G M2M node and M2M Service Provider. Kma is shared between D/G M2M node and NGC. Kma is used for authentication and authorization of M2M applications at the M2M Device/Gateway and for protection of application data traffic ("Machine-to-Machine communications (M2M)," 2011; "Machine-to-Machine communications (M2M)," 2015).

Bootstrapping

In M2M system, the main task of bootstrapping and especially, what is called *service bootstrapping* is provisioning the keys (M2M root keys) into the device or gateway from one side, and in the M2M Authentication server (MAS) from the other side and many other parameters as M2M node ID, SCL (Service Capability layer) ID and a list of NSCL identifiers to the M2M D/G node.

In ETSI M2M specifications, all the available Bootstrapping procedures have been explained in details, from the GBA (Generic Bootstrapping architecture) to EAP (Extensible Authentication Protocol) way of bootstrapping. In this chapter, we opt not to write in details about those procedures (like, Service Bootstrapping), neither about GBA and EAP. Instead, they will be only mentioned as we have done so far, with two figures explaining the bootstrapping (GBA or EAP) as a part of the overall M2M service connection. Figure 6 and Figure 7 are generated based on the standardization drafts presented in ("Machine-to-Machine communications (M2M)," 2011; "Machine-to-Machine communications (M2M)," 2015).

Security of Service Connection

After provisioning the M2M root key to the D/G M2M node, the service connection procedure can take place. The Service connection, as the bootstrap procedure, can have many mechanisms and that depends on the business relation between the mobile operator and the M2M service provider. With business relation between the mobile operator and the M2M operator, "*access network assisted*" bootstrap or service connection is used and this is different than the case when no business relation exists between the mobile operator and the M2M service provider. Service connection procedure is fulfilled through specific steps:

Figure 6. M2M service bootstrap based on the Generic Bootstrapping Architecture. Here, NAF stands for "Network Application Function", BSF stands for "Bootstrapping Server Function", HSS stands for "Home Subscriber Server" and AV means "Authentication Vector"

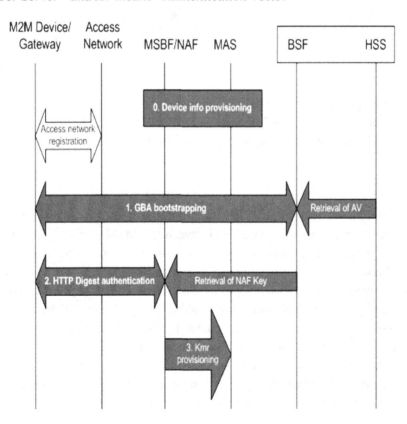

Figure 7. M2M Service Bootstrap based on EAP/PANA (Protocol for Carrying Authentication for Network Access)

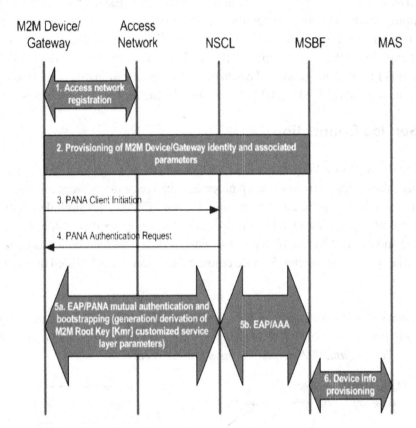

- The mutual authentication of the **mId** end points.
- Agreement of "*Intended to be used*" Keys.
- Establishment of secure session using encryption over **mId**.

mId Interface

There are many levels of security for the mId interface. In some cases, we can rely on the access network security since in this case, a trust relation exists between the M2M service provider and the Mobile operator, and an encryption will be on the access network. From another hand, a secure communication can be established between the D/GSCL and the NSCL using TLS (Transport Layer Security) or IPsec (Internet Protocol Security). *Kmc* or *Kma* shall be used as a shared secret key between the two end-points for performing the end-point authentication. Once a secure channel is established (e.g., a TLS or IPsec tunnel), mId protocols shall be carried over that channel for achieving security. Secure channel can be built only after the M2M Service Connection procedure takes place.

An *object security* level can also be used by securing data at the object (i.e., protocol payload) level. *Channel security* encrypts all the traffic and this is kind of inefficient. This potential inefficiency could be minimized by using security at the same layer as data are transmitted; hence, gaining finer-granularity security over the data. Each data element could be individually integrity-protected and encrypted without any regard to how other data are treated ("Machine-to-Machine communications (M2M)," 2015).

M2M Security Capability (xSEC)

- **Network Security Capability (NSEC):** The NSEC Capability in the NSCL provides the following functionalities:
  - Supporting M2M Service Bootstrap.
  - Supporting key hierarchy realization for authentication and authorization.
  - Performing mutual authentication and key agreement.
  - Verifying the integrity validation status reported by the M2M Device/Gateway and triggering appropriate post validation actions.
- **Gateway SECurity (GSEC) Capability:** In addition to supporting M2M bootstrapping process and key hierarchy realization for authentication and authorization, the other functionalities provided by the GSEC Capability in the GSCL are:
  - Initiating mutual authentication and key agreement.
  - If supported by the M2M Gateway, it should report the integrity validation status to the NSEC and react to post validation actions triggered by NSEC.
  - The GSEC is responsible for the storage and handling of M2M Connection Keys.
- **Device *SECurity (DSEC) Capability*:** In addition to supporting M2M Bootstrap and key hierarchy realization for authentication and authorization, the DSEC Capability in the DSCL provides the following functionalities:
  - Initiating mutual authentication and key agreement.
  - If supported by the M2M Device, it can report the integrity validation status to the NSEC and react to post validation actions triggered by NSEC.
  - The DSEC is responsible for the storage and handling of M2M Connection Keys.

Security Mechanisms at a Glance

All the ETSI-specified security mechanisms could be put together as a part of the overall M2M communication establishment as follows:

- **Application registration:** is the registration of an Application with the SCL that can be on the Device, Gateway or Network side, which will allow the application to use the functions offered by the local M2M SCL.
- **Network bootstrap:** will configure the M2M Device/Gateway with the necessary configuration data to connect and register to the access network (example: from UICC (Universal Integrated Circuit Card))
- **Network registration:** Registration of the Device Gateway with the access network.
- **M2M service bootstrap procedure & M2M service connection:** as were noted before.
- **SCL registration of D/G SCL with NSCL:** After successful M2M Service connection between D/G M2M node and Network node, it is the registration of the SCL of the D/G SCL with the Service Capability Layer on the Network side.

SECURITY THREATS AGAINST M2M

M2M communication will be mainly involved in eHealth applications, intelligent transportation, power generation and distribution, tracking systems, rural area monitoring and many other sectors; therefore, the M2M devices or what is called as the *low-level* of M2M stack, is the main part affected by the posed challenges. On the other hand, the M2M platform, as a core, is also a major target for many security threats and challenges such as viruses or unauthorized access to the offered services and so on.

Since M2M technology still remains as a field of research on various facets of it, we could get increasingly large number of innovative business applications in the coming days. Thus, making a complete list of all the security challenges and threats would be an extremely difficult task, if not impossible.

Security threats and challenges have been indeed studied in some previous works like (John-Green & Watson, 2014; Atamli & Martin, 2014; Rubertis et al., 2013; Singh, Pasquier, Bacon, Ko, & Eyers, 2015; Aris, Oktug, & Yalcin, 2015; Fink, Zarzhitsky, Carroll, & Farquhar, 2015; Nie & Zhai, 2013; Genge, Haller, Gligor, & Beres, 2014; Hossain, Fotouhi, & Hasan, 2015; Schurgot & Shinberg, 2015; Fremantle & Scott, 2015). In a continuous effort, some other works have tried to find enhancements and solutions to the weaknesses in the M2M security systems and proposed various mechanisms and techniques, as security management approach (Jung & Kim, 2013; Huang, Craig, and Yan, 2015), key generation (Granjal, Monteiro, & Silva,, 2013; Qiu & Ma, 2015; Lake, Milito, Morrow, & Vargheese, 2014; Liu, Gu, & Ma, 2015; Hussen et al., 2013), and distribution (Jung, Ahn, Hwang, & Kim, 2012; Shafagh & Hithnawi, 2014; N. Park, J.S. Park, & Kim,, 2014; Inshil, Jiyoung, Shi, & Kijoon, 2014), authentication (Qiu & Ma, 2015; N. Park, J.S. Park, & Kim, 2014; Hu et al., 2012; Kim, Jeong, & Hong, 2014; Doh, Chae, Lim, & Chung, 2015; N. Park, J.S. Park, & Kim, 2015; Jin & Hahm, 2013; Jin, Park, Lee, & Jun, 2013; Sun, Men, Zhao, & Zhou, 2015; Ukil, Bandyopadhyay, Bhattacharyya, Pal, and Bose, 2014; Kim, Jeong, & Hong, 2011) encryption technique (N. Park, J.S. Park, & Kim, 2015). In addition, some works proposed security mechanisms for M2M security, for end-to-end security (Chen, You, Weng, Cheng, & Huang, 2016; Lai, Li, Lu, Shen, & Cao, 2013; W. Zhang, Y. Zhang, Chen, Li, & Wang, 2013; Kothmayr, Hu, Brunig, & Carle, 2012), and other security models related to context awareness (Hu et al., 2012; Lee & Chung, 2012), or related to other techniques as cooperative security (Jung, Kim, & Seoksoo, 2013), distributed approach (Ben, Olivereau, & Laurent, 2012; Karim, Anpalagan, Nasser, Almhana, & Woungang, 2013) and in relation to device cloud (Moon, Lee, Kim, & Choi, 2014; Cagalaban, Ahn, & Kim, 2012; (Sicari, Rizzardi, Coen-Porisini, Grieco, & Monteil, 2015; Anggorojati & Prasad, 2014). Lately, as M2M is being used in different sectors, some works proposed specific security frameworks for different M2M implementation scenarios, as in eHealth (Granjal, Monteiro, & Silva, 2013; Lake, Milito, Morrow, & Vargheese, 2014; Saleem, Derhab, Al-Muhtadi, & Shahzad,, 2015; Choi, Doh, Park, & Chae, 2012), or in transportation (Lee & Kim, 2015; Masek, Muthanna, & Hosek, 2015), metering (Riker et al., 2014), mobile networks (Choi, Han, & Choi, 2015) and many other security frameworks (Mahkonen et al., 2013; Neisse, Steri, Fovino, & Baldini, 2015; Boubakri, Abdallah, & Boudriga, 2014) and mechanisms (Ben, Olivereau, & Laurent, 2012; Anggorojati & Prasad, 2014; Neisse et al., 2014; Gyrard, Bonnet, & Boudaoud, 2014; Farooqi, Khan, Wang, & Lee, 2013).

What we will be doing here is, we will mention all the known security threats and try to clarify the full picture of what M2M communication is facing as security threats. From the next subsection, let us know about the security challenges to the M2M system on the device and gateway level, and then, how those also affect the core or platform level.

Security Threats at the Device Level

Device Compromising

The wide implementation of the devices in different places and the overall system environment make compromising an M2M device an easy task which is not the case in the usual H2H (Human to Human) communication since human is holding the device. One of the general scenarios that we can imagine is some devices are deployed for rural observation and monitoring, so it will take just a little effort by an attacker to get to the physical device and then compromise it. From other hand, many devices will be deployed in indoor environment; therefore, the house owner or others in the house would have the full time to get access to the device.

What would happen if the device is compromised? The list of answers would be very long, which begins with the unauthorized use of the device. A famous case would be what happened in South Africa, as mentioned in ("No stopping," 2015):

As its high walls, electric fences and armed security patrols demonstrate, Johannesburg is well prepared for thwarting the ingenuity of burglars in most situations. But no one thought about traffic lights. Hundreds of lights have been damaged by thieves targeting the machines' SIM cards, which are then used to make mobile phone calls worth millions of South African rand.

In this case, SIM (Subscriber Identity Module) cards were stolen from the implemented smart traffic light devices! As a result, it caused many car crashes and cost thousands of money to fix the whole system. Hence, we learn that there is never an end to the capability of launching an internal attack on the system from the compromised node. This issue then enters into the domain of physical security which becomes more complicated and goes out of the general security issues of M2M or its applications.

Usually, the internal attacks are more dangerous since the other nodes and the system would behave normally with the compromised node as a trusted node and this could cause a significant damage (V.B. Misic & J. Misic, 2014) to the M2M system - even to the M2M area network and to the participating device (especially, in mesh network topology). Different kinds of viruses can also take the compromised node as a bridge to the core platform.

Denial of Service (DoS) Attack

In practicality, a DoS situation can occur due to any kind of incident that diminishes, eliminates, or hinders the normal activities of the network. Say for example, any kind of hardware failure, software bug, resource exhaustion, environmental condition, or any type of complicated interaction of these factors can create *denial of service*. It should be noted that the term 'DoS' indicates to a particular situation in the network and when DoS situation occurs due to an intentional attempt of an adversary, it is called DoS attack (Pathan, 2010a). Although attackers commonly use the Internet to exploit software bugs when making DoS attacks, here we consider primarily protocol- or design-level vulnerabilities (Wood & Stankovic, 2002).

An M2M system can be significantly affected by the DoS attack since such a system depends heavily on the M2M area network. We can imagine a scenario where M2M technology is used for the eHealth application (shown in Figure 8). Let us consider that there are thousands of smart metering devices (M2M

Figure 8. Denial of Service (DoS) attack scenario

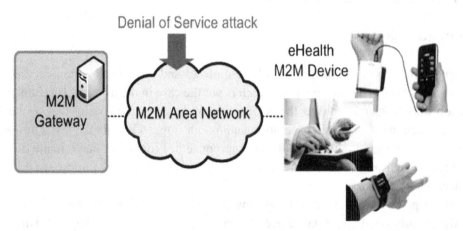

devices) implemented and connected to gateways through an M2M area network. Any jamming on the channel can break the circle and cause DoS; therefore, no information would be transmitted from or to the M2M device and this may threaten a patient's life. In this case and many other similar cases, M2M security challenges could affect human lives directly, not only the security of data or just the privacy issue.

In other situations, depending on the M2M area network topology (where the DoS attack is expected to happen), DoS attack can be much easier to launch. For instance, an access M2M area network based on mesh topology is very susceptible to such attacks ("Denial-of-Service Developments," 2000). Here, any compromised device can launch an internal DoS attack, potentially putting many nodes *out of the service* at the same time.

Viruses

The M2M Platform will be the target of different kinds of computer viruses and malwares (Dagon, Martin, & Starner, 2004) since it holds information as personal information and the most important fact is that it offers services which have good monetary value. Hence, the goal of the attackers can vary, from destroying the platform and putting it *out of service* by manipulating databases to control various functions and services, or by partly controlling the platform, snatching specific information about customers, locations and many other sensitive establishments - even partly controlling the platform to have unauthorized access to various services. This kind of threat (i.e., virus, malware) falls under the category of computer or computing device security (Wang, Streff, & Raman, 2012; Mohammed & Pathan, 2013) and it could really harm any computerized system involved in the M2M system.

M2M INTRUSION DETECTION SYSTEM: MIDS

So far, we have known that the M2M security system standardized by ETSI addresses a big part of the security area and manages many mechanisms for authentication, key provisioning, and other issues. As we have mentioned before, all these mechanisms are still insufficient to protect M2M systems from intrusion attacks. As per our detailed investigation in the area, we have found that though there are some other efforts to device specific IDS for M2M systems (Aris, Oktug, & Yalcin, 2015; Jung & Kim, 2013; Anggorojati & Prasad, 2013), there still remains enough scope of research on M2M security and especially, in the area of Intrusion Detection System (IDS). The way the intrusions are tackled or prevented or detected is not really clear in the ETSI specifications – in fact, we do not have any common scenario yet. Hence, we will address here the IDS for M2M.

After the overview of the M2M system, security system, and security threats for the M2M, in this section, we will try to draw the principle lines of an M2M Intrusion Detection System (MIDS). But, before that, let us have a look at the capabilities and limitations of the M2M devices since any IDS will rely heavily on those participating devices.

Challenges for Security System and for M2M IDS

Due to the heterogeneity and great number of the devices in an M2M system, designing a common platform for intrusion detection system would be very complex. There would be a wide range of devices ranging from the devices with low computational and battery power (Khan, Pathan, & Alrajeh, 2012) to smartphones and handheld or static devices that can have advanced technologies with high computational resources and battery power. The capacity of these devices is a very critical issue because the Device Level will be the actual basis of any kind of security mechanism:

- **Device Battery Power:** Battery power is a very important matter especially for security. First of all, battery power forms the most challenging issue since most of the DoS attacks focus mainly on exhausting the battery power so the device will be off and *out of service*. Second, battery power is related to the computational power or in other words, to the processor capabilities. When the processor is used heavily as in encryption and decryption tasks, the processor would consume more power and therefore, the device battery will run out fast. In the end, designing an M2M Intrusion Detection System must take into consideration the device battery power capability (Pirretti et al., 2006) because the battery power limits the overall available processing time of the device and the computational power of the processor (which is used in encryption and other security related tasks).
- **Computational Power:** The device computational power is a great challenge for the development and practical implementation of a security mechanism/system since the processor at the end would be doing all the ciphering/deciphering and calculations for generating/using keys or running the security codes. Most of the M2M devices except the latest smartphones are either sensors or other similar types of devices with low computational power, often incapable of performing huge and complex cryptographic operations (Azad & Pathan, 2014; Pathan, 2010b) for all the transmitted data.
- **Physical Security of the Device and Security of the Keys:** If someone can access the security keys in the M2M devices, it will be easy for him first to decrypt all the traffic from and to the device and he can send arbitrary data (malicious data) from this device. Hence, physical security of the device plays a role in keeping the implemented keys safe in the device. In addition to thinking about the physical security, the security keys should also be stored in the device in a secure way so that it would be difficult for any attacker to extract the keys, even if he gains physical access to the device (which will be very likely due to the uncontrollable wide implementation of M2M devices). A possible mechanism to ensure this kind of security could be using *tamper-proof* device

that would run self-destruction or erasing operation of memory if opened or touched or broken after deployment or the keys should be stored in a distributed fashion in different separate devices or so. Readers are referred to (Mo et al., 2012; Pathan, 2015) for further reading in this area.

- **Different Kinds of Devices with Different Protocols:** In M2M systems, we will have different kinds of devices and protocols (RFID (Radio-Frequency IDentification), Zigbee, Wi-Fi, etc.) and what is common among them is only the M2M network. Hence, this kind of heterogeneity is also a challenge for designing a common security platform for M2M since every technology has its own security standards and associated mechanisms. Figure 9 shows the pictorial view of the presence of different kinds of technologies (devices and protocols) in the M2M system.

More About MIDS

As we can see in the Figure 10, the supposed M2M security stack is formed from base to top. The Device Level physical security forms the solid ground of the security system since any kind of security system will be weak and vulnerable if the device level is exposed to manipulation and compromise. Hence, the first step would be to find solutions for all the security threats on the device level.

- **Device Compromising and the Physical Security of Implemented Keys:** Many existing solutions for such situations can be used to defend against device compromising, however the issue is that every solution is compatible with the devices of specific configurations and often, the specific way they are used. While many, if not most of those solutions are mainly implementable for the static (i.e., which does not move) devices, only a few may really work in the devices with frequent mobility.
  - ○ **Hardware Security:** There should be strong mechanisms to safeguard and manage digital keys for strong authentication and to provide crypto-processing. M2M device should also

Figure 9. Different technologies in an M2M system at the Device Level

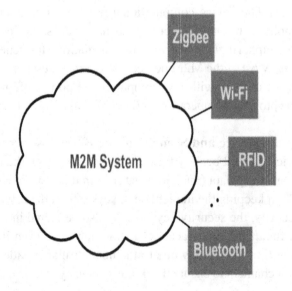

Figure 10. M2M security stack

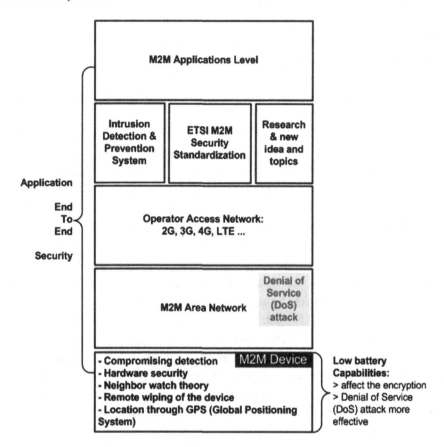

have strong password system which would be capable of protecting the device's secret keys from the well-defined attack/breaking attempts (Mo et al., 2012; Pathan, 2015).

○ **Neighbor Watch Theory:** This method is very effective in case of devices (sensors, actuators or the like) used in a close geographic proximity (e.g., rural regions monitoring, Intelligent transportation devices on roads). These devices can be implemented in an intelligent way in a cluster of 3 devices, where each device will have the responsibility of watching its neighbor by a *Beacon* message and whenever this message is off for a certain time (perhaps, due to the device compromising), a message can be sent to the gateway and then to the IDS server (Song, Xie, Zhu, and Cao, 2007).

● **Remote Device Wiping:** In many cases, the capability of remote wiping of the device can be an acceptable solution for protecting some sensitive information on it. Remote device wiping ("Remote wipe," 2015) refers to a security feature that allows a network administrator (or, device owner) to send a command to a computing device and delete data. It is very useful when a device is lost or stolen to erase all its data and to do a factory reset. Combining this capability with the other mechanisms (mentioned before), we can make it one additional component of the first level of the M2M security stack (see Figure 10).

○ **Devices Locator:** When the neighbor watch theory does not work (for instance, due to the geographical barriers or the way M2M devices are deployed/implemented), *Device locator* through the GPS (Global Positioning System) or through a local station (for tracking system) can protect the device from being manipulated or moved. In case of any unexpected move, the IDS will be alerted through the gateway (Pei, 2012). The majority of the M2M devices are supposed to be static devices and the ones that are mobile can be related to handheld devices or smartphones or such devices. Even so, many M2M devices could afford M2M security services while on the move allowing the location finding algorithms to work properly on the devices.

- **Different Approaches for the IDS:** Intrusion Detection System (IDS) basically refers to any system that detects and warns about illegal breaking into the system and misuse of it, or tries to prevent the entities having legal access from not abusing their privileges (Heady, Luger, Maccabe, & Servilla, 1990; Pathan, 2014). For this reason, the mechanisms in an IDS monitor everything (traffic) to find any potential intrusion. IDSs are mainly based on two types of underlying technologies: the *Misuse based* detection and the *Anomaly based* detection.
  - **Misuse based Detection:** Virus patterns and known threats are recorded in the IDS database, and the IDS searches and scans all the data traffic for a matching of pattern with the database. Once any suspicious data is discovered, an alarm is triggered. The main disadvantage of the misuse based detection is its weakness in discovering new threats (Abduvaliyev et al., 2013; Pathan, 2014; Roesch, 1990; Paxson, 1990).
  - **Anomaly based detection:** In this method, the IDS creates a normal profile for users based on their history of use and then, compare any activity with the usual behavior. Any unexpected change is considered suspicious. This way is very efficient in discovering new attacks and threats but the main disadvantage is that the system needs more computational power, often extra human efforts as well (Paxson, 1990; Chan, Mahoney, & Arshad, 2003).

There can be a third kind of approach, which is called the *Specification based* detection. This is basically a combination of the two major ways of detection, by using manually developed specifications to characterize *normal system behavior*. Table 1 shows a list of IDS frameworks that are somewhat related to the M2M applications and systems. A wide range of techniques are noted for the readers to get relevant references.

The Operational Concept of MIDS

Given the M2M device capabilities or the expected ways the devices will be implemented or deployment, or the different policies of intrusion detection systems that would be employed, the best idea of a standard M2M Intrusion Detection System (MIDS) would be what is close to the reality and could be adapted or adjusted based on the need for specific application scenarios. Hence, what we propose is formulating a general concept of IDS which can combine many other schemes related to intrusion detection or prevention activities. Therefore, hybrid intrusion detection systems (Pathan, 2014; Huh & Hai, 2011) are the best candidates in this direction.

There are a few practical implementation issues here that should be mentioned. First, due to the limited capacities, M2M devices would be incapable of saving the entire malicious data signature (viruses, malware, etc.) neither all the suspicious nodes' IDs (Identities) (to accomplish misuse detection policy

Table 1. Different relevant IDS frameworks at a glance

IDS Title	Used Detection Policy
Hybrid intrusion detection system (Hai, Khan, & Huh,, 2007)	Misuse and anomaly based
Spontaneous Watchdog (Roman, Zhou, & Lopez, 2006)	Based on local-, regional- and central agents in nodes
Cooperative local auditing (Krontiris & Dimitriou, 2007)	Specification based
LIDeA (Krontiris, Dimitriou, & Giannetsos, 2008)	Specification based
Decentralized intrusion detection model (Da Silva et al. 2008)	Specification based
Neighbor-based intrusion detection (Stetsko, Folkman, & Vashek, 2010)	Specification based
Fixed-width clustering (Loo, Ng, Leckie, & Palaniswami, 2010)	Anomaly based
Artificial immune system (Drozda, Schaust, & Szczerbicka, 2010)	Anomaly based
Intrusion aware validation algorithm (Shaikh, Jameel, Auriol, Lee, & Song, 2008)	Anomaly based
Group-based detection scheme (Li, He, & Fu, 2008)	Anomaly based
ANDES algorithm (Gupta, Zheng, & Cheng, 2007)	Anomaly based
Application-independent framework (Zhang, Yu, & Ning, 2008)	Anomaly based
Cumulative summation (Phuong, Hung, Cho, Lee, & Lee, 2006)	Anomaly based
Hierarchical intrusion detection model (Phuong, Hung, Cho, Lee, & Lee, 2006)	Anomaly based
Pair-based approach (K.R. Ahmed, K. Ahmed, S. Munir, & Asad, 2008)	Misuse and Anomaly based
SVELTE (De Almeida, Ribeiro, & Moreno, 2015)	Real time IDS, Misuse and Anomaly based
New IoT IDS (W. Li, Ping, Wu, Pan, & J. Li, 2014)	*K*-nearest neighbor, Misuse and Anomaly based
NAN IDS (Beigi-Mohammadi, J., Misic, H., Khazaei, & V.B. Misic, 2014)	signature and anomaly-based detection systems
Novel IDS for WSN (Karuppiah, Dalfiah, Yuvashri, Rajaram, & Pathan, 2014)	Based on Energy-Efficient Sybil Node Detection Algorithm and Misuse and Anomaly based.
IT-OCSVM, IDS for SCADA (Maglaras, Jiang, & Cruz, 2015)	Combining ensemble methods and social network metrics
IL-IDS (Ren & Gu, 2015)	AI (instance learning) based IDS
IDS for WSN (Wang, Wu, & Chen, 2015)	mathematical morphology

on the low device level). Also, it would be impossible for such a device to scan all the transmitted data, from and to it (to run anomaly detection mechanism). From this point, we can think of defining the role of some kind of local detection agent as mentioned in (Huang, Jasper, & Wicks, 1999) that could be implemented on the M2M device by only affording the low level device security (as we see in the Figure 10, first level). Device compromise detection, neighbor watch, device localization, device wiping, and hardware security will form the main job of this LDA (Local Detection Agent). The local agent will refer to a regional agent (which could be mainly the gateway), and on the network side, the central detection agent will be a *multi-level* priority system.

- Let's begin with the multi-level of priority. The threats or intrusion events/attempts can be disposed on many levels of priorities. Hence, the IDS system will assign to every M2M device or node an ID, and a table containing a combination of the IDs and the current situation.
- The local agent will have various functions like the device compromise detection function, device localization function, hardware security detection function, and many others that can be defined by the operator/administrator. For instance, if device compromise function sends an alert, this will be assigned a high level of priority. Again, if the localization function sends an alert about an unexpected movement of a device, this will be considered a second level priority incident. The levels of priorities can be assigned also by the operator and that depends on the specific M2M system. Those alerts will play a major role in the MIDS decision making process.

Coming back to the hybrid (Pathan, 2014; Huh & Hai, 2011) aspect of MIDS, the system will work on the specification based detection policy. MIDS will be formed by a part working on the anomaly based detection policy which will first build normal profiles for users based on their activity history and daily usage behavior, and when any change in this usual behavior is observed, the distributed local detection agent and regional agent would generate alert and set its priority level. The IDS verification system will then scan the transmitted data from the suspected node or user by applying 2 criteria:

- The amount of transmitted data and comparing it to the usual volume.
- By applying the misuse based policy function for searching about suspicious data (according to the saved malicious and virus patterns)

IDS needs to be also combined with many other procedures that intend to protect the M2M area network from Denial of Service (DoS) attacks and all kinds of *over-the-air* attacks (some issues are mentioned in Section VII), which can be the field of study in others future works. Here, our suggestion is to design a common IDS platform by combining the low level device security based on the M2M security stack presented in this chapter. While this is in essence a foundation step, the concept would have enough scope for expansion by adding new parts and functionalities (as in section VII) and practical implementation.

Now, let us take a look at the way an MIDS (M2M IDS) would work. The MIDS functional blocks are shown in Figure 11. As understood, it's a combination of various sub-blocks and functionalities, including the entities like the local and regional detection agents, the central detection agent, the "*Anomaly Policy*" detection function, the "*Misuse Policy*" detection function, and the MIDS decision function. The Local detection agent discovers an event, as device compromising event or movement of a device, etc. Those events should be defined by the operator/administrator in a way compatible with the nature of M2M system. The local detection agent will generate an alert.

1. This alert with the user ID will be forwarded to the Regional agent (in the gateway).
2. The regional agent then will forward the alert with the user ID to the Central Detection agent.
3. The central detection agent will process the alert and assign to it a certain level of priority and forward it to the MIDS decision function.
4. The MIDS decision function will forward the User ID to the "*Anomaly policy*" detection function which will check up for any change in the user behavior in comparison to its usual activity profile.

Figure 11. MIDS functional blocks

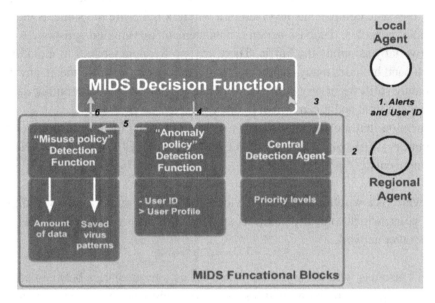

5.   In case of a change in the user profile, The *"Anomaly Policy"* function will forward then the user ID to the *"Misuse Policy"* detection function. This function will scan all the traffic coming from this node based on 2 criteria:

6.   the usual generated amount of data generated by this node and

7.   by searching on any matching with the known stored virus patterns and signatures.

8.   The *"Misuse Policy"* detection function will forward the scan result to the MIDS decision function for further action. The intruder would be then purged our locked within the network based on the employed strategy of tackling with intrusion.

Hence, MIDS decision function will take the decision of allowing the traffic or discarding it.

WIRELESS IDPS: SUPPORTING MIDS AS A LOCAL AGENT

M2M communication will include many kinds of wireless devices and technologies for which we need to talk a bit about the wireless IDPS supporting the MIDS framework. A significant portion of the M2M system may be wireless sensor network or the like. Hence, MIDS framework could work with any wireless IDPS (Intrusion Detection and Prevention System) as well. An IDPS is basically a combination of both *"Intrusion detection"* and *"Intrusion prevention"* mechanisms (W. Ren et al., 2013; Mohammed & Pathan, 2013).

A wireless IDPS (Pathan et al., 2013) monitors wireless network traffic and analyzes wireless networking protocols for identifying malicious behavior. However, it has a limitation that it cannot identify suspicious activity/data in the application or higher-layer network protocols (e.g., TCP, UDP) that the wireless network traffic is transferring. It is most commonly deployed within the range of an organization's wireless network to monitor it, but it can also be deployed to locations where unauthorized wireless networking could occur.

Though due to the transmission methods, wireless network attacks differ often from those on the wired networks, the basic components involved in a wireless IDPS are the same as the network-based IDPS (for example, consoles, database servers, management servers and sensors). A wireless IDPS monitors the network by sampling the traffic. There are two frequency bands to monitor (2.4 GHz and 5 GHz), and each band includes many channels. A software sensor (here, we mean, any kind of sensing mechanism – mainly software or programming application running on a computing device) is used to monitor a channel at a time and it can switch to other channels as needed.

We should mention that most of the WLANs (Wireless LANs) use the Institute of Electrical and Electronics Engineers (IEEE) 802.11 family of WLAN standards. IEEE 802.11 WLANs have two main architectural components:

- A station, which is a wireless end-point device (e.g., laptop computer, personal digital assistant).
- An access point, which logically connects stations with an organization's wired network infrastructure or other network.

Some WLANs also use wireless switches, which act as intermediaries between access points and the wired network. A network based on stations and access points is configured in infrastructure mode; a network that does not use an access point, in which stations connect directly to each other, is configured in ad hoc mode. Nearly all organizational WLANs use infrastructure mode. Each access point in a WLAN has a name assigned to it called a service set identifier (SSID). The SSID allows stations to distinguish one WLAN from another.

Wireless *security sensors* (here, we mean the *software sensor* – i.e., code that senses intrusion or malicious activity) have several available forms. A dedicated sensor of this type is usually passive, performing wireless IDPS functions but not passing traffic from source to destination. Dedicated sensors may be designed for fixed or mobile deployment, with mobile sensors (similar to mobile software robot or so) used primarily for auditing and incident handling purposes (e.g., to locate rogue wireless devices). Sensor software is also available bundled with access points and wireless switches. Some vendors also have host-based wireless IDPS sensor software that can be installed on stations, such as laptops. The sensor software detects station misconfigurations and attacks within range of the stations. This kind of software/application may also be able to enforce security policies on the stations, such as limiting access to wireless interfaces.

If an organization uses WLANs, it most often deploys wireless sensors to monitor the radiofrequency range of the organization's WLANs, which often includes mobile components such as laptops and personal digital assistants (PDAs). Many organizations also use software sensors to monitor areas of their facilities where there should be no WLAN activity, as well as channels and bands that the organization's WLANs should not use, as a way of detecting rogue devices.

Wireless IDPS Security Capabilities

The main advantages of Wireless IDPSs include detection of attacks, misconfigurations, and policy violations at the WLAN protocol level, primarily examining IEEE 802.11 protocol communication. The major limitation of a Wireless IDPS is that it does not examine communications at higher levels (e.g., IP addresses, application payloads). Some products perform only simple signature-based detection, whereas others use a combination of signature-based, anomaly based, and stateful protocol analysis detection techniques. Most of the types of events commonly detected by wireless IDPS sensor software include unauthorized WLANs and WLAN devices and poorly secured WLAN devices (e.g., misconfigured WLAN settings). Additionally, the Wireless IDPSs can detect unusual WLAN usage patterns, which could indicate a device compromise or unauthorized use of the WLAN, and the use of wireless network scanners.

Other types of attacks such as Denial of Service (DoS) conditions, including logical attacks (e.g., overloading access points with large number of messages) and physical attacks (e.g., emitting electromagnetic energy on the WLAN's frequencies to make the WLAN unusable), can also be detected by wireless IDPSs. Some wireless IDPSs can also detect a WLAN device that attempts to spoof the identity of another device.

Another significant advantage is that most wireless IDPS sensors (software) can identify the physical location of a wireless device by using triangulation – estimating the device's approximate distance from multiple sensors from the strength of the device's signal received by each sensor, then calculating the physical location at which the device would be, the estimated distance from each sensor. Handheld IDPS sensors can also be used to pinpoint a device's location, particularly if fixed sensors do not offer triangulation capabilities or if the device is moving.

Wireless IDPS overcome the other types of IDPS by providing more accurate prevention; this is largely due to its narrow focus. Anomaly-based detection methods often generate high false positives, especially if threshold values are not properly maintained. Although many alerts based on benign activities might occur, such as another organization's WLAN being within range of the organization's WLANs, these alerts are not truly false positives because they are accurately detecting an unknown WLAN.

Some tuning and customization are required for the Wireless IDPS technologies to improve their detection accuracy. The main effort required in the Wireless IDPS is in specifying which WLANs, access points, and stations are authorized, and in entering the policy characteristics into the wireless IDPS software. As wireless IDPSs only examine wireless network protocols, not the higher-level protocols (e.g., applications), generally there is not a large number of alert types, and consequently, not many customizations or tunings that are available.

Wireless IDPS sensors provide two types of intrusion prevention capabilities:

- Some sensor software can terminate connections through the air, typically by sending messages to the end points telling them to dissociate the current session and then refusing to permit a new connection to be established.
- Another prevention method is for a sensor to instruct a switch on the wired network to block network activity involving a particular device on the basis of the device's media access control (MAC) address or switch port. However, this technique is only effective for blocking the device's communications on the wired network, not the wireless network.

An important consideration when choosing prevention capabilities is the effect that prevention actions can have on sensor monitoring. For example, if a sensor is transmitting signals to terminate connections, it may not be able to perform channel scanning to monitor other communications until it has completed the prevention action. To mitigate this, some sensors have two radios – one for monitoring and detection, and another for performing prevention actions.

Wireless IDPS Limitations

The wireless IDPSs offer great detection capabilities against authorized activities, but there are some significant limitations. The use of evasion techniques is considered as one of the limitations of some wireless IDPS sensors, particularly against sensor channel scanning schemes. One example is performing attacks in very short bursts on channels that are not currently being monitored. An attacker could also launch attacks on two channels at the same time. If the sensor detects the first attack, it cannot detect the second attack unless it scans away from the channel of the first attack.

We should mention that the wireless IDPSs cannot detect certain types of attacks against wireless networks. An attacker can passively monitor wireless traffic, which is not detectable by wireless IDPSs. If weak security methods are used, for example, Wired Equivalent Privacy (WEP), the attacker can then perform *off-line* processing of the collected traffic to find the encryption key used to provide security for the wireless traffic. With this key, the attacker can decrypt the traffic that was already collected, as well as any other traffic collected from the same WLAN. As the Wireless IDPSs cannot detect certain types of attacks against wireless networks, it cannot fully compensate for the use of insecure wireless networking protocols.

In spite of having the limitations, wireless sensory software could be a good supporting part of the MIDS as M2M system would have significant amount of wireless devices and infrastructure in it. In fact, a wireless sensor software (i.e., wireless IDPS) installed on a wireless device could be the local agent in the MIDS framework combined with other functionalities. Further thoughts and research studies could be performed in this direction in future, for which we have opted to put this section in this chapter. We believe that this area will prosper as fast as the implementation of new M2M-enabled innovations in different sectors of life begins to materialize accompanied by different new security threats in addition to the ones mentioned before.

CONCLUSION

In this chapter, we explained the M2M system and its security challenges. We discussed the security threats that the M2M communication faces and then, highlighted the M2M capabilities to support an Intrusion Detection System. After studying various relevant IDS technologies, we designed a common platform for IDS for M2M system; we suggested an M2M IDS framework combining the device level and wireless IDPS, that may be worked on further towards practical implementation based on various applications and design scenarios emerging for the M2M systems.

REFERENCES

Abduvaliyev, A. Pathan, A.-S.K., Zhou, J., Roman, R., & Wong, W.-C. (2013). On the Vital Areas of Intrusion Detection Systems in Wireless Sensor Networks. *IEEE Communications Surveys & Tutorials, 15*(3), 1223-1237.

Aboelaze, M., & Aloul, F. (2005). Current and future trends in sensor networks: a survey.*Second IFIP International Conference on Wireless and Optical Communications Networks 2005 (WOCN 2005)*, (pp. 551-555). doi:10.1109/WOCN.2005.1436087

Ahmed, K. R., Ahmed, K., Munir, S., & Asad, A. (2008). Abnormal node detection in wireless sensor network by pair based approach using IDS secure routing methodology. *Int J Comput Sci Netw. Sec*, *8*(12), 339–342.

Anggorojati, B., & Prasad, N. R. (2013). An Intrusion Detection game in access control system for the M2M local cloud platform. *2013 19th Asia-Pacific Conference on Communications (APCC)*.

Anggorojati, B., & Prasad, N. R. (2014). Secure capability-based access control in the M2M local cloud platform. *2014-4th International Conference on Wireless Communications, Vehicular Technology, Information Theory and Aerospace & Electronic Systems (VITAE'14)*.

Aris, A., Oktug, S. F., & Yalcin, S. B. O. (2015). Internet-of-Things security: Denial of service attacks.*2015 Signal Processing and Communications Applications Conference (SIU'15)*, (pp. 903-906). doi:10.1109/SIU.2015.7129976

Arnoys, L. (2015). The internet of things: communicating with the cloud, the protocols, security and big data. *NMCT 2015*. Available at: http://hdl.handle.net/10046/1184

Atamli, A. W., & Martin, A. (2014). Threat-Based Security Analysis for the Internet of Things.*2014 International Workshop on Secure Internet of Things (SIoT'14)*. doi:10.1109/SIoT.2014.10

Azad, S., & Pathan, A.-S. K. (Eds.). (2014). Practical Cryptography: Algorithms and Implementations using C++. CRC Press, Taylor & Francis Group.

Barnhart, E. N., & Bokath, C. A. (2011). Considerations for Machine-to-Machine communications architecture and security standardization. *2011 IEEE 5th International Conference on Internet Multimedia Systems Architecture and Application (IMSAA'11)*.

Bartoli, A. (2013). *Security protocols suite for machine-to-machine systems* (Ph.D. Thesis). Universitat Politècnica de Catalunya, Departament d'Enginyeria Telemàtica.

Beigi-Mohammadi, N., Misic, J., Khazaei, H., & Misic, V. B. (2014). An intrusion detection system for smart grid neighborhood area network.*2014 IEEE International Conference on Communications (ICC'14)*. doi:10.1109/ICC.2014.6883967

Ben, S. Y., Olivereau, A., & Laurent, M. (2012). A Distributed Approach for Secure M2M Communications. *2012-5th International Conference on New Technologies, Mobility and Security (NTMS'12)*.

Bojic, I., Granjal, J., Monteiro, E., Katusic, D., Skocir, P., Kusek, M., & Jezic, G. (2014). *Communication and Security in Machine-to-Machine Systems.*Lecture Notes in Computer Science, 8611, 255–281.

Boubakri, W., Abdallah, W., & Boudriga, N. (2014). A chaos-based authentication and key management scheme for M2M communication. *2014 9th International Conference for Internet Technology and Secured Transactions (ICITST'14)*.

Cagalaban, G., Ahn, J. Y., & Kim, S. (2012). A Secure Machine to Machine-Based Framework for Service Provisioning in Cloud Computing Infrastructures. Business, Economics, Financial Sciences, and Management. Springer.

Calhoun, P. R., Zorn, G., Pan, P., & Akhtar, H. (2001). *Diameter Framework Document.* IETF Draft. Retrieved 5 Dec. 2015 from: http://tools.ietf.org/html/draft-calhoun-diameter-framework-09

Cha, I., Shah, Y., Schmidt, A. U., Leicher, A., & Meyerstein, M. V. (2009). Trust in M2M communication. *IEEE Vehicular Technology Magazine, Volume, 4*(3), 69–75. doi:10.1109/MVT.2009.933478

Chan, P. K., Mahoney, M., & Arshad, M. (2003). Learning Rules and Clusters for Anomaly Detection in Network Traffic. In *Managing Cyber Threats*, (pp. 81-99). Academic Press.

Chang, K., Soong, A., Tseng, M., & Xiang, Z. (2011). Global Wireless Machine-to-Machine Standardization. *IEEE Internet Computing, Volume, 15*(2), 64–69. doi:10.1109/MIC.2011.41

Chen, D., & Chang, G. (2012). A Survey on Security Issues of M2M Communications in Cyber-Physical Systems. *Transactions on Internet and Information Systems (Seoul), 6*(1), 24–45.

Chen, H.-C., You, I., Weng, C.-E., Cheng, C. H., & Huang, Y.-F. (2016). A security gateway application for End-to-End M2M communications. *Computer Standards & Interfaces, 44*, 85–93. doi:10.1016/j.csi.2015.09.001

Choi, H. K., Han, C. K., & Choi, D. S. (2015). Improvement of security protocol for Machine Type Communications in LTE-advanced.*Wireless Communications and Mobile Computing Conference 2015 (IWCMC'15).* doi:10.1109/IWCMC.2015.7289270

Choi, Y., Doh, I., Park, S. S., & Chae, K. J. (2012). Security Based Semantic Context Awareness System for M2M Ubiquitous Healthcare Service. In Ubiquitous Information Technologies and Applications. (LNCS), (vol. 214, pp. 187-196). Springer.

Cimler, R., Matyska, J., Balik, L., Horalek, J., & Sobeslav, V. (2015). Security Aspects of Cloud Based Mobile Health Care Application. In *Nature of Computation and Communication.* Springer.

Da Silva, A. P. R., Martins, M. H. T., Rocha, B. P. S., Loureiro, A. A. F., Ruiz, L. B., & Wong, H. C. (2008). Decentralized intrusion detection in wireless sensor networks.*Proceedings of the 1st ACM international workshop on quality of service and security in wireless and mobile networks.*

Dagon, D., Martin, T., & Starner, T. (2004). Mobile phones as computing devices: The viruses are coming! *IEEE Pervasive Computing, Volume, 3*(4), 11–15. doi:10.1109/MPRV.2004.21

De Almeida, F. M., Ribeiro, A. R. L., & Moreno, E. D. (2015). An Architecture for Self-healing in Internet of Things.*UBICOMM 2015: The Ninth International Conference on Mobile Ubiquitous Computing, Systems, Services and Technologies.*

Demblewski, M. (2015). *Security Frameworks for Machine-to-Machine Devices and Networks* (Doctoral dissertation). Nova Southeastern University. Retrieved from: NSUWorks, College of Engineering and Computing.

Denial-of-Service Developments. (2000). *CERT Advisory CA-2000-01*. Retrieved 6 Dec. 2015, from: http://www.cert.org/advisories/CA-2000-01.html

Doh, I., Chae, K., Lim, J., & Chung, M. Y. (2015). *Authentication and Key Management Based on Kerberos for M2M Mobile Open IPTV Security. In Intelligent Automation & Soft Computing* (Vol. 21, pp. 543–558). Taylor & Francis Group.

Dohler, M., Boswarthick, D., & Alonso-Zárate, J. (2012). Machine-to-Machine in Smart Grids & Smart Cities. Technologies, Standards, and Applications. Tutorial Globecom 2012, Anaheim, CA.

Drozda, M., Schaust, S., & Szczerbicka, H. (2010). AIS for misbehaviour detection in wireless sensor networks: performance and design principles. In Congress on evolutionary computation, (pp. 3719-3726).

Duquet, S. (2015). *Smart Sensors: Enabling Detection and Ranging for the Internet of Things and Beyond*. LeddarTech, White paper.

Farooqi, A.H., Khan, F.A., Wang, J., & Lee, S. (2013). A novel intrusion detection framework for wireless sensor networks. *Personal and Ubiquitous Computing*, *17*(5), 907-919.

Fink, G. A., Zarzhitsky, D. V., Carroll, T. E., & Farquhar, E. D. (2015). Security and privacy grand challenges for the Internet of Things.*2015 International Conference on Collaboration Technologies and Systems (CTS'15)*. doi:10.1109/CTS.2015.7210391

Fremantle, P., & Scott, P. (2015). A security survey of middleware for the Internet of Things. *PeerJ PrePrints* 3:e1521. Retrieved 6 Dec. 2015 from: https://peerj.com/preprints/1241/

Genge, B., Haller, P., Gligor, A., & Beres, A. (2014). An Approach for Cyber Security Experimentation Supporting Sensei/IoT for Smart Grid.*2nd International Symposium on Digital Forensics and Security (ISDFS'14)*.

Granjal, J., Monteiro, E., & Silva, J. S. (2013). *Security Issues and Approaches on Wireless M2M Systems. In Wireless Networks and Security Part of the series Signals and Communication Technology* (pp. 133–164). Springer Berlin Heidelberg.

Gupta, S., Zheng, R., & Cheng, A. M. K. (2007). ANDES: an anomaly detection system for wireless sensor networks.*International conference on mobile ad hoc and sensor systems*, (pp. 1–9). doi:10.1109/ MOBHOC.2007.4428636

Gyrard, A., Bonnet, C., & Boudaoud, K. (2014). An Ontology-Based Approach for Helping to Secure the ETSI Machine-to-Machine Architecture.*2014 IEEE International Conference on Internet of Things (iThings), Green Computing and Communications (GreenCom), IEEE and Cyber, and Physical and Social Computing(CPSCom)*. IEEE. doi:10.1109/iThings.2014.25

Hai, T. H., Khan, F., & Huh, E.-N. (2007). Hybrid intrusion detection system for wireless sensor networks. Springer. doi:10.1007/978-3-540-74477-1_36

Hakiri, A., & Berthou, P. (2015). *Leveraging SDN for the 5G Networks. Software Defined Mobile Networks (SDMN): Beyond LTE Network Architecture* (M. Liyanage, A. Gurtov, & M. Ylianttila, Eds.). Chichester, UK: John Wiley & Sons, Ltd. doi:10.1002/9781118900253.ch5

Heady, R., Luger, G., Maccabe, A., & Servilla, M. (1990). *The Architecture of a Network Level Intrusion Detection System. Technical report.* University of New Mexico. doi:10.2172/425295

Hongsong, C., Zhongchuan, F., & Dongyan, Z. (2011). Security and trust research in M2M system.*2011 IEEE International Conference on Vehicular Electronics and Safety (ICVES'11).* doi:10.1109/ICVES.2011.5983830

Hossain, M. M., Fotouhi, M., & Hasan, R. (2015). Towards an Analysis of Security Issues, Challenges, and Open Problems in the Internet of Things.*2015 IEEE World Congress on Services (SERVICES'15).* doi:10.1109/SERVICES.2015.12

Hu, L., Chi, L., Li, H. T., Yuan, W., Sun, Y., & Chu, J. F. (2012). The classic security application in M2M- the authentication scheme of Mobile Payment. *Transactions on Internet and Information Systems (Seoul), 6*(1), 131–146.

Huang, M.-Y., Jasper, R. J., & Wicks, T. M. (1999). A large scale distributed intrusion detection framework based on attack strategy analysis. *Computer Networks, 31*(23–24), 2465–2475. doi:10.1016/S1389-1286(99)00114-0

Huang, X., Craig, P., & Yan, H.L.Z (2015). SecIoT: a security framework for the Internet of Things. *Security and Communication Networks.* DOI: 10.1002/sec.1259

Huh, E.-N., & Hai, T. H. (2011). Lightweight Intrusion Detection for Wireless Sensor Networks. In Intrusion Detection Systems. Academic Press.

Hussen, H. R., Tizazu, G. A., Ting, M., Lee, T., Choi, Y., & Kim, K. H. (2013). SAKES: Secure authentication and key establishment scheme for M2M communication in the IP-based wireless sensor network (6L0WPAN).*2013 Fifth International Conference on Ubiquitous and Future Networks (ICUFN'13),* (pp. 246-251). doi:10.1109/ICUFN.2013.6614820

Inshil, D., Jiyoung, L., Shi, L., & Kijoon, C. (2014). Pairwise and group key setup mechanism for secure machine-to-machine communication. *Science and Information Systems, 11*(3), 1071–1090. doi:10.2298/CSIS130922065D

Jaber, M., Kouzayha, N., Dawy, Z., & Kayssi, A. (2014). On cellular network planning and operation with M2M signalling and security considerations.*2014 IEEE International Conference on Communications Workshops (ICC'14).* doi:10.1109/ICCW.2014.6881236

Jin, B. W., & Hahm, H. (2013). A Design of Advanced Authentication Method for Protection of Privacy in M2M Environment. *International Journal of Smart Home, 7*(5), 145–154. doi:10.14257/ijsh.2013.7.5.15

Jin, B. W., Park, J. P., Lee, K. W., & Jun, M. S. (2013). A Study of Authentication Method for Id-Based Encryption Using In M2M Environment. *Journal of the Korea Academia-Industrial Cooperation Society, 14*(4), 1926–1934.

Jover, R. P. (2015). Security and impact of the IoT on LTE mobile networks. In *Security and Privacy in the Internet of Things (IoT): Models, Algorithms, and Implementations.* CRC Press, Taylor & Francis. Retrieved 6 Dec., 2015 from: http://www.ee.columbia.edu/~roger/LTE_IoT.pdf

Jung, S., Ahn, J. Y., Hwang, D. J., & Kim, S. (2012). A Study on Key Distribution Protocol with Mutual Authentication for M2M Sensor Network. Information, 15, 1229-1240.

Jung, S., Kim, D., & Seoksoo, S. (2013). *Cooperative Architecture for Secure M2M Communication. In Advanced Science and Technology Letters* (Vol. 29, pp. 37–40). SecTech.

Jung, S., & Kim, S. (2013). Hierarchical Security Management for M2M Wireless Sensor Networks. *International Journal of Advancements in Computing Technology, 5*(11), 238–244. doi:10.4156/ijact.vol5.issue11.26

Karim, L., Anpalagan, A., Nasser, N., Almhana, J. N., & Woungang, I. (2013). *An energy efficient, fault tolerant and secure clustering scheme for M2M communication networks. In 2013 IEEE Globecom Workshops* (pp. 677–682). Atlanta, GA: GC Wkshps.

Karuppiah, A. B., Dalfiah, J., Yuvashri, K., Rajaram, S., & Pathan, A.-S. K. (2014). Energy-Efficient Sybil Node Detection Algorithm for Wireless Sensor Networks.*3rd International Conference on Eco-Friendly Computing and Communication Systems (ICECCS 2014).*

Khan, S., Pathan, A.-S. K., & Alrajeh, N. A. (2012). Wireless Sensor Networks: Current Status and Future Trends. Auerbach Publications, CRC Press, Taylor & Francis Group. doi:10.1201/b13092

Kim, J.M., Jeong, H.Y., & Hong, B.H. (2011). A User Authentication Method for M2M Environments. Computer Science and Convergence, *Lecture Notes in Electrical Engineering, 114,* 589-595.

Kim, J.M., Jeong, H.Y., & Hong, B.H. (2014) A study of privacy problem solving using device and user authentication for M2M environments. *Security and Communication Networks, 7*(10, 1528–1535.

Koss, J. (2014). *ETSI Standardizes M2M Communications.* Retrieved 28 Nov. 2015 from: http://www.telit2market.com/wp-content/uploads/2014/10/t2m0510_p038-p039.pdf

Kothmayr, T. D., Hu, W., Brunig, M., & Carle, G. (2012). A DTLS based end-to-end security architecture for the Internet of Things with two-way authentication. *2012 IEEE 37th Conference on Local Computer Networks Workshops (LCN Workshops).*

Krontiris, I., & Dimitriou, T. (2007). Towards intrusion detection in wireless sensor networks. *13th European wireless conference.*

Krontiris, I., Dimitriou, T., & Giannetsos, T. (2008). LIDeA: A distributed lightweight intrusion detection architecture for sensor networks. ACM secure communication.

Lai, C., Li, H., Lu, R., Shen, X. S., & Cao, J. (2013). A unified end-to-end security scheme for machine-type communication in LTE networks.*2013 IEEE/CIC International Conference on Communications in China (ICCC).* doi:10.1109/ICCChina.2013.6671201

Lai, C., Li, H., Zhang, Y., & Cao, J. (2012). Security Issues on Machine to Machine Communications. *Transactions on Internet and Information Systems (Seoul), 6*(2), 498–514.

Lake, D., Milito, R., Morrow, M., & Vargheese, R. (2014). Internet of Things: Architectural Framework for eHealth Security. *Journal of ICT Standardization, 3-4,* 301–328.

Lee, H., & Chung, M. (2012). Context-Aware Security System for the Smart Phone-based M2M Service Environment. *Transactions on Internet and Information Systems (Seoul)*, 6(1), 64–83.

Lee, K.L. & Kim, S.K. (2015). Authentication Scheme based on Biometric Key for VANET Information System in M2M Application Service. *Applied Math and Information Science Journal*, 9(2L), 645-651.

Lee, M. (2013). *M2M and the Internet of Things: How secure is it?* Retrieved 29 Nov. 2015 from: http://www.zdnet.com/article/disgruntled-over-big-data-maybe-its-that-visualization-magic-box-dependence

Li, G., He, J., & Fu, Y. (2008). A group based intrusion detection scheme in wireless sensor networks. *The 3rd international conference on grid and pervasive computing—workshop*, (pp. 286-291).

Li, W., Yi, Wu, Y., Pan, L., & Li, J. (2014). A New Intrusion Detection System Based on KNN Classification Algorithm in Wireless Sensor Network. Journal of Electrical and Computer Engineering.

Liu, L., Gu, M., & Ma, Y. (2015). *Research on the Key Technology of M2M Gateway.* Lecture Notes in Computer Science, 8944, 837–843. doi:10.1007/978-3-319-15554-8_76

Loo, C. E., Ng, M. Y., Leckie, C., & Palaniswami, M. (2010). Intrusion detection for routing attacks in sensor networks. *International Journal of Distributed Sensor Networks*, 2(4), 313–332. doi:10.1080/15501320600692044

Lu, R., Li, X., Liang, X., Shen, X., & Lin, X. (2011). GRS: The green, reliability, and security of emerging machine to machine communications. *IEEE Communications Magazine, Volume*, 49(4), 28–35. doi:10.1109/MCOM.2011.5741143

Machine-to-Machine Communications (M2M) Functional Architecture. (2011). *The European Telecommunications Standards Institute (ETSI), TS 102 690 V1.1.1 (2011-10), 2011*. Retrieved 28 Nov. 2015 from: http://www.etsi.org/deliver/etsi_ts/102600_102699/102690/01.01.01_60/ts_102690v010101p.pdf

Machine-to-Machine Communications (M2M) mIa, dIa and mId Interfaces. (2015). *ETSI TS 102 921 V1.3.1 (2014-09)*. Retrieved 29 Nov., 2015 from: http://www.etsi.org/deliver/etsi_ts/102900_102999/102921/01.03.01_60/ts_102921v010301p.pdf

Machine to Machine Communications. The European Telecommunications Standards Institute (ETSI) standards. (n.d.). Retrieved 28 Nov., 2015 from: http://www.etsi.org/technologies-clusters/technologies/m2m

Maglaras, L. A., Jiang, J., & Cruz, T. G. (2015). Combining ensemble methods and social network metrics for improving accuracy of OCSVM on intrusion detection in SCADA systems. Journal of Information Security and Applications.

Mahkonen, H., Rinta-aho, T., Kauppinen, T., Sethi, M., Kjällman, J., & Salmela, P. (2013). Secure M2M cloud testbed.*Proceedings of the 19th annual international conference on Mobile computing & networking (MobiCom '13)*. ACM. doi:10.1145/2500423.2505294

Maras, M. H. (2015). Internet of Things: security and privacy implications. *International Data Privacy Law*. Retrieved 6 Dec., 2015 from: http://idpl.oxfordjournals.org/content/5/2/99

Masek, P., Muthanna, A., & Hosek, J. (2015). Suitability of MANET Routing Protocols for the Next-Generation National Security and Public Safety Systems. Internet of Things, Smart Spaces, and Next Generation Networks and Systems, Volume 9247 of the series. *Lecture Notes in Computer Science, 9247*, 242–253. doi:10.1007/978-3-319-23126-6_22

Misic, V. B., & Misic, J. (2014). *Machine-to-Machine Communications: Architectures, Technology, Standards, and Applications*. CRC Press.

Mo, Y., Kim, T. H.-H., Brancik, K., Dickinson, D., Lee, H., Perrig, A., & Sinopoli, B. (2012). Cyber–Physical Security of a Smart Grid Infrastructure. *Proceedings of the IEEE, 100*(1), 195-209.

Mohammed, M., & Pathan, A.-S. K. (2013). Automatic Defense against Zero-day Polymorphic Worms in Communication Networks. CRC Press, Taylor & Francis Group. doi:10.1201/b14912

Moon, Y. k., Lee, E. K., Kim, J. J., & Choi, H. R. (2014). *Study on the Container Security Device based on IoT. In Information* (pp. 5425–5433). Tokyo: International Information Institute.

More than 50 billion connected devices. (2011). Ericsson white paper, 28423-3149Uen.

Neisse, R., Fovino, I. N., Baldini, G., Stavroulaki, V., Vlacheas, P., & Giaffreda, R. (2014). A Model-Based Security Toolkit for the Internet of Things. *Availability, Reliability and Security (ARES), 2014 Ninth International Conference on Availability, Reliability and Security (ARES'14)*, (pp. 78 – 87). doi:10.1109/ARES.2014.17

Neisse, R., Steri, G., Fovino, I.N., & Baldini, G. (2015). SecKit: A Model-based Security Toolkit for the Internet of Things. *Computers & Security, 54*, 60–76.

Nie, X., & Zhai, X. (2013) M2M security threat and security mechanism research. *3rd International Conference on Computer Science and Network Technology (ICCSNT 2013)*, (pp. 906-909). doi:10.1109/ICCSNT.2013.6967252

No stopping Johannesburg's traffic light thieves. (2015). Retrieved 30 November, 2015 from: http://www.theguardian.com/world/2011/jan/06/johannesburg-traffic-light-thieves-sim

oneM2M. (2015). Retrieved 29 Nov. 2015 from: http://www.etsi.org/about/what-we-do/global-collaboration/onem2m

Park, N., Park, J. S., & Kim, H. J. (2015). *Inter-Authentication and Session Key Sharing Procedure for Secure M2M/IoT Environment. In Information* (pp. 261–266). Tokyo: International Information Institute.

Park, N., Park, J. S., & Kim, H. K. (2014). *Hash-based authentication and session key agreement Scheme in Internet of Things Environment. In Advanced Science and Technology Letters* (Vol. 62, pp. 9–12). Sensor.

Pathan, A.-S. K. (2015). Securing Cyber Physical Systems. CRC Press, Taylor & Francis Group.

Pathan, A.-S. K. (2010). Denial of Service in Wireless Sensor Networks: Issues and Challenges. In A. V. Stavros (Ed.), *Advances in Communications and Media Research* (Vol. 6). Nova Science Publishers, Inc.

Pathan, A.-S. K. (2010). Major Works on the Necessity and Implementations of PKC in WSN A Beginner's Note. Security of Self-Organizing Networks: MANET, WSN, WMN, VANET. Auerbach Publications, CRC Press, Taylor & Francis Group.

Pathan, A.-S. K. (2014). The State of the Art in Intrusion Prevention and Detection. CRC Press, Taylor & Francis Group. doi:10.1201/b16390

Pathan, A.-S. K., Khanam, S., Saleem, H. Y., & Abduallah, W. M. (2013). Tackling Intruders in Wireless Mesh Networks. In Distributed Network Intelligence, Security and Applications. CRC Press, Taylor & Francis Group.

Pathan, A.-S. K., Monowar, M. M., & Fadlullah, Z. M. (2013). Building Next-Generation Converged Networks: Theory and Practice. CRC Press, Taylor & Francis Group. doi:10.1201/b14574

Paxson, V. (1990). Bro: A system for detecting network intruders in real-time. Computer Networks. *The International Journal of Computer and Telecommunications Networking, 31*(23-24), 2435–2463.

Pei, Y. (2012). A Survey on Localization Algorithms for Wireless Ad Hoc Networks. In Communications and Information Processing. Springer.

Phuong, T. V., Hung, L. X., Cho, S. J., Lee, Y. K., & Lee, S. (2006). An anomaly detection algorithm for detecting attacks in wireless sensor networks. Intelligent and Security Informatics, 735–736.

Pirretti, M., Zhu, S., Vijaykrishnan, N., McDaniel, P., Kandemir, M., & Brooks, R. (2006). The Sleep Deprivation Attack in Sensor Networks: Analysis and Methods of Defense. *International Journal of Distributed Sensor Networks, 2*(3), 267–287. doi:10.1080/15501320600642718

Qiu, Y., & Ma, M. (2015). Security Issues and Approaches in M2M Communications. In Securing Cyber Physical Systems. CRC Press, Taylor & Francis Group.

Remote wipe definition. (2015). *TechTarget*. Retrieved 6 Dec., 2015 from: http://searchmobilecomputing.techtarget.com/definition/remote-wipe

Ren, F., & Gu, Y. (2015). Using Artificial Intelligence in the Internet of Things.ZTE Communications, 13(2).

Ren, W., Yu, L., Ma, L., & Ren, Y. (2013). RISE: A RelIable and SEcure Scheme for Wireless Machine to Machine Communications. *Tsinghua Science and Technology, 18*(1), 100–117. doi:10.1109/TST.2013.6449413

Riker, A., Cruz, T., Marques, B., Curado, M., Simoes, P., & Monteiro, E. (2014). *Efficient and secure M2M communications for smart metering. In 2014 IEEE Emerging Technology and Factory Automation* (pp. 1–7). Barcelona: ETFA. doi:10.1109/ETFA.2014.7005176

Roesch, M. (1999). Snort - Lightweight Intrusion Detection for Networks.*Proceedings of the 13th USENIX conference on System administration (LISA'99)*, (pp. 229-238).

Roman, R., Zhou, J., & Lopez, J. (2006). Applying intrusion detection systems to wireless sensor networks. *3rd IEEE consumer communications and networking conference*, (pp. 640–644).

Roman, R., Zhou, J., & Lopez, J. (2013). On the features and challenges of security and privacy in distributed internet of things. *Computer Networks, 57*(10), 2266–2279. doi:10.1016/j.comnet.2012.12.018

Rubertis, D. A., Mainetti, L., Mighali, V., Patrono, L., Sergi, I., Stefanizzi, M. L., & Pascali, S. (2013). Performance evaluation of end-to-end security protocols in an Internet of Things. *2013 21st International Conference on Software, Telecommunications and Computer Networks (SoftCOM'13).*

Saleem, K., Derhab, A., Al-Muhtadi, J., & Shahzad, B. (2015). *Human-oriented design of secure Machine-to-Machine communication system for e-Healthcare society. In Computers in Human Behavior* (Vol. 51, pp. 977–985). Elsevier.

Satyadevan, S., Kalarickal, B. S., & Jinesh, M. K. (2014). Security, Trust and Implementation Limitations of Prominent IoT Platforms.*Proceedings of the 3rd International Conference on Frontiers of Intelligent Computing: Theory and Applications (FICTA) 2014.*

Schurgot, M. R., & Shinberg, D. A. (2015). Experiments with security and privacy in IoT networks. *2015 IEEE 16th International Symposium on a World of Wireless on Mobile and Multimedia Networks (WoWMoM).*

Shafagh, H., & Hithnawi, A. (2014). Poster Abstract: Security Comes First, a Public-key Cryptography Framework for the Internet of Things.*2014 IEEE International Conference on Distributed Computing in Sensor Systems (DCOSS).* doi:10.1109/DCOSS.2014.62

Shaikh, R. A., Jameel, H., Auriol, B. J., Lee, S., & Song, Y. J. (2008). Trusting anomaly and intrusion claims for cooperative distributed intrusion detection schemes of wireless sensor networks. *The 9th international conference for young computer scientists,* (pp. 2038-2043).

Shih, J.-R., Hu, Y., Hsiao, M.-C., Chen, M.-S., Shen, W.-C., Yang, B.-Y., & Cheng, C.-M. et al. (2013). Securing M2M With Post-Quantum Public-Key Cryptography. *IEEE Journal on Emerging and Selected Topics in Circuits and Systems, Volume, 3*(1), 106–116. doi:10.1109/JETCAS.2013.2244772

Sicari, S., Rizzardi, A., Coen-Porisini, A., Grieco, L. A., & Monteil, T. (2015). Secure OM2M Service Platform. Autonomic Computing (ICAC). *2015 IEEE International Conference on Autonomic Computing (ICAC).* doi:10.1109/ICAC.2015.59

Sicari, S., Rizzardi, A., Grieco, L. A., & Coen-Porisini, A. (2015). Security, privacy and trust in Internet of Things: The road ahead. *Computer Networks.*

Singh, J., Pasquier, T., Bacon, J, Ko, H., & Eyers, D. (2015). Twenty security considerations for cloud-supported Internet of Things. *IEEE Internet of Things Journal.*

Song, H., Xie, L., Zhu, S., & Cao, G. (2007). Sensor node compromise detection: the location perspective. *Proceedings of the 2007 international conference on Wireless communications and mobile computing (IWCMC '07).* doi:10.1145/1280940.1280993

St. John-Green, M., & Watson, T. (2014). Safety and Security of the Smart City - when our infrastructure goes online.*9th IET International Conference on System Safety and Cyber Security.* doi:10.1049/cp.2014.0981

Stetsko, A., Folkman, L., & Vashek, M. (2010). Neighbor-based intrusion detection for wireless sensor networks. *6th IEEE international conference on wireless and mobile communications.*

Sun, X., Men, S., Zhao, C., & Zhou, Z. (2015). A security authentication scheme in machine-to-machine home network service. Security and Communication Networks, 8(16), 2678–2686. doi:10.1002/sec.551

Suo, H., Wan, J., Zou, C., & Liu, J. (2012). Security in the Internet of Things: A Review.*2012 International Conference on Computer Science and Electronics Engineering (ICCSEE)*, (vol. 3, pp. 648-651). doi:10.1109/ICCSEE.2012.373

Swetina, J., Lu, G., Jacobs, P., Ennesser, F., & Song, J. (2014). Toward a standardized common M2M service layer platform: Introduction to oneM2M. *IEEE Wireless Communications, 21*(3), 1536–1284. doi:10.1109/MWC.2014.6845045

Świątek, P., Tarasiuk, H., & Natkaniec, M. (2015). *Delivery of e-Health Services in Next Generation Networks.*Lecture Notes in Computer Science, 9012, 453–462.

Tan, S.K., Sooriyabandara, M., & Fan, Z. (2011). M2M Communications in the Smart Grid: Applications, Standards, Enabling Technologies, and Research Challenges. *International Journal of Digital Multimedia Broadcasting*. doi:10.1155/2011/289015

The Global Wireless M2M Market. (2009). *Berg Insight*. Retrieved 6 Dec. 2015 from: http://www.berginsight.com/ShowReport.aspx?m_m=3&id=95

Ukil, A., Bandyopadhyay, S., Bhattacharyya, A., Pal, A., & Bose, T. (2014). Auth-Lite: Lightweight M2M Authentication reinforcing DTLS for CoAP.*2014 IEEE International Conference on Pervasive Computing and Communications Workshops (PERCOM Workshops)*. doi:10.1109/PerComW.2014.6815204

Wang, Y., Streff, K., & Raman, S. (2012). Smartphone Security Challenges. *IEEE Computer, Volume, 45*(Issue: 12), 52–58. doi:10.1109/MC.2012.288

Wang, Y., Wu, X., & Chen, H. (2015). *An intrusion detection method for wireless sensor network based on mathematical morphology. In Security and Communication Networks*. John Wiley & Sons, Ltd.

Wood, A., & Stankovic, J. A. (2002). Denial of service in sensor networks. *Computer, Volume, 35*(10), 54–62.

Zeadally, S., Pathan, A.-S. K., Alcaraz, C., & Badra, M. (2013). Towards Privacy Protection in Smart Grid. *Wireless Personal Communications, Springer, 73*(1), 23–50. doi:10.1007/s11277-012-0939-1

Zhang, Q., Yu, T., & Ning, P. (2008). A framework for identifying compromised nodes in wireless sensor networks. *ACM Transactions on Information and System Security, XI*(3), 1–37.

Zhang, W., Zhang, Y., Chen, J., Li, H., & Wang, Y. (2013). End-to-end security scheme for Machine Type Communication based on Generic Authentication Architecture. *Cluster Computing, Springer, 16*(4), 861–871. doi:10.1007/s10586-013-0259-6

Chapter 11
Infrequent Pattern Identification in SCADA Systems Using Unsupervised Learning

Mohiuddin Ahmed
UNSW Canberra, Australia

ABSTRACT

In recent years, it has been revealed that these critical infrastructures such as SCADA systems have been the target of cyber-terrorism. In general cyber-attacks are infrequent in nature and hence infrequent pattern identification in SCADA systems is an important research issue. Therefore, design and development of an efficient infrequent pattern detection technique is a research priority. In this chapter, the effectiveness of co-clustering which is advantageous over regular clustering for creating more fine-grained representation of the data and computationally efficient is explored for infrequent pattern identification in SCADA systems. A multi-stage co-clustering based infrequent pattern detection technique is proposed and applied on seven benchmark SCADA datasets which includes practical industrial datasets. The proposed method shows its superiority over existing clustering based techniques in terms of computational complexity which is essential for practical deployment in a SCADA framework.

INTRODUCTION

Nation's critical infrastructures including Energy, Gas and Water networks need advanced monitoring and control for reliable and smooth operation of the whole interconnected complex system. Still today, the Industrial Control Systems (ICS) of these critical infrastructures rely on the Supervisory Control and Data Acquisition (SCADA) systems (Figure 1.) for system wide monitoring and control. Typically, SCADA system includes Remote Terminal Units (RTUs) with Intelligent Electronic Devices (IEDs), Programmable Logic Controllers (PLCs), a telemetry system, a Human Machine Interface (HMI) and a supervisory (computer) system. In a SCADA system, the supervisory system is connected with the RTUs through communication infrastructures. In the SCADA conception, data acquisition is the first task done by the monitoring and sensing devices. For example, in an Energy System Phasor Measurement

DOI: 10.4018/978-1-5225-1829-7.ch011

Units (PMU) measure the Global Positioning System (GPS) synchronised system states, e.g., voltage magnitudes and angles. This information is then sent to the control room. Once data acquisition task is completed, the second task involves with the intelligent decision making in the control centre. Finally, the control decisions are sent to the RTU/PLC to adjust or override the current states. The whole process is a feedback system where all devices and modules play a vital role for information monitoring, processing and control. Due to numerous advantages towards a reliable and efficient system operation, SCADA systems are widely used in different sectors of critical infrastructures. In recent years, SCADA system is facing new type of threats that did not appear before. Often these threats or unusual activities are considered as anomalies, outliers, infrequent patterns. In this chapter, we will use the term infrequent pattern to avoid any ambiguity.

Figure 1. SCADA architecture

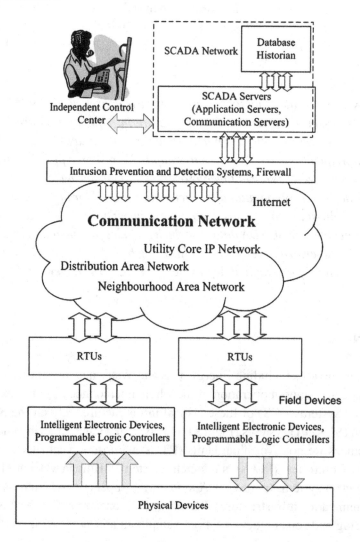

As the primary goal of a SCADA system is to control real-life physical equipment and devices, it differs significantly from conventional information based traffic network (Galloway, B. and Hancke, G. P. (2013)). For example, energy system SCADA can be used to monitor and control the generation plants. SCADA network has its own system requirements and setup. For example, Modbus is commonly used as a SCADA protocol. In recent years, the security requirements of SCADA system is getting more emphasised because of several cyber related threats, especially after the stuxnet virus attack (Ahmed, M., Mahmood, A., and Hu, J. (2015b)). Note, unlike the traditional IT network, the security measures cannot be upgraded so frequently. In other words, most of the SCADA devices/assets have a long life-cycle, e.g., 15-30 years. Besides, the current devices are installed couple of years to decades ago. During that time today's cyber-security threat was not considered. Moreover, it is also not possible to alter all setup to make the network more secured. Hence, new ideas and techniques are required to handle the cyber security issues of a SCADA system. Being a vital part of the nation's critical infrastructure, failure of the SCADA system will cause significant damage in the country's economy and growth. It highlights the needs and importance of research in SCADA security. Novel and practical infrequent pattern detection techniques need to be investigated, which has been the focus of this chapter. Specifically, the contributions of this chapter are as follows:

- An infrequent pattern detection technique for SCADA systems using Multi-Stage Co-Clustering is proposed.
- Proposed method is computationally less expensive compared with the existing clustering based techniques.
- The co-clustering framework has been extended for mixed attributes, e.g., combinations of numerical and categorical attributes.
- Wide ranges of experiments are considered to validate the proposed method using both practical and simulated datasets.

Infrequent Patterns in SCADA Systems

This section discusses the characteristics of some of the common SCADA datasets widely used (Ahmed, M., Anwar, A., Mahmood, A. N., Shah, Z., & Maher, M. J., 2015a), which are also used in this chapter. Figure. 2 displays a simple taxonomy of the infrequent patterns in SCADA systems. The infrequent patterns in the WTP dataset (Lichman, M. (2013)) is caused by the inclement weather. The simulated infrequent patterns in the SimData1,2 contains man-in-the-middle attacks (Suthaharan, Alzahrani, Rajasegarar, Leckie, & Palaniswami, 2010) and in the single-hop, multi-hop (indoor and outdoor) datasets infrequent patterns are injected (Almalawi, Tari, Khalil, & Fahad, 2013). Table 1 displays the main characteristics of these datasets in brief.

BACKGROUND AND LITERATURE REVIEW

In Machine Learning, supervised and unsupervised learning techniques are two widely used knowledge discovery techniques. Supervised learning is the machine learning task of inferring a function from labelled training data. The training data consist of a set of training examples. In supervised learning, each training example consists of an input object and a desired output value. A supervised learning

Table 1. Characteristics of the SCADA datasets

Dataset	Infrequent Pattern (%)	Description
Water Treatment Plant (WTP)	2.5	Contains data of the daily measures of sensors in an urban waste water treatment plant. Stormy weather, solid overloads create the anomalous data in the system.
Single-hop Indoor (SI)	2.65	Two indoor sensor nodes are used to collect the temperature and humidity data for six hours. Anomalies are introduced by using a kettle of hot water in one of the sensors. The simultaneous raise in the temperature and humidity is considered as anomalous in this scenario.
Single-hop Outdoor (SO)	0.63	Two outdoor sensors are used and the same operation is conducted like single-hop indoor data.
SimData1 (Sim1)	0.98	A water distribution system is simulated using the EPANET library (Rossman, L. A. (2010)). Anomalies were created using the man-in-the-middle attacks. In this scenario, water pumps were turned off when the reserve in the tanks is low.
SimData2 (Sim2)	0.95	Similar attacks on another pump and tank of the same distribution system.
Multi-hop Indoor (MI)	2.14	Multi-hop routing is used to create a larger sensor network. Like single-hop indoor dataset, anomalies are introduced using the hot water in the temperature and humidity sensors.
Multi-hop Outdoor (MO)	1.24	In this dataset, outdoor sensors are used to create anomalies using multi-hop routing.

Figure 2. Taxonomy of infrequent patterns in SCADA systems

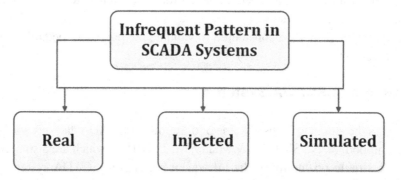

algorithm learns from the training data and creates a knowledge base which can be used for mapping new and unseen data. For example, Support Vector Machine refers to a supervised learning algorithm, where pre-labelled data is required. Labelled data are rare and difficult to find. However, even when pre-labelled data is available, events that are not present in the labelled data, such as zero day attacks in intrusion detection domain, are not handled well. Unsupervised learning tries to find hidden structure in unlabelled data, which distinguishes unsupervised learning from supervised learning. For example, Clustering refers to unsupervised learning algorithms, where pre-labelled data is not required to extract rules for grouping similar data instances. Therefore, unsupervised learning is more suitable for identifying infrequent patterns.

Infrequent pattern detection methods are used to handle different types of anomalous events. To date, these unusual patterns have been handled by three dominant approaches: Supervised, Semi-Supervised and Unsupervised. Supervised and Semi-Supervised approaches both depend on the knowledge from labelled data. The majority of these detection techniques are supervised in nature which relies on labelled training data. This training data is typically expensive to produce. Moreover, these methods have difficulty in detecting new types of pattern. Semi-supervised techniques takes advantage of a small amount of labelled data and create a model for detection. On the other hand, unsupervised detection techniques do not require any training data and capable of detecting previously unseen patterns.

Clustering based Infrequent Pattern Detection

Since the goal of clustering is to group together similar data, it can be used to detect infrequent patterns in a dataset (Ahmed, Mahmood, & Islam, 2016). There are three key assumptions when using clustering to detect anomalies. These are briefly discussed below.

- Clusters of normal data can be created easily, however, any new data that do not fit well with existing clusters of normal data are considered as infrequent. For example, density based clustering algorithms do not include noise inside the clusters (Sander, Ester, Kriegel, & Xu, 1998). Here noise is considered as infrequent.
- When a cluster contains both normal and infrequent data, it has been found that normal data lie close to the nearest cluster centroid but infrequent patterns are far away from the centroids. Under this assumption, infrequent patterns are detected using a score. Svetlona et al (Hautamaki, Cherednichenko, Karkkainen, Kinnunen, & Franti, 2005) presented an algorithm that provides infrequent pattern detection and data clustering simultaneously. The algorithm has two stages. At first, the *k-means* clustering is applied and then a score for each of the data instance is calculated by taking the ratio of an instance's distance to the centroid, and the maximum distance, from the centroid to any other instance. If the score for any instance is greater than a threshold, it is considered as an infrequent pattern and removed from dataset.
- In a clustering where there are clusters of various sizes, smaller and sparser can be considered as infrequent and thicker clusters can be considered normal. The instances belonging to clusters whose size and/or density is below a threshold are considered as infrequent. He et al (He, Z., Xu, X., and Deng, S. (2003)) proposed a definition for cluster based local infrequent patterns. According to their definition, all the data instances in a certain cluster are considered as infrequent rather than a single instance. Amer et al (Amer, M., Goldstein, M., and Abdennadher, S. (2013)) introduced the concept of Local Density which can be considered as a variant. Their proposed score is calculated as the distance to the nearest large cluster divided by the average distance to the cluster centroid of the instances in that large cluster.

Co-Clustering Framework

Co-clustering is an effective way of simultaneous clustering of both rows and columns (Ahmed, M. & Mahmood, A., 2015). Co-clustering creates a set of column clusters of the original columns and a set of row clusters of original row instances (Ahmed, M., Mahmood, A. N., & Maher, M. J., 2015c). Co-clustering also defines a clustering criterion and then optimizes it. However, unlike regular clustering such as *k-means*, co-clustering has significantly lower computational complexity. In a nutshell, co-clustering finds out the subsets of rows and columns simultaneously of a data matrix using a specified criterion, usually distance metric. Co-clustering has been widely applied in various application domain such as text clustering, gene-microarray analysis, natural language processing and many more (Banerjee, A., Dhillon, I., Ghosh, J., Merugu, S., & Modha, D. S., 2007). The benefits of co-clustering over the regular clustering are summarized as follows-

- Simultaneous grouping of both rows and columns can provide a more compressed representation and preserve information contained in the original data.
- Co-clustering can be considered as a dimensionality reduction technique and suitable for creating new features.
- Significant reduction in computational complexity. For example, traditional *k-means* algorithm has the $O(mnk)$ as computational complexity where m = number of rows, n = number of columns and k is the number of clusters. But in co-clustering the computational complexity is $O(mkl+nkl)$, here l is the number of column clusters. Obviously $O(mnk) >> O(mkl+nkl)$.

Information Theoretic Co-Clustering

Information theoretic co-clustering is proposed by Dhillon (Dhillon, Mallela, & Modha, 2003) where the clusters are modelled as the joint probability distribution. According to their approach an optimal co-clustering confirms the loss minimization of `Mutual Information'. Banerjee et al (Banerjee, Dhillon, Ghosh, Merugu, & Modha, 2007) suggested that the information theoretic co-clustering uses the joint probability distribution which may not be known and calculated from contingency table or co-occurrence matrix. Additionally the data used for co-clustering may contain negative entries and distortion measure other than KL-divergence used may be more appropriate. Banerjee et al (Banerjee, Dhillon, Ghosh, Merugu, & Modha, 2007)) extended the information theoretic co-clustering (Dhillon, Mallela, & Modha, 2003) in three directions as follows-

- Nearness is measured by Bregman divergence.
- Allows multiple co-clustering schemes.
- Generalization of maximum entropy approach.

Bregman co-clustering tries to minimize the information loss in the approximation of a data matrix, in terms of a predefined bregman divergence function. For a given co-clustering, a matrix approximation scheme which a class of random variables which store the characteristics of data matrix is defined. The objective function tries to minimize the information loss on the approximation for co-clustering. The authors detected that, the Bregman co-clustering is usable to data with negative values but the data with mixed attributes such as numerical and categorical cannot be handled. It is an important research challenge to handle such data and at the same time using co-clustering to reduce the computational complexity. In the next section, the process of handling mixed attribute data in SCADA systems is discussed.

Co-Clustering Mixed Attribute Data

Since, the co-clustering is used for SCADA data analysis; it is found that, these co-clustering techniques are not using any nearness measures for mixed attribute data instances such as the data matrix with both categorical and numerical data. However, SCADA network instances contain both categorical and numerical data. For example, the protocols of network instances are categorical and port numbers are numerical in nature. In this scenario, the mixed attribute distance measure for co-clustering SCADA data needs to be incorporated. There are various measures for similarity calculation of categorical data (Boriah, S., Chandola, V., and Kumar, V. (2008)) but for simplicity we just consider that, the dissimilarity between two data instances is 1 when they mismatch and zero otherwise. As a whole, for numerical data, Euclidean distance is used and for categorical data the similar data instance has distance zero and dissimilar data has distance one (Ahmed & Mahmood, 2015).

CIISS: CO-CLUSTERING BASED INFREQUENT PATTERN IDENTIFICATION IN SCADA SYSTEMS

Based on the concept of clustering based infrequent pattern detection discussed in previous section, *CIISS* algorithm is built upon the co-clustering framework. The co-clustering framework requires the number of rows and columns as input to create clusters. The *x-means* clustering algorithm (Pelleg, D. and Moore, A. W. (2000)) which is capable of finding out the clusters in a dataset rather than clustering with different number of clusters. The *x-means* algorithm takes input as the dataset and the maximum number of clusters. A heuristic of taking the square root value of half of the data size as the maximum range and two being minimum is well practiced. It is also used as a rule of thumb in order to estimate the number of clusters.

It begins with *(k=2)-means* clustering which is the regular *k-means* clustering to produce two clusters from the dataset. Next, *(k=2)-means* is applied on each of the original clusters. Here the new centroids are moved to a distance proportional to the size of the region in opposite direction. The clustering structure is selected based on the Bayesian Information Criterion (BIC) score. If the BIC score of the original cluster is less than the BIC of *(k=2)-means* clusters, then the original cluster is replaced by them. Else the cluster retrieves its original structure. Finally, the clustering with the best BIC score is considered as the best clustering solution.

According to the SCADA systems description earlier, it is appropriate to apply the clustering based infrequent pattern identification based on the assumption that infrequent clusters are smaller than the normal ones. Based on the type of infrequent patterns in SCADA systems, it is assumed that the infrequent patterns will form a group or cluster. Additionally, considering their percentage in the SCADA systems, it is logical to consider the smallest cluster in the dataset as the cluster containing infrequent patterns. The *CIISS* algorithm applies *x-means* clustering first to find the number of clusters from the dataset and then uses the number of clusters as the number of rows as input to co-clustering framework. For simplicity, number of column cluster is considered one. It is also expected that, the *x-means* will produce clusters which may not segregate the infrequent patterns because; in SCADA systems infrequent patterns might not be much different than the normal behaviour. So, instead of clustering the produced clusters again to find more fine-grained grouping of the data, the number of clusters and apply co-clustering on the dataset. Then, among the clusters produced, the smallest cluster is considered as infrequent. The pseudo code of the proposed algorithm is as follows:

Input: D, dataset
K, maximum number of clusters
c, Number of column for co-clustering.

Output: Candidate Infrequent Patterns
Begin
Let $\{C_1, C_2, ..., C_n\}$ be the output of *x-means(D,K)*
Let $\{C_1, C_2, ..., C_{2n}\}$ be the output of *co-clustering(D,2n,c)*
Candidate Infrequent Patterns ← Smallest Cluster
End

EXPERIMENTAL ANALYSIS

In this section, the experimental analysis is showcased on the SCADA datasets discussed in Introduction. At first, a brief discussion about the evaluation metrics is provided. The accuracy of the proposed approach is measured using the standard confusion metrics. The metrics are listed as True Positive (TP), False Positive (FP), True Negative (TN), False negative (FN). The accuracy is computed using equation (1) as follows.

TP = No. of infrequent patterns correctly identified as infrequent.
FP = No. of Normal data instances incorrectly identified as infrequent.
TN = No. of Normal data correctly identified as normal.
FN = No. of infrequent patterns incorrectly identified as normal.

$$Accuracy = \frac{TP + TN}{TP + TN + FP + FN} \tag{1}$$

Table 2. portrays the accuracy comparison of CIISS and two other clustering based infrequent pattern detection approaches. Interestingly, the CBLOF and LDCOF have slightly better accuracy than the CIISS in four out of seven datasets, in fact it can be considered as similar. But these approaches provide a score for being infrequent to all the data instances and as a result becomes more computationally complex. The complexity analysis is portrayed in Table 3. CIISS reduce the computational complexity far more introducing the concept of co-clustering.

Table 2. Comparison of accuracy in SCADA datasets

Dataset	CBLOF	LDCOF	CIISS
WTP	**97.40**	**97.39**	96.58
Multihop Indoor	97.48	**97.91**	97.48
Multihop Outdoor	98.76	98.76	**99.06**
SimData1	**99.01**	**99.01**	98.17
SimData2	**99.03**	**99.03**	98.17
Singlehop Indoor	97.35	97.41	**98.89**
Singlehop Outdoor	99.36	99.36	**99.84**

Table 3. Comparison of computational complexity. Notes: m= no. of rows, n= no. of columns, k= no. of clusters, l=no. of column clusters

Techniques	Computational Complexity
CBLOF	O(mnk)
LDCOF	O(mnk)
CIISS	O(mkl+nkl)

Combining the computational complexity and the accuracy of the detection methods, an evaluation metric for the infrequent pattern detection methods is proposed as in equation (2). Similar weight to each of the criteria is provided but the complexity is inversely proportional to accuracy because the accuracy is higher the better, the complexity is lower the better. The metric is named as *Overall Performance* based on the combination of accuracy and complexity of the method. A complex method but accurate is not effective than one moderately complex and acceptable accurate method. The performance of proposed **CIISS** method is outdone by others according to accuracy but when comparing with the combination of complexity, it is reflected that the proposed CIISS method is outdoing others. Figure. 3 portrays the comparison according to proposed metric, *overall performance* (OP). Here, we considered the complexity $O(mkl+nkl)$ as 0.5 and $O(mnk)$ as 1.

$$Overall\ Performance = \frac{TP+TN}{TP+TN+FP+FN} + \frac{1}{Complexity} \tag{2}$$

Hit rate is the fraction of the data that are relevant to the query that are successfully retrieved. In the case of anomaly detection, also known as *TPR, Recall*, can be calculated using eq. Figure. 4, displays the hit rate comparison of *CIISS* with the *RANDOM* approach that picks the data instances randomly as infrequent patterns given the number of original infrequent patterns in the dataset.

$$Hit\ Rate = \frac{TP}{TP+FN} \tag{3}$$

CONCLUSION AND FUTURE RESEARCH DIRECTIONS

A novel concept of infrequent pattern detection using unsupervised learning for SCADA system is introduced in this paper. The proposed method is based on a co-clustering approach which is named as CIISS. As CIISS is one of the earliest methods of this kind, the author have implemented and investigated its performance using several real and simulated datasets. From extensive experiments, it can be concluded

Figure 3. Overall Performance Comparison

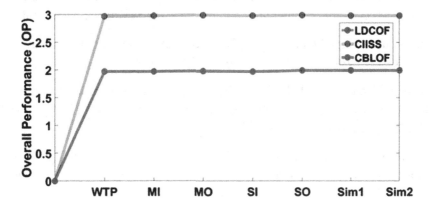

Figure 4. Hit rate Comparison

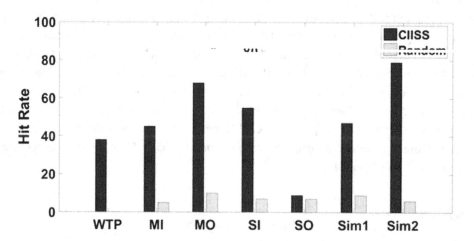

that the proposed method is computationally efficient and capable of producing good quality results. Hence, this information theoretic co-clustering scheme proves its strength for practical deployment in a SCADA environment. Although the current scheme mainly addresses off-line processing of SCADA data, an online method for real-time detection is under preparation.

REFERENCES

Ahmed, M., Anwar, A., Mahmood, A. N., Shah, Z., & Maher, M. J. (2015a). An investigation of performance analysis of anomaly detection techniques for big data in scada systems. *EAI Endorsed Transactions on Industrial Networks and Intelligent Systems*, *15*(3), 1–16.

Ahmed, M., & Mahmood, A. (2015). Network traffic pattern analysis using improved information theoretic co-clustering based collective anomaly detection. In *International Conference on Security and Privacy in Communication Networks*. Springer International Publishing. doi:10.1007/978-3-319-23802-9_17

Ahmed, M., Mahmood, A., & Hu, J. (2015b). A survey of network anomaly detection techniques. *Journal of Network and Computer Applications*, *60*, 19–31. doi:10.1016/j.jnca.2015.11.016

Ahmed, M., Mahmood, A. N., & Islam, M. R. (2016). A survey of anomaly detection techniques in financial domain. *Future Generation Computer Systems*, *55*, 278–288. doi:10.1016/j.future.2015.01.001

Ahmed, M., Mahmood, A. N., & Maher, M. J. (2015c). Scalable Information Systems:*5th International Conference, INFOSCALE 2014*. Springer International Publishing.

Almalawi, A., Tari, Z., Khalil, I., & Fahad, A. (2013). Scadavt-a framework for scada security testbed based on virtualization technology. In *Local Computer Networks (LCN), 2013 IEEE 38th Conference on*. doi:10.1109/LCN.2013.6761301

Amer, M., Goldstein, M., & Abdennadher, S. (2013). Enhancing one-class sup-port vector machines for unsupervised anomaly detection. In *Proceedings of the ACM SIGKDD Workshop on Outlier Detection and Description*. New York, NY: ACM. doi:10.1145/2500853.2500857

Banerjee, A., Dhillon, I., Ghosh, J., Merugu, S., & Modha, D. S. (2007). A generalized maximum entropy approach to bregman co-clustering and matrix approximation. *Journal of Machine Learning Research, 8*, 1919–1986.

Boriah, S., Chandola, V., & Kumar, V. (2008). Similarity measures for cate-gorical data: A comparative evaluation. In *Proceedings of the SIAM International Conference on Data Mining, SDM 2008.*

Dhillon, I. S., Mallela, S., & Modha, D. S. (2003). Information-theoretic co-clustering. In *Proceedings of the Ninth ACM SIGKDD International Conference on Knowledge Discovery and Data Mining.* New York, NY: ACM. doi:10.1145/956750.956764

Galloway, B., & Hancke, G. P. (2013). Introduction to industrial control net-works. *IEEE Communications Surveys and Tutorials, 15*(2), 860–880. doi:10.1109/SURV.2012.071812.00124

Hautamaki, V., Cherednichenko, S., Karkkainen, I., Kinnunen, T., & Franti, P. (2005). Improving k-means by outlier removal. In *Proceedings of the 14th Scandi-navian Conference on Image Analysis.* Berlin:Springer-Verlag. doi:10.1007/11499145_99

He, Z., Xu, X., & Deng, S. (2003). Discovering cluster-based local outliers. *Pattern Recogn. Lett., 24*(9-10), 1641-1650.

Lichman, M. (2013). *UCI machine learning repository.* Academic Press.

Pelleg, D., & Moore, A. W. (2000). X-means: Extending k-means with efficient estimation of the number of clusters. In *Proceedings of the 17th International Conference on Machine Learning.* San Francisco, CA:Morgan Kaufmann Publishers Inc.

Rossman, L. A. (2010). The EPANET Programmer's Toolkit for Analysis of Water Distribution Systems. Academic Press.

Sander, J., Ester, M., Kriegel, H.-P., & Xu, X. (1998). Density-based clustering in spatial databases: The algorithm gdbscan and its applications. *Data Mining and Knowledge Discovery, 2*(2), 169–194. doi:10.1023/A:1009745219419

Chapter 12
CYRAN:
A Hybrid Cyber Range for Testing Security on ICS/SCADA Systems

Bil Hallaq
University of Warwick, UK

Andrew Nicholson
University of Warwick, UK

Richard Smith
De Montfort University, UK

Leandros Maglaras
De Montfort University, UK

Helge Janicke
De Montfort University, UK

Kevin Jones
Airbus Group, UK

ABSTRACT

Cyber Security of ICS/SCADA systems is a major aspect of current research focus. Cyber Ranges and Test-beds can serve as means of vulnerability and threat analysis of real SCADA systems with low costs. Significantly lacking from current research, is detailed documentation of the decision process and the potential difficulties that need to be considered when undertaking the creation of a Cyber Range (CR) in order to facilitate the capture of labelled datasets which is included in this paper. This paper makes several further contributions; a review of Cyber Ranges created by Academic Institutions that influenced the criteria in creating CYRAN, the De Montfort University CYber RANge. The article presents the design implementation, the process of creating effective rules of engagement, the management and running of a Cyber Range Event (CRE) with partners from Industry and Academia and the creation of labelled datasets.

INTRODUCTION

Today Cyber Security is at the top of many government's agendas and extensive research is conducted (Ayres et al., 2016) with the aim of designing solutions that protect against or mitigate cyber attacks (Nickolson et al., 2012). To evaluate such solutions and to increase understanding of how cyber-attacks

DOI: 10.4018/978-1-5225-1829-7.ch012

against organisations evolve and propagate, the replication of realistic attack and defence scenarios is paramount (Hahn et al., 2013). Technical solutions which implement low-level controls such as VPN deployment, data-diodes to ensure unidirectional information flows to the deployment of complex role-based access control mechanisms and federated identity management all serve the purpose of preventing attackers from penetrating the organization defenses. However, the development of security solutions without understanding the concrete threat or the organizations' security behaviour when faced with an incident is lacking a holistic approach to security that must bring together infrastructure, software and human variables. In this work we present the De Montfort University Cyber-Range (CYRAN) providing the infrastructure and resources in terms of scenarios and labelled data-sets to ensure that cyber security solutions are relevant to real world problems and provide insights into how cyber incident response and emergency readiness teams respond to attacks.

One of the earliest works towards the generation of attack datasets was the 1998 Defence Advanced Research Projects Agency (DARPA) in partnership with the Massachusetts Institute of Technologys Lincoln Labs (Lippmann et al., 2002). Their work produced datasets containing simulated data which replicated the traffic of a U.S. Air Force base. They undertook further work in 1999 to extend the previous datasets and released a final extension which addressed specific attack scenarios in 2000. Much research has subsequently been written regarding the shortcomings and usefulness of the DARPA datasets, McHugh (2000), Mahoney (2003), Thomas (2008). Irrespective of these works, these datasets, while innovative at their time, are now nearly 16 years old. As a result they can no longer be considered as representative of modern traffic containing examples of current Advanced Persistent Threats (APT) and Advanced Evasive Threats (AET).

Further work to address the lack of available data-sets was undertaken by Sangster (2009). In order to generate the data, they created a Capture the Flag (CTF) environment, running attack and defense scenarios. The attacking participants were limited to military and government security agencies who launched attacks across a Cyber Range (CR) over a four day period. It is logical to assume that such participants would behave with a nation-state mind set and attack and defend accordingly. Therefore, from a typical corporate enterprise and/or production environment, the subsequent datasets could be potentially viewed as not representative of typical enterprise traffic and related attack types. However, this work clearly proved the efficiency of using CRs to produce unique datasets.

Since the publication of these datasets, there has been little activity to produce and capture datasets that can be shared openly with the wider audience. Rarer still is the ability to find datasets containing traffic and industrial system protocols or specific attacks on Industrial and Automation Control Systems (IACS) and Supervisory Control and Data Acquisition (SCADA) equipment. Yet access to such data is critical to validate and test the research in intrusion detection, networking and general cyber-security, as such systems form an integral part of our IT dependent infrastructure that is increasingly connecting traditional cyber-space with physical systems. This trend is most visible in the move to incorporate and develop the Internet of Things (IoT) for Smart-Grids, Smart-Homes, and Smart-Cities which sees computing becoming pervasive. Often cited for reasons why further work and sharing of data has not been undertaken are the valid concerns around legal and privacy issues and the difficulty in anonymising datasets (Sharma et al., 2014). A further complication is that those who are the data providers, are often not the data producers.

In order to address this gap, we propose CYRAN, a flexible and scalable Hybrid Cyber Range allowing for various types of Cyber Range Events (CRE), such as CTF exercises, training and simulations and serving as a multi-purpose test-bed for cyber activities. This environment facilitates the ability to assume the role of both data producer and data provider, thereby enabling the sharing of datasets and experiences openly with the wider research community.

Motivation and Contributions

The primary motivation of this work is threefold, firstly to build a Hybrid Test Bed which re- quires minimal hardware and infrastructure costs, ensuring key objectives of; scalability, reduced cost, ability to support multiple scenarios, ability to capture enriched datasets and robustness are met. Secondly to be able to support scientifically rigorous cyber-physical security experiments. Thirdly, to openly provide the wider research community with datasets that is the product of running such experiments, essentially being in the unique position of data creator and data provider.

The chapter makes the following contributions:

- It presents CYRAN a flexible and scalable Hybrid Cyber Range. CYRAN can be used in order to conduct cyber-security research, perform cyber threat analysis of systems and evaluate new defense methods and mechanisms.
- It shows how CYRAN supports execution of scientifically rigorous cyber-physical security experiments. CYRAN will be used from students of De Montfort University in the initial stage and from all around the world later for educational purposes.
- It supports the public sharing of data that are collected from these experiments for further analysis, e.g. forensics, causality etc and validation of the results.

CYRAN has already been used twice successfully by conducting two Cyber Range Exercises (CREs). In these exercises different teams from Cardiff University, Lancaster University, De Montfort University and Airbus Group participated. Airbus Group Innovations provided the Production equipment along with knowledge and expertise which was instrumental and ensured it stayed operational during the CRE. The second Cyber Range Exercise was conducted during a UK Cyber Security Challenge bootcamp in August 2015. The Cyber Security Challenge is a series of national competitions, learning programs, and networking initiatives designed to identify, inspire and enable EU citizens resident in the UK to become cyber security professionals. The CYRAN research team of De Montfort University currently working on an expanded suite of scenarios including a Smart Grid, Telecommunication capabilities and an Incident Information System that integrates with Shared Situational Awareness technologies (Hall et al., 2015) that aim at enhancing the decision of CERT teams by providing an increased awareness of the state of environments.

The remainder of this chapter is organized as follows: Section II describes CYRAN's design and architecture. Section III presents the simulation environment and results of CRE conducted. In Section IV we compare CYRAN to the most important works relevant to this chapter, and finally conclude the chapter in Section V where we also outline future work in this area.

CYRAN OVERVIEW

Architecture Principles

Architectural principles for the design of cyber ranges was established by Davis and Magrath (2013) who categorized cyber ranges and test-beds by certain types, namely;

1. Modeling and Simulation,
2. Ad Hoc and
3. Emulation.

Their work elucidates that there is a distinct difference between general Test-beds and Cyber Ranges. A major capability distinction is between the emulation and simulation of network artefacts. Emulation has the objective to model the externally visible behaviour of the components within the system, whereas a simulation has the objective to also model the internal behaviour and state of the components and thus presents a more detailed replica that is based on a different hardware/software solution for the purposes of; scalability, availability, price, or convenience. For the purposes of CYRAN to produce realistic labelled data-sets, a fully functional Cyber Range was required which can both run simulations and emulation. Following Davis and Margraths (2013) classification scheme the next step was to determine the type of CR would be of best use. These considerations are discussed within the remainder of this section. and led to the development of CYRAN as a Hybrid Cyber Range.

Previous works by Bell (2014) and Winter (2012) establish three principle types of cyber-ranges. The first is a physical cyber range for the most realistic perspective as it deploys an exact replication of an entire physical network infrastructure. However, there are several disadvantages which including; significant cost and scalability issues but also the maintenance and change management. The cost of replicating and physical management of an extensive network is very high and is typically only performed for systems that are highly critical and where failures due to changes in configuration as a result of maintenance tasks such as security patching are a high risk to the operating environment or the well-being of people. Even in these settings only those parts of the systems that are critical are usually fully replicated, rather than the overall infrastructure. Scalability is also an issue, since creating new simulations or variations thereof will demand significant work. Within CYRAN, the ability to easily reset the CR after an event is imperative, and can be complex and difficult to achieve with a full replication environment.

The second type of CR is fully virtual where each component is emulated via virtual machines and networking components. This type of set up has several advantages, namely lower capital costs and high scalability thus allowing for the quick creation and addition of new scenarios and environments. Additionally, it can be easily reset allowing it to be returned quickly to its original state. This type of CR is not without its disadvantages though, including; lack of realism, limitations on developing realistic attack scenarios and on modelling equipment behaviour. Finally, completely virtualized environments will not have the same performance as physical systems.

The third option is a hybrid CR, a combination of physical and virtualized components which scale effectively and reflects a best of both worlds approach. A key advantage using a hybrid CR is scalability allowing the easy creation and addition of new scenarios and environments. This type also allows for better performance where needed and is ideal for allowing a mix of high and low impact machines. A further benefit is that improved resiliency testing and simulation of modern infrastructures can be achieved, allowing the incorporation of physical ICS/SCADA systems and thus providing better realism. This method also has some disadvantages, such as the cost element of physical components and that limited resetting and removal of attack artefacts from physical systems may be required. A particular challenge in the development of hybrid CR is the connection and interface between the virtualized components and the physical artefacts that are integrated. Here the move from virtual network solutions to physical networks needs to be seamless and non-detectable by observers that are utilizing the Hybrid CR. Upon review of the three different options it was deemed that the Hybrid CR would provide the most effective architecture and was therefore selected for CYRAN.

The European Union Agency for Network and Information Security (ENISA) provide a list of proactive tools to audit and detect vulnerabilities and prevent incidents. The review of this list helped the decision process in determining some of the most useful aspects that should be included in CYRAN (Table 1)

From the outset CYRANs development had very specific objectives. Namely the contribution of datasets for cyber security research as this is a continued major challenge articulated among other in work by Camp et al. (2009). The headlines of the requests from that publication are presented in the Table 2, along with the feasibility of addressing these within CYRAN.

Communication System

Given the disparate security requirements of ICS and IT systems coupled with the criticality of control systems, a rigorous risk assessment should be conducted prior to interconnecting ICS and business networks. The majority of IT systems are concerned about achieving high performance and throughput while control systems focus on high availability and integrity.

Of the data for continuity of operations. Based on these requirements the scenario developed implemented the Purdue model (Williams, et al. 1994) which uses the concept of zones to subdivide an Enterprise and ICS network into logical segments comprised of systems that perform similar functions or have similar requirements. The architecture of CYRAN uses the concept of zones to split the network into smaller, more focused environments where security controls can be consistently applied.

The communication protocols utilised in CYRAN are; IPv4, IPv6, Profinet and Modbus. The Modbus protocol (Modbus, 2004), was originally developed by Modicon in 1979 which is currently part of the Schneider Electric Group. Modbus is one of the most popular protocols for SCADA applications,

Table 1. ENISA recommendations: CYRAN feasibility

ENISA Recommendations	Feasibility	Comment
Network Auditing	Yes	
Host Auditing	Yes	
Software Auditing	No	Out of scope*
Security Management	Yes	
Network Monitoring	Yes	
Network Intrusion Detection	Yes	
Remote Network Access	Yes	
Secure Tunnels	Yes	

* TOOLS FOR ANALYZING MALWARE COULD BE MADE AVAILABLE SEPARATEY

Table 2. CYRAN: Feasibility against CAMPET AL. requests

Request	Feasibility	Comment
Labeled traffic traces	Yes	
Wireless and cellular network data	No *	Future work
Information about network "agility"	Yes	
URLs received in email	Yes	
Statistical information about email	Yes	
Aggregate statistics about downtime and threats from ISPs	N o	Out of scope
Example hostile workloads for a Web server	Yes	
Malware samples (Centralised Malware Clearing House)	N o	Out of scope
Bug Documentation including regression analysis	N o	Out of scope
Human user event data on various platf orms	Yes	
Data on circumvention of security requirements	Yes	
P ower Grid Related Data	N o	Future work
* Partially		

thanks to its simplicity and ease of use, although it is exposed to different vulnerabilities due to the lack of encryption or any other protection measures.

Physical System

The overall production set attached to CYRAN contained Remote Terminal Units (RTU), Human Machine Interfaces (HMI) and Programmable Logic Controllers (PLC). Open source applications were added such as, a Customer Relationship Management (CRM) system, an Human Resource (HR) Management System, a Finance system, File Storage systems, Blogging Sites and other relevant services that would be found within a typical enterprise network that worked with or utilized production systems.

In order to seed and ensure relevant vulnerabilities were present across the network, several vulnerabilities and threat reports were reviewed. These included The OWASP TOP 10 (Boberski et al., 2010), Qualsys Top 10 (Eschelbeck, 2004), the Common Vulnerabilities and Exposures (CVE) by Mell and Grance (2002), the CISCO 2014 Annual Threat Report, The Microsoft Threat Intelligence Report Volume 16, and other relevant sources. Critical was the ability to capture the data and for that reason the Open Source Intrusion Detection Systems (IDS) Security Onion (Burks et al., 2012) was used. Linked to these vulnerabilities and to key documents hidden throughout the network were a number of hash tokens, used to award a number of points based upon the difficulty of finding the token itself.

The basic hardware configuration of CYRAN includes a physical server which accommodates several virtual servers and numerous desktop and laptop computers in order to provide access to a realistic enterprise network to the end users. Other hardware such as smart switches and wireless routers were incorporated and could be used to extend the network if required. The result of this work produced the minimal base configuration of CYRAN, which could be modified depending upon type of CRE as shown in Figure 1.

Figure 1. CYRAN basic configuration

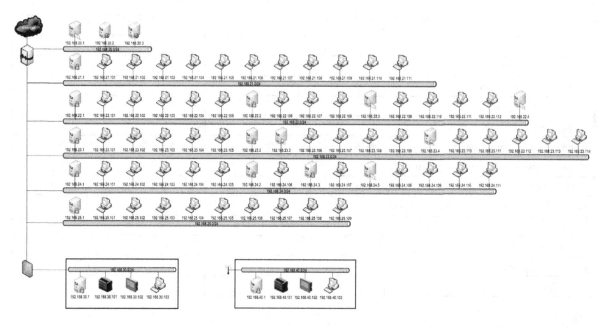

The key aspect was the capability of ensuring the integration of hardware to the virtual environment in a seamless manner, ensuring the transition between hardware and virtualized components was not apparent to those running scenarios across the environment. This helped ensure a level of realism found in real world environments.

Core Features of CYRAN

The core features of CYRAN are:

- It can be run on limited infrastructure, however, allowing for scalability which could include up to 1,000 machines.
- It can be easily redeployed (reset), run multiple scenarios and include a wide range of functionalities.
- CYRAN realistically reflects an enterprise network and the various types of machines and protocols. Included at least one laboratory scale Industrial Control System/SCADA Equipment.
- The ability to incorporate multiple partners with varying skill sets playing various roles.
- Includes the ability to capture not only electronic data, but participants behaviour along with video and voice capture.
- It is robust in the sense that it incurred no interruption in availability during the Cyber
- Range Events.

Additionally, CYRAN is able to easily plug in additional technologies and physical devices and affords flexibility with the capacity to incorporate start up and shut down scripts to provide a different network topology with the minimum of effort whilst successfully deploying a mix of high and low impact machines.

CYRAN EVALUATION AND EXPERIM ENTATION: THE CYBER RANGE EVENT

In this section we describe the first CRE that was conducted using CYRAN in 2013. This event was the first real experiment, performed to evaluate the robustness and efficiency of CYRAN. The second event that took place in the Cyber Security Challenge bootcamp in 2015 was implemented in a similar manner and so is not presented in this chapter. The CRE was made up of over 17 different individuals from a variety of institutions. The membership comprised 4 members for the Blue Team, 5 members for the Red Team, 3 Members for the White Team and 3 members representing management of the production environment sent in by Airbus Group. Additionally a Cyber Psychologist was present to observe and document behavioral dynamics.

The Team breakdown for the CRE (See Figure 3) was as follows:

- De Montfort University (White Team & Blue Team and one Range Monitor)
- Lancaster University (Red Team)
- Cardiff University (Red Team)
- Airbus Group Innovations (Production Management & White Team and one Range Monitor)
- University of Leicester (Behavioural Science and Cyber Psychology observations)

The Red Team undertook the role of attacker. Activities from the Red Team included identifying vulnerabilities, bypassing defences, privilege escalation, Wi-Fi cracking and system attacks, obtaining tokens where successful. Kali-Linux was preconfigured and set-up on dedicated machines, although some attackers preferred to use their own toolsets on personal machines. A separate machine, air-gapped from the range and connected to the Internet was made available for research. The decision to limit internet access was intended to increase co-operation within the red team by introducing the necessity for prioritization of research.

The Blue Team played the role of defenders configured as Security Operations Centre (SOC) analysts and incident responders, with activities including the identification and remediation of the environment. Their remit was to identify weaknesses within the infrastructure and strengthen defenses where possible, identify malicious activity and deploy counter measures where appropriate. To obfuscate some red team traffic generic communication across the network was regularly generated, as an added incentive to the Blue team for accuracy points were deducted for false positive identifications of malicious activity. To aid the Blue team in the identification of Red team activities the Intrusion Detection System (IDS) Security Onion was deployed on dedicated machines with sensors within each subnet. To provide further situational awareness, the AlienVault IDS was deployed on the dedicated ICS subnet to allow focus on malicious activity targeting the real world payloads. Centralized capture information and logs were then provided to the Blue team on request. As with the Red team internet access was limited to a single machine to introduce the requirement of prioritization and role management within the team. As an additional requirement the Blue team were tasked with submitting formal Incident Response. Memos for each action they proposed, to be completed and presented to the White Team for time-stamping and approval. This increased the realism of the scenario, with authorization often required before actions can take place and afforded the white team the capacity to award points to the Blue team for remediating threats whilst still ensuring that some attack vectors remained open to the Red team.

Within the entirety of this project the White Team (WT) had the vast majority of work and undertook several roles. Prior to the event, the WT mapped out the topology and infrastructure, designing and configuring the physical and virtual components within the CR. This included acquiring the necessary equipment, configuring storage, networking, traffic capture, configuring routers, hubs and switches as well as laying network cables and undertaking the creation of VSphere ESXI hosts. During the event, the White Team were in operational control of the CRE, developing the scenario through the use of various 'events' such as providing the Red team with a "found" USB stick containing login credentials and providing guidance to both teams in the event of progress stagnation. They undertook real time activity monitoring during the event (checking bandwidth, resiliency and other critical network functions), were responsible for the capture of activities and logs as well as awarding points where appropriate. To fully scope the engagement, clear documentation was provided detailing the rules of engagement and a waiver to allow the publishing of captured information from the CRE. The WT was also able to play the insider by interacting with the systems internally to simulate rouge activities that are either malicious in nature or simply reflect poor configuration of new services or systems added to the client environment. Further to this, the WT also ensured that all services were running at all times, troubleshooting faults within CYRAN, sensor failures and undertaking the manual provision of network traffic dumps from the central system to the Blue Team when requested.

Critical to the work was ensuring the inclusion of SCADA equipment. The importance of securing SCADA/ICS systems is critical to not only national infrastructure but also for organizations that have production environments or utilize these across various aspects of their networks. The difficulty is obtaining equipment can be difficult. Additionally, replicating some of the more complex equipment can be expensive, limiting the ability for researchers to obtain units for testing. The industry partner, Airbus PLC provided a water pump system and production line, both accurate replicas of traditional systems fabricated on a laboratory scale for portability (See Figure 2). The overall production set attached to CYRAN contained RTUs, HMI's and PLCs.

An additional aspect of the scenario was the inclusion of the Production & Business Management Team made up of solely Airbus Group participants. Their purpose was to increase the realism of the scenario, with members taking the role of various senior members of the business unit and responding to recommendations from a holistic business perspective. They were responsible for ensuring the production systems functioned (See Figure 3) and making business critical decisions when the Blue Team would raise queries relating to the impact of particular mitigation activities they wished to undertake.

As generating attack and defence data was key to achieving the objectives of the CRE, multiple vulnerabilities, with "tokens" were created at various vulnerability points. A scoring server which accumulated scores based on the successful capture or mitigation of these vulnerabilities was added. It

Figure 2. Airbus Water Pump & Assembly Line both attached to CYRAN during the CRE

Figure 3. Cyber range event

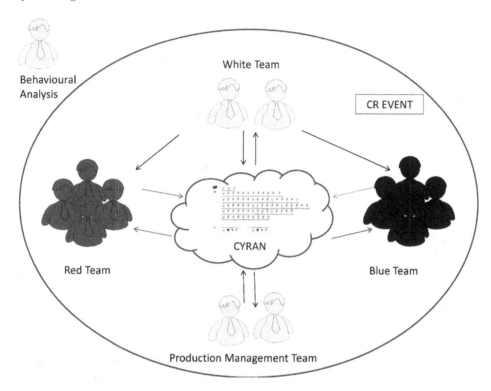

must be noted here that incorporating a level of vulnerabilities within the environment, while trying to balance not making it too easy or too hard. This coupled with ensuring details documentation was created, consumed far greater time than previously anticipated. Researchers undertaking this type of activity should consider this within their planning stages.

Several PCAP files containing traffic across the entire range from both CREs will be made available to the wider scientific community, along with relevant descriptions and related ground truth files (See Figure 4). These datasets will allow the research community to undertake Forensics Analysis, Root Cause Analysis and Incident Investigation and eventually IDS testing (Maglaras et al., 2014).

RELATED WORK

The present work is of relevance to the topics of Cyber-physical test-beds, IDS evaluation datasets, and Cyber Range Exercises. In the rest of this section we briefly and compare the most significant and representative works regarding each topic.

One of the first academic attempts to create a CR with the ability to run on a single device (an important consideration for every Cyber Range is to run on minimal infrastructure) and provided an extensive Graphical User Interface (GUI) was SECUSIM, software developed by the Department of Computer Engineering at Hangkong University in Korea (Park, 2001). With four different levels of expertise, this tool allows those with little expertise to run simulations whilst giving those with greater knowledge the ability to design their own networks and test them against multiple cyber-attacks in a single simulation

Figure 4. Available traffic captures

ceogw000	3/7/2014 3:19 μμ	File	62 KB
dmzgw000	3/7/2014 11:38 πμ	File	97657 KB
dmzgw001	3/7/2014 3:56 μμ	File	93955 KB
eth8000	3/7/2014 11:03 πμ	File	97657 KB
eth8001	3/7/2014 11:35 πμ	File	97657 KB
eth8002	3/7/2014 11:57 πμ	File	97657 KB
eth8003	3/7/2014 12:19 μμ	File	97657 KB
eth8004	3/7/2014 1:45 μμ	File	97658 KB
eth8005	3/7/2014 2:08 μμ	File	97657 KB
eth8006	3/7/2014 3:55 μμ	File	12241 KB
fingw000	3/7/2014 3:56 μμ	File	48951 KB
hrgw000	3/7/2014 3:56 μμ	File	37789 KB
ics1gw000	3/7/2014 3:56 μμ	File	19804 KB
ics2gw000	3/7/2014 3:56 μμ	File	36204 KB
rndgw000	3/7/2014 3:56 μμ	File	3625 KB
worldgw000	3/7/2014 11:36 πμ	File	97657 KB
worldgw001	3/7/2014 3:56 μμ	File	92197 KB

run. SECUSIM includes 20 different attack scenarios which can be deployed to attack over 100 network components. One of the key features that this CR has is the facility to be configured by a single user. Although SECUSIM was a very promising CR, little progress appears to have been made since its initial deployment 13 years ago.

In 2003, the Institute of Security Technology Studies at Dartmouth College developed a cyber-attack simulation tool called NetSim. Similar to other environments, NetSim was a C++ application running on Linux where various device types could be represented along with a few generic attacks. A limitation of NetSim is that the overall architecture of NetSim allows users to take a limited number of realistic remediation actions in response to attacks.

In a later project, Liljenstam (2005) and other researchers at the University of Illinois created the Real-Time Immersive Network Simulation Environment (RINSE). Like SECUSIM it was developed primarily using C++. Although this environment was built to simulate a large scale infrastructure, it has a significant limitation of replicating only two types of cyber-attacks, DDoS and Internet Worm propagation. Sangster et al. (2009), noted that a further drawback to RINSE was its heavy reliance on the use of a command-line interface, instead of a full GUI. which actually was a step backwards from the extensive GUI features included in SECUSIM. An important feature of RINSE was its ability to simulate hundreds of Local Area Networks (LAN) across a virtual Wide Area Network (WAN). Similar in SECUSIM, there appears to be little subsequent work related to this project.

In 2007 researchers from the Rochester Institute of Technology (RIT) presented their work called ARENA. In ARENA a simulation software was used to simulate cyber-attacks against a computer network from an external source such as the internet. One key feature of ARENA, was its ability to make use of pre-scripted attacks which can be predefined within an XML file and then loaded into the simulation environment (Costantini et al., 2007). The other key feature was its focus on the use of Intrusion Detection Sensors which were deployed at various specific places along the network, creating an alert mechanism when specific events are triggered. Again no further work past the one that presents the ARENA exists. However, as the original project was funded in part by the U.S Air Force Research Laboratory (AFRL) it is possible that any subsequent work might have been restricted from public release.

One of the most ambitious and viewed widely as a representative successes of an Academic cyber range is the Michigan Cyber Range (MCR). The level of scale of the MCR is significant as it is dispersed on hardware that runs across three disparate University Campuses in the USA. (Eastern Michigan University, Ferris State University and Northern Michigan University). The infrastructure is broken down into management racks located at each campus, which house up to 10 internal range racks. The management rack contains equipment which can generate traffic via simulation or replay as well as capture traffic. Within the range racks up to 1,000 virtualized nodes are available, allowing the connecting users the ability to attach and run a wide range of networked devices and services. MCR also state that these can run up to 1,000 simultaneous connections. A unique aspect of the Michigan Cyber Range is their representation of a town that is perpetually under siege named "Alphaville". This "town" consists of four virtualized locations, a Library, a School, City Hall and Emergency Services with each location being represented within virtual machines (VMs) configured at various security levels. There appears to be no openly available datasets directly released from MCR.

The DeterLabs Cyber Range infrastructure is supported by a dedicated team aptly named The DE-TER Team at the University of Southern Californias Information Sciences Institute and the University of California at Berkeley. It is a useful example of a federated cyber range which spans across a wide area network containing over 540 high-capacity multi-core server nodes (Benzel et al.. 2011). This Cyber Range has high costing and cannot be portable as CYRAN will be in the final stage of production.

It is well documented that a key reason for the lack of availability is due to the difficulties in ensuring the confidentiality and anonymization of live captured datasets. The most widely used and cited are the Defence Advanced Research Projects Agency (DARPA) datasets compiled conjunction with the Massachusetts Institute of Technology (MIT) Lincoln Lab in 1998, 1999 and 2000 (McHugh 2000). These datasets provided the first systematic approach to attack identification. In the DARPA scenario, labelled data which simulated network traffic of a US Airforce base was generated. In recent years these datasets are still used for research validation primarily because there are few viable alternatives available.

One of the few datasets containing Advanced Persistent Threats (APT) information is the protected Repository for the Defense of Infrastructure against Cyber Threats (PREDICT), main- tained by the US Department of Homeland Security (Scheper, 2015). However, an immediate hurdle is that in order to obtain access to the PREDICT datasets, there are various limitations to whom can gain access, including regional location (of the researcher) limitations. Additionally, there is in place, what some researchers might deem a rather rigid usage restrictions agreement. A further limitation of PREDICT is that data providers can retire datasets making it impossible to reproduce past experiments.

Some publicly available datasets are provided in part as results of Capture the Flag (CTF) competition, however these generally suffer from one of two key difficulties. They are either very large files, frequently not split at the appropriate places to differentiate specific attacks, or they do not provide any details (ground truths) of at least some idea of the type of attacks. They also frequently to not provide specifics of the environment they were generated on and/or the manner in which they were captured. For example the DEFCON 2011 CTF dataset is 246 GB in size split up into over thousands of files. Transferring them in a timely fashion would be the first hurdle let alone identifying the attacks.

The work referenced and undertaken in the Sangster, et al., (2009) paper of the National Cyber Defense Exercise (CDX), provides a good example of how data from a CTF event can be effectively disseminated. It also proved the efficacy of using a CR to produce unique datasets. However, as the attacking participants were all military or national security team members it could be considered as not entirely representative of formal corporate or production traffic It is logical to assume that such participants in the attack would attack and defend based on a nation- state mind set and less as an average cybercriminal or hacktivist. The CDX work is one of the rare examples of a data generator also being the data contributor, a desired aspect for CYRAN. An interesting point within the CDX work, was the requirement for an assortment of virtual environments to be created and provided by other participants for attachment into the core CDX CR. The fact that other partners had provided key components was encouraging for CYRAN as there was a desire to incorporate a subnets provided by Airbus Group or other collaborators in the future.

When it comes to SCADA attack datasets, publicly available ones are rare. The 2011 work from Morris et al. (2011) followed by the 2014 Morris T. and Gao W. (2014) publication, are one of few examples of these being publicly available. These datasets specifically related to critical infrastructure, these are both useful and current. However, the work appears to focus on command injection directly into the Remote Terminal Unit (RTU) and placing greater onus on the identification of potential insider attacks.

One of the most widely reference sources on Internet traffic comes from the Cooperative Association for Internet Data Analysis (CAIDA). It exists with a primary focus on providing a worldwide network framework to allow the study and technical understanding of Internet capacity and usage. CAIDA methodology it to collect and aggregate data from the darknet using the University of California San Diego (UCSD) network telescope. The CAIDA website offers a long list of publications that based on or around the available datasets which are useful. In general though, these datasets are less relevant to this work as they look at large scale internet events. The objective of CYRAN is to be able to produce smaller datasets containing attacks that originate from a simulated version of internet or an outside a network while ensuring they are reflective of the attackers journey once inside the CR. Further drawbacks to CAIDA, is that the many of the datasets which provide attack details, require an account to be established and do not generally provide a ground truth details.

Based on the current work it is concluded that there has been extensive work in the area of simulation and tested environments. With the exception of the Sangster et al. (2009) work, the data generators or those that build the tools and environments, or create CRE are not also the data providers. As stated in the outset of this chapter, the clear objective when developing CYRAN was to create the a Hybrid Cyber Range in order to be able to perform innovative research on the cyber security field, use it for educational purposes and also capture and provide unique datasets from each Cyber Range Event.

CONCLUSION

CYRAN is a realistic environment used for cyber warfare training, cyber resiliency testing and cyber technology development. CYRAN has been developed utilizing a hybrid approach, combining virtualized components with actual physical hardware, facilitating scalability com- bined with robustness and includes but is not limited to the capacity for switches, routers, user terminals with a variety of operating systems, programmable logic controllers, human machine interfaces, geographically distributed networks and virtual private networks.

Scenarios can be developed to better represent operational environments by incorporating physical systems such as control systems and bespoke technologies, providing enhanced re- siliency testing. Once a scenario has been developed Red vs Blue exercises (where one team attack the system and the other attempt to identify and attribute the attacks) can be performed, highlighting areas of weakness likely to be exploited by malicious actors and assessing the level of information required for successful attribution.

CYRAN is a low cost Cyber Range that can be easily used for experiments on realistic scenarios, for various educational and training purposes and for the collection of labelled datasets for further research. CYRAN has already been evaluated in two Cyber Range Events in which attacks were launched against SCADA hardware, while defense mechanisms were deployed on real time. The datasets of these events were collected, labelled and will be made openly available to the wider research community in the near future.

FUTURE WORK

The CYRAN research team is focusing on improving various aspects of the hybrid test-bed. Moving forward CYRAN will be enriched with novel features, such as various telecommunication capabilities, an emulated Banking system, a simulated smart grid, a Virtual Cyber Centre of Operation (Hall et al., 2015), a real time Intrusion Detection System (Maglaras et al., 2016) a honeypot (Doubleday 2016) and several privacy mechanisms (Wagner et al, 2015, Alcaraz et al., 2015). By adding these additional features to CYRAN, new attack scenarios will be easily deployed on the hybrid test-bed, revealing vulnerabilities of the various systems and thus giving the researchers the opportunity of developing innovative defense mechanisms. Of special interest is the deployment of DoS attacks during a CRE event in order to be able to explore different ways of preventing and supressing such kinds of attacks (Belissent 2004). CYRAN will also be used for research purposes inside EU projects, since its capability to be connected to various real world devices to the network makes it ideal for launching attacks and testing the defense mechanisms of various systems.

Plans to produce a portable version of CYRAN are being developed in order easily demonstrate its capabilities and be used as a modern teaching instrument in various cyber security events that take place around Europe. The CYRAN research team is also working towards the capability for researchers to access CYRAN from remote locations. Via such a federated model, researchers all around the world will be given the opportunity to implement various protocols and study their behaviour in a custom tailor-made environment.

REFERENCES

Alcaraz, C., & Zeadally, S. (2015). Critical infrastructure protection: requirements and challenges for the 21st century. *International Journal of critical Infrastructure Protection, 8*, 53-66.

Ayres, N., & Maglaras, L. (2016). *Cyberterrorism targeting general public through social media*. Security Comm. Networks.

Belissent, J. E. (2004). *U.S. Patent No. 6,789,203*. Washington, DC: U.S. Patent and Trademark Office.

Bell, T. E. (2014). *Final Technical Report. Project Boeing SGS*. Seattle, WA: The Boeing Company. doi:10.2172/1177423

Benzel, T. (2011, December). The science of cyber security experimentation: the DETER project. In *Proceedings of the 27th Annual Computer Security Applications Conference* (pp. 137-148). ACM. doi:10.1145/2076732.2076752

Boberski, M. (2010). *The ten most critical Web application security risks. Tech. rep*. OWASP.

Brugger, S. T., & Chow, J. (2007). An assessment of the DARPA IDS Evaluation Dataset using Snort. *UCDAVIS department of Computer Science, 1*(2007), 22.

Burks, D. (2012). *Security Onion.* Available at http://blog.securityonion.net/p/securityonion.html

Camp, J., Cranor, L., Feamster, N., Feigenbaum, J., Forrest, S., Kotz, D.,... Rivest, R. (2009). *Data for cybersecurity research: Process and "wish list"*. Academic Press.

Costantini, K. C. (2007). *Development of a cyber attack simulator for network modeling and cyber security analysis* (Doctoral dissertation). Rochester Institute of Technology.

Davis, J., & Magrath, S. (2013). *A survey of cyber ranges and testbeds (No. DSTO-GD-0771). Defence Science and Technology Organisation.*

Doubleday, H., Maglaras, L., & Janicke, H. (2016). *SSH Honeypot: Building*. Deploying and Analysis.

Eschelbeck, G. (2004). The laws of vulnerabilities. *Black Hat Briefings, 2606.*

Hahn, A., Ashok, A., Sridhar, S., & Govindarasu, M. (2013). Cyber-physical security testbeds: Architecture, application, and evaluation for smart grid. *IEEE Transactions on Smart Grid, 4*(2), 847–855. doi:10.1109/TSG.2012.2226919

Hall, M. J., Hansen, D. D., & Jones, K. (2015, June). Cross-domain situational awareness and collaborative working for cyber security. In *Cyber Situational Awareness, Data Analytics and Assessment (CyberSA), 2015 International Conference on* (pp. 1-8). IEEE. doi:10.1109/CyberSA.2015.7166110

Liljenstam, M., Liu, J., Nicol, D., Yuan, Y., Yan, G., & Grier, C. (2005, June). Rinse: The real-time immersive network simulation environment for network security exercises. In *Workshop on Principles of Advanced and Distributed Simulation (PADS'05)* (pp. 119-128). IEEE. doi:10.1109/PADS.2005.23

Lippmann, R., Haines, J. W., Fried, D. J., Korba, J., & Das, K. (2000). The 1999 DARPA off-line intrusion detection evaluation. *Computer Networks, 34*(4), 579–595. doi:10.1016/S1389-1286(00)00139-0

Maglaras, L. A., Jiang, J., & Cruz, T. (2014). Integrated OCSVM mechanism for intrusion detection in SCADA systems. *Electronics Letters, 50*(25), 1935–1936. doi:10.1049/el.2014.2897

Maglaras, L. A., Jiang, J., & Cruz, T. J. (2016). Combining ensemble methods and social network metrics for improving accuracy of OCSVM on intrusion detection in SCADA systems. *Journal of Information Security and Applications.*

Mahoney, M. V., & Chan, P. K. (2003, September). An analysis of the 1999 DARPA/Lincoln Laboratory evaluation data for network anomaly detection. In *International Workshop on Recent Advances in Intrusion Detection* (pp. 220-237). Springer Berlin Heidelberg. doi:10.1007/978-3-540-45248-5_13

McHugh, J. (2000). Testing intrusion detection systems: A critique of the 1998 and 1999 darpa intrusion detection system evaluations as performed by Lincoln laboratory. *ACM Transactions on Information and System Security*, *3*(4), 262–294. doi:10.1145/382912.382923

Mell, P., & Grance, T. (2002). *Use of the common vulnerabilities and exposures (cve) vulnerability naming scheme (No. NIST-SP-800-51)*. National Inst of Standards and Technology. doi:10.6028/NIST.SP.800-51

Modbus, I. D. A. (2004). *Modbus application protocol specification v1*. Retrieved from www.modbus.org/specs.php

Morris, T., & Gao, W. (2014, March). Industrial Control System Traffic Data Sets for Intrusion Detection Research. In *International Conference on Critical Infrastructure Protection* (pp. 65-78). doi:10.1007/978-3-662-45355-1_5

Morris, T., Srivastava, A., Reaves, B., Gao, W., Pavurapu, K., & Reddi, R. (2011). A control system testbed to validate critical infrastructure protection concepts. *International Journal of Critical Infrastructure Protection*, *4*(2), 88–103. doi:10.1016/j.ijcip.2011.06.005

Nicholson, A., Webber, S., Dyer, S., Patel, T., & Janicke, H. (2012). SCADA security in the light of Cyber-Warfare. *Computers & Security*, *31*(4), 418–436. doi:10.1016/j.cose.2012.02.009

Park, J. S., Lee, J. S., Kim, H. K., Jeong, J. R., Yeom, D. B., & Chi, S. D. (2001, November). Secusim: A tool for the cyber-attack simulation. In *International Conference on Information and Communications Security* (pp. 471-475). Springer Berlin Heidelberg doi:10.1007/3-540-45600-7_53

Sangster, B., O'Connor, T. J., Cook, T., Fanelli, R., Dean, E., Morrell, C., & Conti, G. J. (2009, August). *Toward Instrumenting Network Warfare Competitions to Generate Labeled Datasets*. CSET.

Scheper, C., & Cantor, S. (2015, April). PREDICT: an important resource for the science of security. In *Proceedings of the 2015 Symposium and Bootcamp on the Science of Security* (p. 16). ACM. doi:10.1145/2746194.2746210

Sharma, V., Bartlett, G., & Mirkovic, J. (2014, November). Critter: Content-rich traffic trace repository. In *Proceedings of the 2014 ACM Workshop on Information Sharing & Collaborative Security* (pp. 13-20). ACM.

Thomas, C., Sharma, V., & Balakrishnan, N. (2008, March). Usefulness of DARPA dataset for intrusion detection system evaluation. In *SPIE Defense and Security Symposium* (pp. 69730G-69730G). International Society for Optics and Photonics. doi:10.1117/12.777341

Wagner, I. (2015, May). Genomic privacy metrics: a systematic comparison. In Security and Privacy Workshops (SPW), 2015 IEEE (pp. 50-59). IEEE. doi:10.1109/SPW.2015.15

Williams, T. J. (1994). The Purdue enterprise reference architecture. *Computers in Industry*, *24*(2), 141–158. doi:10.1016/0166-3615(94)90017-5

Chapter 13

A Key Management Scheme for Secure Communications Based on Smart Grid Requirements (KMS–CL–SG)

Bashar Alohali
Liverpool John Moores University, UK

Qi Shi
Liverpool John Moores University, UK

Kashif Kifayat
Liverpool John Moores University, UK

William Hurst
Liverpool John Moores University, UK

ABSTRACT

Over the last decade, Internet of Things (IoTs) have brought radical changes to the means and forms of communication for monitoring and control of a large number of applications including Smart Grid (SG). Traditional energy networks have been modernized to SGs to boost the energy industry in the context of efficient and effective power management, performance, real-time control and information flow using two-way communication between utility provides and end-users. However, integrating two-way communication in SG comes at the cost of cyber security vulnerabilities and challenges. In the context of SG, node compromise is a severe security threat due to the fact that a compromised node can significantly impact the operations and security of the SG network. Therefore, in this chapter, Key Management Scheme for Communication Layer in the Smart Grid (KMS-CL-SG) has proposed. In order to achieve a secure end-to-end communication we assign a unique key to each node in the group.

INTRODUCTION

A SG is a modern electricity supply system. It uses information and communication technology (ICT) to run, monitor and control data between the generation source and the end user. It comprises a set of technologies that uses sensing, embedded processing and digital communications to intelligently control and monitor an electricity grid with improved reliability, security, and efficiency.

DOI: 10.4018/978-1-5225-1829-7.ch013

SGs are classified as Critical Infrastructures. In the recent past, there have been cyber-attacks on SGs causing substantial damage and loss of services. A recent cyber-attack on Ukraine's SG caused over 2.3 million homes to be without power for around six hours (TOMKIW, 2016). Apart from the loss of services, some portions of the SG are yet to be operational, due to the damage caused. SGs also face security challenges such as confidentiality, availability, fault tolerance, privacy, and other security issues. Communication and networking technologies integrated into the SG require new and existing security vulnerabilities to be thoroughly investigated.

Key management is one of the most important security requirements to achieve data confidentiality and integrity in a SG system. It is not practical to design a single key management scheme/framework for all systems, actors and segments in the SG, since the security requirements of various sub-systems in the SG vary. Two specific sub-systems categorized by the network connectivity layer – the Home Area Network (HAN) and the Neighborhood Area Network (NAN) are addressed. Currently, several security schemes and key management solutions for SGs have been proposed. However, these solutions lack better security for preventing common cyber-attacks such as node capture attack, replay attack and Sybil attack. A cryptographic key management scheme that takes into account the differences in the HAN and NAN segments of the SG with respect to topology, authentication and forwarding of data, is proposed. The scheme complies with the overall performance requirements of the SG.

The proposed scheme uses group key management and group authentication in order to address end-to-end security for the HAN and NAN scenarios in a SG, which fulfils data confidentiality, integrity and scalability requirements. The security scheme is implemented in a multi-hop sensor network using TelosB motes and ZigBee OPNET simulation model. In addition, replay attack, Sybil attack and node capture attack scenarios have been implemented and evaluated in a NAN scenario. Evaluation results show that the scheme is resilient against node capture attacks and replay attacks. Smart Meters in a NAN are able to authenticate themselves in a group rather than authenticating one at a time. This significant improvement over existing schemes is discussed with comparisons with other security schemes.

BACKGROUND

The advancement in information and communication technology (ICT) has not only given the world a smart and high-quality life but also an efficient pr system, energy solutions and intelligent homes to live in. Energy is one of the fundamental requirements to fuel the smart technology and so a 'smart' way of living, and electricity is generally used as the primary source of energy.

According to a report by (BP, 2013), worldwide energy consumption is predicted to increase annually by 1.6% from 2011 to 2030, adding 36% to the global energy consumption by the year 2030. In addition to the continuous growing demand for energy and the environmental concerns, efficient and effective power performance and management and pricing are becoming more and more critical requirements. The traditional 20th century power grids are not designed to handle rising power demand, increasing proportion of renewable, fluctuating energy generation, electricity blackout, integration with advanced communication and controls, and smart metering infrastructure. The continually growing dependence on electricity and demand for efficient and reliable energy distribution have been constantly addressed to provide a modernized electric system to ensure efficient and effective power performance and man-agement, real-time bidirectional control and information flow between utility providers and end-users and active monitoring. Therefore, the SG is the future of the power grid; it is designed to meet the future energy requirements that entail capacity, reliability, efficiency, security, sustainability and safety.

To overcome the limitations and challenges experienced by traditional 20th century power grids and to fulfill the requirements of the 21st century, 20th century power grids have started to be replace by a modernized electricity system integrated with advanced communication and controls to enable responsive and resilient energy delivery. This modernized electricity system is known as a Grid System and is also defined as "electricity with a brain", "the energy internet", and "the electronet" ((NIST), 2012).

In this chapter, an overview of the various aspects of the SG including SG technologies, architecture and IoT, Key management in SG and a design description of key management solution for a SG's communication layer is presented. The chapter concludes with a summary of the important points.

Smart Grid: Overview and Characteristics

A Smart Grid comprises a set of technologies that uses sensing, embedded processing and digital communications to intelligently control and monitor an electricity grid with improved reliability, security, and efficiency. It is a meta-system that, unlike current wireless or other computer networks, uses a complex network to communicate with many heterogeneous devices and systems with different sub-systems (E.D. Knapp & Langill, 2011). The complexity of the network is a consequence of the services provided by the Smart Grid and the roles played by each of its functional components. It is divided into seven functional components, namely, Customer, Service Provider, Power Generation, Transmission, Distribution, Operations and Markets. Each of these components serves a specific role and needs to communicate with other components to be able to provide an efficient service. The typical characteristics of a Smart Grid are:

1. Improved reliability, efficiency, security and environment by increasing use of digital information and control systems.
2. Grid operation and resources in dynamic optimization with cyber security.
3. Integrate distributed resources and generation.
4. Integrate distributed demand response.
5. Distribution of intelligent technologies for communication, meter, AMI and substation automation (Y. Xiao, 2013).
6. Integration of intelligent applications and real-time pricing.

The Smart Grid is a modern power electricity system. It operates with sensors, communications, monitoring, automation and computer to achieve safety and security, flexibility, efficiency and reliability in the electricity system. It is an electricity system, which deals with a large number of customers and has an intelligent communications infrastructure. It enables timely, safe, secure and adaptable information flow needed to provide power to the evolving digital economy. There are many benefits of the Smart Grid, such as operation based on real-time data, two-way power flow and renewable power generation.

A Smart Grid can be considered as a heterogeneous network, as shown in Figure 1, based on the integration of multiple networks such as the HANs for effective energy monitoring, control and management at the consumer end; the NAN for providing advance metering infrastructure to meter and monitor the HANs; and the Wide Area Network (WAN) to integrate automation on to the Smart Grid backbone (Meng, Ma, & Chen, 2014). The HAN interconnects to the WAN via a Smart Meter (SM), which is part

Figure 1. The smart grid: A networked view

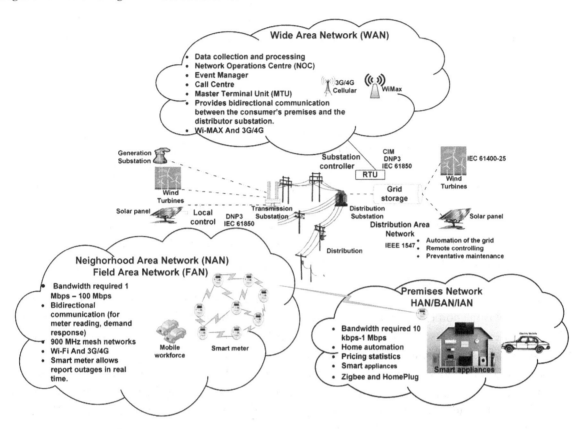

of the NAN. The majority of the devices in the HAN and NAN are wireless communication nodes. The interconnectivity of SMs into the NAN is collectively referred to as advanced metering infrastructure (AMI) and is the focus of this chapter. The NAN is an interconnection of SMs creating a network (with different topologies), consisting of smart meters and gateways that relay data.

Application Layer

The application layer of a Smart Grid generally consists of consumer-end and grid-end applications. At the consumer-end it provides energy usage information, real-time cost, critical peak cost, and automated control for smart devices. At the grid-end, it provides substation monitoring and fault detection, etc. (Iniewski, 2012).

Communication Layer

The Smart Grid is considered to be an intelligent network of metasystems and subsystems providing energy cost-effectively and reliably. It has a hierarchical structure, comprising three areas, HAN, NAN or Field Area Network (FAN) and Wide Area Network (WAN). Smart Grids derive benefit from the fact that homes can be automated using ubiquitous computing and such automation can help in energy monitoring. It is the embedded Internet of Things that provides several services linked to physical devices or resource monitors and enables the management of the energy consumption of devices and appliances. The communication layer consists of three major IP-based and field-level communication networks: wide area networks (WAN), local area networks (LAN) and consumer area networks (CAN). The communication networks are further divided/categorised into more sub-communication networks, as listed below (Iniewski, 2012).

Home Area Network

A HAN is a sub-communication network at the CAN end, which helps to extend the Smart Grid capabilities into a home by exploiting various network technologies/protocols such as IEEE 802.15.4/ZigBee, Wi-Fi, RFID, Ethernet, Z-Wave, HomePlug, Wireless M-Bus, Wavenis (Huq & Islam, 2010). The HAN is sometimes referred as a Business Area Network (BAN) or Industrial Area Network (IAN), as these networks share many common characteristics and design disciplines. A HAN, integrated with sensors and actuators, enables the consumer end to remotely interconnect as well as control various automated smart devices ranging from smart meters to in-house displays, renewable energy sources and storage, to smart appliances such as washing machine, refrigerators, TVs, oven, lights, heating, ventilating, and air conditioning (HVAC), and plugs for electrical cars (Huq & Islam, 2010). One of the important components of a HAN is the home energy management system (HEMS), which enables consumers to monitor how much power their household has consumed. The HAN enables dedicated demand side management (DSM) such as energy efficiency management and demand response through active involvement of power users and consumers (Hossain, Han, & Poor, 2012). A HEMS is the backbone of communication between SM and home appliance. To facilitate the interconnectivity in the HAN with external networks such as NAN, which interconnects smart meters, an energy service interface (ESI) as a HAN gateway has been developed as part of the Utility AMI Open HAN Energy Services Interface.

Neighborhood Area Network

A NAN – sometimes referred to as a FAN or Last Mile Network (LMN)) is a sub-communication network at the LAN end. A NAN, as shown in Figure 1, consists of multiple HANs between the individual service connections to distribute electricity and information (Miller, 2015). The data-aggregator unit (DAU) within the NAN collects the data from HANs with smart meters using network technologies such as WiMax, Zigbee, PLC and ANSI C12 Protocols (Kamto, Qian, Li, & Han, 2016) (Hossain et al., 2012). The NAN behaves as an access network to forward data from consumers to the backhaul enterprise office. In addition to data collection, the DAU also consists of a NAN gateway, which enables NAN connectivity with the HAN and WAN. The NAN is one of the critical components of the SG because it is responsible for transporting huge volumes of data and distributing control signals between utility (service) providers and smart devices connected at the consumer's end.

Wide Area Network

A WAN acts as a bridge between HAN, NAN and utility network and enables connectivity between multiple distribution systems by covering a very large area. Based on various technologies such as Ethernet, cellular network, and broadband networks, WAN provides a backhaul network to connect utility networks to consumers' premises for communication and NAN data transmission (Hossain et al., 2012).

A WAN aggregates data from multiple NANs and relays it to the utility provider's private networks. The utility service provider's WAN is also responsible for delivering a two-way communication network, required for substation communications, power quality monitoring, and distribution automation, while associating aggregation and backhaul for the AMI along with any demand response and demand side management applications (Ho, Gao, Rajalingham, & Le-Ngoc, 2014).

Power Control System Layer

Control systems are computer-based systems and have been of great interest in all types of infrastructure including Smart Grids to monitor and control critical processes and physical utilities. In general, there are two primary types of control system, known as Distributed Control System (DCS) and Supervisory Control and Data Acquisition (SCADA) system. A DCS system is ideal to generate power for small geographic areas whereas SCADA is ideal for large, geographically dispersed distribution operations (Y. Wang, 2013). Therefore, in the context of smart grids, SCADA is a very important component and is discussed below.

Internet of Things (IoT)

Through the years, the era of information technology and pervasiveness of digital technologies has showed an exponential growth, with an increase in the numerous technological improvements available, offering a wealth of new services. Recently, the Internet of Things (IoT) has attracted a great deal of attention, since it involves several applications, including SGs, control systems, remote healthcare, smart mobility, managing traffic flow and so on. In addition, it is expected to grow in popularity in the future. The term IoT was used by Kevin Ashton in 1999 to mean that all things – including physical, digital or any entity that has a chip placed inside it or can be identified via an IP-address – are connected through wired and wireless networks (Gratton, 2013). Basically, it is ubiquitous connectivity with everyday objects communicating and operating constantly. This is leading to a smart world with ubiquitous computing and provides services that enable remote access and intelligent functionality (Chaouchi, 2013). However, over the past decade, the term has been integrated into a wide range of applications such as healthcare, control and monitoring, utilities and transport (Curran, 2014). According to Rose et al. (Rose, Eldridge, & Chapin, 2015), the term Internet of Things can refer to "scenarios where network connectivity and computing capability extends to objects, sensors and everyday items not normally considered computers, allowing these devices to generate, exchange and consume data with minimal human intervention".

Pervasive and ubiquitous sensing enabled by Wireless Sensor Network (WSN) technologies has transformed the way people drive their personal and professional lives. In this technology-oriented globe, WSN technologies are driving the economy and look like they can offer numerous opportunities in various applications by enabling the ability to measure, gather and realize environmental indicators, from mild ecosystems and natural resources, to urban environments and control systems. With the global attention on energy and water management and conservation, the Internet of Things is of great interest to extend the associated benefits of SGs beyond automation, distribution and monitoring (Stackowiak, Licht, Mantha, & Nagode, 2015).

Role of IoT in the Smart Grid

The IoT scope provides three essential layers: perception (sensing layer), reliable transmission (network layer) and intelligent processing (application layer). The IoT enables real-time analysis of big data flows that could improve efficiency, reliability and economy of systems, for example, connecting all appliances in the smart house to save electricity or provide better monitoring. Therefore, the IoT is convenient, sustainable and makes things intelligent everyday of future life (Matin, 2014). From the Smart Grid perspective, the IoT provides a distributed computing intelligence across the whole infrastructure with the help of embedded nodes to achieve an efficient and effective management of Smart Grid infrastructure. From HAN to NAN and WAN to utility providers, the IoT, along with its key technologies such as radio frequency identification (RFID), sensor networks (WSNs), smart technology and nanotechnology, takes a dominant place due to the fact that it helps to provide real-time, accurate and comprehensive communication, data transmission and monitoring over power transmission and distribution (Hua, Junguo, & Fantao, 2014). The growth of the IoT and Smart Grids is mutually supportive. On the one hand, the IoT used in a Smart Grid plays a crucial role to promote the development of Smart Grids and achieve real-time information gathering, monitoring and controlling of important operating parameters (Al-Ali & Aburukba, 2015). On the other hand, the intelligent communication networks have become a driving force towards the development of the IoT network paradigm (Spanò, Niccolini, Di Pascoli, & Iannacconeluca, 2015).

Security Challenges and Attacks in Smart Grid

Recently cyber-attacks on critical infrastructure have highlighted security as a major requirement for Smart Grids (Eric D. Knapp & Samani, 2013). Despite its numerous advantages, there are many security challenges and issues in the Smart Grid, such as access control and identity management, connectivity, privacy, data analysis issues and minimizing cost (Zhong & Hornik, 2013).

The Smart Grid is classified as a critical infrastructure that provides an essential service to users. The challenge in securing the Smart Grid is that the security solutions should be easily deployable, integrable and useable without affecting the performance requirements. Many security solutions have been proposed to fulfil the security requirements of a Smart Grid. However, these solutions are specifically designed for specific security issues, based on a varied set of assumptions, and limited to portions of the functional Smart Grid infrastructure.

Deploying a Smart Grid without adequate security might result in serious consequences such as grid instability, utility fraud, and loss of user information and energy-consumption data (Lv, Mu, & Li, 2014). According to a report published by Krebson Security {krebsonsecurity, APR 12 #85}(krebsonsecurity), the FBI investigated the hacking of Smart Grid meters in Puerto Rico, Brazil. The bureau distributed an intelligence alert about its findings to select industry personnel and law enforcement officials. The FBI said that it believed former employees of the meter manufacturer and employees of the utility company were altering the meters in exchange for cash, and training others to do so because of "the ease of exploitation and economic advantage to the hacker and the electric customer". Therefore, it is important to ensure that the data carried by the Smart Grid system is kept confidential and that no one but the right receiver can access the data (krebsonsecurity).

ATTACKS ON THE SMART GRID

In this section the major challenges faced in securing SGs are explained and then the challenges related to factors that caused recent attacks on SGs. SGs are vulnerable to various threats and attacks like node capture (NC) attacks, denial of service (DoS) attacks, distributed DoS (DDoS) attacks, replay attacks, data injection/alteration attacks, identity spoofing attack, and compromised key attack. Some of the critical attacks are discussed below.

Node Capture Attack

In the Smart Grid context, a node capture (NC) attack is one of the most severe threats due to the unattended nature of the integrated sensor nodes. As the name implies, a NC attack allows an intruder to capture a node and get access to the system by compromising the secure key, node identification, and the data transmitted between node and network (Bharathi, Tanguturi, Jayakumar, & Selvamani, 2012) (Venkatraman, Daniel, & Murugaboopathi, 2013). In the context of HAN and NAN, a node can easily be compromised due to a node capture attack.

Denial of Service (DoS)

The denial of service (DoS) and/or distributed denial of service (DDoS) is a common type of attack on communication networks. The DoS/DDoS attacks target the system availability by thwarting message delivery through delaying, blocking or corrupting the communication between Smart Grid components. The availability of a Smart Grid is its fundamental requirement and therefore the Smart Grid system must be secure enough against the DoS attacks at all communication layers, such as physical layer, MAC layer, network and transport layer (W. Wang & Lu, 2013).

- **Physical Layer:** The data flow between the network components in a Smart Grid significantly relies on the communication channel. If the communication channel between nodes and the control center becomes the target of a DoS attack (i.e. jamming the communication through injecting a large number of packets) by an intruder, then it can significantly affect the power substation system's performance due to delayed delivery of time-critical messages (Liu, Liu, & El Saddik, 2013). Due to the delay-constraint nature of the Smart Grid infrastructure, even a low-level DoS attack (jamming the network to add delay) can cause severe damage to the time-critical communication by adding to the delay.
- **MAC Layer:** In addition to jamming at the physical layer, spoofing (i.e. masquerading as another device to inject fake information) is a relatively severe threat at the MAC layer as it targets both the system's availability and integrity. From the Smart Grid perspective, a compromised node can broadcast fake address resolution protocol (ARP) packets to bring down the connectivity of smart nodes to substation nodes (Premaratne, Samarabandu, Sidhu, Beresh, & Tan, 2010).
- **Network and Transport Layer:** Network and transport layers are vulnerable to DoS threats due to the TCP/IP protocol model and the multi-hop communication. DoS attacks such as distributed traffic flooding and worm propagation over the Internet via network and transport layers can cause severe damage to the entire network (W. Wang & Lu, 2013). In a study by Jin et al.(Jin, Nicol, & Yan, 2011). The impact of a buffer-flooding DoS attack on a DNP3-based SCADA network was

evaluated. DNP3 protocol has been widely used in power SCADA systems to communicate the observed sensor state information to the control center. It is highlighted that SCADA systems are quite vulnerable to DoS attacks like buffer flooding.

In the context of HAN and NAN, a node can easily be compromised due to a node capture attack. The compromised node can be used to trigger a DoS attack, where a compromised node illegitimately sends a large number of malicious packets or performs malicious activity at a rate, which can severely upset the communication between nodes. In the context of HAN/NAN, where multi-hop communication is common, the DoS attack can exhaust nodes' storage, computing and processing capability. The scope of the attack can vary based on the network topologies. It is therefore clear that Smart Grids must be secured to avoid DoS/DDoS attacks.

Sybil Attack

A Sybil is a malicious and masquerading type of attack in which a malicious or compromised node represents multiple forged identifications similar to other normal/honest nodes. The normal nodes, due to their lack of ability to distinguish forged nodes, are misled into communicating with malicious nodes (Taylor & Johnson, 2015). This enables malicious and compromised nodes to attack routing, data aggregation, fault-tolerant schemes, resource allocation and misbehavior detection protocols and sensitive data flowing in the network to damage the system's efficiency, confidentiality and integrity (Golestani Najafabadi, Naji, & Mahani, 2013). Zhang et al. (Zhang, Liang, Lu, & Shen, 2014) discussed three Sybil attack domains, named as community, social and mobile domain, in the context of IoT to define the edge and the capability of the intruder.

In the community Sybil attack, intruders build the connections with the Sybil community with other malicious nodes. In community-level Sybil attacks, the connectivity with normal/honest nodes is not strong, due to limited connectivity. As compared to a community Sybil attack, a social Sybil attack shows that a malicious node can connect with other Sybil nodes as well as with normal/honest nodes. Due to more social connectivity, Sybil social attack is more vulnerable to Smart Grid as AMI is more exposed to the intruder. As compared to both community and social Sybil attacks in the mobile domain is dependent on the dynamic topology due to the node mobility. Due to its dynamic nature, it is less vulnerable to attack compared to community and social Sybil attack as the latter attacks allow intruders to attack a static network.

In the context of the HAN and NAN, a node can easily be compromised due to a node capture attack. The compromised node can be used to trigger a Sybil attack, where a compromised node illegitimately claims multiple identities as Sybil nodes to the HAN and the Gateway. The NAN topology with normal nodes without any compromised node or Sybil attack. Due to a node capture attack a node (SM) that has been compromised, is a threat to the whole NAN topology. The intruder exploits the compromised node to initiate a Sybil attack, where a compromised attack represents the multiple forged identifications as SM w, x, y, and z to other nodes in the NAN to retrieve confidential data, mislead other nodes, severely affect the network traffic and report false readings.

The interconnectivity of SMs in the NAN is collectively referred to as advanced metering infrastructure (AMI) and is vulnerable to Sybil attacks. Detecting and eliminating a Sybil attack quickly and accurately has been a key challenge due to the resource-constrained nature of sensor nodes integrated into the Smart Grid as they present a trade-off between security and adopting learning to defend against a Sybil attack.

The integration of strong cryptography and authentication approaches can be used to prevent a Sybil attack by restricting compromised node from pretending to be legitimate nodes.

Replay Attacks and Data Injections

Intruders can deploy a replay attack by secretly capturing, intercepting and resending (replaying) the data packets back into the system. A message secretly recorded by an intruder can hold secret information, allowing the intruder to intercept/modify by injecting data and then resending the data packet with the same privileges to gain access to the system. In the Smart Grid context, an intruder can secretly record the data transmitted from a consumer to smart meters and evaluate it to get the consumer's power usage routine. Based on the analysis, the intruder can exploit access to the smart meter by injecting the control signals into the system, such as AMI (Tran, Shin, & Lee, 2013)..

Repudiation Attack

Considering the fact that a Smart Grid consists of millions of interconnected devices spread across a large number of locations, one of the fundamental requirements of the energy suppliers and end-consumer value-added energy service is the assurance that data flowing over the communication network is coming from the entities responsible for it. A lack of non-repudiation is one of the major barriers to building a trustworthy Smart Grid as it can cause energy theft, wrong meter readings and so affect the billing information (Z. Xiao, Xiao, & Du, 2013). Therefore, it is vital to have Smart Grid nodes should not be able to repudiate. Repudiation attacks can be controlled by integrating strong cryptography with efficient key management and mutual inspection strategies to ensure that data or control information has been issued by the actual source responsible for that action (Baig & Amoudi, 2013; Z. Xiao et al., 2013)

Eavesdropping Attack

Wireless communication is one of the fundamental forms of communication in smart grids. Wireless communication is carried out in open space and is therefore vulnerable to eavesdropping attacks by an intruder. Eavesdropping attacks can allow intruders to catch sensitive information from smart meters to analyze the consumers' living patterns and damage confidentiality and integrity. Integrating strong cryptography with efficient key management can control such attacks.

KEY MANAGEMENT

As a countermeasure to security threats and to enhance confidentiality, integrity and privacy within Smart Grid systems, encryption and authentication approaches based on cryptography keys are of great interest. The cryptography mechanisms have been categorized as symmetric and asymmetric/public key cryptography. The former mechanism (symmetric cryptography) is based on a single key shared between communication devices whereas the latter mechanism (asymmetric cryptography) is based on a combination of public and private keys. Asymmetric cryptography mechanisms such as RSA (Rivest, Shamir, & Adleman, 1983) and Diffie-Hellman key (Rescorla, 1999) have been considered infeasible for IoT/sensor nodes because of the high computational complexity (Nian, Jinshan, Lin, Jianhua, &

Yanling, 2013). On the other hand, a symmetric cryptography mechanism, based on a single key, is faster and preserves less power; however, it presents the key management with challenges in maintaining confidentiality and integrity.

A secure key, responsible for encrypting and decrypting data, is crucial to ensure secure communication. Unauthorized or illegitimate access to a secure key will result in a vulnerability threat to sensitive information, personal information, billing information, living style, habits and system control. It is, therefore, a secure management and validation of a secret key is a fundamental requirement for key management approaches and to enhance Smart Grid security and establishing a relationship of trust.

Meta-System Interconnections

The Smart Grid is a type of meta-system where a single computing resource composed of a heterogeneous group of autonomous computers (HAN, NAN and WAN) is linked together by a network. The meta-system interconnections raise various challenges, a critical one of which is security, as it opens doors for an intruder to execute an attack from any component of the meta-system. Key management for securing communication between components in a Smart Grid is a fundamental requirement. However, due to the meta-system and heterogeneity of the smart grid, a single key management scheme is not ideal to fit all components (W. Wang & Lu, 2013). Therefore, the security requirement in a meta-system like a Smart Grid must be considered based on the components involved in communication.

In addition to security, interconnections in meta-systems generate exceptional volumes of data, speed and complexity with ad-hoc data exchange in which centralized coordination and control is very difficult to achieve (Wagner, Speiser, & Harth, 2010). The management of metadata in Smart Grid meta-systems is a highly challenging task. A suitable information and communication architecture is required to allow seamless communication and data exchange to avoid data uncertainty, vastness or integration issues.

Key Management Issues in the Smart Grid

Due to a variety of communication components, the Smart Grid has been considered as a heterogeneous network infrastructure and generalized into four layers: application layer, communication layer, power control layer and power system layer. The selection and implementation of cryptography mechanism and thus the key management is vital in the Smart Grid context, due to heterogeneous infrastructure and resource-constrained nature of the integrated nodes. Due to the heterogeneous nature of the network, a single key management approach is not an ideal approach for all networks – such as smart meter, AMI, NAN, and SCADA – in the Smart Grid (Y. Wang, 2013). Therefore, the key management approach must be considered based on the communication network and associated security requirements. According to (Nian et al., 2013), a secure and efficient key management approach is the combination of various processes such as key generation, key distribution, network joining and leaving process, key renewal, revoking and destruction process, additional node joining and replacement. Due to the heterogeneous nature of the network, network topology, transmission pattern and resource-constrained nature of the sensor nodes, key management has been a challenging issue.

Due to the different network topologies of NAN networks (such as star, tree and mesh/partial mesh), the scope of key management varies significantly. The connectivity between neighboring nodes in all three topologies varies significantly, therefore, a secure key management scheme must be able to cope with the appropriate topology while ensuring all the vital processes of a secure and efficient key management approach, such as key generation, key distribution, network joining and leaving process, key renewal, revoking and destruction process, additional node joining and replacement (Kim & Choi, 2012).

In addition to network topology, network transmission (i.e. unicast, multicast and broadcast) can severely weaken the key management approach. A NAN can communicate via unicast, multicast and broadcast transmission; therefore, a key management scheme must be able to cope with all types of communication while maintaining security. In (Nian et al., 2013), a key management scheme based on a key graph was proposed for the AMI considering unicast, multicast and broadcast transmission. The key management scheme provides the key generation, key freshness, authentication and integrity, and forward and backward security. However, it lacks the key distribution, key destruction, key renewal/revoking and node replacement phases to ensure security.

According to (Nian et al., 2013), a secure and efficient key management approach is a combination of various processes such as key generation, key distribution, network joining and leaving process, key renewal, revoking and destruction process, additional node joining and replacement. Considering the fact that a Smart Grid consists of millions of interconnected devices spread across a large number of locations, the key management scheme must be scalable to dynamically adapt the network to integrate all key management processes.

Estimating the Security Requirements

Factors that influence the operational and requirements for the secure scheme to be designed for the NAN scenario are identified. A few of them characterize the NAN from an operational perspective. They are:

1. **Wireless Network:** The predominant means of interconnectivity between SMs is wireless. This implies a shared media and has the associated vulnerabilities such as data capture (snooping), assuming identities (spoofing) and radio signal jamming.
2. **Network Topology:** Radio signal attenuation requires that the SMs be in the radio range of each other. Given the distribution of SMs in a specific area, there might arise a need to use multiple topologies. The topology implementation could even be hierarchical where necessary. The topology within the NAN will therefore be a mix of topologies that could include combinations of star, tree, cluster-tree, partial mesh and mesh. The secure scheme must operate on all topologies. It should be noted that the topology impacts the number of unreachable nodes in the event of failures.
3. **Multi-hop Network:** With the use of multiple topologies, the data from SMs will require multiple hops to reach the data sink. This will imply that the intermediate SMs that perform forwarding upstream or downstream will use more energy compared to the SMs at the bottom of the hierarchy or at one end of the end of the path. There could also be routing overheads that could attribute to higher processing as well as higher path delays.
4. **Grouping SMs and Routing:** It could be logistically useful to group sets of SMs and interconnect such groups. This would enable effective application of policies and controls. The interconnectivity of such groups could again have varied topologies. A topology with multiple hops to the data sink would add routing overheads. Typically, partial mesh topologies are used to interconnect groups so that there is a certain level of link/path redundancies available. The secure scheme must be able to operate across such groups or hierarchies.

5. **Scalability:** Typically, the network scaling in the NAN happens in fairly large numbers (operation-alizing homes in a high-rise or in a condominium, an industrial estate, etc.). The secure scheme must be able to scale sufficiently without having an impact on the memory storage requirements or on the processing requirements on a per SM basis.

Given these characteristics, the security scheme that is designed requires addressing the functional needs as well as the overall security. These, together, form the security requirements of the scheme for the SG. They are:

1. **Authentication:** Individual SMs require to be authenticated by the network when they boot up and begin functioning. The authentication is the primary process for a SM to join an existing group of SMs in a functional network. The authentication is done centrally at an upstream point in the network either located at the closest distribution station or at a centralized location such as the network operations center (NOC) of the network. It is therefore important to ensure that the number of hops in multi-hop topologies is limited so the end-to-end delays are contained.

2. **Use of Symmetric Cryptography:** Symmetric cryptography provides a better cryptographic strength for a given key length. Given the constrained processing and memory resources on the SMs, it is imperative to limit the processing and memory requirements for implementing security. Symmetric cryptography requires lesser processing and memory for encryption and decryption processes, for a given cryptographic strength, compared to asymmetric cryptography. The key management in the secure scheme has to be effective, efficient and resilient since deploying symmetric cryptography requires sharing of keys.

3. **Validated Forwarding:** A low cryptographic overhead could provide a means for validated forwarding of data packets in a multi-hop scenario. An intermediate node could validate a data packet being forwarded through an intermediate SM upstream or downstream. Such a validation could add an extra processing overhead of a message authentication code or an additional round of encryption. Validated forwarding could help in the mitigation of attacks by early detection at such intermediate nodes.

4. **Time Synchronization Between SMs:** Time synchronization between participating SMs in a network enables both data validation as well as the use of time stamps to generate/compute keys without having to share them exclusively on the network. However, time stamp synchronization is an overhead much like the routing overhead, though not as much. While time synchronization provides obvious advantages, it has to deal with the scale of the network as well as ensure that the clock synchronization is kept up with the source. Designing a secure scheme without the need for time synchronization across the entire network would involve lesser overheads and better resilience to failures and restarts of SMs.

5. **Resilience to Attacks:** The secure scheme must be able to mitigate well-known attacks such as replay attacks (man-in-the-middle sniffing packets and replaying them to gain access to the net-work), Sybil attacks (identity spoofing using a compromised SM) and node capture attacks (physical capture of the node).

These are the requirements for the design of the secure scheme for the NAN in the SG.

A KEY MANAGEMENT SCHEME FOR SECURE COMMUNICATIONS BASED ON SMART GRID REQUIREMENTS

The main components in an SG segment are smart meters, which form a large-scale network. Therefore, to manage a large scale SG, organizing the SG into groups of nodes is considered in the proposed scheme. Key management for groups of SMs in a SG has been proposed. In order to achieve a secure end-to-end communication a unique key is assigned to each SM in the group. This unique key is shared only with the utility company server (NOC), and sends encrypted data through other nodes to the NOC without decryption at any intermediate SM. The algorithm proposed is detailed in Figure 2.

Figure 2. The proposed algorithm for the secure scheme

Pre-deployment Phase
Step 1: Formation of the Group GC_g
    // Configure the group controller GC_g ID on the SM; assign a unique serial number SeN
Step 2: Assign unique symmetric key $K_{N_i,NOC}$ to each *Node* N_i
    // must be the same with the NOC key
Step 3: Assign master key MKN_i to N_i
    // N_i is the node ID of the SM, relevant within the group
Step 4: $\forall\ N_i \in GC_g$, do
    Calculate $KN_i = (MKN_i \parallel N_i)$
     //Generate KN_i key
    [End of loop]
Authentication Phase
Step 5: *Authentication Request*: Encrypt SeN with $K_{N_i,NOC}$ to yield Mi; Send Mi, ID and TS (time stamp) to GC_g
Step 6: *Authentication Response*: Receive a key to communicate with the GC_g, KGC_g, from the NOC and generate a new key using KGC_g and the SM's id, ID
Step 7: Authentication Response: Receive a response from the GC_g providing a random seed R' to N_i
Step 8: Authentication Acknowledgement: Send an ACK with ID and TS, encrypted with KGC_g and a message authentication code (MAC) generated using R'
Step 9: GC_g multicasts the SM ID and the random seed to the group to enable communication within the group
    // Random number generated by GC_g to generate a MAC Aut_g
Step 10: $\forall\ N_i \in GC_g$, do
    Calculate $Aut_g = (R' \parallel N_i)$
     //Generate authentication value Aut_g
    [End of loop]
Communication Phase
Step 11: Event data D occurs at N_i
Step 12: Get D at N_i
Step 13: Produce D; Data encrypted using $K_{N_i,NOC}$ which decrypt only in *NOC* using $K_{N_i,NOC}$
    // encrypt D with its unique key $K_{N_i,NOC}$, $E_{K_{N_i,NOC}}(D)$
Step 14: Compute $B = E_{KN_i}(E_{K_{N_i,NOC}}(D), TS_{N_i}, N_i\ ID)$
    // Send $(B, N_i, TS_{N_i}, Aut_g)$ to destination N_i
Step 15: Destination N_i receives messages; validate N_i by generating Aut_g using its locally stored R' and forward B to the next destination N_i or GC_g. Note only the *NOC* can decrypt B
Step 16: GC receives event data, verifies Aut_g, decrypts B, notes down TS_{N_i}, sends $E_{KNOC,GC_g}(E_{K_{N_i,NOC}}(D), ID_{GCg}, TS_{GCg})$ to the NOC
Step 17: NOC returns an ACK to N_i via GC_g, encrypted with $K_{N_i,NOC}$ and $K_{GC_g,NOC}$

Generic Topology

The SMs are organized into groups and each group is designated a group controller (GC). A GC is chosen in a manner that it be in the radio range of the maximum number of nodes in its vicinity. The topology within the group is so formed that nodes that are relatively far away from the GC (typically below a certain threshold received signal value – RSSI – at the GC), use the neighboring nodes to communicate to the GC, rather than directly. GCs, in turn, connect to the NOC via a single hop path or via a multi-hop path.

Authentication of SMs

The communication between the SMs and the NOC occurs in three broad steps. The first is a pre-deployment phase where each of the SMs are configured and initialized with bootstrap information shared with the NOC, such as their identity, initial key and a unique serial number. The NOC uses this information to validate the initial communication of the SM. Secondly, the SM joins the network by authenticating with the NOC. Thirdly, upon successful authentication, the SM and the NOC can communicate mutually. Figure 2 details the elements of each step.

The authentication of an SM proceeds as follows. The interaction is provided in figure 2. $N_i \epsilon\ GC_g$, N_i will encrypt serial number (SeN) that shared with *NOC* using $K_{N_i,NOC}$ and produce m_i. GC_g, checks TS_i and forwards m_i to *NOC* by re-encrypting m_i with a time stamp TS_i using the key $K_{GC_g,NOC}$ shared between *NOC* and group controller GC_g. *NOC* validate N_i by decrypting m_i using $K_{N_i,NOC}$. N_i then receives a master key of GC_g to generate a sharing key between N_i and GC_g. GC_g multicasts a new random number R' for computing keys to generate encrypted messages with a MAC. Note that although time stamps are used, there is no time synchronization within the network; they are viewed loosely as sequence numbers. The NOC always expects a time stamp with a value greater than the one it has recorded from the previous data reception from a particular SM. The difference between the values should not exceed a certain threshold. The threshold is calculated over a period of time, typically as an average of the time stamp differences.

Generating the Key $K_{GC_g,NOC}$

NOC creates a master key K_{NOC} This key will be used to produce keys for each GC_g (GC_1 and GC_2 .. etc.) A unique shared key $K_{GC_g,NOC}$ for each SM GC_g will be generated by applying a one way hash algorithm on the SM ID GC_g and master key K_{NOC} as shown in equation 1. Each GC_g will only be installed with a unique $K_{GC_g,NOC}$

$$K_{GC_g,NOC} = F(\ K_{NOC} \| GC_g\ ) \tag{1}$$

Generating the Key $K_{N_i,NOC}$

A N_i will be able to join the network, if and only it is successfully authenticated and validated by NOC for secure communication. NOC creates a master key K_{NOC}. This key will be used to yield keys for each (N_i and N_j .. etc.) A unique shared key $K_{N_i,NOC}$ for each SM N_i is generated by applying a hash algorithm on the SM ID (N_i) and the master key, K_{NOC}, as shown in equation 2. Each N_i will only be installed with a unique $K_{N_i,NOC}$. A record of each $K_{N_i,NOC}$ will be stored on NOC

$$K_{N_i,NOC} = F(K_{NOC} \| N_i)$$ (2)

where, F () is one-way hash algorithm, $\|$ is the concatenation function.

The authentication of an SM proceeds as follows. The interaction is provided in figure 2. $N_i \in$ GC_g, N_i will encrypt serial number (SeN) that shared with *NOC* using $K_{N_i,NOC}$ and produce m_i GC_g, checks TS_i and forwards m_i to *NOC* by re-encrypting m_i with a time stamp TS_i using the key $K_{GC_g,NOC}$ shared between *NOC* and group controller GC_g. *NOC* validate by decrypting m_i using $K_{N_i,NOC}$. N_i then receives a master key of GC_g to generate a sharing key between N_i and GC_g. GC_g multicasts a new random number R' for computing keys to generate encrypted messages with a MAC. Note that although time stamps are used, there is no time synchronization within the network; they are viewed loosely as sequence numbers. The NOC always expects a time stamp with a value greater than the one it has recorded from the previous data reception from a particular SM. The difference between the values should not exceed a certain threshold. The threshold is calculated over a period of time, typically as an average of the time stamp differences.

Joining and Leaving the Network

There are no specific join and leave phases. Non-receipt of data from an SM for three consecutive data intervals is deemed as an implied "leave". The authentication is typical for any SM joining the network. The NOC and the GC are the active participants in the management of the SMs. The NOC keeps track of all active nodes and when it expects the data from each SM. If it does not receive data from a particular SM for three consecutive intervals, it signals the specific GC about it. If the GC has a similar observation, it simply multicasts a different random number to the group with the ID of the SM to be excluded. Each SM updates its neighbor ID list and does not accept any forwarded data from that node ID. The random number is used to generate the MAC for messages sent from the SMs.

Implementation

The secure scheme for communication layer in a SG is implemented and evaluated the performance. The secure scheme is evaluated on TelosB Figure 8, which is an open-source platform that includes a mote with sensors and the development using the TinyOS platform. TinyOS is a small, open-source, energy-efficient software operating system that supports large-scale, self-configuring sensor networks.

Both TelosB and TinyOS were developed at UC Berkeley. The security scheme in the figure 8 above has been evaluated on a real platform.

Network Topology

To carry out evaluation of proposed scheme, NAN topology partial mesh is considered. The NAN made of (N) nodes is deployed over a region of $A \subseteq R$. Considering that SMs in the AMI are fixed nodes, there is no mobility aspect included. Each mote is equipped with an omni-directional radio with fixed communication range (R) based on the Zigbee standard. The partial mesh topology test bed of NAN, network consists of a GC, intermediate SMs and end devices (SMs).

Measurements

TelosB nodes are deployed as partial mesh topology for NAN. NAN Mesh topology is more flexible as it can allow each mote to choose between multiple routes to transmit/receive data to the target location. It also allows the network to self-heal and search for other paths and so that data can be relayed through.

First, the motes are deployed in a topology with all nodes in a single hop to GC. In this configuration, the network is first base-lined for delays by measuring the single hop RTT. Three measurements, each comprised of a hundred samples were collected and the mean was 26 ms, giving a single hop network delay of 13 ms. The RTT from an end SM to the NOC via the GC and back was measured in a similar manner. This delay, the network delay from the end SM to NOC and back, involving four network hops measured 76.6 ms. Subsequently, the total time taken for authentication (processing delay for encryption and decryption at source, GC and NOC + the network delay for four hops; SM-GC-NOC-GC-SM) in a single-hop-to-GC configuration was measured as 101.3 ms. So, the overheads of encryption and decryption for the authentication phase - the difference of the two measurements – is 24.7 ms, about a 25% delay overhead. These measurements are illustrated in Figure 3.

Figure 3. Estimating the authentication delay overhead

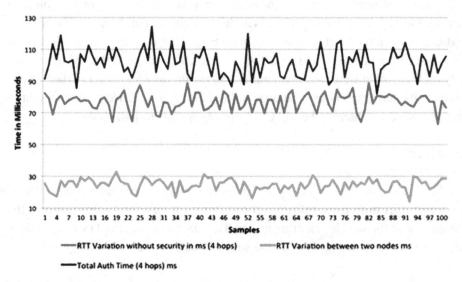

Following this, the delays for the data communication phase were measured. The delays were measured with one, two and three hop configurations to the GC. The overall increase in delay with the addition of each extra hop to the GC was about 30 ms. The average delay for the communication phase in a single-hop-to-GC configuration was about 105 ms. The authentication delay overheads for the communication phase is about 27% when compared with the network delay of 76.6 ms from the earlier measurement. The overheads are relatively high when compared to the authentication phase since the encrypted data messages are tagged with a MAC. The calculation of the keyed hash to generate the MAC contributed to the high delays. Without the MAC, the delays were measured as 88 ms amounting to a delay overhead of 14.3%.

The topology of the motes was changed to a two and three hop configuration to the GC and the delays for the communication phase were measured for these configurations. The comparative measurements are illustrated in Figure 4. Recall that there is one hop from the GC to the NOC. The increase in delay with the increase in hops was somewhat constant. Therefore, an increase in the number of hops to the GC was attempted and delays were measured. It was observed that the delays are fairly linear until a hop count of two but tended to increase rapidly for hops 3 and 4. With 4 and 5 hops to GC, the delays reach over 200 ms. The delays may nor be a serious concern from the perspective of the SG performance requirements. However, with the increasing the hop count within the SM group would imply closer deployment of SMs or an increase in the number of SMs. While the former may not be always practical, increasing the size of the group might lead to routing overheads affecting the performance further. Figure 5 indicates the mean delay measurements with increasing hop count and the standard deviation. Note that as the hop count increases the delay values vary significantly.

In summary, the security scheme was implemented and tested on a cluster-tree (partial-mesh) topology. The SMs (motes) were first pre-configured with the shared keys generated by the NOC. The network was base-lined for network delays by measuring one hop RTT and multiple-hop RTT. The total authentication delay was measured from an end SM and the authentication delay overheads are about 25%, meaning that

Figure 4. Total time for the communication phase with 1, 2 and 3 hops to the GC

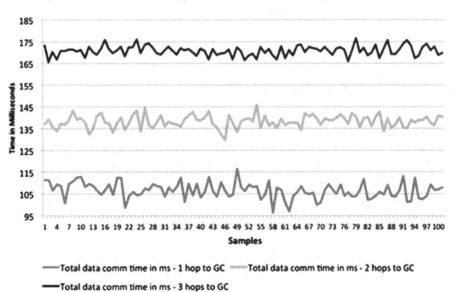

Figure 5. Increase in the communication phase delays with increase in hops to the GC

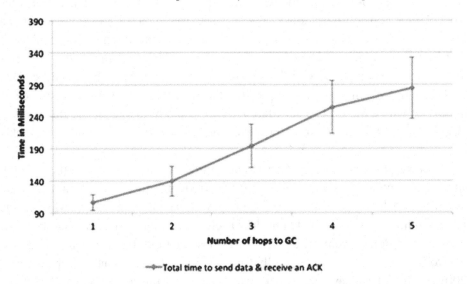

the authentication delay is about a quarter of the total end-to-end delay. The end-to-end delay includes the network delay and the application processing delays on every SM the authentication process involves. The communication phase delay is then measured and the security overheads are about 27%, slightly higher than that for the authentication, due to the higher processing delay on the motes due to the hash computation for the MAC. Finally, the impact of the number of hops to the GC on the communication phase delays was measured. The measurements indicate that delays for one and two hops to the GC are reasonable and have a low variance. From three hops onwards the delay variation is rather high while the increase is delay is close to expected values. With these observations, it is concluded that the number of hops within a group is best limited to two and at most, three.

FUTURE RESEARCH DIRECTIONS

In this section, several research issues have been highlighted for future work.

Prevention in the Wide Area Network (WAN)

It is a core network that covers a broad geographical area and uses communication circuits to connect several subsystems and smart meters with a control centre that is far from the subsystem and customer-side network (Kabalci, 2016). In addition, it has to support the applications and the corresponding requirements in each of the different networks it connects. The WAN can connect using WiMAX, 3G/GSM/LTE or fibre optics. In the WAN, the characteristics and security requirements are fairly complex due to the hosts of grid applications and applications that are related to the operation of a utility, such as SCADA (Berrio & Zuluaga, 2012).

Because WANs have enormous network traffic, traditional security solutions are not efficient for handling such a large data flow. A common issue exists regarding how cryptographic keys can manage a large load of data as well as how to balance the scale of traffic, analysis and data. In addition, logically, the overhead and the load on it increases as the number of hosts increases (Simmhan, Kumbhare, Baohua, & Prasanna, 2011).

Economics and Energy Storage Technology issues

One of the challenges in the development of a Smart Grid is to balance all of the critical variables associated with the dynamic load control powered by ever-increasing renewable sources. The requirement to balance critical variables can be achieved through energy storage technology throughout the smart grid. With the advancement in smart grids, energy storage has become a key technology to develop a low-carbon physical-cyber power system (Venkataramani, Parankusam, Ramalingam, & Wang, 2016). An energy storage system can help to supply more flexibility and balance to the smart grid, providing a back-up to intermittent renewable energy and improving the management of distribution networks, reducing costs and improving energy efficiency and grid management. However, the development and deployment of energy storage technology has various barriers: technological barriers (increasing capacities and efficiencies, developing new technology for local and decentralized systems, integration with smart grid), market and regulatory barriers (creating appropriate market signals and regulations), and strategic barriers (systematic and holistic approach). In addition to that, the main challenge in the development of energy storage is an economic one, which will be a main driver of how quickly, distributed storage solutions are adopted in a smart grid. The economic challenge can vary from case to case depending on various parameters, including where the storage is needed, its generation, transmission, distribution or consumer end.

Big Data Challenges

The upgrade of a traditional power grid into a Smart Grid provides utility service providers with exceptional capabilities for forecasting demand, consumer usage patterns, avoiding blackouts, improving unit assurance, energy market prices, control and maintenance data and more(Joseph, Jasmin, & Chandran, 2015). However, these advancements also generate exceptional volumes of data, speed and complexity, and it is expected that by 2020 the number of smart meters will grow rapidly, for example, to 240 million in Europe, 150 million in North America, 400 million in China and 60 million in Japan. The dynamic nature of the Smart Grid means that it requires constant adjustment based on the real-time information. Therefore, Smart Grid data architecture must be capable of coping with big data volumes for real-time response and sophisticated data analytics (Zhou, Fu, & Yang, 2016).

Substation Distribution/Automation System

This is another important system, which is directly involved in substations towards the consumer and smart meters via AMI. Communication and monitoring systems will incorporate demand response and real-time pricing systems in order to improve the system reliability. Moreover, increasing Smart Grid communication integration through merging the current distinct hardware and software systems decreases cost and lowers redundancy (Bush, 2014).

The substation automation system helps to enhance the system reliability and communication between substations. To ensure a seamless data communication and information exchange across all the distribution networks, the substation automation system is aimed to define the scope to the whole network and provide compatibility with the common information model (CIM) for system reliability and communication (Sauter & Lobashov, 2011). Due to the heterogeneity and interoperability nature of the grid systems, the Common Information Models (CIM) provides a standardized format to allow reliable communication within grid systems (Skopik & Smith, 2015).

CONCLUSION

During the last decade, the SG technology has been considered as progressing in relation to the electricity grid system due to increasing transmission of distribution generation by renewable sources, however, with the added aim to improve the efficiency, reliability and safety of the traditional power grid. In this context, real-time remote data exchange, information about equipment failures, peak usage/limitations and natural accidents are crucial to ensure reliable and real-time identification of possible failures in the SG. It makes cost-effective remote sensing technologies such as IoT crucial for protective, seamless and efficient delivery of power in a SG.

In this chapter, SG technology has been discussed followed by SG architectural layers. The communication layer (HAN, NAN and WAN) has been of great interest as this layer play a crucial role in the deployment of a SG based on the integration of HAN, NAN and WAN. This chapter introduced different SG technologies including AMI, WAMS, and substation distribution systems and so on. Then the SG architecture including an application layer, communication layer and power control system layer is discussed. Finally, the IoT and its role of in the SG is described.

A secure key management scheme for the NAN in the SG is proposed. The scheme is detailed and the interaction between each element in the network is described. An implementation of the secure scheme provides a measure of the overheads due to the implementation of the secure scheme. The measurements are made with different configurations of sensor motes that represent SMs in the SG. The measurements provide a good idea of the number of hops that are ideal within a group of SMs.

Regardless of the improved electricity system reliability and efficiency delivered by SGs, in addition to economical and functional benefits, their deployment and resiliency has been of great concern due to various challenges including vulnerabilities and cyber-threats introduced by integrating emerging ICTs.

REFERENCES

Al-Ali, A., & Aburukba, R. (2015). Role of Internet of Things in the Smart Grid Technology. *Journal of Computer and Communications*, *3*(05), 229–233. doi:10.4236/jcc.2015.35029

Baig, Z. A., & Amoudi, A.-R. (2013). An Analysis of Smart Grid Attacks and Countermeasures. *Journal of Communication*, *8*(8), 473–479. doi:10.12720/jcm.8.8.473-479

Berrio, L., & Zuluaga, C. (2012). *Concepts, standards and communication technologies in smart grid.* Paper presented at the Circuits and Systems (CWCAS), 2012 IEEE 4th Colombian Workshop on.

Bharathi, M. V., Tanguturi, R. C., Jayakumar, C., & Selvamani, K. (2012). *Node capture attack in Wireless Sensor Network: A survey.* Paper presented at the Computational Intelligence & Computing Research (ICCIC), 2012 IEEE International Conference on. doi:10.1109/ICCIC.2012.6510237

BP. (2013). *BP Energy Outlook 2030*. Retrieved 5/2/2016, from http://www.bp.com/content/dam/bp/pdf/energy-economics/energy-outlook-2015/bp-energy-outlook-booklet_2013.pd

Bush, S. F. (2014). *Smart Grid: Communication-Enabled Intelligence for the Electric Power Grid*. Wiley. doi:10.1002/9781118820216

Chaouchi, H. (2013). *The Internet of Things: Connecting Objects*. Wiley. doi:10.1002/9781118600146

Curran, K. (2014). *Recent Advances in Ambient Intelligence and Context-Aware Computing*. IGI Global.

Golestani Najafabadi, S., Naji, H. R., & Mahani, A. (2013). *Sybil attack Detection: Improving security of WSNs for smart power grid application*. Paper presented at the Smart Grid Conference (SGC). doi:10.1109/SGC.2013.6733831

Gratton, D. A. (2013). *The Handbook of Personal Area Networking Technologies and Protocols*. Cambridge University Press. doi:10.1017/CBO9780511979132

Ho, Q.-D., Gao, Y., Rajalingham, G., & Le-Ngoc, T. (2014). *Smart Grid Communications Network (SGCN)*. In Wireless Communications Networks for the Smart Grid (pp. 15–30). Cham: Springer International Publishing.

Hossain, E., Han, Z., & Poor, H. V. (2012). *Smart Grid Communications and Networking*. Cambridge University Press. doi:10.1017/CBO9781139013468

Hua, L., Junguo, Z., & Fantao, L. (2014). Internet of Things Technology and its Applications in Smart Grid. *TELKOMNIKA Indonesian Journal of Electrical Engineering*, *12*(2), 940–946. doi:10.11591/telkomnika.v12i2.4178

Huq, M. Z., & Islam, S. (2010). *Home Area Network technology assessment for demand response in smart grid environment*. Paper presented at the Universities Power Engineering Conference (AUPEC).

Iniewski, L. T. B. K. (2012). *Smart Grid Apllications, Communication and Security*. Hoboken, NJ: New Jersy Wiley.

Jin, D., Nicol, D. M., & Yan, G. (2011). *An event buffer flooding attack in DNP3 controlled SCADA systems*. Paper presented at the Proceedings of the Winter Simulation Conference.

Joseph, S., Jasmin, E. A., & Chandran, S. (2015). Stream Computing: Opportunities and Challenges in Smart Grid. *Procedia Technology*, *21*, 49–53. doi:10.1016/j.protcy.2015.10.008

Kabalci, Y. (2016). A survey on smart metering and smart grid communication. *Renewable & Sustainable Energy Reviews*, *57*, 302–318. doi:10.1016/j.rser.2015.12.114

Kamto, J., Qian, L., Li, W., & Han, Z. (2016). -Augmented Tree for Robust Data Collection in Advanced Metering Infrastructure. *International Journal of Distributed Sensor Networks*, *2016*, 1–13. doi:10.1155/2016/9821289

Kim, J.-Y., & Choi, H.-K. (2012). *An efficient and versatile key management protocol for secure smart grid communications*. Paper presented at the Wireless Communications and Networking Conference (WCNC). doi:10.1109/WCNC.2012.6214081

Knapp, E. D., & Langill, J. (2011). *Industrial Network Security: Securing Critical Infrastructure Networks for Smart Grid, SCADA, and Other Industrial Control Systems*. Syngress.

Knapp, E. D., & Samani, R. (2013). *What is the Smart Grid? In Applied Cyber Security and the Smart Grid* (pp. 1–15). Boston: Syngress. doi:10.1016/B978-1-59749-998-9.00001-3

krebsonsecurity. (n.d.). *FBI: Smart Meter Hacks Likely to Spread*. Retrieved 3/5/2013, from https://krebsonsecurity.com/2012/04/fbi-smart-meter-hacks-likely-to-spread/

Liu, S., Liu, X. P., & El Saddik, A. (2013). *Denial-of-service (DoS) attacks on load frequency control in smart grids*. Paper presented at the Innovative Smart Grid Technologies (ISGT), 2013 IEEE PES.

Lv, X., Mu, Y., & Li, H. (2014). Key management for Smart Grid based on asymmetric key-wrapping. *International Journal of Computer Mathematics*, 92(3), 498–512. doi:10.1080/00207160.2014.917178

Matin, M. A. (2014). *Handbook of Research on Progressive Trends in Wireless Communications and Networking*. IGI Global. doi:10.4018/978-1-4666-5170-8

Meng, W., Ma, R., & Chen, H.-H. (2014). Smart grid neighborhood area networks: A survey. *IEEE Network*, 28(1), 24–32. doi:10.1109/MNET.2014.6724103

Miller, M. (2015). *The Internet of Things: How Smart TVs, Smart Cars, Smart Homes, and Smart Cities Are Changing the World*. Pearson Education.

Nian, L., Jinshan, C., Lin, Z., Jianhua, Z., & Yanling, H. (2013). A Key Management Scheme for Secure Communications of Advanced Metering Infrastructure in Smart Grid. *Industrial Electronics. IEEE Transactions on*, 60(10), 4746–4756. doi:10.1109/TIE.2012.2216237

NIST. (2012). *Smart Grid: A Beginner's Guide*. Retrieved from http://www.nist.gov/smartgrid/beginnersguide.cfm

Premaratne, U. K., Samarabandu, J., Sidhu, T. S., Beresh, R., & Tan, J.-C. (2010). An intrusion detection system for IEC61850 automated substations. *Power Delivery. IEEE Transactions on*, 25(4), 2376–2383.

Rescorla, E. (1999). *Diffie-Hellman key agreement method*. Academic Press.

Rivest, R. L., Shamir, A., & Adleman, L. (1983). A method for obtaining digital signatures and public-key cryptosystems. *Communications of the ACM*, 26(1), 96–99. doi:10.1145/357980.358017

Rose, K., Eldridge, S., & Chapin, L. (2015). *The internet of things: An overview. The Internet Society*. ISOC.

Sauter, T., & Lobashov, M. (2011). End-to-End Communication Architecture for Smart Grids. *IEEE Transactions on Industrial Electronics*, 58(4), 1218–1228. doi:10.1109/TIE.2010.2070771

Simmhan, Y., Kumbhare, A. G., Baohua, C., & Prasanna, V. (2011). *An Analysis of Security and Privacy Issues in Smart Grid Software Architectures on Clouds*. Paper presented at the Cloud Computing (CLOUD), 2011 IEEE International Conference on.

Skopik, F., & Smith, P. D. (2015). *Smart Grid Security: Innovative Solutions for a Modernized Grid*. Elsevier Science.

Spanò, E., Niccolini, L., Di Pascoli, S., & Iannacconeluca, G. (2015). Last-meter smart grid embedded in an Internet-of-Things platform. *Smart Grid. IEEE Transactions on, 6*(1), 468–476.

Stackowiak, R., Licht, A., Mantha, V., & Nagode, L. (2015). *Big Data and The Internet of Things: Enterprise Information Architecture for A New Age.* Apress. doi:10.1007/978-1-4842-0986-8

Taylor, C., & Johnson, T. (2015). *Strong authentication countermeasures using dynamic keying for sinkhole and distance spoofing attacks in smart grid networks.* Paper presented at the Wireless Communications and Networking Conference (WCNC). doi:10.1109/WCNC.2015.7127747

Tomkiw, L. (2016). *Russia-Ukraine Cyberattack Update: Security Company Links Moscow Hacker Group To Electricity Shut Down.* Retrieved 8/1/2016, from http://www.ibtimes.com/russia-ukraine-cyberattack-update-security-company-links-moscow-hacker-group-2256634

Tran, T.-T., Shin, O.-S., & Lee, J.-H. (2013). *Detection of replay attacks in smart grid systems.* Paper presented at the Computing, Management and Telecommunications (ComManTel), 2013 International Conference on. doi:10.1109/ComManTel.2013.6482409

Venkataramani, G., Parankusam, P., Ramalingam, V., & Wang, J. (2016). A review on compressed air energy storage–A pathway for smart grid and polygeneration. *Renewable & Sustainable Energy Reviews, 62*, 895–907. doi:10.1016/j.rser.2016.05.002

Venkatraman, K., Daniel, J. V., & Murugaboopathi, G. (2013). Various attacks in wireless sensor network: Survey. *International Journal of Soft Computing and Engineering, 3*(1).

Wagner, A., Speiser, S., & Harth, A. (2010). *Semantic web technologies for a smart energy grid: Requirements and challenges.* Paper presented at the Proceedings of the 2010 International Conference on Posters & Demonstrations Track.

Wang, W., & Lu, Z. (2013). Cyber security in the Smart Grid: Survey and challenges. *Computer Networks, 57*(5), 1344–1371. doi:10.1016/j.comnet.2012.12.017

Wang, Y. (2013). Smart grid, automation, and scada systems security. *Security and Privacy in Smart Grids*, 245-268.

Xiao, Y. (2013). *Security and Privacy in Smart Grids.* Taylor & Francis. doi:10.1201/b15240

Xiao, Z., Xiao, Y., & Du, D. H.-C. (2013). Non-repudiation in neighborhood area networks for smart grid. *Communications Magazine, IEEE, 51*(1), 18–26. doi:10.1109/MCOM.2013.6400434

Zhang, K., Liang, X., Lu, R., & Shen, X. (2014). Sybil Attacks and Their Defenses in the Internet of Things. *Internet of Things Journal, IEEE, 1*(5), 372–383. doi:10.1109/JIOT.2014.2344013

Zhong, Q. C., & Hornik, T. (2013). *Control of Power Inverters in Renewable Energy and Smart Grid Integration.* Wiley.

Zhou, K., Fu, C., & Yang, S. (2016). Big data driven smart energy management: From big data to big insights. *Renewable & Sustainable Energy Reviews, 56*, 215–225. doi:10.1016/j.rser.2015.11.050

Section 4
Smart Energy and Network Management

Chapter 14

Modelling Software–Defined Wireless Sensor Network Architectures for Smart Grid Neighborhood Area Networks

Nazmus S. Nafi
RMIT University, Australia

Khandakar Ahmed
RMIT University, Australia

Mark A. Gregory
RMIT University, Australia

ABSTRACT

In a smart grid machine to machine communication environment, the separation of the control and data planes in the Software Defined Networking (SDN) paradigm increases flexibility, controllability and manageability of the network. A fully integrated SDN based WSN network can play a more prominent role by providing 'last mile' connectivity while serving various Smart Grid applications and offer improved security, guaranteed Quality of Service and flexible interworking capabilities. Hence, more efforts are required to explore the potential role of SDN in Smart Grid communications and thereby ensure its optimum utilization. In this chapter we provide a description of how SDN technology can be used in WSN with an emphasis on its end-to-end network architecture. We then present its novel application to Advanced Metering Infrastructure, Substation Automation, Distributed Energy Resources, Wide Area Measurement Systems, and Roaming of Electric Vehicles in Smart Grids.

INTRODUCTION

Research into Smart Grid (SG) communication networks aims to identify an integrated approach that leverages communication technologies and standards whilst focusing on the management and control of systems found in the existing power grids. Machine to Machine (M2M) communication protocols and standards provide a starting point for the broader development of SG communication networks that can

DOI: 10.4018/978-1-5225-1829-7.ch014

be enhanced by abstracting high-level network functionalities. A one stop communication solution is yet to be developed that facilitates reliable and efficient traffic exchange between the different SG domains and supports the deployment of diverse communication network services and applications. Software Defined Networking (SDN) provides a separation of traffic control and the systems that transfer traffic across the network (Yan, Yu, Gong, & Li, 2016). SDN is an approach to the management and control of communication networks that provides a higher level of abstraction of network functionality that is appropriate for use in SGs. SDN provides an efficient, secure, reliable, cheap and flexible topology for SG communications. An SDN based communication architecture for SGs provides the flexibility and low cost necessary to support the transition from the existing power grids to SGs. Another feature of a potential SDN implementation for SG communications is the optional use of different communication technologies for traffic control and traffic transmission systems. Selection of the appropriate communication technologies will depend on the traffic model developed for each of the SG domains. Multiple applications can be incorporated utilizing SDN that has different traffic patterns, processing priorities, and data expiration times.

The future SG is expected to have high system resilience in order to manage a large number of M2M devices that can introduce greater risk of sudden failures or malicious attacks. The pervasive use of new software in different SG domains endangers the power grid by introducing inconsistencies leading to vulnerability. The adaptive network configuration capability of the SDN paradigm would be beneficial for SG as the diverse network can be managed from a single control point. The non-adaptive network configuration of existing M2M networks does not allow run-time modifications or network device configuration to react to sudden attacks. Also, bandwidth demand could increase rapidly with the introduction of new and diverse SG applications. Correspondingly, the horizon for unexpected attacks on future SG networks is likely to increase, though this is mitigated to some extent with SDN because the physical layer switches forward packets based on flow table entries that are set by controllers over separate secure channels.

Wireless Sensor Networks (WSN) have evolved utilizing ubiquitous wireless communication technologies that provide high-speed, low cost and secure M2M communication (Gungor, Lu, & Hancke, 2010). Among the contemporary communication technologies, WSN is particularly suited for use with SG communication networks because of its design for low energy consumption, easy deployment, and Quality of Service (QoS). WSN supports continuous innovation, reduced equipment costs, and open standards that reduce the need for a single vendor solution. For potential SG operators, WSN is an attractive alternative to wireline communication technologies for M2M. A fully integrated SDN based WSN for SG communication networks can offer more than just last-mile connectivity and WSN based radio networks provide SG operators with:

- State-of-the-art Authentication, Authorization and Accounting (AAA) capabilities for real-time energy metering and implementation of various demand response programs;
- Smooth interworking with the existing wired communication infrastructure for substation and feeder automation;
- Flexible network topologies that are used to connect distributed energy resources and perform a wide range of distribution management functions;
- Remote sensor networks for wide area monitoring applications; and
- Real-time data applications for facility coverage, asset tracking and workforce management applications.

In this chapter, a high-level study of SDN based WSN technology is provided with a particular focus on a network architecture for SG Neighborhood Area Network (SGNAN) M2M communication and SG applications. The rest of the chapter is organized as follows. Section 2 provides a brief overview of an SDN based WSN network and describes its end-to-end SGNAN network architecture. Section 3 presents its novel application to Advanced Metering Infrastructure (AMI), Substation Automation, Distributed Energy Resources, Wide Area Measurement System, and Electric Vehicle management as a power source in SGs. Section 4 provides a description of the simulation model of an SDN WSN for SGs implemented in Castalia. Section 5 presents conclusions and opportunities for future work.

SDN BASED WSN FOR SG NAN

In recent times, SDN has become a key focus for the communication network research industry. Both academic and industrial experts are deeply motivated by the future prospects of the SDN paradigm. The need for gaining more controllability and manageability over the network is the main driving force behind the initiative to convert existing networks to next generation SDN networks. Due to a separation between the data and control planes, SDN offers more manageable network features when compared with conventional networks. Rapid growth in data usage and the emergence of smart technologies thrived an exponential roll out of network devices over the past decade. Accommodating a large number of network services and applications is a challenge that is best met with the shift to SDN. Also, proprietary network equipment makes it difficult to implement hardware and software updates in a multi-vendor provisioned network. With SDN, the entire network can be controlled using a single secure monitoring and management platform. Also, SDN facilitates software updates, including network service updates, without directly intervening or physically configuring the network devices. The network can be configured, monitored and controlled using a hierarchy of SDN controllers regardless of vendor specific network devices. In most of the literature, SDN has been designed to utilize the OpenFlow protocol (Chaparadza et al., 2013). The OpenFlow framework was proposed by the Open Networking foundation (Open Networking Foundation, 2013) to develop and test new control mechanisms for large networks. The framework defines a packet forwarding model, flow table generation and update mechanism. The protocol specifically establishes communication between the SDN controller and OpenFlow enabled switches. In an OpenFlow based SDN network, multiple flow tables can be installed or programmed onto a switch via the controller. Packets arriving at the switch match their header field information with the flow entries stored in the flow table. Packets are forwarded based on the action defined by the flow entry. In the case of a flow miss scenario, the switch sends a flow request to the controller and based on the flow command received from the controller the packets are forwarded to the destination. However, OpenFlow based SDN is one of the basic solutions derived from the wide horizon of the SDN paradigm.

The power grid today, in most regions of the world, operates using a hierarchical structure where the power flow is unidirectional from generation to consumer premises. The power grid control center has very limited real-time information about the grid components. Thus, it's hard to assess the dynamicity of the power grid environment. Also, due to increased demand for low cost green power, renewable energy sources are becoming more popular and the power grid increasingly needs to accommodate this growing number of renewable energy sources. The benefit of this wide scale integration of renewable energy resources will only be realized if synchronization and load management through bi-directional power supply can be enabled. Synchronization of Distributed Energy Resources (DERs) and smart load management require advanced monitoring and control systems. The operational grid parameters including current, voltage and frequency should be monitored and stabilized to optimize the demand supply profile.

The modern SG is destined to enable bidirectional power and information flow between the grid equipment. Deploying M2M communication within the SG is performed via developing separate network domains such as Home Area Networks (HANs), Neighborhood Area Networks (NANs) and Wide Area Networks (WANs) (Reduan H. Khan & Khan, 2013). In a SG communication network, thousands of M2M devices will be operating in a periodic, semi-periodic or stochastic manner. A massive amount of traffic is expected to be disseminated throughout the network based on the SG application requirement. The diverse traffic patterns need to be handled carefully as there will be multiple applications running with varied delay requirements.

Figure 1 shows the power system sections and corresponding communication networks used to serve each section. The control center Local Area Network (LAN) in the generation and transmission domains is built upon the legacy communication infrastructure. Generally, large substations reside within these domains and a backbone connects the substations to the control center. The backbone is created based on third party networks using wired infrastructure such as copper cables, fibers or digital subscriber line (DSL). On the other side, customer premise, distributions substation, and feeder comprise the distribution domain and cover a large geographic area. A wide area communication network is used to control and monitor the power grid equipment in the distribution domain. Also, a WAN is used to establish the connection between the distribution domain and the control center. The WAN provides a 'last mile' connection to the end users so that several potential SG applications (e.g. demand response, smart load management, smart billing etc.) can be deployed. According to the IEEE 2030 ("IEEE Guide for Smart Grid Interoperability of Energy Technology and Information Technology Operation with the Electric Power System (EPS), End-Use Applications, and Loads," 2011). The NAN is a subnetwork of the WAN and located within the customer premises. There are two more subnetworks within the WAN which are the Field Area Network (FAN) and Workforce Mobile Network (WMN). The FAN is used to monitor and control substation and feeder equipment whereas the WMN is used for troubleshooting and maintenance activity. The control center's backbone communication infrastructure can be connected to the WAN via a backhaul network.

Figure 1. Power system and communication network architecture

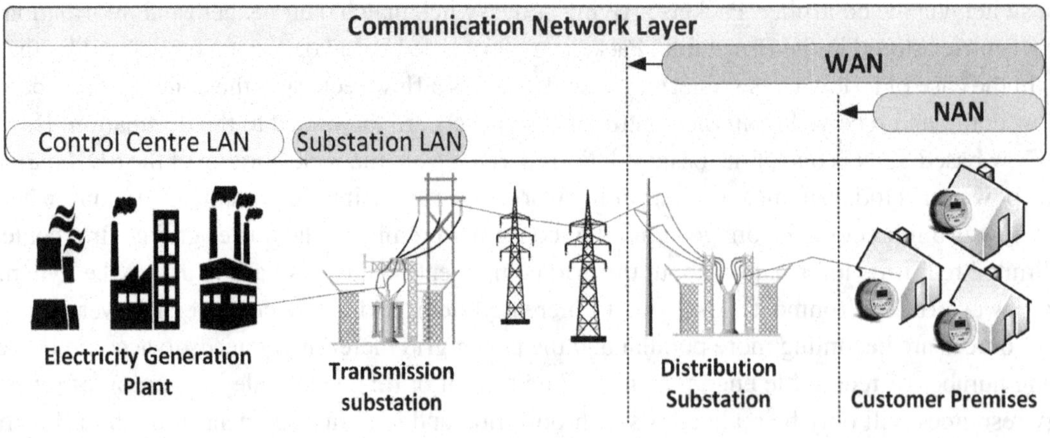

SDN NAN ARCHITECTURE BASED ON WSN

The NAN of the SG communication network comprises of a large number of smart meters. The NAN can be referred to as a logical representation of AMI (Zhou, Hu, & Qian, 2012). As a basic component of a NAN, smart meters provide various types of information on the consumption and power quality and also perform a few load balancing tasks. Interestingly, private networks like the HAN can be connected to a NAN via smart meters acting as an Energy Service Interface (ESI). A number of SG applications such as Plugged in Electric Vehicle (PEVs) charging and discharging, remote load balancing and load management, synchronization of distributed energy resources, in-home consumption monitoring and control system etc. can be deployed via AMI infrastructure. Figure 2 represents the logical configuration of a NAN in a SG. A single smart meter or a Data Aggregation Point (DAP) connected to multiple smart meters may act as an end point of the NAN. With a backbone network the NAN is connected to the control center Meter Data Management System (MDMS).

It's important to determine the appropriate communication technology when modeling the NAN. A couple of important factors need to be taken into consideration while developing the network solution for this section of the SG. In a SG AMI system, the periodicity of the packet transmission can be random, semi-periodic or fully periodic. Based on the type of application, a packet can be categorized as a delay tolerant or delay sensitive packet. In the case of a stochastic delay sensitive application, the packet need to be delivered to the destination within a strict delay boundary with high accuracy. For a delay tolerant packet, the network reliability should be very high so that there is minimal information loss during packet transmission. While keeping the aforementioned requirements in mind, WSN can be considered to be an appropriate solution among the existing wireless solutions for modeling SG NAN as

Figure 2. Smart grid neighborhood area network

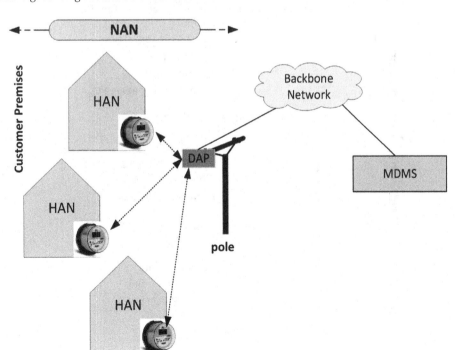

it also includes inherent support for sensors and data collection. This is due to the basic characteristics of WSN, where a large number of short range sensor nodes create a mesh network and collect data such as voltage, current, and frequency. The sensor nodes in a WSN operate using very low power at a minimal cost. Also, sensor nodes are small in size and able to operate under extreme weather conditions with self-configuring features. While deploying the WSN nodes in a high voltage environment it is likely that insulation would be needed and this can be either retrofitted or built into the WSN nodes. Hence, WSN can be used as a key enabler for many SG applications such as demand response, PEVs and load management at the customer premises.

There are three different operational frequency bands defined by the IEEE 802.15.4 standard. The first one operates between 868.0 and 868.6MHz in Europe with only one channel. The second one operates between 902.0 and 928.0MHz in the USA with 10 channels and the third one operates between 2.4 and 2.4835GHz worldwide with 16 channels ("IEEE Standard for Local and metropolitan area networks Part 15.4: Low-Rate Wireless Personal Area Networks (LR-WPANs)Amendment 5: Physical Layer Specifications for Low Energy, Critical Infrastructure Monitoring Networks," 2013). The third spectrum band is unlicensed and an unlimited number of applications can be deployed where the maximum transmit power can be up to 1W (Suciu, 2010). Based on the routing capability two types of devices are defined by the IEEE 802.15.4 that are full-function devices (FFD) and reduced function devices (RFD). The FFD has the capability to act as a coordinator router. In a SDN based scenario, the FFD device can act as the switch. On the other hand, the RFD can act as an end device, which only transmits sensor data to the FFD device. The 2.4GHz band operates with OQPSK chip modulation where the data rate is 250Kbps.

Figure 3. Logical architecture of smart grids using a SDN paradigm

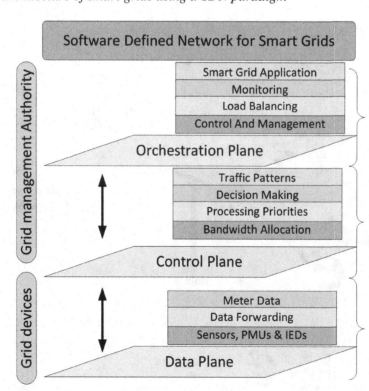

In the case of a SG NAN environment, the smart meters would be equipped with RFDs and the network can be configured with different topologies depending on the SG application.

SDN based SGs aim to eliminate the existing challenges in the SG communication network. Grid equipment like sensors, Intelligent Electronic Devices (IEDs), and Phasor Measurement Units (PMUs) transfer information over the data plane of the SDN based SG. The network devices are scattered among different domains of the power system. Grid information such as voltage, current, consumption data, and temperature are forwarded to specific destination according to decision information supplied via the control plane. Figure 3 stretches our understanding on the logical architecture of SGs using the SDN paradigm. The orchestration plane handles the monitoring, control and management capabilities. From this plane the grid authority can define, install, operate and manage new SG network services and applications. Based on the application set defined by the orchestration plane, the control plane handles the data plane. The control plane configures the data rate, allocates bandwidth for each application, sets the priority based on delay sensitivity, creates and maintains the flow table and deploys flow information switches. As our scope of this chapter is limited to analyze the network configuration of a SDN based NAN, we will focus on the customer premises of the power grid.

Development of a SDN based NAN will depend on vast number of sensors deployed via complex networking into the customer premises of the SG. To enable increased SG traffic generated from AMI applications, the network should be scalable, efficient and easily manageable. Most of the available underlying SG communications capability is hardware-centric and purposefully designed for a particular set of applications. The major challenge of NANs is the limited flexibility to install and update new applications. Physical intervention in network device configuration increases physical and financial costs. With a SDN based NAN controller, network devices at the NAN can be programmed remotely and new network services and applications can be configured without intervening with the physical sensor devices or smart meters. Also, with the retrieved control and monitoring data set new AMI applications can be modelled. Figure 4 presents a conceptual network architecture of SDN based NAN. In this case the smart meters' act as the end devices that generate the sensor data. The distributed NAN controllers (controller 1 and 2 in Figure 4) are coordinated via a single NAN controller which is further connected to a DAP. Sensor data is aggregated via the distributed controllers. A DAP is connected to each distributed controller. The aggregated data is processed through the controller and based on the application definition the controller generates the flow information to send the data to the MDMS. As the data layer and control layers are separated the proposed SDN based NAN, the MDMS can deploy SG applications by pushing the application onto the NAN controller. Based on the application the NAN controller can send specific instructions to distributed controllers.

According to the IEEE 802.15.4g task group (TG4g), ("IEEE Standard for Local and metropolitan area networks--Part 15.4: Low-Rate Wireless Personal Area Networks (LR-WPANs) Amendment 3: Physical Layer (PHY) Specifications for Low-Data-Rate, Wireless, Smart Metering Utility Networks," 2012) the widely accepted topology for sensor nodes in a SG environment is a mesh configuration. The proposed traffic model follows TG4g specifications for supporting a large number of network devices with minimum infrastructure. SDN traffic modelling in the NAN domain is dependent on the characteristic of the AMI applications. The most common AMI applications are Demand response (DR), Micro-grid management, Advanced Meter Reading (AMR) and distributed energy resources (DERs). An AMR application collects periodic meter readings from the smart meters and sends the data to the MDMS. The meter reading data contains various power grid performance details including connectivity information and meter health status. The AMR data also can be generated at usual grid events. For example, in case

Figure 4. Conceptual network architecture of SDN based NAN

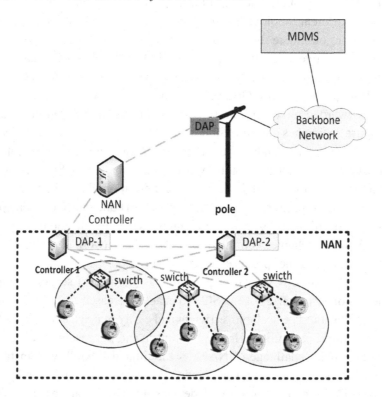

of a blackout event in a suburb all of the smart meters will send the last gasp message to the control center. However, there are two critical aspects of this event. First, smart meters run on electrical power and will have to rely on the capacitive charge after the blackout event occurs to transmit the last gasp message. There will be a very strict delay boundary depending on the capacitor characteristics. Second, a sudden burst of data sent via a large number of smart meters will increase the collision rate and may end up causing congestion resulting in temporary network failure. Thus SDN based NAN should be robust enough to accommodate major SG applications following proper delay specifications.

Traffic Model

Figure 5 shows the traffic dissemination model of the proposed SDN based NAN. The operational devices of the SDN network can be classified in five categories. These are Smart Meters, NAN switches, NAN controller, Controller at Utility center and grid equipment such as circuit breakers, grid relays or switches. Measurements from a smart meter installed at a NAN can be considered as raw data and based on the information several SG applications can be modelled. Any newly developed application can be deployed from the SDN controller and in this case, the NAN controller is responsible for the deployed SG application.

Primarily, NAN applications can be divided into the two categories: delay sensitive and delay tolerant. Delay sensitive applications require guaranteed packet delivery to the destination within a strict delay boundary. Whereas, in the case of a delay tolerant application, the main objective is limited reliable and successful message transmission. The time constraint is much more flexible for delay tolerant packets.

Figure 5. Traffic dissemination model

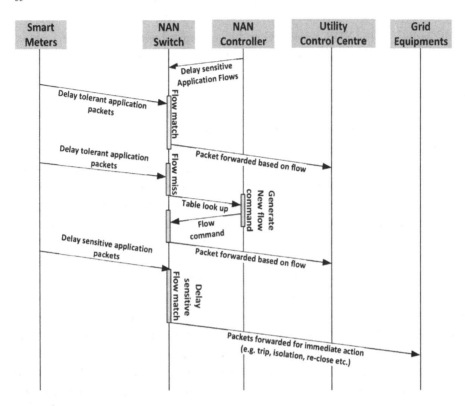

Considering these requirements, the proposed SDN based NAN adopted intelligent and interesting techniques to handle the different application types.

Most of the common delay tolerant applications running on the NAN domain would be predefined by the NAN controller. In other words, the NAN switches will have predefined flow tables to forward the common delay tolerant applications. If a delay tolerant application packet is received at the switch it attempts to find instructions for how to handle the flow in the flow table, then the switch directly forwards the packets to the destination if permitted. If the first delay tolerant packet is forwarded to the utility control center based on the flow table entries. However, for delay tolerant packets with no initial flow entry, the switch sends a request packet to the controller to get additional flow information for the new packet type. Upon receiving the new flow command from the controller, the NAN switch forwards the packet. It is interesting to notice that to get a new flow command additional flow setup time is needed. So, if there is any unknown application deployed at any instance, the total end-to-end packet forwarding delay will be increased due to the flow setup process. On the other hand, delay sensitive applications are stochastic in manner and mostly event based. Also, these application packets need to be delivered within a specific time constraint. Thus, it's inevitable to have predefined flows for such applications. If a delay sensitive packet is received at the switch, the NAN switch classifies the particular packet as a top priority message and forwards it to the destination. In most circumstances a delay sensitive packet will be forwarded to the grid equipment or to control center for immediate action.

POTENTIAL SDN BASED SG APPLICATION MODELS

To illustrate the ability of the SDN based SG end-to-end architecture to address various SG network services and applications, several novel usage scenarios are outlined in this section.

Advanced Metering Infrastructure

AMI refers to a group of smart energy meters that use two-way communication to send meter readings and receive control signals in real-time (R. H. Khan & Khan, 2012). AMI smart meters remove the need to send staff to take meter readings at premises and permit measurements to be taken more frequently, which facilitates early satisfaction of changes to demand response and early tampering detection leading to fraud reduction. Demand response enables the utility operator to optimally balance power generation and consumption either by offering dynamic pricing or by implementing various load control programs (Liu, Liu, Wang, Zomaya, & Hu, 2015). The SDN paradigm can provide an integrated AMI solution as shown in Figure 6.

As shown in Figure 6, a SDN enabled AMI smart meter is connected with the switch via a wireless link. The smart meter sends meter readings to the Billing Server over the uplink and receives control signals from the Supervisory Control & Data Acquisition (SCADA) Server over the downlink from the network control center. The switch adjacent to the smart meter filters application related information from the data packets prior to sending them to the AAA server.

The AAA server authenticates the meter and authorizes energy flow for each of the connected loads. The Billing Server provides real-time pricing and energy consumption information on the meter's display so that the customers can regulate their own consumption. In addition, the SCADA Server executes load-control programs by sending control signals to the target appliance(s) via the smart meter.

Substation Automation

Substation automation refers to the monitoring, control, and communication functions on substation and feeder equipment such as supervisory control of circuit breakers, load tap changers (LTCs), regulators,

Figure 6. Integrated advanced metering infrastructure using wireless technology

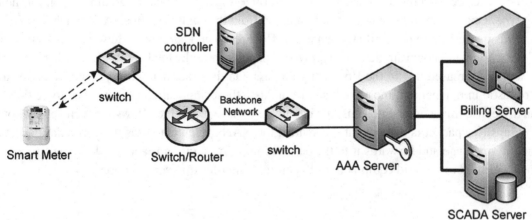

reclosers, sectionalizers, switches and capacitor banks. The utility operators are expected to use standardized communication protocols like IEC61850 to support various distribution automation functions (Mackiewicz, 2006).

The IEC61850 protocol is based on interoperable IEDs that interact with each other, either within a substation (e.g. protection signals to circuit breakers) or on feeders (e.g. automated reclosers and switches along a feeder responding to isolate a fault). The IEC61850 protocol runs over a commercial communication network including Ethernet. A consolidated SDN network can connect all the substations with each other and with the control center and thereby extend the domain of the automation functions from a single substation to the whole transmission and distribution network. A SDN based heterogeneous network (HetNet) could connect the substations using already available wireline infrastructure such as DSL, fiber, and coaxial cables in conjunction with the newly deployed wireless networks (Pirak, Sangsuwan, & Buayairaksa, 2014). In this case the SDN controller will provide authentication, security and QoS to substation IEDs irrespective of the access network technology.

In case of wireline connectivity, the interworking between the communication network and the IEC61850 substation bus can be performed by an Ethernet switch that aggregates the data from substation IEDs and transfers it to the controller as shown in Figure 7.

The SDN controller provides a transparent IP connectivity between the substation IEDs and the SCADA servers of the control center. The AAA server provides authentication services to the IEDs and the policy server enforces QoS profiles such that the control signals get higher priority than the statistical and monitoring information. The servers in the utility control center can also provide a single control and communication platform to the SG via the SDN controller. The convergence of control and communication entities can further reduce the latency of delay sensitive control signals and thus provide faster response to the fault conditions.

Distributed Energy Resources

Distributed Energy Resources (DER) are small sources of power generation and/or storage that are often connected to the distribution system. In order to facilitate the large scale integration of DERs into

Figure 7. Substation Connectivity using SDN wireline access network interworking

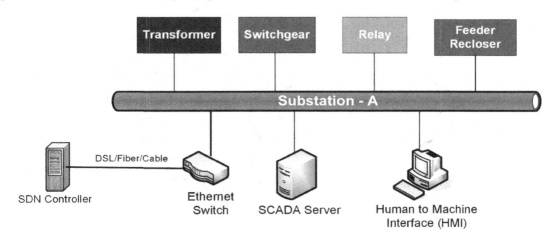

SGs requires a robust communication network to connect the DER sites and perform a variety of active distribution management functions (Guobin, Moulema, & Wei, 2013).

Since the DERs are typically located within various business, residential and industry premises over a large geographic area the Long Term Evaluation – Advanced (LTE-A) Femtocell provides a suitable wireless communications system to connect the locally dispersed sites with sufficient capacity and coverage. LTE-A Femtocells are specialized low-cost and low-power home base stations that connect user terminals to the LTE-A core network using a locally available broadband connection (Ginting, Fahmi, & Kurniawan, 2015). Since Femtocells are placed in the customer premises and uses third party broadband connections, the cost of network deployment is reduced to a large extent. Figure 8 illustrates the remote DER connectivity with LTE-A Femtocells.

To ensure network security, the Femtocells should be configured in Private Access Mode so that only pre-configured users have access to the network (Das, Chandhar, Mitra, & Ghosh, 2011). In addition, the extensive user authentication and data encryption techniques of the LTE-A network should be used in order reduce the security threats associated with using a third party network for backbone connectivity.

Wide Area Measurement System

WAMS refers to an advanced sensing and measurement system that continuously monitors power grid performance and provides operators with high-quality data and analysis tools (National Energy Technology Laboratory (NETL) of U.S. Department of Energy (DOE), 2007). In a WAMS, the system state and power quality information is obtained from the state measurement modules based on the PMU. The results from the PMUs are then combined with a Control Center Network (CCN) in order to display the system stability measures in real-time and a SCADA system for remote monitoring and control. PMUs utilize the Global Positioning System (GPS) to provide a time-stamp for each phasor measurement (Hadley, McBride, Edgar, O'Neil, Johnson, 2007).

As PMUs are scattered throughout the power system, WSNs are an appropriate option to collect real-time information. Data from the WSNs can be conveyed to the CCN via LTE-A base stations (eNodeBs)

Figure 8. Connectivity of distributed energy resources using LTE-A Femtocells

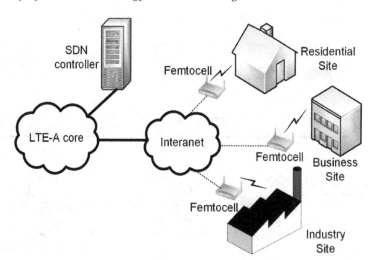

connected in a mesh topology. LTE-A serves as a wireless access network technology to integrate the sensor sub-networks and for connecting the WSN to the CCN.

In addition, the Mobile Management Entity (MME) can act as the Phasor Data Concentrator (PDC) for the PMUs and provide a secondary clock reference along with the GPS. One concern for this WSN-LTE-A hybrid network is that the security of the overall system depends on the security of each network component. Therefore, the AAA server in the LTE core should periodically authenticate all the WSN entities along with the end PMU devices. Figure 9 shows the connectivity of PMUs using remote WSN and LTE-A.

Plug-in Electric Vehicle Roaming

PEVs are regular hybrid vehicles that have a large high-capacity battery bank. The vehicles draw power from the grid during off peak hours to charge the batteries and provide power back to the grid during peak hours. Thus they can play a key role in balancing power generation and consumption (Kennel, D, x00F, rges, & Liu, 2013). Since the PEVs are highly mobile, integrating them into the SG can be a major challenge.

Figure 9. Wide area measurement using LTE-A connected wireless sensor networks

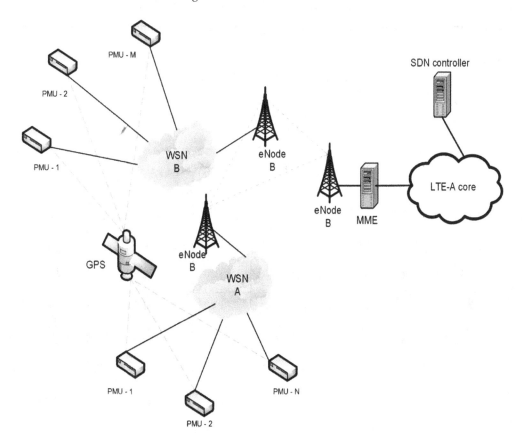

The advanced roaming model of a LTE-A network architecture can enable utility operators to allow flexible charging and de-charging of PEVs anytime, anywhere and in any utility network using an on-board smart meter. Figure 10 shows the roaming scenario of a PEV with an on-board LTE-A smart meter.

The charging station is located within the visited LTE-A network and the smart meter in the PEV authenticates itself and sends metering information to the AAA and Billing Servers of its home network. Communication between the home and visited networks is carried out using the AAA proxy servers located at the edge of each network. The visited network provides network access to the PEV and the inter-operator billing is settled later using a potentially standardized roaming agreement.

SIMULATION MODEL

Most of the AMI applications including PEV, AMR and DR require two-way communication between the devices and the utility control centers. The main objectives are ensuring efficient energy consumption and optimal utilization of energy resources via customer participation. These are considered to be important SG applications. A SDN based NAN using WSN should support an enormous number of M2M devices. The M2M devices installed at the NAN domain collect measurements form residential or commercial buildings and send the information to a DAP using frequent low data rate transmissions. As a result, the medium access channel could become overwhelmed with a large number of access requests. For example, in an event of outage, all the M2M devices could try to send an event report simultaneously which could increase the network access load exponentially and lead to network failure.

Figure 10. Roaming of electric vehicles using SDN and LTE-A

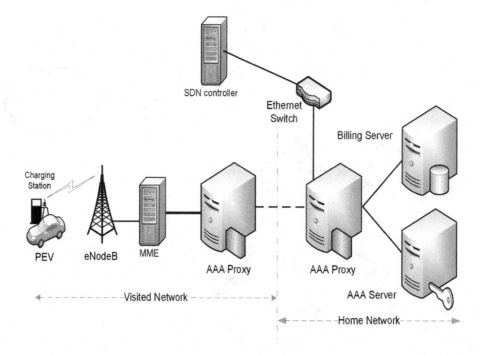

A Software Defined WSN (SDWSN) based NAN simulation model was developed in Castalia v3.2 (Boulis, 2011), which is built on top of OMNet++ (OMNet++, 2016). It was assumed that the smart meters installed at the premises operate using the CC2530 specification, which supports the IEEE 802.15.4 Zigbee protocol operating on the 2.4 GHz band. The CC2530 is a popular commercial Zigbee system that was developed by Texas Instruments. A Castalia node consists of five modules including Sensor Manager, Application, Communications, Resource Manager and Mobility Manager. The Communication module is a composite module and consists of three sub-modules including Routing, MAC and Radio. The node sensing property is handled by the sensor manager, which maintains the interaction between the physical process module and a number of sensor modules. A range of wireless channel modules are available in Castalia to simulate real world wireless communication networks. The module interfaces enable information flow between the physical processes and the wireless channels.

Two simulations were conducted with the AMI application characteristics in the NAN domain. First, a generic SDN based AMI application was considered where small data bursts (100 bytes) are sent from the smart meters to the Utility control center. The data burst transmission intensity followed an exponential distribution. Further, the reporting cycle was varied from 1 min to 5 min. A total number of 1200 smart meters were considered where 120 SDN switches were uniformly distributed. We also assume that delay sensitive applications like PEV charging/discharging and DR are also accommodated in the reporting interval. Next we observed the effect of the traffic loads on the proposed SDN based NAN.

In the second simulation scenario, a power outage event was considered. It was assumed that a group of smart meters will transmit the 'last gasp' message asynchronously within an interval of 10 sec. The number of affected smart meters was varied between 400 to 1200 (Golla, Bell, Lin, Himayat, Talwar & Johnsson, 2010) with a step of 100 and effects analyzed to evaluate the SDN based NAN. As the 'last gasp' message is a type of delay sensitive SG application, the flows were predefined via the SDN controller and stored in the associated switches. The flush out time for this application packet was set to infinity due to random generation nature of the packets. Moreover, any predefined delay sensitive application packets are placed into a priority queue for immediate forwarding.

Results from the first simulation trial are presented in Figure 11 and the average end-to-end delay of both delay tolerant and delay sensitive applications are plotted against the reporting interval. The end-to-end delay increases as the reporting interval decreases, which is due to the high number of smart meters trying to deliver the packets within a shorter period to the switch as it attempts to forward the packets to the destination. However, with a reporting interval of 1 min, the proposed model successfully delivered the delay tolerant packets with a 97% success rate, as shown in Figure 12. The delay boundary for most of the delay sensitive applications varies between 70-100 msec (Gungor et al., 2013). The proposed network model supports all of the major delay sensitive SG applications and successfully disseminates the packets within a strict delay boundary. As shown in Figure 12, the success rate is 100% for all types of application packets when the reporting interval is equal to or greater than 3 min.

From the second simulation results, we plotted the success rate and associated end-to-end packet delay of the 'last gasp' messages against a varying number of affected smart meters. Figure 13 shows the uplink delay of AMI traffic in the proposed SDN network. Results show that the SDN based NAN could provide support for 900 affected smart meters with 100% success rate. The success rate starts to fall as more affected smart meters try to send the 'last gasp' message within a small interval of 10 sec. The smart meters are supposed to run on their capacitive power after the outage event and transmit the packet with the remaining capacitive power. Based on the outcome derived from the second simulation

Figure 11. Average delay of AMI traffic in SDN based NAN

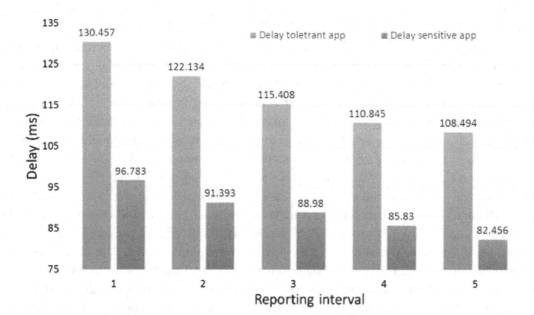

Figure 12. Success rate of AMI traffic in SDN based NAN

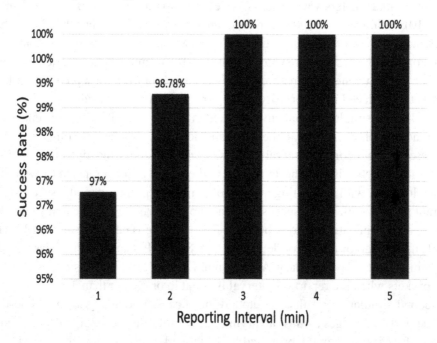

it is evident that the proposed model can successfully deliver the outage event messages within the required delay boundary. However, successful reception of outage alarms reduces as the number of smart meters increase. Accordingly, the end-to-end delay for outage alarm delivery gets higher as more smart meters get installed on the network. Based on the simulation statistics it would be interesting to develop

Figure 13. Uplink delay of AMI traffic in SDN based NAN

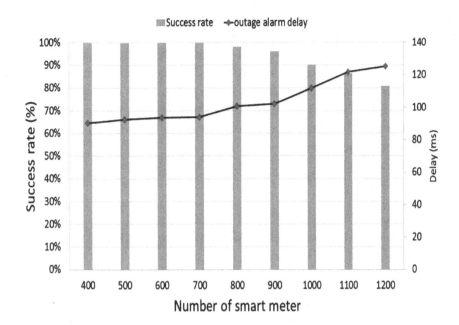

an analytical model to derive the maximum number of smart meters operating with a 100% success rate while delivering an outage alarm. To keep the focus of the simulation model limited, this issue is left as a future research interest.

CONCLUSION

The SDN paradigm has been designed to separate the control and data planes to create a robust framework for communication networks that support bandwidth-intensive, real-time applications. The flexible SDN architecture simplifies interworking, roaming, network service and application delivery. Thus, a fully integrated SDN network has the ability to support various SG network services and applications that have diverse communication needs in terms of capacity, coverage and QoS.

In this paper, we have provided a high level study of an end-to-end SDN based SG network architecture that highlights the further application to key SG applications. An end-to-end SDN based NAN can be used to provide an integrated AMI network that can perform various demand response programs effectively and efficiently. It can connect different substations using its flexible interworking capability with wired and wireless technologies and thus leverage the substation automation function domain from a single substation within the power system. In addition, it can connect the dispersed DERs using LTE-A Femtocells and PMUs using WSN via its backbone network. It can also facilitate PEV roaming using its advanced roaming capabilities. This list of scenarios is not exhaustive and we expect that several more scenarios will also emerge. SDN could be a key enabler for future 5G networks and the Internet of Things (IoT). Aligned with this shift to introduce flexibility and programmability into networks, the future of SGs could significantly benefit through the smart utilization of the SDN paradigm.

The continuation of this research will include development of protocols and schemes to support various SDN network services and applications for SGs including the ones discussed in this chapter. In a SG environment, multiple SDN controllers could be required to cover a large geographical area. A future research interest aims to identify an optimal number of distributed controllers for common SDN based topologies. Limited work has been observed on SDN controller to controller communication in a multi-domain scenario and future SGs would require multi-domain communication to integrate the end-to-end power grid communication network. A SDN based heterogeneous communication network architecture for distributed SGs would rely upon the successful incorporation of multi-domain SDN controller to controller communication.

REFERENCES

Boulis, A. (2011). *Castalia User Manual*. Retrieved from: https://castalia.forge.nicta.com.au/index.php/en/documentation.html

Chaparadza, R., Meriem, T. B., Radier, B., Szott, S., Wodczak, M., Prakash, A., & Mihailovic, A. (2013, December 9-13). *SDN enablers in the ETSI AFI GANA Reference Model for Autonomic Management & Control (emerging standard), and Virtualization impact. Paper presented at the 2013 IEEE Globecom Workshops (GC Wkshps)*.

Das, S. S., Chandhar, P., Mitra, S., & Ghosh, P. (2011, September 5-8). Issues in Femtocell Deployments in Broadband OFDMA Networks: 3GPP-LTE a Case Study. *Paper presented at the Vehicular Technology Conference (VTC Fall)*. IEEE.

Ginting, D., Fahmi, A., & Kurniawan, A. (2015, November 25-26). Performance evaluation of inter-cell interference of LTE-A system using carrier aggregation and CoMP techniques. *Paper presented at the 2015 9th International Conference on Telecommunication Systems Services and Applications (TSSA)*.

Golla, R., Bell, W., Lin, M., Himayat, N., Talwar, S., & Johnsson, K. (2010). Power outage alarm for smart metering applications IEEE 802.16p Task Group.

Gungor, V. C., Lu, B., & Hancke, G. P. (2010). Opportunities and Challenges of Wireless Sensor Networks in Smart Grid. *IEEE Transactions on Industrial Electronics*, *57*(10), 3557–3564. doi:10.1109/TIE.2009.2039455

Gungor, V. C., Sahin, D., Kocak, T., Ergut, S., Buccella, C., Cecati, C., & Hancke, G. P. (2013). A Survey on Smart Grid Potential Applications and Communication Requirements. *IEEE Transactions on Industrial Informatics*, *9*(1), 28–42. doi:10.1109/TII.2012.2218253

Guobin, X., Moulema, P., & Wei, Y. (2013, May 21-23). Integrating distributed energy resources in smart grid: Modeling and analysis. *Paper presented at the Energytech*. IEEE.

Hadley, M., McBride, J., Edgar, T., O'Neil, L., & Johnson, J. (2007). *Securing Wide Area Measurement Systems. Pacific Northwest National Laboratory to U.S. Department of Energy (DOE)*. Retrieved from http://www.energy.gov/sites/prod/files/oeprod/DocumentsandMedia/8-Securing_WAMS.pdf

IEEE. (2011). *IEEE Guide for Smart Grid Interoperability of Energy Technology and Information Technology Operation with the Electric Power System (EPS), End-Use Applications, and Loads.* Std 2030-2011. doi:10.1109/IEEESTD.2011.6018239

IEEE. (2012). IEEE Standard for Local and metropolitan area networks--Part 15.4: Low-Rate Wireless Personal Area Networks (LR-WPANs) Amendment 3: Physical Layer (PHY) Specifications for Low-Data-Rate, Wireless, Smart Metering Utility Networks IEEE Std 802.15.4g-2012 (Amendment to IEEE Std 802.15.4-2011). doi:10.1109/IEEESTD.2012.6190698

IEEE. (2013). IEEE Standard for Local and metropolitan area networks Part 15.4: Low-Rate Wireless Personal Area Networks (LR-WPANs) Amendment 5: Physical Layer Specifications for Low Energy, Critical Infrastructure Monitoring Networks. IEEE Std 802.15.4k-2013 (Amendment to IEEE Std 802.15.4-2011 as amended by IEEE Std 802.15.4e-2012, IEEE Std 802.15.4f-2012, IEEE Std 802.15.4g-2012, and IEEE Std 802.15.4j-2013). doi:10.1109/IEEESTD.2013.6581828

Kennel, F., Gorges, D., & Liu, S. (2013). Energy Management for Smart Grids with Electric Vehicles Based on Hierarchical MPC. *IEEE Transactions on Industrial Informatics*, 9(3), 1528-1537. doi:10.1109/TII.2012.2228876

Khan, R. H., & Khan, J. Y. (2012, November 5-8). A heterogeneous WiMAX-WLAN network for AMI communications in the smart grid. *Paper presented at the 2012 IEEE Third International Conference on Smart Grid Communications (SmartGridComm).*

Khan, R. H., & Khan, J. Y. (2013). A comprehensive review of the application characteristics and traffic requirements of a smart grid communications network. *Computer Networks*, 57(3), 825–845. doi:10.1016/j.comnet.2012.11.002

Liu, L., Liu, Y., Wang, L., Zomaya, A., & Hu, S. (2015). Economical and Balanced Energy Usage in the Smart Home Infrastructure: A Tutorial and New Results. *IEEE Transactions on Emerging Topics in Computing*, 3(4), 556–570. doi:10.1109/TETC.2015.2484839

Mackiewicz, R. E. (2006, May 21-24). Overview of IEC 61850 and Benefits. *Paper presented at the 2005/2006 IEEE/PES Transmission and Distribution Conference and Exhibition.*

National Energy Technology Laboratory to U.S. Department of Energy. (2007). *A Compendium of Modern Grid Technologies.* Retrieved from https://www.netl.doe.gov/File%20Library/research/energy%20efficiency/smart%20grid/whitepapers/Compendium-of-Modern-Grid-Technologies.pdf

OMNet++ (2016). *OMNet++ user manual.* Retrieved from https://omnetpp.org/doc/omnetpp/User-Guide.pdf

Open Networking Foundation. (2013). *Openflow Switch Specification, version 1.3.0 (Wire Protocol 0x05),* Retrieved from https://www.opennetworking.org/images/stories/downloads/sdn-resources/onf-specifications/openflow/openflow-spec-v1.4.0.pdf

Pirak, C., Sangsuwan, T., & Buayairaksa, S. (2014, March 19-21). Recent advances in communication technologies for smart grid application: A review. *Paper presented at the 2014 International Electrical Engineering Congress (iEECON).*

Suciu, D. (2010). A study of RF link and coverage in Zigbee. *Scientific Bulletin of the Petru Maior*, 7(1).

Yan, Q., Yu, F. R., Gong, Q., & Li, J. (2016). *Software-Defined Networking (SDN) and Distributed Denial of Service (DDoS) Attacks in Cloud Computing Environments: A Survey*, Some Research Issues, and Challenges. *IEEE Communications Surveys and Tutorials*, 18(1), 602–622. doi:10.1109/COMST.2015.2487361

Zhou, J., Hu, R. Q., & Qian, Y. (2012). Scalable Distributed Communication Architectures to Support Advanced Metering Infrastructure in Smart Grid. *IEEE Transactions on Parallel and Distributed Systems*, 23(9), 1632–1642. doi:10.1109/TPDS.2012.53

Chapter 15
Smart Energy and Cost Optimization for Hybrid Micro–Grids:
PV/ Wind/ Battery/ Diesel Generator Control

Imene Yahyaoui
Federal University of Espírito Santo, Brazil

Fernando Tadeo
University of Valladolid, Spain

Rachid Ghraizi
Indra, Spain

Marcelo Eduardo Vieira Segatto
Federal University of Espírito Santo, Brazil

ABSTRACT

This chapter is concerned with the energy management of a hybrid micro-grid composed of photovoltaic/ wind/ battery bank and diesel generator, which is used to supply domestic loads. Hence, a control strategy is proposed to manage the power flow between the power sources and the loads, which ensures the maximization of the renewable sources use, and therefore the minimization of the battery bank and diesel generator use. The control strategy allows the installation operating cost to be minimized and the safe operating for the battery bank to be guaranteed. The strategy is tested using measured data of some climatic parameters of the target area, showing its efficiency in fulfilling the fixed objectives.

INTRODUCTION

Electrical energy is a vital input for the social and economic developments, for which the demand has significantly increased (Lund et al., 2015; Santamouris et al., 2015). However, due to the instability in the fossil fuel prices and the increase in the greenhouse gas emissions, renewable energy sources are best placed to solve these issues (Jacobson et al., 2015; Mathiesen et al., 2015). Since renewable energies depend on the climatic parameters, characterized by their intermittence, it is necessary then to optimize

DOI: 10.4018/978-1-5225-1829-7.ch015

and to use smart strategies (Østergaard et al., 2016; Narimani et al., 2015), which can be applied in micro-grids, including smart grids (Mathiesen et al., 2015; Pouresmaeil et al., 2015). Fortunately, the continuous advances in computer hardware and software are allowing researchers to deal with smart grids systems. This is performed by applying optimization and energy management strategies to the renewable and sustainable energy field, in such a way to ensure the optimum use of the generated energy, to provide the energy needed to the loads, and to guarantee a safe and secure operation for the whole smart grids system (Oró et al., 2015; Sonnenschein et al., 2015). Establishing an energy management strategy for smart grids systems is essential, since it allows the system autonomy and the continuity in the power supply to be ensured, thanks to the use of operational planning network through two-way power flow and communication (Farhadi et al., 2015; Zhao et al., 2015). Moreover, these strategies allow looking out the system security, by detecting defaults when occur, predicting energy generation and consumption from the one hand, and fulfill the energy demands whenever and wherever are needed from the other one (Aman et al., 2015; Sabo et al., 2016).

Hence, in this research chapter, a strategy for the optimum energy control of a hybrid system composed of photovoltaic (PV) panels, a wind turbine, a lead- acid batteries bank, a diesel generator which supply a variable domestic load, is proposed and discussed in depth (Figure 1). The proposed Energy Management strategy (EMS) is based on several considerations related with the electricity generation, maintenance, components replacements and fuel price costs. Therefore, a cost function is introduced and minimized in order to optimize the involvement degrees of each power source, by comparing, at each sample time, the power sources combinations costs while supplying the domestic loads. The electricity generation cost includes the components operation, maintenance, fuel and replacement costs of the system parts studied during 20 years. The proposed strategy aims to guarantee the system operation continuity; in such a way the load is always supplied. Secondly, it ensures the system safe operation, since it respects constraints that allow extending the components lifetime. Furthermore, the EMS aims to minimize the use of the diesel generator to emergency and strictly required cases and maximize the use of the renewable energy for the domestic load power supply. Nevertheless, these components can be used in case of defaults in some components, or in case of non-availability of the renewable energies. Therefore, the battery bank and/ or the diesel generator takes part in generating the power needed to supply the domestic loads. Consequently, the proposed energy strategy allows guaranteeing the smart grid security operation and to supply an energy flow with the network settings including a protection system.

The proposed EMS is tested using measured data of climatic parameters of the target area (Medjez El Beb: Northern Tunisia, latitude: 36.39°, longitude: 9.6°), showing the efficiency of the proposed optimization method in minimizing the electricity generation cost, from the one hand, ensuring a safe operation for the system components, and providing the loads with the needed energy, from the other one.

Background

Hybrid renewable energy systems are becoming popular, especially for remote area, thanks to advances in renewable energy technologies. However, renewable energies, especially PV and wind energy are characterized by their intermittence, since they extremely depend on the climatic parameters, namely the solar radiation G, the ambient temperature T_a and the wind speed V. Therefore, the discontinuity in the power generation often involves reliability problems associated with their operation for micro-grid systems. This issue is more complicated, if several systems are interconnected between each other, as

Figure 1. Scheme of the proposed photovoltaic system connected to a single-phase grid utility

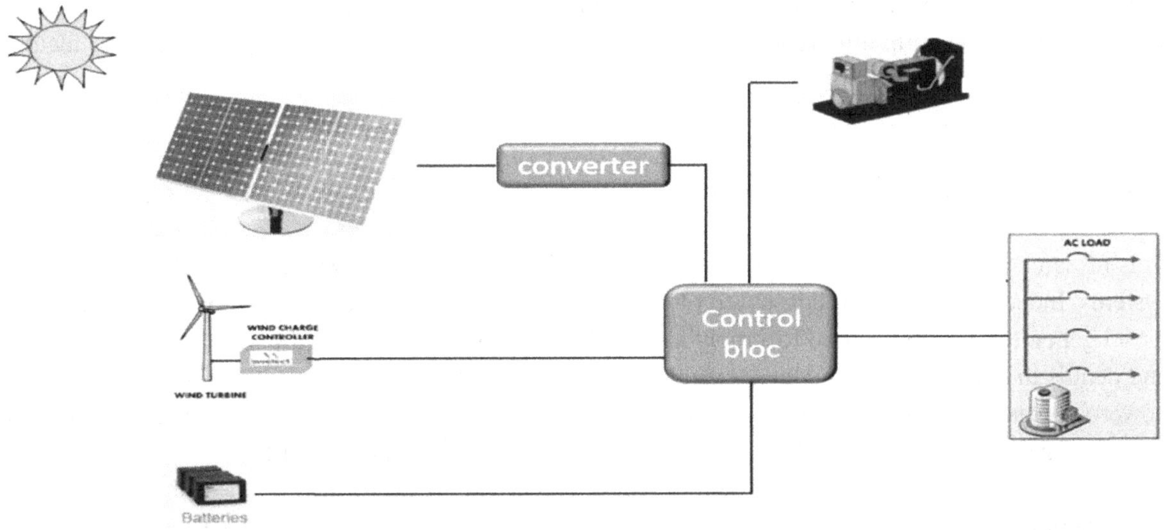

in the case of smart grids, for which this chapter concentrates. Thus, to face this issue, many research works focused in enhancing the renewable sources efficiency, such as establishing techniques for accurately predicting the powers generated, and reliably integrate them with other conventional sources, namely storing energy devices (Choubin et al., 2016; Mohanty et al., 2016). Other works, concentrated in extracting the maximum of power generated by these sources and enhancing the hybrid system components efficiency, by studying the design techniques, as it has been studied by Rezk et al., 2015 and Yahyaoui et al., 2016a.

Additionally, multi-objective algorithms have been proposed, in order to optimize the mix of the renewable system. In fact, these research works focused in maximizing their contributions to the peak load, while minimizing the combined intermittence, at a minimum cost, and minimizing the total greenhouse gas emissions of the system during its lifetime (Feng et al., 2016). For instance, some researchers applied the Particle Swarm Optimization (PSO) approach, to solve this issue (Chen et al., 2014). Indeed, they concluded that its performance is better than the conventional optimization techniques (Chen et al., 2014). Other researchers use the Genetic Algorithm (GA) to solve the economic environmental dispatching of a hybrid power system, including the wind and solar thermal energies throughout the useful life of the installation and the pollutant emissions (Carlucci et al., 2015). GA has also been mixed with the simplex, to optimize a hybrid system coupled to PV, a battery and a fuel cell for stand-alone street lighting systems, considering the monthly average solar irradiation and the wind speed data (Hamdy et al., 2016). The results obtained when designing a photovoltaic–wind–diesel system demonstrate the practical utility of the design method used.

Moreover, some other research works concentrate on optimization techniques which are based on the artificial intelligence tools, including the Artificial Neural Network (ANN) (Bhandari et al., 2015) and Fuzzy logic (Yahyaoui et al., 2014; Suganthi et al., 2015; Balaman et al., 2016). These techniques gave good results, since they hold the uncertain renewable energy supplies, load demands and the non-linear characteristics of some components that constitute the system. Further, some authors have dealt with determining the optimal combination of renewable energy technologies. Indeed, the renewable energy resources safe operation has been taken into account, in addition to the technology characterization, and economic parameters, namely the installation, maintenance and replacement costs. Moreover, some authors studied the optimum composition of hybrid systems, considering socio-demographic factors algorithm (Tito, S et al., 2016).

MAIN FOCUS OF THE CHAPTER

This research chapter focuses on the energy optimization of a typical hybrid plant used in smart grids systems. Indeed, the system is composed of PV panels, a wind turbine, a lead- acid battery bank, and a diesel generator, which are used to supply a variable domestic load. Hence, the present work proposes and details in depth an Energy Management Strategy (EMS), to optimize the powers generated by the power sources, maximize the renewable sources use and to minimize the use of the battery bank and the diesel generator. Moreover, the EMS aims to guarantee a safe operation of the system components and the continuity in the loads power supply. These objectives are performed by the minimization of a cost function, in which the power generation cost, the battery depth of discharge (dod) and the energetic balance are considered. This strategy is important for smart grids system security, since it can be used to supervise smart grids systems from both the energetic and the economic points of view.

Issues, Controversies, Problems

The energy management in hybrid systems faces two issues: first, the optimization strategy should take into account all the system components nonlinearities, from the one hand, and the loads power demand, from the other one. This includes the system components operation under uneven climatic parameters changes (namely the solar radiation, the wind speed, etc.). Additionally, the EMS is a multi-objective function, which includes energetic and economic objectives and criteria, in addition to taking into account a safe operation of the system elements. Since the proposed plant is the heart of smart grids systems, therefore, several issues and criteria interconnected are included in this proposed EMS (energetic and economic). Sure, to solve it, a powerful and reliable tool should be used. In this research chapter, the Genetic Algorithm (GA) is chosen, to perform the proposed strategy. The solution is tested for a typical hybrid plant, which can be then generalized for more sophisticated systems, namely the smart grids systems.

Numbered Lists

The following numbered lists are proposed, in such a way to describe in a coherent and comprehensive manner the topic proposed in this research chapter. Indeed, the chapter begins by describing the models of the system components. Then, the EMS adopted for the cost optimization of the hybrid plant is detailed. After that, the simulation results of the components models used and then the energy management algorithm are presented and explained in depth. Finally, the chapter ends by conclusions, in which the authors mention the impact of the proposed strategy for smart grids security systems. The numbered list is explained now:

1. System Components Modelling
   a. Photovoltaic panels
   b. Incremental conductance for MPPT
   c. Battery bank
   d. Wind turbine
   e. Diesel generator
2. Energy Management Strategy (EMS)
   a. Investment cost
   b. Production cost
   c. Use cost
3. Application to a Case Study
   a. Results of the system components models
   b. Energy management strategy and interpretation
4. Conclusions
5. Acknowledgements
6. References

SOLUTIONS AND RECOMMENDATIONS

System Components Modelling

Photovoltaic Panels

The earth surface receives approximatively 1.79 10^8 kWh of solar energy, which is equivalent to a continuous power of 1.729 10^{17} W. however, 23% of this energy is reflected directly back into space, 29% is absorbed in the atmosphere and converted to heat radiated within the infrared spectrum. The remaining 48% of the energy is used to supply the hydrological cycles and photosynthesis (Yahyaoui, 2016c). Taking into account the alternations of day and night and cloudy periods, the peak power is estimated to be 1kW (Yahyaoui, c, 2016). The solar energy is converted to electricity using PV arrays. In the literature, several models have been studied to model the PV panels. Indeed, some models consider the two diodes model (Chin, et al., 2016). Other models characterize the PV panels by yield (Fernández et al., 2015; Steiner et al., 2015). In this research chapter, the photovoltaic panel is modelled using the one-diode non-linear model (Hasan et al., 2016). This model depends on the solar radiation G *(t)*, the ambient temperature $T_a(t)$ at the panel surface, and the panel parameters namely the number of photovoltaic cells connected in series, the short- circuit current and the open- circuit voltage at the reference temperature. The model evaluates the photovoltaic current $I_c(t)$ and power $P_{pv}(t)$. The adopted model is described by (1)-(6) (Hasan et al., 2016).

$$I_c = I_{ph}(t) - I_r(t)\left(\exp\left(\frac{V_c(t) + R_s I_c(t)}{V_{t\_T_a}} \right) - 1 \right) - \frac{V_c(t) + R_s I_c(t)}{R_p} \tag{1}$$

$$I_{ph}(t) = \frac{G(t)}{G_{ref}} I_{sc}(t) \qquad (2)$$

$$I_{sc}(t) = I_{sc\_T_{ref}} \left(1 + a\left(T_a(t) - T_{ref}\right)\right) \qquad (3)$$

$$I_r(t) = I_{r\_T_{ref}} \left(\frac{T_a(t)}{T_{ref}}\right)^{\frac{3}{n}} \exp\left(\frac{-qV_g}{nK_B}\left(\frac{1}{T_a(t)} - \frac{1}{T_{ref}}\right)\right) \qquad (4)$$

$$I_{r\_T_{ref}} = \frac{I_{sc\_T_{ref}}}{\exp\left(\dfrac{qV_{c\_T_{ref}}}{nK_BT_{ref}}\right) - 1} \qquad (5)$$

where: $T_a(t)$: the ambient temperature at the panel surface (K),

$G(t)$: the solar radiance at the panel surface (W/m²),

$I_c(t)$: the estimated photovoltaic cell current (A),

$I_{ph}(t)$: the generated photo-current at G (A),

$I_r(t)$: the reverse saturation current at T_a (A),

$V_c(t)$: the open circuit voltage of the photovoltaic cell (V),

R_s: the serial resistance of the photovoltaic module (Ω),

V_{t_Ta}: the thermal potential at the ambient temperature (V),

R_p: the parallel resistance of the photovoltaic module (Ω),

G_{ref}: the solar radiation at reference conditions (W/m^2),

$I_{sc}(t)$: the short circuit current for T_a (A),

$I_{sc\_T_{ref}}$: the short circuit current per cell at the reference temperature T_{ref} (A),

a: the temperature coefficient for the short circuit current (K^{-1}),

$I_{r\_T_{ref}}$: the reverse saturation current for T_{ref} (A),

n: the quality factor,

q: the electron charge (C),

V_g: the Gap energy (e.V),

K_B: the Boltzmann coefficient (J/K),

$V_{c\_T_{ref}}$: the open circuit voltage per cell at T_{ref} (V).

Hence, the photovoltaic power P_{pv} generated by the panel is then described by (Yahyaoui et al., 2014; Hasan et al., 2016; Yahyaoui et al., 2016b):

$$P_{pv}(t) = n_s n_p V_c(t) \left(I_{ph}(t) - I_r(t) \left(\exp\left(\frac{V_c(t) + R_s I_c(t)}{V_{t\_T_a}} \right) - 1 \right) - \frac{V_c(t) + R_s I_c(t)}{R_p} \right) \qquad (6)$$

where:

n_s : the number of serial photovoltaic cells,

n_p : the number of parallel photovoltaic modules.

Incremental Conductance for MPPT

Climatic parameters, namely the solar radiance and the ambient temperature, are intermittent; in such a way that they change continually during the day, which therefore affect the PV power generated by the PV arrays. Consequently, it is necessary to use techniques that track the maximum power point, called Maximum Power Point Tracking (MPPT) methods (Yahyaoui et al., 2016a). In this sense, several methods for MPPT have been studied in depth namely, the Perturb and Observe (Muthuramalingam et al., 2014), the Look up Table (Ozdemir et al., 2014), Fuzzy logic (Boukenoui, et al., 2016) and the incremental conductance methods for MPPT (Bizon, 2016). In fact, they all differ in complexity and tracking accuracy, but they require sensing the PV current and voltage, using the off-the–shelf hardware. Thanks to its good efficiency and reliability, in this research chapter, the incremental conductance algorithm for MPPT is used to track the MPP generated by the photovoltaic panels, and to generate the control signal for the boost converter (Bizon, 2016; Yahyaoui et al., 2016a) (Figure 2). In fact, this method consists in using the current ripple in the chopper output I_{pv}, to maximize the panel power P_{pv}, using the relation between the current and voltage continuously identified online (Bizon, 2016, Yahyaoui et al., 2016a). Indeed, the algorithm tests the actual conductance $-\dfrac{I_{pv}}{V_{pv}}$ and the incremental conductance $\dfrac{dI_{pv}}{dV_{pv}}$ as follows (Bizon, 2016; Yahyaoui et al., 2016a):

If $\dfrac{dI_{pv}}{dV_{pv}} \succ -\dfrac{I_{pv}}{V_{pv}}$, then the operating point is on the left of the MPP, so $\qquad (7)$

α is varied to increase V_{pv}.

If $\dfrac{dI_{pv}}{dV_{pv}} \prec -\dfrac{I_{pv}}{V_{pv}}$, then the operating point is on the right of the MPP, so $\qquad (8)$

α is varied to decrease V_{pv}.

If $\dfrac{dI_{pv}}{dV_{pv}} \approx -\dfrac{I_{pv}}{V_{pv}}$, then the operating point is in the MPP, $\qquad (9)$

So, the value of α is maintained.

where dI_{pv} and dV_{pv} are the PV current and voltage variations, respectively.

Thus, the duty cycle α, used to generate the PWM signal for the DC- DC converter control, is calculated using (10) (Bizon, 2016; Yahyaoui et al., 2016a):

$$\frac{V_{DC}}{V_{pv}} = \frac{1}{1-\alpha} \tag{10}$$

Battery Bank

It is well known that renewable energy sources generate electrical energy intermittently. Therefore, the use of an energy storage device, in which the excess of the photovoltaic energy generated is stored, is necessary. This stored energy can be extracted when the power generated by the renewable energy sources is not sufficient to supply the load with power. Generally, batteries are used to save energy (Burgos et al., 2015; Yahyaoui et al., 2016). Lead-acid batteries are among the most common energy saving devices. A battery type is composed of positive and negative electrodes separated by an electrolyte. It is used to convert the chemical energy to electric energy thanks to oxidoreduction reactions (Burgos et al., 2015; Yahyaoui, 2016c). Some researchers developed models for the battery characteristics, to describe the battery State Of Charge (SOC) or its depth of discharge (dod). In this sense, linear modeling methods, namely the Coulometric, the open-circuit voltage method, and the non-linear dynamic modeling method have been developed (Burgos et al., 2015; Yahyaoui, 2016c). In this research chapter, a non-linear model for the lead- acid battery is used to model the battery bank behavior (Yahyaoui et al., 2016b). In addition to its simplicity, both the battery current and voltage are used to describe preciously the battery bank's behavior during charging and discharging. Its performance is evaluated by the depth of discharge dod. To evaluate it, the stored charge in the battery C_R is first determined by (Yahyaoui et al., 2014):

Figure 2. Scheme of the control principle of the DC- DC converter for MPPT

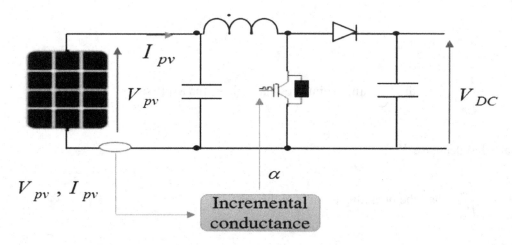

$$C_{R(k)} = C_{R(k-1)} + \frac{\partial k}{3600} I_{bat_{(k)}}^{k_p} \tag{11}$$

where ∂k is the time between instant k-1 and k and k_p is the Peukert coefficient.

Hence, the depth of discharge dod is given by (Yahyaoui et al., 2016b):

$$dod_{(k)} = 1 - \frac{C_{R_{(k)}}}{C_p} \tag{12}$$

where C_p is the Peukert capacity, considered constant (A.h).

Wind Turbine

Wind is a physical phenomenon in the nature. As it knows; it is the result of the differential pressure between warm and cool areas in the atmosphere that produces the constantly movements of the air masses (Krishnamoorthy et al., 2014; Lanzafame et al., 2014; Yahyaoui, 2016c). The electricity generated from wind is created by a turbine that converts a portion of the kinetic energy from the wind into a mechanical energy, which is available on a generator shaft (Lanzafame et al., 2014; Yahyaoui, 2016c). This mechanical energy runs the wind turbine and thus, allows electric energy to be generated (Yahyaoui, 2016c). World wind energy resources are substantial, and in many areas, such as the USA and Northern Europe, could in theory supply all of the electricity demands. However, the intermittent character of the wind resources and the necessity of long distances for energy transmission are considered the main disadvantages of the wind energy (Krishnamoorthy et al., 2014; Yahyaoui, 2016c). The wind turbine creates a wind energy deficit between the wind leaving the turbine (known as wake) and the wind arriving in front of the turbine. Hence, a reduction of power output is produced at downwind turbines (Krishnamoorthy et al., 2014; Lanzafame et al., 2014). In this research chapter, the wind turbine power P_W is modelled by a non- linear expression, which essentially depends on the wind speed v and the blades' pitch angle β, as it is described now (Krishnamoorthy et al., 2014; Lanzafame et al., 2014):

$$P_W = \frac{1}{2} \rho A C_p(\lambda_1) v^3 \tag{13}$$

where ρ is the air density (kg. m^{-3}), A is the surface of the

Turbine blades (m^2) and C_p is the power coefficient (Lanzafame et al., 2014):

$$C_p(\lambda_1) = 0.5176 \left(\frac{116}{\lambda_i} - 0.4\beta - 5 \right) e^{\frac{-21}{\lambda_i}} + 0.0068 \lambda_1 \tag{14}$$

$$\frac{1}{\lambda_i} = \frac{1}{\lambda_1 + 0.08\beta} - \frac{0.035}{\beta^3 + 1} \tag{15}$$

and:

$$\lambda_1 = \frac{\Omega R}{v} \tag{16}$$

where: R is the helix radius (m) and Ω is the angular mechanic speed (rad. s^{-1}).

Diesel Generator

Typical diesel generator is composed of three main components, which are the diesel engine, the synchronous generator and the excitation system (Figure 3) (Salazar et al., 2015; Yahyaoui et al., 2016d). In fact, the first component (the diesel engine) is composed of the current driver, the actuator, the engine and the flywheel, as it is described in Figure 4 (Salazar et al., 2015; Yahyaoui et al., 2016d). Indeed, the current driver, which is presented by a constant K_3, converts the fuel flow into a mechanical torque. Moreover, the speed of the engine is controlled by the actuator, which relates the fuel intake. Therefore, the fuel rack position depends on the input current, which determines the fuel amount φ, injected into the combustion chamber (Graciano et al., 2015, Yahyaoui et al., 2016d). The third element of the diesel engine consists of the combustion system, which is designed by the Engine block in Figure 4 (Graciano et al., 2015; Salazar et al., 2015). Consequently, the movement of the piston during the power strokes produces the crankshaft drive and the mechanical torque T_{mech}, which is generated by the injection of the fuel ignited by the compressed hot air in the combustion chamber. Finally, the flywheel comprises the engine inertia dynamics, the damping factor (K_D) and the loaded alternator.

The rotor angular velocity w_r and the mechanical torque T_{mech} relation is given by (Salazar et al., 2015):

$$2H \frac{d\Delta w_r}{dt} = T_{mech} - T_{sg} - K_D \Delta w_r \tag{17}$$

$$\frac{d\delta}{dt} = w_0 \Delta w_r \tag{18}$$

$$\Delta w_r = w_r - 1 \tag{19}$$

where the time t is in seconds (s), the rotor angle δ is in radian, the rated generator speed w_0 is in rad/s, Δw_r is the speed deviation (pu), w_r is the rotor angular velocity (pu), T_{sg} is the generator torque (pu) and H is the inertia constant.

Using the Park transformation, the synchronous generator is modeled as follows (Salazar et al., 2015):

Figure 3. Block diagram of the diesel generator

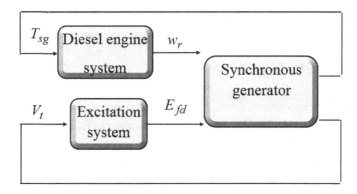

$$V_d = E''_d - R'_s I_d + X''_q I_q \tag{20}$$

$$V_q = E''_q - R'_s I_q - X''_d I_d \tag{21}$$

where R'_s is the armature resistance, I_q and I_d are the currents flowing in the stator windings, the $X''_{d,q}$ are the so-called subs transient d and q-axis reactance and $E''_{d,q}$ are given by:

$$E''_d = \frac{\left(X_q - X''_q\right)}{1 + \tau''_{q0} s} I_q \tag{22}$$

$$E''_q = \frac{1}{1 + \tau''_{d0} s} E'_q - \frac{\left(X'_d - X''_d\right)}{1 + \tau''_{d0} s} I_d \tag{23}$$

where:

$X_{d,q}$ and $X'_{d,q}$: the synchronous and transient reactances,

$\tau''_{d,q0}$: the open circuit sub transient time constants,

and E'_q is given by:

$$E'_q = \frac{1}{\left(\dfrac{X_d - X''_d}{X'_d - X''_d}\right) + \tau'_{d0} s} E_{fd} + \frac{\left(\dfrac{X_d - X'_d}{X'_d - X''_d}\right)}{\left(\dfrac{X_d - X''_d}{X'_d - X''_d}\right) + \tau'_{d0} s} E''_q \tag{24}$$

where: E_{fd} is the exciter field voltage and τ'_{d0} is the open circuit transient time constant.

The excitation block supplies and automatically adjusts the field current of the synchronous generator, by applying control and protective functions required to the satisfactory performance of the system (Salazar et al., 2015; Yahyaoui, 2016c).

Energy Management Strategy

Since the hybrid system is composed of several non –linear components that supply a variable domestic load, then it is necessary to use an Energy Management Strategy (EMS) that controls the energy flow between the power sources and the load. Thus, in this research chapter, the aim of the EMS is to optimize the operational costs of the hybrid installation, guarantee the loads' power supply and ensure a safe operation for the lead- acid battery bank, using the powers P_{pv}, P_w, P_{bat} and P_G, generated by the photovoltaic panels, the wind turbine, the battery bank and the diesel engine, respectively, the power consumed by the variable domestic loads P_L, from the one hand, and the installation operation cost, from the other one, as it is described in Figure 5.

In fact, the EMS consists in evaluating, at each sample time, the optimum power sources combination that minimizes the cost of the power production, as it is explained in Figure 6. Indeed, since the system is composed of five components, then it can be modeled by fives power sources, as it is described by equation (25):

$$V(t) = \begin{bmatrix} v_1(t) \\ v_2(t) \\ v_3(t) \\ v_4(t) \\ v_5(t) \end{bmatrix} = \begin{bmatrix} P_{PV}(t) \\ P_W(t) \\ P_{bat}(t) \\ P_G(t) \\ P_L(t) \end{bmatrix} \tag{25}$$

Figure 4. Block diagram of the diesel engine

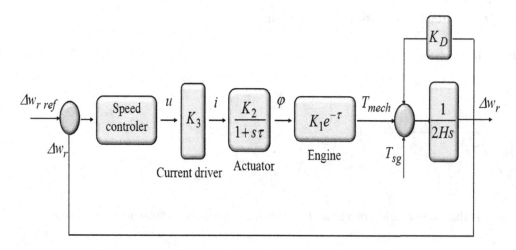

Thus, for each sample time, the state vector $\alpha(t)$ describes the contribution of each power source for supplying the domestic load with power, as it is given by equation (26):

$$\alpha(t) = \begin{bmatrix} \alpha_{PV}(t) \\ \alpha_{W}(t) \\ \alpha_{bat}(t) \\ \alpha_{G}(t) \end{bmatrix} \tag{26}$$

Hence, during the optimization, the power sources provide to the loads the needed power, which must fulfill the following condition (equation (27)), which ensure the continuity of the power supply of the domestic load:

$$\alpha_{PV}P_{PV}(t) + \alpha_{W}P_{W}(t) + \alpha_{bat}P_{bat}(t) + \alpha_{G}P_{G}(t) - P_{L}(t) = 0 \tag{27}$$

where:

α_{PV}, α_{W}, α_{bat}, and α_{G} are the power contribution of the PV panel, the wind turbine, the battery bank and the diesel generator, respectively, to supply the load.

Therefore, for an installation composed of N components, the objective function to be minimized is defined as the absolute minimum of the total micro grid cost, as it is described by equation (28). The minimization of this function allows then providing the load by the needed power, while maintaining a safe operation of the system elements. In the present research chapter, this cost function is minimized using the Genetic Algorithm tool (GA), since it as good performance and easy in application (Sakellaridis et al., 2015).

Figure 5. Synoptic scheme of the proposed approach

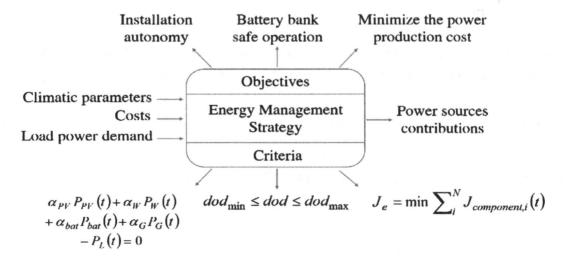

$$J_e = \min \sum_i^N J_{component,i}(t) \qquad (28)$$

The EMS objective evaluates and minimizes the objective function $J(t)$ for 20 years of the system operation. Thus, it must include the investment, the production and the use costs, $J_I(t)$, $J_P(t)$ and $J_U(t)$, respectively, during this period. It is described by equation (29) (Sakellaridis et al., 2015):

$$J_{component}(t) = J_I(t) + J_P(t) + J_U(t) \qquad (29)$$

These costs are detailed now in depth.

Investment Cost

The investment cost $J_I(t)$ describes the cost of the maximum power $P_{PV}, P_W, P_{conv}, P_{bat}$ provided by its system's components. This cost includes the buying and implementation costs, J_{Ic} and J_{Ie}, respectively:

$$J_I(t) = J_{Ic} + \frac{1}{8760} J_{Ie} t \qquad (30)$$

where J_{Ie} is evaluated during N_a amortization years (20 years in this research work), characterized by its maximum energetic capacity, P_{max}, which is described by equation (31) (Sakellaridis et al., 2015):

$$J_{Ie}(t) = \frac{1}{(1+\xi)^{N_a} - 1} \left[J(P_{max}) - J_{Ic} \right] \xi (1+\xi)^{N_a} \qquad (31)$$

where ξ is the annual interest rate.

Production Cost

The production cost $X_P(t)$ depends on the power generated by a power source $X_P(t)$ of the hybrid system elements and its maximum X_{Pmax} at instant t. It is given by the equation (32) as follows:

$$J_P(t) = \sum_0^t \alpha_P \left[X_{Pmax}, sign(X_P(\tau)), t \right] X_P(\tau) \Delta \tau \qquad (32)$$

where α_P is the per unit element energetic cost (€ kWh).

a.   Use cost

The use cost $J_u(t)$ includes the annual up keeping and maintenance costs, $J_u(t)$ and $J_M(t)$, respectively. Indeed, the maintenance cost describes the usury and the maximum installation production P_{max}, and it is given by equation (33) (Sakellaridis et al., 2015):

$$J_U(t) = \frac{\beta_a(P_{max})}{8760}t + \sum_0^t \gamma_a |X_E(\tau)|\Delta\tau \tag{33}$$

where:

β_a: the annual mean cost up keeping coefficient,

γ_a: the mean usury cost.

Consequently, the total cost $J_{PV}(t)$ that corresponds to the photovoltaic panel is expressed by (Sakellaridis et al., 2015):

$$J_{PV}(t) = J_{I_{PV}}\left(P_{P_{PV}}, t, N_a, \delta_a\right) + \frac{\beta_{PV}P_{P_{pv}}}{8760}t \tag{34}$$

The total cost $J_W(t)$ for the wind turbine is given by equation (35) as follows:

$$J_W(t) = J_{I_W}\left(P_{P_W}, t, N_a, \delta_a\right) + \frac{\beta_W P_{P_W}}{8760}t + \sum_0^t \gamma_W\left(P_{P_W}\right)P_W(\tau)\Delta\tau \tag{35}$$

While the total cost $J_{bat}(t)$ that corresponds to the battery bank is expressed by equation (36):

$$J_{bat}(t) = J_{I_{bat}}\left(P_{P_{bat}}, t, N_a, \delta_a\right) + \frac{\beta_{bat}P_{P_{bat}}}{8760}t + \sum_0^t \gamma_{bat}\left|P_{P_{bat}}(\tau)\right|\Delta\tau \tag{36}$$

The cost related to the inverter is given by equation (37):

$$J_{conv}(t) = J_{I_{conv}}\left(P_{P_{conv}}, t, N_a, \xi\right) \tag{37}$$

Therefore, the total cost function J includes the operation, maintenance, fuel and replacement costs, and it is given by equation (38), as follows (Sakellaridis et al., 2015; Yahyaoui et al., 2016d):

$$J(t) = J_{I_{PV}}\left(P_{P_{PV}}, t, N_a, \delta_a\right) + J_{I_W}\left(P_{P_W}, t, N_a, \delta_a\right) + J_{I_{bat}}\left(P_{P_{bat}}, t, N_a, \delta_a\right) + J_{I_{conv}}\left(P_{P_{conv}}, t, N_a, \delta_a\right)$$
$$+ \frac{t}{8760}\left[\beta_W P_{P_W} + \beta_{PV}P_{P_{PV}} + \beta_{bat}P_{P_{bat}}\right] + \sum_0^t \gamma_W P_{P_W}P_W(\tau)\Delta\tau + \sum_0^t \gamma_{bat}\left|P_{bat}(\tau)\right|\Delta\tau \tag{38}$$

The EMS used to minimize the cost C_{glob} of the hybrid plant composed of the PV panels, the wind turbine, the battery bank and the diesel generator, perform the optimization over a fixed duration T_f, taking into account the following constraints expressed by equation (39) (Figure 6):

$$\begin{cases} P_L(t) = \alpha_{PV}P_{PV}(t) + \alpha_W P_W(t) + \alpha_{bat}P_{bat}(t) + \alpha_G P_G(t) \\ dod_{min} \le dod(t) \le dod_{max} \end{cases}$$

$$\forall t \in [0, T_f]$$

(39)

In fact, the management strategy consists in maximizing the use of the renewable energy sources (the PV panels and the wind turbine) (Figure 6). If excess of renewable energy is generated, then the excess is saved in the battery bank in case it is discharged. When the renewable energy generated is not sufficient to supply the load, thus if the battery is charged, then it participates in supplying the domestic loads with power, otherwise, the diesel generator is switched on and it complete the missing power. This is described by Figure 6.

Application to a Case Study

Results of the System Components Models

The models of the system components are first tested using measured data of the solar radiation G, the ambient temperature T_a and the wind speed V, that correspond to a sunny day of the target site (Northern Tunisia, latitude: 36.39°, longitude: 9.6°). The simulation results of the photovoltaic panels, the wind

Figure 6. Energy management strategy principle

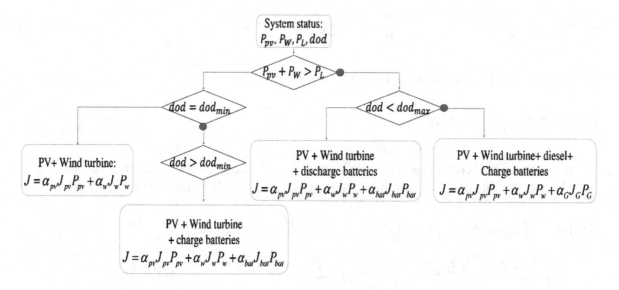

turbine and the diesel engine models are given in Figure 7 to Figure 11 respectively. Figure 7 shows that the variation of the solar radiation G affects significantly the PV current generated. Similarly, the wind turbine power increases when the wind speed increases, as it is shown it Figure 8 and 9.

Energy Management Strategy and Interpretation

The algorithm is tested by simulation using the climatic parameters data, which are the solar radiation G, the ambient temperature T_a and the wind speed V of the target area (Northern Tunisia, latitude: 36.39°, longitude: 9.6°). The powers P_{pv} and P_W generated respectively by the PV panels and the wind turbine, that corresponds to the climatic parameters are presented in Figure 12 and Figure 13.

The EMS is tested by simulation using Matlab- Simulink. The obtained results show that the algorithm always ensures the load power supply, a safe operation of the battery bank and the minimization of the

Figure 7. Photovoltaic module generation variation following the solar radiation and the ambient temperature changes

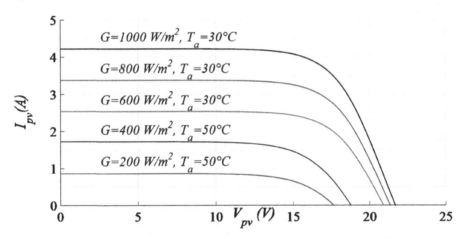

Figure 8. Wind power coefficient variation following the pitch angle

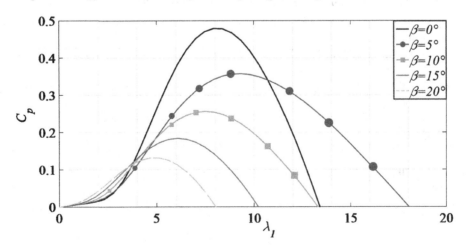

Figure 9. Wind power variation following the wind speed

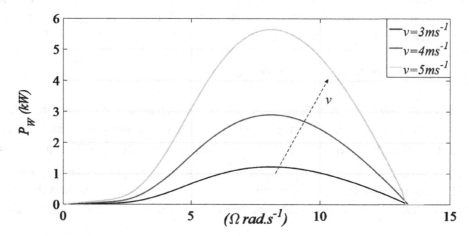

Figure 10. Stator terminal voltage of the diesel engine

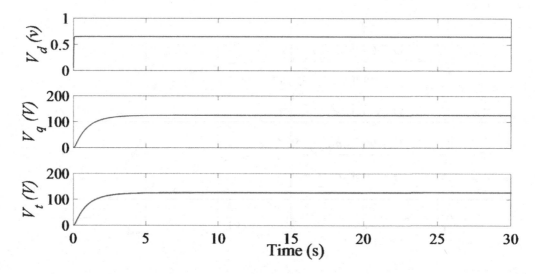

Figure 11. Power, torque and rotor angular velocity of the diesel engine

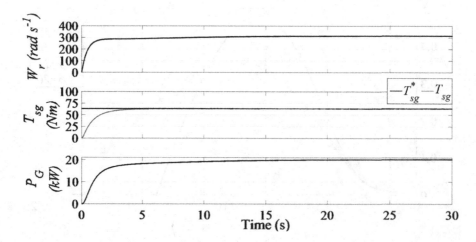

genset use. In fact, Figure 14 shows that during the night, the wind turbine and the battery bank supply the load with power, since the wind turbine generates insufficient power to the domestic load power supply and the battery bank is charged. This is presented by the EMS response at t_1. Then, when the PV panels start generating the PV power, the renewable power source and the battery bank, together supply the load with the needed electrical power. Figure 14 also shows that, when this generated power is insufficient for the domestic load power supply, therefore the diesel generator is switched on and all the components participate to supply the load, as it is shown at the EMS response at t_1.

In addition, it is clear that the battery depth of discharge (dod) is always maintained between the maximum and minimum limits (0.02 and 0.8). Thus, this allows the battery bank to be protected against charges excess and deep discharges, and the excess of the renewable energy generated to be stored and then used to supply the domestic loads when it is needed.

Figure 12. Climatic parameters of a sunny day

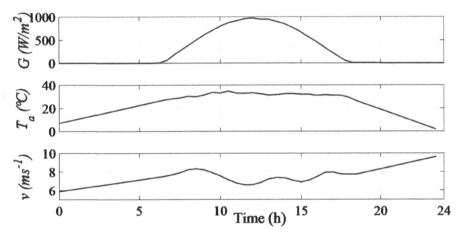

Figure 13. Generated powers from renewable sources

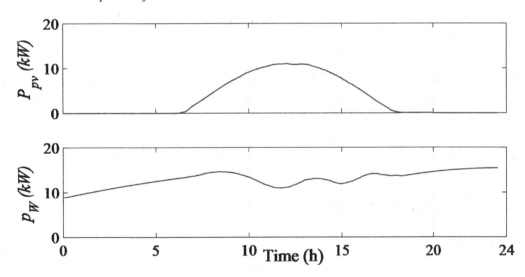

Figure 14. Power sources contributions to the load power supply

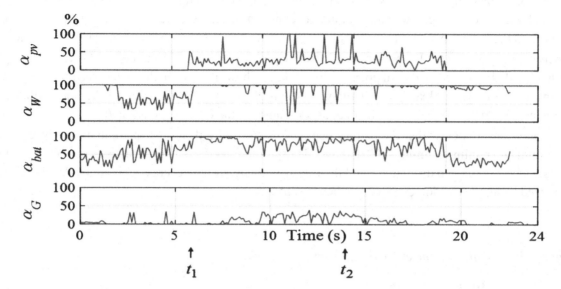

Figure 15. EMS objectives fulfillment: batteries safe operation and loads power supply

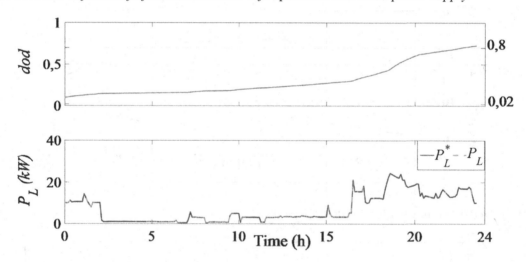

Consequently, using an appropriate EMS applied to the GA, it has been demonstrated the efficiency and the reliability of the EMS proposed in maintaining the domestic loads supplied continually, with taking into account of criteria related to the system components safe operation. Moreover, the EMS allows maximizing the use of the renewable energies and minimizing the use of the battery bank and the diesel generator. Consequently, this affects the system cost operation studied for twenty years.

FUTURE RESEARCH DIRECTIONS

Following the developed work in this chapter, it has been proved the efficiency and the reliability of the EMS in fulfilling the energetic and economic objectives planned for the hybrid installation destined

Figure 16. Contribution of each power source for the loads power supply

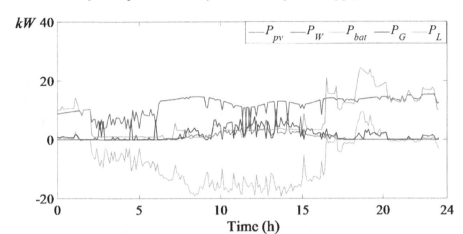

Table 1. Explanation of the used symbols and their definitions

Symbol	Definition	Symbol	Definition
a	Temperature coefficient for the short circuit current (K^{-1})	R_p	Parallel resistance of the photovoltaic module (Ω)
A	Wind turbine blades (m²)	R_s	Serial resistance of the photovoltaic module (Ω)
C_p	Peukert capacity (A.h)	R_s'	Armature resistance (Ω)
C_R	Stored charge in the battery bank (A. h)	S_1, S_2	Inverter control signals
E_{fd}	Exciter field voltage (V)	T_{sg}	Diesel generator torque (pu)
$\dfrac{dI_{pv}}{dV_{pv}}$	Incremental conductance (1/Ω)	V_{dq}	Direct and quadratic voltage, respectively (V)
G	Solar radiation (W/m²)	$V_c(t)$	Open circuit voltage of the photovoltaic cell (V),
G_{ref}	Solar radiation at reference conditions (W/ m^2)	V_{t_Ta}	Thermal potential at the ambient temperature (V)
H	inertia constant	V_g	Gap energy (e.V)
I_{bat}	Battery current (A)	V_r	Modulation wave amplitude (V)
$I_c(t)$	Estimated photovoltaic cell current (A)	$V_{c\_T_{ref}}$	Open circuit voltage per cell at T_{ref} (V)
I_{dq}	Direct and quadratic currents, respectively (A)	α	Chopper duty cycle

continued on following page

Table 1. Continued

Symbol	Definition	Symbol	Definition
		V_c	Carrier wave amplitude (V)
$I_{ph}(t)$	generated photo-current at G (A)	VOC	Voltage Oriented Control
$I_r(t)$	Reverse saturation current at T_a (A)	$X_{d,q}, X'_{d,q}$	Synchronous and transient reactances
$I_{sc}(t)$	Short circuit current for T_a (A)	ζ	Damping ratio
$I_{sc\_T_{ref}}$	Short circuit current per cell at the reference temperature T_{ref} (A)	w_n	Natural frequency (Hz)
$I_{r\_T_{ref}}$	Reverse saturation current for T_{ref} (A)	w_r	Rotor angular velocity (pu)
$-\dfrac{I_{pv}}{V_{pv}}$	Actual conductance (1/Ω)	β	Pitch angle (°)
K_B	Boltzmann coefficient (J/K)	ρ	Air density (kg. m^{-3}),
MPPT	Maximum Power Point Tracking	Ω	Angular mechanic speed (rad. s^{-1})
n_p	Number of parallel photovoltaic modules	φ	Fuel amount (m³)
P	Active power (W)	δ	Rotor angle (radian)
P_W	Wind power (W)	Δw_r	Speed deviation (pu)
P_{pv}	Photovoltaic power (W)	τ'_{d0}	Open circuit transient time constant
Q	Reactive power (VAR)	$\tau''_{d,q0}$	Open circuit sub transient time constants
Q	Electron charge (C)	$\alpha_{PV}, \alpha_W, \alpha_{bat}, \alpha_G$	Sources contribution in the load supply
R	Helix radius (m)		

to supply a variable domestic load. This approach can be applied for other applications, including grid connected systems (hybrid or renewable). Moreover, this work can be also performed using other optimization methods and tools, namely the Artificial Neural Network, the Fuzzy logic, etc. Consequently, in the future, the present work can be extended and applied to several applications, since it is simple, easy to develop and practical.

CONCLUSION

An Energy Management Strategy that consists in minimizing a cost function of a hybrid system is proposed and tested. The system supplies a variable domestic load via the contribution of the micro-grid elements, which is composed of photovoltaic panels, a wind turbine, a battery bank and a genset. The EMS allows providing the domestic load with the power in demand and ensures a safe operation for the battery bank. The EMS minimizes a cost function that takes into account of the operation, maintenance and production costs during twenty years of operation. The EMS efficiency is tested by simulation and gives good results. The reliability of the studied EMS is important and encouraging, since it can be applied in real–time to more sophisticated systems that are constituted of various interconnected micro-grids, as it is the case of smart grids systems. Moreover, this strategy showed its efficiency, since it has been tested using measured data. Thus, it is powerful and reliable, especially in cases of non-availability of sufficient renewable energy to supply the loads with the needed power. Consequently, this approach contributes to the security of micro-grids and hence, for the smart grids too.

ACKNOWLEDGMENT

Dr. Yahyaoui is funded by the project 0838/2015 from the Brazilian Foundation for Research and Innovation of Espiritu Santo (FAPES) and a grant from CAPES/Brazil. Pr. Tadeo is partially supported by the seventh Framework program FP7, under grant agreement N° 288145, within the ocean of tomorrow joint call 2011. Dr. M. E. V. Segatto is partially supported by CNPq/Brazil (CNPq 307470/2012-1).

REFERENCES

Aman, S., Simmhan, Y., & Prasanna, V. K. (2015). Holistic measures for evaluating prediction models in smart grids. *IEEE Transactions on Knowledge and Data Engineering*, 27(2), 475–488. doi:10.1109/TKDE.2014.2327022

Balaman, Ş. Y., & Selim, H. (2016). Sustainable design of renewable energy supply chains integrated with district heating systems: A fuzzy optimization approach. *Journal of Cleaner Production*.

Bhandari, B., Lee, K. T., Lee, G. Y., Cho, Y. M., & Ahn, S. H. (2015). Optimization of hybrid renewable energy power systems: A review. *International Journal of Precision Engineering and Manufacturing-Green Technology*, 2(1), 99–112. doi:10.1007/s40684-015-0013-z

Bizon, N. (2016). Global Extremum Seeking Control of the power generated by a Photovoltaic Array under Partially Shaded Conditions. *Energy Conversion and Management*, 109, 71–85. doi:10.1016/j.enconman.2015.11.046

Boukenoui, R., Salhi, H., Bradai, R., & Mellit, A. (2016). A new intelligent MPPT method for stand-alone photovoltaic systems operating under fast transient variations of shading patterns. *Solar Energy*, 124, 124–142. doi:10.1016/j.solener.2015.11.023

Burgos, C., Sáez, D., Orchard, M. E., & Cárdenas, R. (2015). Fuzzy modelling for the state-of-charge estimation of lead-acid batteries. *Journal of Power Sources, 274*, 355–366. doi:10.1016/j.jpowsour.2014.10.036

Carlucci, S., Cattarin, G., Causone, F., & Pagliano, L. (2015). Multi-objective optimization of a nearly zero-energy building based on thermal and visual discomfort minimization using a non-dominated sorting genetic algorithm (NSGA-II). *Energy and Building, 104*, 378–394. doi:10.1016/j.enbuild.2015.06.064

Chen, G., Liu, L., Song, P., & Du, Y. (2014). Chaotic improved PSO-based multi-objective optimization for minimization of power losses and L index in power systems. *Energy Conversion and Management, 86*, 548–560. doi:10.1016/j.enconman.2014.06.003

Chin, V. J., Salam, Z., & Ishaque, K. (2016). An accurate modelling of the two-diode model of PV module using a hybrid solution based on differential evolution. *Energy Conversion and Management, 124*, 42–50. doi:10.1016/j.enconman.2016.06.076

Choubin, B., Khalighi-Sigaroodi, S., Malekian, A., & Kişi, Ö. (2016). Multiple linear regression, multilayer perceptron network and adaptive neuro-fuzzy inference system for forecasting precipitation based on large-scale climate signals. *Hydrological Sciences Journal, 61*(6), 1001–1009. doi:10.1080/026266 67.2014.966721

Farhadi, M., & Mohammed, O. (2015). Adaptive energy management in redundant hybrid DC microgrid for pulse load mitigation. *IEEE Transactions on Smart Grid, 6*(1), 54–62. doi:10.1109/TSG.2014.2347253

Feng, L., Mears, L., Beaufort, C., & Schulte, J. (2016). Energy, economy, and environment analysis and optimization on manufacturing plant energy supply system. *Energy Conversion and Management, 117*, 454–465. doi:10.1016/j.enconman.2016.03.031

Fernández, E. F., Pérez-Higueras, P., Almonacid, F., Ruiz-Arias, J. A., Rodrigo, P., Fernandez, J. I., & Luque-Heredia, I. (2015). Model for estimating the energy yield of a high concentrator photovoltaic system. *Energy, 87*, 77–85. doi:10.1016/j.energy.2015.04.095

Graciano, V., Vargas, J. V., & Ordonez, J. C. (2015). Modeling and simulation of diesel, biodiesel and biogas mixtures driven compression ignition internal combustion engines. *International Journal of Energy Research.*

Hamdy, M., Nguyen, A. T., & Hensen, J. L. (2016). A performance comparison of multi-objective optimization algorithms for solving nearly-zero-energy-building design problems. *Energy and Building, 121*, 57–71. doi:10.1016/j.enbuild.2016.03.035

Hasan, M. A., & Parida, S. K. (2016). An overview of solar photovoltaic panel modeling based on analytical and experimental viewpoint. *Renewable & Sustainable Energy Reviews, 60*, 75–83. doi:10.1016/j. rser.2016.01.087

Jacobson, M. Z., Delucchi, M. A., Cameron, M. A., & Frew, B. A. (2015). Low-cost solution to the grid reliability problem with 100% penetration of intermittent wind, water, and solar for all purposes. *Proceedings of the National Academy of Sciences of the United States of America, 112*(49), 15060–15065. doi:10.1073/pnas.1510028112 PMID:26598655

Krishnamoorthy, H. S. G., Pawan, P. N., & Pitel, I. J. (2014). Wind Turbine Generator–Battery Energy Storage Utility Interface Converter Topology With Medium-Frequency Transformer Link. *IEEE Transactions on Power Electronics*, *29*(8), 4146–4155. doi:10.1109/TPEL.2013.2295419

Lanzafame, R., Stefano, M., & Messina, M. (2014). 2D CFD modeling of H-Darrieus wind turbines using a transition turbulence mode. *Energy Procedia*, *45*, 131–140. doi:10.1016/j.egypro.2014.01.015

Lund, P. D., Lindgren, J., Mikkola, J., & Salpakari, J. (2015). Review of energy system flexibility measures to enable high levels of variable renewable electricity. *Renewable & Sustainable Energy Reviews*, *45*, 785–807. doi:10.1016/j.rser.2015.01.057

Mathiesen, B. V., Lund, H., Connolly, D., Wenzel, H., Østergaard, P. A., Möller, B., & Hvelplund, F. K. et al. (2015). Smart Energy Systems for coherent 100% renewable energy and transport solutions. *Applied Energy*, *145*, 139–154. doi:10.1016/j.apenergy.2015.01.075

Mohanty, S., Patra, P. K., & Sahoo, S. S. (2016). Prediction and application of solar radiation with soft computing over traditional and conventional approach–A comprehensive review. *Renewable & Sustainable Energy Reviews*, *56*, 778–796. doi:10.1016/j.rser.2015.11.078

Muthuramalingam, M., & Manoharan, P. S. (2014). Comparative analysis of distributed MPPT controllers for partially shaded stand alone photovoltaic systems. *Energy Conversion and Management*, *86*, 286–299. doi:10.1016/j.enconman.2014.05.044

Oró, E., Depoorter, V., Garcia, A., & Salom, J. (2015). Energy efficiency and renewable energy integration in data centres. Strategies and modelling review. *Renewable & Sustainable Energy Reviews*, *42*, 429–445. doi:10.1016/j.rser.2014.10.035

Østergaard, P. A., Lund, H., & Mathiesen, B. V. (2016). Smart energy systems and 4th generation district heating. *International Journal of Sustainable Energy Planning and Management*, *10*, 1–2.

Ozdemir, S., Altin, N., & Sefa, I. (2014). Single stage three level grid interactive MPPT inverter for PV systems. *Energy Conversion and Management*, *80*, 561–572. doi:10.1016/j.enconman.2014.01.048

Pouresmaeil, E., Mehrasa, M., & Catalão, J. P. (2015). A multifunction control strategy for the stable operation of DG units in smart grids. *IEEE Transactions on Smart Grid*, *6*(2), 598–607. doi:10.1109/TSG.2014.2371991

Rezk, H., & Eltamaly, A. M. (2015). A comprehensive comparison of different MPPT techniques for photovoltaic systems. *Solar Energy*, *112*, 1–11. doi:10.1016/j.solener.2014.11.010

Sabo, M. L., Mariun, N., Hizam, H., Radzi, M. A. M., & Zakaria, A. (2016). Spatial energy predictions from large-scale photovoltaic power plants located in optimal sites and connected to a smart grid in Peninsular Malaysia. *Renewable & Sustainable Energy Reviews*, *66*, 79–94. doi:10.1016/j.rser.2016.07.045

Sakellaridis, N. F., Spyridon, R. I., Antonopoulos, A. K., Mavropoulos, G. C., & Hountalas, D. T. (2015). Development and validation of a new turbocharger simulation methodology for marine two stroke diesel engine modelling and diagnostic applications. *Energy*, *91*, 952–966. doi:10.1016/j.energy.2015.08.049

Salazar, J., Tadeo, F., & Prada, C. (2015). Modelling of diesel generator sets that assist off-grid renewable energy micro grids. *Renewable Energy and Sustainable Development*, *1*, 72–80.

Santamouris, M., Cartalis, C., Synnefa, A., & Kolokotsa, D. (2015). On the impact of urban heat island and global warming on the power demand and electricity consumption of buildings—A review. *Energy and Building*, *98*, 119–124. doi:10.1016/j.enbuild.2014.09.052

Sonnenschein, M., Lünsdorf, O., Bremer, J., & Tröschel, M. (2015). Decentralized control of units in smart grids for the support of renewable energy supply. *Environmental Impact Assessment Review*, *52*, 40–52. doi:10.1016/j.eiar.2014.08.004

Steiner, M., Siefer, G., Hornung, T., Peharz, G., & Bett, A. W. (2015). YieldOpt, a model to predict the power output and energy yield for concentrating photovoltaic modules. *Progress in Photovoltaics: Research and Applications*, *23*(3), 385–397. doi:10.1002/pip.2458

Suganthi, L., Iniyan, S., & Samuel, A. A. (2015). Applications of fuzzy logic in renewable energy systems–a review. *Renewable & Sustainable Energy Reviews*, *48*, 585–607. doi:10.1016/j.rser.2015.04.037

Tito, S. R., Lie, T. T., & Anderson, T. N. (2016). Optimal sizing of a wind-photovoltaic-battery hybrid renewable energy system considering socio-demographic factors. *Solar Energy*, *136*, 525–532. doi:10.1016/j.solener.2016.07.036

Yahyaoui, I. (2016c). Specifications of Photovoltaic Pumping Systems in Agriculture: Sizing, Fuzzy Energy Management and Economic Sensitivity Analysis. Elsevier science. ISBN: 9780128120392.

Yahyaoui, I., Chaabene, M., & Tadeo, F. (2016). a). Evaluation of Maximum Power Point Tracking algorithm for off-grid photovoltaic pumping. *Sustainable Cities and Society*, *25*, 65–73. doi:10.1016/j.scs.2015.11.005

Yahyaoui, I., Ghraizi, R., & Tadeo, F. (2016d). Operational cost optimization for renewable energy microgrids in Mediterranean climate.*Proceedings of the International Renewable Energy Conference (IREC)*. doi:10.1109/IREC.2016.7478881

Yahyaoui, I., Sallem, S., Kamoun, M. B. A., & Tadeo, F. (2014). A proposal for off-grid photovoltaic systems with non-controllable loads using fuzzy logic. *Energy Conversion and Management*, *78*, 835–842. doi:10.1016/j.enconman.2013.07.091

Yahyaoui, I., Yahyaoui, A., Chaabene, M., & Tadeo, F. (2016). b). Energy management for a stand-alone photovoltaic-wind system suitable for rural electrification. *Sustainable Cities and Society*, *25*, 90–101. doi:10.1016/j.scs.2015.12.002

Zhao, B., Xue, M., Zhang, X., Wang, C., & Zhao, J. (2015). An MAS based energy management system for a stand-alone microgrid at high altitude. *Applied Energy*, *143*, 251–261. doi:10.1016/j.apenergy.2015.01.016

Chapter 16
Feasibility Study of Renewable Energy Integrated Electric Vehicle Charging Infrastructure

Azhar Ul-Haq
University of New Brunswick, Canada

Marium Azhar
École de Technologie Supérieure, Canada & Lahore College for Women University, Pakistan

ABSTRACT

This chapter presents a detailed study of renewable energy integrated charging infrastructure for electric vehicles (EVs) and discusses its various aspects such as siting requirements, standards of charging stations, integration of renewable energy sources for powering up charging stations and interfacing devices between charging facilities and smart grid. A smart charging station for EVs is explained along with its essential components and different charging methodologies are explained. It has been recognized that the amalgamation of electric vehicles in the transportation sector will trigger power issues due to the mobility of vehicles beyond the stretch of home area network. In this regard an information and communication technology (ICT) based architecture may support EVs management with an aim to enhance the electric vehicle charging and energy storage capabilities with the relevant considerations. An ICT based solution is capable of monitoring the state of charge (SOC) of EV batteries, health and accessible amount of energy along with the mobility of EVs.

INTRODUCTION

Concept of smart cities envisages diffusion of plug-in hybrid electric vehicles that utilize electric power to run. Electric vehicles have gained attention of various researchers and stake-holders evaluating their potential benefits such as zero carbon emission and reducing dependency on fuel for the greater penetration of plug-in hybrid electric vehicles. Penetration of PHEV/EVs will definitely help overcome likely shortage of oil resources due to tremendously increasing consumption of fuel. In order to have acceptable market of electric vehicles, charging infrastructure is required to be deployed optimally keeping focus

DOI: 10.4018/978-1-5225-1829-7.ch016

on cost concerns. An economic deployment of charging stations added with low costs onboard power electronics along with vehicles' battery technology may be the major certain factors in the success of electric mobility i.e. PHEV running. While building charging infrastructure, a care is to be taken that charging stations' standards and power rating must be synchronized with the type of electric vehicle. It is estimated that the sale of EVs is expected to increase as high as 64% by 2030. As per the expectations, making diffusion of EVs practicable, in future, more focus is needed to be paid on the development of appropriate charging facility for EVS recharging. Concentration of the present research community is to reduce recharging time of vehicle's battery by supplying fairly high voltage &current rating.

However, high power supply to charging station may cause grid stability problem during high demand hours so it may require additional power generation to satisfy the power demand during peak load hours (Gil & Taiber, 2014). Therefore, impact of charging station load on the power grid and rate of vehicle charging is to be taken into account carefully while designing the charging station. Additionally, in view of optimal development of charging infrastructure, various energy storage technologies such as batteries, super capacitors, flywheels and etc. are under evaluation contributing in optimization of EV charging station. Simultaneously, distribution power generation (DPG) has received wide attention because of its advantages in terms of attention cutting down transmission investment, decreased operating cost and less losses in transmitting electric power with the improved grid stability during peak hours (Begovic, Pregelj, Rohatgi & Novosel, 2001; Lasseter, 2006). However, DPG system must stop its operation in case a power system failure is determined otherwise it may add negative impact on the power grid (ISC Committee, 2003). In this regard, concept of micro- grid has emerged to ensure reliable operation of the power grid (Tuttle & Baldick, 2012). In order to support economic deployment of EVs, mileage of e-vehicles needs to be enlarged and utilities may be required to design power infrastructure around the recharging station rescheduling provision of supply offering high quality of service in terms of reliability, continuity, low delay, and security.

With the advent of EVs, will be a rising need for technologies that achieve an intelligent and improved management of all energy resources. Technologies based strategies such as demand based pricing are assumed to be effective in dynamic shapes of power usage. Demand based pricing of power is anticipated to become the typical mechanism for pricing in smart grids to uphold the system secure and unfailing at low cost. From the user's viewpoint an EV is the most promising electric load in this assimilated optimization practice of energy resources due to its high power requirements and bidirectional (V2G) features. An accurate identification of EVs features such as parking status, location, and its energy storage capacity are vital to devise an efficient algorithm. In the residential consumers' perspective, the key goal is cost reduction. Though, for the utilities, following objectives are of extreme importance; deployment and costs reduction, load balancing, mitigation of distribution losses and operation of grid reliability. In this wake, Information and Communication Technology (ICT) based solutions obtain and archives the relevant feature and objectives. All the information will be utilized in amalgamation with the dynamic tariffs, preferences of users and requirements of comfort in terms of operation of appliances through appropriate algorithms that will deliver optimized choices in a household energy management systems (EMS).

In view of limited EV driving range, a significant research is concentrated on EV wireless charging with an aim of extending the driving range of EVs. Assuming scenario of a highway that connects two main cities with one EV charging lane. This charging lane has many charging mats beneath the road. When an EV reaches a charging mat, it will be wirelessly recharged for that moment. In this regard, a few research projects are evaluating the viability of such dynamic charging mechanism, and it is predicted that ICT may play a vital role in this environment.

Charging process of a single EV cannot recompense grid oscillations and it may be controlled through an ICT based central operator that can respond to varying grid operating conditions. A number of e-services for grid are discussed which are based on an ICT architecture with specific communication protocols. In view of smart load management an ICT based ICT solutions may be used to aggregate a great number of charge stations.

The extensive penetration of EVs integrally relies on the collaboration between the EVs and the grid. The tie connecting them is pervasive network. Usually, such network is built on heterogeneous architecture, which involves all the advanced communication equipment. In its architecture level, many tools, controllers, sensors, and computers are unified and accessible via the Internet. At the practical level, networks such as Zigbee, WiMAX, WiFi, and cognitive networks are all practicable for assisting the information gathering and communication in several scenarios. A theoretical framework of smart grid with communication technologies is depicted in Figure 1. Though equipping the smart grid with numerous communication technologies improve the efficiency and flexibility of the grid, the suscepti-bilities that exist in communication systems are subjected to safety risks in the power system. Thus, it is important to discuss the cyber security issues against the EVs network, then emphasis given on the wireless security techniques to ensure secure communication among the EVs and system.

In this chapter readers will find a comprehensive discussion on various issues and challenges related to possible pervasion of EVs and their charging infrastructure to recharge EVs. A substantial consideration is given to ICT based EVs integration in the smart grid with the relevant issues and ICT based solutions.

Figure 1. The EV integrated smart grid with communication technologies

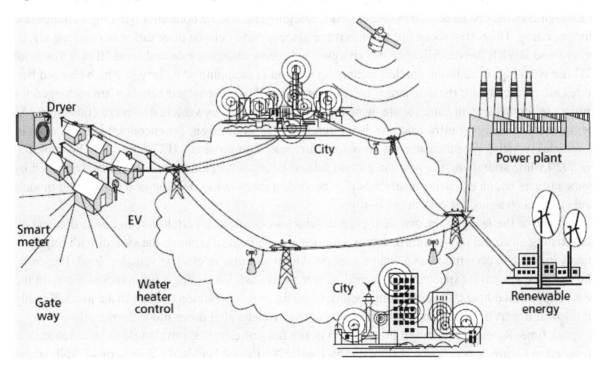

We shall have a detailed look on different charging standards with its pros & cons and feasibility measurement in terms of siting requirements and siting points for installation of charging stations, smart grid and electric vehicle integration, possible and appropriate energy resources, power electronics interface with EVs and their charging facilities, distributed power generation and electric vehicle's integration, positive and negative impact of electro-mobility on distribution network. The chapter also contains detailed description on the concept of smart charging station. Furthermore, a case study is carried out in view of possible impact on vehicle owners and their preferences about optimal and user friendly deployment of electric vehicles in which some important results are concluded based on the hypothesis statistics obtained from the conducted survey in a town Fredericton.

SMART GRID AND EVs CHARGING

Concept of smart cities envisages diffusion of plug-in hybrid electric vehicles for greener reliable and efficient transportation system, a future vision of smart grid paradigm is shown in Figure 2 It is a visible fact that electric vehicles diffusion in the market greatly depends on the uniform, secure, reliable and robust presence of charging infrastructure. Thus, installation of charging station and its related issues are discussed to provide an understanding regarding feasibility of possible pervasion of electric vehicles on the road. Electric vehicles may cause the power grid to be over stress and can have negative impact on the grid stability because they are likely to be charged in the existing distribution network. In the proceeding section it will be shown that such EVs will need large amount of power and it is worth noting that amount of EVs penetration will define the level of impact on the power grid and charging requirements. It is well recognized that for greater pervasion of plug-in vehicles in transportation network, it is necessary to develop charging infrastructure with defined charging standards and methods. Although EVs may be recharged by outlet, fast recharging can also be done supplying high voltage and current rating. The SAE- 'society of automotive engineers' have defined three different charging levels; level-I and level-II are described as AC charging with slow charging rate and level-III is defined for DC fast charging. In addition, another recharging method is swapping of battery in which charged batteries are replaced with the discharged batteries and then these discharged batteries are recharged for future use. In this system batteries are owned by operators and not by vehicle owners or consumers. As deployment of charging infrastructures is the fundamental requirement for encouraging the uptake of e-vehicles reducing greenhouse gases emission. European Commission's (EC) strategy to be deployed by 2020 while addressing the grid integration related issues. Charging points are being developed by some utilities but an extensive research is also needed to carry out to develop grid connection models and efficient charging network in the Europe.

In view of the fact that uncontrolled plug-in vehicles could cause certain rise in power demand on the existing electrical power infrastructure. Utilities are required to upgrade the system with improvements in order to accommodate negative impacts due to addition in electric vehicles' load. Presently, the designed system is expected to meet peak power which lasts for around a few hundred hours, in the rest off-peak load hours, the generating facilities remain in rest condition and are made available only to respond to part time peak load demand hours or even remain shut down mode during off-

peak time. Research and development trend in the field of charging infrastructure for e-vehicles is depicted in Figure 3. A research carried out by Pacific Northwest National Laboratories-PNNL stated

Figure 2. Future vision of smart grid paradigm

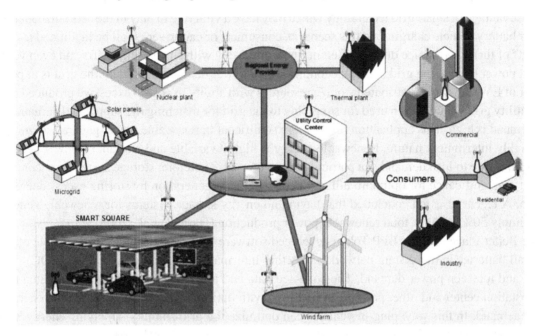

that idle generating capacity of electrical power can be exploited to supply 70% of e-vehicles powering them up which is equivalent to around 175 million plug-in vehicles.

However, rigorous control and management are key factors in achieving the optimized charging of e- vehicle's battery. In this regard, principles of smart grid technology may be applied to centrally manage and control the recharging of e-vehicles with existing generation, transmission &distribution and communication network (Bahn, Marcy, Vaillancourt & Waaub, 2013).

Applying smart grid principles would enhance systems' capability of power generation and power consumption bridging effective communication among nodes of the network and help make decisions

Figure 3. Research and trends

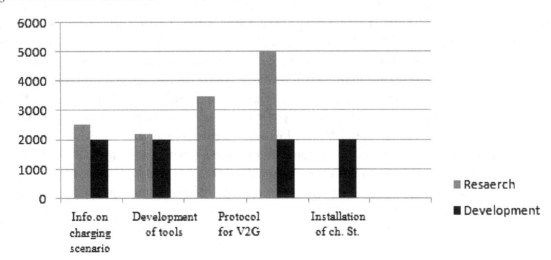

about generation and consumption matching supply and demand. Timely varying price system is the salient advantage of smart grid technology which may have a vital role to play in the centralized management of battery vehicle charging. In this scenario, consumers or car drivers shall be facilitated to choose the tariff of their own choice during different times of the day with fluctuating tariffs and even vehicles can sell power back to the grid at better economy when power demand or load on the grid is at peak. A number of EVs can act as distributed storage resources with ability to absorb excessive produced energy in the utility grid which is then used for supplying to the grid for matching the supply and demand when load demand is high. This application seems more significant in renewable power generation in view of their highly intermittent nature. Renewable energy is highly variable and amount of power generation may be opposite to load demand at a particular time interval. Therefore, storage systems are considered of primary significance for optimum utilization of renewable generation by storing excess energy production. A recent research concluded that having no energy storage systems for renewable generation would imply 50% dump of total renewable power production (Harnad et al., 2008).

The Better Place Project- BPP Tokyo developed software for e-vehicle smart grid capable of monitoring all batteries in the system network, collecting information about state of charge (SOC) of each battery and foreseen power demand. The collected data and information can be communicated to utility, substation center and other partners in real-time with optimized allocation of available energy and supply demand. In this way, plug-in vehicles can optimize the grid stability supplying energy back to the grid during peak load hours (Guille & Gross, 2009). The existing technology allows consumers to supply extra power from the stored electricity system back to the utility grid with bi-directional advanced metering infrastructure-AMI. Utilizing plug-in vehicles as storage devices would save the cost of backup storage capacity keeping the system standby in order to respond to immediate increase in load avoiding transients and failures on the power grid (Ul-Haq et al., 2013)

Vehicle-to-Grid Technology

Electric vehicles can be designed in such a way that they can transfer power back to the grid, this technology is known as Vehicle-to-Grid (V2G). Normally, AC power from utility grid is utilized to charge battery vehicles. On contrary, in V2G technology, DC power drawn by the vehicle' battery need to be converted into AC power for connecting to the power grid. To obtain the required rating of current and voltage individual cells of battery are connected in parallel/series configuration. Power electronics' unique behavior in V2G technology is that it must be capable of bidirectional power transfer i.e. either drawing power from the grid while recharging battery of the vehicle or supplying power to the grid upon power demand. The V2G operation can help resolve frequency variation and voltage regulation issues in distributed power generation applications with effective demand side management. Additionally, large number of EVs can serve as energy storage devices, particularly in case of renewable generation, when the generation is fairly high and load demand is low. System operators can control V2G operation for power transfer to the utility grid, when required. During low power demand time vehicle's driver can recharge batteries to full utilizing excess power generation to run vehicle's electric motor for the vehicle traction saving consumption of fuel. A number of vehicles parked at public places could be employed to deliver electric power to the grid when power demand is high and thus offsetting start-up of additional generators to supply the instantly increased load. Such a setup is considered an isolated system operator-ISO.

A plug-in vehicle with V2G technology configuration must have following three elements;

1. It must be connected with the power grid for electric power transfer,
2. Precision metering and
3. Control and communication facility with operator.

However, a V2G service is likely to be carried out for a few hours so the economic benefit is limited. Recently published research report "Public Utilities Fortnightly" by Denholm suggest that V2G technology mostly refers to auxiliary services. Vehicles with V2G system use high energy & power battery system and a bidirectional power converter. Typically, a V2G system uses Li-ion or Ni metal battery pack.

CHARGING METHODOLOGIES OF EVs

Quality of service of a recharging station is measured in terms of how fast the vehicles' battery is charged and discharged, provision of electric supply for recharging EVs, delay in accepting charging request by vehicle owner, long term effect on battery performance, and pricing. Charging capability of battery as defined in the SAE J1772 standard for e-vehicles (SAE Standard,2010; Kissel, 2011) is as follows:

-   **Slow Charging - Level 1:** Supplying AC energy to the on-board charger of the vehicle of rating of 120V/16 A for charging 1.92 kW battery with charging time of 10 hours
-   **Standard Charging - Level 2:** Implies AC energy to the on-board charger of the vehicle of voltage of 208-240 V and current of 12-80 A for 2.5-19.2 kW with charging time of 8 hours at most
-   **Fast Charging - Level 3:** Using DC energy from an off-board charger, in DC charging there is no minimum energy requirement but the maximum current may be 400 A and 240 kW with charging time of 20-30 minutes, (Quebec Construction Code, 2010; Hydro Quebec, 2012).

Level-1 charging may be suitable at homes where vehicles are normally parked for 8-10 hours during night through many of the electrical circuits near parking supply up to 120 Volt, a rate that is only required for level-1 charging. Use of a 120 Volt outlet requires no special EV supply equipment and therefore, Level-1 charging is considered to be suitable at home garages. Electric vehicle can be easily plugged-in in the normal house socket as it requires normal AC supply. On the other hand, fast-charging may not be installed at home garages because of its special requirements of supply equipment and high current rating and safety measures. It is expected that mostly recharging will occur at home even if there is a sufficient public charging station network. It does not necessarily mean that there is no or lower need of public charging stations because many residences do not have adequate facilities for recharging EVs. Level-2 electric vehicle supply equipment does operate on circuits with a capacity similar to those that run appliances, such as clothes dryers and electric ovens. It is suggested that EV drivers that travel long distances on regular basis and have high capacity batteries should use Level-2 charging station. However, installation costs can easily exceed the cost of the level-1 EV supply equipment itself. As Level-2 charging typically takes around 4-6 hours to recharge an EV, so it may be useful to install level-2 charging at workplaces, factories and etc. DC fast charging is different from Level-1 and Level-2 charging because of substantial difference in charging duration. Power load and high current rating required by DC fast charging seem impossible to be drawn at home garages and also it requires dedicated circuit and panel to supply DC supply to electric vehicles because existing electrical panel and circuitry does not ensure that the panel at homes has the electrical load capacity for provision of DC fast charging. Drivers would require DC fast charging facility for quick recharging of their cars and will plug in for approximately 10 minutes to 30 minutes and will likely stay near the vehicle. Suggested potential locations for DC fast charging include restaurants, stores, coffee shops and shopping malls. A detailed description of locating the charging station is given in following section.

Locating Charging Stations

Electric vehicles need recharging facility on time and on site for their reliable and smooth operation. Therefore, it is necessary to install charging infrastructure at residences, work places, parking sites and other public places. It seems more convenient that majority vehicles are recharged during night using AC charging either level-II or the level-II (SAE Standard, 2010). People only lacking charging facility at night cannot coincide with the option of charging at home. On the other hand, commercial vehicles need to be equipped with charging infrastructure, at day times as well, at public places and employment centers. In this section we shall take a quick look on different siting requirements for installing charging station (Haq, Chadhry & Saleemi, 2013).

1.   Charging Facility at Residential Garages

A large number of electric vehicles are assumed to be charged at homes during night. According to web-based study, conducted in 2010, 81% vehicles are recharged at homes (Yilmaz & Krein, 2013). It is expected that future studies will also validate the previous concept that mostly e-vehicles recharging will be done at homes. As a matter of fact, many residence sites do not have appropriate charging facility.

A recent survey in the north America have concluded that almost 50% of the residential garages have no required charging facility for recharging battery of e-vehicles within every 30 feet (Tuttle & Baldick, 2012). As per report of December 2011 by EV Project, vehicle drivers plugged in their car for charging for an average duration of 7 hours a day whereas the actual duration of charging was low around 2.5 hours a day (Dyke, Schofield & Barnes, 2010).

On the other hand, level-II charging at night may be workable for the vehicle owners who do not travel for more than 40 miles. While siting an electric vehicle supply equipment at different places e.g. at garage, vehicle parking or any other place, issues related to mounting the charging inlet on the vehicle and length of e-vehicle's charging cord are to be taken into account irrespective of what charging level is being installed. Supplying equipment should be able to minimize the hazardous tripping of charging cable balancing the safety measures.

Multi-Unit Residential Complex

For multi-unit housing building, charging sockets can be installed at specific parking location close to each unit distribution point. In fact, a few parking plots at multi-unit housing complex have electrical outlets. According to a recent survey report, only 17% vehicles owners in the North America have available electrical outlets near their apartment's garages (Smart & Schey, 2012). Mostly parking places at apartment complex have 120V available and are suitable to support level 1 charging method. A proper location may be a common point where all energy meters are mounted. Generally, charging outlets can

Figure 4. Flow diagram showing procedure for installing charging facility

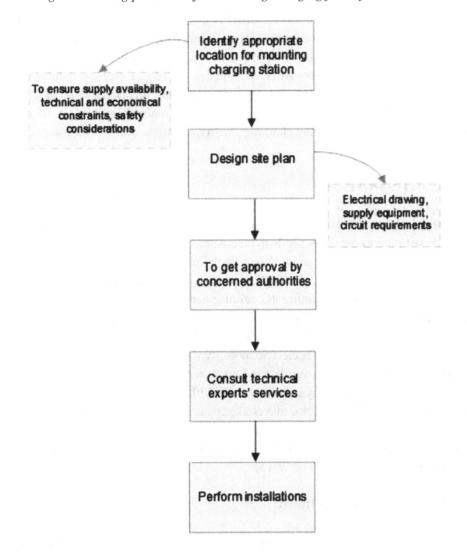

be located at common distribution point at each housing complex and then it may further be distributed to individual homes with required e-vehicles supply equipment. Some housing buildings are flexible in exchanging parking places. Parking facility in multi-unit buildings is either included in the house property or maybe not. All these scenarios affect siting of e-vehicle charging station and the charging level to be employed.

Charging Station at Public Places

EV charging stations are to be located on various places owned by government, private or any other organizations. Generally, those EV owners prefer to recharge their electric vehicles at the public places, who do not have either adequate charging facility at their own homes or have depleted car battery during day time. All the three charging methods; Level- I, Level-II, and Level-III DC fast charging may be installed at specific public places as per vehicles' needs. Electric vehicles' supply equipment for Level-I &Level-II charging and DC fast charging- Level-III is different with different specifications because all three levels use different voltage and current level offering different charging time. In case of level-I and level- II charging, a vehicle will be left for at least 2-6 hours for recharging, so in this case charging station need to be located at such places where people can afford to wait for a number of hours e.g. at work places, employment centers and etc. Whereas, DC fast charging can be done in up to 30 minutes, therefore, this type of charging can be suitable at commercial places, shopping malls and etc. A flow diagram, showing procedure for locating charging facility, is shown in the Figure 4.

ICT AND EVs INTEGRATION

To support e-vehicles' smooth driving, provision of recharging facility on-time on-place with high quality of service with the lower delay needs to be ensured. Vehicles are needed to equipped with new navigation and infotainment devices as well as with wireless communication technology to support Vehicle to charging station Infrastructure (V2I) and charging station Infrastructure to Vehicle (I2V) communication provided by 3G and future 4G cellular networks. Updated onboard information about the status and location of a charging station in terms of number of available free plugs and average waiting time at the station is likely to be provided in future electric vehicles' network. In this way such communication infrastructure optimizes electric mobility with reduced search time for charging station, price information depending on the power demand for better economy with reduced trip time. An effective communication infrastructure may help cooperate within network of EVs to utilize electric power charging infrastructure efficiently (Sortomme et al., 2011; Martinez et al., 2011). Authors explore the role of modern communication technologies as an integral part of smart grid for effective demand side management while matching supply and load on the power grid with reflection of real-time dynamic pricing signal (Gungor et al., 2011; 2012; 2013).

ICT Based EVs Load Management

In view of smart load management an ICT based ICT solutions may be used to aggregate a great number of charge stations.

For this purpose, the central operator (CO) is assumed to be linked with a pool of EV charging stations. The station sends information about current charging processes to CO, which can thereby assume reliable estimation of charging processes. Conversely, CO is linked with the grid objects to deliver balancing power and demand on behalf of the EVs charging network. For a a sustainable penetration of EVs, the smart load management plays an inevitable role to guarantee grid stability and provides an opportunity for EVs by participating in e-service such as provision of power balancing purposes and clearing forecast errors of renewable energy generation. The amount of energy compensation is exchanged with the Balancing Authority (BR) and does not stand liable to a lower energy quantity. For comprehension of e-services, it is assumed that regulatory necessities are determined and the CO has thorough knowledge of grid operating conditions where EV charging stations are installed. Additionally, in order to reduce the danger of inadequate accessibility of connected EVs the CO may be able to group a number of renewable energy resources. An ICT based scheme to aggregate a large number of charging stations with energy balancing e-service is shown in Figure 5.

Figure 5. e-service for energy balancing

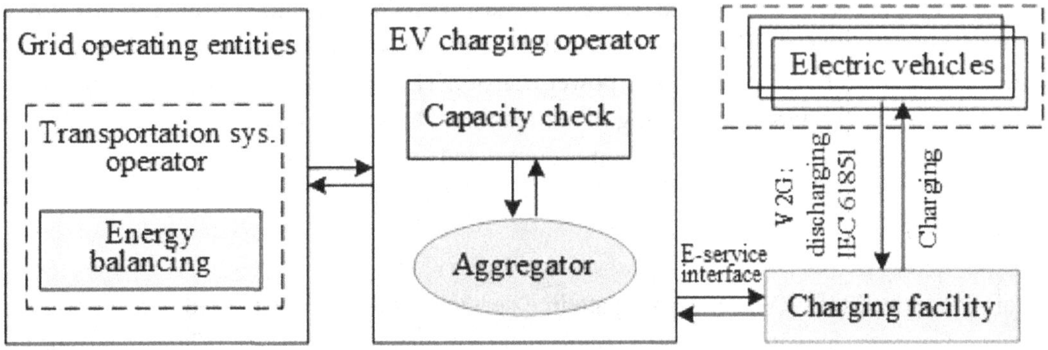

To control EVs charging, there are two key Types of protocol that are present amid the charging stations and EVs. One is a Low-Level Communication which is based on a PWM technique and the second one is based on IP communication. In the V2G Communication Interface, that is presently standardized as IEC 15118 is proposed. For communication from CO to the transmission system operator the Merit Order List Server interface is a potential protocol to comprehend control of EV charging.

IEC 61851-1 is a low-level protocol that can serve between the charging station and EVs. It guarantees personal safety, since interruption of the charging plug found to be very fast and the charging can be interrupted. Alternatively, standard IEC 61851-1 permits two parameters an exchange between the charging stations and EVs. The first constraint is the state of EV, whether it is connected and prepared to recharge before plugging in the power supply and the second parameter is the charging current that is delivered by the charging point over the duty cycle of PWM. The duty cycle is examined by the EV charger and the permissible charging current of is attuned. In order to control the charging processes, CO can adjust the duty cycle within the charging station to either decrease or increase the EV charging current. Therefore, the e-services can be taken with the support of IEC 61851-1. A duty cycle of 5% prompts the EV charging to shift to IEC 15118 for charging.

Standard IEC 15118 can also perform the e-service by a simple low level communication. However, the IEC 61851-1 does not offer an information related to the charging process such as amount of energy or time of departure. Though, this fact is valuable for the purpose of capacity analysis of CO to foresee the power available for the provision of e-service. Thus, standard ISO/IEC 15118 is proposed for realization of the e-service.

The Working Group describing the ISO/IEC 15118 published an International Standard Draft for charge control mechanisms, which is capable for customer-friendly balancing procedures with the plug & charge principle. Furthermore, IEC 15118 provides authentication mechanisms necessarily for the public space. In this regard, a part of the IEC 15118 DIS (JWG, n. d.) describes numerous message arrangements, which can be further distributed into three stages including charge, pre-charge, and post-charge phase. The pre-charge stage is analogous to setting up a charge, where, communication between EV and EV charging facility is recognized. Moreover, details of payment and service are exchanged. All charging parameters are communicated from EV to the facility which determines the bounds for a charging process. In case of AC charging the Charging request contains the parameters, amount of power, time of departure, EV maximum voltage, maximum and minimum permissible current. The EV charging facility responds to the request containing the charging parameters and its charging schedule.

After the necessary information is exchanged for scheduling of charging, the EV conducts a charging profile to the charging station through a delivery request while taking into account the limits from the module of maximum schedule. This sequence signifies the evolution to the phase of charging. The EV is informed about and it begins the electric power transfer. The charging stage includes repeating messages about the status of charging, allowing meter reading. During the phase of post-charging; transfer of energy is ended and the recognized session is completed.

E-Services for EVs

It is certainly assumed that EVs can participate in e-services as they are activated considering the user convenience. The e-services are established by the means of standard protocols. When a charging process is initialized, the EV charging facility offers a schedule of charging including charging parameters and a list of schedule time interval and maximum power values.

Based on the given information, EVs reserve a charging profile through a power delivery request to the charging station. It encompasses various entries of profile including profile of charging start and charging maximum power transfer. When, the CO makes a request of energy allocation to signal the charging station, it calculates the scheduling of charge and a updated charging parameters. Afterward, the EV regulates the charging profile. In order to enable an end-to-end communication from the charging station to an EV for controlling mechanisms, all protocols need to cooperate with each other. In the balancing power e-service, EVs offer compensation of energy in case of forecast errors of renewable resource. The CO negotiates the amount of energy compensation and offers a general agreement. Though, there is no standard protocol on the communication interface between the operator and user and it may become more prevalent with higher penetration of renewable energy resources. There is need of an interface for automatic provisioning of power balancing. In order to avoid interoperability issues, ICT has greater role to play. The provision of energy balancing is offered between operator and the EV users. For this purpose, the operator transmits a request for negotiation including its prospects for the balancing of energy. For cumulative result of all EV charging facilities, charging profile is adapted to ensure energy balancing through the response activation. In the consequence of power balancing processing, an accounting between the operator and the EV user is exchanged through the sequential accounting messages.

ICT Integrated Dynamic EV Charging

A dynamic EV charging infrastructure requires the ICT based implementation to manage the track users, process charging requests and billing issues. Guiding the electric vehicles to the charging track will be sustained by a system of navigation with an ability to inform the user about the position of the track, the charging price and the accessibility of the charging mats to the vehicle. The navigation scheme will compute the an efficient a charging plan for an EV trip. The charging lane will be controlled and accessed through by an appropriate algorithm that would further notify the nearby EV about the charging mat location and status of availability (Smiai et al, 2015).

This section presents a state-of-the-art study of the relevant ICT based solutions for dynamic charging of EVs in the following fields including; EV identification, User accounts management, booking and billing, guidance to charging track that contains charging pads, assistance while driving and Dynamic routing.

EV charging infrastructure requires to identify pre-booked or authorized EVs in order to trigger the charging process. Two distinguished identification levels include the recognition of the EVs near approaching the charging track. For this identification, two methods can be applied: the automatic Plate Recognition (APR) a short-range communications (SRC). The APR is the abstraction of the license plate of vehicle information from a sequence of images. The extracted data can be exploited with through a database in numerous applications, for example, an automated payment system (parking fee payment), monitoring systems for the surveillance of traffic. A camera is used by an APR system to catch the image of the vehicle's plate. Where, the quality of the taken images is an important factor in the attainment of the APR. Under diverse environmental situations, the APR is supposed to treat the license plates rapidly. As the license plates in different region exhibit different colors, languages and or fonts; a single background color or images can exist in vehicle's plates. Some other environmental factors such as dirt and lighting can impede the Plates, thus, the APR system must be mature enough to support the need of EV charging.

The short-range communications (SRC) is a cluster of radio channels which is designed for vehicle-to-vehicle and vehicle-to-infrastructure wireless communications setup (Tsai, 2014). These two communication links have numerous objectives including, its intention to improve the awareness of car driver about the nearby environment (position of pedestrians, vehicles, and obstacles). Those are aimed at rapid dissemination of emergency in order to promptly trigger an appropriate measure. It is meant to communicate the drivers about nearby construction works, traffic flow and speed limits. Road operators are allowed to obtain information about the vehicles on road. SRC may also be used for toll collection in several countries and it can be considered to support the identifications of EVs dynamic charging. Its experimentation will disclose the necessary alterations over state-of-the-art.

Identification of EVs near Charging Track: based on the length of charging mate, EVs exact location can be identified and for this, there is need for an authentication protocol to validate an EV's identity in 10 ms only so that it allows enough time for the process of energy transfer. The systems may be designed in such a way that it reaches rapid authentication being based on symmetric keys and location of the EV:

- **Managing User Accounts and Billing:** EV charging infrastructure will require a system to identify its users to allow them to reserve charging points and to be billed. An EV driver may use dissimilar charging tracks during a trip and the system must be capable enough to create a user account that is interoperable among energy retailers. The system should be able provide a bill specifying the charging facility operator and the bill of the consumed energy. The system should permit the connection of EVs to a credit card holder through an automates payment systems of the energy delivered. Through enabling the reservation of the charging point will assure that the charging track is well-matched with the charging system and contain sufficient power to recharge an EV. It is interesting to employ a system that will grip reservation the EV users.
- **EVs Guidance to the Charging Track:** An EV driver is required to be directed towards the available and compatible charging tracks and it should be notified via precise signs and messages. Various variable message signs (VMS) can serve this purpose. VMS can communicate traffic and roadway info to drivers and is considered a component of an intelligent transportation. It can be used to supply traffic information, such as traffic conditions, accidents, special announcements, construction works, alternative routes, speed limits, and etc. A vital application of VMS is the source of authentic message and the motorists to fulfil the exhibited guidelines. This VMS is of the great concern for the road operators when deviation is required under the conditions of conges-

tion. A VMS system does assist to ease traffic problems by reducing the travel time while meeting driver's demand, (Ettelt et al., 2014).

- **EV Driving Assistance:** An EV is required to bring into line its receiving coil (through which wireless charging is performed) with the power transmitting coil to increase efficiency of energy transfer while keeping the charging track to realize this process. This alignment usually depends on on a camera which is placed behind the shield mirror to perceive the appropriate lane. The process of alignment of the coils can automatically correct the vehicle path while using a path prediction algorithm to inform the EV driver before leaving the lane. In order to correct the trajectory of EV, the location of the vehicle and charging mat may be measured using various techniques given in (Sukprasert, Nguyen & Fujimoto, 2014). The lane sensing mechanism may be based on the infrared sensor, nonetheless there is concern of accuracy in bad weather conditions. An infrared sensor is a cheaper device and is not much affected by reduced visibility, but it is unable foresee a lane departure. When a departing lane is detected, a departure warning may be transmitted via visual or audio system.

Dynamic Routing of EVs

EV dynamic routing is meant to guide an EV driver to facilitate the planning of charging events while travelling. The routing system enables the EV user to select a route and with specific charging lanes drive on. In the driving state, the routing system must point out the charging track and notify the driver about its current position. The will be informed about the availability of the charging mats so that an EV can be recharges upon reaching onto an available charging mat. For this purpose, web mapping programs based solutions such as Google Maps can be used to devise a routing application for the EV dynamic routing system. In this regard, web mapping offers several advantages over traditional mapping applications and is a low price solution, as web server, and hardware tools are relatively cheap. Products can be dispersed and replicated at very limited expenditures. The web maps also allow a greater cooperation among the users. The web based maps can offer real-time information about the availability of charging lane, pricing, and probable time to reach a destination in real-time traffic conditions (Yang et al., 2015; Neaimeh et al., 2013). As fact of matter, modeling the problem of possible routing is a challenging task because of the cost factor due to complex net of roads with several charging lanes. An EV dynamic charging process is depicted in Figure 6.

The cost allocated to a road does not only depend on the existence of a charging track/lane but also on the preference of an EV driver during a travel. Algorithms for dynamic routing of EVs needs to be studied in detail, so that the calculated route considers the destination, arrival time, and budget for recharging. In order to estimate and decide whether to consider a charging track requires a comprehensive research. For example, a charging track may inform the driver about its unavailability if there are many requests for reservation during congested traffic conditions.

An additional important feature includes the development of a dedicated human-machine interface. In general, a human-machine interface should be capable to deliver the real-time information in accordance with the driver's workload so that one can concentrate on the road conditions (Bellotti et al, 2005). Smart devices should be correctly unified with the other systems of the vehicle and human-machine interface should be user-centric.

An advanced assistance system can take advantage of the relevant research & development in order to warn an EV driver of early dangers for prevention of collisions with the other vehicles. The driving range depends on the human-machine interface (HMI) that arouses an EV driver to utilize the regenerative braking while driving to the nearer charging track when needed (Stromberg et al, 2011). Similarly, a driver will be provided with an HMI for charging monitoring, authorization, and interruption in case of poor rate of energy transfer. Moreover, a driver will be able to reserve a charging track through a minimum interaction with an HMI.

Cyber Security for EVs Charging Network

A massive use of EVs and the efficient and secure management of huge power requirements will certainly call for advanced communication technologies that may ensure no suffer from possible cyber-attacks. Cyber-attacks in a communication network of a smart grid environment may cause disastrous harm to the extremely inter-reliant users of the smart grid.

Security Risks in Electric Vehicles Charging Network

The cyber security concerns in communication system can be classified into three types: confidentiality, authenticity, and integrity, (Qiu et al., 2012). An important one is the obtainability of the service. The loss of availability may arise the loss of ability to retort to uncertainties in the real-time power demand.

Figure 6. Dynamic charging process

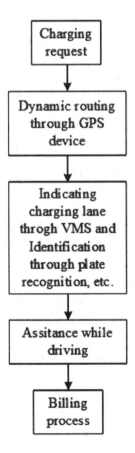

In terms of EVs, loss of connection with the grid may lead to an inadequate charging. It may be perceived that a criminal could disturb the recharging process of police vehicles by interrupting the communication link among the police vehicles and the grid before committing a bank robbery, and similarly, a hacker can paralyze EVs in large area by directing the EV management station. A robber can make the system to deny a service from several remote devices. It may hack some civil PCs and launch the attack through worthless messages from manipulated computers. The central computer system can be overcome by the enormous messages. In case of an emergency in the smart grid, the controller cannot not be able to retort to it rapidly. Such attacks require the attacker to hack many computers and to be capable of personating someone else. As fact of the matter, an attack can be easier in a wireless communication system due to the its widespread broadcasting nature. All the attacker would know the band of a wireless system and distance from the receiver, as usually such information is known to a common man. Using this information, the attacker can jam the signal at the receiver by releasing a arbitrary signal into the air and the jammed signal is unidentifiable by the receiver. Such a jamming attack can be conducted at numerous levels and situations. At the user level, a jamming attack interrupts the information channel among the home applications and the grid, which may cause ailment in the home electricity while rendering a substantial area into a running state. An accurate information cannot be conveyed to the major controller.

Another vulnerability is the confidentiality and management of information. The attackers can enter the controlling computer to acquire sensitive information files, such as the design of the grid. At the user level, the confidentiality of the household user could be investigated by intercepting the exchange of messages between different appliances and the information accumulators (Bauer, Stockinger & Lukowicz, 2009). Moreover, integrity and authenticity of message must also be secure. Integrity of information defends a message from being modified. A modified message can deceive the central controller to make incorrect operations causing harm to the power system and accidents. For instance, an attacker may amend a message to distort the balancing system. Such probable attacks are important to the safety of the grid.

As a communication setup for the smart grid contains both wireless and wired networks, the schemes that are perfect for the wired networks are not much applicable to the wireless network. The confidentiality of wireless communication network is weaker than that of the wired systems. All security schemes are based on a protected secret key. Though, in the wireless scenarios, it is much expensive and unreasonable to attain a key from a reliable authority. This discussion also focused on introducing a key generation technique and an anti-jamming protocols. A few wireless schemes are categorized on the properties of a channel.

- **Randomness of Channel:** As the fading along a channel is random in nature due to propagation, its parameters including phase and amplitude a signal at the receiver is projected to fluctuation. Multipath propagation of a beacon signal causes an eavesdropper to work through information of diverse phases and amplitudes of the signal.
- **Variation in Channel:** A signal from a transmitter reaches the receiver with varying parameters, as the receiver is placed at a half wavelength. It happens because the propagation path between the receivers and transmitter are different due to the environmental conditions.
- **Channel Reciprocity:** The channel parameters are similar for the transceivers at the ends of wireless link because the propagation path of the signal is the same. This property ensures that the transceivers can attain the agreement from the randomness of the channel. The channel based key agreement influences the phase and amplitude of the channel to produce secret keys, the methods along this course are mainly divided into two classes including the signal strength based

method (Jana et al, 2009). phase information based approach. These two approaches share mutual techniques.

- **Anti-Jamming in EVs Network:** In order prevent a jamming attack there is need to design an algorithm in consideration of such attacks. There are several anti-jamming communication techniques such as frequency-hopping spread spectrum, direct-sequence spread spectrum, and uncoordinated frequency hopping. However, these anti-jamming systems are not appropriate for the cognitive radio network because these techniques consider the sender, receiver, and jammer only. However, the presence of the primary users is not ignorable in this network setting. These techniques require a reliable authority to allocate the random noise code firmly. Such authority may not be always available in various scenarios. In this section, we present a jamming-resilient DSA protocol for cognitive radio networks.

Lets' assume there are a few primary users including cellular stations, TV stations and, a jammer and secondary users including EVs, charging facilities, and network nodes. The primary users (PUs) become active on their own channels these channels will be busy, else, they remain idle. The transition of state at each channel can be molded as based on Markov chain. Where, SUs, sender, and receiver, are equipped with numerous radios that allow each of them to communicate several channels at the same time.

In order to safeguard the PU from being affected by the nodes of cognitive radio, the system ensues in a time positioned manner. In the first part of the time slot, the PUs send a channel-preserving signal to indicate occupation of their channels. The SUs sense this signal and keep silent on the occupied channels in this time slot. In the second part of the time slot, the PUs access the channels they preserved, and the SUs access the channels they sensed to be idle. In the last part of the time slot, the cognitive receiver replies with an acknowledgment (ACK) to the cognitive sender. We assume the jammer does not interfere with the users because of the penalty for being situated. The jammer is equipped with many radios and can pick a jamming feature. Types of jammers include: A static jammer which locks/jams a particular set of channels all times. A random jammer arbitrarily selects channels to lock in different time slot and adaptive jammer picks stations in accordance with the history information.

RENEWABLE ENERGY SOURCES FOR EVs CHARGING

Supplying EVs charging stations by renewable energy generation make the environment clean. Two popular natural renewable resources- wind & solar power are the main energy sources for supporting EV's' load. However, their intermittent output can be managed by the taking electricity from the power grid during peak hours.

Wind Power

There are various technologies to transform wind energy into electric power such as wind mills, wind turbines, wind pumps and etc. Generating electric power from wind is much developed and mature renewable technology at present. Generally, large wind farms supply power to electric power transmission network whereas small-scale wind power generation supplies power to the local isolated locations. Wind energy is vastly distributed, renewable and environment friendly clean with zero carbon gases emission. With advent of wind generators, wind energy cost becomes lower up to around 4% per unit generation depending on the nature of project. Thus wind energy is considered to be a very economic as compared to fossil fuel and thermal power station. In practice, intermittency and non- dispatch able characteristics of wind power generation are required to be managed in such a way that demand and supply must be matched, in fact, until now highly variable nature of wind power is the grave challenge to integrate it with the power system.

Solar Power

In solar power generation photovoltaic panels convert radiation from sunlight into electricity. Following steps define the principle of electricity generation using photovoltaic.

1. Semiconducting material inside the photovoltaic absorb the photon from sunlight and
2. Electrons escape from atoms and start moving in a single direction due to particular composition of photovoltaic (Smart, Bradley, & Salisbury, 2014).

There are two basic systems for utilizing the electricity generated by photovoltaic panel based grid connected and stand-alone. Electric energy is stored and then used upon local demand in the stand alone system. Whereas, in grid connected system, the photovoltaic is connected to the electric power grid via power converter and other metering equipment. Thus, solar power production can be utilized either on-site when demanded or supplied to the power grid selling to utilities. Solar energy is also an intermittent in nature i.e. power is only produced when solar radiations are available. Thus power demand may be fulfilled by other power sources such as wind power and traditional generators. Solar energy generation has been growing continuously since 2000. 100% production was record in 2008 and has become the fastest rising energy generation technology (Chow, 2010). A charging station supplied by solar or wind energy is depicted in the Figure 7. Distributed power generation (DPG) is small-scale power generation that produces electric power up to some MW using a variety of generating technologies e.g. photovoltaic, wind turbines, diesel engines, fuel cells and etc. Generally, DPG becomes part of the power grid at substation or distribution level (Mousazadeh et al, 2009). Distributed power generation can either operated by utilities or independent individual and it provides with various benefits like low carbon emission, better economy, secure and reliable power generation and the better power quality provision.

A fairly large DPG unit is dispatchable with capability of communication with central control utilities. However small-scale DPG units are neither monitored nor controlled by central utilities. Though distributed renewable power generation seems more attractive as compared with traditional power generation methods but in actual it is still much expensive and require considerable subsidies for better economy. Moreover, DPG can cause the voltage regulation problem over distribution feeder length. DPG as an independent small-scale system may be suitable on highways for powering the e-vehicle charging station. Electric Power Research Institute has concluded in the recent study that if electric vehicles uptake become 50% of the total transportation on the road, additional power generation capacity may not be more than 8% of the existing power generation capacity if mostly vehicles are recharged overnight i.e. during off peak hours (Roberts, 2009). Vehicle to Grid system (V2G) enables e-vehicles to supply power to utility via grid during peak load hours when the vehicle battery is fully charged. The amount of power stored in vehicle's battery depends on capacity and technology of the battery used. In V2G system DC Power is converted into AC power at fixed frequency when power is back delivered to the grid and Power electronics topology & applied control strategies determine that whether the supplied

Figure 7. Charging station supplied by renewable energy resources

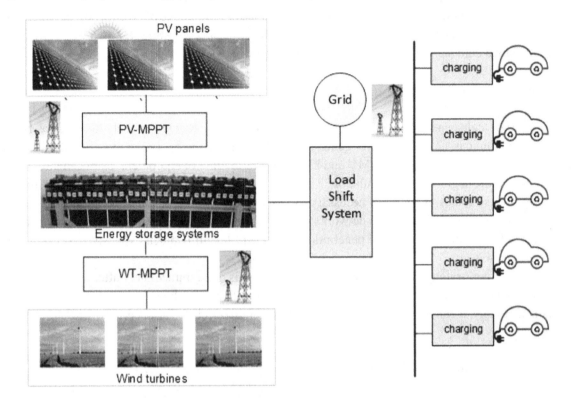

current is constant or variable. V2G system is an alternative to enhance the small-scale distributed power generation to support the grid during peak hours. V2G technology is under evaluation by the utilities and other stakeholders like Xcel and PG&E. A typical form of an EV is supplied by the motor control system and vehicle's battery for wheel traction. Most EVs use permanent magnet which can also recharge the battery in generator mode. As motor becomes generator during regenerative braking during slow motion of vehicle supplying power to the batteries and when battery gets fully charged, friction brakes are applied to stop the car. A smart charging station architecture in shown in Figure 8.

EV CHARGING STRATEGIES

Three different EV charging strategies including uncontrolled EV charging, tariff based EV charging and controlled EV charging are considered in this in this study and those are illustrated in the following subsections. In the uncontrolled charging strategy, EV charging can be freely done without any incentives for charging and restrictions. Thus, EV charging is considered a normal load like other electrical loads. In this charging plan, EVs can be connected and charged, whenever and whenever needed. It starts getting charged to its full battery storage capacity when an EV is plugged-in. In this charging mode EVs owner assume electricity tariff to be constant for all day/night. Because, they are not given advantage of economic tariff during valley hours even when the grid operating conditions are flexible for bearing increase in the economic energy consumption and thus EVs are charged as per need. On the other hand, in tariff based EV charging strategy, an EV is assumed to be recharged when grid and the distribution system operating conditions are some favorable, on the contrary of uncontrolled charging in which EVs were free to be recharged anywhere any time. While, the controlled EV charging (CEVC) is meant to manage EV load demand to avoid stress on the power grid.

Uncontrolled EV Charging

In case of large-scale penetration of EVs, an uncontrolled charging strategy is likely to arouse technical as well as economic issues in the power generation system and on the operation of utility grid in terms of voltage drop, voltage imbalance at MV and LV level, overloading of equipment, extra generation cost during peak hours, degradation of insulation of the power cables, heating of equipment and etc. In order to deal with these issues, it becomes necessary to upgrade the present power generation system, grid expansion, up-gradation of electrical networks in such a way that these are made capable of adapting the expected load demand due to EV penetration. However, this all is much expensive requiring huge investments.

In this charging strategy, it is supposed that EV charging is done immediately after a journey is performed but depending on the state of charge (SOC) of the battery of vehicle.

Mathematically, it can be written as in Eq. (1) (Mirzaei, Kazemi, & Homaee, 2014):

$$SOC_{bat} = \begin{cases} \left(1 - \dfrac{d}{AER}\right) & d \leq AER, d \geq AER \\ 0 \end{cases} \tag{1}$$

where, d is the distance covered by an EV during a day and AER represents all electric range of the electric vehicle.

EVs number being charged at hour h can be found as given in Eq. (2):

$$EV_{Nr(\max)} = \sum_{t(h)=1}^{24} \left(EV_{C_{t(h)}}^{HS} + EV_{C_{t(h)}}^{WP} + EV_{C_{t(h)}}^{PP} \right) * EV_{PL} \tag{2}$$

$EV_{C_{t(h)}}^{HS}$ = EV charging at home through normal socket at hour h

$EV_{C_{t(h)}}^{WP}$ = EV charging at work place/commercial place at hour h

$EV_{C_{t(h)}}^{PP}$ = EV charging at public place at hour h

EV_{PL} = EV penetration level

$EV_{Nr(\max)}$ = Maximum number of EVs to be recharged at hour h

Sum of the power drawn from the LV distribution network for charging all ranges of EVs can be expressed as in Eq. (3) and power required to charge $EV_{Nr(\max)}$ can be calculated using Eq. (4):

$$P_{EV_{Nr(\max)}} = EV_{Nr(\max)} * P_{C(h)EV} \tag{3}$$

$$P_{EV_{Nr(\max)}} = \sum_{t(h)=1}^{24} \left\{ \left(EV_{C_{t(h)}}^{HS} + EV_{C_{t(h)}}^{PP} \right) * P_{C(h)EV} \right\} * EV_{PL} \tag{4}$$

$P_{EV_{Nr(\max)}}$ = Active power required to charge $EV_{Nr(\max)}$ and $P_{C(h)EV}$ represents amount of power required to charge an EV

Tariff Based EV Charging

This charging strategy is based on a fact that price of electricity is not fixed all the times, i.e. the electricity price goes lower or higher depending on the grid operating conditions. In this regard, EVs owner can be informed about the tariff so that they might be willing to recharge their vehicle during valley hours. However, optimality of this charging strategy depend on EVs driver's willingness that whether they are attracted by low tariff policy or not and in this way a part of the load of EV charging is shifted towards optimal charging scenario.

In this case, sum of the power drawn from the LV distribution network for charging all ranges of EVs can be expressed as in Eq. (5) and power required to charge $EV_{Nr(\max)}$ can be calculated using Eq. (6)

$$P_{EV_{c(h)}^{HS}} \leq \sum_{t(h)=1}^{24} \left(EV_{C_{t(h)}}^{HS} + P_{C(h)EV} \right) * EV_{PL} \tag{5}$$

$$P_{EV_{c(h)}^{PP}} \leq \sum_{t(h)=1}^{24} \left(EV_{C_{t(h)}}^{PP} + P_{C(h)EV} \right) * EV_{PL} \tag{6}$$

$$P_{EV_{Nr(\max)}} \leq \sum_{t(h)=1}^{24} \left\{ \left(EV_{C_{t(h)}}^{HS} + EV_{C_{t(h)}}^{PP} \right) * P_{C(h)EV} \right\} * EV_{PL} \tag{7}$$

It should be noted that in case of large-scale penetration of EVs, given that economic signal is provided to consumers, if large number of EVs are connected for recharging at the same time then it could also cause the utility grid to reach its beyond normal load conditions.

Controlled EV Charging

The controlled EV (CEVC) charging is meant to manage EV load demand to avoid stress on the power grid. The upper limit is considered with perspective of daily load curve (Arancibia & Strunz, 2012). In order to prevent overloading of feeder, EV charging is allowed when maximum power demand on a load node is less than the threshold value otherwise EV drivers are directed to the nearest available charging slot. At hour h, total power demand including EV load demand, as given in Eq. (8) is compared with maximum permissible power supply from a node as given in Eq. (9), while the charging request is accepted if total demand is less than maximum allowable value.

$$P_{NL_o} = \sum_{t(h)=1}^{24} P_{NL_t(h)} \tag{8}$$

$$P_{NL_o} \leq \sum_{t(h)=1}^{24} \left\{ \left(EV_{C_{t(h)}}^{HS} + EV_{C_{t(h)}}^{PP} \right) * P_{C(h)EV} \right\} * EV_{PL} \tag{9}$$

$$P_{NL_o} < P_{NL\max}$$

$$otherwise, \; P_{C(h)EV} = 0$$

where, P_{NL_o} stands for total power demand at a node load R after accession of EVs, $P_{NL\max}$ represents maximum power demand that can be fed at hour h, and $P_{C(h)EV}$ is the amount of power for recharging EVs.

POWER QUALITY IMPACT OF EVS ON DISTRIBUTION NETWORK

A typical EV is equipped with a battery bank which can store energy up to tens of kWh (Li & Zhang, 2012), it implies that a battery EV requires fairly high amount of energy from distribution network for its operation, (Clement-Nyns, Van Reusel & Driesen, 2007).

Popularization of EVs is becoming high rather than discussing their negative impact on electrical distribution system and it is assumed that the distribution system is capable enough to support EVs' load, and it is not true in real. However, recently, some considerations have been made to discuss limitations of distribution network capacity for EV charging (Richardson, Flynn & Keane, 2012' Tikka, Lassila, Haakana & Partanen, 2011). Several studies have been carried out to assess EVs´ impact on the power grid (Camus, Silva, Farias & Esteves, 2009; Kempton & Tomic, 2005; Sortomme et al, 2011) and other studies about EVs´ impact on the power distribution system are described in (Orr, Emanuel & Pileggi, 1984; Zhao, Prousch, Hubner & Moser, 2010). Large-scale integration of EVs put certain impact on the power system infrastructure, mainly on LV power distribution system (Clement-Nyns, Haeson, & Driesen, 2010). As EV load is directly interfaced with the distribution network for former´s charging. EVs may affect the power system multifariously. Impact of EV charging load on the operation of power distribution system can be broadly considered in terms of technical concerns and economic issues. EV battery chargers are equipped with power electronic components for recharging EVs and former are characterized as non-linear loads or distorting loads which introduce harmonics in the system. Importantly, presence of voltage unbalance in the system induces non-characteristic triplet current harmonics e.g. 3rd and 9th harmonics adding them with characteristic harmonics of power converters. In power electronic interfaced loads, a small increase in voltage unbalance may cause input current to become significantly unbalanced that causes change its waveform into single-pulse waveform from a double-pulse waveform due to asymmetrical conduction of power electronic (Von Jouanne & Banerjee, 2001). Excessive flow of phase currents in a three phase system due to the voltage unbalance may cause circuits of overload-protection to trip (Pillay & Manyage, 2001). As harmonic injection in the system causes an increase in phase currents so it leads to increased lines losses and overloading of cables. In the technical context, mostly loads connected to the system need an appropriate level of power quality and such loads may fail to function properly in case of variations in the fundamental parameters of power system i.e. voltage, frequency and or current and consequently, some of components e.g. transformers, motors and may face reduced lifespan. There are different power quality indices to be quantified including, voltage unbalances, harmonic contents, frequency variations, voltage drop and etc. (Statistisches, 2008).

Quantity of power quality indices is restricted by a number of relevant standards. Generally, a specific system is considered and studied, for evaluation of any power quality index, that is aimed at identifying potential problems and causes of the issues in the system because power quality depends on various factors ranging from power generation site to the point of ultimate consumption and the elements connected to it throughout. Thus, envisaged EVs´ impact on power distribution system include increased power flow in power cables, distribution lines, transformer overloading, harmonic distortion, voltage drop, voltage unbalance and etc. (Dugan, McGranaghan & Beaty, 1996). Additionally, EVs are characterized as a single phase load in a three phase distribution system and it is well known fact that presence of large single phase loads, and their uneven distribution on each phase causes voltage unbalance in the system. Nature of voltage unbalance can be conceptualized as an unequal magnitudes or phase angles of voltages in a three phase system (under-voltages and over-voltages) and or uneven harmonic distortion among the phases.

Voltage unbalance can occur in both; an urban residential distribution network, where heavy single phase loads are imposed, and in rural distribution system with fairly long power distribution lines (Farmer, Hines, Dowds & Blumsack, 2010; von Jouanne & Banerjee, 2000). Voltage unbalance is a severe power quality problem which is detrimental to both; equipment and the power system. Voltage unbalance produces negative sequence components in the system that is harmful to all poly-phase loads especially induction machines. Presence of negative sequence voltage components leads to large amount of current unbalance of the order of 6-10 times of voltage unbalance percent due to low negative sequence impedance in the power circuit (Lee, Venkataramanan & Jahns, 2008). Some of its common effects include increased losses, extra heating, vulnerability of the system to faults because an unbalanced system might not be capable of transferring emergency loads (Lee, 1999). Voltage unbalance can also negatively affect induction machines, power electronic based equipment including power converters and adjustable speed drives. Operating an induction motor in VU scenario, may cause to produce air gap flux that generates reverse torque and hence the net (positive) torque is reduced which ultimately degrades efficiency of the machine and decreases motor life or it can even lead to permanent damage of the motor (Anwari & Hiendro, 2010; Faiz, Ebrahimpour & Pillay, 2004). Therefore, it becomes quiet important to identify and determine the presence of VU in the circuit in order to deal with it timely for trouble free operation of the power system and the connected loads.

In view of large-scale penetration of unevenly distributed heavy single phase load of EVs in the distribution network, The EU Electricity Directive (Directive 2009/72, 2009) distribution system operators (DSOs) are held responsible for up-gradation of the network to support EV charging load even though they are not fully able to curtail or regulate frequency and duration of EVs charging. Consequently, up-gradation of the network planning and expansion may become complicated due this high uncertainty. Thus impact assessment of EVs on low voltage distribution network should be focused to reduce the degree of uncertainty in the system. This section aims at summarizing power quality index including voltage drop, unbalance and harmonic contamination in a three phase distribution system, associated with uneven EV charging. Relevant studies in most of previous works have been based on small-scale distribution networks with emphasis on industrial networks. Rather industrial power networks are observed with their own power supply system with specifically characterized loads. On contrary, a residential distribution system is meant to feed a variety of consumers with their diverse types of loads and even a slight distortion in the system may arise customer's dissatisfaction.

Power Quality Index Due to EVs Load

Large-scale integration of EVs put certain impact on the power system infrastructure, mainly on LV power distribution system. As EV load is directly interfaced with the distribution network for former´s charging. EVs may affect the power system multifariously. Impact of EV charging load on the operation of power distribution system is illustrated in Figure 8.

- **Economic Concerns:** EV battery chargers are equipped with power electronic components for recharging EVs and former are characterized as non-linear loads or distorting loads which introduce harmonics in the system. Importantly, presence of voltage unbalance in the system induces non-characteristic triplet current harmonics e.g. 3rd and 9th harmonics adding them with characteristic harmonics of power converters. In power electronic interfaced loads, a small increase in voltage unbalance may cause input current to become significantly unbalanced that causes change its waveform into single-pulse waveform from a double-pulse waveform due to asymmetrical conduction of power electronic elements. Excessive flow of phase currents in a three phase system due to the voltage unbalance may circuits of overload-protection to trip [64]. As harmonic injection in the system causes an increase in phase currents so it leads to increased lines losses and overloading of cables. Harmonic contamination induced by VU in the distribution network alters reactive power circulation abnormally and voltage regulation problems that badly affects working efficiency of distribution transformer and results in the decreased life of machines. Where, increased line losses, de-rating of induction machines, decreased efficiency and reduced life of power equipment are described as an economic concern for DSOs. Thus VU caused by uneven single phase load of EVs is quite harmful to economy of a distribution network.
- **Technical Concerns:** In the technical context, a power quality problem can be defined as, manifestation of any problem in voltage, current or frequency of the power system that results in malfunctioning of equipment. Since a decade, power quality has been gaining due attention because of to its effects on components in the power system. Mostly, loads connected to the system need an appropriate level of power quality and such loads may fail to function properly in case of variations in the fundamental parameters of power system i.e. voltage, frequency and or current and consequently, some of components e.g. transformers, motors and may face reduced lifespan. Thus, it is quite important to assess power quality index. There are different power quality indices to be quantified including, voltage unbalances, harmonic contents, frequency variations, voltage drop and etc. Quantity of power quality indices is restricted by a number of relevant standards. Generally, a specific system is considered and studied, for evaluation of any power quality index, that is aimed at identifying potential problems and causes of the issue in the system because power quality depends on various factors ranging from power generation site to the point of ultimate consumption and the elements connected to it throughout.

Figure 8. Concerns on the operation of distribution network due to EV charging load

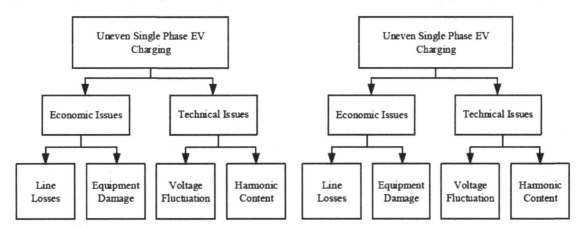

Low Voltage Distribution Networks

The impact of connection of EV charging load on low voltage distribution system is of great concern because of latter's specific characteristics. As an LV distribution system is characterized with varying loads, unbalanced phase voltages, higher value of resistances on its branches, low reactance values, i.e. small ratio of X/R with radial structure as compared to medium voltage (MV) networks so it exhibits power quality problems. As fact of matter, low voltage networks are termed as the weaker portion of electrical power system. It implied that in case of even small variation in demand-supply could arouse worse effects in the power distribution system. It can be explained in view of a fact that the LV distribution lines have limited capacity of the connected equipment with impedance from HV/MV lines which results in problematic power supply with large impedance.

Taking this into account, an LV distribution system is expected to suffer a significant impact following a future scenario with large scale EV integration, which can affect system performance. Therefore, a detailed analysis is required in terms of evaluating the quality of supply and identifying in anticipation technical limitations and possible problems that may arise in face of increasing EV integration in LV grids. The related technical issues, as mentioned in introduction part must be properly addressed and specific actions to avoid or at least reduce technical violations must be developed. In this context, an EV impact analysis for LV distribution grids is required in order to identify the impact of EV connection to the network and to provide the means to deal with them.

In order to analyze the impacts of EV connection on the technical operation of LV distribution grids, a steady-state tool should be used. The tool should be able to take into account the specific characteristics of LV distribution systems with EV integration, especially the fact that LV grids are generally unbalanced and, more importantly, it must be able to model and implement the EV demand for different scenarios. For this reason, a specific tool may be adopted in order to perform a required task in the following sequence:

- Define EV demand, charging method and mobility
- Run an LV three-phase power flow routine
- Verify the main technical constraints of the system (namely system losses, voltage profiles)

- Provide supply quality and system performance parameters and indexes calculation (namely voltage imbalances and load imbalances)
- Compile the results from different scenarios

The entire process is shown in the flow chart in Figure 9 and the description is explained below.

A power flow routine be developed in order to be capable of dealing with the specificity of LV distribution networks, mainly the existence of three unbalanced phases plus a neutral conductor and lines with a low X/R ratio. This routine will enable the analysis of the steady-state behavior of a LV network and dealing with single-phase loads and different micro-generation technologies. A first version of the algorithm was developed in (Madureira, 2012) as a microgrid analysis tool, and extended to four-wire systems in (Ciric, Feltrin & Ochoa, 2003) being used for three-phase, four-wire and radial distribution networks. Moreover, although designed for radial distribution networks, it may be adapted for weakly meshed networks. However, this is no obstacle since the test-networks to be used are typical LV distribution grids and therefore with a radial structure.

Figure 9. Flow-chart for EV impact analysis on LV grid

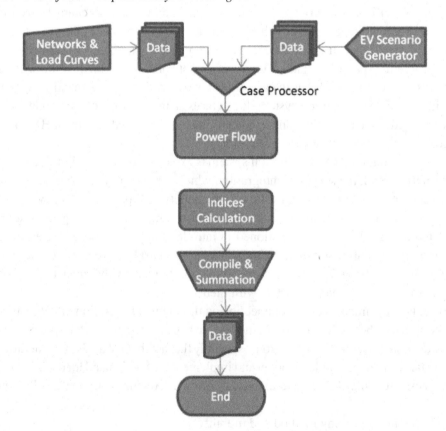

HARMONIC CONTAMINATION DUE TO EVS

Generally, harmonics originate from power electronic interfaced loads. Harmonic in the power system may cause significant problems in the form of excessive heating of AC electric machines, transformers and occurrence of resonance in the system, thus posing technical as well as economic concerns (IEEE, 1993). As electric vehicles are connected to the distribution system though power electronic interface so these represent an addition of non-linear load in the system. A harmonic pattern provided by any non-linear load means a specific harmonic content and its quantitative amount is expressed as total harmonic distortion (THD).

In view of a fact that a distribution system is supposed to feed a number of linear and non-linear loads connected to it, the system modeling is carried out with harmonic current sources. The *hth* harmonic of the non-linear load at load bus k with real power and reactive power is taken as given in Eq. (9):

$$I_k^h = c(h)I_k^1 \tag{9}$$

In Eq. (9), c (h) is obtained by dividing h harmonic to the fundamental value. Voltage at bus k is found as given in Eq. (10).

$$|V_k| = \left(\sum_{h=2}^{H} |V_k^h|^2\right)^2 \tag{10}$$

Total current and voltage harmonic distortion *(THD)i*, *(THD)v* can be expressed as given in Eq. (11) and (12).

$$THD_i = \sqrt{\frac{\sum_{h=2}^{H}\left(I_k^h\right)^2}{I_k^1}} \tag{11}$$

$$THDv = \sqrt{\frac{\sum_{h=2}^{H}\left(V_k^h\right)^2}{V_k^1}} \tag{12}$$

Where h represents harmonic order, H is the highest number of harmonic, *Ih* is the RMS value of the h harmonic component and *I1* is the fundamental frequency component. Typically, an EV charging is done via two power converters including AD-DC power converter that exchanges power between charger and the grid and DC/DC power converter that controls battery charging. Harmonics caused by EV charging are mainly related to interfacing circuit topology connecting to the network. For instance, employing uncontrolled diode rectifier would provide high amount of harmonics in the AC network. However, there has been rapid evolution of robust topologies and control schemes of power converters with better features such as rectifiers for Power Factor Correction (PFC) (Ciric, Feltrin & Ochoa, 2003; Masoum, Deilami &Islam, 2010).

Relevant Standards to Restrict Harmonics

In view of EV integration in the system and the related harmonics effect include current harmonic content that is injected into the power grid and voltage harmonics caused by distorted current into the system.

Quantitative amount of current harmonics into the power grid are defined by a number of standards. IEC 61000, part 3-2, states allowable limits for current harmonics for electrical equipment with maximum input phase current of 16 A connected to a public power distribution system. Considering EVs to be of class A, Table-I below contains the allowable harmonics for each group (Abidin, 2006).

Allowable current harmonic distortion is also specified by Standard IEEE 519-1992. Application of this standard varies depending on the size of electric circuit and the short-circuit current at common coupling point (PCC). This standard also defines some limits for current harmonics in transmission systems. On the other hand, most popular standards for limiting voltage harmonics are IEC 61000 and EN 50160 that define maximum possible values. According to EN 50160, Total Harmonic Distortion (THD) in an LV or MV systems should not be more than 8% under normal operation.

Standard IEC 61000-2-2 also states that voltage THD at the buses carrying up to 69 kV must remain below 5%. As this work deals with single phase charging EV charging of rating 3.7 kW for each EV so charging current for an EV charging should not be considered beyond 16 A per phase.

CASE STUDY

Author carried out a case study in a city town of Fredericton by conducting a survey, constructing hypothesis statistics and concluded at simulations. Fredericton is somewhat by hilly town with windy environment. The case study is carried out considering parking times and parking spaces at shopping centers, industries, factories, offices and university parking areas.

The survey shows that mostly people park their cars in the parking slots approximately from 8:00 to 17:00 Fredericton almost remains shiny from 7:00 to 16:00 hours in the winter season and from 6:00 to 17:00 in summer. The study has been conducted taking into account these and some other factors for feasibility study of installation of smart charging stations using renewable resources. Following factors are included in the case study; parking routines of vehicle owners, parking hours, vehicle types and model, routes adopted for fuel/gas filling, willingness of people to accept EV, average distance that a vehicle covers daily, weather conditions of Fredericton, installation of solar panels on roof top of parking plots,

Table 1. Limits for current harmonic set by IEC 61000-3-2 for equipment with maximum input current of 16 A

Harmonic Order	Harmonics
2, 3	1.08, 2.3
4, 5	0.43, 1.14
6, 7	0.30, 0.77
9	0.40
$15 \leq n \leq 39$	0.15*15/n
$8 \leq n \leq 40$	0.23*8/n

charging stations installation powered by wind generation, utilization cost comparison among diesel, benzene, electricity and other fuels, environmental impacts such as CO2 emission & air pollution and impact on the existing power infrastructure. The survey conducted was based on collected opinion of people considering above mentioned factors. The survey statistics indicate that almost all people welcome take up of e-vehicles and prefer renewable resources to supply charging stations.

The idea which was supported by majority people is install a carport with solar panels and in this way cars can be recharges while parked at parking slots. It is worth mentioning here charging station should be installed keeping in view the routines of distance travelled by vehicles and then charging facility should be made avail- able on respective routes with specific distance between two charging points. The survey shows that 50% people live within 10km from their working place, 30% people reside within circumference of 20-25km from work place and almost 15- 25% people are required to cover a distance of more than 15km daily.

Frequency of charging vehicles is given in the table A. Parking habits of vehicle owners is as follow; 60% vehicle owners park their cars at work places from 9:00 to17:00 daily excluding weekends, 20% people park their cars from 11:00 am to 19:00 at their business centers and almost 10-20% people leave their cars at different parking places for 3-4 hours. The concept of installing solar panels on canopy of parking sites, it is necessary that are covered by solar panels and area of top roof of the parking lots should be matched in such a way that solar power generation capacity could fulfill the power demand by the vehicles under the canopy. In this regard we consider parking area of our faculty of engineering at Head Hall, Fredericton. Collected statistics show that there are almost 750 students and 110 people in staff. See table B and C The covered area of parking is around 2042.2 m/square for around 137 cars and if we install solar panels on the roof of parking area, the generated power will be around 2.1MW. For that, almost 40 to 45 e-vehicles can be serviced simultaneously. If level-2 standard charging is installed which for which charging time is 4-6 hours. It means that around 100 cars can be recharged in a day while the cars are parked at parking place.

Hypothesis Statistics

Testing Hypothesis (Phase-I): The hypothesis statistics are obtained in the basis of con- ducted survey at the Faculty of Engineering at Head Hall, Fredericton. See Table 2 and 3.

Testing Hypothesis (Phase-II): Phase-II of hypothesis testing was carried out to test the feasibility of installation of charging station at a shopping mall of Fredericton, Regent Mall. Statistics show that city shopping center is the most crowded place in the daily evening particularly at weekend timing from 16:00 to 8:00. The hypothesis is created to install e-vehicle charging station supplied by wind

Table 2. Testing Hypothesis: Requirements of EV recharging

No. of Participants	Frequency Recharging Requirement	
	Freq. of Recharging (/day)	**Percentage (%)**
25	Once	70
55	Twice	15
37	thrice	8
27	Upon requirement	7

Table 3. Testing Hypothesis: Locating charging stations and charging timings

Locating Charging Stations		Charging Timings		Vehicles	
Locations	**(%)**	**Utilization Timings**	**(%)**	**in Use (%)**	
Offices	40	Till Noon	70	Suzuki	55
Universities	30	Evening	23	BMW	20
Commercial centers	20	Night	15	Toyota	15
	10	Randomly	2	others	10

power generation. According to obtained statistics almost 70-90 cars parked in the parking area require approximately 3-4MW electric power if all the vehicles are plugged-in simultaneously. Thus, the area available for parking and installation of wind turbines for the required power generation must be matched, approximate figures are mentioned above. The produced results based on the obtained statistical data are shown in Figures 10, 11 and 12.

CONCLUSION

The chapter focuses on e-vehicle charging infrastructure discussing its multi-dimensional implications on the power grid and vehicle owners to analyze and evaluate the performance of charging stations to keep stress on the grid to a minimum, general charging methodology is described with respect to charging and

Figure 10. Classification of participants

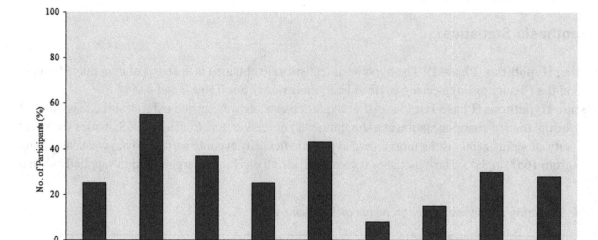

Figure 11. Response of satisfaction level for installing charging infrastructure

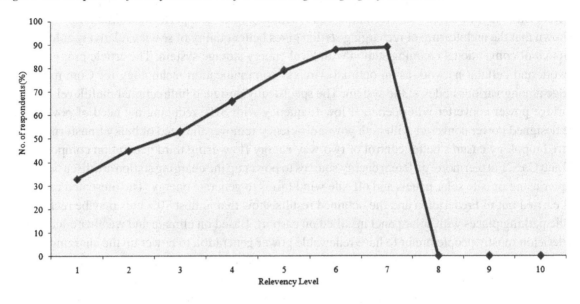

Figure 12. Response of integration level for installing charging infrastructure

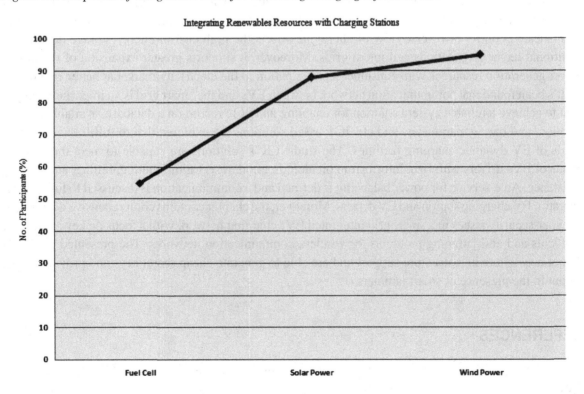

traffic characteristics, cost parameters, load management and V2G operation. In this chapter, we identified different flaws in the conventional techniques and methodologies, and performed simulation in which it is shown that the architecture of recharging station gives better quality of service relatively at lower cost than that of conventional charging station with local energy storage system. The article proposes mesh network and cellular network as an optimal wireless communication technology for Communication Bridge among various nodes of the system. The specifically designed bidirectional multilevel cascaded H-bridge power converter will operate at low frequency with SHE reducing the need of power filter. The designed power converter with high power efficiency removes the need of bulky transformers. The desired topology ensures better control of two-way energy flow using third generation component e.g. SiC and GaN. Furthermore, different energy sources to power up the charging station are discussed in this chapter using on-site solar panels and off-site wind farms to generate energy. The presented case study was carried out in Fredericton and the obtained results show that almost 70% cars may be recharged at public parking places with solar panel installed on carport. Based on climate and weather conditions in Fredericton mostly people prefer to have renewable power generation to power up the charging stations and almost 90% vehicle owners showed their will to accept electric vehicles for mobility. Moreover, power electronics configuration is also presented in the paper for all ranges of EVs. Finally, the chapter gives the reader an insight into diverse aspects and challenges faced by popularization and acceptance of electric vehicles on road. Using electric vehicles as an energy storage devices facilitate integration and sustainability of renewable energy resources. High power multilevel power converter becomes best suitable for quick recharging method- level 3 fast charging. It helps grid stabilization, optimum power factor control and reduces harmonic content. The scheme offers full exploitation of V2G operation with sophisticated control of reverse flow of energy. It offsets the high cost of energy storage devices for traditional recharging stations and micro grids. Moreover, it supports greater expansion of renewable power generation resources with consumer's participation in the electricity market at better economy.

It's been found that communication network between EVs and the smart grid is an important component to achieve a reliable system solution for enabling an EV to record on a database, available energy, location, and battery parameters and etc. ICT based solutions are explored that to fulfill the structural needs of EV dynamic charging facilities. The studied ICT solutions are capable to meet the requirements of EVs drivers with firm information on identification, reservation, routing, billing, and driving assistance. An e-service for power balancing is defined and a communication is discussed to link central operator, EV charging station and EV drivers. Moreover, the chapter contains comprehensive description of cyber-security issues in a smart grid integrated EVs charging network with a focus on key agreement protocols and anti-jamming protocols for wireless communication networks. The presented protocols do not necessitate infrastructure support and are able to generate cheap secret keys and provide robust output in the presence of smart jammers.

REFERENCES

Abidin, M. N. Z. (2006). *IEC 61000-3-2 Harmonics Standards Overview*. Edison, NJ, USA: Schaffner EMC Inc.

Anwari, M., & Hiendro, A. (2010). New unbalance factor for estimating performance of a three-phase induction motor with under-and overvoltage unbalance. *IEEE Transactions on Energy Conversion, 25*(3), 619–625. doi:10.1109/TEC.2010.2051548

Arancibia, A., & Strunz, K. (2012, March). Modeling of an electric vehicle charging station for fast DC charging. *Proceedings of the2012 IEEE InternationalElectric Vehicle Conference (IEVC)* (pp. 1-6). IEEE. doi:10.1109/IEVC.2012.6183232

Bahn, O., Marcy, M., Vaillancourt, K., & Waaub, J. P. (2013). Electrification of the Canadian road transportation sector: A 2050 outlook with TIMES-Canada. *Energy Policy, 62,* 593–606. doi:10.1016/j.enpol.2013.07.023

Bauer, G., Stockinger, K., & Lukowicz, P. (2009, September). Recognizing the use-mode of kitchen appliances from their current consumption. *Proceedings of theEuropean Conference on Smart Sensing and Context* (pp. 163-176). Springer Berlin Heidelberg. doi:10.1007/978-3-642-04471-7_13

Begović, M., Pregelj, A., Rohatgi, A., & Novosel, D. (2001). Impact of renewable distributed generation on power systems.*Proceedings of the 34th Hawaii international conference on system sciences* (pp. 654-663). doi:10.1109/HICSS.2001.926265

Bellotti, F., De Gloria, A., Montanari, R., Dosio, N., & Morreale, D. (2005). COMUNICAR: Designing a multimedia, context-aware human-machine interface for cars. *Cognition Technology and Work, 7*(1), 36–45. doi:10.1007/s10111-004-0168-9

Camus, C., Silva, C. M., Farias, T. L., & Esteves, J. (2009, March). Impact of Plug-in Hybrid Electric Vehicles in the Portuguese electric utility system. *Proceedings of the2009 International Conference on Power Engineering, Energy and Electrical Drives* (pp. 285-290). IEEE. doi:10.1109/POWERENG.2009.4915184

Chow, T. T. (2010). A review on photovoltaic/thermal hybrid solar technology. *Applied Energy, 87*(2), 365–379. doi:10.1016/j.apenergy.2009.06.037

Ciric, R. M., Feltrin, A. P., & Ochoa, L. F. (2003). Power flow in four-wire distribution networks-general approach. *IEEE Transactions on Power Systems, 18*(4), 1283–1290. doi:10.1109/TPWRS.2003.818597

Ciric, R. M., Feltrin, A. P., & Ochoa, L. F. (2003). Power flow in four-wire distribution networks-general approach. *IEEE Transactions on Power Systems, 18*(4), 1283–1290. doi:10.1109/TPWRS.2003.818597

Clement-Nyns, K., Haesen, E., & Driesen, J. (2010). The impact of charging plug-in hybrid electric vehicles on a residential distribution grid. *IEEE Transactions on Power Systems, 25*(1), 371–380. doi:10.1109/TPWRS.2009.2036481

Clement-Nyns, K., Van Reusel, K., & Driesen, J. (2007, January). The consumption of electrical energy of plug-in hybrid electric vehicles in Belgium.*Proceedings of EET-European Ele-Drive Transportation conference* (p. 10).

Committee, I. S. C. (2003). *IEEE standard for interconnecting distributed resources with electric power systems.* New York, NY: Institute of Electrical and Electronics Engineers.

Dugan, R. C., McGranaghan, M. F., & Beaty, H. W. (1996). Electrical power systems quality. New York, NY: McGraw-Hill.

Dyke, K. J., Schofield, N., & Barnes, M. (2010). The impact of transport electrification on electrical networks. *IEEE Transactions on Industrial Electronics, 57*(12), 3917–3926. doi:10.1109/TIE.2010.2040563

Electric Vehicle Charging Station Technical Installation Guide. (2012). 1st ed.). Hydro-Québec.

Enjeti, P. N., & Choudhury, S. A. (1993). A new control strategy to improve the performance of a PWM AC to DC converter under unbalanced operating conditions. *IEEE Transactions on Power Electronics, 8*(4), 493–500. doi:10.1109/63.261020

Ettelt, D., Rey, P., Jourdan, G., Walther, A., Robert, P., & Delamare, J. (2014). 3D magnetic field sensor concept for use in inertial measurement units (IMUs). *Journal of Microelectromechanical Systems, 23*(2), 324–333. doi:10.1109/JMEMS.2013.2273362

European Communities. (2009). Directive 2009/72/EC Concerning Common Rules for the Internal Market in Electricity and Repealing Directive 2003/54/EC.

Faiz, J., Ebrahimpour, H., & Pillay, P. (2004). Influence of unbalanced voltage on the steady-state performance of a three-phase squirrel-cage induction motor. *IEEE Transactions on Energy Conversion, 19*(4), 657–662. doi:10.1109/TEC.2004.837283

Farmer, C., Hines, P., Dowds, J., & Blumsack, S. (2010, January). Modeling the impact of increasing PHEV loads on the distribution infrastructure. *Proceedings of the 2010 43rd Hawaii International Conference on System Sciences (HICSS)* (pp. 1-10). IEEE. doi:10.1109/HICSS.2010.277

Gil, A., & Taiber, J. (2014). A Literature Review in Dynamic Wireless Power Transfer for Electric Vehicles: Technology and Infrastructure Integration Challenges. In *Sustainable Automotive Technologies 2013* (pp. 289–298). Springer International Publishing. doi:10.1007/978-3-319-01884-3_30

Guille, C., & Gross, G. (2009). A conceptual framework for the vehicle-to-grid (V2G) implementation. *Energy Policy, 37*(11), 4379–4390. doi:10.1016/j.enpol.2009.05.053

Gungor, V. C., Sahin, D., Kocak, T., Ergut, S., Buccella, C., Cecati, C., & Hancke, G. P. (2011). Smart grid technologies: communication technologies and standards. *IEEE transactions on Industrial informatics, 7*(4), 529-539.

Gungor, V. C., Sahin, D., Kocak, T., Ergut, S., Buccella, C., Cecati, C., & Hancke, G. P. (2012). Smart grid and smart homes: Key players and pilot projects. *IEEE Industrial Electronics Magazine, 6*(4), 18–34. doi:10.1109/MIE.2012.2207489

Gungor, V. C., Sahin, D., Kocak, T., Ergut, S., Buccella, C., Cecati, C., & Hancke, G. P. (2013). A survey on smart grid potential applications and communication requirements. *IEEE Transactions on Industrial Informatics, 9*(1), 28–42. doi:10.1109/TII.2012.2218253

Haq, A. U., Chadhry, M. J., & Saleemi, F. (2013, November). A smart charging station for EVs with evaluation of different energy storage technologies. *Proceedings of the 2013 IEEE Conference on Clean Energy and Technology (CEAT)* (pp. 248-253). IEEE. doi:10.1109/CEAT.2013.6775635

Harnad, S., Brody, T., Vallieres, F., Carr, L., Hitchcock, S., Gingras, Y., & Hilf, E. R. et al. (2008). The access/impact problem and the green and gold roads to open access: An update. *Serials Review, 34*(1), 36–40. doi:10.1080/00987913.2008.10765150

IEEE. (1993, April). Recommended Practices and Requirements for Harmonic Control in Electrical Power Systems, IEEE Std. 519-1992.

Jana, S., Premnath, S. N., Clark, M., Kasera, S. K., Patwari, N., & Krishnamurthy, S. V. (2009, September). On the effectiveness of secret key extraction from wireless signal strength in real environments. *Proceedings of the 15th annual international conference on Mobile computing and networking* (pp. 321-332). ACM. doi:10.1145/1614320.1614356

ISO. (n. d.). JWG ISO/TC22/SC, ISO/IEC 15118-2 DIS: Vehicle-to-Grid Communication Interface.

Kempton, W., & Tomić, J. (2005). Vehicle-to-grid power fundamentals: Calculating capacity and net revenue. *Journal of Power Sources*, *144*(1), 268–279. doi:10.1016/j.jpowsour.2004.12.025

Kissel, G. (2011). Presentation of Standard J1772. *Proceedings of the EPRI Infrastructure Working Council Conf.*

Lasseter, R. H. (2006, March). The role of distributed energy resources in future electric power systems. *Proceedings of the Energy Systems Seminar*, University of Wisconsin.

Lee, C. Y. (1999). Effects of unbalanced voltage on the operation performance of a three-phase induction motor. *IEEE Transactions on Energy Conversion*, *14*(2), 202–208. doi:10.1109/60.766984

Lee, K., Venkataramanan, G., & Jahns, T. M. (2008). Modeling effects of voltage unbalances in industrial distribution systems with adjustable-speed drives. *IEEE Transactions on Industry Applications*, *44*(5), 1322–1332. doi:10.1109/TIA.2008.2002277

Lewandowski, C., Böcker, S., & Wietfeld, C. (2013, December). An ICT solution for integration of Electric Vehicles in grid balancing services. *Proceedings of the 2013 International Conference on Connected Vehicles and Expo (ICCVE)* (pp. 195-200). IEEE. doi:10.1109/ICCVE.2013.6799792

Li, G., & Zhang, X. P. (2012). Modeling of plug-in hybrid electric vehicle charging demand in probabilistic power flow calculations. *IEEE Transactions on Smart Grid*, *3*(1), 492–499. doi:10.1109/TSG.2011.2172643

Madureira, A. G. (2012). Coordinated and optimized voltage management of distribution networks with multi-microgrids. Retrieved from https://repositorio-aberto.up.pt/bitstream/10216/58358/1/000143265.pdf

Martinez, F. J., Toh, C. K., Cano, J. C., Calafate, C. T., & Manzoni, P. (2011). A survey and comparative study of simulators for vehicular ad hoc networks (VANETs). *Wireless Communications and Mobile Computing*, *11*(7), 813–828. doi:10.1002/wcm.859

Masoum, M. A., Deilami, S., & Islam, S. (2010, July). Mitigation of harmonics in smart grids with high penetration of plug-in electric vehicles. *Proceedings of the IEEE PES General Meeting* (pp. 1-6). IEEE. doi:10.1109/PES.2010.5589970

Mirzaei, M. J., Kazemi, A., & Homaee, O. (2014). RETRACTED: Real-world based approach for optimal management of electric vehicles in an intelligent parking lot considering simultaneous satisfaction of vehicle owners and parking operator. *Energy*, *76*, 345–356. doi:10.1016/j.energy.2014.08.026

Mousazadeh, H., Keyhani, A., Javadi, A., Mobli, H., Abrinia, K., & Sharifi, A. (2009). A review of principle and sun-tracking methods for maximizing solar systems output. *Renewable & Sustainable Energy Reviews, 13*(8), 1800–1818. doi:10.1016/j.rser.2009.01.022

Neaimeh, M., Hill, G. A., Hübner, Y., & Blythe, P. T. (2013). Routing systems to extend the driving range of electric vehicles. *IET Intelligent Transport Systems, 7*(3), 327–336. doi:10.1049/iet-its.2013.0122

Orr, J. A., Emanuel, A. E., & Pileggi, D. J. (1984). Current harmonics, voltage distortion, and powers associated with electric vehicle battery chargers distributed on the residential power system. *IEEE Transactions on Industry Applications, IA-20*(4), 727–734. doi:10.1109/TIA.1984.4504481

Pillay, P., & Manyage, M. (2001). Definitions of voltage unbalance. *IEEE Power Engineering Review, 21*(5), 50–51. doi:10.1109/39.920965

Qiu, M., Su, H., Chen, M., Ming, Z., & Yang, L. T. (2012). Balance of security strength and energy for a PMU monitoring system in smart grid. *IEEE Communications Magazine, 50*(5), 142–149. doi:10.1109/MCOM.2012.6194395

Québec Construction Code. (2010). Chapter V – Electricity, Canadian Electrical Code, Part One with Québec Amendments, Canadian Standards Association, Standard C22.10-10, 21st edition Sec. 86.

Richardson, P., Flynn, D., & Keane, A. (2012). Optimal charging of electric vehicles in low-voltage distribution systems. *IEEE Transactions on Power Systems, 27*(1), 268–279. doi:10.1109/TPWRS.2011.2158247

Roberts, B. (2009). Capturing grid power. *IEEE Power and Energy magazine, 7*(4), 32-41.

SAE. (2010). SAE Standard J1772-2010, SAE Electric Vehicle and Plug in Hybrid Vehicle Conductive Charge Coupler.

Smart, J., Bradley, T., & Salisbury, S. (2014). Actual Versus Estimated Utility Factor of a Large Set of Privately Owned Chevrolet Volts. *SAE International Journal of Alternative Powertrains, 3*(1), 30-35.

Smart, J., & Schey, S. (2012). Battery electric vehicle driving and charging behavior observed early in the EV project. *SAE International Journal of Alternative Powertrains, 1*(1), 27-33.

Smiai, O., Bellotti, F., De Gloria, A., Berta, R., Amditis, A., Damousis, Y., & Winder, A. (2015, August). Information and communication technology research opportunities in dynamic charging for electric vehicle. *Proceedings of the 2015 Euromicro Conference on Digital System Design (DSD)* (pp. 297-300). IEEE. doi:10.1109/DSD.2015.111

Sortomme, E., Hindi, M. M., MacPherson, S. J., & Venkata, S. S. (2011). Coordinated charging of plug-in hybrid electric vehicles to minimize distribution system losses. *IEEE transactions on smart grid, 2*(1), 198-205.

Sortomme, E., Hindi, M. M., MacPherson, S. J., & Venkata, S. S. (2011). Coordinated charging of plug-in hybrid electric vehicles to minimize distribution system losses. *IEEE transactions on smart grid, 2*(1), 198-205.

Statistisches Bundesamt. (n. d.). Fachserie 15 Heft 1, EVS 2008. Retrieved from http://www.destatis.de/

Strömberg, H., Andersson, P., Almgren, S., Ericsson, J., Karlsson, M., & Nåbo, A. (2011, November). Driver interfaces for electric vehicles.*Proceedings of the 3rd International Conference on Automotive User Interfaces and Interactive Vehicular Applications* (pp. 177-184). ACM.

Sukprasert, P., Nguyen, B. M., & Fujimoto, H. (2014, December). Estimation of lateral displacement of electric vehicle to an alignment of wireless power transmitters. *Proceedings of the 2014 IEEE/SICE International Symposium on System Integration (SII)* (pp. 542-547). IEEE. doi:10.1109/SII.2014.7028097

Tikka, V., Lassila, J., Haakana, J., & Partanen, J. (2011, December). Case study of the effects of electric vehicle charging on grid loads in an urban area. *Proceedings of the 2011 2nd IEEE PES International Conference and Exhibition on Innovative Smart Grid Technologies (ISGT Europe)* (pp. 1-7). IEEE. doi:10.1109/ISGTEurope.2011.6162667

Tsai, J. L. (2014). An improved cross-layer privacy-preserving authentication in WAVE-enabled VANETs. *IEEE Communications Letters, 18*(11), 1931–1934. doi:10.1109/LCOMM.2014.2323291

Tuttle, D. P., & Baldick, R. (2012). The evolution of plug-in electric vehicle-grid interactions. *IEEE Transactions on Smart Grid, 3*(1), 500–505. doi:10.1109/TSG.2011.2168430

Tuttle, D. P., & Baldick, R. (2012). The evolution of plug-in electric vehicle-grid interactions. *IEEE Transactions on Smart Grid, 3*(1), 500–505. doi:10.1109/TSG.2011.2168430

Ul-Haq, A., Buccella, C., Cecati, C., & Khalid, H. A. (2013, June). Smart charging infrastructure for electric vehicles. *Proceedings of the 2013 International Conference on Clean Electrical Power (ICCEP)* (pp. 163-169). IEEE. doi:10.1109/ICCEP.2013.6586984

Von Jouanne, A., & Banerjee, B. (2001). Assessment of voltage unbalance. *IEEE Transactions on Power Delivery, 16*(4), 782–790. doi:10.1109/61.956770

von Jouanne, A., & Banerjee, B. B. (2000). *Voltage unbalance: Power quality issues, related standards and mitigation techniques. Electric Power Research Institute.* Palo Alto, CA: EPRI Final Rep.

Yang, H., Yang, S., Xu, Y., Cao, E., Lai, M., & Dong, Z. (2015). Electric vehicle route optimization considering time-of-use electricity price by learnable Partheno-Genetic algorithm. *IEEE Transactions on Smart Grid, 6*(2), 657–666. doi:10.1109/TSG.2014.2382684

Yilmaz, M., & Krein, P. T. (2013). Review of battery charger topologies, charging power levels, and infrastructure for plug-in electric and hybrid vehicles. *IEEE Transactions on Power Electronics, 28*(5), 2151–2169. doi:10.1109/TPEL.2012.2212917

Zhao, L., Prousch, S., Hübner, M., & Moser, A. (2010, April). Simulation methods for assessing electric vehicle impact on distribution grids. In *IEEE PES T&D 2010* (pp. 1–7). IEEE. doi:10.1109/TDC.2010.5484386

Chapter 17
Enabling Publish/Subscribe Communication for On-the-Move Electric Vehicle Charging Management

Yue Cao
Northumbria University, UK

Tong Wang
Harbin Engineering University, China

Yunfeng Wang
Harbin Engineering University, China

ABSTRACT

The introduction of Electric Vehicle (EVs) has a great potential for the reductions of carbon emissions and air pollution. Whereas, EVs are more likely to run out of energy and need to be charged during their journeys. This is mainly due to the limited EV battery capacity and long trip distance in big cities. Practically, this concern could be substantially improved by recharging EVs' electricity at deployed public Charging Stations (CSs) during journeys. However, even if the flexibility of public CSs could be improved and adjusted following the rapid growth of EVs, major technical challenges and contributions in this chapter involve decision making intelligence for the selection of CSs as charging plans, and the provisioning communication infrastructure for secure information dissemination within network.

INTRODUCTION

As the emerging key urban infrastructures, the Smart Grid and Intelligent Transportation Systems (ITS) have been playing increasing important roles in modern cities. This enables Electric Vehicles (EVs) that are expected to be widely adopted as individual, commercial, and public vehicle fleets. The application of EVs (Schewel & Kammen, 2010) has been recognized as a significant transportation option to reduce

DOI: 10.4018/978-1-5225-1829-7.ch017

CO2 emissions and has attracted numerous attentions from both academia and industry. It is anticipated that EVs will represent a sizeable portion of the US national transportation fleet, with around 50% of new electric car sales by 2050 (Top 10 Electric Car Makers for 2010 and 2011). However, adopting EVs will pose new challenges to the electricity grid, particularly in terms of EV charging management. For example, a large number of EVs charging demands would result in unbalanced charging load at different CSs in power grid.

In addition to the use case considering home-based EV charging overnight, recent research works have also investigated the development of public Charging Station (CSs) in order to provide charging services during EV journeys. These public CSs are typically deployed at places where there is high concentration of EVs such as shopping mall parking places. In this case, on-the-move EVs requesting charging services during their journeys have the opportunity to select the best CS for charging, e.g., to experience a minimized charging waiting time. However, due to the relatively long charging time for EVs, how to optimally manage EV charging requests has become a critical issue. This is mainly because:

- How to manage EV charging according to their requests will have strong impact on charging efficiency at the CS side. This is particularly the case where a grid operator deploys multiple CSs and aims to optimize (e.g. balance) the charging demands across them.
- In addition, individual EVs can also benefit from smart charging scheduling in order to minimize their waiting time before being served.

In general, whenever an EV on the road requires charging, it needs to communicate with the grid or other third party who is interested in charging management, in order to be aware of its charging plan. The setting of EV charging use case in smart grid also introduces some unique security challenges, e.g., in public smart charging of EVs, where the sudden availability of charge details introduces a new incentive for attacks. This requires a design of more secure, resilient, scalable, and flexible than conventional information systems.

Driven by these requirements, this chapter introduces a Publish/Subscribe (P/S) enabled communication mode, in which different stakeholders in the ecosystem (e.g. EVs, CSs and the centralized controller implementing charging management) can exchange information based on dedicated topics depending on their interest for information subscription, instead of relying on the conventional point-to-point communication system. Also, due to decoupling between publishers and subscribers through the P/S paradigm, the end-to-end connections between CSs and EVs are avoided. As a result, the system benefits from scalability (i.e., the number of connections at CS sides does not depend on the number of EVs) and efficiency (i.e., fast connection establishment and reduced bandwidth usage), as the benefits of P/S based communication between CSs and EVs against point-to-point communication.

BACKGROUND

Charging Methodologies

EVs sales are approximately doubling each year. It is important to make intelligent choices for different charging methodologies. One major challenge with EVs is range anxiety. At present, the charging methods can be divided into conventional charging and fast charging. The battery operates with DC whereas the electric utility grid operates with AC. Consequently, a conversion between these two has to take place when power is transferred between the battery and grid. The current question (Wu et al., 2011) is as follows: where should the AC-DC conversion occur? With a DC based CS, the AC-DC conversion takes place in the CS itself, off-board the EV, whereas AC based CSs transfer grid AC power directly to the EV's on-board converters. In other words, an AC based CS does not require power conversion, whereas DC based CS requires power electronics to convert AC to DC, which adds to the configuration cost, weight and complexity.

The work (J. Johansen) discusses conventional charging is a means of mitigating range anxiety, while lowering total cost of EV roll-outs. The benefit of conventional charging is that it allows EVs to charge from an inexpensive AC based CS, by feeding power directly from the electric grid to EVs. Conventional charging costs a long time, has low safety and may emerge gas in charging process (Budhia et al., 2011). Fast charging has improved the charging efficiency, as it allows EVs to charge from a DC based CS (Christen et al., 2015). One reason for showing interest in fast charging is its potential for mitigating range anxiety. When drivers can charge their EVs in 30-60 minutes, then longer trips are made possible because EVs can be charged without inconvenient waiting times.

Types of EVs

Different types of EVs are discussed in (Soares et al., 2013). Firstly, a Battery Electric Vehicle (BEV) runs entirely on a battery and electric drive train, without a conventional internal combustion engine. This kind of EVs must be plugged into an external source of electricity to recharge their batteries. Because of the limited capacity of batteries, the industry has proposed a novel solution centered on the use of "swapping stations" at which depleted batteries can be exchanged for recharged ones in the middle of long trips (Mak et al., 2013). Secondly, Plug-in Hybrid Electric Vehicle (PHEV) runs mostly on battery that is recharged by plugging into the power grid. PHEV is also equipped with an internal combustion engine that can recharge the battery and/or to replace the electric drive train when the battery is low and more power is required. Its engine and the motor can simultaneously turn the transmission, which powers the wheels (Penina et al., 2010). Fuel-cell EVs create electricity from hydrogen and oxygen. Because of these vehicles' efficiency and water-only emissions, some experts consider these cars to be the best type of EVs, even though they are still in development phase.

EV Charging Use Cases

The idea of EV charging management has been investigated for two use cases: Parking Mode and On-the-move Mode.

Parking Mode

Majority of previous works address this use case (concerning when/whether to charge EVs), where EVs have already been parking at homes/CSs. For a detailed survey of this use case, we recommend the readers to refer to (Mukherjee & Gupta, 2014; Rigas, Ramchurn, & Bassiliades, 2015). Here, we briefly summarize these works as follows:

- Schedule and control the charging/discharging of EVs, with different durations such that grid constraints are maintained. This benefits grid such that peaks and possible overloads of the electricity network may be avoided. Meanwhile, the renewable energy could be brought as it is complementary to power grid.

Researchers in (Clement-Nyns, Haesen, & Driesen, 2010) propose a dynamic programming solution that estimates the charging schedule for uncertain EVs charging demand, for the sake of minimizing peaks and carbon taxes. In comparison, the same problem is solved with a decentralized algorithm where each EV computes its own schedule, whereas without addressing prediction error (Anh, Li & Peng, 2011). Another decentralized scheme considers transformer limits and imbalance costs that are caused by uncertain changes in production and consumption (Vandael, Boucké, Holvoet, Craemer, & Deconinck, 2010). Above solutions typically ignore the fact that ultimately, EVs may be powered using uncontrollable renewable energy sources (e.g., wind or solar). Researchers in (Caramanis & Foster, 2009) propose a scheduling scheme according to the availability of energy, while guaranteeing EVs' intended journeys can be met. Another work (Saber & Venayagamoorthy, 2012) exploits particle swarm optimization for charge scheduling that takes the uncertainties of renewable power generation. The hourly wind schedules based on a 30-min persistence prediction by adding uncertain error to the average wind power generation is proposed in (Sortomme & El-Sharkawi, 2011), while the random wind availabilities are handled deterministically in (Awami & Sortomme, 2012).

- Address pricing issue in order to encourage EVs not to charge during periods of high demand.

Researchers (Erol-Kantarci & Mouftah, 2010) propose a scheme based on forecast of the energy prices in time of the charging period. While that work assumes energy demands that are centrally known and can be used for scheduling, this is less robust to failures. With this concern, a decentralized solution is proposed in (Vaya & Andersson, 2012), where EVs react to a price signal broadcast by the utility a day-ahead. The scheme in (Bayram, Michailidis, Papapanagiotou, & Devetsikiotis, 2013) fixes prices for a certain number of EVs that charge at one charging point, and once this threshold is reached, the system enables EVs to charge at other points. Note that the game theory is also studied for the performance of CSs and EVs individually, by predicting the Nash equilibrium of the game (Escudero-Garzas & Seco-Granados, 2012).

On-the-Move Mode

A few works have been studied to manage the EV drivers' charging plans, where they are on-the-move. Three technique branches have been studied:

- Route EVs to minimize energy loss and maximize energy harvested during a trip, such that the time spent to fully recharge EVs is minimized.

Some previous works (Eisner, Funke, & Storandt, 2011; Sachenbacher, Leucker, Artmeier, & Haselmayr, 2011) just focus on calculating the most energy-efficient routes. In contrary, the work in (Storand 2012) takes into account time constraints of the driver by attempting to balance the travel time against energy consumption and the number of demand recharging events, and further brings the battery swap stations instead of conventional plug-in charging stations (Storand & Funke, 2012).

- Deploy CSs such that EVs can access CSs within their driving ranges. Besides, the capabilities of CSs to handle peak demands are taken into account, due to different number of EV arrivals at different times.

Initial work (Storandt & Funke, 2013) on CSs placement assumes the energy consumption for return trips between pairwise nodes is never larger than an EV's battery capacity. Recent work proposed by (Funke, Nusser, & Storandt, 2014) assumes that, given any shortest path between any two nodes, there are a lot of stations for an EV to have enough energy to go on its journey (assuming it starts with a fully charged battery). Different from where to deploy CSs, the work (Bayram, Michailidis, & Devetsikiotis, 2013) addresses EVs' arrival and introduces a scheme to minimize the electric power delivered to the station, as well as the number of charging slots that must be installed in the station.

- Select the appropriate CS as charging plan, meaning to select the CS which is not highly congested, so as to experience a minimized charging waiting time. This cannot be overlooked as it is the most important feature of a vehicle in future smart city, especially for fast charging.

The works in (Yang, Cheng, Hsu, Gan, & Lin, 2013; Cao, Wang, & Kamel, 2014; Weerdt, Stein, Gerding, Robu, & Jennings, 2015) implement charging plans for all EVs based on the minimized queuing time. Further results in (Gharbaoui et al., 2012) show that considering number of other EVs parking at the CS outperforms that considering the distance to the CS, achieves a shorter charging waiting time particularly given a high EV density. In (Hausler, Crisostomi, Schlote, Radusch, & Shorten, 2014), the CS with a higher capability to accept charging requests from EVs will advertise this service with a higher frequency, while EVs sense this service with a decreasing function of their current battery level. Further to these, the EV's charging reservation (Qin & Zhao, 2011; Cao, Wang, Kamel, & Kim, 2015; Cao, Wang, Kim, & Ge, 2015) is brought into system, in order to further improve performance. Further to these, an advanced work (Wang, Liang, Zhang, Deng, & Shen, 2014) jointly combines the issue from energy scheduling as well as CS selection, through a point-to-point Vehicle-to-X (V2X) communication framework.

Cyber Security in EV Charging System

Since the computer science and wireless networks have the specificities, such as relatively easy access to the network nodes and open communication media, the communication involved in EV charging management can be subject to cyber-attacks, especially the data transmission in wireless networks, which is inherently public. Furthermore, GA coordinates a large number of data from CSs and manages charging for on-the-move EVs, by collecting smart meters data, transferring the utility instruction and information via WAN. The potential attacks can be middleman-attack, spoofing etc. The most effective way for preventing malicious attacks from the communication network is cryptography. For instance, HAN and Zigbee use Advanced Encryption Standard (AES, 2001) encryption.

Generally, there exist three main types of attacks in smart grids, including vulnerability, intentional, and false data injection attacks.

- The first type of attack is associated with the failure of network devices or communication channels, and deterioration of feedback signals within control processes. The work (Chaudhry et al., 2012) discusses the security issues of EVs as distributed nodes in a data communication network and review some of the potential vulnerabilities in the EVs infrastructure. Vulnerability attacks can be protected by fault diagnosis and localization methods.
- Intentional attacks can be caused by paralyzing a part of the network nodes, if an adversary has knowledge about the network topology. False data injection attacks aim at the manipulation of smart meter measurement to affect the smart grid operations, mostly the economic variables (Chen, Cheng, & Chen, 2012).
- Intrusion Detection Methods (IDMs) are utilized to analyse the measurement data to detect any possible cyber-attacks on the operation of smart grid systems (Arvani & Rao, 2014). In addition, the work (Su, Qiu, & Wang, 2012) introduces two types of security protocols: key agreement from wireless channel estimation and jamming-resilient communication.

EV CHARGING MANAGEMENT SYSTEM

Network Entities

Most of literature works on EV charging management rely on a centralized controller, e.g., Global Aggregator (GA) to implement the management operation. Generally, three major network entities are involved in the charging system:

- **Electric Vehicle (EV):** Each EV is with a Status Of Charge (SOC). If the ratio between its current energy and maximum energy is below the value of SOC, EV starts to negotiate with the GA to find an appropriate CS for charging planning.
- **Charging Station (CS):** Each CS is located at a certain location to charge EVs in parallel, based on multiple charging slots. Its condition information (number of EVs already parking at the CS and their charging time) is monitored by the GA, through reliable channel like cellular network or wired line communication.
- **Global Aggregator (GA):** It is a centralized entity to manage charging for EVs on-the-move. Here, the CSs' condition information will be collected to make CS-selection decision.

Centralized vs. Distributed Charging Manner

In general, the on-the-move EV charging management can be executed in both centralized and distributed manners. Generally, the common practice is that, an EV which requests charging would travel towards the one with the least load (referred to minimum waiting time at CS) or with the closest distance (the geographic distance measured from this EV to CS).

- With the centralized manner, the charging management is executed by the GA or other third party who is interested in charging management. However, this suffers from much privacy concern, because the EV status information (e.g., location and ID) has to release to the GA.

- The distributed manner benefits from a low privacy sensitivity, where the charging management is executed by EV individually (using accessed condition information from CSs). Therefore, there is no necessity for EV to release its status information.

System Cycle

Figure 1 describes four phases within the EV charging management cycle:

- **Driving Phase:** The EV is travelling towards its trip destination.
- **Where to Charge Phase:** The EV reaching a threshold on its residual battery volume, requires a charging service. The corresponding decision maker (involved in centralized /distributed charging manner) then implements the decision on where to charge.
- **When/Whether to Charge Phase:** Upon arrival at the selected CS, the underlying charging scheduling concerning when/whether to charge EVs, is implemented by CS itself or other entities with the eligibility. For example, in case of the First Come First Serve (FCFS) policy, the EV with an earlier arrival time will be scheduled with a higher charging priority.
- **Battery Charging Phase:** The EV is being charged via the plug-in charger at CS. Upon departure (fully or not fully charged due to certain parking duration), the EV resumes its mobility and turns to Driving Phase.

Publish/Subscribe (P/S) Communication Paradigm

With both manners, necessary information needs to be disseminated to corresponding entities involved in charging management. The accuracy of information plays an important role on the charging management. In general, the cellular network communication (with a ubiquitous communication range) is applied for the centralized management manner. While heterogeneous network communications, e.g.,

Figure 1. Overview of EV charging system cycle

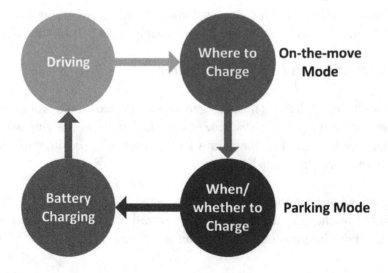

WiFi, WiMAX or even Delay/Disruption Tolerant Networking (DTN) (Cao & Sun, 2013) can be applied for distributed management manner.

Contrary to above classical host based communication mode which uses location specific IP addresses to identify a receiver (with point-to-point communication paradigm), the Publish/Subscribe (P/S) communication paradigm (Eugster, Felber, Guerraoui, & Kermarrec, 2003) allows event distribution from publisher (event producer) to subscriber (event consumer) without the use of any explicit IP address. Here, the event distribution is based on declared subscribers' interests. This mechanism mainly offers communications decoupled in space that subscribers do not need to know the IP address of publishers and vice-versa), and potentially in time if the system is able to store events for clients which are temporally disconnected, such as the intermittent connection resulting from rapid topology changes and sparse network density in DTNs.

The P/S communication paradigm also gains the standard security, namely the decoupling of clients and subscribers. Having no direct communication between clients and between clients and subscribers lessens the attack surface of network entities. The most important security aspect that P/S communication paradigm offers lies in the resilience and availability guarantees, along with those cyber security technologies introduced previously in EV charging use case. In the following sections, such P/S communication paradigm is provisioned for centralized and distributed charging manners.

P/S COMMUNICATION FRAMEWORK FOR CENTRALIZED EV CHARGING MANAGEMENT

Topics Defined for Basic Charging Service

Under this scenario, the GA is the decision maker and manages EV charging in a centralized way. Specifically, the GA as the subscriber receives published information from both CSs and EVs, in order to perform optimized charging management. This is the common practice based on most of the existing works in the literature. In this case, EVs as publishers publish their requests for charging, including the information about current location, residual energy, expected charging duration etc. Meanwhile, CSs also publish their current conditions (e.g. expected waiting time and available energy) to the GA. Three topics can are defined as follows to enable the basic charging management:

- **CS_Condition_Update:** This topic is used by individual CSs to periodically publish their own condition to the GA, where CSs are topic publishers and the GA is the sole subscriber. A publication message from the CS includes the ID of the CS, together with necessary information about its conditions including current charging load, waiting time and available energy.
- **EV_Charging_Request:** This topic is used by individual EVs to publish their charging requests to the GA, in which case the EVs are topic publishers and the GA is the sole subscriber. A publication message from the EV includes the EV ID, together with its current location, velocity and residual energy. Note that any EV cannot become a subscriber of this topic as it is not supposed to know about the information on other EVs' charging requests, for the benefit of security and privacy purposes.
- **EV_Charging_Arrangement:** When the GA has made a decision on which CS to serve an EV's charging request, a charging reply needs to be sent back to that pending EV, including the location

of the allocated CS. In this case, the "EV_Charging_Arrangement" topic bound to this particular EV is used, with the GA being the publisher and this specific EV needs charging being the sole subscriber of the topic.

Then EVs are notified by the GA through the topic of "EV_Charging_Arrangement" about which CS to travel for charging. Based on an example in Figure 2, the EV which requests charging, namely EV_r, publishes its charging request to the GA (in step 1). According to recently received CS conditions, the GA optimally manages the EV request to one of the CSs according to specific strategies such as the one with the lowest charging load, by replying this decision to that EV_r (in step 2).

Topics Defined for Reservation Charging Service

Above procedures present essential steps to arrange charging plan for an EV needs charging service. However, since the number of EVs parking at a CS is fluctuated depending on the EVs' arrival, such uncertainty inevitably has influence on charging management. As such, a potential charging hotspot may happen if many EVs travel towards the same CS for charging, due to that the decision just considers the local condition of CSs. In this context, it is suggested EVs should further report their charging reservations, including when they will arrive at their selected CSs and how long their charging time will be at there. Here, the "EV_Charging_Reservation" topic bounds to the EV acknowledges the arrangement from the GA, with GA being the subscriber and that EV (received charging arrangement from the GA) being the publisher.

Given an example in Figure 2, by monitoring the condition information of CSs, through topic based P/S communication, the compulsory step 1 and step 2 explicitly support the basic charging service. Upon that, in step 3, the EV which has accepted the charging arrangement (implemented by the GA), further publishes its charging reservation back to GA. By jointly utilizing the knowledge from CSs and EVs (with intention on where to charge), a future status (e.g., Expected Waiting Time illustrated in Figure 3) of CSs can be estimated. Therefore, the CS which will be overloaded is not arranged as other EVs' charging plans. Such a way can minimize a potential charging hotspot at CS, which minimizes the

Figure 2. Example of basic and reservation based charging management in centralized manner

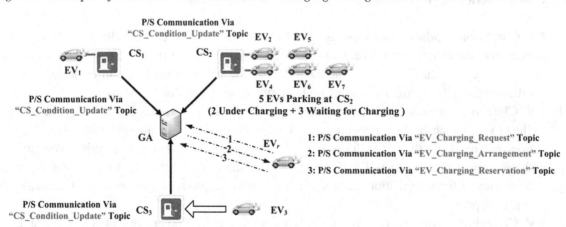

charging waiting time for EVs as well as balance the electricity usage across all CSs in networks. An overview of knowledge required for estimating the expected waiting time of the EV needs charging is presented in Figure 3.

Enabling Charging Management under Mobility Uncertainty

While the simple scenario described above is based on an ideal situation without considering dynamic traffic conditions. Specifically, once an EV has received the information from the GA with an identified CS for serving its charging request, due to traffic congestion it might be the case that the EV will not be able to arrive at the selected CS, such that the original management can be disrupted. As such, a more advanced scheme is to allow EVs to publish their updated conditions (if necessary) to the GA which is then able to manage the request based on the latest situation.

Here, the mobility uncertainty refers to the situation that there is several traffic jams happen in a city. An EV within a certain range of traffic jam has to slow down its speed, while it will accelerate its speed once leaving from the range of that traffic jam. In particular, an EV may temporarily stop for a while, if it is close to the traffic central. In such case, an EV only resumes its movement once the closest traffic jam disappears.

Due to the mobility uncertainty, the variation of EV moving speed will inevitably affect the arrival time at the CS, and the electricity consumption for travelling towards that CS. In this case, the EV can publish updated charging reservation to the GA which then may identify an alternative CS for providing the charging service, via the "EV_Reservation_Update" topic, where the publisher is the EV has made charging reservation and the sole subscriber is the GA. Note that the "EV_Charging_Arrangement" topic is also used here, for acknowledging an updated charging arrangement from the GA back to that EV.

Figure 3. Knowledge required for estimating expected waiting time in reservation mode

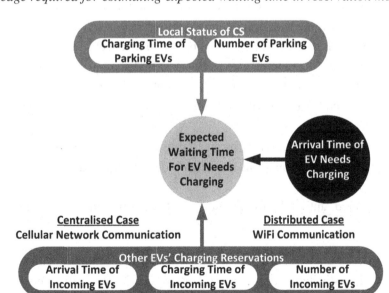

Table 1. Topic used for centralized EV charging

Topic	Publisher	Subscriber	Description
EV_Charging_Request	The EV with charging request	GA	EV provides its status information, such as SOC and location, for GA to select the appropriate CS for that EV.
EV_Charging_Arrangement	GA	The EV sent charging request	GA publishes its selected CS to the EV sending charging request. Also used for information update (if necessary) due to follow-up EV uncertainty on the road.
CS_Condition_Update	CSs	GA	GA needs periodical condition information from CSs to make selection decision for incoming EV charging requests.
EV_Charging_Reservation	The EV acknowledges decision from the GA	GA	EV publishes its arrival time (when it will reach that CS) and expected charging time (how long it will need to charge at that CS) at the selected CS (decided by the GA)
EV_Reservation_Update	The EV made reservation	GA	EV publishes updated charging reservation to the GA, to check the fitness of preference about where to charge

As an example in Figure 4, each EV has its individual parking duration at a CS, and in particular, an EV may depart from a CS before being fully charged. Then a typical procedure for tackling the mobility uncertainty is listed as follows:

1. For each on-the-move EV needs charging, namely, EV_r publishes its charging request to the GA.
2. The GA then compiles a list of CSs and ranks the most appropriate one, where the decision in relation to the best one is sent back to EV_r.
3. EV_r further publishes its reservation information in relation to this decided CS, including its arrival time, expected charging time and parking duration at this CS.
4. While travelling towards the decided CS, EV_r periodically checks whether that currently selected CS is still a better choice, by publishing a reservation update request to the GA.
5. The GA then compares a cost in relation to the currently selected CS as well as that of other CSs. If the currently selected CS is not with the minimum cost, the GA will inform EV_r about a new CS-selection decision.
6. EV_r then cancels its previous reservation and publishes the reservation information in relation to the newly selected CS, then changes its movement towards that place.

Steps 4 to 6 are repeated, until EV_r finally reaches a CS through this periodical operation.

Case Study

A case study has been investigated in (Cao, Wang, Kim, & Ge, 2014), under the scenario illustrated in Figure 5, with 4500×3400 m² area shown as the down town area of Helsinki city in Finland. Here, 240 EVs with [5~15] m/s variable moving speed are initialized in the network. The configuration of EVs

Figure 4. Example of handling mobility uncertainty in reservation mode

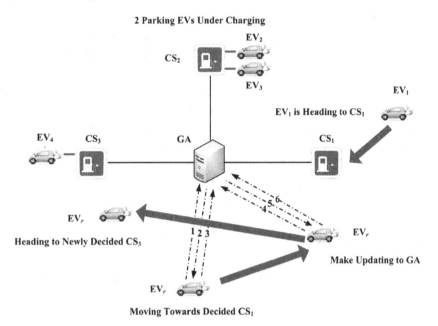

follows the charging specification {Maximum Electricity Capacity (MEC), Max Travelling Distance (MTD), Status Of Charge (SOC)}. There are three types of EVs, which are Coda Automotive ("www.codaautomotive.com.") {33.8 kWh, 193 km, 30%}, Wheego Whip ("www.wheego.net.") {30 kWh, 161 km, 40%} and Hyundai BlueOn ("wikipedia.org/wiki/Hyundai BlueOn") {16.4 kWh, 140 km, 50%}. Each type is with 80 EVs.

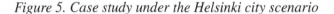

Figure 5. Case study under the Helsinki city scenario

Besides, 7 CSs are provided with sufficient electric energy and 3 charging slots through entire simulation, using the fast charging rate of 62 kW. If the ratio between its current energy and maximum energy is below the value of SOC, the EV would travel towards a decided CS for charging. Here, the shortest path towards CS is formed considering road topology. Particularly, 30 randomly generated accidents happen for every 900s in the city, and the warning distance is 300m. Therefore, each EV will adjust its moving speed, if the distance between its location and an accident place is smaller than 300m.

The average waiting time reflects the average period between the time an EV arrives at the selected CS and the time it fully finishes recharging its battery, considering the full charging cannot be finished within parking duration. Researchers have provided a comparison with four CS-selection schemes:

Proposed-1: The CS-selection scheme tackling the mobility uncertainty (Cao, Wang, Kim, & Ge, 2015).

Proposed-2: The CS-selection scheme without tackling the mobility uncertainty, but with charging reservation feature (Cao, Wang, Kim, & Ge, 2015).

Compared-1: The CS-selection is based on the minimum queuing time at a CS (Cao, Wang, & Kamel, 2014).

Compared-2: The CS-selection is based on the closest distance between the EV sending charging request and a CS (Yang, Cheng, Hsu, Gan, & Lin, 2013).

The result in Figure 6 shows that a longer parking duration increases the average waiting time. This is because more EVs will stay at CSs until being fully recharged, as such a total waiting time considering all parking EVs will be increased. Particularly, the Proposed-2 (without reservation updating) still achieves a better performance, than the CS-selection schemes based on local queueing time and distance. Further to this, since EVs with uncertain mobility benefit from the reservation updating, the Proposed-1 dynamically adjusts charging plan.

Figure 6. Average waiting time vs. parking duration

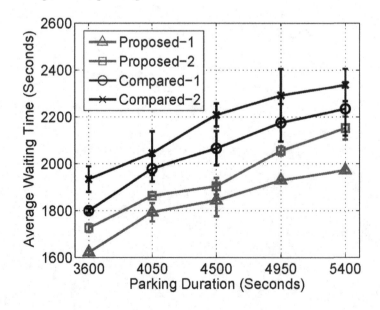

Since the EV charging plan is coordinated by reporting reservation as well as reservation updating, Proposed-2 achieves a higher number of charged EVs in Figure 7, where the version without reservation updating is the secondary, due to not adjusting CS-selection decision. Here, the CS-selection scheme based on the closest distance is the worst, because it does not consider how many EVs are parking at a CS. Thus a closer CS does not mean it is occupied by a less number of EVs. Of course, a longer parking duration leads to a higher number of charged EVs, as more EVs can be fully recharged.

P/S COMMUNICATION FRAMEWORK FOR DISTRIBUTED EV CHARGING MANAGEMENT

Compared to centralized charging management, an alternative system without necessarily relying on the GA (that is responsible for scheduling EV charging requests) is to implement charging management in a distributed manner. In the latter case, each EV locally operates their decisions on where to charge individually, based on the received CSs condition information. In the following parts of this section, a dedicated communication framework to support this distributed charging manner is introduced.

Topics Defined for Basic Charging Service

In order to enabling the distributed charging management, the Road Side Units (RSU) (Rashidi, Batros, Madsen, Riaz, & Paulin, 2012) is introduced which behave as an intermediate entity for bridging the information flow exchange between EVs on the road and the grid infrastructure CSs, through wireless communications. The actual realization of RSUs can be based on existing wireless communication technologies such as cellular base stations or WiFi access points. It is worth mentioning that different

Figure 7. Number of fully charged EVs vs. parking duration

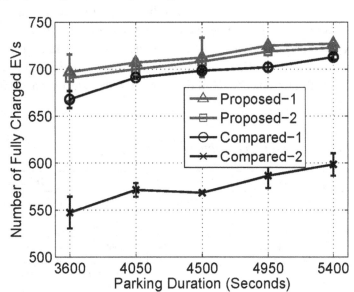

types of realization of RSUs (in particular the radio transmission coverage) will affect the actual charging information due to the information freshness related to the data exchange between EVs and the grid.

Again, the P/S mechanism is applied to disseminate necessary information of CSs to EVs. Those EVs subscribing to such information could then make their individual decisions to select a desired CS for charging, according to received information such as expected waiting time. In this scenario, since there is no central entity such as a GA that is responsible for scheduling EV charging requests, load demand optimization on the CS side will become a much more challenging issue. Specifically, the possibility that EVs receive the published information from CS will directly impact the overall charging performance. In this basic scenario, a single topic is defined for individual CSs to publish their conditions to EVs, illustrated in Table 2.

Communication Framework Provisioning

Since simple broadcasting of published CS condition information to EVs on the road through cellular networks may be deemed to be expensive, and also that such information does not need to "ubiquitously" accessible to EVs on the road. As such it is more desirable to deploy low-cost RSUs with limited radio coverage (e.g. either through road side WiFi hotspots or only through a selected subset of cellular base stations). In this case, only when an EV is in RSU radio coverage, it receives published conditions of CSs (Zeng, Leng, & Zhang, 2013).

However, the provisioning of RSUs can potentially influence the actual charging performance due to information freshness on the CS condition available to EVs. More specifically, since EVs are not able to obtain the up-to-date CS condition publications if they are not in the radio coverage of RSUs, delay can be introduced before they receive the message. From provisioning strategy point of view, a key technical issue is how to determine the optimized density of RSU coverage in public in order to achieve the best trade-off between charging efficiency and infrastructure cost minimization.

With this concern in mind, two complementary communication modes are introduced herein, namely Push and Pull Modes, in order to enable the required information dissemination operation.

- In Push Mode, CSs periodically publish their condition information to nearby RSUs, from which the data is directly disseminated to the on-the-move EVs within the radio coverage of those RSUs.
- In Pull Mode, the CS condition information is periodically published to the RSUs with data storage space and gets cached there. When an EV enters the radio coverage of a RSU which holds the message, it can query through that RSU in order to fetch the latest cached information. For each

Table 2. Topics used for distributed EV charging management

Topic	Publisher	Subscriber	Description
CS_Condition_Update	CSs	EVs	CS periodically publish its local condition information (basic charging service only) and anonymous other EVs reservations.
EV_Charging_Reservation	The EV decided which CS to charge	The selected CS by EV	EV publishes its arrival time (when it will reach that CS) and expected charging time (how long it will need to charge at that CS) at the selected CS (decided by EV individually)

CS, whenever a new publication of the condition information becomes available, the RSU will replace the old values cached in the past with the new data.

It can be inferred that, in the Push Mode, if the radio coverage is not ubiquitous (e.g. the WiFi scenario in which the communication is disruptive, which means that there is no ubiquitous network access for on-the-move EVs), an EV may miss the published information while it traverses the radio coverage of that RSU (depending on the CS publication frequency), thus affecting the received information freshness. As such, a key technical challenge is the RSU deployment strategies, which is also linked to the control of CS information publication frequency for enabling optimized EV charging performances on both the CS and the EV sides. In other words, both the RSU provisioning strategy and the control of CS condition publication can influence the information freshness on the EV side which will actually affect the actual charging performance on both the CS side (e.g. load demand) and the EV side (e.g. waiting time).

Analysis of Two Communication Modes

Under the Push Mode as shown in Figure 8, the EV, as subscriber, passively receives information from a nearby RSU. This happens when the EV is within the radio coverage of that RSU, as given by $D < R$. Here, D is the distance between RSU and EV, while R is the radius of RSU radio coverage. Note that the RSU under this mode will not cache any historical information received from CS, thus a communicating EV cannot obtain any information if CSs are not currently publishing its information.

Under the Pull Mode, each RSU locally caches the information from a CS as the historical record. The EV with L radius coverage initially sends an explicit query to the RSU, when their current distance is smaller than the minimum value between their radio coverage, as given by $D < Min(R, L)$. In general, the condition $L < R$. holds true because the RSU is with much larger transmission range. Upon receiving this query, the RSU then sends its latest cached information to that EV, as shown in Figure 8. Different from passively receiving information for multiple times from each RSU under the Push Mode, here, each EV can only obtain the information from RSU only once.

Practically, there is no overlap between the radio coverage of two adjacent RSUs, for instance in the WiFi scenario where the radio coverage is not ubiquitous. Figure 9 provides an example with 2 RSUs with adjacent distance S for analysis purpose, where T is the EV speed, R is the radio coverage range of RSU, L is the radio coverage range of EV, and F is just the distance from the starting point to the centre of first RSU.

Given that there are N RSUs with equal adjacent distance S on a straight road, the probability P_{push} that an EV can get information from at least one RSU under the Push Mode is given by:

$$P_{push} \leq 1 - \left(1 - \frac{F+R}{V \times T}\right)\left(1 - \frac{4R^2}{V \times T \times S}\right)^{(N-1)}$$

It is observed that the probability that an EV getting information relies on a larger radio coverage and number of RSUs in general. Meanwhile, a more frequent update interval and slower EV moving speed also improve such probability. Recall that since there is no overlap between the radio coverage of two adjacent RSUs, thus a closer distance S is beneficial to increase P_{push} as well.

Figure 8. Overview of push mode and pull mode

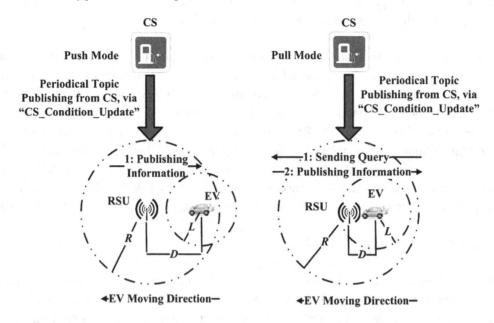

Figure 9. Analysis model with 2 RSUs

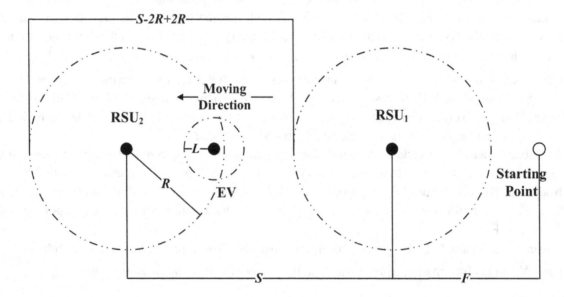

In Pull Mode, since the EV has to send query to the RSU for requesting the information, the radio coverage of EV needs to be taken into account. Different from that under the Push Mode, the probability that an EV obtains information is gradually increased when passing through more RSUs, due to the caching nature of RSUs. In this case, this given probability depends on whether the RSU has the historical record about the CS when communicating with the EV. Inherently, a longer elapsed travelling time indicates a higher probability, as the RSU has more chance to cache the historical information of CS. Then, P_{pull} is given by:

$$P_{pull} \leq 1 - \prod_{i=1}^{N} \left\{ 1 - \left[\frac{(i-1) \times S + F + L}{V \times T} \right] \right\}$$

It is observed that increasing the radio coverage of EV improves P_{pull} to obtain information from RSUs. Similar to that under the Push Mode, the influence of V and T are also applicable in this case. However, since it is beneficial to wait for a longer time to cache the historical information of CS under the Pull Mode, a larger S is desirable.

Recall that the radio coverage between two adjacent RSUs is not ubiquitous, thus the condition $2R \leq S$ is given. Then the upper bound of P_{push} is converted as:

$$
\begin{aligned}
P_{push}^{upper} &= 1 - \left(1 - \frac{F+R}{V \times T} \right) \left(1 - \frac{4R^2}{V \times T \times S} \right)^{(N-1)} \\
&\leq 1 - \left(1 - \frac{F+R}{V \times T} \right) \left(1 - \frac{S^2}{V \times T \times S} \right)^{(N-1)} \\
&= 1 - \left(1 - \frac{F+R}{V \times T} \right) \left(1 - \frac{S}{V \times T} \right)^{(N-1)}
\end{aligned}
$$

Next, the upper bound of P_{pull} can be converted as:

$$
\begin{aligned}
P_{pull}^{upper} &= 1 - \prod_{i=1}^{N} \left\{ 1 - \left[\frac{(i-1)S + F + L}{V \times T} \right] \right\} \\
&\leq 1 - \left(1 - \frac{F+L}{V \times T} \right) \prod_{i=2}^{N-1} \left\{ 1 - \left[\frac{(2-1)S + F + L}{V \times T} \right] \right\} \\
&= 1 - \left(1 - \frac{F+L}{V \times T} \right) \left(1 - \frac{S + F + L}{V \times T} \right)^{(N-1)}
\end{aligned}
$$

Based on the above, it is observed that if configuring $R = L$ for fair comparison, the Pull Mode always achieves a higher probability to obtain information from RSUs than Push Mode. For a detailed derivation, we recommend the readers to refer to (Cao, Wang & Kamel, 2014).

Case Study

In Figure 10, the default scenario with 4500×3400 m² area is shown as the down town area of Helsinki city in Finland. Here, 100 EVs with [30-50] km/h variable moving speed are initialized in the network. All EVs are with the Wheego Whip (www.wheego.net) EV type, with SOC = 40%.

Considering these 100 EVs in network, 5 CSs are provided with 3000 kWh electric energy and 3 charging slots through entire simulation, using the fast charging rate of 62 kW. Under this configura-

Figure 10. The Helsinki city with RSUs deployed

tion, the charging management is essential as some EVs have to wait additional time for charging, until charging services for other EVs in front of the queue at a CS are finished. For the purpose of fairness, 300m radio coverage is applied for 7 RSUs and 100 EVs, where all EVs continually receive information regardless of their SOC. The default update interval (publication frequency) of CS is 100s while simulation time is 43200s = 12 hours.

All CSs are connected with each RSU through dedicated and reliable communication channels. While each EV communicates with RSUs to gather status information about all CSs. The EV reaching a threshold on its residual battery charge applies a pre-defined policy to select a dedicated CS for charging, using the information obtained from RSU. Note this EV might have received information for several times when it is reaching the threshold for requesting charging. Here, each EV selects a dedicated CS within the EV reachability, based on the minimum waiting time. Since EVs' decision making is always based on the latest published information, the information freshness (which affects the actual charging performance) effectively depends on how often the periodically published information is received by the on-the-move EVs. Finally, upon reaching the selected CS, EVs are then scheduled based on a policy, e.g., the First Come First Serve (FCFS) priority for charging.

The charging system based on an Ideal Case is also evaluated, that each EV could obtain the CS instantaneous queuing time by sending request and receiving decision reply from a global controller. This is the common framework applied by previous works, performing in a centralized way. The Push and Pull Modes however are with a distributed nature, where the CS-selection is made by each EV locally.

In addition to average waiting time and number of charged EVs described previously, two metrics are given:

- **Average Information Freshness:** The average value of the difference between the current waiting time at CS side and that recorded at EV side, only calculated when an EV makes an individual selection decision.
- **Utilization of CSs:** The amount of consumed electric energy calculated at CS side.

Influence of CS Update Interval

In Figure 11, the Push Mode results in poor information freshness than the Pull Mode, based on the analysis aforementioned.

In Figure 12 and Figure 13, with an infrequent update interval of CS, all EVs in the network experience an increased average waiting time, the number of charged EVs in network is reduced. This is due to the fact that using outdated information affects the computation at the EV side to make selection decision. In other words, the number of EVs waiting at CS, as estimated at the EV side when making decision, may be significantly different from that at the CS side. Thus, with an increased update interval, there will be a huge difference between that performance given 100s and 900s interval.

In particular, by relying on the direct communication between CSs and EVs in Ideal Case, the obtained information is the same as the status of CSs. As such, the performance under the Ideal Case achieves the best performance, particularly when both Push and Pull Modes are based on 900s update interval.

In Figure 14, it is observed that CS update interval also has influence on the utilization of CSs. This is because that the poor information freshness yields EVs to make inaccurate selection decision, as such the electric energy at some CSs may not be utilized for charging. The above observation becomes more significantly given 900s update interval.

Figure 11. Influence of CS update interval vs. average information freshness

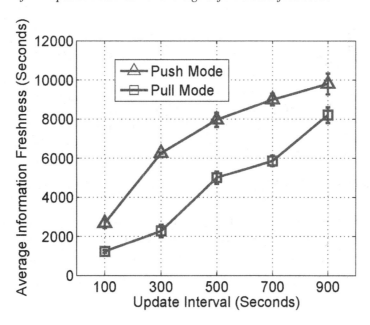

Figure 12. Influence of CS update interval vs. average waiting time

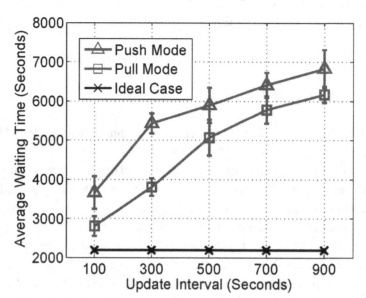

Figure 13. Influence of CS update interval vs. number of charged EVs

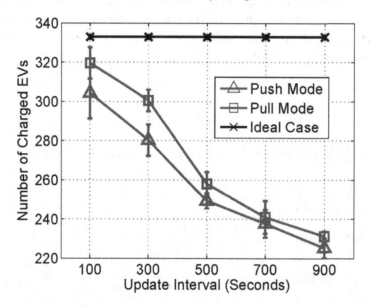

Influence of RSUs Provisioning

In this case, RSU7, RSU8, RSU10, RSU11 in Figure 10 are removed, while CS update interval and radio coverage range are fixed to be 100s and 300m respectively. In Figure 15 and Figure 16, it is observed that reducing the number of RSUs somehow degrades performance, compared to that given 7 RSUs case.

Figure 14. Influence of CS update interval vs. utilizations of CSs

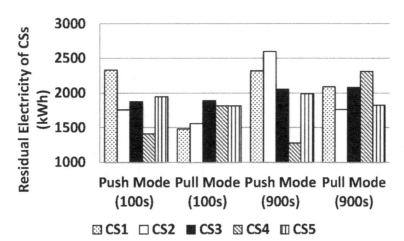

Figure 15. RSUs provisioning vs. average waiting time

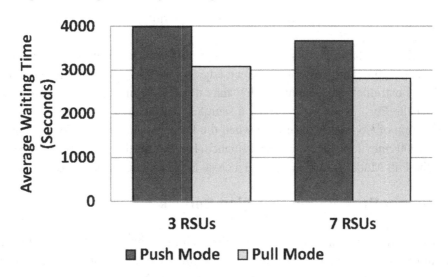

Summary of Results

Above results provides two key observations to guide communication framework provisioning.

1. A worse information freshness results in an increased average waiting time, as EVs using relatively outdated information for selecting CS would yield unbalanced charging demand among all CSs in the network.
2. The main advantage of using the Pull Mode is the flexibility and higher utilization of CSs given sparsely deployed RSUs, with the expense of caching overhead to maintain CS condition information.

The advantage of the P/S enabled distributed charging system is the scalability, where any available RSU in network would continually bridge information disseminated from CS to EV, if some other RSUs

Figure 16. RSUs provisioning vs. number of charged EVs

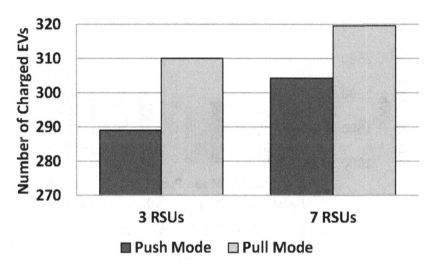

fail to work. This is different from the Ideal Case where the charging management would not be operated if the centralized controller fails.

Although with the advantage in terms of application, a major concern is how frequent the information should be published, as the radio coverage between adjacent RSUs is not ubiquitous. In the worst case if the publication is extremely infrequent, the EV may not obtain any information from passed RSUs particularly under the Push Mode. In contrast, a seamless publication is whereas costly as the fresh condition information of CS is only necessary when the EV needs to select a CS. Here, increasing the update interval to 900s inevitably degrades performance. In contrast, the performance given 100s update interval (under the Pull Mode) is able to achieve a close performance based on Ideal Case.

Topics Defined for Reservation Charging Service

Above analysis and results have already shown that the caching nature under the Pull Mode is beneficial for improving information freshness at EV side. For enabling the reservation based charging management, as already discussed in centralized charging system, those EVs which are in the status of travelling towards their selected CSs for charging will publish their reservation information to their selected CSs.

In case of distributed charging management, such reservation information publication from EVs to CSs is bridged by RSUs. In particular, each CS will publish its predicted condition information according to the received EV reservations, and such information publication has anonymous EV IDs and their current locations considering the privacy issue. This anticipated information including when an EV will arrive and how long it will need to fully recharging its battery, are used for other on-the-move EVs to estimate the expected waiting time at a CS in the near future.

Signaling Sequences

The entire timing sequences for on-the-move EV charging under the Pull Mode enabled charging reservation system, namely Advanced Pull Mode (shown in Figure 17) are listed as follows:

1. An EV accesses CS condition information from RSUs, by referring to the Pull Mode.
2. Given a low electricity status, the EV selects where to charge using its accessed information.
3. If this EV (which has made decision on where to charge) encounters any RSU on the road, the EV will publish its charging reservation to its selected CS, through the encountered RSU.

Data Format for CS Publication

Since the decision is made at EV side, there is a privacy concern if releasing the IDs of other EVs included in their charging reservations. With this concern, each CS will integrate the information in relation to a number of EVs which reserve at here for charging, with the CS local information for publication. As

Figure 17. Time sequences of advanced pull mode

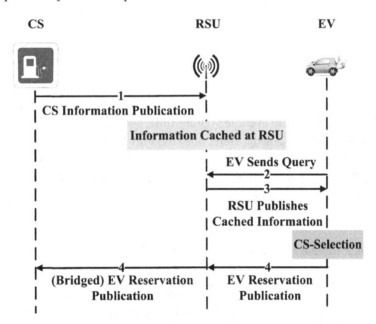

Table 3. Format of information published from CS side

CS ID
CS$_3$
Instantaneous Queuing Time
3060s
Available Charging Time Per Charging Slot
[3300s, 3950s, 4210s]
Reservation Information

Reservation Entry	Arrival Time	Reserved Charging Time
1	3500s	730s
2	4700s	700s

observed from the format in Table 3 format of information published from cs side, the IDs of those EVs reserving for charging at CS are hidden. As such, the EV subscribing to the CS publication will not obtain any knowledge about who else has reserved for charging, since only a list of entries containing the arrival time and reserved charging time upon that arrival are received.

In addition, the published arrival time does not disclose the EV's location. This is because the arrival time is estimated depending on the location of EV and its corresponding speed at that time, whereas this information will not be released through any communication.

One concern of such reservation reporting is that it is inherently entitled with a possibility to introduce system instability through service attacks against CSs, since EVs send reservation information to CSs for future charging. The assumption that reservation information is trustworthy is vulnerable without ensuring the integrity of messages from EVs to CSs on end-to-end aspects. E.g., forged or wrong reservation information are continuously delivered to CSs through RSUs, CSs will compute quite imprecise estimation for charging available time and advertise imprecise information to EVs through RSUs. The general secured vehicular communication framework (Kargl, et al., 2008) can be applied to enable secured delivery of EV reservation requests towards CSs.

Case Study

Based on the same scenario illustrated in Figure 10, in Figure 18, it is observed that increasing the number of charging slots reduces the average waiting time, since the parallel charging process enables more EVs can be charged simultaneously. Here, both the Pull Mode and Advanced Pull Mode achieve the best performance given 100s update interval, compared to that given 900s update interval. This is because that a frequent information publication improves the information freshness at EV side to make accurate CS-selection decision, in particular the reservation in relation to a CS as well as its local in-

Figure 18. Performance comparison regarding average waiting time

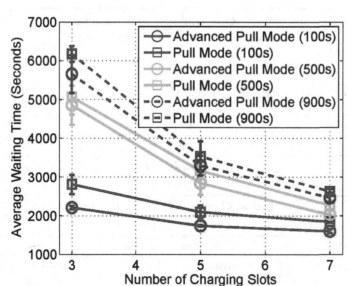

Figure 19. Performance comparison regarding number of charged EVs

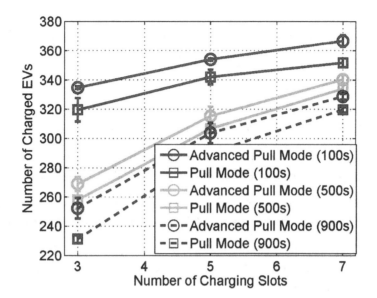

formation are received with a more recent value. Compared to the original Pull Mode by only using CS instantaneous queuing information, using EVs' reservation information improves the average waiting time, by considering EVs' future movement to select the CS with the minimum expected waiting time.

Of course, applying more charging slots improves performance for both of them. The observation in Figure 19 shows that the Advanced Pull Mode charges more number of EVs than that under original Pull Mode. Note that more fresh information is beneficial to make accurate decision, as such the performance given 100s update interval achieves the highest value.

CONCLUSION

In this chapter, the P/S driven communication framework is presented to support on-the-move EV charging management. The centralized charging manner relies on GA to globally process the published request published from all EVs, and make decision on which CS should travel for charging. Regarding the distributed charging manner where each EV could make their individual decision for selecting CS, the RSU is applied to bridge the information published from CS to EVs. The benefit of applying charging reservation is further introduced, with the improvement at EV side in terms of reduced charging waiting time, and CS side in terms of increased number of charged EVs. By modifying the content for information publication, the proposed P/S communication framework can also support the battery swap or the pricing issues. Of course, factors such as EV driver's pattern, EV classification, trip type and purpose could be further taken into account for management aspect, based on the enabled P/S communication framework.

REFERENCES

Advanced encryption standard (AES) (2001). National Institute for Standards and Technology.

Ahn, C., Li, C.-T., & Peng, H. (2011). Decentralized charging algorithm for electrified vehicles connected to smart grid.*Proc. of ACC (pp. 3924–3929).*

Al-Awami, A. T., & Sortomme, E. (2012, March). Coordinating vehicle-to-grid services with energy trading. *IEEE Trans. Smart Grid, 3*(1), 453–462. doi:10.1109/TSG.2011.2167992

Arvani, A., & Rao, V. S. (2014). Detection and protection against intrusions on smart grid systems. *International Journal of Cyber-Security and Digital Forensics, 3*(1), 38–48. doi:10.17781/P001273

Bayram, G. Michailidis, & M. Devetsikiotis. (2013, October). Electric power resource provisioning for large scale public EV charging facilities. *Proc. IEEE Int. Conf. SmartGridComm* (pp. 133–138).

Bayram, I., Michailidis, G., Papapanagiotou, I., & Devetsikiotis, M. (2013, Dec). Decentralized control of electric vehicles in a network of fast charging stations.*Proc. IEEE GLOBECOM* (pp. 2785–2790). doi:10.1109/GLOCOM.2013.6831496

Budhia, M., Covic, G. A., & Boys, J. T. (2011). Design and optimization of circular magnetic structures for lumped inductive power transfer systems. *IEEE Transactions on Power Electronics, 26*(11), 3096–3108. doi:10.1109/TPEL.2011.2143730

Cao, Y., & Sun, Z. (2013). Routing in Delay/Disruption Tolerant Networks: A Taxonomy, Survey and Challenges. *IEEE Communications Surveys and Tutorials, 15*(2), 654–677. doi:10.1109/SURV.2012.042512.00053

Cao, Y., Wang, N., & Kamel, G. (2014). Publish/subscribe communication framework for managing electric vehicle charging. *Proceedings ofIEEE ICCVE' 14.*

Cao, Y., Wang, N., Kamel, G., & Kim, Y.-J. (2015). An Electric Vehicle Charging Management Scheme Based on Publish/Subscribe Communication Framework. *IEEE Systems Journal, PP*(99), 1–14.

Cao, Y., Wang, N., Kim, Y.-J., & Ge, C. (2015). *A Reservation Based Charging Management for On-the-move EV Under Mobility Uncertainty.* IEEE Online GreenComm. doi:10.1109/OnlineGreen-Com.2015.7387372

Caramanis, M., & Foster, J. (2009). Management of electric vehicle charging to mitigate renewable generation intermittency and distribution network congestion. *Proc. 48th IEEE CDC/28th CCC* (pp. 4717–4722).

Chaudhry, H., & Bohn, T. (2012, January). Security concerns of a plug-in vehicle. *Proceedings of the 2012 IEEE PES Innovative Smart Grid Technologies (ISGT).*

Chen, P. Y., Cheng, S. M., & Chen, K. C. (2012). Smart attacks in smart grid communication networks. *IEEE Communications Magazine, 50*(8), 24–29. doi:10.1109/MCOM.2012.6257523

Christen, D., Jauch, F., & Biel, J. (2015, September). Ultra-fast charging station for electric vehicles with integrated split grid storage. *Proceedings of the 2015 17th European Conference on Power Electronics and Applications (EPE'15)*. doi:10.1109/EPE.2015.7309322

CleanFleet Report. (2011). Top 10 Electric Car Makers for 2010 and 2011. Retrieved from http:www. cleanfleetreport.com/clean-fleet-articles/topelectric-cars-2010

Clement-Nyns, K., Haesen, E., & Driesen, J. (2010, February). The impact of charging plug-in hybrid electric vehicles on a residential distribution grid. *IEEE Transactions on Power Systems*, *25*(1), 371–380. doi:10.1109/TPWRS.2009.2036481

CodaAutomotive. (n. d.). Retrieved from www.codaautomotive.com

de Weerdt, M., Stein, S., Gerding, E., Robu, V., & Jennings, N. (2015). Intention-Aware Routing of Electric Vehicles. *IEEE Transactions on Intelligent Transportation Systems*, PP(99), 1–11.

Eisner, J., Funke, S., & Storandt, S. (2011). Optimal route planning for electric vehicles in large networks. *Proc. 25th Conf. AAAI* (pp. 1108–1113).

Erol-Kantarci, M., & Mouftah, H. T. (2010). Prediction-based charging of PHEVs from the smart grid with dynamic pricing. *Proc. IEEE 35th Conf. LCN* (pp. 1032–1039).

Escudero-Garzas, J., & Seco-Granados, G. (2012, Jan). Charging station selection optimization for plug-in electric vehicles: An oligopolistic game-theoretic framework.*Proc. IEEE PES ISGT*. doi:10.1109/ ISGT.2012.6175791

Eugster, P. T., Felber, P. A., Guerraoui, R., & Kermarrec, A.-M. (2003, June). The Many Faces of Publish/ Subscribe. *ACM Computing Surveys*, *35*(2), 114–131. doi:10.1145/857076.857078

Funke, S., Nusser, A., & Storandt, S. (2014). Placement of loading stations for electric vehicles: No detours necessary!*Proc. 28th AAAI Conf.* (pp. 417–423).

Gharbaoui, M., Valcarenghi, L., Bruno, R., Martini, B., Conti, M., & Castoldi, P. (2012, March). An Advanced Smart Management System for Electric Vehicle Recharge. *Proceedings of IEEE IEVC*, Greenville, SC, USA.

Gonzalez Vaya, M., & Andersson, G. (2012). Centralized and decentralized approaches to smart charging of plug-in vehicles. *Proc. IEEE Power Energy Soc. Gen. Meet.*

Hausler, F., Crisostomi, E., Schlote, A., Radusch, I., & Shorten, R. (2014, April). Stochastic Park-and-Charge Balancing for Fully Electric and Plug in Hybrid Vehicles. *IEEE Transactions on Intelligent Transportation Systems*, *15*(2), 895–901. doi:10.1109/TITS.2013.2286266

Johansen, J. (n. d.). Fast-charging electric vehicles using ac [Master Thesis].

Kargl, F., Papadimitratos, P., Buttyan, L., Muter, M., Schoch, E., Wiedersheim, B., & Hubaux, J.-P. et al. (2008, November). Secure Vehicular Communication Systems: Implementation, Performance, and Research Challenges. *IEEE Communications Magazine*, *46*(11), 110–118. doi:10.1109/MCOM.2008.4689253

Mak, H. Y., Rong, Y., & Shen, Z. J. M. (2013). Infrastructure planning for electric vehicles with battery swapping. *Management Science*, *59*(7), 1557–1575. doi:10.1287/mnsc.1120.1672

J. Mukherjee, & A. Gupta. (2014). A Review of Charge Scheduling of Electric Vehicles in Smart Grid. *IEEE Systems Journal*, PP(99), 1–13.

Penina, N., Turygin, Y.V. & Racek, V. (2010, June). Comparative analysis of different types of hybrid electric vehicles. *Proceedings of the 2010 13th International Symposium MECHATRONIKA* (pp. 102-104).

Qin, H., & Zhang W. (2011, September). Charging Scheduling with Minimal Waiting in a Network of Electric Vehicles and Charging Stations. in ACM VANET' 11, Las Vegas, Nevada, USA.

Rashidi, M., Batros, I., Madsen, T., Riaz, M., & Paulin, T. (2012, October). Placement of Road Side Units for Floating Car Data Collection in Highway Scenario. Proceedings of IEEE ICUM' 12, Petersburg, Russia.

Rigas, E., Ramchurn, S., & Bassiliades, N. (2015, August). Managing Electric Vehicles in the Smart Grid Using Artificial Intelligence: A Survey. *IEEE Transactions on* Intelligent Transportation Systems, *16*(4), 1619–1635.

Saber, A., & Venayagamoorthy, G. (2012, March). Resource scheduling under uncertainty in a smart grid with renewables and plug-in vehicles. *IEEE Syst. J.*, *6*(1), 103–109. doi:10.1109/JSYST.2011.2163012

Sachenbacher, M., Leucker, M., Artmeier, A., & Haselmayr, J. (2011). Efficient energy-optimal routing for electric vehicles. *Proc. 25th Conf. AAAI* (pp. 1402–1407).

Schewel, L., & Kammen, D. M. (2010). Smart Transportation: Synergizing Electrified Vehicles and Mobile Information Systems. Environment. *Science and Policy for Sustainable Development*, *52*(5), 24–35. doi:10.1080/00139157.2010.507143

Soares, F. J., Almeida, P. M. R., Lopes, J. A. P., Garcia-Valle, R., & Marra, F. (2013). State of the Art on Different Types of Electric Vehicles. In Electric Vehicle Integration into Modern Power Networks. doi:10.1007/978-1-4614-0134-6_1

Sortomme, E., & El-Sharkawi, M. A. (2011, March). Optimal charging strategies for unidirectional vehicle-to-grid. *IEEE Trans. Smart Grid*, *2*(1), 131–138. doi:10.1109/TSG.2010.2090910

Storandt, S. (2012). Quick and energy-efficient routes: Computing constrained shortest paths for electric vehicles. *Proc. 5th ACM SIGSPATIAL IWCTS* (pp. 20–25). doi:10.1145/2442942.2442947

Storandt, S., & Funke, S. (2012). Cruising with a battery-powered vehicle and not getting stranded. *Proc. 26th Conf. AAAI '12* (pp. 1628–1634).

Storandt, S., & Funke, S. (2013). Enabling e-mobility: Facility location for battery loading stations. *Proc. 27th Conf. AAAI* (pp. 1341–1347).

Su, H., Qiu, M., & Wang, H. (2012). Secure wireless communication system for smart grid with rechargeable electric vehicles. *IEEE Communications Magazine*, *50*(8), 62–68. doi:10.1109/MCOM.2012.6257528

Vandael, S., Boucké, N., Holvoet, T., De Craemer, K., & Deconinck, G. (2011). Decentralized coordination of plug-in hybrid vehicles for imbalance reduction in a smart grid. *Proc. of the 10th Int. Conf. Auton. Agents Multiagent* (pp. 803–810).

Wang, M., Liang, H., Zhang, R., Deng, R., & Shen, X. (2014, July). Mobility-Aware Coordinated Charging for Electric Vehicles in VANET-Enhanced Smart Grid. *IEEE Journal on Selected Areas in Communications*, *32*(7), 1344–1360. doi:10.1109/JSAC.2014.2332078

WheeGo. (n. d.). Retrieved from www.wheego.net

Wikipedia. (n. d.). Hyundai Blue On. Retrieved from www.wikipedia.org/wiki/HyundaiBlueOn

Wu, H. H., Gilchrist, A., Sealy, K., Israelsen, P., & Muhs, J. (2011, May). A review on inductive charging for electric vehicles.*Proceedings of the 2011 IEEE International Electric Machines & Drives Conference* (pp. 143-147).

Yang, S.-N., Cheng, W.-S., Hsu, Y.-C., Gan, C.-H., & Lin, Y.-B. (2013, June). Charge Scheduling of Electric Vehicles in Highways. *Elsevier Mathematical and Computer Modelling*, *57*(1112), 2873–2882. doi:10.1016/j.mcm.2011.11.054

Zeng, M., Leng, S., & Zhang, Y. (2013, June). Power Charging and Discharging Scheduling for V2G Networks in the Smart Grid. Proceedings of IEEE ICC' 13, Budapest, Hungary.

Chapter 18

Smart Control Strategy for Small-Scale Photovoltaic Systems Connected to Single-Phase Grids:
Active and Reactive Powers Control

Imene Yahyaoui
Federal University of Espírito Santo, Brazil

Fernando Tadeo
University of Valladolid, Spain

Marcelo Eduardo Vieira Segatto
Federal University of Espírito Santo, Brazil

ABSTRACT

This research chapter is concerned with the control of a photovoltaic powered plant connected to a single-phase grid. The system is equipped with dc–dc converters, which allow the panels' maximum power point to be tracked, and the voltage at their terminals to be regulated. Power is injected into the grid using an adequate control of a single-phase inverter connected to a filter and loads. In this research chapter, the active and reactive powers are controlled using the Voltage Oriented Control strategy, taking into account the grid and the loads characteristics. The control strategy is tested by simulation, and the obtained results prove its performance even under solar radiation change.

DOI: 10.4018/978-1-5225-1829-7.ch018

INTRODUCTION

Smart grids systems face challenges related to performing reliable operating, following the systems demands and the generated power by the sources (Gungor et al., 2013). This means that in these types of systems, which are based on highly controllable supply, they have to match a largely uncontrolled demand. Moreover, the variability in the climatic parameters, namely the solar radiation, makes necessary using reliable control strategies that ensure a safe operation for the power sources, from the one hand, and provide the loads with the power in need, from the other one (Penner, 2014). However, with the dual concerns of climate change and energy security, this can cause problems with the conventional system balancing methodologies, since penetration levels of energy sources and the loads demands are variable, in addition to its dependency on intermittent climatic parameters (Sivarasu et al., 2015; Yahyaoui, 2016b).

Fortunately, smart grids are characterized by their potential to mitigate these types of issues, since on one hand, they generally include flexible energy management strategies and power distribution, and on the other, they are able to make the system operating on both the supply-side and the demand-side (Logenthiran et al., 2012). This can be achieved in many ways from active demand-side management to temporary storage technologies, whether dedicated to electricity or sourced through a symbiotic supply (such as electric vehicles).

Moreover, smart grids systems encompass a wide range of technologies and applications, which include advanced metering infrastructures, that facilitate remote disconnection/ reconnection of consumers, load control, detection and response to outages, energy theft responsiveness, and monitoring of power quality and consumption (Valverde et al., 2016). They are also equipped with distribution, outage management and geographic information systems and advanced intelligent electronics devices. All of this equipment is to ensure a safe operating for the system and fulfilling the load demand in power (Siano et al., 2014).

Photovoltaic (PV) energy represents one of the main energy sources in smart grids systems, as well as wind turbine and fuel cells (Phuangpornpitak et al., 2013; Yahyaoui, 2016b). In smart grids plants, the power generated in excess can be stored or injected into the grid. In this case, PV grid connected systems must be associated to control strategies, which are needed to regulate the powers flow, following the grid restrictions and constraints. This is relevant, to not perturb the grid operation, the grid power quality, namely the frequency and the power factor, and to maintain a continuous and stable power supply for the loads (Reddy et al., 2014).

Generally, three- phase PV grid connected systems are used to inject power into the grids (Pattnaik et al., 2016). These type of grids are well studied in the literature, for which several control techniques are conceived. However, few research works focus on single- phase grids, since they are used in small-scale plants (Romero-Cadaval et al., 2013).

Thus, this research is concerned with the development of a control strategy for a PV single-phase system connected to the grid. The PV panels are coupled to boost converter, a single-phase inverter that injects the power converted from DC to AC into the grid (Figure 1).

The present work is organized as follows: first, the components models are explained in Section 1. Section 2 describes the strategy proposed to control the active and reactive powers. The results and discussion are detailed in Section 4. Finally, conclusions are presented in Section 5.

Figure 1. Scheme of the proposed photovoltaic system connected to a single-phase grid utility

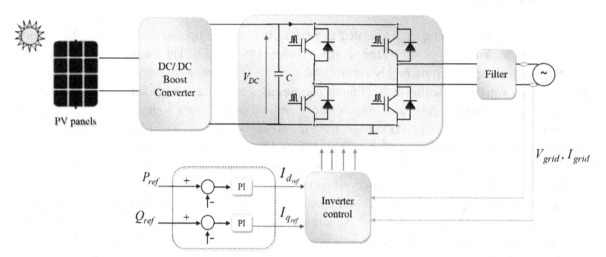

BACKGROUND

In the last few decades, more interest is focused on the electricity supply and infrastructure (Hertwich et al., 2015). This is justified by the fact that electricity usage is in continuous increase, and it is also very fluctuating (Moss, 2016). Thus, nowadays, the introduction of renewable sources, namely PV panels, wind turbines and fuel cells, for electricity generation becomes important, due to the instability of the fuel price (Mathiesen et al., 2015; Yahyaoui, 2016b). However, these renewable resources are intermittent and very sensitive to climatic parameters. Additionally, the generation patterns resulting from these renewable sources may have some similarities with the electricity demand patterns, but they are in general far from being equal. Hence, one of the solution for this issue is to generate electricity using these renewable sources, and injecting it into the grid, as the case of PV grid connected systems (Twidell, 2015).

In fact, PV energy is widely used to generate electricity for isolated plants as well as grid connected systems (Fahrenbruch, 2012). Indeed, several works are concerned with PV energy, namely those that deal with the PV power modelling (Qi et al., 2014), system sizing (Kaplani et al., 2012), climatic parameters that affect the PV operation prediction (Moballegh et al., 2014) and PV systems control (Von Appen et al., 2014). In this sense, several researchers focus on the control of three-phase systems connected to the grid (Song et al., 2013). However, few are those that concentrate on single- phase PV grid- connected systems (Gu et al., 2013). Among them, some researchers detail some models of these grids. Other works deal with the control, detailing the filters choice or the power control strategies (Pena-Alzola et al., 2013). In fact, several control strategies are conceived for such systems, namely the Current Hysteresis Control (CHC) (Swain et al., 2013). Other techniques use resonant PI regulator (Bergna et al., 2012) and the Voltage Oriented Control (VOC) (Ferreira et al., 2013). Indeed, the CHC requires the knowledge of the parameters of the load (Monfared et al., 2012, a). Resonant regulators have been used to control the three- phase grid connected systems: synchronous frame current regulators allow conventional compensation strategies to be used, to achieve zero steady-state error (Castilla et al., 2013).

In this work, the VOC is used to control the single-phase inverter, since this strategy allows the active and reactive powers to be controlled separately (Monfared et al., 2012, b). In fact, in this paper research, the active power P is controlled by adjusting the direct current I_d to its reference I_{dref} using a PI regulator (Monfared et al., 2012, a). The direct current reference I_{dref} is obtained by the DC voltage at the chopper outputs $\left(V_{DC}\right)$. The reactive power Q is controlled by regulating the power factor, which is ensured by correcting the error between the quadrature current I_q and its reference I_{qref} (Majumder, 2013).

To perform these two control loops, it is necessary to decouple the direct and the quadrature currents components. However, since the single– phase grid has one conductor phase and its neutral, it is necessary then to create a fictitious phase, which is orthogonal to the real phase, in order to perform the Park transformation in the frame (αβ-dq).

In the literature, several methods, that allow the fictitious phase to be created, are studied in depth. They allows generating an orthogonal fictitious phase to the real phase variable. These methods include the transport delay (Mnider et al., 2016), Hilbert transformation (Monfared et al., 2014), all-pass filter (Ramezani et al., 2016), and SOGI (Rashed et al., 2013) methods.

The method used in this research is to introduce a phase shift of 90° with respect to the real phase variable (Han et al., 2016). Then, the Phase Locked Loop (PLL) method is used to synchronize the rotating reference frame d, q with the grid voltage. Then, the voltages and currents fed by inverter are filtered using a filter connected between the inverter and the grid.

MAIN FOCUS OF THE CHAPTER

The dependence of PV plants connected to the grid on the climatic parameters, and especially the solar radiation, is considered their basic inconvenient, since, due to the absence of energy storage elements, this can generate significant issues for the PV grid connected systems, and also for the distribution networks, which can affect both the grid frequency and the voltage. Thus, the main solution is to develop control strategies, which maintain the system operating safely, even under extreme climatic conditions, namely the rapid change in the solar radiation. Thus, the present chapter is concerned with a control strategy of a specific type of PV grid connected plant, which is the single- phase PV systems. The studied system is composed of photovoltaic panels, which are connected to DC-DC converter, which allows the Maximum Power Point (MPP) to be tracked. The system components are connected to a single- phase inverter, which converts the DC signals to AC, suitable to the grid power supply requirements (frequency, voltage and current). Hence, using the Voltage Oriented Control (VOC) method for decoupling the voltage and current into their direct and quadrature components, it is possible then to control the active and reactive powers, by adjusting the direct and the quadrature currents to their references, using the convenient regulators. Therefore, in the present chapter, an appropriate control strategy for the active and reactive powers of a PV plant connected to a single- phase grid is explained in depth. Then, its reliability is tested by simulation using Matlab- Simulink.

Issues, Controversies, Problems

For the control of a PV single-phase grid connected system, two issues are faced: first, since a PV single-phase system is composed of one phase conductor with neutral return, two orthogonal signals are needed, to extend the synchronous (d, q) reference frame control strategies to a single-phase system. Hence, a second fictitious phase should be properly generated, to model a single-phase circuit as an equivalent virtual two-phase circuit. Second, the inverter operation must be synchronized to the grid, following its requirements. Thus, the inverter outputs must be synchronized in phase, as well in frequency, with the fundamental component of the grid voltage.

Numbered Lists

The following numbered lists is proposed, in such a way to describe in a coherent and comprehensive manner the topic proposed in this research chapter. In fact, the chapter begins by describing the models of the system components. Then, the control strategies adopted for the active and reactive powers of the PV single- phase grid connected system are explained in depth. After that, the obtained results are presented and explained. Finally, the chapter ends by conclusions, in which the authors mention the impact of the proposed strategy for smart grids security systems. The numbered list is explained now:

1. System Components Modelling:
    a. Photovoltaic panels
    b. Incremental conductance for MPPT
    c. Single- phase inverter
2. Principle of the Control Strategy:
    a. Principle of the fictitious phase generation
    b. Principle of the Voltage Oriented Control method
    c. Principle of the single- phase inverter synchronization to the grid
    d. Principle of the direct and quadrature currents control loops
3. Results and Discussion,
4. Conclusion.

SOLUTIONS AND RECOMMENDATIONS

System Components Modelling

Photovoltaic Panels

The photovoltaic panel is modelled using the one-diode non-linear model, which considers the PV cells as a current source in parallel with a diode. These components are linked to serial and parallel resistance, which describe the resistance resultant by the contact between the wafers and electric conductors, and the defects during recombination phenomena, respectively (Ciulla et al., 2014). This model depends on the solar radiation $G(t)$, the ambient temperature $T_a(t)$ at the panel surface, and the panel parameters namely the number of photovoltaic cells connected in series, the short- circuit current and the open-circuit voltage at the reference temperature. The model evaluates the photovoltaic current $I_c(t)$ and power $P_{pv}(t)$ (Laudani et al., 2014). The adopted model is described by (1)-(6) (Siddique et al., 2013; Yahyaoui, 2016b):

$$I_c = I_{ph}(t) - I_r(t)\left[\exp\left(\frac{V_c(t) + R_s I_c(t)}{V_{t\_T_a}}\right) - 1\right] - \frac{V_c(t) + R_s I_c(t)}{R_p} \tag{1}$$

$$I_{ph}(t) = \frac{G(t)}{G_{ref}} I_{sc}(t) \tag{2}$$

$$I_{sc}(t) = I_{sc\_T_{ref}}\left(1 + a\left(T_a(t) - T_{ref}\right)\right) \tag{3}$$

$$I_r(t) = I_{r\_T_{ref}}\left(\frac{T_a(t)}{T_{ref}}\right)^{\frac{3}{n}} \exp\left(\frac{-qV_g}{nK_B}\left(\frac{1}{T_a(t)} - \frac{1}{T_{ref}}\right)\right) \tag{4}$$

$$I_{r\_T_{ref}} = \frac{I_{sc\_T_{ref}}}{\exp\left(\frac{qV_{c\_T_{ref}}}{nK_B T_{ref}}\right) - 1} \tag{5}$$

where:

$T_a(t)$: the ambient temperature at the panel surface (K),

$G(t)$: the solar radiance at the panel surface (W/m²),

$I_c(t)$: the estimated photovoltaic cell current (A),

$I_{ph}(t)$: the generated photo-current at G (A),

$I_r(t)$: the reverse saturation current at T_a (A),

$V_c(t)$: the open circuit voltage of the photovoltaic cell (V),

R_s: the serial resistance of the photovoltaic module (Ω),

V_{t_Ta}: the thermal potential at the ambient temperature (V),

R_p: the parallel resistance of the photovoltaic module (Ω),

G_{ref}: the solar radiation at reference conditions (W/m^2),

$I_{sc}(t)$: the short circuit current for T_a (A),

$I_{sc\_T_{ref}}$: the short circuit current per cell at the reference temperature T_{ref} (A),

a: the temperature coefficient for the short circuit current (K^{-1}),

$I_{r\_T_{ref}}$: the reverse saturation current for T_{ref} (A),

n: the quality factor,

q: the electron charge (C),

V_g : the Gap energy (e.V),

K_B : the Boltzmann coefficient (J/K),

$V_{c\_T_{ref}}$: the open circuit voltage per cell at T_{ref} (V).

A photovoltaic cell produces low electrical current and voltage. Hence, it is necessary to connect several PV cells to increase first the PV voltage, by connecting n_s PV cells in series, which gives the PV module. Then, depending on the application, these PV modules are connected in series and/ or in parallel, using n_p modules in parallel, and hence obtaining the PV panel. Therefore, the power P_{pv} generated by the PV panel is then described by (Yahyaoui et al., 2014; Yahyaoui et al., 2016, a; Guenounou et al., 2016):

$$P_{pv}\left(t\right) = n_s n_p V_c\left(t\right) \left(\begin{array}{c} I_{ph}\left(t\right) - I_r\left(t\right) \left(\exp\left(\dfrac{V_c\left(t\right) + R_s I_c\left(t\right)}{V_{t\_T_a}} \right) - 1 \right) \\ -\dfrac{V_c\left(t\right) + R_s I_c\left(t\right)}{R_p} \end{array} \right) \tag{6}$$

where:

n_s : the number of serial photovoltaic cells,

n_p : the number of parallel photovoltaic modules.

Incremental Conductance for MPPT

The photovoltaic panel has non-linear characteristic for the voltage- current, as it has been seen in the PV panel-modelling paragraph. In addition, the PV power generated depends on the climatic parameters, namely the solar radiation and the ambient temperature. However, there exists only one point, called Maximum Power Point (MPP), on the power–voltage curve, for which the PV power generated is maximum. Indeed, the MPP varies with the climatic conditions, which are intermittent. Additionally, PV energy conversion is very low (14% for monocrystalline PV panels), and mismatch between source and load characteristics causes significant power losses (Rauschenbach, 2012). Consequently, maximization of power output with greater efficiency is very important, in such a way to use all the power generated by the PV panel. Thus, Maximum power point tracking (MPPT) is a technique employed to extract maximum power available from the PV module (Kheldoun et al., 2016). The MPPT allows the PV operating voltage corresponding to the MPP to be tracked and the operating point at MPP to be maintained, in such a way to extract maximum power from the PV array (Fathabadi, 2016).

In the literature, several conventional MPPT techniques have been studied. Hence, the selection of a particular MPPT technique is a confusing task, since each technique has its advantages and drawbacks. Among the MPPT methods, researchers studied the Perturb and Observe (P&O) method, which consists in perturbing the PV array voltage and seeing its effect on the PV power generated, (Bizon, 2016). However, the P&O technique has a problem of oscillations around the MPP, due to which there is considerable loss of PV power. In addition, the response of P&O algorithm is slow under fast changing environmental conditions, especially in the solar radiation (Zainuri et al., 2014). Another method used for MPPT is the Look up Table method, which consists in attributing a power value for each set of solar radiation and temperature (Malathy et al., 2013). The look-up table principle is considered the main drawback of this MPP method, since it considers all the climatic parameters by intervals, which causes losses of power. Additionally, Fuzzy logic method is used for MPPT (Hussamo et al., 2013). In fact, this method consists in deducing, using the expert knowledge and fuzzy rules, the duty cycle, which is used to control the DC- DC converter (Muthuramalingam et al., 2014). The main disadvantage of this method is that it requires big database, and that it depends on the expert knowledge. Other method for the MPP is the incremental conductance method, which consists in seeing the effect of perturbation in the PV voltage on the PV current (Bizon, 2016). This MPPT method has the advantages of P&O MPPT method. In addition to that, it is characterized by its ability to detect the solar radiation change, by testing the PV current variation (Tey et al., 2014; Yahyaoui, 2016b).

Thus, MPPT algorithms differ in complexity and tracking accuracy, but they all require the sensing of the PV current and voltage using the off-the–shelf hardware. Thanks to its efficiency, in this chapter, the incremental conductance algorithm for MPPT is used to track the MPP of the photovoltaic panels, and generate the control signal for the boost converter (Tey et al., 2014, Yahyaoui et al., 2016, b) (Figure 2). In fact, this method uses the current ripple in the chopper output I_{pv}, to maximize the panel power P_{pv} using the relation between the current and voltage continuously identified online (Yahyaoui et al., 2016, b). Indeed, the algorithm tests the actual conductance $-\dfrac{I_{pv}}{V_{pv}}$ and the incremental conductance $\dfrac{dI_{pv}}{dV_{pv}}$ as follows (Ali et al., 2015, a & b; Yahyaoui et al., 2016, b):

If $\dfrac{dI_{pv}}{dV_{pv}} \succ -\dfrac{I_{pv}}{V_{pv}}$, then the operating point is on the left of the MPP, so α is varied to increase V_{pv}.

$$(7)$$

If $\dfrac{dI_{pv}}{dV_{pv}} \prec -\dfrac{I_{pv}}{V_{pv}}$, then the operating point is on the right of the MPP, so α is varied to decrease V_{pv}.

$$(8)$$

If $\dfrac{dI_{pv}}{dV_{pv}} \approx -\dfrac{I_{pv}}{V_{pv}}$, then the operating point is in the MPP, so, the value of α is maintained. $\quad(9)$

where dI_{pv} and dV_{pv} are the PV current and voltage variations, respectively.

Thus, the duty cycle α, used to generate the PWM signal for the MOSFET switching, is calculated using (10) (Ali et al., 2015, a; Yahyaoui et al., 2016, b):

$$\frac{V_{dc}}{V_{pv}} = \frac{1}{1-\alpha} \qquad (10)$$

Figure 2. Scheme of the control principle of the DC-DC converter for MPPT

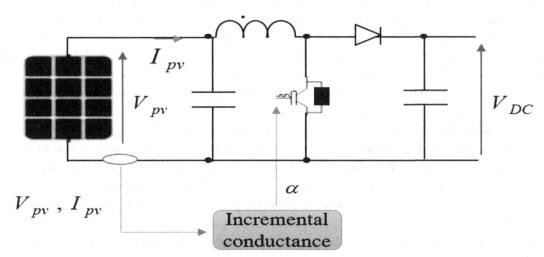

Single-Phase Inverter

Inverters that connect PV panels to the grid involve major tasks. The first is to convert DC signals to AC, and then inject the sinusoidal current into the grid. Hence, it must also be able to detect an islanding situation, and respond appropriately to persons and equipment protection. In this research, a full bridge inverter composed of two legs is used to convert DC voltage and current to AC voltage and current (Figure 3). Hence, a PWM signal is generated to control the switchers. Indeed, the control signal PWM is obtained by comparing the modulating waves, which is characterized by the frequency f_r and the amplitude V_r, with the carrier wave, characterized by a frequency $f_p >> f_r$, and the amplitude V_p f_p (Chang et al., 2014). The first leg is controlled by a signal $V_{mod\,ulation}$, while the second leg is controlled by $-V_{mod\,ulation}$. Hence, the PWM signals obtained and used to control the switchers are characterized by the frequency f_p (Chang et al., 2014) (Figure 4).

Figure 3. Scheme of the single-phase full bridge inverter

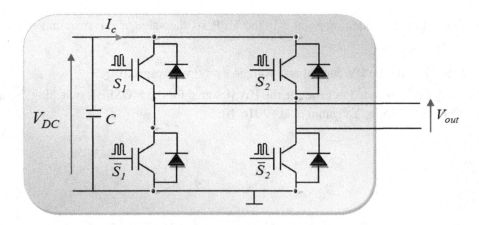

The switches T_1, T_1', T_2 and T_2' are connected as follows:

- If $V_{\mathrm{mod}\,ulation} > V_{carrier}$, then T_1 is on.
- If $V_{\mathrm{mod}\,ulation} < V_{carrier}$, then T_1' is on.
- If $-V_{\mathrm{mod}\,ulation} > V_{carrier}$, then T_2 is on.
- If $-V_{\mathrm{mod}\,ulation} < V_{carrier}$, then T_2' is on.

Hence, the inverter output voltage is evaluated by:

$$V_{out}(t) = V_{AN}\left(t\right) - V_{BN}\left(t\right) \tag{11}$$

Principle of the Control Strategy

Principle of the Fictitious Phase Generation

As it has previously been explained, the single-phase circuit has one phase conductor with a neutral return. In order to extend the synchronous (d, q) reference frame control strategies to single-phase systems, two orthogonal signals are needed. Hence, a second fictitious phase should be properly generated, to model a single-phase circuit as an equivalent virtual two-phase circuit. In the literature, several works for generating the fictitious phase are studied, including the transport delay (Martin-Martinez et al., 2013), Hilbert transformation (Saitou et al., 2002), all-pass filter (Kwon et al., 2001), and SOGI (Ciobotaru et al., 2006) methods have been conceived. In fact, for the Hilbert transformation, due to its huge sensitivity to input disturbances and frequency fluctuations, it has found no industrial acceptance. On the other hand, the original transformation brings non-causality and is not practically realizable. All-pass filter (APF) method for fictitious phase generation approximates the response of the Hilbert transformation and can be easily implemented in discrete platforms. This method has been proven to be an attractive solution. Usually the second phase is implemented by using a first-order APF with the following transfer function. The transport delay method consists in performing a phase shift of 90°, with respect to the fundamental frequency of the input signal. This can be realized through the use of a first-in-first-out memory, with the delay adjusted to one fourth the number of total samples of a cycle of the fundamental frequency (Monfared, 2012).

Consequently, all fictitious phase generation techniques are frequency dependent, so problems can occur when the grid frequency has fluctuations. Usually these techniques receive a frequency feedback from the PLL block to boost the performance. In this research, the transport delay method is used to generate the fictitious phase, since it is simple and can be implemented by digital controllers without the need for tuning any parameters (Monfared, 2012) (Figure 5).

Principle of the Voltage Oriented Control Method

The Voltage Oriented control (VOC) is an indirect method for the direct and quadrature currents control. In fact, it consists in regulating the active and reactive currents, by orienting the current vector following the line voltage vector. Indeed, the VOC is performed in the direct-quadrature (d, q) synchronous refer-

Figure 4. Generation of the PWM signal for the single-phase inverter control

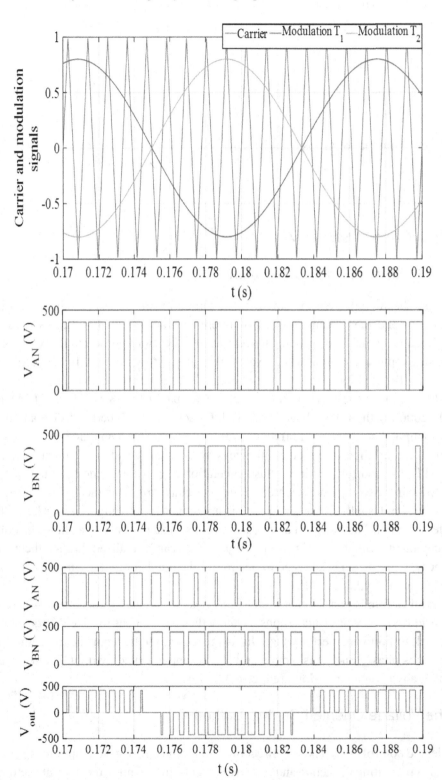

Figure 5. Transport delay method to generate the fictitious phase signal

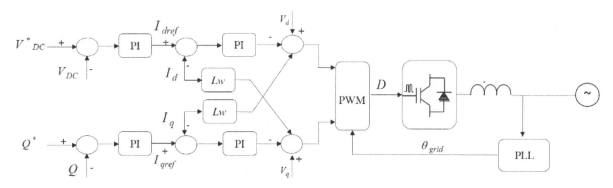

ence frame, where the error between the direct $\left(I_d\right)$ and quadrature $\left(I_q\right)$ components of the AC current and their reference values are fed to PI controllers (Blaabjerg et al., 2006; Monfared, 2012; Khajehoddin et al., 2013). Hence, the PI regulators generate the reference voltage components for the direct and quadrature voltages V_d and V_q, which are applied to the single- phase inverter, using a PWM modulator. Therefore, the currents and voltages are transformed to the synchronous reference frame, where the zero steady-state error is ensured using proportional-integral (PI) controllers. Thus, the internal current control loops ensure high dynamics and static performance, although its dependency on the applied current control strategy and the connected AC network conditions (Figure 6).

The closed transfer function of the d-q current loops is given by:

$$\frac{I_d\left(s\right)}{I_{d,ref}\left(s\right)} = \frac{I_q\left(s\right)}{I_{q,ref}\left(s\right)} = \frac{k_p s + k_i}{Ls^2 + \left(k_p + R\right)s + k_i} \tag{12}$$

where I_{dq} and $I_{dq,ref}$ are respectively, the measured and reference currents.

Hence, using the standard form for the second-order transfer function, the damping ratio ζ and the natural frequency w_n are deduced (13- 14):

Figure 6. Block-diagram of the VOC for single-phase inverter

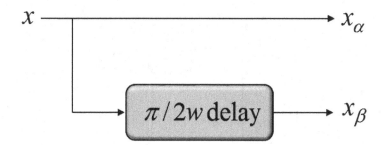

$$\zeta = \frac{k_p + R}{2\sqrt{k_i L}} \qquad (13)$$

and:

$$w_n = \sqrt{\frac{k_i}{L}} \qquad (14)$$

Hence, the current controllers gains are evaluated by (15- 16):

$$k_p = 2\xi w_n L - R \qquad (15)$$

$$k_i = L w_n^{2} \qquad (16)$$

Principle of the Single-Phase Inverter Synchronization to the Grid

The phase synchronization consists in detecting the signal error of the phase angle at the input and the output, using the phase detection. Then, the corrected signal is filtered. This allows the voltage-controlled oscillator to generate the output signal, and thus correcting the phase error and maintaining the synchronism.

Hence, the PI controller sets the reference signal of the quadrature voltage V_q to zero (Figure 7).

In the literature, several synchronization techniques are conceived. However, they differ in the manner of implementation. For instance, single-phase PLLs are divided into the transport delay-based (Mnider et al., 2016), Hilbert transformation-based (Monfared et al., 2014), all pass filter-based (Ramezani et al., 2016), and SOGI (Rashed et al., 2013) and SOGI PLL (Rashed et al., 2013). Currently, the synchronous reference frame PLL (SRF-PLL) is the most common technique used for single phase grid synchronization. In case of single- phase synchronization (SF-PLL), without harmonic distortions or unbalance and with a high bandwidth, the phase synchronization provides a fast and precise detection of the phase and amplitude of the utility voltage vector. If high-order harmonics distort the utility voltage, the SF-PLL

Figure 7. Block diagram for the synchronization principle

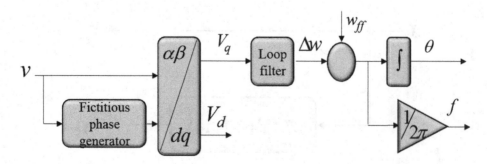

Figure 8. Block diagram for the frequency and phase generation

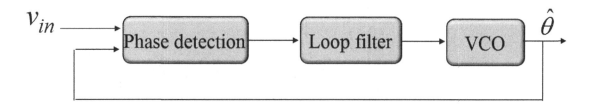

operates when it is reduced at the cost of the PLL response speed reduction, to reject and/ or cancel out the effect of these harmonics on the voltage. Hence, the SF- PLL generates a synchronized voltage output, eliminating high order- harmonics, since the 90-degree-shifted orthogonal component of the single phase input signal is created (Figure 8).

Principle of the Direct and Quadrature Currents Control Loops

Two current loops are used to control the direct and quadrature grid currents, I_d and I_q, respectively, which allows the active and reactive powers to be controlled (Pattnaik et al., 2016). In fact, these components are compared with their respective reference components I_{dref} and I_{qref}, and then, the resultant errors are injected to the PI regulators, in such a way to generate the control signals of the single- phase inverter. Hence, the AC signals are generated, following the grid characteristics (frequency and phase). Indeed, the direct current component controls the grid active power flow, while the quadrature component is used to regulate the reactive power flow between the PV plant and the grid. Hence, a voltage loop, which regulates the mean and measured voltages at the boost outputs, is used to generate the reference of the direct current I_{dref}. While, the quadrature current reference I_{qref} is generated by the phase control loop. The DC bus voltage is maintained constant by a voltage loop, which allows the continuous active power flow between the PV array and the grid, to be controlled. Thus, the PI regulator uses the difference between the reference and measured signals of the DC voltage, to generate the reference signal of the direct current I_{dref} (17):

$$C_{DC}\frac{dV_{DC}}{dt} = \frac{P_{pv} - P_{grid}}{V_{DC}} \tag{17}$$

The reactive power is adjusted by the power coefficient control. In fact, it is ensured by generating the reference signal of the reactive current component I_{qref}, thanks to a PI regulator. A simplified block diagram of the reactive power control loop is described by Figure 9.

Figure 9. Block diagram of the reactive power control

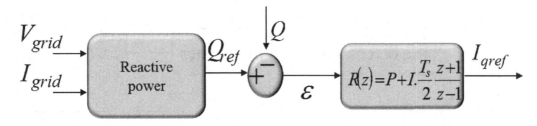

RESULTS AND DISCUSSION

The VOC control reliability for the single-phase PV system connected to the grid is tested by simulation, using Matlab- Simulink software (Figure 1). The system is composed of photovoltaic panels, a boost converter, which allows the voltage at the PV outputs to be regulated and the MPP to be tracked, a single- phase inverter equipped with its control block, a filter and a single- phase grid.

The PV panel is modeled according to the specification of the commercial PV panel from Trina Solar. The DC link capacitor considered in this research is of 100 µF, and the AC filter is characterized by its parameters $L = 16.8$ mH and $R = 33$ Ω. The input transformer provides a 120 V peak at its terminals. The modulation of each cell is done using unipolar Sinusoidal Pulse Width Modulation (SPWM) generated by comparing a triangular signal with frequency $f_r = 3.780$ kHz to the carrier sinusoidal signal with a frequency $f_c = 60$ Hz. The simulation is carried out in Matlab–Simulink, where the converter is modeled according to (11). The operation of the single-phase inverter is simulated for three different operating conditions, as shown in Figure 10. In the first one, the solar radiation is equal to 500 W/m². At $t = 2$ s, the solar radiation increases to 1000 W/m². Finally, at $t = 4$ s, the solar radiation decreases from 1000 W/m² to 500 W/m².

First, the incremental conductance for MPPT is tested using a variation of the solar radiation (Figure 10- Figure 11). The results show that the incremental conductance algorithm use for MPPT, allows the MPP to be tracked perfectly, since the instantaneous and the incremented impedance $-\dfrac{I_{pv}}{V_{pv}}$ and $\dfrac{dI_{pv}}{dV_{pv}}$, respectively, are the same and equal to zero. The incremental conductance algorithm for MPPT gives good results, even when the solar radiation changes. Thus, the MPPT gives references around the optimum point, and the corresponding duty cycle α, which is used to control the switcher of the boost chopper, is generated (Figure 11).

The voltage at the chopper output is regulated using a PI regulator. Figure 12 shows that it follows the voltage reference, in the three operating conditions. The regulation of the voltage V_{DC} at the chopper outputs allows the reference direct current I_{dref} to be generated, which is used to control the measured direct current I_d, and hence the system active power (Figure 13). The regulation of the reactive power Q is performed by generating the reference quadrature current I_{qref}, using the regulation principle explained in Figure 9. This current is used to regulate the measured quadrature current I_q, which follows its reference, as it is shown in Figure 13.

Figure 10. Photovoltaic panel characteristics

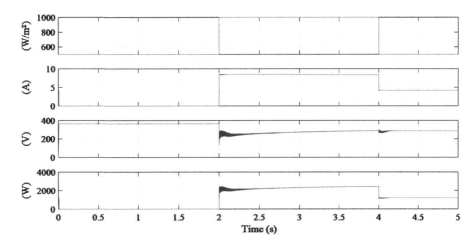

Figure 11. Results for incremental conductance MPPT

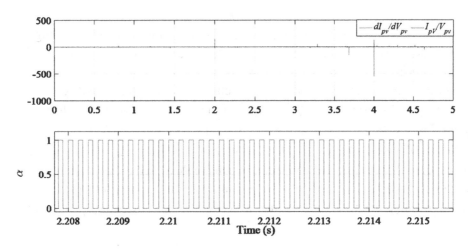

Figure 12. Output voltage at the boost converter terminals

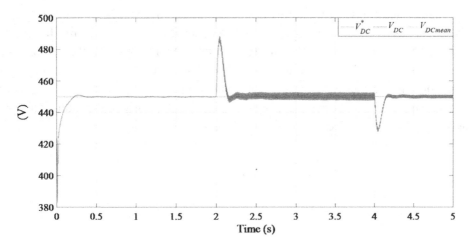

Figure 13. Direct and quadrature currents characteristics

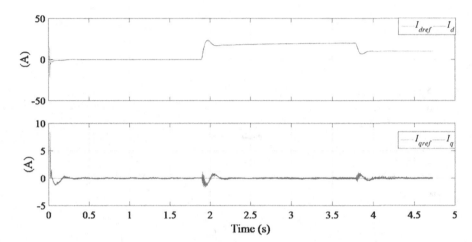

The direct and quadrature currents are used to generate the direct and quadrature voltages, which are the components of the inverter voltage, and to deduce the modulation index of the PWM signal, which control the single- phase inverter. The voltage at the inverter terminals is given by Figure 14, and the corresponding modulation index is depicted in Figure 15. The control of the single- phase inverter allows the grid-voltage and current to be in phase (Figure 16).

The regulation of the direct and quadrature currents allows the active and reactive powers to be regulated. The measured powers P and Q, depicted in Figure 17 and Figure 18, show that they follow their references P_{ref} and Q_{ref}.

Hence, following the detailed study, the VOC method for controlling the single- phase inverters allows generating the signals that controls the converter, which are then used to control the active and reactive powers, using PI controllers. The method is simple and the simulation results proves the reliability of the technique in fulfilling the grid requirements, which are the grid frequency, voltage and current.

FUTURE RESEARCH DIRECTIONS

This work can be applied for several photovoltaic applications. Hence, in a future work, the authors aim to use the obtained results in studying the effect of intermittent changes of the climatic parameters in the performance of single- phase grid connected inverters. More precisely, the authors aim to study the voltage regulation for small and medium scales PV plants. In addition, it is possible to study the frequency regulation during constant, variable solar radiations and even during shading, which affects the PV panels operation. The authors are concerned also with the study of the faults diagnosis of such plants, in such a way to enhance the photovoltaic efficiency.

Figure 14. Voltage at the single-phase inverter terminals

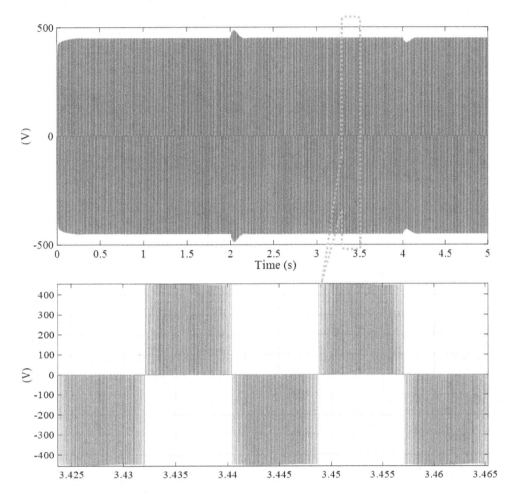

Figure 15. PWM signal for the inverter control

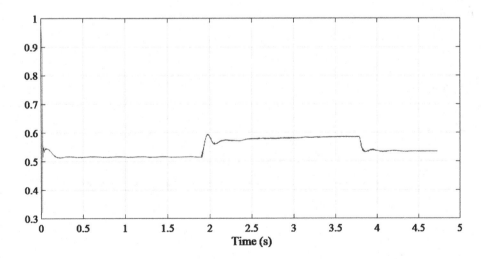

Figure 16. Grid voltage and current

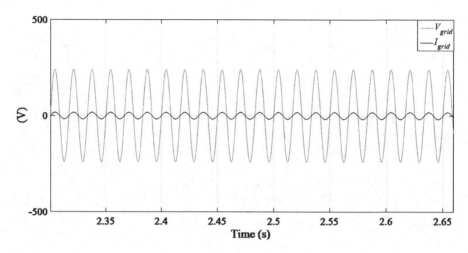

Figure 17. Active power control results

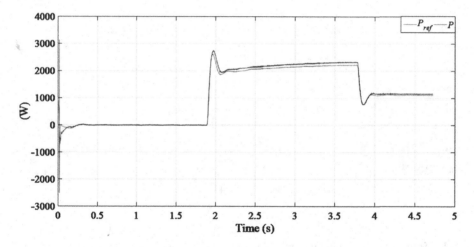

Figure 18. Reactive power control results

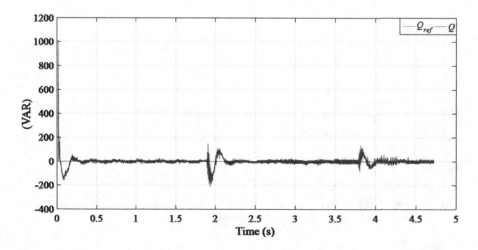

Table 1. Explanation of the used symbols and their definitions

Symbol	Definition	Symbol	Definition
a	Temperature coefficient for the short circuit current $\left(K^{-1} \right)$	k_p, k_i	Current controller gains
AC	Alternative current	n_p	Number of parallel photovoltaic modules
DC	Direct Current	P	Active power (W)
$\dfrac{dI_{pv}}{dV_{pv}}$	Incremental conductance (1/Ω)	P_{pv}	Photovoltaic power (W)
G	Solar radiation (W/m²)	Q	Reactive power (VAR)
G_{ref}	Solar radiation at reference conditions (W/m^2)	q	Electron charge (C)
f_c	Carrier wave frequency (Hz)	R_p	Parallel resistance of the photovoltaic module (Ω)
f_r	Modulation wave frequency (Hz)	R_s	Serial resistance of the photovoltaic module (Ω),
$I_c\left(t \right)$	Estimated photovoltaic cell current (A)	$V_c\left(t \right)$	Open circuit voltage of the photovoltaic cell (V),
$I_{dq}, I_{dq,ref}$	Measured and reference direct and quadratic currents, respectively (A)	V_{t_Ta}	Thermal potential at the ambient temperature (V)
I_{grid}, V_{grid}	Grid current and voltage (A, V)	V_g	Gap energy (e.V)
$I_{ph}\left(t \right)$	generated photo-current at G (A)	V_r	Modulation wave amplitude (V)
$I_r\left(t \right)$	Reverse saturation current at T_a (A)	$V_{c\_T_{ref}}$	Open circuit voltage per cell at T_{ref} (V)
$I_{sc}\left(t \right)$	Short circuit current for T_a (A)	α	Chopper duty cycle
$I_{sc\_T_{ref}}$	Short circuit current per cell at the reference temperature T_{ref} (A)	V_c	Carrier wave amplitude (V)
$I_{r\_T_{ref}}$	Reverse saturation current for T_{ref} (A)	VOC	Voltage Oriented Control
$-\dfrac{I_{pv}}{V_{pv}}$	Actual conductance (1/Ω)	ζ	Damping ratio
K_B	Boltzmann coefficient (J/K)	w_n	Natural frequency (Hz)

CONCLUSION

In this chapter, a practical strategy for a single- phase PV system connected to the grid is studied in depth. This study demonstrated the relevance of the active and reactive powers control, to provide power quality that follows the parameters required by the grid. This is important, since it ensures the grid security, and thus, it can be applied in smart grid systems. The control strategy concept used the Voltage Oriented Control (VOC) method, to control the system active and reactive powers. Following the above conducted studies, it has been proven that the VOC allows the active and reactive powers to be controlled by regulating the errors between the direct and quadrature currents and their references, using simple PI regulators. Moreover, this research shows that the VOC allows the voltage and current of the grid to be in phase. Hence, one can conclude that VOC presents good results in controlling a single- phase PV plant connected to the grid. To evaluate the reliability of the adopted control strategy, it was tested even during solar radiation change, and the results prove its good efficiency. Hence, this is important for the smart grids safe operation and security, since the climatic parameters variability can affect significantly the smart grids operation, and therefore the distribution network and the power quality and continuity during the power supply.

ACKNOWLEDGMENT

Dr. Yahyaoui is funded by the project 0838/2015 from the Brazilian Foundation for Research and Innovation of Espiritu Santo (FAPES) and a grant from CAPES/Brazil. Pr. Tadeo is partially supported by the seventh Framework program FP7, under grant agreement N° 288145, within the ocean of tomorrow joint call 2011. Dr. M. E. V. Segatto is partially supported by CNPq/Brazil (CNPq 307470/2012-1).

REFERENCES

Ali, A., Wang, Y., Li, W., & He, X. (2015a). Implementation of simple moving voltage average technique with direct control incremental conductance method to optimize the efficiency of DC microgrid. *Proceedings of the 2015 International Conference on Emerging Technologies (ICET)* (pp. 1-5). IEEE.

Ali, A., Li, W., & He, X. (2015b). Simple Moving Voltage Average Incremental Conductance MPPT Technique with Direct Control Method under No uniform Solar Irradiance Conditions. *International Journal of Photoenergy*.

Bergna, G., Suul, J. A., Berne, E., Egrot, P., Lefranc, P., Vannier, J. C., & Molinas, M. (2012, October). Mitigating DC-side power oscillations and negative sequence load currents in modular multilevel converters under unbalanced faults-first approach using resonant PI. *Proceedings of the 38th Annual Conference on IEEE Industrial Electronics Society IECON '12* (pp. 537-542). IEEE. doi:10.1109/IECON.2012.6388769

Bizon, N. (2016). Global Extremum Seeking Control of the power generated by a Photovoltaic Array under Partially Shaded Conditions. *Energy Conversion and Management, 109*, 71–85. doi:10.1016/j.enconman.2015.11.046

Castilla, M., Miret, J., Camacho, A., Matas, J., & de Vicuña, L. G. (2013). Reduction of current harmonic distortion in three-phase grid-connected photovoltaic inverters via resonant current control. *IEEE Transactions on Industrial Electronics*, *60*(4), 1464–1472. doi:10.1109/TIE.2011.2167734

Chang, C. H., Lin, Y. H., Chen, Y. M., & Chang, Y. R. (2014). Simplified reactive power control for single-phase grid-connected photovoltaic inverters. *IEEE Transactions on Industrial Electronics*, *61*(5), 2286–2296. doi:10.1109/TIE.2013.2271600

Ciulla, G., Brano, V. L., Di Dio, V., & Cipriani, G. (2014). A comparison of different one-diode models for the representation of I–V characteristic of a PV cell. *Renewable & Sustainable Energy Reviews*, *32*, 684–696. doi:10.1016/j.rser.2014.01.027

Fahrenbruch, A., & Bube, R. (2012). *Fundamentals of solar cells: photovoltaic solar energy conversion*. Elsevier.

Fathabadi, H. (2016). Novel photovoltaic based battery charger including novel high efficiency step-up DC/DC converter and novel high accurate fast maximum power point tracking controller. *Energy Conversion and Management*, *110*, 200–211. doi:10.1016/j.enconman.2015.12.025

Ferreira, A., Carvalho, A., Martins, A. P., Pereira, F., & Sobrado, V. (2013). Dynamic Performance of Voltage Oriented Control Method Applied in a Voltage Source Converter. *Proceedings of studECE '13*.

Fox-Penner, P. (2014). *Smart Power Anniversary Edition: Climate Change, the Smart Grid, and the Future of Electric Utilities*. Island Press.

Gu, B., Dominic, J., Lai, J. S., Chen, C. L., LaBella, T., & Chen, B. (2013). High reliability and efficiency single-phase transformerless inverter for grid-connected photovoltaic systems. *IEEE Transactions on Power Electronics*, *28*(5), 2235–2245. doi:10.1109/TPEL.2012.2214237

Guenounou, A., Malek, A., & Aillerie, M. (2016). Comparative performance of PV panels of different technologies over one year of exposure: Application to a coastal Mediterranean region of Algeria. *Energy Conversion and Management*, *114*, 356–363. doi:10.1016/j.enconman.2016.02.044

Gungor, V. C., Sahin, D., Kocak, T., Ergut, S., Buccella, C., Cecati, C., & Hancke, G. P. (2013). A survey on smart grid potential applications and communication requirements. *IEEE Transactions on Industrial Informatics*, *9*(1), 28–42. doi:10.1109/TII.2012.2218253

Han, Y., Luo, M., Zhao, X., Guerrero, J. M., & Xu, L. (2016). Comparative Performance Evaluation of Orthogonal-Signal-Generators-Based Single-Phase PLL Algorithms—A Survey. *IEEE Transactions on Power Electronics*, *31*(5), 3932–3944. doi:10.1109/TPEL.2015.2466631

Hertwich, E. G., Gibon, T., Bouman, E. A., Arvesen, A., Suh, S., Heath, G. A., & Shi, L. et al. (2015). Integrated life-cycle assessment of electricity-supply scenarios confirms global environmental benefit of low-carbon technologies. *Proceedings of the National Academy of Sciences of the United States of America*, *112*(20), 6277–6282. doi:10.1073/pnas.1312753111 PMID:25288741

Houssamo, I., Locment, F., & Sechilariu, M. (2013). Experimental analysis of impact of MPPT methods on energy efficiency for photovoltaic power systems. *International Journal of Electrical Power & Energy Systems*, *46*, 98–107. doi:10.1016/j.ijepes.2012.10.048

Kaplani, E., & Kaplanis, S. (2012). A stochastic simulation model for reliable PV system sizing providing for solar radiation fluctuations. *Applied Energy*, *97*, 970–981. doi:10.1016/j.apenergy.2011.12.016

Kheldoun, A., Bradai, R., Boukenoui, R., & Mellit, A. (2016). A new golden section method-based maximum power point tracking algorithm for photovoltaic systems. *Energy Conversion and Management*, *111*, 125–136. doi:10.1016/j.enconman.2015.12.039

Laudani, A., Fulginei, F. R., & Salvini, A. (2014). High performing extraction procedure for the one-diode model of a photovoltaic panel from experimental I–V curves by using reduced forms. *Solar Energy*, *103*, 316–326. doi:10.1016/j.solener.2014.02.014

Logenthiran, T., Srinivasan, D., & Shun, T. Z. (2012). Demand side management in smart grid using heuristic optimization. *IEEE Transactions on Smart Grid*, *3*(3), 1244–1252. doi:10.1109/TSG.2012.2195686

Majumder, R. (2013). Reactive power compensation in single-phase operation of microgrid. *IEEE Transactions on Industrial Electronics*, *60*(4), 1403–1416. doi:10.1109/TIE.2012.2193860

Malathy, S., & Ramaprabha, R. (2013). Maximum Power Point Tracking Based on Look up Table Approach. *Advanced Materials Research*, *768*, 124–130. doi:10.4028/www.scientific.net/AMR.768.124

Mathiesen, B. V., Lund, H., Connolly, D., Wenzel, H., Østergaard, P. A., Möller, B., & Hvelplund, F. K. et al. (2015). Smart Energy Systems for coherent 100% renewable energy and transport solutions. *Applied Energy*, *145*, 139–154. doi:10.1016/j.apenergy.2015.01.075

Mnider, A. M., Atkinson, D. J., Dahidah, M., Zbede, Y. B., & Armstrong, M. (2016, March). A programmable cascaded LPF based PLL scheme for single-phase grid-connected inverters. *Proceedings of the 2016 7th International Renewable Energy Congress (IREC)* (pp. 1-6). IEEE. doi:10.1109/IREC.2016.7478935

Moballegh, S., & Jiang, J. (2014). Modeling, prediction, and experimental validations of power peaks of PV arrays under partial shading conditions. *IEEE Transactions on Sustainable Energy*, *5*(1), 293–300. doi:10.1109/TSTE.2013.2282077

Monfared, M., & Golestan, S. (2012). a). Control strategies for single-phase grid integration of small-scale renewable energy sources: A review. *Renewable & Sustainable Energy Reviews*, *16*(7), 4982–4993. doi:10.1016/j.rser.2012.04.017

Monfared, M., Golestan, S., & Guerrero, J. M. (2014). Analysis, design, and experimental verification of a synchronous reference frame voltage control for single-phase inverters. *IEEE Transactions on Industrial Electronics*, *61*(1), 258–269. doi:10.1109/TIE.2013.2238878

Monfared, M., Sanatkar, M., & Golestan, S. (2012). b). Direct active and reactive power control of single-phase grid-tie converters. *IET Power Electronics*, *5*(8), 1544–1550. doi:10.1049/iet-pel.2012.0131

Moss, T., & Marvin, S. (2016). *Urban infrastructure in transition: networks, buildings and plans.* Routledge.

Muthuramalingam, M., & Manoharan, P. S. (2014). Comparative analysis of distributed MPPT controllers for partially shaded standalone photovoltaic systems. *Energy Conversion and Management*, *86*, 286–299. doi:10.1016/j.enconman.2014.05.044

Pattnaik, S., Dash, R., Swain, S. C., & Mohapatra, P. (2016, March). Control of active and reactive power of a three phase grid connected photovoltaic system. *Proceedings of the2016 International Conference on Circuit, Power and Computing Technologies (ICCPCT)* (pp. 1-6). IEEE. doi:10.1109/ICCPCT.2016.7530227

Pena-Alzola, R., Liserre, M., Blaabjerg, F., Sebastián, R., Dannehl, J., & Fuchs, F. W. (2013). Analysis of the passive damping losses in LCL-filter-based grid converters. *IEEE Transactions on Power Electronics*, *28*(6), 2642–2646. doi:10.1109/TPEL.2012.2222931

Phuangpornpitak, N., & Tia, S. (2013). Opportunities and challenges of integrating renewable energy in smart grid system. *Energy Procedia*, *34*, 282–290. doi:10.1016/j.egypro.2013.06.756

Qi, J., Zhang, Y., & Chen, Y. (2014). Modeling and maximum power point tracking (MPPT) method for PV array under partial shade conditions. *Renewable Energy*, *66*, 337–345. doi:10.1016/j.renene.2013.12.018

Ramezani, M., Golestan, S., & Li, S. (2016, May). Non-frequency sensitive all-pass filter based single-phase PLLs. Proceedings of the 2016 IEEE/PES Transmission and Distribution Conference and Exposition (T&D) (pp. 1-5). IEEE. doi:10.1109/TDC.2016.7519933

Rashed, M., Klumpner, C., & Asher, G. (2013). Repetitive and resonant control for a single-phase grid-connected hybrid cascaded multilevel converter. *IEEE Transactions on Power Electronics*, *28*(5), 2224–2234. doi:10.1109/TPEL.2012.2218833

Rauschenbach, H. S. (2012). *Solar cell array design handbook: the principles and technology of photovoltaic energy conversion*. Springer Science & Business Media.

Reddy, K. S., Kumar, M., Mallick, T. K., Sharon, H., & Lokeswaran, S. (2014). A review of Integration, Control, Communication and Metering (ICCM) of renewable energy based smart grid. *Renewable & Sustainable Energy Reviews*, *38*, 180–192. doi:10.1016/j.rser.2014.05.049

Romero-Cadaval, E., Spagnuolo, G., Franquelo, L. G., Ramos-Paja, C. A., Suntio, T., & Xiao, W. M. (2013). Grid-connected photovoltaic generation plants: Components and operation. *IEEE Industrial Electronics Magazine*, *7*(3), 6–20. doi:10.1109/MIE.2013.2264540

Siano, P. (2014). Demand response and smart grids—A survey. *Renewable & Sustainable Energy Reviews*, *30*, 461–478. doi:10.1016/j.rser.2013.10.022

Siddique, H. A. B., Xu, P., & De Doncker, R. W. (2013, June). Parameter extraction algorithm for one-diode model of PV panels based on datasheet values. *Proceedings of the 2013 International Conference on Clean Electrical Power (ICCEP)* (pp. 7-13). IEEE. doi:10.1109/ICCEP.2013.6586957

Sivarasu, S. R., Sekaran, E. C., & Karthik, P. (2015). Development of renewable energy based microgrid project implementations for residential consumers in India: Scope, challenges and possibilities. *Renewable & Sustainable Energy Reviews*, *50*, 256–269. doi:10.1016/j.rser.2015.04.118

Song, Z., Xia, C., & Liu, T. (2013). Predictive current control of three-phase grid-connected converters with constant switching frequency for wind energy systems. *IEEE Transactions on Industrial Electronics*, *60*(6), 2451–2464. doi:10.1109/TIE.2012.2225394

Swain, S., Panda, P. C., & Subudhi, B. D. (2013). A Comparative Study of Two Control Strategies for Three Phase Shunt Active Power Filter using Adaptive Hysteresis Band Current Controller.

Tey, K. S., & Mekhilef, S. (2014). Modified incremental conductance MPPT algorithm to mitigate inaccurate responses under fast-changing solar irradiation level. *Solar Energy*, *101*, 333–342. doi:10.1016/j.solener.2014.01.003

Twidell, J., & Weir, T. (2015). *Renewable energy resources*. Routledge.

Twining, E., & Holmes, D. G. (2003). Grid current regulation of a three-phase voltage source inverter with an LCL input filter. *IEEE Transactions on Power Electronics*, *18*(3), 888–895. doi:10.1109/TPEL.2003.810838

Valverde, L., Rosa, F., Bordons, C., & Guerra, J. (2016). Energy Management Strategies in hydrogen Smart-Grids: A laboratory experience. *International Journal of Hydrogen Energy*, *41*(31), 13715–13725. doi:10.1016/j.ijhydene.2016.05.279

Von Appen, J., Stetz, T., Braun, M., & Schmiegel, A. (2014). Local voltage control strategies for PV storage systems in distribution grids. *IEEE Transactions on Smart Grid*, *5*(2), 1002–1009. doi:10.1109/TSG.2013.2291116

Yahyaoui, I., Chaabene, M., & Tadeo, F. (2016). b). Evaluation of Maximum Power Point Tracking algorithm for off-grid photovoltaic pumping. *Sustainable Cities and Society*, *25*, 65–73. doi:10.1016/j.scs.2015.11.005

Yahyaoui, I., Sallem, S., Kamoun, M. B. A., & Tadeo, F. (2014). A proposal for off-grid photovoltaic systems with non-controllable loads using fuzzy logic. *Energy Conversion and Management*, *78*, 835–842. doi:10.1016/j.enconman.2013.07.091

Yahyaoui, I., Tadeo, F., & Segatto, M. V. (2016a). Energy and water management for drip-irrigation of tomatoes in a semi-arid district. *Agricultural Water Management*.

Yahyaoui, I. (2016b). *Specifications of photovoltaic pumping systems in agriculture: Sizing, fuzzy energy management and economic sensitivity analysis*. Elsevier Science.

Zainuri, M. A. A. M., Radzi, M. A. M., Soh, A. C., & Rahim, N. A. (2014). Development of adaptive perturb and observe-fuzzy control maximum power point tracking for photovoltaic boost dc-dc converter. *IET Renewable Power Generation*, *8*(2), 183–194. doi:10.1049/iet-rpg.2012.0362

Compilation of References

Abduvaliyev, A. Pathan, A.-S.K., Zhou, J., Roman, R., & Wong, W.-C. (2013). On the Vital Areas of Intrusion Detection Systems in Wireless Sensor Networks. *IEEE Communications Surveys & Tutorials*, *15*(3), 1223-1237.

Abidin, M. N. Z. (2006). *IEC 61000-3-2 Harmonics Standards Overview*. Edison, NJ, USA: Schaffner EMC Inc.

Aboelaze, M., & Aloul, F. (2005). Current and future trends in sensor networks: a survey.*Second IFIP International Conference on Wireless and Optical Communications Networks 2005 (WOCN 2005)*, (pp. 551-555). doi:10.1109/WOCN.2005.1436087

Abuadbba, A., & Khalil, I. (2015). Wavelet based steganographic technique to protect household confidential information and seal the transmitted smart grid readings. *Information Systems*, *53*, 224–236. Retrieved from http://www.sciencedirect.com/science/article/pii/S0306437914001355 doi:10.1016/j.is.2014.09.004

Advanced encryption standard (AES) (2001). National Institute for Standards and Technology.

Ahmed, K. R., Ahmed, K., Munir, S., & Asad, A. (2008). Abnormal node detection in wireless sensor network by pair based approach using IDS secure routing methodology. *Int J Comput Sci Netw. Sec*, *8*(12), 339–342.

Ahmed, M., Anwar, A., Mahmood, A. N., Shah, Z., & Maher, M. J. (2015a). An investigation of performance analysis of anomaly detection techniques for big data in scada systems. *EAI Endorsed Transactions on Industrial Networks and Intelligent Systems*, *15*(3), 1–16.

Ahmed, M., & Mahmood, A. (2015). Network traffic pattern analysis using improved information theoretic co-clustering based collective anomaly detection. In *International Conference on Security and Privacy in Communication Networks*. Springer International Publishing. doi:10.1007/978-3-319-23802-9_17

Ahmed, M., Mahmood, A. N., & Hu, J. (2016). A survey of network anomaly detection techniques. *Journal of Network and Computer Applications*, *60*, 19–31. doi:10.1016/j.jnca.2015.11.016

Ahmed, M., Mahmood, A. N., & Islam, M. R. (2016). A survey of anomaly detection techniques in financial domain. *Future Generation Computer Systems*, *55*, 278–288. doi:10.1016/j.future.2015.01.001

Ahmed, M., Mahmood, A. N., & Maher, M. J. (2015c). Scalable Information Systems:*5th International Conference, INFOSCALE 2014*. Springer International Publishing.

Ahn, C., Li, C.-T., & Peng, H. (2011). Decentralized charging algorithm for electrified vehicles connected to smart grid. *Proc. of ACC (pp. 3924–3929)*.

Al-Ali, A., & Aburukba, R. (2015). Role of Internet of Things in the Smart Grid Technology. *Journal of Computer and Communications*, *3*(05), 229–233. doi:10.4236/jcc.2015.35029

Al-Awami, A. T., & Sortomme, E. (2012, March). Coordinating vehicle-to-grid services with energy trading. *IEEE Trans. Smart Grid*, *3*(1), 453–462. doi:10.1109/TSG.2011.2167992

Alcaraz, C., & Zeadally, S. (2015). Critical infrastructure protection: requirements and challenges for the 21st century. *International Journal of critical Infrastructure Protection, 8*, 53-66.

Alcaraz, C., Agudo, I., Nuñez, D., & Lopez, J. (2011). Managing incidents in smart grids á la cloud. In The IEEE Cloud-Com 2011 (pp. 527–531). IEEE Computer Society.

Alcaraz, C., Cazorla, L., & Fernandez, G. (2015). Context-awareness using anomaly-based detectors for Smart grid do-mains. In *The 9th International Conference on Risks and Security of Internet and Systems* (vol. 8924, pp. 17–34). Springer.

Alcaraz, C., Lopez, J., & Choo, K-K. (2016). Dynamic restoration in interconnected RBAC-based cyber-physical control systems. In *14th International Conference on Security and Cryptography (SECRYPT 2016)* (*vol. 4*, pp. 19-27). SCITEPRESS.

Alcaraz, C., & Lopez, J. (2010). A security analysis for wireless sensor mesh networks in highly critical systems. *IEEE Transactions on Systems, Man and Cybernetics. Part C, Applications and Reviews, 40*(4), 419–428. doi:10.1109/TSMCC.2010.2045373

Alcaraz, C., & Lopez, J. (2012). Analysis of requirements for critical control systems. *International Journal of Critical Infrastructure Protection, 5*(3-4), 137–145. doi:10.1016/j.ijcip.2012.08.003

Alcaraz, C., Lopez, J., & Wolthunsen, S. (2016). Policy enforcement system for secure interoperable control in distrib-uted Smart Grid systems. *Network and Computer Applications, Elsevier, 59*, 301–314. doi:10.1016/j.jnca.2015.05.023

Ali, A., Wang, Y., Li, W., & He, X. (2015a). Implementation of simple moving voltage average technique with direct control incremental conductance method to optimize the efficiency of DC microgrid. *Proceedings of the 2015 International Conference on Emerging Technologies (ICET)* (pp. 1-5). IEEE.

Ali, A., Li, W., & He, X. (2015b). Simple Moving Voltage Average Incremental Conductance MPPT Technique with Direct Control Method under No uniform Solar Irradiance Conditions. *International Journal of Photoenergy*.

Al-Kuwaiti, M., Kyriakopoulos, N., & Hussein, S. (2009). A comparative analysis of network dependability, fault-toler-ance, reliability, security, and survivability. *IEEE Communications Surveys and Tutorials, 11*(2), 106–124. doi:10.1109/SURV.2009.090208

Almalawi, A., Tari, Z., Khalil, I., & Fahad, A. (2013). Scadavt-a framework for scada security testbed based on virtualiza-tion technology. In *Local Computer Networks (LCN), 2013 IEEE 38th Conference on.* doi:10.1109/LCN.2013.6761301

Aman, S., Simmhan, Y., & Prasanna, V. K. (2015). Holistic measures for evaluating prediction models in smart grids. *IEEE Transactions on Knowledge and Data Engineering, 27*(2), 475–488. doi:10.1109/TKDE.2014.2327022

Amer, M., Goldstein, M., & Abdennadher, S. (2013). Enhancing one-class sup-port vector machines for unsupervised anomaly detection. In *Proceedings of the ACM SIGKDD Workshop on Outlier Detection and Description*. New York, NY: ACM. doi:10.1145/2500853.2500857

Amoah, R., Camtepe, S., & Foo, E. (2016). *Securing DNP3 Broadcast Communications in SCADA Systems. IEEE Transactions on Industrial Informatics*.

Anggorojati, B., & Prasad, N. R. (2013). An Intrusion Detection game in access control system for the M2M local cloud platform. *2013 19th Asia-Pacific Conference on Communications (APCC)*.

Anggorojati, B., & Prasad, N. R. (2014). Secure capability-based access control in the M2M local cloud platform. *2014-4th International Conference on Wireless Communications, Vehicular Technology, Information Theory and Aerospace & Electronic Systems (VITAE'14).*

Anwari, M., & Hiendro, A. (2010). New unbalance factor for estimating performance of a three-phase induction motor with under-and overvoltage unbalance. *IEEE Transactions on Energy Conversion, 25*(3), 619–625. doi:10.1109/TEC.2010.2051548

Apostol, K. (2012). *Brute-force attack.* Salu Publishing.

Arancibia, A., & Strunz, K. (2012, March). Modeling of an electric vehicle charging station for fast DC charging. *Proceedings of the 2012 IEEE International Electric Vehicle Conference (IEVC)* (pp. 1-6). IEEE. doi:10.1109/IEVC.2012.6183232

Aravinthan, V., Namboodiri, V., Sunku, S., & Jewell, W. (2011). Wireless AMI Application and Security for Controlled Home Area Networks. *IEEE Power and Energy Society General Meeting.*

Aris, A., Oktug, S. F., & Yalcin, S. B. O. (2015). Internet-of-Things security: Denial of service attacks. *2015 Signal Processing and Communications Applications Conference (SIU'15)*, (pp. 903-906). doi:10.1109/SIU.2015.7129976

Arnoys, L. (2015). The internet of things: communicating with the cloud, the protocols, security and big data. *NMCT 2015*. Available at: http://hdl.handle.net/10046/1184

Arvani, A., & Rao, V. S. (2014). Detection and protection against intrusions on smart grid systems. *International Journal of Cyber-Security and Digital Forensics, 3*(1), 38–48. doi:10.17781/P001273

Assante, M. J. (2016). *Confirmation of a Coordinated Attack on the Ukrainian Power Grid.* Retrieved from SANS Industrial Control Systems Security Blog: https://ics.sans.org/blog

Atamli, A. W., & Martin, A. (2014). Threat-Based Security Analysis for the Internet of Things. *2014 International Workshop on Secure Internet of Things (SIoT'14)*. doi:10.1109/SIoT.2014.10

Ayres, N., & Maglaras, L. (2016). *Cyberterrorism targeting general public through social media.* Security Comm. Networks.

Ayres, N., & Maglaras, L. A. (2016). Cyberterrorism targeting the general public through social media. *Security Comm. Networks*. doi:10.1002/sec.1568

Azad, S., & Pathan, A.-S. K. (Eds.). (2014). Practical Cryptography: Algorithms and Implementations using C++. CRC Press, Taylor & Francis Group.

Badra, M., & Zeadally, S. (2013, April). Key management solutions in the smart grid environment. In *Wireless and Mobile Networking Conference (WMNC), 2013 6th Joint IFIP* (pp. 1-7). IEEE. doi:10.1109/WMNC.2013.6549050

Bagai, R., Tang, & Kim. (2013). Effectiveness of Probabilistic Attacks on Anonymity of Users Communicating via Multiple Messages. *Systems Journal, IEEE, 7*(2), 199-210.

Bahn, O., Marcy, M., Vaillancourt, K., & Waaub, J. P. (2013). Electrification of the Canadian road transportation sector: A 2050 outlook with TIMES-Canada. *Energy Policy, 62*, 593–606. doi:10.1016/j.enpol.2013.07.023

Baig, Z. A., & Amoudi, A.-R. (2013). An Analysis of Smart Grid Attacks and Countermeasures. *Journal of Communication, 8*(8), 473–479. doi:10.12720/jcm.8.8.473-479

Bajracharya, C., & Rawat, D. B. (2016). Dynamic spectrum access enabled home area networks for smart grid communications. *Int. J. Smart Grid and Green Communications, 1*(2), 130–142. doi:10.1504/IJSGGC.2016.078946

Balaman, Ş. Y., & Selim, H. (2016). Sustainable design of renewable energy supply chains integrated with district heating systems: A fuzzy optimization approach. *Journal of Cleaner Production.*

Banerjee, A., Dhillon, I., Ghosh, J., Merugu, S., & Modha, D. S. (2007). A generalized maximum entropy approach to bregman co-clustering and matrix approximation. *Journal of Machine Learning Research*, 8, 1919–1986.

Bansal, S., Sharma, S., & Trivedi, I. (2012). A detailed review of fault tolerance techniques in distributed systems. *International Journal on Internet and Distributed Computing Systems*, 1(1), 33–39.

Barbosa, R. R. R., & Pras, A. (2010, June). Intrusion detection in SCADA networks. In *IFIP International Conference on Autonomous Infrastructure, Management and Security* (pp. 163-166). Springer Berlin Heidelberg.

Barnhart, E. N., & Bokath, C. A. (2011). Considerations for Machine-to-Machine communications architecture and security standardization. *2011 IEEE 5th International Conference on Internet Multimedia Systems Architecture and Application (IMSAA'11).*

Bartoli, A. (2013). *Security protocols suite for machine-to-machine systems* (Ph.D. Thesis). Universitat Politècnica de Catalunya, Departament d'Enginyeria Telemàtica.

Bauer, G., Stockinger, K., & Lukowicz, P. (2009, September). Recognizing the use-mode of kitchen appliances from their current consumption. *Proceedings of theEuropean Conference on Smart Sensing and Context* (pp. 163-176). Springer Berlin Heidelberg. doi:10.1007/978-3-642-04471-7_13

Bayat, M., Arkian, H. R., & Aref, M. R. (2015). A revocable attribute based data sharing scheme resilient to DoS attacks in smart grid. *Wireless Networks*, 21(3), 871–881. doi:10.1007/s11276-014-0824-9

Bayram, G. Michailidis, & M. Devetsikiotis. (2013, October). Electric power resource provisioning for large scale public EV charging facilities. *Proc. IEEE Int. Conf. SmartGridComm* (pp. 133–138).

Bayram, I., Michailidis, G., Papapanagiotou, I., & Devetsikiotis, M. (2013, Dec). Decentralized control of electric vehicles in a network of fast charging stations.*Proc. IEEE GLOBECOM* (pp. 2785–2790). doi:10.1109/GLOCOM.2013.6831496

Begović, M., Pregelj, A., Rohatgi, A., & Novosel, D. (2001). Impact of renewable distributed generation on power systems.*Proceedings of the 34th Hawaii international conference on system sciences* (pp. 654-663). doi:10.1109/HICSS.2001.926265

Beigi-Mohammadi, N., Mišić, J., Khazaei, H., & Mišić, V. B. (2014). An intrusion detection system for smart grid neighborhood area network. In *Proceedings of IEEE International Conference on Communications (ICC)*. Sydney: IEEE. doi:10.1109/ICC.2014.6883967

Belissent, J. E. (2004). *U.S. Patent No. 6,789,203*. Washington, DC: U.S. Patent and Trademark Office.

Bellotti, F., De Gloria, A., Montanari, R., Dosio, N., & Morreale, D. (2005). COMUNICAR: Designing a multimedia, context-aware human-machine interface for cars. *Cognition Technology and Work*, 7(1), 36–45. doi:10.1007/s10111-004-0168-9

Bell, T. E. (2014). *Final Technical Report. Project Boeing SGS.* Seattle, WA: The Boeing Company. doi:10.2172/1177423

Ben, S. Y., Olivereau, A., & Laurent, M. (2012). A Distributed Approach for Secure M2M Communications. *2012-5th International Conference on New Technologies, Mobility and Security (NTMS'12).*

Benmalek, M., & Challal, Y. (2015, August). eSKAMI: Efficient and Scalable multi-group Key management for Advanced Metering Infrastructure in Smart Grid. In Trustcom/BigDataSE/ISPA, 2015 IEEE (Vol. 1, pp. 782-789). IEEE.

Benzel, T. (2011, December). The science of cyber security experimentation: the DETER project. In *Proceedings of the 27th Annual Computer Security Applications Conference* (pp. 137-148). ACM. doi:10.1145/2076732.2076752

Berger, L. T., & Iniewski, K. (Eds.). (April2012). *Smart Grid - Applications, Communications and Security.* John Wiley and Sons.

Bergna, G., Suul, J. A., Berne, E., Egrot, P., Lefranc, P., Vannier, J. C., & Molinas, M. (2012, October). Mitigating DC-side power oscillations and negative sequence load currents in modular multilevel converters under unbalanced faults-first approach using resonant PI. *Proceedings of the 38th Annual Conference on IEEE Industrial Electronics Society IECON '12* (pp. 537-542). IEEE. doi:10.1109/IECON.2012.6388769

Berrio, L., & Zuluaga, C. (2012). *Concepts, standards and communication technologies in smart grid.* Paper presented at the Circuits and Systems (CWCAS), 2012 IEEE 4th Colombian Workshop on.

Bessani, A., Veronese, G., Correia, M., & Lung, L. (2009). Highly-resilient services for critical infrastructures. In *Proceedings of the Embedded Systems and Communications Security Workshop.*

Bhaiji, Y. (2008). *Network Security Technologies and Solutions.* CCIE Professional Development Series.

Bhandari, B., Lee, K. T., Lee, G. Y., Cho, Y. M., & Ahn, S. H. (2015). Optimization of hybrid renewable energy power systems: A review. *International Journal of Precision Engineering and Manufacturing-Green Technology, 2*(1), 99–112. doi:10.1007/s40684-015-0013-z

Bharathi, M. V., Tanguturi, R. C., Jayakumar, C., & Selvamani, K. (2012). *Node capture attack in Wireless Sensor Network: A survey.* Paper presented at the Computational Intelligence & Computing Research (ICCIC), 2012 IEEE International Conference on. doi:10.1109/ICCIC.2012.6510237

Bizon, N. (2016). Global Extremum Seeking Control of the power generated by a Photovoltaic Array under Partially Shaded Conditions. *Energy Conversion and Management, 109*, 71–85. doi:10.1016/j.enconman.2015.11.046

Boberski, M. (2010). *The ten most critical Web application security risks. Tech. rep.* OWASP.

Bohli, J.-M., Sorge, C., & Ugus, O. (2010). A privacy model for smart metering. In Communications workshops (ICC), 2010 IEEE international conference on (pp. 1–5). doi:10.1109/ICCW.2010.5503916

Bojic, I., Granjal, J., Monteiro, E., Katusic, D., Skocir, P., Kusek, M., & Jezic, G. (2014). *Communication and Security in Machine-to-Machine Systems.* Lecture Notes in Computer Science, 8611, 255–281.

Boriah, S., Chandola, V., & Kumar, V. (2008). Similarity measures for cate-gorical data: A comparative evaluation. In *Proceedings of the SIAM International Conference on Data Mining, SDM 2008.*

Boubakri, W., Abdallah, W., & Boudriga, N. (2014). A chaos-based authentication and key management scheme for M2M communication. *2014 9th International Conference for Internet Technology and Secured Transactions (ICITST'14).*

Bou-Harb, E., Fachkha, C., Pourzandi, M., Debbabi, M., & Assi, C. (2013). Communication security for smart grid distribution networks. *IEEE Communications Magazine, 51*(1), 42–49. doi:10.1109/MCOM.2013.6400437

Boukenoui, R., Salhi, H., Bradai, R., & Mellit, A. (2016). A new intelligent MPPT method for stand-alone photovoltaic systems operating under fast transient variations of shading patterns. *Solar Energy, 124*, 124–142. doi:10.1016/j.solener.2015.11.023

Boulis, A. (2011). *Castalia User Manual.* Retrieved from: https://castalia.forge.nicta.com.au/index.php/en/documentation.html

Bowen, J., & Stavridou, V. (1993). Safety-critical systems. Formal Methods and Standards. *Software Engineering Journal, 8*(4), 189209. doi:10.1049/sej.1993.0025

BP. (2013). *BP Energy Outlook 2030.* Retrieved 5/2/2016, from http://www.bp.com/content/dam/bp/pdf/energy-economics/energy-outlook-2015/bp-energy-outlook-booklet_2013.pd

Brugger, S. T., & Chow, J. (2007). An assessment of the DARPA IDS Evaluation Dataset using Snort. *UCDAVIS department of Computer Science, 1*(2007), 22.

Budhia, M., Covic, G. A., & Boys, J. T. (2011). Design and optimization of circular magnetic structures for lumped inductive power transfer systems. *IEEE Transactions on Power Electronics, 26*(11), 3096–3108. doi:10.1109/TPEL.2011.2143730

Budka, K. C., Deshpande, J. G., & Thottan, M. (2014). *Communication Networks for Smart Grids.* Springer-Verlag London. doi:10.1007/978-1-4471-6302-2

Burgos, C., Sáez, D., Orchard, M. E., & Cárdenas, R. (2015). Fuzzy modelling for the state-of-charge estimation of lead-acid batteries. *Journal of Power Sources, 274*, 355–366. doi:10.1016/j.jpowsour.2014.10.036

Burks, D. (2012). *Security Onion.* Available at http://blog.securityonion.net/p/securityonion.html

Burman, P. (1989). A comparative study of ordinary cross-validation, v-fold cross-validation and the repeated learning-testing methods. *Biometrika, 76*(3), 503–514. doi:10.1093/biomet/76.3.503

Bush, S. F. (2014). *Smart Grid: Communication-Enabled Intelligence for the Electric Power Grid.* Wiley. doi:10.1002/9781118820216

Cagalaban, G., Ahn, J. Y., & Kim, S. (2012). A Secure Machine to Machine-Based Framework for Service Provisioning in Cloud Computing Infrastructures. Business, Economics, Financial Sciences, and Management. Springer.

Calhoun, P. R., Zorn, G., Pan, P., & Akhtar, H. (2001). *Diameter Framework Document.* IETF Draft. Retrieved 5 Dec. 2015 from: http://tools.ietf.org/html/draft-calhoun-diameter-framework-09

Camp, J., Cranor, L., Feamster, N., Feigenbaum, J., Forrest, S., Kotz, D., ... Rivest, R. (2009). *Data for cybersecurity research: Process and "wish list".* Academic Press.

Campbell, C., Cristianini, N., & Shawe-Taylor, J. (1999). Dynamically adapting kernels in support vector machines. *Advances in Neural Information Processing Systems, 11*, 204–210.

Camus, C., Silva, C. M., Farias, T. L., & Esteves, J. (2009, March). Impact of Plug-in Hybrid Electric Vehicles in the Portuguese electric utility system. *Proceedings of the 2009 International Conference on Power Engineering, Energy and Electrical Drives* (pp. 285-290). IEEE. doi:10.1109/POWERENG.2009.4915184

Cao, Y., Wang, N., & Kamel, G. (2014). Publish/subscribe communication framework for managing electric vehicle charging. *Proceedings of IEEE ICCVE' 14.*

Cao, Y., Wang, N., Kamel, G., & Kim, Y.-J. (2015). An Electric Vehicle Charging Management Scheme Based on Publish/Subscribe Communication Framework. *IEEE Systems Journal*, PP(99), 1–14.

Cao, L., & Gu, Q. (2002). Dynamic support vector machines for non-stationary time series forecasting. *Intelligent Data Analysis, 6*(1), 67–83.

Cao, Y., & Sun, Z. (2013). Routing in Delay/Disruption Tolerant Networks: A Taxonomy, Survey and Challenges. *IEEE Communications Surveys and Tutorials, 15*(2), 654–677. doi:10.1109/SURV.2012.042512.00053

Cao, Y., Wang, N., Kim, Y.-J., & Ge, C. (2015). *A Reservation Based Charging Management for On-the-move EV Under Mobility Uncertainty.* IEEE Online GreenComm. doi:10.1109/OnlineGreenCom.2015.7387372

Caramanis, M., & Foster, J. (2009). Management of electric vehicle charging to mitigate renewable generation intermittency and distribution network congestion. *Proc. 48th IEEE CDC/28th CCC* (pp. 4717–4722).

Cárdenas, A., Amin, S., Lin, Z., Huang, Y., Huang, C., & Sastry, S. (2011). Attacks against process control systems: Risk assessment, detection, and response. In *The 6th ACM Symposium on Information, Computer and Communications Security* (pp. 355–366). ACM.

Carlucci, S., Cattarin, G., Causone, F., & Pagliano, L. (2015). Multi-objective optimization of a nearly zero-energy building based on thermal and visual discomfort minimization using a non-dominated sorting genetic algorithm (NSGA-II). *Energy and Building, 104,* 378–394. doi:10.1016/j.enbuild.2015.06.064

Castilla, M., Miret, J., Camacho, A., Matas, J., & de Vicuña, L. G. (2013). Reduction of current harmonic distortion in three-phase grid-connected photovoltaic inverters via resonant current control. *IEEE Transactions on Industrial Electronics, 60*(4), 1464–1472. doi:10.1109/TIE.2011.2167734

CEN-CENELEC-ETSI. (2014, December). *Smart grid information security.* Author.

Cha, I., Shah, Y., Schmidt, A. U., Leicher, A., & Meyerstein, M. V. (2009). Trust in M2M communication. *IEEE Vehicular Technology Magazine, Volume, 4*(3), 69–75. doi:10.1109/MVT.2009.933478

Chan, P. K., Mahoney, M., & Arshad, M. (2003). Learning Rules and Clusters for Anomaly Detection in Network Traffic. In *Managing Cyber Threats,* (pp. 81-99). Academic Press.

Chang, C. H., Lin, Y. H., Chen, Y. M., & Chang, Y. R. (2014). Simplified reactive power control for single-phase grid-connected photovoltaic inverters. *IEEE Transactions on Industrial Electronics, 61*(5), 2286–2296. doi:10.1109/TIE.2013.2271600

Chang, K., Soong, A., Tseng, M., & Xiang, Z. (2011). Global Wireless Machine-to-Machine Standardization. *IEEE Internet Computing, Volume, 15*(2), 64–69. doi:10.1109/MIC.2011.41

Chaouchi, H. (2013). *The Internet of Things: Connecting Objects.* Wiley. doi:10.1002/9781118600146

Chaparadza, R., Meriem, T. B., Radier, B., Szott, S., Wodczak, M., Prakash, A., & Mihailovic, A. (2013, December 9-13). *SDN enablers in the ETSI AFI GANA Reference Model for Autonomic Management & Control (emerging standard), and Virtualization impact. Paper presented at the 2013 IEEE Globecom Workshops (GC Wkshps).*

Chaudhry, H., & Bohn, T. (2012, January). Security concerns of a plug-in vehicle. *Proceedings of the 2012 IEEE PES Innovative Smart Grid Technologies (ISGT).*

Chen, B.-L., Kuo, W.-C., & Wuu, L.-C. (2014). Robust smart-card-based remote user password authentication scheme. *International Journal of Communication Systems, 27*(2), 377–389. doi:10.1002/dac.2368

Chen, D., & Chang, G. (2012). A Survey on Security Issues of M2M Communications in Cyber-Physical Systems. *Transactions on Internet and Information Systems (Seoul), 6*(1), 24–45.

Chen, G., Liu, L., Song, P., & Du, Y. (2014). Chaotic improved PSO-based multi-objective optimization for minimization of power losses and L index in power systems. *Energy Conversion and Management, 86,* 548–560. doi:10.1016/j.enconman.2014.06.003

Chen, H.-C., You, I., Weng, C.-E., Cheng, C. H., & Huang, Y.-F. (2016). A security gateway application for End-to-End M2M communications. *Computer Standards & Interfaces, 44,* 85–93. doi:10.1016/j.csi.2015.09.001

Chen, P. Y., Cheng, S. M., & Chen, K. C. (2012). Smart attacks in smart grid communication networks. *IEEE Communications Magazine*, *50*(8), 24–29. doi:10.1109/MCOM.2012.6257523

Chess, B., & McGraw, G. (2004). Static analysis for security. *IEEE Security and Privacy*, *2*(6), 76–79. doi:10.1109/MSP.2004.111

Cheung, J. C., Chim, T., Yiu, S., Hui, L. C., & Li, V. O. (2011). Credential-based Privacy-preserving Power Request Scheme for Smart Grid Network.*IEEE Global Telecommunications Conference (GLOBECOM)*. doi:10.1109/GLOCOM.2011.6134566

Chin, V. J., Salam, Z., & Ishaque, K. (2016). An accurate modelling of the two-diode model of PV module using a hybrid solution based on differential evolution. *Energy Conversion and Management*, *124*, 42–50. doi:10.1016/j.enconman.2016.06.076

Cho, S., Li, H., & Choi, B. J. (2014). Palda: Efficient privacy-preserving authentication for lossless data aggregation in smart grids. In Smart grid communications (smartgridcomm), 2014 IEEE international conference on (pp. 914–919).

Choi, Y., Doh, I., Park, S. S., & Chae, K. J. (2012). Security Based Semantic Context Awareness System for M2M Ubiquitous Healthcare Service. In Ubiquitous Information Technologies and Applications. (LNCS), (vol. 214, pp. 187-196). Springer.

Choi, H. K., Han, C. K., & Choi, D. S. (2015). Improvement of security protocol for Machine Type Communications in LTE-advanced.*Wireless Communications and Mobile Computing Conference 2015 (IWCMC'15)*. doi:10.1109/IWCMC.2015.7289270

Choi, J., Shin, I., Seo, J., & Lee, C. (2011). An Efficient Message Authentication for Non-repudiation of the Smart Metering Service. In *Proceedings of First ACIS/JNU International Conference on Computers, Networks, Systems and Industrial Engineering (CNSI)*. Korea, Jeju Island: IEEE. doi:10.1109/CNSI.2011.28

Choubin, B., Khalighi-Sigaroodi, S., Malekian, A., & Kişi, Ö. (2016). Multiple linear regression, multi-layer perceptron network and adaptive neuro-fuzzy inference system for forecasting precipitation based on large-scale climate signals. *Hydrological Sciences Journal*, *61*(6), 1001–1009. doi:10.1080/02626667.2014.966721

Chow, T. T. (2010). A review on photovoltaic/thermal hybrid solar technology. *Applied Energy*, *87*(2), 365–379. doi:10.1016/j.apenergy.2009.06.037

Christen, D., Jauch, F., & Biel, J. (2015, September). Ultra-fast charging station for electric vehicles with integrated split grid storage. *Proceedings of the 2015 17th European Conference on Power Electronics and Applications (EPE'15)*. doi:10.1109/EPE.2015.7309322

Christin, D., Reinhardt, A., Mogre, P., & Steinmetz, R. (2009). Wireless sensor networks and the internet of things: Selected challenges. In *8th GI/ITG KuVS Fachgespr¨ach Drahtlose Sensornetze*.

Cimler, R., Matyska, J., Balik, L., Horalek, J., & Sobeslav, V. (2015). Security Aspects of Cloud Based Mobile Health Care Application. In *Nature of Computation and Communication*. Springer.

Ciric, R. M., Feltrin, A. P., & Ochoa, L. F. (2003). Power flow in four-wire distribution networks-general approach. *IEEE Transactions on Power Systems*, *18*(4), 1283–1290. doi:10.1109/TPWRS.2003.818597

Ciulla, G., Brano, V. L., Di Dio, V., & Cipriani, G. (2014). A comparison of different one-diode models for the representation of I–V characteristic of a PV cell. *Renewable & Sustainable Energy Reviews*, *32*, 684–696. doi:10.1016/j.rser.2014.01.027

CleanFleet Report. (2011). Top 10 Electric Car Makers for 2010 and 2011. Retrieved from http:www.cleanfleetreport. com/clean-fleet-articles/topelectric-cars-2010

Clement-Nyns, K., Haesen, E., & Driesen, J. (2010). The impact of charging plug-in hybrid electric vehicles on a residential distribution grid. *IEEE Transactions on Power Systems, 25*(1), 371–380. doi:10.1109/TPWRS.2009.2036481

Clement-Nyns, K., Van Reusel, K., & Driesen, J. (2007, January). The consumption of electrical energy of plug-in hybrid electric vehicles in Belgium.*Proceedings of EET-European Ele-Drive Transportation conference* (p. 10).

CodaAutomotive. (n. d.). Retrieved from www.codaautomotive.com

Committee, I. S. C. (2003). *IEEE standard for interconnecting distributed resources with electric power systems.* New York, NY: Institute of Electrical and Electronics Engineers.

Cook, A., Nicholson, A., Janicke, H., Maglaras, L., & Smith, R (2016). Attribution of Cyber Attacks on Industrial Control System. *EAI Transactions on Industrial Networks and Intelligent Systems*, 1-15.

Cormen, T., Leiserson, C., Rivest, R., & Stein, C. (2009). *Introduction to Algorithms* (3rd ed.). Cambridge, MA: The MIT Press.

Costantini, K. C. (2007). *Development of a cyber attack simulator for network modeling and cyber security analysis* (Doctoral dissertation). Rochester Institute of Technology.

Coyne, E., & Weil, T. (2013). ABAC and RBAC: Scalable, flexible, and auditable access management. *IT Professional, 15*(3), 14–16. doi:10.1109/MITP.2013.37

Cruz Cruz, T., Proença, J., Simões, P., Aubigny, M., Ouedraogo, M., Graziano, A., & Yasakhetu, L. (2014, July). Improving cyber-security awareness on industrial control systems: The CockpitCI approach. In *13th European Conference on Cyber Warfare and Security ECCWS-2014*(p. 59).

Curran, K. (2014). *Recent Advances in Ambient Intelligence and Context-Aware Computing.* IGI Global.

Cyber Security Working Group. (2010). The Smart Grid Interoperability Panel - Guidelines for smart grid cyber security. *NISTIR, 7628*, 1–597.

Da Silva, A. P. R., Martins, M. H. T., Rocha, B. P. S., Loureiro, A. A. F., Ruiz, L. B., & Wong, H. C. (2008). Decentralized intrusion detection in wireless sensor networks.*Proceedings of the 1st ACM international workshop on quality of service and security in wireless and mobile networks.*

Dagon, D., Martin, T., & Starner, T. (2004). Mobile phones as computing devices: The viruses are coming! *IEEE Pervasive Computing, Volume, 3*(4), 11–15. doi:10.1109/MPRV.2004.21

Das, S. S., Chandhar, P., Mitra, S., & Ghosh, P. (2011, September 5-8). Issues in Femtocell Deployments in Broadband OFDMA Networks: 3GPP-LTE a Case Study. *Paper presented at the Vehicular Technology Conference (VTC Fall).* IEEE.

Dasgupta, D., & Gonzalez, F. A. (2001, May). An intelligent decision support system for intrusion detection and response. In *International Workshop on Mathematical Methods, Models, and Architectures for Network Security* (pp. 1-14). Springer Berlin Heidelberg. doi:10.1007/3-540-45116-1_1

Davis, J., & Magrath, S. (2013). *A survey of cyber ranges and testbeds (No. DSTO-GD-0771). Defence Science and Technology Organisation.*

De Almeida, F. M., Ribeiro, A. R. L., & Moreno, E. D. (2015). An Architecture for Self-healing in Internet of Things.*UBI-COMM 2015: The Ninth International Conference on Mobile Ubiquitous Computing, Systems, Services and Technologies.*

de Weerdt, M., Stein, S., Gerding, E., Robu, V., & Jennings, N. (2015). Intention-Aware Routing of Electric Vehicles. *IEEE Transactions on Intelligent Transportation Systems*, PP(99), 1–11.

Dehlawi, Z., & Abokhodair, N. (2013). Saudi Arabia's response to cyber conflict: A case study of the Shamoon malware incident. In *Proceedings of IEEE International Conference on Intelligence and Security Informatics (ISI)*. Seattle, WA: IEEE. doi:10.1109/ISI.2013.6578789

Demblewski, M. (2015). *Security Frameworks for Machine-to-Machine Devices and Networks* (Doctoral dissertation). Nova Southeastern University. Retrieved from: NSUWorks, College of Engineering and Computing.

Demertzis, F. F., Karopoulos, G., Xenakis, C., & Colarieti, A. (2015). Self-organised Key Management for the Smart Grid. In Ad-hoc, Mobile, and Wireless Networks (pp. 303-316). Springer International Publishing. doi:10.1007/978-3-319-19662-6_21

Denial-of-Service Developments. (2000). *CERT Advisory CA-2000-01*. Retrieved 6 Dec. 2015, from: http://www.cert.org/advisories/CA-2000-01.html

Detken, K.-O., Genzel, C.-H., & Jahnk, M. (2014). Integrity protection in a smart grid environment for wireless access of smart meters. *Wireless Systems within the Conferences on Intelligent Data Acquisition and Advanced Computing Systems: Technology and Applications (IDAACS-SWS), 2nd International Symposium on*, (pp. 79-86).

Dhillon, I. S., Mallela, S., & Modha, D. S. (2003). Information-theoretic co-clustering. In *Proceedings of the Ninth ACM SIGKDD International Conference on Knowledge Discovery and Data Mining*. New York, NY: ACM. doi:10.1145/956750.956764

Doh, I., Chae, K., Lim, J., & Chung, M. Y. (2015). *Authentication and Key Management Based on Kerberos for M2M Mobile Open IPTV Security. In Intelligent Automation & Soft Computing* (Vol. 21, pp. 543–558). Taylor & Francis Group.

Dohler, M., Boswarthick, D., & Alonso-Zárate, J. (2012). Machine-to-Machine in Smart Grids & Smart Cities. Technologies, Standards, and Applications. Tutorial Globecom 2012, Anaheim, CA.

Domingo-Ferrer, J., & Torra, V. (2008). *A Critique of k-Anonymity and Some of Its Enhancements*. Academic Press.

Doubleday, H., Maglaras, L., & Janicke, H. (2016). *SSH Honeypot: Building*. Deploying and Analysis.

Drozda, M., Schaust, S., & Szczerbicka, H. (2010). AIS for misbehaviour detection in wireless sensor networks: performance and design principles. In Congress on evolutionary computation, (pp. 3719-3726).

Du, J., & Qian, M. (2012, August). Research and application on LTE technology in smart grids. In *Communications and Networking in China (CHINACOM), 2012 7th International ICST Conference on* (pp. 76-80).

Duan, X., & Wang, X. (2015). Authentication handover and privacy protection in 5G hetnets using software-defined networking. *IEEE Communications Magazine*, *53*(4), 28–35. doi:10.1109/MCOM.2015.7081072

Dugan, R. C., McGranaghan, M. F., & Beaty, H. W. (1996). Electrical power systems quality. New York, NY: McGraw-Hill.

Duncan, G., & Fienberg, S. (1998). Obtaining information while preserving privacy: A Markov perturbation method for tabular data. In Statistical Data Protection, (pp. 351–362).

Duquet, S. (2015). *Smart Sensors: Enabling Detection and Ranging for the Internet of Things and Beyond*. LeddarTech, White paper.

Dyke, K. J., Schofield, N., & Barnes, M. (2010). The impact of transport electrification on electrical networks. *IEEE Transactions on Industrial Electronics*, *57*(12), 3917–3926. doi:10.1109/TIE.2010.2040563

East, S., Butts, J., Papa, M., & Shenoi, S. (2009). A Taxonomy of Attacks on the DNP3 Protocol. In C. Palmer, & S. Shenoi (Eds.), Critical Infrastructure Protection III (pp. 67-81). Springer Berlin Heidelberg. doi:10.1007/978-3-642-04798-5_5

Efthymiou, C., & Kalogridis, G. (2010). Smart grid privacy via anonymization of smart metering data. In *Smart grid communications (smartgridcomm), 2010 first IEEE international conference on* (pp. 238–243). doi:10.1109/SMART-GRID.2010.5622050

Eisner, J., Funke, S., & Storandt, S. (2011). Optimal route planning for electric vehicles in large networks.*Proc. 25th Conf. AAAI* (pp. 1108–1113).

Electric Vehicle Charging Station Technical Installation Guide. (2012). 1st ed.). Hydro-Québec.

Enjeti, P. N., & Choudhury, S. A. (1993). A new control strategy to improve the performance of a PWM AC to DC converter under unbalanced operating conditions. *IEEE Transactions on Power Electronics, 8*(4), 493–500. doi:10.1109/63.261020

Erol-Kantarci, M., & Mouftah, H. T. (2010). Prediction-based charging of PHEVs from the smart grid with dynamic pricing. *Proc. IEEE 35th Conf. LCN* (pp. 1032–1039).

Eschelbeck, G. (2004). The laws of vulnerabilities. *Black Hat Briefings, 2606.*

Escudero-Garzas, J., & Seco-Granados, G. (2012, Jan). Charging station selection optimization for plug-in electric vehicles: An oligopolistic game-theoretic framework.*Proc. IEEE PES ISGT.* doi:10.1109/ISGT.2012.6175791

Eskin, E., Arnold, A., Prerau, M., Portnoy, L., & Stolfo, S. (2002). A geometric framework for unsupervised anomaly detection. In Applications of data mining in computer security (pp. 77-101). Springer US. doi:10.1007/978-1-4615-0953-0_4

Esmalifalak, M., Liu, L., Nguyen, N., Zheng, R., & Han, Z. (2014). Detecting Stealthy False Data Injection Using Machine Learning in Smart Grid. *IEEE Systems Journal, (99),* 1-9.

Ettelt, D., Rey, P., Jourdan, G., Walther, A., Robert, P., & Delamare, J. (2014). 3D magnetic field sensor concept for use in inertial measurement units (IMUs). *Journal of Microelectromechanical Systems, 23*(2), 324–333. doi:10.1109/JMEMS.2013.2273362

Eugster, P. T., Felber, P. A., Guerraoui, R., & Kermarrec, A.-M. (2003, June). The Many Faces of Publish/Subscribe. *ACM Computing Surveys, 35*(2), 114–131. doi:10.1145/857076.857078

European Commission. (2009). *Smart grids and meters*. Retrieved from http://ec.europa.eu/energy/en/topics/markets-and-consumers/smart-grids-and-meters

European Communities. (2009). Directive 2009/72/EC Concerning Common Rules for the Internal Market in Electricity and Repealing Directive 2003/54/EC.

Evans, M., Maglaras, L. A., He, Y., & Janicke, H. (2016). Human Behaviour as an aspect of Cyber Security Assurance. *arXiv preprint arXiv:1601.03921*

Fahrenbruch, A., & Bube, R. (2012). *Fundamentals of solar cells: photovoltaic solar energy conversion.* Elsevier.

Faiz, J., Ebrahimpour, H., & Pillay, P. (2004). Influence of unbalanced voltage on the steady-state performance of a three-phase squirrel-cage induction motor. *IEEE Transactions on Energy Conversion, 19*(4), 657–662. doi:10.1109/TEC.2004.837283

Falliere, N., Murchu, L., & Chien, E. (2011). *W32.Stuxnet Dossier.* Symantec.

Fangfang, W., Huazhong, W., Dongqing, C., & Yong, P. (2013). *Substation Communication Security Research Based on Hybrid Encryption of DES and RSA* (pp. 437–441). Intelligent Information Hiding and Multimedia Signal Processing. doi:10.1109/IIH-MSP.2013.115

Fan, Z., Kulkarni, P., Gormus, S., Efthymiou, C., Kalogridis, G., Sooriyabandara, M., & Chin, W. H. et al. (2012). Smart Grid Communications: Overview of Research Challenges, Solutions, and Standardization Activities. *IEEE Communications Surveys and Tutorials*, 21–38.

Farash, M. S., & Ahmadian-Attari, M. (2014). A Pairing-free ID-based Key Agreement Protocol with Different PKGs. *International Journal of Network Security*, *16*(2), 143–148.

Farhadi, M., & Mohammed, O. (2015). Adaptive energy management in redundant hybrid DC microgrid for pulse load mitigation. *IEEE Transactions on Smart Grid*, *6*(1), 54–62. doi:10.1109/TSG.2014.2347253

Farmer, C., Hines, P., Dowds, J., & Blumsack, S. (2010, January). Modeling the impact of increasing PHEV loads on the distribution infrastructure. *Proceedings of the 2010 43rd Hawaii International Conference on System Sciences (HICSS)* (pp. 1-10). IEEE. doi:10.1109/HICSS.2010.277

Farooq, H., & Jung, L. T. (2014). Choices available for implementing smart grid communication network. In *Proceedings ofInternational Conference on Computer and Information Sciences (ICCOINS)*. IEEE.

Farooqi, A.H., Khan, F.A., Wang, J., & Lee, S. (2013). A novel intrusion detection framework for wireless sensor networks. *Personal and Ubiquitous Computing*, *17*(5), 907-919.

Fathabadi, H. (2016). Novel photovoltaic based battery charger including novel high efficiency step-up DC/DC converter and novel high accurate fast maximum power point tracking controller. *Energy Conversion and Management*, *110*, 200–211. doi:10.1016/j.enconman.2015.12.025

Feng, T., Wang, C., Zhang, W., & Ruan, L. (2008). Confidentiality protection for distributed sensor data aggregation. In *Infocom 2008. the 27th conference on computer communications*. IEEE. doi:10.1109/INFOCOM.2008.20

Feng, L., Mears, L., Beaufort, C., & Schulte, J. (2016). Energy, economy, and environment analysis and optimization on manufacturing plant energy supply system. *Energy Conversion and Management*, *117*, 454–465. doi:10.1016/j.enconman.2016.03.031

Fernandes, E., Jung, J., & Prakash, A. (2016). *Security Analysis of Emerging Smart Home Applications*. Retrieved from https://cdn2.vox-cdn.com/uploads/chorus_asset/file/6410049/Paper27_SP16_CameraReady_SmartThings_Revised_1_.0.pdf

Fernández, E. F., Pérez-Higueras, P., Almonacid, F., Ruiz-Arias, J. A., Rodrigo, P., Fernandez, J. I., & Luque-Heredia, I. (2015). Model for estimating the energy yield of a high concentrator photovoltaic system. *Energy*, *87*, 77–85. doi:10.1016/j.energy.2015.04.095

Ferreira, A., Carvalho, A., Martins, A. P., Pereira, F., & Sobrado, V. (2013). Dynamic Performance of Voltage Oriented Control Method Applied in a Voltage Source Converter. *Proceedings of studECE '13*.

Fienberg, S. E., Makov, E. U., & Steel, R. J. (1998). Disclosure Limitation using Perturbation and Related Methods for Categorical Data. *Journal of Official Statistics*, *14*, 485–502.

Fink, G. A., Zarzhitsky, D. V., Carroll, T. E., & Farquhar, E. D. (2015). Security and privacy grand challenges for the Internet of Things.*2015 International Conference on Collaboration Technologies and Systems (CTS'15)*. doi:10.1109/CTS.2015.7210391

Finster, S. (2013). Smart meter speed dating, short-term relationships for im- proved privacy in smart metering. In Smart grid communications (smart- gridcomm), 2013 IEEE international conference on (pp. 426–431).

Finster, S., & Baumgart, I. (2013). Elderberry: A peer-to-peer, privacy-aware smart metering protocol. In Infocom, 2013 proceedings IEEE (pp. 3411– 3416).

Finster, S., & Baumgart, I. (2014). Privacy-Aware Smart Metering: A Survey. *IEEE Communications Surveys and Tutorials, 16*(3), 1732–1745. doi:10.1109/SURV.2014.052914.00090

Finster, S., & Baumgart, I. (2015). Privacy-aware smart metering: A survey. *IEEE Communications Surveys and Tutorials, 17*(2), 1088–1101. doi:10.1109/COMST.2015.2425958

FIPS PUB 200. (2006). *Minimum Security Requirements for Federal Information and Information Systems.* Federal Information Processing Standards Publication.

Fox-Penner, P. (2014). *Smart Power Anniversary Edition: Climate Change, the Smart Grid, and the Future of Electric Utilities.* Island Press.

Fremantle, P., & Scott, P. (2015). A security survey of middleware for the Internet of Things. *PeerJ PrePrints* 3:e1521. Retrieved 6 Dec. 2015 from: https://peerj.com/preprints/1241/

Friedman, J., Hastie, T., & Tibshirani, R. (2001). The elements of statistical learning (Vol. 1). Springer.

Fung, B. C. M., Wang, K., Chen, R., & Yu, P. S. (2010, June). Privacy-preserving data publishing: A survey of recent developments. *ACM Computing Surveys, 42*(4), 14. doi:10.1145/1749603.1749605

Funke, S., Nusser, A., & Storandt, S. (2014). Placement of loading stations for electric vehicles: No detours necessary! *Proc. 28th AAAI Conf.* (pp. 417–423).

Galloway, B., & Hancke, G. P. (2013). Introduction to industrial control net-works. *IEEE Communications Surveys and Tutorials, 15*(2), 860–880. doi:10.1109/SURV.2012.071812.00124

Gao, Q. (2012). Biometric authentication in Smart Grid. In *Proceedings of International Energy and Sustainability Conference (IESC).* New York, NY: IEEE.

Gao, W., Morris, T., Reaves, B., & Richey, D. (2010, October). On SCADA control system command and response injection and intrusion detection. *IneCrime Researchers Summit, 2010*, 1–9.

Garcia, F. D., & Jacobs, B. (2011). Privacy-friendly energy-metering via homomorphic encryption. In *Security and trust management* (pp. 226–238). Springer. doi:10.1007/978-3-642-22444-7_15

Garrett, K., Talluri, S. R., & Roy, S. (2015). On vulnerability analysis of several password authentication protocols. *Innovations in Systems and Software Engineering, 11*(3), 167–176. doi:10.1007/s11334-015-0250-x

Gaur, S., Moh, M., & Balakrishnan, M. (December2013). Hiding behind the Clouds: Efficient, Privacy-Preserving Queries via Cloud Proxies. In *Proc. of International Workshop on Cloud Computing Systems, Networks, and Applications.* doi:10.1109/GLOCOMW.2013.6825035

Genge, B., Haller, P., Gligor, A., & Beres, A. (2014). An Approach for Cyber Security Experimentation Supporting Sensei/IoT for Smart Grid. *2nd International Symposium on Digital Forensics and Security (ISDFS'14).*

Gharavi, H., & Hu, B. (2013). 4-way handshaking protection for wireless mesh network security in smart grid. In *Proceedings of IEEE Global Communications Conference (GLOBECOM).* Atlanta, GA: IEEE. doi:10.1109/GLOCOM.2013.6831169

Gharbaoui, M., Valcarenghi, L., Bruno, R., Martini, B., Conti, M., & Castoldi, P. (2012, March). An Advanced Smart Management System for Electric Vehicle Recharge. *Proceedings of IEEE IEVC,* Greenville, SC, USA.

Gil, A., & Taiber, J. (2014). A Literature Review in Dynamic Wireless Power Transfer for Electric Vehicles: Technology and Infrastructure Integration Challenges. In *Sustainable Automotive Technologies 2013* (pp. 289–298). Springer International Publishing. doi:10.1007/978-3-319-01884-3_30

Ginting, D., Fahmi, A., & Kurniawan, A. (2015, November 25-26). Performance evaluation of inter-cell interference of LTE-A system using carrier aggregation and CoMP techniques. *Paper presented at the 2015 9th International Conference on Telecommunication Systems Services and Applications (TSSA)*.

Glazer, A., Lindenbaum, M., & Markovitch, S. (2013). q-ocsvm: A q-quantile estimator for high-dimensional distributions. In Advances in Neural Information Processing Systems (pp. 503-511).

Golestani Najafabadi, S., Naji, H. R., & Mahani, A. (2013). *Sybil attack Detection: Improving security of WSNs for smart power grid application.* Paper presented at the Smart Grid Conference (SGC). doi:10.1109/SGC.2013.6733831

Golla, R., Bell, W., Lin, M., Himayat, N., Talwar, S., & Johnsson, K. (2010). Power outage alarm for smart metering applications IEEE 802.16p Task Group.

Gonzalez Vaya, M., & Andersson, G. (2012). Centralized and decentralized approaches to smart charging of plug-in vehicles. *Proc. IEEE Power Energy Soc. Gen. Meet.*

Gözde, H., Taplamacıoğlu, M. C., Arı, M., & Shalaf, H. (2015, April). 4G/LTE technology for smart grid communication infrastructure. In Smart Grid Congress and Fair (ICSG), 2015 3rd International Istanbul (pp. 1-4).

Graciano, V., Vargas, J. V., & Ordonez, J. C. (2015). Modeling and simulation of diesel, biodiesel and biogas mixtures driven compression ignition internal combustion engines. *International Journal of Energy Research.*

Granelli, F., Domeniconi, D., Da Fonseca, N. L., & Tsetsgee, B. (2014, July). On the Usage of WiFi and LTE for the Smart Grid. In *2014 7th International Conference on Ubi-Media Computing and Workshops*. doi:10.1109/U-MEDIA.2014.49

Granjal, J., Monteiro, E., & Silva, J. S. (2013). *Security Issues and Approaches on Wireless M2M Systems. In Wireless Networks and Security Part of the series Signals and Communication Technology* (pp. 133–164). Springer Berlin Heidelberg.

Gratton, D. A. (2013). *The Handbook of Personal Area Networking Technologies and Protocols.* Cambridge University Press. doi:10.1017/CBO9780511979132

Greveler, U., Justus, B., & Loehr, D. (2012). *Multimedia Content Identification Through Smart Meter Power Usage Profiles.* CPDP.

Grochocki, D. (2012). AMI threats, intrusion detection requirements and deployment recommendations. *InProceedings of IEEE Third International Conference on Smart Grid Communications (SmartGridComm)*. Taiwan: IEEE. doi:10.1109/SmartGridComm.2012.6486016

Gu, B., Dominic, J., Lai, J. S., Chen, C. L., LaBella, T., & Chen, B. (2013). High reliability and efficiency single-phase transformerless inverter for grid-connected photovoltaic systems. *IEEE Transactions on Power Electronics*, 28(5), 2235–2245. doi:10.1109/TPEL.2012.2214237

Guenounou, A., Malek, A., & Aillerie, M. (2016). Comparative performance of PV panels of different technologies over one year of exposure: Application to a coastal Mediterranean region of Algeria. *Energy Conversion and Management*, 114, 356–363. doi:10.1016/j.enconman.2016.02.044

Guille, C., & Gross, G. (2009). A conceptual framework for the vehicle-to-grid (V2G) implementation. *Energy Policy*, 37(11), 4379–4390. doi:10.1016/j.enpol.2009.05.053

Gungor, V. C., Sahin, D., Kocak, T., Ergut, S., Buccella, C., Cecati, C., & Hancke, G. P. (2011). Smart grid technologies: communication technologies and standards. *IEEE transactions on Industrial informatics, 7*(4), 529-539.

Gungor, V. C., Lu, B., & Hancke, G. P. (2010). Opportunities and Challenges of Wireless Sensor Networks in Smart Grid. *IEEE Transactions on Industrial Electronics, 57*(10), 3557–3564. doi:10.1109/TIE.2009.2039455

Gungor, V. C., Sahin, D., Kocak, T., Ergut, S., Buccella, C., Cecati, C., & Hancke, G. P. (2012). Smart grid and smart homes: Key players and pilot projects. *IEEE Industrial Electronics Magazine, 6*(4), 18–34. doi:10.1109/MIE.2012.2207489

Gungor, V. C., Sahin, D., Kocak, T., Ergut, S., Buccella, C., Cecati, C., & Hancke, G. P. (2013). A Survey on Smart Grid Potential Applications and Communication Requirements. *IEEE Transactions on Industrial Informatics, 9*(1), 28–42. doi:10.1109/TII.2012.2218253

Guobin, X., Moulema, P., & Wei, Y. (2013, May 21-23). Integrating distributed energy resources in smart grid: Modeling and analysis. *Paper presented at the Energytech*. IEEE.

Gupta, S., Zheng, R., & Cheng, A. M. K. (2007). ANDES: an anomaly detection system for wireless sensor networks. *International conference on mobile ad hoc and sensor systems*, (pp. 1–9). doi:10.1109/MOBHOC.2007.4428636

Gyrard, A., Bonnet, C., & Boudaoud, K. (2014). An Ontology-Based Approach for Helping to Secure the ETSI Machine-to-Machine Architecture. *2014 IEEE International Conference on Internet of Things (iThings), Green Computing and Communications (GreenCom), IEEE and Cyber, and Physical and Social Computing(CPSCom)*. IEEE. doi:10.1109/iThings.2014.25

Hadley, M., McBride, J., Edgar, T., O'Neil, L., & Johnson, J. (2007). *Securing Wide Area Measurement Systems. Pacific Northwest National Laboratory to U.S. Department of Energy (DOE)*. Retrieved from http://www.energy.gov/sites/prod/files/oeprod/DocumentsandMedia/8-Securing_WAMS.pdf

Hahn, A., Ashok, A., Sridhar, S., & Govindarasu, M. (2013). Cyber-physical security testbeds: Architecture, application, and evaluation for smart grid. *IEEE Transactions on Smart Grid, 4*(2), 847–855. doi:10.1109/TSG.2012.2226919

Hai, T. H., Khan, F., & Huh, E.-N. (2007). Hybrid intrusion detection system for wireless sensor networks. Springer. doi:10.1007/978-3-540-74477-1_36

Hakiri, A., & Berthou, P. (2015). *Leveraging SDN for the 5G Networks. Software Defined Mobile Networks (SDMN): Beyond LTE Network Architecture* (M. Liyanage, A. Gurtov, & M. Ylianttila, Eds.). Chichester, UK: John Wiley & Sons, Ltd. doi:10.1002/9781118900253.ch5

Hall, M. J., Hansen, D. D., & Jones, K. (2015, June). Cross-domain situational awareness and collaborative working for cyber security. In *Cyber Situational Awareness, Data Analytics and Assessment (CyberSA), 2015 International Conference on* (pp. 1-8). IEEE. doi:10.1109/CyberSA.2015.7166110

Hamdy, M., Nguyen, A. T., & Hensen, J. L. (2016). A performance comparison of multi-objective optimization algorithms for solving nearly-zero-energy-building design problems. *Energy and Building, 121*, 57–71. doi:10.1016/j.enbuild.2016.03.035

Han, Y., Luo, M., Zhao, X., Guerrero, J. M., & Xu, L. (2016). Comparative Performance Evaluation of Orthogonal-Signal-Generators-Based Single-Phase PLL Algorithms—A Survey. *IEEE Transactions on Power Electronics, 31*(5), 3932–3944. doi:10.1109/TPEL.2015.2466631

Haq, A. U., Chadhry, M. J., & Saleemi, F. (2013, November). A smart charging station for EVs with evaluation of different energy storage technologies. *Proceedings of the 2013 IEEE Conference on Clean Energy and Technology (CEAT)* (pp. 248-253). IEEE. doi:10.1109/CEAT.2013.6775635

Harish, P. D., & Roy, S. (2014, May). Energy oriented vulnerability analysis on authentication protocols for cps. In *Distributed Computing in Sensor Systems (DCOSS), 2014 IEEE International Conference on* (pp. 367-371). IEEE. doi:10.1109/DCOSS.2014.52

Harnad, S., Brody, T., Vallieres, F., Carr, L., Hitchcock, S., Gingras, Y., & Hilf, E. R. et al. (2008). The access/impact problem and the green and gold roads to open access: An update. *Serials Review*, *34*(1), 36–40. doi:10.1080/0098791 3.2008.10765150

HART Communication Foundation IEC 62591. (2010). *Industrial communication networks Wireless communication network and communication profiles WirelessHART*. Retrieved on May, 2016, from http://www.hartcomm.org/

Hasan, M. A., & Parida, S. K. (2016). An overview of solar photovoltaic panel modeling based on analytical and experimental viewpoint. *Renewable & Sustainable Energy Reviews*, *60*, 75–83. doi:10.1016/j.rser.2016.01.087

Hassan, R., Abdallah, M., & Radman, G. (2012). Load shedding in smart grid: A reliable efficient Ad-Hoc broadcast algorithm for smart house. In *Proceedings of IEEE Southeastcon*. IEEE. doi:10.1109/SECon.2012.6196919

Hausler, F., Crisostomi, E., Schlote, A., Radusch, I., & Shorten, R. (2014, April). Stochastic Park-and-Charge Balancing for Fully Electric and Plug in Hybrid Vehicles. *IEEE Transactions on Intelligent Transportation Systems*, *15*(2), 895–901. doi:10.1109/TITS.2013.2286266

Hautamaki, V., Cherednichenko, S., Karkkainen, I., Kinnunen, T., & Franti, P. (2005). Improving k-means by outlier removal. In *Proceedings of the 14th Scandi-navian Conference on Image Analysis*. Berlin: Springer-Verlag. doi:10.1007/11499145_99

He, W., Liu, X., Nguyen, H., Nahrstedt, K., & Abdelzaher, T. (2007). PDA: Privacy-preserving data aggregation in wireless sensor networks. In *Infocom 2007. 26th IEEE international conference on computer communications* (pp. 2045–2053).

He, Z., Xu, X., & Deng, S. (2003). Discovering cluster-based local outliers. *Pattern Recogn. Lett.*, *24*(9-10), 1641-1650.

Heady, R., Luger, G., Maccabe, A., & Servilla, M. (1990). *The Architecture of a Network Level Intrusion Detection System. Technical report.* University of New Mexico. doi:10.2172/425295

Hellemans. (2016). Europe Bets €1 Billion on Quantum Tech. *IEEE Spectrum*.

Hertwich, E. G., Gibon, T., Bouman, E. A., Arvesen, A., Suh, S., Heath, G. A., & Shi, L. et al. (2015). Integrated life-cycle assessment of electricity-supply scenarios confirms global environmental benefit of low-carbon technologies. *Proceedings of the National Academy of Sciences of the United States of America*, *112*(20), 6277–6282. doi:10.1073/pnas.1312753111 PMID:25288741

Holfeld, B., Jaeckel, S., Thiele, L., Wirth, T., & Scheppelmann, K. (2015, May). Smart grid communications: LTE outdoor field trials at 450 MHz. In *2015 IEEE 81st Vehicular Technology Conference (VTC Spring)* (pp. 1-5).

Hong, J., Suh, E., & Kim, S. (2009). Context-aware systems. *Expert Systems with Applications*, *36*(4), 8509–8522. doi:10.1016/j.eswa.2008.10.071

Hongsong, C., Zhongchuan, F., & Dongyan, Z. (2011). Security and trust research in M2M system. *2011 IEEE International Conference on Vehicular Electronics and Safety (ICVES'11)*. doi:10.1109/ICVES.2011.5983830

Ho, Q.-D., Gao, Y., Rajalingham, G., & Le-Ngoc, T. (2014). *Smart Grid Communications Network (SGCN). In Wireless Communications Networks for the Smart Grid* (pp. 15–30). Cham: Springer International Publishing.

Hossain, E., Han, Z., & Poor, H. V. (2012). *Smart Grid Communications and Networking*. Cambridge University Press. doi:10.1017/CBO9781139013468

Hossain, M. M., Fotouhi, M., & Hasan, R. (2015). Towards an Analysis of Security Issues, Challenges, and Open Problems in the Internet of Things. *2015 IEEE World Congress on Services (SERVICES'15)*. doi:10.1109/SERVICES.2015.12

Houle, K. J., Weaver, G. M., Long, N., & Thomas, R. (2001). *Trends in denial of service attack technology.* Retrieved from: https://resources.sei.cmu.edu/asset_files/WhitePaper/2001_019_001_52491.pdf

Houssamo, I., Locment, F., & Sechilariu, M. (2013). Experimental analysis of impact of MPPT methods on energy efficiency for photovoltaic power systems. *International Journal of Electrical Power & Energy Systems, 46*, 98–107. doi:10.1016/j.ijepes.2012.10.048

Hoyos, J., Dehus, M., & Brown, T. X. (2012). *Exploiting the GOOSE protocol: A practical attack on cyber-infrastructure.* IEEE Globecom Workshops.

Hu & Gharavi. (2014). Smart Grid Mesh Network Security Using Dynamic Key Distribution With Merkle Tree 4-Way Handshaking. *IEEE Transactions on Smart Grid, 5*. doi: 10.1109/TSG.2013.2277963

Hua-jin, W., Hu, & Liu. (2010). Distributed Mining of Association Rules Based on Privacy-Preserved Method. *Information Science and Engineering (ISISE),2010International Symposium on.*

Hua, L., Junguo, Z., & Fantao, L. (2014). Internet of Things Technology and its Applications in Smart Grid. *TELKOMNIKA Indonesian Journal of Electrical Engineering, 12*(2), 940–946. doi:10.11591/telkomnika.v12i2.4178

Huang, X., Craig, P., & Yan, H.L.Z (2015). SecIoT: a security framework for the Internet of Things. *Security and Communication Networks.* DOI: 10.1002/sec.1259

Huang, M.-Y., Jasper, R. J., & Wicks, T. M. (1999). A large scale distributed intrusion detection framework based on attack strategy analysis. *Computer Networks, 31*(23–24), 2465–2475. doi:10.1016/S1389-1286(99)00114-0

Huh, E.-N., & Hai, T. H. (2011). Lightweight Intrusion Detection for Wireless Sensor Networks. In Intrusion Detection Systems. Academic Press.

Hu, L., Chi, L., Li, H. T., Yuan, W., Sun, Y., & Chu, J. F. (2012). The classic security application in M2M- the authentication scheme of Mobile Payment. *Transactions on Internet and Information Systems (Seoul), 6*(1), 131–146.

Huq, M. Z., & Islam, S. (2010). *Home Area Network technology assessment for demand response in smart grid environment.* Paper presented at the Universities Power Engineering Conference (AUPEC).

Hussen, H. R., Tizazu, G. A., Ting, M., Lee, T., Choi, Y., & Kim, K. H. (2013). SAKES: Secure authentication and key establishment scheme for M2M communication in the IP-based wireless sensor network (6L0WPAN).*2013 Fifth International Conference on Ubiquitous and Future Networks (ICUFN'13)*, (pp. 246-251). doi:10.1109/ICUFN.2013.6614820

Hwang, T. (2009). OFDM and its wireless applications: A survey. *IEEE Transactions on Vehicular Technology, 58*(4), 1673–1694. doi:10.1109/TVT.2008.2004555

IEC 61850: Communication networks and systems for power utility automation. (n.d.). International Electrotechnical Commission Std.

IEC 61850-7-420. (2009). *Basic communication structure - Distributed Energy Resources logical nodes.* International Electrotechnical Commission.

IEC-62351. (2007). *IEC-62351 (1-8): Information security for power system control operations, international electrotechnical commission.* Retrieved in May 2016, from http://www.iec.ch/smartgrid/standards/

IEEE 1646. (2004). IEEE Standard Communication Delivery Time Performance Requirements for Electric Power Substation Automation.

IEEE 802.11s. (2011). *Part11: Wireless LAN medium access control (MAC) (PHY) specifications amendment 10: Mesh networking.* IEEE Press.

IEEE Standard 802.15.4-2006. (2006). *Wireless medium access control and physical layer specifications for low-rate wireless personal area networks.* IEEE.

IEEE. (1993, April). Recommended Practices and Requirements for Harmonic Control in Electrical Power Systems, IEEE Std. 519-1992.

IEEE. (2011). *IEEE Guide for Smart Grid Interoperability of Energy Technology and Information Technology Operation with the Electric Power System (EPS), End-Use Applications, and Loads.* Std 2030-2011. doi:10.1109/IEEESTD.2011.6018239

IEEE. (2012). IEEE Standard for Local and metropolitan area networks--Part 15.4: Low-Rate Wireless Personal Area Networks (LR-WPANs) Amendment 3: Physical Layer (PHY) Specifications for Low-Data-Rate, Wireless, Smart Metering Utility Networks IEEE Std 802.15.4g-2012 (Amendment to IEEE Std 802.15.4-2011). doi:10.1109/IEEESTD.2012.6190698

IEEE. (2013). IEEE Standard for Local and metropolitan area networks Part 15.4: Low-Rate Wireless Personal Area Networks (LR-WPANs) Amendment 5: Physical Layer Specifications for Low Energy, Critical Infrastructure Monitoring Networks. IEEE Std 802.15.4k-2013 (Amendment to IEEE Std 802.15.4-2011 as amended by IEEE Std 802.15.4e-2012, IEEE Std 802.15.4f-2012, IEEE Std 802.15.4g-2012, and IEEE Std 802.15.4j-2013). doi:10.1109/IEEESTD.2013.6581828

IEEE-USA Board of Directors. (2010). *Building a Stronger and Smarter Electrical Energy Infrastructure.* Author.

Iniewski, L. T. B. K. (2012). *Smart Grid Apllications, Communication and Security.* Hoboken, NJ: New Jersy Wiley.

Inshil, D., Jiyoung, L., Shi, L., & Kijoon, C. (2014). Pairwise and group key setup mechanism for secure machine-to-machine communication. *Science and Information Systems*, *11*(3), 1071–1090. doi:10.2298/CSIS130922065D

Ipakchi, A., & Albuyeh, F. (2009). Grid of the future. *IEEE Power and Energy Magazine*, *7*(2), 52–62. doi:10.1109/MPE.2008.931384

Irfan, A., Taj, N., & Mahmud, S. A. (2015). A Novel Secure SDN/LTE Based Architecture for Smart Grid Security. In *Proceedings of IEEE International Conference on Computer and Information Technology; Ubiquitous Computing and Communications; Dependable, Autonomic and Secure Computing; Pervasive Intelligence and Computing (CIT/IUCC/DASC/PICOM).* Liverpool, UK: IEEE. doi:10.1109/CIT/IUCC/DASC/PICOM.2015.112

ISA100. 11a - IEC 62734. (2009). *Wireless systems for industrial automation: Process control and related applications.* Retrieved on May 2016, from http://www.isa.org/

ISO. (n. d.). JWG ISO/TC22/SC, ISO/IEC 15118-2 DIS: Vehicle-to-Grid Communication Interface.

J. Mukherjee, & A. Gupta. (2014). A Review of Charge Scheduling of Electric Vehicles in Smart Grid. *IEEE Systems Journal*, PP(99), 1–13.

Jaber, M., Kouzayha, N., Dawy, Z., & Kayssi, A. (2014). On cellular network planning and operation with M2M signalling and security considerations.*2014 IEEE International Conference on Communications Workshops (ICC'14).* doi:10.1109/ICCW.2014.6881236

Jacobson, M. Z., Delucchi, M. A., Cameron, M. A., & Frew, B. A. (2015). Low-cost solution to the grid reliability problem with 100% penetration of intermittent wind, water, and solar for all purposes. *Proceedings of the National Academy of Sciences of the United States of America*, *112*(49), 15060–15065. doi:10.1073/pnas.1510028112 PMID:26598655

Jana, S., Premnath, S. N., Clark, M., Kasera, S. K., Patwari, N., & Krishnamurthy, S. V. (2009, September). On the effectiveness of secret key extraction from wireless signal strength in real environments.*Proceedings of the 15th annual international conference on Mobile computing and networking* (pp. 321-332). ACM. doi:10.1145/1614320.1614356

Jawurek, M., Johns, M., & Rieck, K. (2011). Smart metering de- pseudonymization. In *Proceedings of the 27th annual computer security applications conference* (pp. 227–236).

Jiang, J., & Yasakethu, L. (2013, October). Anomaly detection via one class svm for protection of scada systems. In *Cyber-Enabled Distributed Computing and Knowledge Discovery (CyberC), 2013 International Conference on* (pp. 82-88). IEEE. doi:10.1109/CyberC.2013.22

Jia, W., Zhu, H., Cao, Z., Dong, X., & Xiao, C. (2014). Human-Factor-Aware Privacy-Preserving Aggregation in Smart Grid. *IEEE Systems Journal, 8*(2), 598–607. doi:10.1109/JSYST.2013.2260937

Jin, D., Nicol, D. M., & Yan, G. (2011). *An event buffer flooding attack in DNP3 controlled SCADA systems.* Paper presented at the Proceedings of the Winter Simulation Conference.

Jin, B. W., & Hahm, H. (2013). A Design of Advanced Authentication Method for Protection of Privacy in M2M Environment. *International Journal of Smart Home, 7*(5), 145–154. doi:10.14257/ijsh.2013.7.5.15

Jin, B. W., Park, J. P., Lee, K. W., & Jun, M. S. (2013). A Study of Authentication Method for Id-Based Encryption Using In M2M Environment. *Journal of the Korea Academia-Industrial Cooperation Society, 14*(4), 1926–1934.

Johansen, J. (n. d.). Fast-charging electric vehicles using ac [Master Thesis].

Joseph, S., Jasmin, E. A., & Chandran, S. (2015). Stream Computing: Opportunities and Challenges in Smart Grid. *Procedia Technology, 21*, 49–53. doi:10.1016/j.protcy.2015.10.008

Jover, R. P. (2015). Security and impact of the IoT on LTE mobile networks. In *Security and Privacy in the Internet of Things (IoT): Models, Algorithms, and Implementations.* CRC Press, Taylor & Francis. Retrieved 6 Dec., 2015 from: http://www.ee.columbia.edu/~roger/LTE_IoT.pdf

Jung, S., Ahn, J. Y., Hwang, D. J., & Kim, S. (2012). A Study on Key Distribution Protocol with Mutual Authentication for M2M Sensor Network. Information, 15, 1229-1240.

Jung, S., Kim, D., & Seoksoo, S. (2013). *Cooperative Architecture for Secure M2M Communication. In Advanced Science and Technology Letters* (Vol. 29, pp. 37–40). SecTech.

Jung, S., & Kim, S. (2013). Hierarchical Security Management for M2M Wireless Sensor Networks. *International Journal of Advancements in Computing Technology, 5*(11), 238–244. doi:10.4156/ijact.vol5.issue11.26

Kabalci, Y. (2016). A survey on smart metering and smart grid communication. *Renewable & Sustainable Energy Reviews, 57*, 302–318. doi:10.1016/j.rser.2015.12.114

Kaku, M. (2008). *Physics of the Impossible.* New York: Anchor Books.

Kalogridis, G., Efthymiou, C., Denic, S., Lewis, T., & Cepeda, R. (2010). Privacy for smart meters: Towards undetectable appliance load signatures. In IEEE SmartGridComm (pp. 232–237). IEEE.

Kamto, J., Qian, L., Li, W., & Han, Z. (2016). -Augmented Tree for Robust Data Collection in Advanced Metering Infrastructure. *International Journal of Distributed Sensor Networks, 2016*, 1–13. doi:10.1155/2016/9821289

Kaplani, E., & Kaplanis, S. (2012). A stochastic simulation model for reliable PV system sizing providing for solar radiation fluctuations. *Applied Energy, 97*, 970–981. doi:10.1016/j.apenergy.2011.12.016

Kapoor, A., & Moh, M. (2015). Implementation and evaluation of the DFF protocol for Advanced Metering Infrastructure (AMI) networks. *Proceedings of 11th IEEE International Conference on Design of Reliable Communication Networks.*

Kargl, F., Papadimitratos, P., Buttyan, L., Muter, M., Schoch, E., Wiedersheim, B., & Hubaux, J.-P. et al. (2008, November). Secure Vehicular Communication Systems: Implementation, Performance, and Research Challenges. *IEEE Communications Magazine*, *46*(11), 110–118. doi:10.1109/MCOM.2008.4689253

Kargupta, H., Datta, S., Wang, Q., & Ravikumar, K. (2003). *Random Data Perturbation Techniques and Privacy Preserving Data Mining*. Paper from the IEEE International Conference on Data Mining, Orlando, FL.

Karim, L., Anpalagan, A., Nasser, N., Almhana, J. N., & Woungang, I. (2013). *An energy efficient, fault tolerant and secure clustering scheme for M2M communication networks. In 2013 IEEE Globecom Workshops* (pp. 677–682). Atlanta, GA: GC Wkshps.

Karnouskos, S. (2011). Stuxnet worm impact on industrial cyber-physical system security. In *Proceedings of 37th Annual Conference on IEEE Industrial Electronics Society (IECON 2011)*. Melbourne, Vic: IEEE. doi:10.1109/IECON.2011.6120048

Karuppiah, A. B., Dalfiah, J., Yuvashri, K., Rajaram, S., & Pathan, A.-S. K. (2014). Energy-Efficient Sybil Node Detection Algorithm for Wireless Sensor Networks.*3rd International Conference on Eco-Friendly Computing and Communication Systems (ICECCS 2014).*

Katzir, L., & Schwartzman, I. (2011). Secure firmware updates for smart grid Devices. *Innovative Smart Grid Technologies (ISGT Europe),2nd IEEE PES International Conference and Exhibition on*, (pp. 1-5).

Kazienko, J. F., Silva Filho, P. R., Moraes, I. M., & Albuquerque, C. V. (2015). On the Performance of a Secure Storage Mechanism for Key Distribution Architectures in Wireless Sensor Networks. *International Journal of Distributed Sensor Networks*, *2015*, 1–14. doi:10.1155/2015/392495

Kempton, W., & Tomić, J. (2005). Vehicle-to-grid power fundamentals: Calculating capacity and net revenue. *Journal of Power Sources*, *144*(1), 268–279. doi:10.1016/j.jpowsour.2004.12.025

Kenkre, P. S., Pai, A., & Colaco, L. (2015). Real time intrusion detection and prevention system. In *Proceedings of the 3rd International Conference on Frontiers of Intelligent Computing: Theory and Applications (FICTA) 2014* (pp. 405-411). Springer International Publishing. doi:10.1007/978-3-319-11933-5_44

Kennel, F., Gorges, D., & Liu, S. (2013). Energy Management for Smart Grids with Electric Vehicles Based on Hierarchical MPC. *IEEE Transactions on Industrial Informatics*, *9*(3), 1528-1537. doi:10.1109/TII.2012.2228876

Khaitan, S. K., McCalley, J. D., & Liu, C. C. (2015). *Cyber Physical Systems Approach to Smart Electric Power Grid*. Springer-Verlag Berlin Heidelberg. doi:10.1007/978-3-662-45928-7

Khan, L., Awad, M., & Thuraisingham, B. (2007). A new intrusion detection system using support vector machines and hierarchical clustering. *The VLDB Journal—The International Journal on Very Large Data Bases*, *16*(4), 507-521.

Khan, R. H., & Khan, J. Y. (2012, November 5-8). A heterogeneous WiMAX-WLAN network for AMI communications in the smart grid. *Paper presented at the 2012 IEEE Third International Conference on Smart Grid Communications (SmartGridComm).*

Khan, S., Pathan, A.-S. K., & Alrajeh, N. A. (2012). Wireless Sensor Networks: Current Status and Future Trends. Auerbach Publications, CRC Press, Taylor & Francis Group. doi:10.1201/b13092

Khan, R. H., & Khan, J. Y. (2013). A comprehensive review of the application characteristics and traffic requirements of a smart grid communications network. *Computer Networks*, *57*(3), 825–845. doi:10.1016/j.comnet.2012.11.002

Khaund, K. (2015). *Cybersecurity in Smart Buildings*. Frost & Sullivan Collaborative Industry Perspective. Retrieved from http://23873b0b5ea986687186-fddd749ce937721293aa13aa786d4227.r31.cf1.rackcdn.com/Documentation/Cybersecurity%20in%20Smart%20Buildings_White%20Paper.pdf

Kheldoun, A., Bradai, R., Boukenoui, R., & Mellit, A. (2016). A new golden section method-based maximum power point tracking algorithm for photovoltaic systems. *Energy Conversion and Management, 111*, 125–136. doi:10.1016/j.enconman.2015.12.039

Kildall, G. A. (1973, October). A unified approach to global program optimization. In *Proceedings of the 1st annual ACM SIGACT-SIGPLAN symposium on Principles of programming languages* (pp. 194-206). ACM. doi:10.1145/512927.512945

Kim, J.M., Jeong, H.Y., & Hong, B.H. (2011). A User Authentication Method for M2M Environments. Computer Science and Convergence, *Lecture Notes in Electrical Engineering, 114,* 589-595.

Kim, J.M., Jeong, H.Y., & Hong, B.H. (2014) A study of privacy problem solving using device and user authentication for M2M environments. *Security and Communication Networks, 7*(10, 1528–1535.

Kim, J.-Y., & Choi, H.-K. (2012). *An efficient and versatile key management protocol for secure smart grid communications.* Paper presented at the Wireless Communications and Networking Conference (WCNC). doi:10.1109/WCNC.2012.6214081

Kim, Kim, Lim, Ko, & Lee. (2012). Improving the Reliability of IEEE 802.11s Based Wireless Mesh Networks for Smart Grid Systems. *Journal of Communications and Networks, 14*(6).

Kim, B. G., Zhang, Y., van der Schaar, M., & Lee, J. W. (2014). Dynamic pricing for smart grid with reinforcement learning. In *Proceedings of IEEE Conference on Computer Communications Workshops (INFOCOM WKSHPS)*. Toronto, ON: IEEE. doi:10.1109/INFCOMW.2014.6849306

Kim, J. C., & Kim, T. H. (2014). Implementation of Secure IEC 61850 Communication. *CIRED Workshop.*

Kim, J., & Bentley, P. J. (2001, July). An evaluation of negative selection in an artificial immune system for network intrusion detection. In *Proceedings of GECCO* (pp. 1330-1337).

Kim, M. J., & Kang, D. K. (2010). Ensemble with neural networks for bankruptcy prediction. *Expert Systems with Applications, 37*(4), 3373–3379. doi:10.1016/j.eswa.2009.10.012

Kissel, G. (2011). Presentation of Standard J1772. *Proceedings of the EPRI Infrastructure Working Council Conf.*

Knapp, E. D., & Langill, J. (2011). *Industrial Network Security: Securing Critical Infrastructure Networks for Smart Grid, SCADA, and Other Industrial Control Systems.* Syngress.

Knapp, E. D., & Samani, R. (2013). *What is the Smart Grid? In Applied Cyber Security and the Smart Grid* (pp. 1–15). Boston: Syngress. doi:10.1016/B978-1-59749-998-9.00001-3

Knight, J., & Strunk, E. (2004). Achieving critical system survivability through software architectures. In *Architecting Dependable Systems II* (Vol. 3069, pp. 51–78). Springer. doi:10.1007/978-3-540-25939-8_3

Knorr, E. M., & Ng, R. T. (1997, August). *A Unified Notion of Outliers: Properties and Computation* (pp. 219–222). KDD.

Koss, J. (2014). *ETSI Standardizes M2M Communications.* Retrieved 28 Nov. 2015 from: http://www.telit2market.com/wp-content/uploads/2014/10/t2m0510_p038-p039.pdf

Kothmayr, T. D., Hu, W., Brunig, M., & Carle, G. (2012). A DTLS based end-to-end security architecture for the Internet of Things with two-way authentication. *2012 IEEE 37th Conference on Local Computer Networks Workshops (LCN Workshops).*

Kounev, V., Lévesque, M., Tipper, D., & Gomes, T. (2016). Reliable Communication Networks for Smart Grid Transmission Systems. *Journal of Network and Systems Management, 24*(3), 629–652. doi:10.1007/s10922-016-9375-y

Kowalenko (2010). The Smart Grid: A Primer. *The Institute, IEEE.*

Kozen, D. (1997). *Automata and Computability.* Ithaca, NY: Springer. doi:10.1007/978-1-4612-1844-9

Krawczyk, B., & Woźniak, M. (2014). Diversity measures for one-class classifier ensembles. *Neurocomputing, 126,* 36–44. doi:10.1016/j.neucom.2013.01.053

krebsonsecurity. (n.d.). *FBI: Smart Meter Hacks Likely to Spread.* Retrieved 3/5/2013, from https://krebsonsecurity.com/2012/04/fbi-smart-meter-hacks-likely-to-spread/

Krishnamoorthy, H. S. G., Pawan, P. N., & Pitel, I. J. (2014). Wind Turbine Generator–Battery Energy Storage Utility Interface Converter Topology With Medium-Frequency Transformer Link. *IEEE Transactions on Power Electronics, 29*(8), 4146–4155. doi:10.1109/TPEL.2013.2295419

Krontiris, I., & Dimitriou, T. (2007). Towards intrusion detection in wireless sensor networks. *13th European wireless conference.*

Krontiris, I., Dimitriou, T., & Giannetsos, T. (2008). LIDeA: A distributed lightweight intrusion detection architecture for sensor networks. ACM secure communication.

Kursawe, K., Danezis, G., & Kohlweiss, M. (2011). Privacy-friendly aggregation for the smart-grid. In Privacy enhancing technologies (pp. 175–191). doi:10.1007/978-3-642-22263-4_10

Kush, N., Ahmed, E., Branagan, M., & Foo, E. (2014). Poisoned GOOSE: Exploiting the GOOSE Protocol. *Proceedings of the Twelfth Australasian Information Security Conference,* (pp. 17-22).

Kushner, D. (2013). The real story of stuxnet. *IEEE Spectrum, 50*(3), 48–53. doi:10.1109/MSPEC.2013.6471059

Kuzlu, M., & Pipattanasomporn, M. (2013). Assessment of communication technologies and network requirements for different smart grid applications. In Innovative Smart Grid Technologies (pp. 1–6).

Lai, C., Li, H., Lu, R., Shen, X. S., & Cao, J. (2013). A unified end-to-end security scheme for machine-type communication in LTE networks. *2013 IEEE/CIC International Conference on Communications in China (ICCC).* doi:10.1109/ICCChina.2013.6671201

Lai, C., Li, H., Zhang, Y., & Cao, J. (2012). Security Issues on Machine to Machine Communications. *Transactions on Internet and Information Systems (Seoul), 6*(2), 498–514.

Lake, D., Milito, R., Morrow, M., & Vargheese, R. (2014). Internet of Things: Architectural Framework for eHealth Security. *Journal of ICT Standardization, 3-4,* 301–328.

Lanzafame, R., Stefano, M., & Messina, M. (2014). 2D CFD modeling of H-Darrieus wind turbines using a transition turbulence mode. *Energy Procedia, 45,* 131–140. doi:10.1016/j.egypro.2014.01.015

Lasseter, R. H. (2006, March). The role of distributed energy resources in future electric power systems. *Proceedings of the Energy Systems Seminar,* University of Wisconsin.

Laudani, A., Fulginei, F. R., & Salvini, A. (2014). High performing extraction procedure for the one-diode model of a photovoltaic panel from experimental I–V curves by using reduced forms. *Solar Energy, 103,* 316–326. doi:10.1016/j.solener.2014.02.014

Lee, K.L. & Kim, S.K. (2015). Authentication Scheme based on Biometric Key for VANET Information System in M2M Application Service. *Applied Math and Information Science Journal*, *9*(2L), 645-651.

Lee, M. (2013). *M2M and the Internet of Things: How secure is it?* Retrieved 29 Nov. 2015 from: http://www.zdnet. com/article/disgruntled-over-big-data-maybe-its-that-visualization-magic-box-dependence

Lee, W. B., Chen, T. H., Sun, W. R., & Ho, K. I. J. (2014, May). An S/Key-like one-time password authentication scheme using smart cards for smart meter. In *Advanced Information Networking and Applications Workshops (WAINA), 2014 28th International Conference on* (pp. 281-286). IEEE.

Lee, C. Y. (1999). Effects of unbalanced voltage on the operation performance of a three-phase induction motor. *IEEE Transactions on Energy Conversion*, *14*(2), 202–208. doi:10.1109/60.766984

Lee, E. K., Gerla, M., & Oh, S. Y. (2012). Physical layer security in wireless smart grid. *IEEE Communications Magazine*, *50*(8), 46–52. doi:10.1109/MCOM.2012.6257526

Lee, E.-K., Oh, S. Y., & Gerla, M. (2011). Frequency Quorum Rendezvous for Fast and Resilient Key Establishment under Jamming Attack. *Mobile Computing and Communications Review*, *14*(4), 1–3. doi:10.1145/1942268.1942270

Lee, H., & Chung, M. (2012). Context-Aware Security System for the Smart Phone-based M2M Service Environment. *Transactions on Internet and Information Systems (Seoul)*, *6*(1), 64–83.

Lee, K., Venkataramanan, G., & Jahns, T. M. (2008). Modeling effects of voltage unbalances in industrial distribution systems with adjustable-speed drives. *IEEE Transactions on Industry Applications*, *44*(5), 1322–1332. doi:10.1109/TIA.2008.2002277

Lee, S., Bong, J., Shin, S., & Shin, Y. (2014). A security mechanism of Smart Grid AMI network through smart device mutual authentication. In *Proceedings of the International Conference on Information Networking (ICOIN2014)*. IEEE.

Lewandowski, C., Böcker, S., & Wietfeld, C. (2013, December). An ICT solution for integration of Electric Vehicles in grid balancing services. *Proceedings of the 2013 International Conference on Connected Vehicles and Expo (ICCVE)* (pp. 195-200). IEEE. doi:10.1109/ICCVE.2013.6799792

Li & Sarkar. (2006). A Tree-Based Data Perturbation Approach for Privacy-Preserving Data Mining. *Knowledge and Data Engineering, IEEE Transactions on, 18*(9), 1278-1283.

Li, F., Luo, B., & Liu, P. (2010). Secure information aggregation for smart grids using homomorphic encryption. In *Smart grid communications (smartgridcomm), 2010 first IEEE international conference on* (pp. 327–332). doi:10.1109/SMARTGRID.2010.5622064

Li, G., He, J., & Fu, Y. (2008). A group based intrusion detection scheme in wireless sensor networks. *The 3rd international conference on grid and pervasive computing—workshop*, (pp. 286-291).

Li, K. L., Huang, H. K., Tian, S. F., & Xu, W. (2003, November). Improving one-class SVM for anomaly detection. In *Machine Learning and Cybernetics, 2003 International Conference on* (Vol. 5, pp. 3077-3081). IEEE.

Li, T., & Li, N. (2008). Injector: Mining background knowledge for data anonymization. In ICDE.

Li, W., Yi, Wu, Y., Pan, L., & Li, J. (2014). A New Intrusion Detection System Based on KNN Classification Algorithm in Wireless Sensor Network. Journal of Electrical and Computer Engineering.

Lichman, M. (2013). *UCI machine learning repository*. Academic Press.

Li, G., & Zhang, X. P. (2012). Modeling of plug-in hybrid electric vehicle charging demand in probabilistic power flow calculations. *IEEE Transactions on Smart Grid*, *3*(1), 492–499. doi:10.1109/TSG.2011.2172643

Li, H., & Han, Z. (2011). Manipulating the Electricity Power Market via Jamming the Price Signaling in Smart Grid. *IEEE International Workshop on Smart Grid Communications and Networks*. doi:10.1109/GLOCOMW.2011.6162363

Li, H., Lu, R., Zhou, L., Yang, B., & Shen, X. (2013). An Efficient Merkle-Tree-Based Authentication Scheme for Smart Grid. *IEEE Systems Journal*, *8*(2), 655–663. doi:10.1109/JSYST.2013.2271537

Liljenstam, M., Liu, J., Nicol, D., Yuan, Y., Yan, G., & Grier, C. (2005, June). Rinse: The real-time immersive network simulation environment for network security exercises. In *Workshop on Principles of Advanced and Distributed Simulation (PADS'05)* (pp. 119-128). IEEE. doi:10.1109/PADS.2005.23

Li, N., Li, T., & Venkatasubramanian, S. (2010). Closeness: A New Privacy Measure for Data Publishing. *IEEE Transactions on Knowledge and Data Engineering*, *22*(7), 943–956. doi:10.1109/TKDE.2009.139

Lippmann, R., Haines, J. W., Fried, D. J., Korba, J., & Das, K. (2000). The 1999 DARPA off-line intrusion detection evaluation. *Computer Networks*, *34*(4), 579–595. doi:10.1016/S1389-1286(00)00139-0

Li, Q., Ross, C., Yang, J., Di, J., Balda, J. C., & Alan, H. (2015). The effects of flooding attacks on time-critical communications in the smart grid. *Innovative Smart Grid Technologies Conference (ISGT)*. IEEE Power & Energy Society. doi:10.1109/ISGT.2015.7131802

Lisovich, M. A., Mulligan, D. K., & Wicker, S. B. (2010). Inferring Personal Information from Demand-Response Systems. *IEEE Security and Privacy*, *8*(1), 11–20. doi:10.1109/MSP.2010.40

Li, T., Li, N., & Zhang, J. (2009). Modeling and integrating background knowledge in data anonymization. In ICDE. doi:10.1109/ICDE.2009.86

Liu, Q., Shen, H., & Sang, Y. (2014). A Privacy-Preserving Data Publishing Method for Multiple Numerical Sensitive Attributes via Clustering and Multi-sensitive Bucketization. *Parallel Architectures, Algorithms and Programming (PAAP),2014 Sixth International Symposium on*.

Liu, S., Liu, X. P., & El Saddik, A. (2013). *Denial-of-service (DoS) attacks on load frequency control in smart grids*. Paper presented at the Innovative Smart Grid Technologies (ISGT), 2013 IEEE PES.

Liu, H., Chen, Y., Chuah, M. C., & Yang, J. (2013). Towards self-healing smart grid via intelligent local controller switching under jamming. In *Proceedings of IEEE Conference on Communications and Network Security (CNS)*. Washington, DC: IEEE.

Liu, J., Lu, Y.-H., & Koh, C.-K. (2010). *Performance analysis of arithmetic operations in homomorphic encryption*. *Purdue University e-Pubs*. ECE Technical Reports.

Liu, L., Gu, M., & Ma, Y. (2015). *Research on the Key Technology of M2M Gateway*. Lecture Notes in Computer Science, 8944, 837–843. doi:10.1007/978-3-319-15554-8_76

Liu, L., Liu, Y., Wang, L., Zomaya, A., & Hu, S. (2015). Economical and Balanced Energy Usage in the Smart Home Infrastructure: A Tutorial and New Results. *IEEE Transactions on Emerging Topics in Computing*, *3*(4), 556–570. doi:10.1109/TETC.2015.2484839

Liu, X., Zhang, Y., Wang, B., & Wang, H. (2014). An anonymous data aggregation scheme for smart grid systems. *Security and Communication Networks*, *7*(3), 602–610. doi:10.1002/sec.761

Li, X., Wang, L., & Sung, E. (2008). AdaBoost with SVM-based component classifiers. *Engineering Applications of Artificial Intelligence*, *21*(5), 785–795. doi:10.1016/j.engappai.2007.07.001

Logenthiran, T., Srinivasan, D., & Shun, T. Z. (2012). Demand side management in smart grid using heuristic optimization. *IEEE Transactions on Smart Grid, 3*(3), 1244–1252. doi:10.1109/TSG.2012.2195686

Loo, C. E., Ng, M. Y., Leckie, C., & Palaniswami, M. (2010). Intrusion detection for routing attacks in sensor networks. *International Journal of Distributed Sensor Networks, 2*(4), 313–332. doi:10.1080/15501320600692044

Lopes, Y., Muchaluat-Saade, D. C., Fernandes, N. C., & Fortes, M. Z. (2015). Geese: A traffic generator for performance and security evaluation of IEC 61850 networks. *IEEE 24th International Symposium on Industrial Electronics (ISIE)*, (pp. 687-692).

Lopes, Y., Fernandes, N. C., Bastos, C. A., & Muchaluat-Saade, D. C. (2015). SMARTFlow: a solution for autonomic management and control of communication networks for smart grids.*Proceedings of the 30th Annual ACM Symposium on Applied Computing*, (pp. 2212-2217). doi:10.1145/2695664.2695733

Lüders, S. (2011). Why Control System CyberSecurity Sucks. *GovCERT.NL Symposium*.

Lu, M., Shi, Z., Lu, R., Sun, R., & Shen, X. S. (2013). PPPA: A practical privacy-preserving aggregation scheme for smart grid communications. In *Proceedings of IEEE/CIC International Conference on Communications in China (ICCC)*. IEEE. doi:10.1109/ICCChina.2013.6671200

Lund, P. D., Lindgren, J., Mikkola, J., & Salpakari, J. (2015). Review of energy system flexibility measures to enable high levels of variable renewable electricity. *Renewable & Sustainable Energy Reviews, 45*, 785–807. doi:10.1016/j.rser.2015.01.057

Lu, R., Liang, X., Li, X., Lin, X., & Shen, X. (2012). EPPA: An efficient and privacy-preserving aggregation scheme for secure smart grid communications. Parallel and Distributed Systems. *IEEE Transactions on, 23*(9), 1621–1631.

Lu, R., Lin, X., Shi, Z., & Shen, X. (2013). EATH: An efficient aggregate authentication protocol for smart grid communications. In *Proceedings of IEEE Wireless Communications and Networking Conference (WCNC)*. IEEE. doi:10.1109/WCNC.2013.6554840

Lu, R., Li, X., Liang, X., Shen, X., & Lin, X. (2011). GRS: The green, reliability, and security of emerging machine to machine communications. *IEEE Communications Magazine, Volume, 49*(4), 28–35. doi:10.1109/MCOM.2011.5741143

Lu, Z., Lu, X., Wang, W., & Wang, C. (2010). Review and evaluation of security threats on the communication networks in the smart grid. In *Proceedings of MILITARY COMMUNICATIONS CONFERENCE (MILCOM 2010)*. San Jose, CA: IEEE. doi:10.1109/MILCOM.2010.5679551

Lv, X., Mu, Y., & Li, H. (2014). Key management for Smart Grid based on asymmetric key-wrapping. *International Journal of Computer Mathematics, 92*(3), 498–512. doi:10.1080/00207160.2014.917178

Ma, J., & Perkins, S. (2003, July). Time-series novelty detection using one-class support vector machines. In *Neural Networks, 2003.Proceedings of the International Joint Conference on* (Vol. 3, pp. 1741-1745). IEEE. doi:10.1109/IJCNN.2003.1223670

Machanavajjhala, A., Gehrke, J., Kifer, D., & Venkitasubramaniam, M. (2006). L-diversity: Privacy beyond k-anonymity. In *Proc. 22nd Intnl. Conf. Data Engg. (ICDE)*. doi:10.1109/ICDE.2006.1

Machine to Machine Communications. The European Telecommunications Standards Institute (ETSI) standards. (n.d.). Retrieved 28 Nov., 2015 from: http://www.etsi.org/technologies-clusters/technologies/m2m

Machine-to-Machine Communications (M2M) Functional Architecture. (2011). *The European Telecommunications Standards Institute (ETSI), TS 102 690 V1.1.1 (2011-10), 2011*. Retrieved 28 Nov. 2015 from: http://www.etsi.org/deliver/etsi_ts/102600_102699/102690/01.01.01_60/ts_102690v010101p.pdf

Machine-to-Machine Communications (M2M) mIa, dIa and mId Interfaces. (2015). *ETSI TS 102 921 V1.3.1 (2014-09)*. Retrieved 29 Nov., 2015 from: http://www.etsi.org/deliver/etsi_ts/102900_102999/102921/01.03.01_60/ts_102921v010301p.pdf

Mackiewicz, R. E. (2006, May 21-24). Overview of IEC 61850 and Benefits. *Paper presented at the 2005/2006 IEEE/PES Transmission and Distribution Conference and Exhibition*.

Madureira, A. G. (2012). Coordinated and optimized voltage management of distribution networks with multi-microgrids. Retrieved from https://repositorio-aberto.up.pt/bitstream/10216/58358/1/000143265.pdf

Maglaras, L. A. & Jiang, J. (2015). A novel intrusion detection method based on OCSVM and K-means recursive clustering. *EAI Transactions on Security and Safety*, 1-10.

Maglaras, L. A., & Jiang, J. (2014, August). Ocsvm model combined with k-means recursive clustering for intrusion detection in scada systems. In *Heterogeneous Networking for Quality, Reliability, Security and Robustness (QShine), 2014 10th International Conference on* (pp. 133-134). IEEE. doi:10.1109/QSHINE.2014.6928673

Maglaras, L. A., Jiang, J., & Cruz, T. G. (2015). Combining ensemble methods and social network metrics for improving accuracy of OCSVM on intrusion detection in SCADA systems. Journal of Information Security and Applications.

Maglaras, L. A., Jiang, J., & Cruz, T. J. (2016). Combining ensemble methods and social network metrics for improving accuracy of OCSVM on intrusion detection in SCADA systems. *Journal of Information Security and Applications*.

Maglaras, L. A., & Jiang, J. (2014). A real time OCSVM Intrusion Detection module with low overhead for SCADA systems. *International Journal of Advanced Research in Artificial Intelligence*, 3(10).

Maglaras, L. A., & Jiang, J. (2014, August). Intrusion detection in scada systems using machine learning techniques. In *Science and Information Conference (SAI)* (pp. 626-631). IEEE doi:10.1109/SAI.2014.6918252

Maglaras, L. A., Jiang, J., & Cruz, T. (2014). Integrated OCSVM mechanism for intrusion detection in SCADA systems. *Electronics Letters*, 50(25), 1935–1936. doi:10.1049/el.2014.2897

Mahkonen, H., Rinta-aho, T., Kauppinen, T., Sethi, M., Kjällman, J., & Salmela, P. (2013). Secure M2M cloud testbed. *Proceedings of the 19th annual international conference on Mobile computing & networking (MobiCom '13)*. ACM. doi:10.1145/2500423.2505294

Mahoney, M. V., & Chan, P. K. (2003, September). An analysis of the 1999 DARPA/Lincoln Laboratory evaluation data for network anomaly detection. In *International Workshop on Recent Advances in Intrusion Detection* (pp. 220-237). Springer Berlin Heidelberg. doi:10.1007/978-3-540-45248-5_13

Majumder, R. (2013). Reactive power compensation in single-phase operation of microgrid. *IEEE Transactions on Industrial Electronics*, 60(4), 1403–1416. doi:10.1109/TIE.2012.2193860

Mak, H. Y., Rong, Y., & Shen, Z. J. M. (2013). Infrastructure planning for electric vehicles with battery swapping. *Management Science*, 59(7), 1557–1575. doi:10.1287/mnsc.1120.1672

Malathy, S., & Ramaprabha, R. (2013). Maximum Power Point Tracking Based on Look up Table Approach. *Advanced Materials Research*, 768, 124–130. doi:10.4028/www.scientific.net/AMR.768.124

Manandhar, K., & Cao, X., Fei Hu & Liu, Y. (2014). Combating False Data Injection Attacks in Smart Grid using Kalman Filter. In *Proceedings of International Conference on Computing, Networking and Communications (ICNC)*. Honolulu, HI: IEEE. doi:10.1109/ICCNC.2014.6785297

Maras, M. H. (2015). Internet of Things: security and privacy implications. *International Data Privacy Law*. Retrieved 6 Dec., 2015 from: http://idpl.oxfordjournals.org/content/5/2/99

Marmol, F. G., Sorge, C., Ugus, O., & Ṕerez, G. M. (2012). Do not snoop my habits: preserving privacy in the smart grid. *Communications Magazine, IEEE, 50*(5), 166–172.

Martin, D. J., Kifer, D., Machanavajjhala, A., Gehrke, J., & Halpern, J. Y. (2007). Worst-Case Background Knowledge for Privacy-Preserving Data Publishing. *ICDE 2007. IEEE 23rd International Conference on*.

Martinez, F. J., Toh, C. K., Cano, J. C., Calafate, C. T., & Manzoni, P. (2011). A survey and comparative study of simulators for vehicular ad hoc networks (VANETs). *Wireless Communications and Mobile Computing, 11*(7), 813–828. doi:10.1002/wcm.859

Masek, P., Muthanna, A., & Hosek, J. (2015). Suitability of MANET Routing Protocols for the Next-Generation National Security and Public Safety Systems. Internet of Things, Smart Spaces, and Next Generation Networks and Systems, Volume 9247 of the series. *Lecture Notes in Computer Science, 9247*, 242–253. doi:10.1007/978-3-319-23126-6_22

Masoum, M. A., Deilami, S., & Islam, S. (2010, July). Mitigation of harmonics in smart grids with high penetration of plug-in electric vehicles. *Proceedings of the IEEE PES General Meeting* (pp. 1-6). IEEE. doi:10.1109/PES.2010.5589970

Mathiesen, B. V., Lund, H., Connolly, D., Wenzel, H., Østergaard, P. A., Möller, B., & Hvelplund, F. K. et al. (2015). Smart Energy Systems for coherent 100% renewable energy and transport solutions. *Applied Energy, 145*, 139–154. doi:10.1016/j.apenergy.2015.01.075

Matin, M. A. (2014). *Handbook of Research on Progressive Trends in Wireless Communications and Networking*. IGI Global. doi:10.4018/978-1-4666-5170-8

McBride, A. J., & McGee, A. R. (2012). Assessing smart Grid security. *Bell Labs Technical Journal, 17*(3), 87–103. doi:10.1002/bltj.21560

McDaniel, P., & McLaughlin, S. (2009). Security and Privacy Challenges in the Smart Grid. *IEEE Security and Privacy, 7*(3), 75–77. doi:10.1109/MSP.2009.76

McGhee, J., & Goraj, M. (2010). Smart High Voltage Substation Based on IEC 61850 Process Bus and IEEE 1588 Time Synchronization. *Smart Grid Communications (SmartGridComm), First IEEE International Conference on*, (pp. 489-494).

McHugh, J. (2000). Testing intrusion detection systems: A critique of the 1998 and 1999 darpa intrusion detection system evaluations as performed by Lincoln laboratory. *ACM Transactions on Information and System Security, 3*(4), 262–294. doi:10.1145/382912.382923

Mell, P., & Grance, T. (2002). *Use of the common vulnerabilities and exposures (cve) vulnerability naming scheme (No. NIST-SP-800-51)*. National Inst of Standards and Technology. doi:10.6028/NIST.SP.800-51

Menahem, E., Rokach, L., & Elovici, Y. (2013, October). Combining one-class classifiers via meta learning. In *Proceedings of the 22nd ACM international conference on Conference on information & knowledge management* (pp. 2435-2440). ACM doi:10.1145/2505515.2505619

Meng, W., Ma, R., & Chen, H. H. (2014). Smart grid neighborhood area networks: A survey. *IEEE Network, 28*(1), 24–32. doi:10.1109/MNET.2014.6724103

Merkle, R. (1979). *Secrecy Authentication and Public Key Systems*. Information Systems Laboratory, Stanford Electronics Laboratories. Retrieved from http://www.merkle.com/papers/Thesis1979.pdf

Miller, M. (2015). *The Internet of Things: How Smart TVs, Smart Cars, Smart Homes, and Smart Cities Are Changing the World*. Pearson Education.

Mirzaei, M. J., Kazemi, A., & Homaee, O. (2014). RETRACTED: Real-world based approach for optimal management of electric vehicles in an intelligent parking lot considering simultaneous satisfaction of vehicle owners and parking operator. *Energy, 76*, 345–356. doi:10.1016/j.energy.2014.08.026

Mishra, S., Dinh, T. N., Thai, M. T., Seo, J., & Shin, I. (2016). Optimal packet scan against malicious attacks in smart grids. *Theoretical Computer Science, 609*, 606–619. doi:10.1016/j.tcs.2015.07.054

Misic, V. B., & Misic, J. (2014). *Machine-to-Machine Communications: Architectures, Technology, Standards, and Applications*. CRC Press.

Mnider, A. M., Atkinson, D. J., Dahidah, M., Zbede, Y. B., & Armstrong, M. (2016, March). A programmable cascaded LPF based PLL scheme for single-phase grid-connected inverters. *Proceedings of the 2016 7th International Renewable Energy Congress (IREC)* (pp. 1-6). IEEE. doi:10.1109/IREC.2016.7478935

Moballegh, S., & Jiang, J. (2014). Modeling, prediction, and experimental validations of power peaks of PV arrays under partial shading conditions. *IEEE Transactions on Sustainable Energy, 5*(1), 293–300. doi:10.1109/TSTE.2013.2282077

Modbus, I. D. A. (2004). *Modbus application protocol specification v1*. Retrieved from www.modbus.org/specs.php

Mohammed, M., & Pathan, A.-S. K. (2013). Automatic Defense against Zero-day Polymorphic Worms in Communication Networks. CRC Press, Taylor & Francis Group. doi:10.1201/b14912

Mohanty, S., Patra, P. K., & Sahoo, S. S. (2016). Prediction and application of solar radiation with soft computing over traditional and conventional approach–A comprehensive review. *Renewable & Sustainable Energy Reviews, 56*, 778–796. doi:10.1016/j.rser.2015.11.078

Molina-Markham, A., Shenoy, P., Fu, K., Cecchet, E., & Irwin, D. (2010). Private Memoirs of a Smart Meter. *Proceedings of the 2nd ACM Workshop on Embedded Sensing Systems for Energy-Efficiency in Building*, (pp. 61-66). doi:10.1145/1878431.1878446

Monfared, M., & Golestan, S. (2012). a). Control strategies for single-phase grid integration of small-scale renewable energy sources: A review. *Renewable & Sustainable Energy Reviews, 16*(7), 4982–4993. doi:10.1016/j.rser.2012.04.017

Monfared, M., Golestan, S., & Guerrero, J. M. (2014). Analysis, design, and experimental verification of a synchronous reference frame voltage control for single-phase inverters. *IEEE Transactions on Industrial Electronics, 61*(1), 258–269. doi:10.1109/TIE.2013.2238878

Monfared, M., Sanatkar, M., & Golestan, S. (2012). b). Direct active and reactive power control of single-phase grid-tie converters. *IET Power Electronics, 5*(8), 1544–1550. doi:10.1049/iet-pel.2012.0131

Monroe, C., & Kim, J. (2013, March). Scaling the Ion Trap Quantum Processor. *Science, 339*(6124), 1164–1169. doi:10.1126/science.1231298 PMID:23471398

Montenegro, G., Kushalnagar, N., Hui, J., & Culler, D. (2007). *RFC 4944: Transmission of IPv6 packets over IEEE 802.15.4 networks*. RFC.

Moon, Y. k., Lee, E. K., Kim, J. J., & Choi, H. R. (2014). *Study on the Container Security Device based on IoT. In Information* (pp. 5425–5433). Tokyo: International Information Institute.

Moore, R. A., Jr. (1996). Controlled data-swapping techniques for masking public use microdata sets. Statistical Research Division Report Series RR 96-04. U.S. Bureau of the Census.

More than 50 billion connected devices. (2011). Ericsson white paper, 28423-3149Uen.

Morris, T., & Gao, W. (2014, March). Industrial Control System Traffic Data Sets for Intrusion Detection Research. In *International Conference on Critical Infrastructure Protection* (pp. 65-78). doi:10.1007/978-3-662-45355-1_5

Morris, T., Srivastava, A., Reaves, B., Gao, W., Pavurapu, K., & Reddi, R. (2011). A control system testbed to validate critical infrastructure protection concepts. *International Journal of Critical Infrastructure Protection, 4*(2), 88–103. doi:10.1016/j.ijcip.2011.06.005

Moss, T., & Marvin, S. (2016). *Urban infrastructure in transition: networks, buildings and plans.* Routledge.

Mousazadeh, H., Keyhani, A., Javadi, A., Mobli, H., Abrinia, K., & Sharifi, A. (2009). A review of principle and sun-tracking methods for maximizing solar systems output. *Renewable & Sustainable Energy Reviews, 13*(8), 1800–1818. doi:10.1016/j.rser.2009.01.022

Mo, Y., Kim, T. H.-H., Brancik, K., Dickinson, D., Lee, H., Perrig, A., & Sinopoli, B. (2012). Cyber–Physical Security of a Smart Grid Infrastructure.*Proceedings of the IEEE, 100*(1), 195-209.

Mukkamala, S., Janoski, G., & Sung, A. (2002). Intrusion detection using neural networks and support vector machines. In *Neural Networks, 2002. IJCNN'02.Proceedings of the 2002 International Joint Conference on* (Vol. 2, pp. 1702-1707). IEEE. doi:10.1109/IJCNN.2002.1007774

Muñoz, M., Moh, M., & Moh, T.-S. (2014). Improving Smart Grid Authentication using Merkle Trees.*Proc. IEEE International Conference on Parallel and Distributed Systems.* doi:10.1109/PADSW.2014.7097884

Muñoz, M., Moh, M., & Moh, T.-S. (2014). Improving Smart Grid Security using Merkle Trees.*IEEE Conference on Communications and Network Security* (CNS). doi:10.1109/CNS.2014.6997535

Muthuramalingam, M., & Manoharan, P. S. (2014). Comparative analysis of distributed MPPT controllers for partially shaded stand alone photovoltaic systems. *Energy Conversion and Management, 86,* 286–299. doi:10.1016/j.enconman.2014.05.044

Naehrig, M., Lauter, K., & Vaikuntanathan, V. (2011). Can homomorphic encryption be practical? In *Proceedings of the 3rd acm workshop on cloud computing security workshop* (pp. 113–124). doi:10.1145/2046660.2046682

Namboodiri, V., Aravinthan, V., Mohapatra, S. N., Karimi, B., & Jewell, W. (2014). Toward a Secure Wireless-Based Home Area Network for Metering in Smart Grids. *IEEE Systems Journal, 8*(2), 509–520. doi:10.1109/JSYST.2013.2260700

National Energy Technology Laboratory to U.S. Department of Energy. (2007). *A Compendium of Modern Grid Technologies.* Retrieved from https://www.netl.doe.gov/File%20Library/research/energy%20efficiency/smart%20grid/whitepapers/Compendium-of-Modern-Grid-Technologies.pdf

National Institute of Standards and Technology. (2010). *NIST Framework and Roadmap for Smart Grid Interoperability Standards (NIST Special Publication 1108).* U.S. Department of Commerce.

Neaimeh, M., Hill, G. A., Hübner, Y., & Blythe, P. T. (2013). Routing systems to extend the driving range of electric vehicles. *IET Intelligent Transport Systems, 7*(3), 327–336. doi:10.1049/iet-its.2013.0122

Neisse, R., Fovino, I. N., Baldini, G., Stavroulaki, V., Vlacheas, P., & Giaffreda, R. (2014). A Model-Based Security Toolkit for the Internet of Things. *Availability, Reliability and Security (ARES),2014 Ninth International Conference on Availability, Reliability and Security (ARES'14),* (pp. 78 – 87). doi:10.1109/ARES.2014.17

Neisse, R., Steri, G., Fovino, I.N., & Baldini, G. (2015). SecKit: A Model-based Security Toolkit for the Internet of Things. *Computers & Security, 54,* 60–76.

Nian, L., Jinshan, C., Lin, Z., Jianhua, Z., & Yanling, H. (2013). A Key Management Scheme for Secure Communications of Advanced Metering Infrastructure in Smart Grid. *Industrial Electronics. IEEE Transactions on, 60*(10), 4746–4756. doi:10.1109/TIE.2012.2216237

Nicanfar, H., Jokar, P., Beznosov, K., & Leung, V. (2014). Efficient authentication and key management mechanisms for smart grid communications. *Systems Journal, IEEE, 8*(2), 629–640. doi:10.1109/JSYST.2013.2260942

Nicanfar, H., Jokar, P., Beznosov, K., & Leung, V. C. (2014). *Efficient Authentication and Key Management Mechanisms for Smart Grid Communications. IEEE Systems Journal.*

Nicholson, A., Webber, S., Dyer, S., Patel, T., & Janicke, H. (2012). SCADA security in the light of Cyber-Warfare. *Computers & Security, 31*(4), 418–436. doi:10.1016/j.cose.2012.02.009

Nie, X., & Zhai, X. (2013) M2M security threat and security mechanism research.*3rd International Conference on Computer Science and Network Technology (ICCSNT 2013)*, (pp. 906-909). doi:10.1109/ICCSNT.2013.6967252

NIST 7628 Revision 1. (2014). *Guidelines for Smart Grid Cyber Security.* Retrieved from http://nvlpubs.nist.gov/nist-pubs/ir/2014/NIST.IR.7628r1.pdf

NIST 7628. (2010). *Guidelines for Smart Grid Cyber Security.* Retrieved from http://www.nist.gov/smartgrid/upload/nistir-7628_total.pdf

NIST. (2012). *Smart Grid: A Beginner's Guide.* Retrieved from http://www.nist.gov/smartgrid/beginnersguide.cfm

NIST. (2014). *NIST Framework and Roadmap for Smart Grid Interoperability Standards, Release 3.0.* NIST.

No stopping Johannesburg's traffic light thieves. (2015). Retrieved 30 November, 2015 from: http://www.theguardian.com/world/2011/jan/06/johannesburg-traffic-light-thieves-sim

OMNet++ (2016). *OMNet++ user manual.* Retrieved from https://omnetpp.org/doc/omnetpp/UserGuide.pdf

oneM2M. (2015). Retrieved 29 Nov. 2015 from: http://www.etsi.org/about/what-we-do/global-collaboration/onem2m

Open Networking Foundation. (2013). *Openflow Switch Specification, version 1.3.0 (Wire Protocol 0x05)*, Retrieved from https://www.opennetworking.org/images/stories/downloads/sdn-resources/onf-specifications/openflow/openflow-spec-v1.4.0.pdf

Oró, E., Depoorter, V., Garcia, A., & Salom, J. (2015). Energy efficiency and renewable energy integration in data centres. Strategies and modelling review. *Renewable & Sustainable Energy Reviews, 42*, 429–445. doi:10.1016/j.rser.2014.10.035

Orr, J. A., Emanuel, A. E., & Pileggi, D. J. (1984). Current harmonics, voltage distortion, and powers associated with electric vehicle battery chargers distributed on the residential power system. *IEEE Transactions on Industry Applications, IA-20*(4), 727–734. doi:10.1109/TIA.1984.4504481

Østergaard, P. A., Lund, H., & Mathiesen, B. V. (2016). Smart energy systems and 4th generation district heating. *International Journal of Sustainable Energy Planning and Management, 10*, 1–2.

Ovidiu, V., Harrison, M., Vogt, H., Kalaboukas, K., Tomasella, M., Wouters, K., Gusmeroli, S., & Haller, S. (2009). Internet of things strategic research roadmap. *European Commission - Information Society and Media DG.*

Ozdemir, S., Altin, N., & Sefa, I. (2014). Single stage three level grid interactive MPPT inverter for PV systems. *Energy Conversion and Management, 80*, 561–572. doi:10.1016/j.enconman.2014.01.048

Pai, S., Meingast, M., Roosta, T., Bermudez, S., Wicker, S. B., Mulligan, D. K., & Sastry, S. (2009). Transactional confidentiality in sensor networks. *IEEE Security and Privacy, 6*(4), 28–35. doi:10.1109/MSP.2008.107

Pappu, V., Carvalho, M., & Pardalos, P. M. (2013). *Optimization and Security Challenges in Smart Power Grids*. Springer-Verlag Berlin Heidelberg. doi:10.1007/978-3-642-38134-8

Park, J. S., Lee, J. S., Kim, H. K., Jeong, J. R., Yeom, D. B., & Chi, S. D. (2001, November). Secusim: A tool for the cyber-attack simulation. In *International Conference on Information and Communications Security* (pp. 471-475). Springer Berlin Heidelberg doi:10.1007/3-540-45600-7_53

Park, N., Park, J. S., & Kim, H. J. (2015). *Inter-Authentication and Session Key Sharing Procedure for Secure M2M/IoT Environment. In Information* (pp. 261–266). Tokyo: International Information Institute.

Park, N., Park, J. S., & Kim, H. K. (2014). *Hash-based authentication and session key agreement Scheme in Internet of Things Environment. In Advanced Science and Technology Letters* (Vol. 62, pp. 9–12). Sensor.

Pathan, A.-S. K. (2010). Major Works on the Necessity and Implementations of PKC in WSN A Beginner's Note. Security of Self-Organizing Networks: MANET, WSN, WMN, VANET. Auerbach Publications, CRC Press, Taylor & Francis Group.

Pathan, A.-S. K. (2014). The State of the Art in Intrusion Prevention and Detection. CRC Press, Taylor & Francis Group. doi:10.1201/b16390

Pathan, A.-S. K. (2015). Securing Cyber Physical Systems. CRC Press, Taylor & Francis Group.

Pathan, A.-S. K., Khanam, S., Saleem, H. Y., & Abduallah, W. M. (2013). Tackling Intruders in Wireless Mesh Networks. In Distributed Network Intelligence, Security and Applications. CRC Press, Taylor & Francis Group.

Pathan, A.-S. K., Monowar, M. M., & Fadlullah, Z. M. (2013). Building Next-Generation Converged Networks: Theory and Practice. CRC Press, Taylor & Francis Group. doi:10.1201/b14574

Pathan, A.-S. K. (2010). Denial of Service in Wireless Sensor Networks: Issues and Challenges. In A. V. Stavros (Ed.), *Advances in Communications and Media Research* (Vol. 6). Nova Science Publishers, Inc.

Pattnaik, S., Dash, R., Swain, S. C., & Mohapatra, P. (2016, March). Control of active and reactive power of a three phase grid connected photovoltaic system. *Proceedings of the 2016 International Conference on Circuit, Power and Computing Technologies (ICCPCT)* (pp. 1-6). IEEE. doi:10.1109/ICCPCT.2016.7530227

Paxson, V. (1990). Bro: A system for detecting network intruders in real-time. Computer Networks. *The International Journal of Computer and Telecommunications Networking, 31*(23-24), 2435–2463.

Pei, Y. (2012). A Survey on Localization Algorithms for Wireless Ad Hoc Networks. In Communications and Information Processing. Springer.

Pejanovic-Djurisic, M., Kocan, E., & Prasad, R. (2012). *OFDM Based Relay Systems for Future Wireless Communications*. River Publishers.

Pelleg, D., & Moore, A. W. (2000). X-means: Extending k-means with efficient estimation of the number of clusters. In *Proceedings of the 17th International Conference on Machine Learning*. San Francisco, CA:Morgan Kaufmann Publishers Inc.

Pena-Alzola, R., Liserre, M., Blaabjerg, F., Sebastián, R., Dannehl, J., & Fuchs, F. W. (2013). Analysis of the passive damping losses in LCL-filter-based grid converters. *IEEE Transactions on Power Electronics, 28*(6), 2642–2646. doi:10.1109/TPEL.2012.2222931

Penina, N., Turygin, Y.V. & Racek, V. (2010, June). Comparative analysis of different types of hybrid electric vehicles. *Proceedings of the 2010 13th International Symposium MECHATRONIKA* (pp. 102-104).

Petukhov, A., & Kozlov, D. (2008). *Detecting security vulnerabilities in web applications using dynamic analysis with penetration testing. Computing Systems Lab.* Department of Computer Science,Moscow State University.

Phuangpornpitak, N., & Tia, S. (2013). Opportunities and challenges of integrating renewable energy in smart grid system. *Energy Procedia, 34*, 282–290. doi:10.1016/j.egypro.2013.06.756

Phuong, T. V., Hung, L. X., Cho, S. J., Lee, Y. K., & Lee, S. (2006). An anomaly detection algorithm for detecting attacks in wireless sensor networks. Intelligent and Security Informatics, 735–736.

Pillay, P., & Manyage, M. (2001). Definitions of voltage unbalance. *IEEE Power Engineering Review, 21*(5), 50–51. doi:10.1109/39.920965

Pirak, C., Sangsuwan, T., & Buayairaksa, S. (2014, March 19-21). Recent advances in communication technologies for smart grid application: A review. *Paper presented at the 2014 International Electrical Engineering Congress (iEECON).*

Pirretti, M., Zhu, S., Vijaykrishnan, N., McDaniel, P., Kandemir, M., & Brooks, R. (2006). The Sleep Deprivation Attack in Sensor Networks: Analysis and Methods of Defense. *International Journal of Distributed Sensor Networks, 2*(3), 267–287. doi:10.1080/15501320600642718

Portnoy, L., Eskin, E., & Stolfo, S. (2001). Intrusion detection with unlabeled data using clustering. In *Proceedings of ACM CSS Workshop on Data Mining Applied to Security* (DMSA-2001).

Pothamsetty, V., & Malik, S. (2009). *Smart grid leveraging intelligent communications to transform the power infrastructure.* CISCO.

Pouresmaeil, E., Mehrasa, M., & Catalão, J. P. (2015). A multifunction control strategy for the stable operation of DG units in smart grids. *IEEE Transactions on Smart Grid, 6*(2), 598–607. doi:10.1109/TSG.2014.2371991

Premaratne, U. K., Samarabandu, J., Sidhu, T. S., Beresh, R., & Tan, J.-C. (2010). An intrusion detection system for IEC61850 automated substations. *Power Delivery. IEEE Transactions on, 25*(4), 2376–2383.

Qi, J., Zhang, Y., & Chen, Y. (2014). Modeling and maximum power point tracking (MPPT) method for PV array under partial shade conditions. *Renewable Energy, 66*, 337–345. doi:10.1016/j.renene.2013.12.018

Qin, H., & Zhang W. (2011, September). Charging Scheduling with Minimal Waiting in a Network of Electric Vehicles and Charging Stations. in ACM VANET' 11, Las Vegas, Nevada, USA.

Qiu, Y., & Ma, M. (2015). Security Issues and Approaches in M2M Communications. In Securing Cyber Physical Systems. CRC Press, Taylor & Francis Group.

Qiu, M., Su, H., Chen, M., Ming, Z., & Yang, L. T. (2012). Balance of security strength and energy for a PMU monitoring system in smart grid. *IEEE Communications Magazine, 50*(5), 142–149. doi:10.1109/MCOM.2012.6194395

Québec Construction Code. (2010). Chapter V – Electricity, Canadian Electrical Code, Part One with Québec Amendments, Canadian Standards Association, Standard C22.10-10, 21st edition Sec. 86.

Rahimi, F. A., Lauby, M. O., Wrubel, J. N., & Lee, K. L. (1993). Evaluation of the transient energy function method for on-line dynamic security analysis. *Power Systems. IEEE Transactions on, 8*(2), 497–507.

Rahimi, S., Chan, A. D., & Goubran, R. A. (2011). Usage Monitoring of Electrical Devices in a Smart Home.*33rd Annual International Conference of the IEEE EMBS.* doi:10.1109/IEMBS.2011.6091313

Ramezani, M., Golestan, S., & Li, S. (2016, May). Non-frequency sensitive all-pass filter based single-phase PLLs. Proceedings of the 2016 IEEE/PES Transmission and Distribution Conference and Exposition (T&D) (pp. 1-5). IEEE. doi:10.1109/TDC.2016.7519933

Rashed, M., Klumpner, C., & Asher, G. (2013). Repetitive and resonant control for a single-phase grid-connected hybrid cascaded multilevel converter. *IEEE Transactions on Power Electronics*, *28*(5), 2224–2234. doi:10.1109/TPEL.2012.2218833

Rashidi, M., Batros, I., Madsen, T., Riaz, M., & Paulin, T. (2012, October). Placement of Road Side Units for Floating Car Data Collection in Highway Scenario. Proceedings of IEEE ICUM' 12, Petersburg, Russia.

Rastogi, V., Suciu, D., & Hong, S. (2007). The boundary between privacy and utility in data publishing. In *Proceedings of the 33rd International Conference on Very Large Data Bases* (VLDB) (pp. 531–542).

Rauschenbach, H. S. (2012). *Solar cell array design handbook: the principles and technology of photovoltaic energy conversion*. Springer Science & Business Media.

Rawat, D. B., & Bajracharya, C. (2015, April). Cyber security for smart grid systems: Status, challenges and perspectives. In SoutheastCon 2015 (pp. 1-6).

Rawat, D. B., & Bajracharya, C. (2015). Detection of false data injection attacks in smart grid communication systems. *IEEE Signal Processing Letters*, *22*(10), 1652–1656. doi:10.1109/LSP.2015.2421935

Rawat, D. B., Rodrigues, J. J., & Stojmenovic, I. (Eds.). (2015). *Cyber-physical systems: from theory to practice*. CRC Press. doi:10.1201/b19290

Reddy, K. S., Kumar, M., Mallick, T. K., Sharon, H., & Lokeswaran, S. (2014). A review of Integration, Control, Communication and Metering (ICCM) of renewable energy based smart grid. *Renewable & Sustainable Energy Reviews*, *38*, 180–192. doi:10.1016/j.rser.2014.05.049

Reed, J. H., & Gonzalez, C. R. A. (2012). Enhancing Smart Grid cyber security using power fingerprinting: Integrity assessment and intrusion detection. In *Proceedings of Future of Instrumentation International Workshop (FIIW)*. Gatlinburg, TN: IEEE. doi:10.1109/FIIW.2012.6378346

Reiss, S. P. (1984). Practical data-swapping: The first steps. *ACM Trans. Datab. Syst.*, *9*(1), 20–37.

Reiter, J. P. (2002). Satisfying Disclosure Restrictions with Synthetic Data Sets. *Journal of Official Statistics*, *18*, 531–543.

Remote wipe definition. (2015). *TechTarget*. Retrieved 6 Dec., 2015 from: http://searchmobilecomputing.techtarget.com/definition/remote-wipe

Ren, F., & Gu, Y. (2015). Using Artificial Intelligence in the Internet of Things.ZTE Communications, 13(2).

Ren, W., Yu, L., Ma, L., & Ren, Y. (2013). RISE: A Rellable and SEcure Scheme for Wireless Machine to Machine Communications. *Tsinghua Science and Technology*, *18*(1), 100–117. doi:10.1109/TST.2013.6449413

Rescorla, E. (1999). *Diffie-Hellman key agreement method*. Academic Press.

Rezk, H., & Eltamaly, A. M. (2015). A comprehensive comparison of different MPPT techniques for photovoltaic systems. *Solar Energy*, *112*, 1–11. doi:10.1016/j.solener.2014.11.010

Richardson, P., Flynn, D., & Keane, A. (2012). Optimal charging of electric vehicles in low-voltage distribution systems. *IEEE Transactions on Power Systems*, *27*(1), 268–279. doi:10.1109/TPWRS.2011.2158247

Rieffel, E., & Polak, W. (2011). *Quantum Computing, A Gentle Introduction*. Cambridge, MA: The MIT Press.

Rigas, E., Ramchurn, S., & Bassiliades, N. (2015, August). Managing Electric Vehicles in the Smart Grid Using Artificial Intelligence: A Survey. *IEEE Transactions on* Intelligent Transportation Systems, *16*(4), 1619–1635.

Riker, A., Cruz, T., Marques, B., Curado, M., Simoes, P., & Monteiro, E. (2014). *Efficient and secure M2M communications for smart metering. In 2014 IEEE Emerging Technology and Factory Automation* (pp. 1–7). Barcelona: ETFA. doi:10.1109/ETFA.2014.7005176

Rivest, R. L., Shamir, A., & Adleman, L. (1983). A method for obtaining digital signatures and public-key cryptosystems. *Communications of the ACM, 26*(1), 96–99. doi:10.1145/357980.358017

Roberts, B. (2009). Capturing grid power. *IEEE Power and Energy magazine, 7*(4), 32-41.

Rodofile, N. R., Radke, K., & Foo, E. (2015). Real-Time and Interactive Attacks on DNP3 Critical Infrastructure Using Scapy.*Proceedings of the 13th Australasian Information Security Conference (AISC)*, pp. 67-70.

Roesch, M. (1999). Snort: Lightweight Intrusion Detection for Networks. *LISA*, 229-238.

Roesch, M. (1999). Snort - Lightweight Intrusion Detection for Networks.*Proceedings of the 13th USENIX conference on System administration (LISA'99)*, (pp. 229-238).

Roman, R., Zhou, J., & Lopez, J. (2006). Applying intrusion detection systems to wireless sensor networks. *3rd IEEE consumer communications and networking conference*, (pp. 640–644).

Roman, R., Zhou, J., & Lopez, J. (2013). On the features and challenges of security and privacy in distributed internet of things. *Computer Networks, 57*(10), 2266–2279. doi:10.1016/j.comnet.2012.12.018

Romero-Cadaval, E., Spagnuolo, G., Franquelo, L. G., Ramos-Paja, C. A., Suntio, T., & Xiao, W. M. (2013). Grid-connected photovoltaic generation plants: Components and operation. *IEEE Industrial Electronics Magazine, 7*(3), 6–20. doi:10.1109/MIE.2013.2264540

Rose, K., Eldridge, S., & Chapin, L. (2015). *The internet of things: An overview. The Internet Society.* ISOC.

Rosen, K. (1995). *Discrete Mathematics And Its Applications* (3rd ed.). New York: McGraw-Hill, Inc.

Rossman, L. A. (2010). The EPANET Programmer's Toolkit for Analysis of Water Distribution Systems. Academic Press.

Roy, S., Das, A. K., & Li, Y. (2011). Cryptanalysis and security enhancement of an advanced authentication scheme using smart cards, and a key agreement scheme for two-party communication. In *Performance Computing and Communications Conference (IPCCC), 2011 IEEE 30th International.* IEEE. doi:10.1109/PCCC.2011.6108113

Rubertis, D. A., Mainetti, L., Mighali, V., Patrono, L., Sergi, I., Stefanizzi, M. L., & Pascali, S. (2013). Performance evaluation of end-to-end security protocols in an Internet of Things. *2013 21st International Conference on Software, Telecommunications and Computer Networks (SoftCOM'13).*

Ruchika, M. (2013). *Schemes for surviving advanced persistent threats* (Dissertation). Faculty of the Graduate School of the University at Buffalo, State University of New York.

Ruj, S., & Nayak, A. (2013). A Decentralized Security Framework for Data Aggregation and Access Control in Smart Grids. *IEEE Transactions on Smart Grid, 4*(1), 196–205. doi:10.1109/TSG.2012.2224389

Rumney, M. (Ed.). (2013). *LTE and the evolution to 4G wireless: Design and measurement challenges.* John Wiley & Sons. doi:10.1002/9781118799475

Russo, A., & Sabelfeld, A. (2010). Dynamic vs. static flow-sensitive security analysis. In *Computer Security Foundations Symposium (CSF), 2010 23rd IEEE*, (pp. 186–199). IEEE.

Saber, A., & Venayagamoorthy, G. (2012, March). Resource scheduling under uncertainty in a smart grid with renewables and plug-in vehicles. *IEEE Syst. J., 6*(1), 103–109. doi:10.1109/JSYST.2011.2163012

Sabo, M. L., Mariun, N., Hizam, H., Radzi, M. A. M., & Zakaria, A. (2016). Spatial energy predictions from large-scale photovoltaic power plants located in optimal sites and connected to a smart grid in Peninsular Malaysia. *Renewable & Sustainable Energy Reviews, 66*, 79–94. doi:10.1016/j.rser.2016.07.045

Sachenbacher, M., Leucker, M., Artmeier, A., & Haselmayr, J. (2011). Efficient energy-optimal routing for electric vehicles.*Proc. 25th Conf. AAAI* (pp. 1402–1407).

Sadeghi, A. R., Wachsmann, C., & Waidner, M. (2015, June). Security and privacy challenges in industrial internet of things. In *Proceedings of the 52nd Annual Design Automation Conference* (p. 54). ACM. doi:10.1145/2744769.2747942

SAE. (2010). SAE Standard J1772-2010, SAE Electric Vehicle and Plug in Hybrid Vehicle Conductive Charge Coupler.

Sakellaridis, N. F., Spyridon, R. I., Antonopoulos, A. K., Mavropoulos, G. C., & Hountalas, D. T. (2015). Development and validation of a new turbocharger simulation methodology for marine two stroke diesel engine modelling and diagnostic applications. *Energy, 91*, 952–966. doi:10.1016/j.energy.2015.08.049

Salazar, J., Tadeo, F., & Prada, C. (2015). Modelling of diesel generator sets that assist off-grid renewable energy micro grids. *Renewable Energy and Sustainable Development, 1*, 72–80.

Saleem, K., Derhab, A., Al-Muhtadi, J., & Shahzad, B. (2015). *Human-oriented design of secure Machine-to-Machine communication system for e-Healthcare society. In Computers in Human Behavior* (Vol. 51, pp. 977–985). Elsevier.

Samarati, P. (2001). Protecting respondents identities in microdata release. *IEEE Transactions on Knowledge and Data Engineering, 13*(6), 1010–1027. doi:10.1109/69.971193

Sander, J., Ester, M., Kriegel, H.-P., & Xu, X. (1998). Density-based clustering in spatial databases: The algorithm gdbscan and its applications. *Data Mining and Knowledge Discovery, 2*(2), 169–194. doi:10.1023/A:1009745219419

Sangster, B., O'Connor, T. J., Cook, T., Fanelli, R., Dean, E., Morrell, C., & Conti, G. J. (2009, August). *Toward Instrumenting Network Warfare Competitions to Generate Labeled Datasets.* CSET.

Santamouris, M., Cartalis, C., Synnefa, A., & Kolokotsa, D. (2015). On the impact of urban heat island and global warming on the power demand and electricity consumption of buildings—A review. *Energy and Building, 98*, 119–124. doi:10.1016/j.enbuild.2014.09.052

Santhanam, L., Xie, B., & Agrawal, D. (2008). Secure and Efficient Authentication in Wireless Mesh Networks using Merkle Trees.*33rd IEEE Conference on Local Computer Networks.* doi:10.1109/LCN.2008.4664310

Sarathy, R., & Muralidhar, K. (2010). Some additional insights on applying differential privacy for numeric data. *Proceeding PSD'10 Proceedings of the 2010 international conference on Privacy in statistical databases* (pp. 210-219). doi:10.1007/978-3-642-15838-4_19

Satyadevan, S., Kalarickal, B. S., & Jinesh, M. K. (2014). Security, Trust and Implementation Limitations of Prominent IoT Platforms.*Proceedings of the 3rd International Conference on Frontiers of Intelligent Computing: Theory and Applications (FICTA) 2014.*

Sauter, T., & Lobashov, M. (2011). End-to-End Communication Architecture for Smart Grids. *IEEE Transactions on Industrial Electronics, 58*(4), 1218–1228. doi:10.1109/TIE.2010.2070771

Saxena, N., & Choi, B. J. (2015). State of the Art Authentication, Access Control, and Secure Integration in Smart Grid. *Energies, 8*(10), 11883–11915. doi:10.3390/en81011883

Scheme, B. T. (2009). LTE: The evolution of mobile broadband. *IEEE Communications Magazine, 45.*

Scheper, C., & Cantor, S. (2015, April). PREDICT: an important resource for the science of security. In *Proceedings of the 2015 Symposium and Bootcamp on the Science of Security* (p. 16). ACM. doi:10.1145/2746194.2746210

Schewel, L., & Kammen, D. M. (2010). Smart Transportation: Synergizing Electrified Vehicles and Mobile Information Systems. Environment. *Science and Policy for Sustainable Development, 52*(5), 24–35. doi:10.1080/00139157.2010.507143

Schneier, B. (1996). *Applied Cryptography* (2nd ed.). New York: Wiley & Sons Inc.

Schölkopf, B., Platt, J. C., Shawe-Taylor, J., Smola, A. J., & Williamson, R. C. (2001). Estimating the support of a high-dimensional distribution. *Neural Computation, 13*(7), 1443–1471. doi:10.1162/089976601750264965 PMID:11440593

Schurgot, M. R., & Shinberg, D. A. (2015). Experiments with security and privacy in IoT networks. *2015 IEEE 16th International Symposium on a World of Wireless on Mobile and Multimedia Networks (WoWMoM)*.

Sectoral e-Business Watch. (2009). *Case study: Smart grid journey at Austin Energy, Texas, USA*. Author.

Seferian, V., Kanj, R., Chehab, A., & Kayssi, A. (2014). PUF and ID-based key distribution security framework for advanced metering infrastructures. In Smart grid communications (smartgridcomm), 2014 IEEE international conference on (pp. 933–938).

Selga, J. M., Zaballos, A., & Navarro, J. (2013). Solutions to the Computer Networking Challenges of the Distribution Smart Grid. *IEEE Communications Letters, 17*(3), 588–591. doi:10.1109/LCOMM.2013.020413.122896

Shafagh, H., & Hithnawi, A. (2014). Poster Abstract: Security Comes First, a Public-key Cryptography Framework for the Internet of Things. *2014 IEEE International Conference on Distributed Computing in Sensor Systems (DCOSS)*. doi:10.1109/DCOSS.2014.62

Shaikh, R. A., Jameel, H., Auriol, B. J., Lee, S., & Song, Y. J. (2008). Trusting anomaly and intrusion claims for cooperative distributed intrusion detection schemes of wireless sensor networks. *The 9th international conference for young computer scientists*, (pp. 2038-2043).

Shang, W., Li, L., Wan, M., & Zeng, P. (2015, December). Industrial communication intrusion detection algorithm based on improved one-class SVM. In *2015 World Congress on Industrial Control Systems Security (WCICSS)* (pp. 21-25). IEEE. doi:10.1109/WCICSS.2015.7420317

Sharma, K., & Saini, L. M. (2015). Performance analysis of smart metering for smart grid: An overview. *Renewable & Sustainable Energy Reviews, 49*, 720–735. doi:10.1016/j.rser.2015.04.170

Sharma, V., Bartlett, G., & Mirkovic, J. (2014, November). Critter: Content-rich traffic trace repository. In *Proceedings of the 2014 ACM Workshop on Information Sharing & Collaborative Security* (pp. 13-20). ACM.

Shih, J.-R., Hu, Y., Hsiao, M.-C., Chen, M.-S., Shen, W.-C., Yang, B.-Y., & Cheng, C.-M. et al. (2013). Securing M2M With Post-Quantum Public-Key Cryptography. *IEEE Journal on Emerging and Selected Topics in Circuits and Systems, Volume, 3*(1), 106–116. doi:10.1109/JETCAS.2013.2244772

Shor, P. (1997, October). Polynomial-Time Algorithms for Prime Factorization and Discrete Logarithms on a Quantum Computer. *SIAM Journal on Computing, 26*(5), 1484–1509. doi:10.1137/S0097539795293172

Siano, P. (2014). Demand response and smart grids—A survey. *Renewable & Sustainable Energy Reviews, 30*, 461–478. doi:10.1016/j.rser.2013.10.022

Sicari, S., Rizzardi, A., Coen-Porisini, A., Grieco, L. A., & Monteil, T. (2015). Secure OM2M Service Platform. Autonomic Computing (ICAC). *2015 IEEE International Conference on Autonomic Computing (ICAC)*. doi:10.1109/ICAC.2015.59

Sicari, S., Rizzardi, A., Grieco, L. A., & Coen-Porisini, A. (2015). Security, privacy and trust in Internet of Things: The road ahead. *Computer Networks*.

Siddique, H. A. B., Xu, P., & De Doncker, R. W. (2013, June). Parameter extraction algorithm for one-diode model of PV panels based on datasheet values. *Proceedings of the 2013 International Conference on Clean Electrical Power (ICCEP)* (pp. 7-13). IEEE. doi:10.1109/ICCEP.2013.6586957

Siddiqui, F., Zeadally, S., Alcaraz, C., & Galvao, S. (2012). Smart grid privacy: Issues and solutions.*21st International Conference on Computer Communications and Networks (ICCCN)*.

Siddiqui, M. S., & Huong, C. S. (2007). Security Issues in Wireless Mesh Networks.*International Conference on Multimedia and Ubiquitous Engineering (MUE)*.

Simmhan, Y., Kumbhare, A. G., Baohua, C., & Prasanna, V. (2011). *An Analysis of Security and Privacy Issues in Smart Grid Software Architectures on Clouds*. Paper presented at the Cloud Computing (CLOUD), 2011 IEEE International Conference on.

Singh, J., Pasquier, T., Bacon, J, Ko, H., & Eyers, D. (2015). Twenty security considerations for cloud-supported Internet of Things. *IEEE Internet of Things Journal*.

Sivarasu, S. R., Sekaran, E. C., & Karthik, P. (2015). Development of renewable energy based microgrid project implementations for residential consumers in India: Scope, challenges and possibilities. *Renewable & Sustainable Energy Reviews*, *50*, 256–269. doi:10.1016/j.rser.2015.04.118

Skopik, F., & Smith, P. D. (2015). *Smart Grid Security: Innovative Solutions for a Modernized Grid*. Elsevier Science.

Smart, J., & Schey, S. (2012). Battery electric vehicle driving and charging behavior observed early in the EV project. *SAE International Journal of Alternative Powertrains*, *1*(1), 27-33.

Smart, J., Bradley, T., & Salisbury, S. (2014). Actual Versus Estimated Utility Factor of a Large Set of Privately Owned Chevrolet Volts. *SAE International Journal of Alternative Powertrains*, *3*(1), 30-35.

Smiai, O., Bellotti, F., De Gloria, A., Berta, R., Amditis, A., Damousis, Y., & Winder, A. (2015, August). Information and communication technology research opportunities in dynamic charging for electric vehicle. *Proceedings of the 2015 Euromicro Conference on Digital System Design (DSD)* (pp. 297-300). IEEE. doi:10.1109/DSD.2015.111

Soares, F. J., Almeida, P. M. R., Lopes, J. A. P., Garcia-Valle, R., & Marra, F. (2013). State of the Art on Different Types of Electric Vehicles. In Electric Vehicle Integration into Modern Power Networks. doi:10.1007/978-1-4614-0134-6_1

Sobajic, D. J., & Pao, Y.-H. (1989). Artificial neural-net based dynamic security assessment for electric power systems. *Power Engineering Review, IEEE*, *9*(2), 55–55. doi:10.1109/MPER.1989.4310480

Song, H., Xie, L., Zhu, S., & Cao, G. (2007). Sensor node compromise detection: the location perspective.*Proceedings of the 2007 international conference on Wireless communications and mobile computing (IWCMC '07)*. doi:10.1145/1280940.1280993

Song, X., Fan, G., & Rao, M. (2008). Svm-based data editing for enhanced one-class classification of remotely sensed imagery. *IEEE Geoscience and Remote Sensing Letters*, *5*(2), 189–193. doi:10.1109/LGRS.2008.916832

Song, Z., Xia, C., & Liu, T. (2013). Predictive current control of three-phase grid-connected converters with constant switching frequency for wind energy systems.*IEEE Transactions on Industrial Electronics*, *60*(6), 2451–2464. doi:10.1109/TIE.2012.2225394

Sonnenschein, M., Lünsdorf, O., Bremer, J., & Tröschel, M. (2015). Decentralized control of units in smart grids for the support of renewable energy supply. *Environmental Impact Assessment Review, 52,* 40–52. doi:10.1016/j.eiar.2014.08.004

Sortomme, E., Hindi, M. M., MacPherson, S. J., & Venkata, S. S. (2011). Coordinated charging of plug-in hybrid electric vehicles to minimize distribution system losses. *IEEE transactions on smart grid, 2*(1), 198-205.

Sortomme, E., & El-Sharkawi, M. A. (2011, March). Optimal charging strategies for unidirectional vehicle-to-grid. *IEEE Trans. Smart Grid, 2*(1), 131–138. doi:10.1109/TSG.2010.2090910

Sowmyarani, C. N. (2012). Article: Survey on Recent Developments in Privacy Preserving Models. *International Journal of Computers and Applications, 38*(9), 18–22. doi:10.5120/4636-6884

Spanò, E., Niccolini, L., Di Pascoli, S., & Iannacconeluca, G. (2015). Last-meter smart grid embedded in an Internet-of-Things platform. *Smart Grid. IEEE Transactions on, 6*(1), 468–476.

St. John-Green, M., & Watson, T. (2014). Safety and Security of the Smart City - when our infrastructure goes online. *9th IET International Conference on System Safety and Cyber Security.* doi:10.1049/cp.2014.0981

Stackowiak, R., Licht, A., Mantha, V., & Nagode, L. (2015). *Big Data and The Internet of Things: Enterprise Information Architecture for A New Age.* Apress. doi:10.1007/978-1-4842-0986-8

Stajic, J. (2013, March). The Future of Quantum Information Processing. *Science, 339*(6124), 1163. doi:10.1126/science.339.6124.1163 PMID:23471397

Stallings, W. (1999). *Cryptography and Network Security* (2nd ed.). Upper Saddle River, NJ: Prentice Hall.

Stamp, M. (2011). *Information Security Principles and Practices* (2nd ed.). Hoboken, NJ: Wiley & Sons Inc. doi:10.1002/9781118027974

Statistisches Bundesamt. (n. d.). Fachserie 15 Heft 1, EVS 2008. Retrieved from http://www.destatis.de/

Steiner, M., Siefer, G., Hornung, T., Peharz, G., & Bett, A. W. (2015). YieldOpt, a model to predict the power output and energy yield for concentrating photovoltaic modules. *Progress in Photovoltaics: Research and Applications, 23*(3), 385–397. doi:10.1002/pip.2458

Stetsko, A., Folkman, L., & Vashek, M. (2010). Neighbor-based intrusion detection for wireless sensor networks. *6th IEEE international conference on wireless and mobile communications.*

Storandt, S., & Funke, S. (2012). Cruising with a battery-powered vehicle and not getting stranded. *Proc. 26th Conf. AAAI '12* (pp. 1628–1634).

Storandt, S. (2012). Quick and energy-efficient routes: Computing constrained shortest paths for electric vehicles. *Proc. 5th ACM SIGSPATIAL IWCTS* (pp. 20–25). doi:10.1145/2442942.2442947

Storandt, S., & Funke, S. (2013). Enabling e-mobility: Facility location for battery loading stations. *Proc. 27th Conf. AAAI* (pp. 1341–1347).

Strömberg, H., Andersson, P., Almgren, S., Ericsson, J., Karlsson, M., & Nåbo, A. (2011, November). Driver interfaces for electric vehicles. *Proceedings of the 3rd International Conference on Automotive User Interfaces and Interactive Vehicular Applications* (pp. 177-184). ACM.

Suciu, D. (2010). A study of RF link and coverage in Zigbee. *Scientific Bulletin of the Petru Maior, 7*(1).

Suganthi, L., Iniyan, S., & Samuel, A. A. (2015). Applications of fuzzy logic in renewable energy systems–a review. *Renewable & Sustainable Energy Reviews, 48,* 585–607. doi:10.1016/j.rser.2015.04.037

Su, H., Qiu, M., & Wang, H. (2012). Secure wireless communication system for smart grid with rechargeable electric vehicles. *IEEE Communications Magazine, 50*(8), 62–68. doi:10.1109/MCOM.2012.6257528

Sukprasert, P., Nguyen, B. M., & Fujimoto, H. (2014, December). Estimation of lateral displacement of electric vehicle to an alignment of wireless power transmitters. *Proceedings of the 2014 IEEE/SICE International Symposium on System Integration (SII)* (pp. 542-547). IEEE. doi:10.1109/SII.2014.7028097

Sun, X., Men, S., Zhao, C., & Zhou, Z. (2015). A security authentication scheme in machine-to-machine home network service. Security and Communication Networks, 8(16), 2678–2686. doi:10.1002/sec.551

Sun, X., Wang, H., & Li, J. (2009). Achieving P-Sensitive K-Anonymity via Anatomy. *ICEBE '09. IEEE International Conference on e-Business Engineering.*

Sun, C.-C., Liu, C.-C., & Xie, J. (2016). *Cyber-Physical System Security of a Power Grid: State-of-the-Art.* Electronics.

Suo, H., Wan, J., Zou, C., & Liu, J. (2012). Security in the Internet of Things: A Review.*2012 International Conference on Computer Science and Electronics Engineering (ICCSEE)*, (vol. 3, pp. 648-651). doi:10.1109/ICCSEE.2012.373

Swain, S., Panda, P. C., & Subudhi, B. D. (2013). A Comparative Study of Two Control Strategies for Three Phase Shunt Active Power Filter using Adaptive Hysteresis Band Current Controller.

Sweeney, L. (2002). k-ANONYMITY: A Model for Protecting Privacy. *International Journal of Uncertainty, Fuzziness and Knowledge-based Systems, 10*(5), 557–570. doi:10.1142/S0218488502001648

Swetina, J., Lu, G., Jacobs, P., Ennesser, F., & Song, J. (2014). Toward a standardized common M2M service layer platform: Introduction to oneM2M. *IEEE Wireless Communications, 21*(3), 1536–1284. doi:10.1109/MWC.2014.6845045

Świątek, P., Tarasiuk, H., & Natkaniec, M. (2015). *Delivery of e-Health Services in Next Generation Networks.*Lecture Notes in Computer Science, 9012, 453–462.

Syverson, P. (1994). A taxonomy of replay attacks [cryptographic protocols]. In *Computer Security Foundations Workshop VII, 1994. CSFW7. Proceedings*, (pp. 187–191). IEEE.

Talluri, S. R., & Roy, S. (2014). Cryptanalysis and security enhancement of two advanced authentication protocols. In Advanced Computing, Networking and Informatics (vol. 2, pp. 307–316). Springer. doi:10.1007/978-3-319-07350-7_34

Tan, S.K., Sooriyabandara, M., & Fan, Z. (2011). M2M Communications in the Smart Grid: Applications, Standards, Enabling Technologies, and Research Challenges. *International Journal of Digital Multimedia Broadcasting.* doi:10.1155/2011/289015

Tanenbaum, A. (1990). *Structured Computer Organization* (3rd ed.). Englewood Cliffs, NJ: Prentice Hall.

Tax, D. M. (2001). One-class classification. TU Delft, Delft University of Technology.

Taylor, C., & Johnson, T. (2015). *Strong authentication countermeasures using dynamic keying for sinkhole and distance spoofing attacks in smart grid networks.* Paper presented at the Wireless Communications and Networking Conference (WCNC). doi:10.1109/WCNC.2015.7127747

Tey, K. S., & Mekhilef, S. (2014). Modified incremental conductance MPPT algorithm to mitigate inaccurate responses under fast-changing solar irradiation level. *Solar Energy, 101*, 333–342. doi:10.1016/j.solener.2014.01.003

The Edison Foundation. (2014, September). *Utility-scale smart meter deployments: Building block of the evolving power grid* (Tech. Rep.). The Edison Foundation.

The Global Wireless M2M Market. (2009). *Berg Insight*. Retrieved 6 Dec. 2015 from: http://www.berginsight.com/ShowReport.aspx?m_m=3&id=95

The Wall Street Journal. (2016). *China's Latest Leap Forward Isn't Just Great—It's Quantum. Beijing launches the world's first quantum-communications satellite into orbit*. Retrieved 8/17/2016 from: http://www.wsj.com/articles/chinas-latest-leap-forward-isnt-just-greatits-quantum-1471269555

Thomas, C., Sharma, V., & Balakrishnan, N. (2008, March). Usefulness of DARPA dataset for intrusion detection system evaluation. In *SPIE Defense and Security Symposium* (pp. 69730G-69730G). International Society for Optics and Photonics. doi:10.1117/12.777341

Tikka, V., Lassila, J., Haakana, J., & Partanen, J. (2011, December). Case study of the effects of electric vehicle charging on grid loads in an urban area. *Proceedings of the 2011 2nd IEEE PES International Conference and Exhibition on Innovative Smart Grid Technologies (ISGT Europe)* (pp. 1-7). IEEE. doi:10.1109/ISGTEurope.2011.6162667

Tito, S. R., Lie, T. T., & Anderson, T. N. (2016). Optimal sizing of a wind-photovoltaic-battery hybrid renewable energy system considering socio-demographic factors. *Solar Energy*, *136*, 525–532. doi:10.1016/j.solener.2016.07.036

Tomkiw, L. (2016). *Russia-Ukraine Cyberattack Update: Security Company Links Moscow Hacker Group To Electricity Shut Down*. Retrieved 8/1/2016, from http://www.ibtimes.com/russia-ukraine-cyberattack-update-security-company-links-moscow-hacker-group-2256634

Tran, T.-T., Shin, O.-S., & Lee, J.-H. (2013). *Detection of replay attacks in smart grid systems*. Paper presented at the Computing, Management and Telecommunications (ComManTel), 2013 International Conference on. doi:10.1109/ComManTel.2013.6482409

Treaster, M. (2005). *A survey of fault-tolerance and fault-recovery techniques in parallel systems*. CoRR, abs/cs/0501002.

Tsai, J. L. (2014). An improved cross-layer privacy-preserving authentication in WAVE-enabled VANETs. *IEEE Communications Letters*, *18*(11), 1931–1934. doi:10.1109/LCOMM.2014.2323291

Tseng, H. R. (2012, April). A secure and privacy-preserving communication protocol for V2G networks. In *Wireless Communications and Networking Conference (WCNC)* (pp. 2706-2711). IEEE. doi:10.1109/WCNC.2012.6214259

Tsoumakas, G., Katakis, I., & Vlahavas, I. (2004, September). Effective voting of heterogeneous classifiers. In *European Conference on Machine Learning* (pp. 465-476). Springer Berlin Heidelberg.

Tuttle, D. P., & Baldick, R. (2012). The evolution of plug-in electric vehicle-grid interactions. *IEEE Transactions on Smart Grid*, *3*(1), 500–505. doi:10.1109/TSG.2011.2168430

Twidell, J., & Weir, T. (2015). *Renewable energy resources*. Routledge.

Twining, E., & Holmes, D. G. (2003). Grid current regulation of a three-phase voltage source inverter with an LCL input filter. *IEEE Transactions on Power Electronics*, *18*(3), 888–895. doi:10.1109/TPEL.2003.810838

U.S. Department of Energy. (2010). *Communication requirements of smart grid*. Author.

U.S.-Canada Power System Outage Task Force. (2004). *Final Report on the August 14, 2003 Blackout in the United States and Canada: Causes and Recommendations*. Retrieved from: http://energy.gov/sites/prod/files/oeprod/DocumentsandMedia/BlackoutFinal-Web.pdf

Ukil, A., Bandyopadhyay, S., Bhattacharyya, A., Pal, A., & Bose, T. (2014). Auth-Lite: Lightweight M2M Authentication reinforcing DTLS for CoAP.*2014 IEEE International Conference on Pervasive Computing and Communications Workshops (PERCOM Workshops)*. doi:10.1109/PerComW.2014.6815204

Ul-Haq, A., Buccella, C., Cecati, C., & Khalid, H. A. (2013, June). Smart charging infrastructure for electric vehicles. *Proceedings of the 2013 International Conference on Clean Electrical Power (ICCEP)* (pp. 163-169). IEEE. doi:10.1109/ICCEP.2013.6586984

United Nations General Assembly. (1987). Towards Sustainable Development, Commission on Environment and Development: Our Common Future. Document, A/42/427. Author.

Unnthorsson, R., Runarsson, T. P., & Jonsson, M. T. (2003, August). Model selection in one-class SVMs using rbf kernels. In *Proc. 16th Int. Congress and Exhibition on Condition Monitoring and Diagnostic Engineering Management.* doi:10.1109/iThings/CPSCom.2011.34

Ur-Rehman, O., Zivic, N., & Ruland, C. (2015). Security issues in smart metering systems. *Smart Energy Grid Engineering (SEGE), IEEE International Conference on*, (pp. 1-7).

Valverde, L., Rosa, F., Bordons, C., & Guerra, J. (2016). Energy Management Strategies in hydrogen Smart-Grids: A laboratory experience. *International Journal of Hydrogen Energy, 41*(31), 13715–13725. doi:10.1016/j.ijhydene.2016.05.279

Vandael, S., Boucké, N., Holvoet, T., De Craemer, K., & Deconinck, G. (2011). Decentralized coordination of plug-in hybrid vehicles for imbalance reduction in a smart grid. *Proc. of the 10th Int. Conf. Auton. Agents Multiagent* (pp. 803–810).

Varodayan, D., & Khisti, A. (2011). Smart meter privacy using a rechargeable battery: Minimizing the rate of information leakage.*IEEE International Conference on Acoustics, Speech and Signal Processing (ICASSP).* doi:10.1109/ICASSP.2011.5946886

Vasilomanolakis, E., Karuppayah, S., Mühlhäuser, M., & Fischer, M. (2015). Taxonomy and survey of collaborative intrusion detection. *ACM Computing Surveys, 47*(4), 55. doi:10.1145/2716260

Venkataramani, G., Parankusam, P., Ramalingam, V., & Wang, J. (2016). A review on compressed air energy storage– A pathway for smart grid and polygeneration. *Renewable & Sustainable Energy Reviews, 62*, 895–907. doi:10.1016/j.rser.2016.05.002

Venkatraman, K., Daniel, J. V., & Murugaboopathi, G. (2013). Various attacks in wireless sensor network: Survey. *International Journal of Soft Computing and Engineering, 3*(1).

Vetter, B., Ugus, O., Westhoff, D., & Sorge, C. (2012). Homomorphic primitives for a privacy-friendly smart metering architecture. In Secrypt (pp. 102– 112).

Viinikka, J., Debar, H., Mé, L., & Séguier, R. (2006, March). Time series modeling for IDS alert management. In *Proceedings of the 2006 ACM Symposium on Information, computer and communications security* (pp. 102-113). ACM. doi:10.1145/1128817.1128835

Von Appen, J., Stetz, T., Braun, M., & Schmiegel, A. (2014). Local voltage control strategies for PV storage systems in distribution grids. *IEEE Transactions on Smart Grid, 5*(2), 1002–1009. doi:10.1109/TSG.2013.2291116

Von Jouanne, A., & Banerjee, B. (2001). Assessment of voltage unbalance. *IEEE Transactions on Power Delivery, 16*(4), 782–790. doi:10.1109/61.956770

von Jouanne, A., & Banerjee, B. B. (2000). *Voltage unbalance: Power quality issues, related standards and mitigation techniques. Electric Power Research Institute.* Palo Alto, CA: EPRI Final Rep.

Vora, P. L. (2007). An Information-Theoretic Approach to Inference Attacks on Random Data Perturbation and a Related Privacy Measure. *Information Theory, IEEE Transactions on, 53*(8), 2971-2977.

Wagner, A., Speiser, S., & Harth, A. (2010). *Semantic web technologies for a smart energy grid: Requirements and challenges*. Paper presented at the Proceedings of the 2010 International Conference on Posters & Demonstrations Track.

Wagner, I. (2015, May). Genomic privacy metrics: a systematic comparison. In Security and Privacy Workshops (SPW), 2015 IEEE (pp. 50-59). IEEE. doi:10.1109/SPW.2015.15

Wang, Y. (2013). Smart grid, automation, and scada systems security. *Security and Privacy in Smart Grids*, 245-268.

Wang, M., Liang, H., Zhang, R., Deng, R., & Shen, X. (2014, July). Mobility-Aware Coordinated Charging for Electric Vehicles in VANET-Enhanced Smart Grid. *IEEE Journal on Selected Areas in Communications*, *32*(7), 1344–1360. doi:10.1109/JSAC.2014.2332078

Wang, W., & Lu, Z. (2013). Cyber security in the Smart Grid: Survey and challenges. *Computer Networks*, *57*(5), 1344–1371. doi:10.1016/j.comnet.2012.12.017

Wang, X., & Yi, P. (2011, December). Security Framework for Wireless Communications in Smart Distribution Grid. *IEEE Transactions on Smart Grid*, *2*(4), 809–818. doi:10.1109/TSG.2011.2167354

Wang, Y., Streff, K., & Raman, S. (2012). Smartphone Security Challenges. *IEEE Computer, Volume*, *45*(Issue: 12), 52–58. doi:10.1109/MC.2012.288

Wang, Y., Wong, J., & Miner, A. (2004, June). Anomaly intrusion detection using one class SVM. In *Information Assurance Workshop, 2004. Proceedings from the Fifth Annual IEEE SMC* (pp. 358-364). IEEE. doi:10.1109/IAW.2004.1437839

Wang, Y., Wu, X., & Chen, H. (2015). *An intrusion detection method for wireless sensor network based on mathematical morphology. In Security and Communication Networks*. John Wiley & Sons, Ltd.

Wei-Chi, K., & Chang, S.-T. (2005). Impersonation attack on a dynamic id-based remote user authentication scheme using smart cards. *IEICE Transactions on Communications*, *88*(5), 2165–2167.

Wei-Chi, K., Hao-Chuan, T., & Tsaur, M.-J. (2004). Stolen-verifier attack on an efficient smart card-based one-time password authentication scheme. *IEICE Transactions on Communications*, *87*(8), 2374–2376.

Wei, M., & Wang, W. (2016). Data-centric threats and their impacts to real-time communications in smart grid. *Computer Networks*, *104*, 174–188. doi:10.1016/j.comnet.2016.05.003

WELMEC. (2010, May). *Guideline on time depending consumption measurements for billing purposes* (interval metering). Author.

WheeGo. (n. d.). Retrieved from www.wheego.net

Wikipedia. (n. d.). Hyundai Blue On. Retrieved from www.wikipedia.org/wiki/HyundaiBlueOn

Wilhoit, K. (2013). *The SCADA That Didn't Cry Wolf*. BlackHat Security Conference.

Williams, T. J. (1994). The Purdue enterprise reference architecture. *Computers in Industry*, *24*(2), 141–158. doi:10.1016/0166-3615(94)90017-5

Wong, R., Moh, T.-S., & Moh, M. (2012). Efficient Semi-Supervised Learning BitTorrent Traffic Detection: An Extended Summary. In *Proc. of 13th Int. Conf on Distributed Computing and Networking – ICDCN 2012 (LNCS)*, (vol. 7129). Springer. doi:10.1007/978-3-642-25959-3_40

Wood, A., & Stankovic, J. A. (2002). Denial of service in sensor networks. *Computer, Volume*, *35*(10), 54–62.

Wood, B. (2000). An insider threat model for adversary simulation. SRI International. *Research on Mitigating the Insider Threat to Information Systems, 2*, 1–3.

Woo, P. S., Kim, B. H., & Hur, D. (2015). Towards Cyber Security Risks Assessment in Electric Utility SCADA Systems. *Journal of Electrical Engineering and Technology, 10*(3), 888–894. doi:10.5370/JEET.2015.10.3.888

Wu, H. H., Gilchrist, A., Sealy, K., Israelsen, P., & Muhs, J. (2011, May). A review on inductive charging for electric vehicles. *Proceedings of the 2011 IEEE International Electric Machines & Drives Conference* (pp. 143-147).

Wu, Y., Lau, V. K. N., Tsang, D. H. K., Qian, L., & Meng, L. (2012). Optimal exploitation of renewable energy for residential smart grid with supply-demand model. In *proceedings of 7th International ICST Conference on Communications and Networking in China (CHINACOM)*. IEEE.

Xia, J., & Wang, Y. (2012). Secure key distribution for the smart grid. Smart Grid. *IEEE Transactions on, 3*(3), 1437–1443.

Xiao, Y. (2013). *Security and Privacy in Smart Grids*. Taylor & Francis. doi:10.1201/b15240

Xiao, Z., Xiao, Y., & Du, D. H. (2013). Non-repudiation in neighborhood area networks for smart grid. *IEEE Communications Magazine, 51*(1), 18–26. doi:10.1109/MCOM.2013.6400434

Xu & Wang. (2013). Wireless Mesh Network in Smart Grid: Modeling and Analysis for Time Critical Communications. *IEEE Transactions on Wireless Communications, 12*(7), 3360 – 3371.

Xu, Y., & Fischione, C. (2012, May). Real-time scheduling in LTE for smart grids. In *Communications Control and Signal Processing (ISCCSP), 2012 5th International Symposium on* (pp. 1-6). doi:10.1109/ISCCSP.2012.6217872

Xu, L., & Wu, F. (2015). An improved and provable remote user authentication scheme based on elliptic curve cryptosystem with user anonymity. *Security and Communication Networks, 8*(2), 245–260. doi:10.1002/sec.977

Yahyaoui, I. (2016c). Specifications of Photovoltaic Pumping Systems in Agriculture: Sizing, Fuzzy Energy Management and Economic Sensitivity Analysis. Elsevier science. ISBN: 9780128120392.

Yahyaoui, I. (2016b). *Specifications of photovoltaic pumping systems in agriculture: Sizing, fuzzy energy management and economic sensitivity analysis*. Elsevier Science.

Yahyaoui, I., Chaabene, M., & Tadeo, F. (2016). a). Evaluation of Maximum Power Point Tracking algorithm for off-grid photovoltaic pumping. *Sustainable Cities and Society, 25*, 65–73. doi:10.1016/j.scs.2015.11.005

Yahyaoui, I., Ghraizi, R., & Tadeo, F. (2016d). Operational cost optimization for renewable energy microgrids in Mediterranean climate. *Proceedings of the International Renewable Energy Conference (IREC)*. doi:10.1109/IREC.2016.7478881

Yahyaoui, I., Sallem, S., Kamoun, M. B. A., & Tadeo, F. (2014). A proposal for off-grid photovoltaic systems with non-controllable loads using fuzzy logic. *Energy Conversion and Management, 78*, 835–842. doi:10.1016/j.enconman.2013.07.091

Yahyaoui, I., Tadeo, F., & Segatto, M. V. (2016a). Energy and water management for drip-irrigation of tomatoes in a semi-arid district. *Agricultural Water Management*.

Yahyaoui, I., Yahyaoui, A., Chaabene, M., & Tadeo, F. (2016). b). Energy management for a stand-alone photovoltaic-wind system suitable for rural electrification. *Sustainable Cities and Society, 25*, 90–101. doi:10.1016/j.scs.2015.12.002

Yan, Y., Qian, Y., Sharif, H., & Tipper, D. (2012). A survey on smart grid communication infrastructures: Motivations, requirements and challenges. *IEEE Communications Surveys & Tutorials*, (99), 1–16.

Yang, H.-S., Kim, S.-S., & Jang, H.-S. (2012). Optimized Security Algorithm for IEC 61850 Based Power Utility System. *Journal of Electrical Engineering & Technology*, *7*(3), 443–450. doi:10.5370/JEET.2012.7.3.443

Yang, H., Yang, S., Xu, Y., Cao, E., Lai, M., & Dong, Z. (2015). Electric vehicle route optimization considering time-of-use electricity price by learnable Partheno-Genetic algorithm. *IEEE Transactions on Smart Grid*, *6*(2), 657–666. doi:10.1109/TSG.2014.2382684

Yang, L., & Li, F. (2013). Detecting false data injection in smart grid in-network aggregation. In *Proceedings of IEEE International Conference on Smart Grid Communications (SmartGridComm)*. Vancouver, Canada: IEEE. doi:10.1109/SmartGridComm.2013.6687992

Yang, L., & Moh, M. (2011). Dual Trust Secure Protocol for Cluster-Based Wireless Sensor Networks. In *Proc. IEEE 45th Asilomar Conference on Signals, Systems and Computers*. doi:10.1109/ACSSC.2011.6190298

Yang, S.-N., Cheng, W.-S., Hsu, Y.-C., Gan, C.-H., & Lin, Y.-B. (2013, June). Charge Scheduling of Electric Vehicles in Highways. *Elsevier Mathematical and Computer Modelling*, *57*(1112), 2873–2882. doi:10.1016/j.mcm.2011.11.054

Yang, Y., McLaughlin, K., Sezer, S., Littler, T., Im, E. G., Pranggono, B., & Wang, H. F. (2014). Multiattribute SCADA-specific intrusion detection system for power networks. *IEEE Transactions on Power Delivery*, *29*(3), 1092–1102. doi:10.1109/TPWRD.2014.2300099

Yan, Q., Yu, F. R., Gong, Q., & Li, J. (2016). *Software-Defined Networking (SDN) and Distributed Denial of Service (DDoS) Attacks in Cloud Computing Environments: A Survey*, Some Research Issues, and Challenges. *IEEE Communications Surveys and Tutorials*, *18*(1), 602–622. doi:10.1109/COMST.2015.2487361

Yan, Y., Hu, R. Q., Das, S. K., Sharif, H., & Qian, Y. (2013). An efficient security protocol for advanced metering infrastructure in smart grid. *IEEE Network*, *27*(4), 64–71. doi:10.1109/MNET.2013.6574667

Yan, Y., Qian, Y., Sharif, H., & Tipper, D. (2012). A Survey on Smart Grid Communication Infrastructures: Motivations, Requirements and Challenges. *IEEE Communications Surveys and Tutorials*, 5–20.

Yan, Y., Qian, Y., Sharif, H., & Tipper, D. (2012, January). A Survey on Cyber Security for Smart Grid Communications. *Communication Surveys and Tutorials, IEEE*, *14*(4), 998–1010. doi:10.1109/SURV.2012.010912.00035

Yasinsac, A. (2001). Dynamic analysis of security protocols. In *Proceedings of the 2000 workshop on New security paradigms*, (pp. 77–87). ACM.

Yilmaz, M., & Krein, P. T. (2013). Review of battery charger topologies, charging power levels, and infrastructure for plug-in electric and hybrid vehicles. *IEEE Transactions on Power Electronics*, *28*(5), 2151–2169. doi:10.1109/TPEL.2012.2212917

Yip, S. C., Wong, K., Phan, R. C. W., Tan, S. W., Ku, I., & Hew, W. P. (2014). A Privacy-Preserving and Cheat-Resilient electricity consumption reporting Scheme for smart grids. In *Proceedings of International Conference on Computer, Information and Telecommunication Systems (CITS)*. IEEE doi:10.1109/CITS.2014.6878971

Yoo, H., & Shon, T. (2015). Novel Approach for Detecting Network Anomalies for Substation Automation based on IEC 61850. *Multimedia Tools and Applications*, *74*(1), 303–318. doi:10.1007/s11042-014-1870-0

Yuan, Y., Yang, J., Zhang, J., Lan, S., & Zhang, J. (2011). Evolution of privacy-preserving data publishing. In *Anti-Counterfeiting, Security and Identification (ASID),2011IEEE International Conference on.*

Yu, R., Zhang, Y., Gjessing, S., Yuen, C., Xie, S., & Guizani, M. (2011). Cognitive radio based hierarchical communications infrastructure for smart grid. *IEEE Network*, *25*(5), 6–14. doi:10.1109/MNET.2011.6033030

Zaballos, A., Vallejo, A., & Selga, J. M. (2011). Heterogeneous communication architecture for the smart grid. *IEEE Network*, *25*(5), 30–37. doi:10.1109/MNET.2011.6033033

Zainuri, M. A. A. M., Radzi, M. A. M., Soh, A. C., & Rahim, N. A. (2014). Development of adaptive perturb and observe-fuzzy control maximum power point tracking for photovoltaic boost dc-dc converter. *IET Renewable Power Generation*, *8*(2), 183–194. doi:10.1049/iet-rpg.2012.0362

Zeadally, S., Pathan, A., Alcaraz, C., & Badra, M. (2012). Towards privacy protection in smart grid. *Wireless Personal Communications*, *73*(1), 23–50. doi:10.1007/s11277-012-0939-1

Zeng, M., Leng, S., & Zhang, Y. (2013, June). Power Charging and Discharging Scheduling for V2G Networks in the Smart Grid. Proceedings of IEEE ICC' 13, Budapest, Hungary.

Zhang, K., Lu, R., Liang, X., Qiao, J., & Shen, X. (2013, Aug). PARK: A privacy-preserving aggregation scheme with adaptive key management for smart grid. In Communications in China (ICCC), 2013 IEEE/CIC international conference on (p. 236-241). doi:10.1109/ICCChina.2013.6671121

Zhang, K., Liang, X., Lu, R., & Shen, X. (2014). Sybil Attacks and Their Defenses in the Internet of Things. *Internet of Things Journal, IEEE*, *1*(5), 372–383. doi:10.1109/JIOT.2014.2344013

Zhang, Q., Yu, T., & Ning, P. (2008). A framework for identifying compromised nodes in wireless sensor networks. *ACM Transactions on Information and System Security*, *XI*(3), 1–37.

Zhang, R., Zhang, S., Lan, Y., & Jiang, J. (2008). Network anomaly detection using one class support vector machine. In *Proceedings of the International MultiConference of Engineers and Computer Scientists* (Vol. 1).

Zhang, W., Zhang, Y., Chen, J., Li, H., & Wang, Y. (2013). End-to-end security scheme for Machine Type Communication based on Generic Authentication Architecture. *Cluster Computing, Springer*, *16*(4), 861–871. doi:10.1007/s10586-013-0259-6

Zhang, Y., Sun, W., Wang, L., Wang, H., Green, R. II, & Alam, M. (2011). A multi-level communication architecture of smart grid based on congestion aware wireless mesh network. *43rd North American Power Symposium (NAPS)*.

Zhang, Y., Wang, L., Sun, W., Green, R. C., & Alam, M. (2011). Artificial immune system based intrusion detection in a distributed hierarchical network architecture of smart grid. In *Proceedings of IEEE Power and Energy Society General Meeting*. Detroit, MI: IEEE. doi:10.1109/PES.2011.6039697

Zhao, B., Xue, M., Zhang, X., Wang, C., & Zhao, J. (2015). An MAS based energy management system for a stand-alone microgrid at high altitude. *Applied Energy*, *143*, 251–261. doi:10.1016/j.apenergy.2015.01.016

Zhao, F., Hanatani, Y., Komano, Y., Smyth, B., Ito, S., & Kambayashi, T. (2012). Secure authenticated key exchange with revocation for smart grid. In *Proceedings of IEEE PES conference on Innovative Smart Grid Technologies (ISGT)*. Washington, DC: IEEE.

Zhao, L., Prousch, S., Hübner, M., & Moser, A. (2010, April). Simulation methods for assessing electric vehicle impact on distribution grids. In *IEEE PES T&D 2010* (pp. 1–7). IEEE. doi:10.1109/TDC.2010.5484386

Zhong, Q. C., & Hornik, T. (2013). *Control of Power Inverters in Renewable Energy and Smart Grid Integration*. Wiley.

Zhou, J., Hu, R. Q., & Qian, Y. (2012). Scalable Distributed Communication Architectures to Support Advanced Metering Infrastructure in Smart Grid. *IEEE Transactions on Parallel and Distributed Systems*, *23*(9), 1632–1642. doi:10.1109/TPDS.2012.53

Zhou, K., Fu, C., & Yang, S. (2016). Big data driven smart energy management: From big data to big insights. *Renewable & Sustainable Energy Reviews*, *56*, 215–225. doi:10.1016/j.rser.2015.11.050

ZigBee Alliance. (2008). *ZigBee Specifications 053474r17*. Retrieved from http://www.zigbee.org/

ZigBee Alliance. (2010). *Zigbee specifications*. Retrieved in May 2016, from http://www.zigbee.org/

About the Contributors

Mohamed Amine Ferrag received the Bachelor's degree (June,2008), Master's degree (June,2010) and Ph.D. degree (June,2014) from Badji Mokhtar- Annaba University, Algeria, all in Computer Science. Since October 2014, he is an assistant professor at the Department of Computer Science, Guelma University, Algeria. He is also affiliated as a Researcher member with Networks and Systems Laboratory, Annaba University, Algeria. His research interests include wireless network security, network coding security, and applied cryptography. He is currently serving on various editorial positions like Editorial Board Member in International Journal of Information Security and Privacy (IGI Global) and International Journal of Internet Technology and Secured Transactions (Inderscience Publishers). He has served as an Organizing Committee Member in numerous international conferences like ICNAS'13, ICNAS'15, ASD'16. He has served as TPC Member in ANT'15, IEEE GlobeCom'15, CyberSec'16, IEEE ANTS'16, IEEE ICEMIS'16, etc. Mohamed Amine is member of the IEEE Technical Committee on Security & Privacy, and member of the IEEE Cybersecurity Community. He received some awards for his reviewing activities.

Ahmed Ahmim received the Bachelor's degree (June, 2007), Master's degree (June, 2009) and PhD (October, 2014) from Badji Mokhtar-Annaba University, Algeria, all in Computer Science. He has been an Assistant Professor at the Department of Mathematics and Computer Science, University of Larbi Tebessi, Algeria, since May 2015. He is also affiliated as a Researcher member (Since October 2010) with Networks and Systems Laboratory – LRS, Badji Mokhtar – Annaba University, Algeria. His research interests include wireless network security, network coding security, and applied cryptography. He has served as an Organizing Committee Member, and Technical Program Committee (TPC) member in numerous international conferences like ICNAS'13, ICNAS'15, IT4OD'16, PAIS'2016.

* * *

Khandakar Ahmed is a Lecturer at School of IT & Engineering, Melbourne Institute of Technology, Melbourne, Australia and currently an affiliated researcher, Australia-India Research Centre for Automation Software Engineering (AICAUSE), RMIT University, Melbourne, Australia. He received his PhD from RMIT University, Melbourne, Australia in December, 2014 and M.Sc. in Networking and e-Business Centred Computing (NeBCC) from the consortia of University of Reading, UK; Aristotle University of Thessaloniki, Greece; and University of Charles III de Madrid, Spain. Dr. Ahmed has authored or co-authored more than 30 publications in the form of journal Article, peer reviewed conference proceedings, book chapter, and book. He has also worked as the reviewer for many Journals including

Parallel and Distributed Computing (JPDC), Journal of Computer Networks (ComNet) and Journal of Ad-hoc Networks. His research interest includes Software Defined Wide Area Network, Software Defined Wireless Network, Wireless Sensor Network, Smart-Grid and Cloud Networks.

Mohiuddin Ahmed is working in the arena of Data Mining, Machine Learning and Cyber Security towards his Ph.D. degree at the UNSW, Canberra. He received his Bachelor of Science degree in Computer Science and Information Technology from Islamic University of Technology, Bangladesh, in 2011.

Rami Haidar Ahmad is a Telecom Engineer (Master) working in research and consultancy especially in the security field related to Internet of Things , cyber security and Telecommunication in general. Holding a Bachelor degree (2006) and a Master degree (2008) in Telecom engineering from the Lebanese International University and was a Ph.D. student at the Technical university of Berlin (2012-2014). Participating in many seminars and conferences and giving consultancy for private companies and official sectors about cyber security and new technology security challenges. Interested in academic publications as tutorials, books, book chapters and scientific papers. Located in Lebanon.

Cristina Alcaraz, Ph.D., is a Senior Researcher in Computer Science at the University of Malaga. She was awarded her PhD in Computer Science by the University of Malaga in 2011, and visited Royal Holloway, University of London in 2012 - 2014 and the U.S. National Institute of Standards and Technology (NIST) in 2011 - 2012. She has also been involved in European and national research projects, focusing on topics related to CIP (security in SCADA systems, cyber-physical systems and Smart Grids). She serves on multiple international conference committees and on Editorial Boards of journals related to CIP and information security (e.g., International Journal of Critical Infrastructure Protection (IJCIP), Telecommunication Systems (TELS), Ad Hoc Networks or Industrial Integration and Management (JIIM), amongst others).

Bashar Alohali is a PhD research student in Network Security at Liverpool John Moores University. His fields of interest are smart grid and cyber security, computer forensics, computer networks and security, sensor-based applications for smart cities, critical infrastructure protection and cloud computing. He obtained his master's degree in computer systems security from the University of Glamorgan in 2011.

Marium Azhar is working as Postdoctoral Researcher in Electrical Engineering Department in École de technologie supérieure, Montreal, Canada and has been Assistant Professor in Lahore College for Women University, Lahore, Pakistan. She obtained her Ph.D. in Electrical and Information Engineering in November 2015 and her research area is wireless communication technologies with its applications and security in smart grid.

Yue Cao received his PhD degree from the Institute for Communication Systems (ICS) formerly known as Centre for Communication Systems Research, at University of Surrey, Guildford, UK in 2013. Further to his PhD study, he was a Research Fellow at the ICS. Since October 2016, he has been the Lecturer in Department of Computer and Information Sciences, at Northumbria University, Newcastle upon Tyne, UK. His research interests focus on Delay/Disruption Tolerant Networks, Electric Vehicle (EV) charging management, Information Centric Networking (ICN), Device-to-Device (D2D) communication and Mobile Edge Computing (MEC).

Andrew Crampton has been researching in the areas of Computational Mathematics, Machine Learning and Approximation Theory since completing his PhD at the University of Huddersfield in 2002. His is currently the Acting Head of Department at Huddersfield University and is the Subject Area Leader for Computing and Information Systems within the Department of Informatics.

Tiago Bornia de Castro received a degree in Telecommunications Engineering from the Fluminense Federal University in 2013. Currently, he is in the Electrical and Telecommunications Engineering master's program at Fluminense Federal University.

Vitor Farias graduated in Telecommunications Engineering from Universidade Federal Fluminense (2013). He is currently a graduate student in Telecommunications Engineering from UFF and participates Fibre project, funded by RNP. He has experience in Telecommunications Engineering area, acting on the following topics: Reliability Engineering, IEC61850 and Future Internet.

Natalia Castro Fernandes received the electronics and computer engineering degree, M.Sc. degree, and D.Sc. degree in electrical engineering from Universidade Federal do Rio de Janeiro (UFRJ), Rio de Janeiro, Brazil, in 2006, 2008, and 2011, respectively. She has been an assistant professor at the Telecommunications Engineering Department since 2012 and she is currently deputy head of this department. Alumni Association of the Polytechnic School (A3P) has awarded her with the A3P prize of Greater Accumulated Income Ratio in the course of Electronic Engineering at UFRJ in 2007. In addition, she received a grant from the FAPERJ, a government-funding agency, called FAPERJ Nota 10, which is dedicated for the best Ph.D. students of State of Rio de Janeiro from 2010 until 2011. She also received the Marechal-do-Ar Casimiro Montenegro Filho award, promoted by the Brazilian Department of Strategic Issues (SAE) from the Presidency of Federative Republic of Brazil, in 2012, for her PhD. thesis results. Other awards were also received due to recent works with her advised students. She has coordinated research projects funded by Brazilian agencies and she has already participated in Europe-Brazil collaboration projects, such as FIBRE and Horizon. In addition, she is coordinating the technical development in the holographic telemedicine project with Brazilian Army. Her major research interests are in network security, future Internet, smart grids, and telemedicine. She has published 5 journal papers, 7 book chapters, and 37 conference papers. She has supervised 7 master students and she is currently supervising 2 PhD students and 6 master students.

Sowmyarani C N is currently working as Associate Professor in the Department of Computer Science and Engineering at RVCE, India. She was with MSRIT, India as Assistant Professor. She has her M.E. degree from UVCE, Bangalore University, India. Ph.D. degree from VTU, India. Her focused areas are, Privacy Preserving data Publishing, Information Retrieval, Computer Security and Privacy. She has published number of International journals and Conference papers in the focused areas.

Rachid Ghraizi performed his PhD in Process and Systems Engineering at the Systems and Automatic Engineering department (ISA), University of Valladolid, Spain. Also at the same department he received a diploma in advanced studies in the field of Process and Systems Engineering. He received his B. Eng in Automation and Industrial Electronics (1996) and master degrees in Automatic Control (2000) from the Department of Automatic and Computer Science, Higher Polytechnic Institute (ISPJAE). Havana, Cuba. He worked and works currently as a specialist in power generation as thermosolar, hydroelectric plants, and combined cycle. He worked at the ISA department as a researcher. His interests were the supervision of industrial controllers and he performed different methods in this field. He worked as a teacher and researcher at the ISPJAE at the department of Automatic and Computer Science, ISPJAE. She is a reviewer for prestigious scientific journals, such as Agricultural Water Management and others.

Mark A. Gregory is a Fellow of the Institute of Engineers Australia and a Senior Member of the IEEE. Mark A Gregory received a PhD from RMIT University, Melbourne, Australia in 2008, where he is a Senior Lecturer in the School of Engineering. In 2009, he received an Australian Learning and Teaching Council Citation for an outstanding contribution to teaching and learning. He is the Managing Editor of two international journals (AJTDE and IJICTA) and the General Co-Chair of ITNAC. Research interests include telecommunications, network design and technical risk.

Helge Janicke is heading De Montfort University's Software Technology Research Laboratory and the Cyber Security Centre. He is the Interim Head of School of Computer Science and Informatics. Dr. Janicke was awarded his PhD in Computer Science in 2007 and worked on Cyber Security with organisations such as QinetiQ, Ministry of Defence and General Dynamics UK as part of the DIF-DTC consortium. His interests are covering formal verification techniques and their application to Cyber Security, SCADA and Industrial Control System Security as well as aspects of Cyber Warfare. He is working with Airbus Group and established DMU's Airbus Group Centre of Excellence in SCADA Cyber Security and Forensics Research in 2013. He is a general chair of the International Symposium on SCADA and Industrial Control Systems Cyber Security Research (ICS-CSR). He is Editor-in-Chief for the Journal of Security and Safety (EAI) and serves on the editorial board and as reviewer of international journals.

Kevin Jones is the Head of 'Product and Cyber Security' at Airbus Group Innovations, a Global network of; teams, projects, and collaborations undertaking research, innovation, and state of the art cyber security solutions in support of Airbus Group. He holds a BSc in Computer Science and MSc in Distributed Systems Integration from De Montfort University, Leicester where he also obtained his PhD: A Trust Based Approach to Mobile Multi-Agent System Security in 2010. He is active in the cyber security research community and holds a number of patents within the domain. He has many years experience in consultancy to aid organisations in cyber security topics and currently acts as an executive consultant to the Airbus Group on matters of cyber security across multiple domains and platforms. Kevin is a frequent public speaker on cyber security topics in addition to an advisor to numerous cyber security research programmes and events. He is an advocate and champion for cyber security in academia, for cyber skills, and for multi-disciplinary research.

Georgios Karopoulos received a Diploma of Information and Communication Systems Engineer in 2003, a M.Sc. in Information and Communication Systems Security in 2005, and a Ph.D. in Computer Network Security in 2009, from the department of Information and Communication Systems Engineering, University of the Aegean, Greece. Currently, he is a Marie Curie fellow researcher at the department of Informatics and Telecommunications of the National and Kapodistrian University of Athens, Greece. In the past, he has held positions as a postdoctoral researcher at IIT-CNR (Italy) in 2010-2011 and JRC (Italy) in 2012-2014, as well as an adjunct lecturer at the University of the Aegean (department of Information and Communication Systems Engineering) in 2010. He is a reviewer of international journals and conferences and has served as a technical program committee member in international conferences in security and networking. His research interests are in the areas of network security, smart grid security and Critical Infrastructure protection, and he has published in conferences and scientific journals in the above areas.

Yona Lopes is a Brazilian computer scientist and Ph.D. student at Universidade Federal Fluminense. She received her degree in electrical engineering in 2010, and her master degree in telecommunication engineering from Fluminense Federal University in 2013. Her research focuses on smart grid, IEC 61850 and Software Defined Networks (SDN). Yona is visiting professor at INFNET and INATEL university and automation professor at SEL-university. In addition, she received a grant from the FAPERJ, a government-funding agency, called FAPERJ Nota 10, which is dedicated for the best Ph.D. students of State of Rio de Janeiro in 2016.

Javier Lopez is Full Professor in the Computer Science Department and Head of NICS Labs at University of Malaga. His activities are mainly focused on network security and CIIP, leading a number of national and international research projects. Prof. Lopez is the Co-Editor in Chief of International Journal of Information Security (IJIS) and Spanish representative in the IFIP TC-11 on Security and Protection in Information Systems. Additionally, he is a member of several journal Editorial Boards, like IEEE Wireless Communications, IEEE Internet of Things, Computers & Security and Journal of Computer Security, amongst others.

Leandros Maglaras received the B.Sc. degree from Aristotle University of Thessaloniki, Greece in 1998, M.Sc. in Industrial Production and Management from University of Thessaly in 2004 and M.Sc. and PhD degrees in Electrical & Computer Engineering from University of Volos, in 2008 and 2014 respectively. He is currently a Lecturer in the School of Computer Science and Informatics at the De Montfort University, U.K. During 2014 he was a Research Fellow in the Department of Computer at the University of Surrey, U.K. He has participated in various research programs investigating vehicular and ICT technologies (C4C-project.eu, reduction-project.eu), sustainable development (islepact.eu, Smile-gov), cyber security (cockpitci.eu, fastpass-project.eu) and optimization and prediction of the dielectric behavior of air gaps (optithesi.webs.com). He serves on the Editorial Board of several International peer-reviewed journals such as Wiley Journal on Security & Communication Networks, EAI Transactions on e-Learning and EAI Transactions on Industrial Networks and Intelligent Systems. He is general (co-)Chair of INISCOM 2016, a new, annual, EAI and Springer sponsored conference on industrial networks and intelligent systems. He is an author of more than 50 papers in scientific magazines and conferences and is a senior member of IEEE. His research interests include wireless sensor networks and vehicular ad hoc networks. He is currently invited as visiting professor the Shenzhen University for June of 2016 in order to perform research and give seminar lectures on the Research Institute for Future Media Computing.

João Pedro Marques studies Telecommunications Engineering since 2012 at Universidade Federal Fluminense. He has been participating of the Cientific Initiation Programm since 2015.

Melody Moh obtained her MS and Ph.D., both in computer science, from Univ. of California - Davis. She joined San Jose State University in 1993, and has been a Professor since Aug 2003. Her research interests include cloud computing, software defined networks, mobile, wireless networking, and security/privacy for cloud and network systems. She has published over 130 refereed papers in international journals, conferences and as book chapters, and has consulted for various companies.

Débora Christina Muchaluat-Saade received a computer engineering degree, and M.Sc. and D.Sc. degrees in computer science from PUC-Rio, Brazil, in 1992, 1996 and 2003, respectively. Since 2002, she has been an associate professor at Universidade Federal Fluminense (UFF). She has coordinated several research projects funded by Brazilian agencies. Her major research interests are computer networks, smart grids, multimedia communications and telemedicine applications.

Melesio Muñoz holds a master's degree in computer science from San Jose State University and two bachelor's degrees from University of California, Santa Cruz, in computer science and in history. His professional and research interests are related to information security on the future electrical power, i.e., the Smart Grid. He has held positions in the software industry and in research astronomy, and for the last ten years he has worked in the electrical construction industry as well as taught in community colleges.

Nazmus Shaker Nafi received the B.Eng. (Hons.) degree in Communication from the International Islamic University Malaysia (IIUM), in 2010, and the M.Phil. degree in Computer engineering from the University of Newcastle, Newcastle, NSW, Australia, in 2013. Currently, he is a Ph.D. candidate in the RMIT University, Melbourne, VIC, Australia. His current research interests include SG communication systems, wireless network architecture, Machine to Machine, Software Defined Networks and Internet of Things.

Andrew Nicholson is a lead engineer working in cyber security. He is broadly interested in topics of attack attribution, application security and visualisation.

Julia Noce is a Computer Science student in Universidade Federal Fluminense. She has been participating of the Scientific Initiation Program since 2015.

Christoforos Ntantogian received his B.Sc. degree in Computer Science and Telecommunications in 2004 and his M.Sc. degree in Computer Systems Technology in 2006 both from the Department of Informatics and Telecommunications, University of Athens. In 2009 he received his Ph.D. from the University of Athens (Department of Informatics and Telecommunications). Currently, he is an adjunct lecturer at the Department of Digital Systems of the University of Piraeus. He has participated in numerous projects realized in the context of EU Programs (ACTS, IST, AAL, DGHOME, H2020) as well as National Programs (Greek). His research interests lie in the intersection of system/software security, data analysis and applied mathematics to develop practical systems with security.

Al-Sakib Khan Pathan received Ph.D. degree (MS leading to Ph.D.) in Computer Engineering in 2009 from Kyung Hee University, South Korea. He received B.Sc. degree in Computer Science and Information Technology from Islamic University of Technology (IUT), Bangladesh in 2003. He is currently an Associate Professor at the Computer Science and Engineering department, Southeast University, Bangladesh. From August 2010 to July 2015, he served as an Assistant Professor at Computer Science department at IIUM, Malaysia. Even before that, till June 2010, he was an Assistant Professor at Computer Science and Engineering department, BRAC University, Bangladesh and also worked as a Researcher at Networking Lab, Kyung Hee University, South Korea from September 2005 to August 2009. His research interests include wireless sensor networks, network security, and e-services technologies. Currently he is also working on some multidisciplinary issues. He is a recipient of several awards/best paper awards and has many publications in these areas. He has served as a Chair, Organizing Committee Member, and Technical Program Committee (TPC) member in numerous international conferences/workshops like GLOBECOM, ICC, LCN, GreenCom, AINA, WCNC, HPCS, ICA3PP, IWCMC, VTC, HPCC, etc. He was awarded the IEEE Outstanding Leadership Award and Certificate of Appreciation for his role in IEEE GreenCom'13 conference. He is currently serving on various editorial positions like Editor-in-Chief of International Journal of Communication Networks and Information Security, Deputy Editor-in-Chief of International Journal of Computers and Applications, Taylor & Francis, Associate Technical Editor of IEEE Communications Magazine, Editor of Ad Hoc and Sensor Wireless Networks, Old City Publishing, and International Journal of Sensor Networks, Inderscience Publishers, Associate Editor of International Journal of Computational Science and Engineering, Inderscience, Guest Editor of many special issues of top-ranked journals, and Editor/Author of 15 published books. One of his books has been included twice in Intel Corporation's Recommended Reading List for Developers, 2nd half 2013 and 1st half of 2014; 3 books were included in IEEE Communications Society's (IEEE ComSoc) Best Readings in Communications and Information Systems Security, 2013, 2 other books were indexed with all the titles (chapters) in Elsevier's acclaimed abstract and citation database, Scopus, in February 2015 and a seventh book is translated to simplified Chinese language from English version. Also, 2 of his journal papers and 1 conference paper were included under different categories in IEEE Communications Society's (IEEE ComSoc) Best Readings Topics on Communications and Information Systems Security, 2013. He also serves as a referee of many prestigious journals. He received some awards for his reviewing activities like: one of the most active reviewers of IAJIT three times, in 2012, 2014, and 2015; Outstanding Reviewer of Elsevier Computer Networks (July 2015) and Elsevier JNCA (November 2015); recognized reviewer status of Elsevier Computers & Electrical Engineering (March 2014), Elsevier Ad Hoc Networks journal (April 2014), Elsevier FGCS (October 2014), just to mention a few. As part of his academic duties, he has so far supervised 2 PhD students to completion. He is a Senior Member of the Institute of Electrical and Electronics Engineers (IEEE), USA and several IEEE technical committees.

Dayananda Pruthviraja is currently working as an Associate Professor in the Deprtment of ISE at JSSATE. He has Obtained Ph.D. degree from VTU and M.Tech degree from RVCE. His focus area is Information Retrieval. He was with MSRIT, Bengaluru, India in Department of ISE as an Assistant Professor. He has published international journals and conference papers in the field of Information retrieval.

Danda B. Rawat is an Associate Professor in the Department of Electrical Engineering & Computer Science at Howard University, Washington, DC, USA. Prior to Howard University, he was with the College of Engineering & Information Technology of Georgia Southern University, Statesboro, GA as a faculty member until 2016. Dr. Rawat's research focuses on wireless communication networks, cyber security, cyber physical systems, Internet of Things, big data analytics, wireless virtualization, software-defined networks, smart grid systems, wireless sensor networks, and vehicular/wireless ad-hoc networks. His research is supported by US National Science Foundation, University Sponsored Programs and Center for Sustainability grants. Dr. Rawat is the recipient of NSF Faculty Early Career Development (CAREER) Award. Dr. Rawat has published over 120 scientific/technical articles and 8 books. He has been serving as an Editor/Guest Editor for over 10 international journals. He serves as a Web-Chair for IEEE INFO-COM 2016/2017, served as a Student Travel Grant Co-chair of IEEE INFOCOM 2015, Track Chair for Wireless Networking and Mobility of IEEE CCNC 2016, Track Chair for Communications Network and Protocols of IEEE AINA 2015, and so on. He served as a program chair, general chair, and session chair for numerous international conferences and workshops, and served as a technical program committee (TPC) member for several international conferences including IEEE INFOCOM, IEEE GLOBECOM, IEEE CCNC, IEEE GreenCom, IEEE AINA, IEEE ICC, IEEE WCNC and IEEE VTC conferences. He is the recipient of Outstanding Research Faculty Award (Award for Excellence in Scholarly Activity) 2015, Allen E. Paulson College of Engineering and Technology, GSU among others. He is the Founder and Director of the Cyber-security and Wireless Networking Innovations (CWiNs) Research Lab. He received the Ph.D. in Electrical and Computer Engineering from Old Dominion University, Norfolk, Virginia. Dr. Rawat is a Senior Member of IEEE and member of ACM and ASEE. He served as a Vice Chair of the Executive Committee of the IEEE Savannah Section and Webmaster for the section from 2013 to 2017.

Swapnoneel Roy is an Assistant Professor of Computer Science and Information Technology at the UNF School of Computing. Dr. Roy's primary research focus is in cybersecurity. He has taught five upper-level undergraduate courses, and one graduate course covering various topics of cybersecurity. Additionally, he has directed 11 Master's theses, most of which explores problems in cybersecurity. Dr. Roy has published a lot of work in cybersecurity, most of which have resulted from the research conducted with students. He has successfully undertaken two research projects being awarded grant money for them. The first one was an industrial project with Johnson & Johnson Visioncare, while the second one was a state level grant from the Florida Center for cybersecurity at USF. Dr. Roy has also represented UNF at various national and international conferences in cybersecurity. He has also been interviewed on different topics by different media on various topics in cybersecurity. Dr. Roy has also assisted his students to receive scholarships and awards to pursue research and travel to conferences on cybersecurity. He serves as the faculty advisor of the Association of Information Technology Professionals (AITP) Club of the School of Computing, which has conducted hackathon events on campus, and participated in national programming contests.

Marcelo E. V. Segatto received the B. Sc. Degree in electrical engineering from the Federal University of Espírito Santo (UFES), Vitória, Brazil in 1991, the M.Sc. Degree also in electrical engineering from State University of Campinas (UNICAMP), Campinas, Brazil in 1994, and the Ph.D. from the Imperial College of Science, Technology and Medicine, London, UK, in 2001. He joined UFES, Department of the Electrical Engineering as an Assistant Professor in 1994 acting as its Head from 2012 to 2016. During his Ph.D, he worked as researcher at British Telecom Labs (BT Labs) and Corning Labs, both in Ipswich, England. He is a member of the Optical Society of America (OSA), the Brazilian Society of Microwaves and Optoelectronics (SBMO, Electromagnetics (SBMag) and Telecommunications (SBrT). From 2000 up to 2015, he has acted as consultant and carried out several transfer technology projects for a number of companies linked to the Information and Communication Technology and Electrical Engineering such as Petrobras, Eletronorte, Eletrosul, PADTEC S/A and several startup companies.

Also in 2015, he acted as a member of the postgraduate program of Electrical Engineering at UFES with research interests concentrated in optical communications including devices, systems and networks, optical sensors, network sensors, broadband powerline communication.

Richard Smith is a Senior Lecturer at De Montfort University and interim head of the Cyber Security Centre. His research currently focuses on Industrial Control System and satellite security having previously worked extensively with the European Space agency and NASA, as both technical lead and prime for global international consortia. He has worked on contracts worth over €2 million with teams comprising partners from both academia and industry, producing scientific results far exceeding original expectations which led to numerous CCNs to expand the remit of projects such as River & Lake, hosted by DMU on behalf of ESA. He was Project Leader and lead developer for the ESA ACE2 Global Digital Elevation Model project. ACE2 has been used in the processing chains for multiple satellites and is currently being incorporated on-board the €305 million Sentinel-3 satellite. In this scope he has been responsible for ensuring the data integrity of commercially sensitive satellite mission datasets, ensuring the raw data are only accessible to those pre-approved by ESA. He has brought his experience of the space industry into the cyber threat domain and is currently lead researcher on the ASSESS project, investigating embedded satellite security and is developing the Framework for the Assessment of Satellite Threats (FAST), a new security framework focusing on the requirements and environment of the space sector.

Fernando Tadeo is Professor of the School of Engineering at the University of Valladolid since 2010. He graduated from the same university, in Physics in 1992, and in Electronic Engineering in 1994. After completing an M.Sc. in Control Engineering in the University of Bradford, U.K., he went back to Valladolid, where he got his Ph.D. degree. His main interest area is Advanced Process Control, focused on applications in Desalination and Renewable Energies (Wind, Solar and Osmotic).

Gurbakshish Singh Toor received his B.E. in Electronics and Communication engineering from Panjab University, India in 2013. He is currently a MEng student at Nanyang Technological University Singapore. His research interests include cyber security, smart grids, wireless communication and networking technologies.

Azhar Ul-Haq is working as a Postdoctoral Research Fellow in the Department of Electrical and Computer Engineering of University of New Brunswick, Canada. He obtained Ph.D. degree in Electrical Engineering from University of L'Aquila Italy in March 2016 and had been exchange student Department of Electrical and Computer Engineering of University of University of Waterloo. His research interests fall in the area of photovoltaic powered electric vehicles (EVs) smart charging in smart grid environment and shift and control of residential and commercial loads, peak power redistribution.

Tong Wang is an Associate Professor & PhD supervisor at Information and Communication Engineering College, Harbin Engineering University, China. He received Doctor's degree in Computer Application from Harbin Engineering University in 2006. His research interests include Wireless Network, Vehicular ad-hoc Network and Internet of Things.

Yunfeng Wang is the Ph.D. at information and communication engineering Collage, Harbin Engineering University, China. His research interests include Caching and D2D in 5G.

Christos Xenakis received his B.Sc degree in computer science in 1993 and his M.Sc degree in telecommunication and computer networks in 1996, both from the Department of Informatics and Telecommunications, University of Athens, Greece. In 2004 he received his Ph.D. from the University of Athens (Department of Informatics and Telecommunications). From 1998 – 2001 he was with a Greek telecoms system development firm, where he was involved in the design and development of advanced telecommunications subsystems. From 1996 – 2007 he was a member of the Communication Networks Laboratory of the University of Athens. Since 2007 he is a faculty member of the Department of Digital Systems of the University of Piraeus, Greece, where currently is an Associate Professor, a member of the Systems Security Laboratory and the director of the Postgraduate Degree Programme, on "Techno-economics Management and Digital Systems Security". He has participated in numerous projects realized in the context of EU Programs (ACTS, ESPRIT, IST, AAL, DGHOME, Marie Curie, Horizon2020) as well as National Programs (Greek). He is the project manager of the ReCRED project funded by Horizon2020 and the technical manager of the UINFC2 project funded by DGHOME/ISEC. His research interests are in the field of systems, networks and applications security. He has authored more than 70 papers in peer-reviewed journals and international conferences.

Imene Yahyaoui received her B. Eng and master degrees in electrical engineering and renewable energies from the National School of Engineering of Sfax, Tunisia in 2011. She performed her PhD in Systems and Process Engineering and at the Systems Engineering and Automatic department (ISA), at the Industrial Engineering School of Valladolid, Spain until 2015. She is currently performing her postdoc researches at the Electric Department of the Federal University of Espírito Santo, Brasil. Her interests are in renewable energy applications, SMART grids and power electronics. She is a member in international congress organization committees, author of many scientific articles in high quality journals and has three books with Elsevier. She is a reviewer for prestigious scientific journals, such as Energy Conversion and Management, applied energy, applied thermal energy, sustainable cities and society, Renewable and Sustainable Energy journals and so many others.

Index

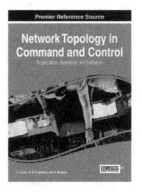

Printed in the United States
By Bookmasters